THE SPANISH BOURBONS

The History of a Tenacious Dynasty

THE SPANISH BOURBONS

THE HISTORY
OF A TENACIOUS DYNASTY

by John D. Bergamini

G. P. PUTNAM'S SONS   *New York*

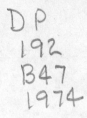

Contents

Republic and Monarchist Intrigues: Alfonso and Ena's separation in exile—Paris meetings of King Alfonso and Don Jaime—Alfonso Carlos, the new pretender—Constitution of 1931 and radical reforms—Sanjurjo revolt—renunciations of Alfonso's older sons in favor of Don Juan—political swing to the right—the disorders of 1934—the Popular Front victory of 1936—General Franco's pronunciamiento. 3. The Civil War: class, ideological, geographical, and international dimensions of the conflict—King Alfonso in Rome—Don Juan's efforts to join Franco—Franco's coup at the expense of the Carlists—siege of Madrid—the Carlist Francis Xavier and Franco—death of Prince Alfonso in Miami—birth of Don Juan Carlos—end of the Civil War and its costs.

Illustrations will be found following page 222

THE SPANISH BOURBONS

The History of a Tenacious Dynasty

Prologue:
Invaders and Dynasts
Before the Bourbons

THE first Bourbon King of Spain, the sixteen-year-old Felipe V, reluctantly forsook the salons and gardens of Versailles on December 4, 1700, rode south on a white horse to the Pyrenees and beyond, and entered a jubilant Madrid after a journey of fifty days. One of Felipe's legacies to the capital was the vast Baroque Oriente Palace, and it was from his study here that the last Bourbon, the forty-four-year-old Alfonso XIII, heard the hooting, cursing crowds outside and decided to abandon Spain on April 14, 1931, leaving on so few hours' notice that the family photographs still remain on the tables for the tourist to view today. Alfonso made a three-day trip by motorcar, warship, and train to Paris, where he distractedly took up the exile's vigil in the nightclubs.

In their more than two centuries of rule the Spanish Bourbons faced and surmounted other crises and disasters. They met utter humiliation and imprisonment at the hands of Napoleon in 1808, only to return in triumph in 1814. The crown was contested by a niece and an uncle after 1833, causing no less than three civil wars, but the dynasty survived. A Bourbon queen and all her family were deposed by a popular revolution in 1868; her son was serenely restored to the throne in 1875 after the country had experimented with successively another royal house and a republic. Originally French but soon determinedly Spanish, the Bourbons always came back. Now again their immediate destiny is to preside over the uncertain future following the death of General Franco.

It is necessary to differentiate the Spanish Bourbons first of all from the senior line of French Bourbons, who have not ruled in that country since 1848 but who still boast royal pretenders. Then, there are the junior lines of Parma and Naples Bourbons, deposed in 1860 and likewise with present-day claimants. All the Bourbon royal houses have intermarried frequently, producing a complicated genealogy and hundreds of living descendants. The dimly known founder of the illustrious family was Aimon, lord of Bourbonnais, a barony south of Paris, the largest in ninth-century France. His descendants married into French royalty and were styling themselves . Dukes of Bourbon by the thirteenth century. The first Bourbon who actually sat on the throne of the Capets, the statesmanlike Henry IV, was originally leader of the Huguenots in the French religious strife of the sixteenth century, but on becoming monarch, he converted to Catholicism, making the celebrated quip "Paris is worth a mass." His successor, Louis XIII, was a memorable king only by virtue of the greatness of his minister Cardinal Richelieu, who made France the first power in Europe. Then came the incomparable Louis XIV, who in the course of a reign of sixty-two years brought it about that his grandson became King Felipe V of Spain.

That first Bourbon who journeyed from France to Spain in 1700 found his country administratively disorganized, economically backward, and culturally stagnant. Compared to the bureaucratic machine at Versailles, Spain's political institutions were antiquated. There was no middle class in Spain such as was leading France to prosperity and eventually to revolution. By even French standards Spain was religion-ridden. In making their imprint on Spain over the next centuries, and a considerable imprint it was, the Bourbon kings would be competing with the strange and unique forces of earlier Spanish history.

It was long before archaeologists, to say nothing of royalty, found vestiges of the first known inhabitants of the peninsula, the Iberians coming from Africa after 3000 B.C. Later Spain was overrun from the north, and to this day can be seen the Celtic admixture in the population—fair-skinned, light-eyed, and even blond types, especially in the Basque provinces. After 800 B.C. appeared the Phoenicians, who established trading centers such as Cádiz, reputedly the oldest continuously inhabited city in Europe and later the Bourbons' major naval base. Subsequent Greek colonies left few lasting monuments in Spain, but the Carthaginians after 300 B.C. contributed city names such as Cartagena (New Carthage), the port from which Alfonso sailed away forever in 1931, and Barcelona (named for Hamilcar Barcas, Hannibal's father), the last stronghold of the Bourbons' Hapsburg rivals for the throne in the early eighteenth century.

Pamplona, through which Felipe V passed in 1700, was named for the Roman general Pompey, Julius Caesar's unsuccessful foe, and in Segovia the young king saw the great double arched aqueduct, an architectural reminder of the centuries of Roman rule. At times Roman Spain had almost seemed to dominate the mother country rather than vice versa, being the birthplace of such powerful emperors as Trajan and Hadrian and of such cultural lights as the two Senecas. The two most significant Roman contributions to Spain were the language and Christianity. Pious Spaniards accepted the legend that St. James himself preached and converted in the north of their country, and after the miraculous discovery of his bones on a hillside in Galicia the city of Santiago de Compostela (St. James of the field of stars) became the greatest pilgrimage center of Christendom in medieval times.

The Bourbons' first royal predecessors in Spain were the kings of the Visigoths, after these barbarians invaded the peninsula A.D. 414 (coming on the heels of the Vandals, who gave their name to Andalusia and then crossed over to Africa). The Visigothic monarchy, with its capital at Toledo, was elective rather than hereditary, producing the spectacle of thirty kings in three centuries, few of whom died in bed, a lesson that Spanish monarchists ponder to this day. Other than being an ethnic drop in the bucket, the Visigoths left little mark on Spain, unlike, say, the contemporary Franks in France or the Anglo-Saxons in England. The oppressiveness of the Visigothic rule explains in great measure why the Spanish peoples welcomed new African conquerors, the Moslems, or Moors.

The Moorish conquest of Spain after 711 was virtually total, and Moorish rule of all or parts of Spain continued for almost eight centuries. The Bourbons would find that Arab influences were what made Spain so un-French, so un-European. The first capital of the Moorish kingdom or caliphate was at Córdoba, which became the largest city in Europe west of Constantinople and certainly the most civilized, with its libraries, observatories, schools, and hospitals. In the twelfth century Córdoba was surpassed by Seville in size and cultural splendor. Later Christian rulers of Spain would not destroy but merely appropriate in awe such magnificent buildings as Córdoba's Great Mosque, the largest outside Mecca, and Seville's Alcázar, a palace and gardens of unusual magnificence (the present pretender Don Juan played here in the 1920's). Architecturally, the Moorish imprint on Spain could not be mistaken by an eighteenth-century Bourbon any more than by a twentieth-century tourist. It is less easy to appreciate the tremendous Moorish contributions to the economic system. Most difficult and most important to understand are the counteractions the Moors produced in Christian Spain.

The Asturias, an inaccessible and mountainous area in the northwest of Spain which once long before resisted Roman control, was also the first focus of Christian resistance to Moslem rule. In 718 the tribes of this stubborn pocket raised a new leader named Pelayo upon a shield, and in 722 he led them to a resounding victory over a Moorish expedition in the valley of Covadonga. The man whom Arab historians myopically dismissed as "a savage ass named Pelayo" was actually to give birth to a great and lasting dynasty, for Pelayo's daughter married a local chieftain named Alfonso, who was to be the first of a long bloodline of King Alfonsos, ending with the unlucky thirteenth in 1931. The bravery of the mountaineers has been commemorated by titling the heir to the throne Prince of the Asturias, the Spanish equivalent of Prince of Wales. Recent Bourbon kings have also favored the title Count of Covadonga as an incognito when traveling abroad on private missions.

The Christian reconquest of Spain occupied the entire Middle Ages. From the remote fastness of the Asturias and Galicia the subjects of Pelayo's successors ventured south and east onto the plains of León, and later they settled Castile, the "land of castles" so named for the lines of strongholds built to resist Moorish efforts at resubjugation. Not until 1085 did the Christians reach the center of the peninsula and capture a major Moorish city, Toledo falling in that year to an Alfonso VI who made it capital of New Castile. A contemporary of this king, his sometime ally and his sometime enemy, was the renowned El Cid. This double-dealing but romantic and successful adventurer sought to enlist as soldiers "those who want to stop their toil and get rich." The antiwork spirit and abhorrence of manual labor and business activity came to motivate Castilian conquistadores both in the reconquest and later in the New World. The crusading spirit, a kind of holy war fanaticism in imitation of the Moslems, was the other great legacy of the medieval Spanish experience.

The reconquest also shaped the social structure. The crown granted huge blocs of newly won lands to the church, four military orders, and great nobles. In time 2 or 3 percent of the population owned 97 percent of the soil. The most important nobles became known as the grandees (*grandes* in Spanish). One of the treasured privileges of the grandees that the first Bourbon found singular was the right to keep their hats on in the presence of the king. Another thing that amazed the Frenchman was the sheer number of the lesser nobles, the hidalgos. Hundreds of thousands of hidalgos, even if later reduced to poverty, jealously guarded the appellation "Don" and the right to display coats of arms on their houses, all in recognition of military services dating from the reconquest.

Briefly it seemed that Castile's destiny might lie in southern France when in the twelfth century a King Alfonso VIII married Eleanor, daughter of King Henry II of England, and gained Aquitaine as her dowry, but Aquitaine was given away as the dowry of a Spanish princess in turn, and Castile's drive southward recommenced. The turning point in the great contest of Christian and Moorish Spaniards was the Battle of Las Navas de Tolosa in 1212. After Alfonso VIII and his knights won a stunning victory, it fell to a Fernando III to capture Córdoba in 1236 and Seville in 1248, the latter city becoming capital of a kingdom that embraced Old and New

Castile, as well as all Andalusia except Moorish Granada. For these conquests and for acts of piety Ferdinand III was called the Saint and was later canonized as San Fernando. Another landmark event of his reign was the first meeting of the Castilian Cortes in 1250, a parliament which predated the English one by fifteen years but which subsequently failed to develop the power of its counterpart to defy royal arbitrariness. The Castilian tradition of a relatively strong monarchy was to be appropriated appreciatively by the Bourbons.

While Castile grew mighty in northern, central, and southern Spain, the Christian kingdom of Aragón flourished in the east. Actually, this realm, united under its own line of kings, was composed of three kingdoms: Aragón itself, landlocked and pastoral; Catalonia, with its prosperous trading center Barcelona; and Valencia, rich in ports and agriculture, newly conquered from the Moors in the thirteenth century. The eastern kingdoms were unique for their business enterprise, which encompassed the whole Mediterranean, and for their strong constitutionalism, which involved *fueros* (tax exemptions and other rights) being jealously maintained against royal encroachment by their three Cortes. The "oath of the Aragonese" the later Bourbon rulers were to find less picturesque than galling: "We who are as good as you swear to you who are no better than we to accept you as our king and sovereign lord, provided you observe our liberties, but if not, not."

"The most glorious epoch" in the history of Spain was the reign of Fernando and Isabel, to state the view of the noted nineteenth-century American historian William Prescott, a view shared by virtually every Spanish historian. The clandestine marriage of the wily Fernando and the high-minded Isabel in 1469 began the train of events which brought about the union of Aragón and Castile (Isabel was actually something of a usurper in Castile, but she, like the contemporary Tudors, had able literary apologists). Then, the conquest of Moorish Granada completed the unification of Spain in 1492, the same year Christopher Columbus laid the foundations of the vast Spanish overseas empire, which the Bourbons inherited virtually intact. Fernando and Isabel were tireless legislators of mercantilism, determined practitioners of royal absolutism, and successful pursuers of marriage and military diplomacy, so that Spain emerged as the leading power in Europe. They were also responsible for the establishment of the Inquisition and the expulsion of the Jews, Spain's natural middle class. These two actions, which many later historians see as blots on their memory, if not disastrous mistakes, earned Fernando and Isabel in their lifetimes the appellation "Catholic Monarchs" from the Spanish profligate Pope Alexander VI (all subsequent Spanish rulers, including the Bourbons, are referred to in diplomatic correspondence as "Catholic Majesty").

The era of unleashed energies and great deeds continued under the illustrious king known to the Spanish as Carlos I but better remembered in history as the Holy Roman Emperor Charles V. The coming of the first Bourbon in 1700 was prefigured in 1517, when Carlos of Hapsburg, seventeen, first landed in Spain, a complete stranger to his subjects but in time the founder of a new dynasty. Carlos was the son of Fernando and Isabel's sole heir, Juana the Mad, and of Philip of Burgundy (his premature death drove the wife to complete insanity and seclusion in a cloister until her death in 1555). From his parents and grandparents Carlos inherited the greatest conglomeration of territories ever before controlled by a single ruler—the Austrian dominions in central Europe, the Netherlands, various duchies in Italy, Aragón, Castile, and the New World. To rule this vast empire, Carlos set up a complicated system of government, involving first of all a number of central councils, such as the Council of Castile or the Council of the Indies or the Council of Finance, and then nine viceroys for the outlying realms, such as the viceroy of Naples or the viceroy of Mexico. "No states were more governed in the sixteenth century than those of the King of Spain." They were well governed too, in terms of peace and public order, for a long time, but eventually the administrative system became inefficient, corrupt, and utterly exasperating to its Bourbon inheritors. Imposing as his power and works were, Carlos I ended up abdicating in frustration and exhaustion, a victim of Hapsburg melancholia. All his reign he had had to fight France (for a brief while in 1525 he held the French king prisoner in a small castle in the little known town of Madrid). All his reign he had to counter the depredations of the Ottoman Turks in central Europe and in the Mediterranean. All his reign he had to confront the new disruptiveness of the Protestant Reformation, especially in Germany. For such staggering missions, largely borne by Spain, it did not even suffice that the amount of bullion flowing in from the Americas rose from 1,000,000 pesos at the beginning of the reign to 12,000,000 at the end.

The second Hapsburg, Felipe II (Philip II), who came to the throne in 1556, was another giant among Renaissance rulers and essentially another "splendid failure." Royal bureaucrat that he was ("no secretary in the world uses more paper than his majesty"), Felipe II was responsible for giving Spain its modern capital Madrid, choosing for efficiency's sake not a venerable metropolis like Seville but a small town in the very geometric center of the peninsula. The "royal kill-joy," according to the American visitor John Hay three centuries later, "delighted in having the dreariest capital in Europe." Even though Madrid grew from a few thousand people to 150,000 by 1700, industry and suburbs did not surround the city until very recent times, so that the capital did seem a place stuck in the middle of nowhere, the domain of courtiers and clerks in Felipe's time and later of politicians and their hangers-on in the Bourbon era. Thirty miles north of Madrid Felipe built the forbiddingly gray and harshly symmetrical Escorial, "the grandest ideal of majesty and ennui the world has ever seen," again according to Hay. Besides being a museum and a monastery (the king's cell was his office), the Escorial became the mausoleum of the Hapsburg and Bourbon royalty. Two empty niches remain in the burial chamber of the kings.

The great successes of the reign of Felipe II were the defeat of the Turkish naval might at Lepanto in 1571 and the annexation of Portugal in 1580, adding its huge overseas empire to Spain's own. The great disasters were the revolt of the Spanish Netherlands after 1568, depriving the crown of its richest realm, and the annihilation of the Spanish Armada sent against Protestant England in 1588, a drama in which the military, commercial, and religious future of the whole world was at stake. Among the unfortunate results of the king's four marriages were a heart-broken Mary Tudor (the Prado Museum has an entrancing portrait of this English Queen of Spain), a deranged monster as firstborn son who had to be done away with (the Don Carlos of opera), and a sickly and unpromising heir.

Hapsburg Spain went from the heights of power in the sixteenth century to the depths of degradation in the seventeenth. The first two rulers were the colorless, vice-less Felipe III (1598–1621) and the colorless, vice-ridden Felipe IV (1621–1665). Both let themselves be controlled by *validos*, or favorites, who, if not completely self-seeking, were less than able. The domination of favorites was a Hapsburg legacy some of the Bourbons unwisely perpetuated. The costs of royal incompetence were staggering: recurrent state bankruptcies; the loss of Portugal; revolts in Naples and Catalonia; humiliation at the outcome of the Thirty Years' War in Germany; and repeated defeats on land and sea by the Netherlands, England, and France, the rising powers which Spain insanely chose to fight, often simultaneously. Militarily Spain became the laughingstock of Europe, a condition from which the new dynasty would briefly rescue it. A measure of the nation's near collapse was the population decline from 9,000,000 to 6,000,000 between 1500 and 1700.

Paradoxically, the golden age of Spanish arts and letters continued well into the seventeenth century. If the reign of Felipe II had its El Greco and St. Teresa, the later era had its Velázquez (who did for the Hapsburgs in portraiture what Goya would do for the Bourbons) and its Cervantes (his *Don Quixote* remains the most widely read novel ever written).

For all the universality of appeal of such giants as Velázquez and Cervantes, their works show an acute awareness that their native country was in trouble, that its great days were over, and that it pursued unhealthy illusions. After the Armada and other defeats seemed to reveal that Spaniards were not God's chosen but God's damned, the nation's intellectuals began to indulge in earnest speculation about the reasons for Spain's precipitous decline, the same basic subject which has preoccupied historians more than any other aspect of the country's past. This earlier soul-searching aided the Bourbons more than they admitted when they set out to revitalize Spain in the eighteenth century.

It once was fashionable for the French-thinking rulers and their advisers to put down Spain's ills simply to "superstition, sloth, and ignorance." At best these pejoratives are only useful categorizations for more fundamental problems. Superstition in Spaniards, symbolized by the Inquisition, was also accompanied by a heroic crusading zeal which led them to overcommit themselves both in Europe and in the New World—that is, to pursue the dream of "universality," this being the main cause of Spain's failure, according to the widely admired historian Salvador de Madariaga. Sloth in the Spaniards, which reflects a historically conditioned distaste for making money, was also the accident of New World riches imposed on an unbalanced, backward, and mismanaged economy. Ignorance in Spaniards often took the form of suspiciousness of European ideas, but more important were the stupidity and unwillingness to change of the ruling classes. The enlightened Bourbons of the next period could and did reverse the processes of decline; the less than brilliant ones still a century later failed to keep pace with history and brought about the near ruin of both country and dynasty.

All royal families are alternately heroic and outrageous, and their human condition written large is in itself interesting, provoking both thought and titillation. The Bourbons have their full share of the noble and vicious, the banal and the bizarre. The melancholic monarch, the enlightened despot, the cuckold, the tyrant, the nymphomaniac, and the playboy are not the sum of Spanish history, or even necessarily the heart of it, but they are unquestionably a vital feature of it.

I.
The Crisis of 1700–1714:
The Crown Disputed

1. The Last Gasps of the Old Dynasty

THE reign of the last surviving male Spanish Hapsburg, Carlos II, was the very nadir of the nation's fortunes. It has been characterized as "the monarchy without a monarch." His life despaired of from the moment of birth, Carlos confounded all by living for thirty-nine years. His two marriages meant the year-to-year possibility of an heir, but Europe's kings expected otherwise and began maneuvers to divide up the Spanish empire. His death caused a world war, in the course of which the Bourbon dynasty secured possession of the throne of Spain.

The father of Carlos II, Felipe IV, had been anything but backward in providing for the succession to say nothing of indulging his own sexual appetites, which were extraordinary, with upwards of thirty royal bastards as proof. By his first Portuguese wife Felipe IV had a daughter and son who lived beyond infancy. The marriage of the daughter, named María Teresa, to Louis XIV of France turned out to be a crux of history later, but at the time Spain's expectations centered on the son, named Baltasar Carlos, a sturdy lad with a steady gaze judging from the charming Velázquez portrait of him at age fourteen. Then suddenly he was dead at seventeen. His father remarried, to the son's intended and his own niece, María Ana of the Austrian Hapsburgs being only thirteen at the time of the first negotiations. Six of the first eight children of María Ana and Felipe IV died at childbirth or soon after. A surviving daughter, Margarita, also delightfully captured by Velázquez as a doll-like princess in pinks and blues, eventually married the Holy Roman Emperor Leopold I, with the result of adding Austrian pretensions to the Spanish throne to those of the French. A son,

21

optimistically named Felipe Prospero, was born in 1657, only to expire from compounded ailments at age four. A few days later in 1661 Queen María Ana gave birth to another boy, Carlos. The baby, representing the last fling of a libertine father and the lingering hope of Spain, was born without complications, perhaps thanks to the presence of such sacred relics in the delivery room as three thorns from Christ's crown, two nails from the Cross, a piece of the Virgin's mantle, and the cane of Santo Domingo.

The official gazette told the world that the new royal infant was "most beautiful in features, large head, dark skin, and somewhat over plump." A skeptical Louis XIV questioned both the health of the baby and its sex. His agent in Madrid duly reported to Versailles that Carlos was "very feeble" and subject to rashes and suppurations, a general prognosis which proved correct. On the death of Felipe IV in 1665 the four-year-old succeeded him as Carlos II. The underdeveloped child king had to be presented to the notables of the realm supported on strings held by a nurse. He remained something of a puppet for the rest of his days.

Carlos grew up to be a near monster and imbecile, the victim of two centuries of Hapsburg interbreeding, the like of which in history one has for comparison only the Ptolemaic pharaohs. Four generations of Carlos' direct predecessors—that is, Felipe IV, Felipe III, Felipe II, and Carlos I—had all married cousins or nieces. Analytically, the king's father and mother would each have 8 ancestors in the third generation, 16 in the fourth, and 32 in the fifth, for a total of 56 relationships each or 112 together. In the case of Carlos these 112 family relationships were shared by only 38 individuals.

It is not difficult to trace back the poisoned genes that made Carlos a feebleminded grotesque. On the Spanish side, Isabel of Castile was a healthy aberration, descended as she was from a schizophrenic mother and a degenerate father. Her daughter, Juana the Mad, proved to be dementia personified. Yet, incredibly, seven of Carlos' eight grandparents claimed descent from this mad queen. On the Hapsburg side of Carlos' genealogy, Isabel's contemporary the Emperor Maximilian was notoriously eccentric, as well as being facially misshapen. The Strigel portrait of the emperor and his children shows a bizarre collection of jutting jaws and gaping mouths. Maximilian's Burgundian wife contributed a family predisposition to outsized, pendant lower lips. The dynasty came to suffer from acrocephaly, an endocrine dysfunction that produced not only physical deformity but also tendencies toward epilepsy, nervousness, and melancholy, all of which were evident in some degree in Carlos' renowned ancestors Carlos I and Felipe II and in an extreme degree in Felipe II's ill-fated monster son Don Carlos. The family ugliness compounded with each generation, and so it came to be that Carlos looked "like a caricature" of the dynastic portraits—pale, wild-eyed, and with his chin taking up fully one-third of his long, narrow head. Wigs hid the fact that he was nearly bald above his huge forehead.

Carlos' jaw stuck out so far that his teeth did not meet, and not being able to chew properly, he satisfied a ravenous appetite by swallowing food whole, thus adding indigestion to a long catalogue of physical ailments. The king was subject to fits and seizures; he suffered fainting spells and was often prostrated for days on end. These conditions and Carlos' rashes, discharges, and eruptions were treated by an endless succession of Spanish and foreign doctors, but to little avail. Faith healers and exorcists were also called in, for in time the court became convinced that a monarch so hideously afflicted could only be bewitched. "Carlos the Bewitched" was, indeed, his most familiar sobriquet during his time. A modern scholar suggests that the ulcers, diseased bones, and other disorders point to congenital syphilis, a result of Felipe IV's escapades in Madrid's slums.

Carlos' health was such a preoccupation that his education suffered completely. Elderly courtiers, superstitious nurses, and a bizarre collection of dwarfs were his only childhood companions. He grew up barely able to write and ignorant of all books except devotional tracts. Feebleminded and rachitic, Carlos was largely incapable of ruling. Yet he was expected to rule, even to save, his long-suffering nation. "A sub-human person always treated as superhuman," Carlos was at once pathetic and heroic, for he always tried to act the king and did his best to ensure the succession, which—and this was his great importance—was entirely at his discretion, his last word, his will, his say-so, if not actually his seed.

During Carlos' minority and also well into his majority Spain was misgoverned by his ignorant and selfish mother, Queen María Ana of Austria, and her favorites. No Cortes were summoned, and the councils devoted themselves to petty intrigues, while the economy went from stagnation to collapse. "It would be difficult to describe to its full extent the disorder in the government of Spain," wrote the French ambassador in 1668, adding that lack of money caused the prisons to be unstaffed and therefore unfilled. His English counterpart reported to London: "This country is in a most miserable condition. No head to govern, and every man in office does what he pleases without fear of being called to account." A Venetian envoy observed: "From the poor to the rich everyone devours the estate of the King, some taking little bites, the nobility large ones, and the greatest enormous portions. . . . Many think it is a miracle that the Monarchy is still in existence." Still another witness noted that "of the gold of the treasure fleet only a fraction ever reaches the Treasury. It is remarkable that the kingdom is able to carry on at all." In the view of a modern historian, the reign of the miserable Carlos II exposed the "moral and intellectual bankruptcy of the Castilian ruling class" and "at a moment when it could least be afforded."

More military defeats were in store for the exhausted country, as its armies went unpaid and its navy rotted down to a handful of serviceable vessels. Louis XIV of France, making arrogant territorial claims in the name of his Spanish wife, annexed a large portion of Flanders, including Lille, after the War of Devolution of 1667–1668, and later Carlos' brother-in-law seized Franche-Comté in 1674. On the Spanish Main the pirates united for the first time under Henry Morgan, and in 1671 they sacked Panama, earning Morgan not punishment but knighthood and the governorship of Jamaica from the English king, the namesake of Spain's own, Charles II.

For many Spaniards the only ray of hope in these years of degradation lay in the king's half brother, the bastard Don Juan of Austria. Son of Felipe IV by an actress and thus fortunately only half Hapsburg, Don Juan had displayed bravery, energy, and intelligence in his military and administrative career, but he was weak of will. In the first of three coups, Don Juan made a show of force against the regent in 1669, drove her rapacious confessor from the country, and then retired to become viceroy of Aragón. Again in 1675, when Carlos II was declared of age, Don Juan tried secretly to separate the king from his mother's influence. Finally, in 1677 the bastard prince marched another army to Madrid, exiled the queen mother's new favorite to the Philippines, and announced an ambitious program of reforms, which soon were dropped. Don Juan abruptly died in 1679, "the first of that long series of flashy leaders from whom the Castilians, expecting everything, obtained nothing." He represented two precedents from which the Bourbons would suffer: the popular general trying to change the government by a manifesto and the outlying provinces interfering in the affairs of Madrid.

The king's marriage to a French princess was an achievement of Don Juan, who just before his death negotiated the match against the Austrian preferences of the queen mother. Marriage seemed to be one subject that really aroused Carlos II. He angrily rejected the idea of waiting for a nine-year-old Hapsburg archduchess to grow up and he declared himself infatuated with the portrait of Marie Louise, daughter of the Duke of Orléans (the effeminate "Monsieur," brother of Louis XIV) and Henrietta of England (the unhappy daughter of the tragic Charles I). Ironically, Louis XIV, who in twenty years would settle for nothing less than all Spain, approved the Spanish alliance but "without any question whatsoever of fortresses or territory, as he would not give up so much as one garden for his niece's marriage, as it mattered very little to him whether she married into Spain or not." Despite this French refusal of concessions, the Spanish ambassador advised consent to the match, for the princess was "of remarkable artistry and physique, tall in proportions, graceful, and well modeled with dark eyes and hair, and most to the point apt for immediate fertilization, according to the information I have received."

The marriage was first celebrated by proxy at Fontainebleau, in the course of which one thousand ortolans were served to the guests on plates of gold and silver. Spain could not even afford a suitable carriage to accommodate its new queen, to say nothing of decent roads, so that Marie Louise was brought into the country in a litter and was wed to Carlos in a miserable village near Burgos. It was a royal custom to grant tax exemption to the town of the king's wedding so that the choice of a large Spanish city would have been ruinous financially. Despite the unfortunate preliminaries, the royal marriage appeared felicitous. Now called María Luisa, the queen was indeed exceedingly pretty, as well as being pleasure-loving. The king's health was never better. The couple shared a devotion to hunting by day and to musical performances by night. María Luisa patiently played cards for the smallest stakes with her childlike husband, who in turn took actions to relax Spanish etiquette.

The marriage of Carlos II and María Luisa soured when it became apparent that they were not going to have any children. The disappointment of their sex life not only embittered them but engaged the attention of the whole court, much of the population of Madrid, and the major chancelleries of Europe. Everything and everyone were blamed. The French queen's riding horses was one natural criticism by prudish Spaniards. Another easy explanation was that Louis XIV of France had ulterior designs and was sending his niece abortifacients and sexual depressants disguised as aphrodisiacs. Bewitchment of both the royal couple was expounded. Nobody dared suggest that the king was at fault. If Carlos had at least cheated on his wife, there might have been proof of something. Fragments of diplomatic dispatches and modern sophistication combine to suggest that the king was not impotent, nor the queen unwilling, but that mutual ignorance of the sex act prevented procreation. Carlos' problem was praecatio ejacualis; the royal couple, however active in bed, never experienced truly mutual coitus. The king preoccupied himself more and more with hunting, and the queen let herself get fat. She kept her lucrative position, as well as her influence over him, by occasionally announcing pregnancies. Nor was María Luisa beyond saying that she had been distressed to the point of abortion when she did not have her way.

Queen María Luisa died suddenly in February, 1689, following a gastric upset. Her Spanish doctors blamed it on her exotic French diet. The French, notably her famous letter-writing stepmother, "Madame," were absolutely sure that she was poisoned, poisoned by the Austrian party at court, headed, of course, by the queen mother. Modern historians variously interpret the evidence. Spanish scholars accuse foreign scholars of indulging in the *leyenda negra,* the black legend that Spaniards are so cruel and benighted as to be capable of anything. A recent British biographer of Carlos does find very suspicious evidence of the Austrian ambassador's foreknowledge of the queen's demise, as well as his satisfaction from it.

There was no question in the Council of State but that Carlos II should remarry as soon as possible so as to give Spain an heir. By now the question of the succession to the Spanish empire was crucial to European diplomacy. Louis XIV had long since written off the possibility of Carlos' producing a successor and thought more in terms of taking Spain for a Bourbon prince by force. Other considerations led Louis XIV to begin a Rhine campaign in 1688, which in turn freed William of Orange to invade England and depose the Catholic James II. The new Netherlands-English ruler, William III, therewith took the lead in forming the League of Augsburg of 1688 to counter French aggression in Europe. Having fought and lost so many wars to France in the seventeenth century, Spain unhesitatingly joined in the new war, which dragged on painfully for all concerned until 1697. The upshot was that Carlos married a bride favored by the anti-French party and that the bride had to be conveyed to Spain by sea in an English warship.

Carlos' second wife was Mariana of Neuburg, a princess of the electoral palatine whose main distinction was that her sister was the wife of the Holy Roman Emperor Leopold I. The king had said of her portrait that "nobody could call her ugly," and he decided that she looked fecund. The story of this marriage was that of the first all over again: the childless bride became frustrated and embittered, alternately announcing pregnancies and miscarriages; the king sulked and languished physically; and the court and the foreign ambassadors indulged in intrigue and talk again of witchcraft plots.

With Carlos' health deteriorating and with no prospective heir, the main concern of the various factions at court became that of persuading the king to designate in a will one of his collateral relatives as his successor. Carlos balked, however, even flew into rages, since any suggestion of his making a will seemed an affront to his virility. Nonetheless, everyone else preoccupied themselves with the several living contenders to the throne and their complicated claims. Two noisy claimants were generally ignored: the King of Portugal and the Duke of Savoy. The three prime candidacies represented the royal houses of France, Austria, and Bavaria.

The French case rested on the fact that both Louis XIII and Louis XIV had wed Spanish princesses, even though these at the times of their marriages renounced any future claims to the Spanish throne. The fine print of the Treaty of the Pyrenees of 1659, which sealed the end of a long war through the marriage of Louis XIV and Carlos' sister María Teresa, provided that her renunciation was valid only on the payment of a large dowry, and this was set at a figure ridiculously more than a bankrupt Spain could afford and was currently in complete default. Moreover, the renunciations in general were made in the spirit of keeping Spain and France from being ruled by a single monarch; the accession of a younger son would not cause this problem. Accordingly, in the most legalistic and even religious terms, Europe's most powerful monarch put forth his second grandson, Philip of Anjou (born 1683) as the rightful successor. Since France was again at war with Spain, there were few voices at the court to support Louis.

The Austrian Hapsburg monarchs had also married daughters of Felipe III and Felipe IV; these princesses' renunciations had been less explicit. The current Emperor Leopold I maintained that his first wife, Margarita, another sister of Carlos II, had resigned her rights directly to him and indirectly to his son by a third wife, the Archduke Charles (born 1685). The Austrian case was tirelessly and vociferously upheld by Carlos' queen, Mariana of Neuburg, sister of the latter empress.

The third claim also derived from the Infanta María Antonia: her surviving daughter by Leopold I married the Electoral Prince of Bavaria, and this couple's son, the Electoral Prince Joseph Ferdinand (born 1692), was impartially considered to have the best title to the Spanish throne. The cause of the electoral prince was dearest to the heart of a very influential person, his grandmother the Queen Mother María Ana. She used every resource in her power to secure her royal son's nomination of this heir, while her daughter-in-law, the queen, and the barely represented French interest did everything possible to block it.

The death of the queen mother in May, 1696, accomplished what she had not been able to do in her lifetime. She passed on as a result of a huge cancerous tumor in her breast, despite the incessant prayers of the king, who had never shaken off the spell of her influence. Himself gravely debilitated again and his wife's counterinfluence temporarily removed by a near fatal illness, Carlos II was induced by the Council of State secretly to will the Spanish empire to the Bavarian prince in the fall of 1696. The king's condition was so serious that his doctors ordered him not to sleep with his wife.

Although French troops captured Barcelona in the summer, the War of the League of Augsburg was over in September, 1697. By the Treaty of Ryswick Spain received very generous terms from Louis XIV, who had higher future stakes in view and was once again in a position to send an ambassador to Madrid to pursue them. Carlos II recovered from his worst ailments and was permitted to resume intercourse. Curiously beloved, the long-suffering monarch was joyously received that fall by the city of Toledo in a festive round of bullfights and balls, and even the queen seemed popular. It was now her turn to change the succession picture, not by giving birth but by going over to the French. Feeling slighted by the Austrian party and above all fearing the prospect of retirement to a nunnery, Queen Mariana grasped avidly at the French ambassador's hints that she could remain queen by espousing the Bourbon cause, perhaps even the Bourbon claimant himself. These behind-doors dealings became an open secret at court and were duly related to London by Ambassador Alexander Stanhope, who also reported that Carlos II had taken a turn for the worse and looked like a "ghost." The French ambassador was given instructions by his king to cultivate the goodwill of the nobility and the populace and, more important, to bribe the governors of the northern fortresses in the event of the king's death and the subsequent entry of Philip of Anjou into Spain.

Louis XIV showed himself capable of pursuing more than one Spanish policy, for in October, 1698, the European capitals in general and Madrid in particular were stunned to learn that France had joined its traditional enemies, England and the Netherlands, in a treaty of partition of the Spanish realms. It was agreed that Spain itself, the Spanish Netherlands, and the Indies would go to the electoral prince, while the Archduke Charles would be compensated with the duchy of Milan and France would gain Naples, Sicily, parts of Tuscany, and the Pyrenean province of Guipúzcoa. Since a new general conflict seemed unthinkable, Europe relaxed in the belief that the question of the Spanish succession had been rationalized and internationalized.

The partitioning powers had not taken into account Spain and its king, to whom the totality of the Spanish dominions was a sacred unity, a "seamless garment" like the robe of Christ. As Stanhope wrote home, "they will rather deliver themselves up . . . to the devil, so they may go all together, than be dismembered." Carlos II was provoked in November, 1698, to name once again the Bavarian prince sole heir to all his domains. As always when he was aroused by a decision, the king's health improved.

A few months later came the news of the sudden death of the Bavarian prince in February, 1699, making nonsense of both the partition treaty and Carlos' will. There was hardly time to speculate whether the prince had died from smallpox or from mischief, as Europe's diplomats returned to the succession problem. Perhaps it was national frustration more than anything else—frustration in the loss of the fantasy of a secured future under a rightful king—that led to the great street riots in Madrid and Valladolid in April, 1699. Carlos was forced to dismiss unpopular officials, and the price of food was lowered. While the ownership of Spain's royal prerogatives was being debated by the courtiers, the people of the country were suffering perhaps more so than ever in their history. By midsummer the king was observed to be "sensibly worse and worse" by Stanhope, who said he "staggered all the way" at the Corpus Christi procession. Then, there was another dramatic recovery, to the point that the English ambassador reported: "His Catholic Majesty . . . has the same looks I remember him in the time of his best health." Some observers linked this to the official discovery and burning of some malevolent charms—dolls studded with nails.

The next development was a Second Partition Treaty signed between England and France in March, 1700, to which the Netherlands acceded. Again the Spanish empire was to be divided; Spain and the Indies were accorded the Archduke Charles, with the provision that they would never come into the possession of the Austrian line of Hapsburgs; Naples and Sicily, parts of Tuscany, and Guipúzcoa again went to France, plus the duchy of Lorraine (the Duke of Lorraine being awarded Milan in exchange). This treaty, provocative of events even though it came to naught, contained two great ironies. Louis XIV, mistakenly despairing of securing the whole Spanish inheritance, made the unwitting move that did eventually gain him all. Leopold I, confident of winning all, refused to accept the part accorded to him by the treaty and ended up with nothing.

Once again the willingness of its fellow powers to dismember its empire threw Spain into turmoil and its king into tantrums. Popular rage was directed especially at the treachery of Louis XIV, and the Austrian party seemed in the ascendancy. There were rumors of a new royal will naming the archduke sole heir. The queen, who had returned to the Austrian cause, complicated things by announcing a new pregnancy, soon proved false as so often before. When the king's health again became desperate, the Council of State supplicated for a new royal will, only to be informed by the king that its own decision was solicited. The council's deliberations came back again and again to a single question: what country had the power to keep the empire intact? An overwhelming majority decided that France alone had the might to defend, as well as the greatest potential to harm, Spain itself and its outlying dominions, like the Netherlands and Milan. The Pope, asked for his advice, supported this decision. Accordingly, on October 3 Carlos II secretly named the Bourbon Philip of Anjou heir to all his dominions. The desperate king, who previously had opened the tombs of his ancestors in the Escorial seeking some sign, now broke down in tears at the thought that he was betraying Hapsburg family traditions.

A month later, on November 1, Carlos was dead, overwhelmed at age thirty-nine by his hideous afflictions. He had kept the world waiting so long, and yet his passing was too sudden, in that the powers had not agreed on the way to compromise and peace. He had tried his best but left a prostrate Spain with an uncertain future.

Following the king's death, the Duke of Abrantes appeared outside the bedchamber where an assemblage awaited to hear the royal will. The French ambassador advanced toward the duke with smiling confidence, but the Spaniard passed him with a look of disdain and went over to embrace the Austrian ambassador with the greatest respect and affection. Abrantes maliciously repeated his gesture, then said, "Sir, it is with the greatest pleasure—Sir, it is with the greatest satisfaction—for my whole life—I take my leave of the most illustrious House of Austria."

2. Felipe of Bourbon Versus Carlos of Hapsburg

It was a splendidly memorable scene even by the theatrical standards of the court of Versailles during the long and eventful reign of the Sun King. The great folding doors of the royal office were thrown open, and Louis XIV appeared with his grandson before the expectant assemblage in the grand saloon. "Gentlemen, you see here the King of Spain," Louis announced solemnly. "His descent called him to this Crown; the deceased king so ordered it by his testament; the whole nation desired it and earnestly entreated me to give my assent; such was the will of Heaven. I have fulfilled it with joy."

Turning to Philip, *le grand monarque* continued: "Be a good Spaniard; that is now your first duty; but remember that you are born a Frenchman and maintain the unity between the two nations; this is the way to make them happy and to preserve the peace of Europe." The animated murmurs of the crowd became cheers, which Louix XIV acknowledged gravely, and then he again addressed his grandson with carefully chosen words: "Let us now give thanks to God. May it please Your Majesty to attend mass." They swept out with graceful dignity, the sixteen-year-old on the right of the sixty-two-year-old, an honor reserved to foreign monarchs. The day was November 16, 1700.

A brief while before, Louis XIV had summoned the Spanish ambassador to be the first to salute the new monarch, who would reign with the title Felipe V. Overwhelmed with feeling, the Marquis of Castel dos Ruis fell to his knees and exclaimed: "What a pleasure. There are no longer any Pyrenees. They have sunk into the ground and we now form a single nation." The ambassador meant only to emphasize the prospects of peace between the traditionally hostile nations. For much of Europe, however, the ringing phrase *il n'y a plus des Pyrénées* had the ominous implication of an intended fusion of the huge power of France with the huge extent of the

Spanish empire, to the complete detriment of the balance of power. Spaniards too might ponder how close their association with France was to be and where it might lead them. In December that same year Louis had the Parlement de Paris register a patent whereby Felipe kept conditional rights to the throne of France. Was this a Bourbon defiance of the world or just a wise precaution?

Louis' decision to accept on behalf of Felipe had been made only after many agitated sessions of the king's council, some of which met in the apartments of his mistress, Madame de Maintenon. He later confided to a relative that he would be blamed whatever he did. When the courier from Madrid arrived with the news of Carlos' death and will, it was known that the Spanish government had given him orders to proceed to Vienna with the same offer of all or nothing, if Versailles refused. Yet going back on the Partition Treaty negotiated in good faith but months before would incur against France the active hostility of England and the Netherlands in addition to the implacable enmity of the Austrian Hapsburgs. To honor the Partition Treaty, however, would mean extensive military measures to force it on Spain, without any assurance that the maritime powers would aid France in this. A major war seemed inevitable one way or the other, so that it was really just a choice of causes. Not only was the cause of Felipe V the most profitable for France, but also it was legally just in terms of the testament of Carlos II and logically consistent with the Spanish marriage designs of Louis' ancestors.

Felipe V set out for his new kingdom on December 4, fifteen days before his seventeenth birthday. His grandfather, whom he now was supposed to address as "My Brother," escorted him as far as Sceaux, and his two brothers rode with him to the Pyrenees, where they took leave with tearful embraces, at once joyful and fearful for Felipe's future. The young king crossed the Spanish frontier on January 28, 1701, and was greeted at Fuenterrabía by the French ambassador, the Duc Henri d' Harcourt, who among other pieces of advice warned Felipe against the possibility of his being poisoned. Fear of death from what he ate became a lifelong obsession of this monarch, who nonetheless was tactful enough from the first to affect a delight in Spanish-style cooking. His new subjects responded with enthusiasm as Felipe made his slow progress south toward the capital. He passed through the city of Burgos in Old Castile with its particularly magnificent Gothic cathedral, through Segovia with its Roman aqueduct, and over the Guadarrama Mountain divide to Felipe II's grim Escorial palace in New Castile. He entered Madrid on February 18 to such great acclaim that many people were crushed to death in the uproar. As heralds cried out, "Castile, Castile, Castile, for the King Don Felipe, master of these realms," the Bourbon took up residence in the Buen Retiro Palace of his

Hapsburg predecessors. His accession was likewise proclaimed in Milan, Naples, Brussels, and the colonial American capitals.

Spain, so dazzled by the recent crowding of events, now took stock of its new king and his background. Felipe V was a quarter Spanish through his grandmother María Teresa; from her he undoubtedly inherited a somewhat gaping mouth and, more important, the Hapsburg melancholy, which eventually he was to express to a greater degree than any of his predecessors. From Louis XIV he acquired the handsomeness and dignity of bearing notable in all the great king's grandchildren. The influences of his immediate parents were uncertain. His father, Louis, *Le Grand Dauphin*, had been deliberately excluded from affairs of state and had grown to be a cynic, a glutton, and a profligate. Perhaps, Felipe's decided indolence was traceable to the parent described in these words by "Madame," his diarist aunt: "He carried idleness to extremes . . . he would have preferred his ease to all the kingdoms and empires." Nonetheless, *Le Grand Dauphin* came to take pride in the fact that he alone was in a position to say "the king, my father, the king, my son." Felipe's mother, the mousy and sickly María Ana of Bavaria, also had a tendency to melancholy. According to "Madame" again, she was driven to an early death by the unkindness of the French court as surely "as if they had shot her with a pistol." As for Felipe's brothers, they were quite unlike him: the elder, the Duke of Burgundy, was hearty and imperious; the younger, the Duke of Berri, was lighthearted and insinuating. Felipe, serious, quiet, and reserved, was the most Spanish in character.

For all his illustrious genealogy, Felipe V at seventeen was largely a cipher, an awkward, shy, somewhat morose youth, pale but decidedly handsome, blond like the last king. Since younger brothers of the heir of France could cause trouble, he had been educated only with a view to piety, submissiveness, and the drawing-room graces. Hunting seemed his sole passion, and he might throw tantrums or sulk if a meeting of the council interfered with this pleasure. He had been made to promise by his advisers at the outset that he would attend to state business four hours a day, that he would receive dignitaries regularly, and that he would dine in state on occasion, a practice that his grandfather considered essential public relations for royalty. Early in his stay in Madrid Felipe refused to be present at an auto-da-fé intended to be in his honor, an action which could be interpreted as either stubbornness or as the first glimmer of a resolve not to cater to the less enlightened customs of his new kingdom. Likewise, he insisted on the French courtesy of lifting or removing his hat to all people, offending some of the rank-obsessed grandees but delighting many of the less high and mighty.

After encountering their new king a few times, Spanish officials and courtiers complained that he did not talk to them. It turned out not to be the language barrier, as suspected, but simply the fact that Felipe did not like to talk, whether in French or in Spanish. He could remain silent for days. He did let his mouth hang open frequently and had to be gently told to close it, a reminder he took docilely. Characterized by an almost total timidity, the well-intentioned youth was at no pains, however, to conceal his boredom much of the time. The king obviously led an interior life.

Whatever the original intention of Louis XIV, the laziness and inexperience of his grandson opened the way to French interference in all aspects of Spanish affairs. The French monarch soon surmised that Felipe even let his French tutor help with his royal duties, for there exists this schoolboyish letter from Madrid to Versailles: "It is true that Louville helps me write my letters, but I do not know how you found out. . . . I give them to him privately, and he corrects them for me and returns them. What forces me to work thus is my lack of confidence in myself and my little experience with writing letters on affairs." The letters from grandfather to grandson became voluminous, and it was not long before Louis XIV was instructing the new French ambassador to Felipe's court "to be minister for his Catholic Majesty." Spaniards continued to occupy the main offices of state, but Louis XIV in Versailles came to supervise the award of positions in Madrid. Not a few of his envoys sat on the Council of State. Frenchmen were accorded the privileges of grandees of Spain. A French-born official named Jean Orry was given supreme authority over taxes and finances, which he found in hopeless disorder and immediately set out to reform. A rationalist French passion for uniformity and centralization was to become the hallmark of Bourbon rule in Spain when the eighteenth century is considered as a whole.

An assembly of notables, more a national assembly than a traditional Castilian Cortes, was summoned as of May, 1701, and they duly swore allegiance to Felipe V and voted a subsidy. Because extended debates could prove embarrassing, the young king prorogued the session, announcing that his impending marriage made it necessary for him to leave Castile. He set off to greet his bride in September. The king's reception in traditionally separatist Catalonia was cool, but after his arrival in Barcelona on October 1 he swore to maintain the *fueros* of the realm and granted other privileges freely, so that the Catalan Cortes was induced to respond with a generous money gift.

Felipe's marriage was entirely arranged and dictated by his grandfather. The bride was the barely thirteen-year-old María Luisa of Savoy, chosen primarily because of the key position of her father, Duke Victor Amadeus, on the diplomatic chessboard. Seasickness forced the princess to give up a water voyage to Barcelona, and she came by way of France. The marriage was celebrated at the small town of Figueras outside Barcelona in November, 1701. Several contretemps marred the occasion. At the wedding banquet the Spanish servants deliberately spilled all the French dishes prepared especially to please the foreign queen. Deprived at the frontier of the company of her Savoyard ladies-in-waiting, the bride became petulant and frightened, refusing to undress when the time came. The king was advised to avenge his hurt by declining the bridal bed the second night, and María Luisa gave in from shame the third.

The royal teen-agers soon revealed unexpected and important dimensions to their characters. Felipe, to whom nothing seemed of interest except riding and shooting, proved to be a passionate slave of lovemaking. "From his first leap into the marriage bed his uxoriousness provoked titters throughout Europe." María Luisa, seemingly the most giddy and frivolous of queens, soon revealed a kind of wisdom and a taste for politics. Under the tutelage of her chief lady-in-waiting, the Princess of Ursins, she emerged the more decisive voice of the royal couple. Louis XIV was to pay María Luisa a kind of compliment a few years later when, thwarted by her in some matter, he complained of her presumption at such a young age "to govern a vast disorganized monarchy."

It was not long before everyone recognized that the Princess of Ursins was the real ruler of Spain, and she retained this eminence over thirteen years. Of an aristocratic French family, she and her first husband were forced to flee the country because of a duel. Widowed, she shone in the high society of Rome and married an elderly member of the Orsini family, who left her his title, in due course Frenchified to Ursines (and later Anglicized to Ursins). Subsequently in France she became intimate with Madame de Maintenon, the influential mistress of Louis XIV, and that king came to appreciate her diplomatic talents and saw to her appointment as mentor to the young Queen of Spain. On the verge of sixty when she came, the Princess of Ursins was a woman of tremendous charm and grace, with expressive blue eyes and a taste for décolletage. She became the center of all the intrigues at court. Resented by some Spanish officials, she was at pains not to offend patriotic sensibilities. Frequently at odds with successive French ambassadors, who lacked her gift for public relations, she once suffered a brusque recall by Louis XIV only to return in triumph after the urgent pleas of the Spanish royal couple. She served her monarchs well, revealing a great grasp of public business, but personal ambition was eventually her downfall.

The internal affairs of Felipe's court mattered very little at this time, for his very right to rule was about to be contested by the European powers. In the history books the great conflict is known as the War of the Spanish

Succession, and it lasted until 1713. The war had various beginnings in various regions. As early as February, 1701, French troops had seized and manned the barrier fortresses in the Spanish Netherlands, a typically high-handed move by Louis XIV in disregard of both his grandson's prerogatives and the sensibilities of France's neighbors. In May, 1701, the illustrious Hapsburg general Prince Eugene led an army into northern Italy and by a series of skillful maneuvers entrenched himself in Lombardy despite the efforts of a French army to drive the Austrians out. In the middle of this game was the duchy of Savoy: hence Felipe was married to María Luisa, and her father came in on the French side. The war took on truly continental and, indeed, world dimensions only after England, the Netherlands, and the Holy Roman Empire signed the Treaty of The Hague in September, 1701, and formed the Grand Alliance dedicated to securing at least part of the Spanish inheritance for the Austrian Hapsburgs, to furthering the commercial interests of the maritime powers, and to humbling Louis XIV.

England, the chief sustainer of the War of the Spanish Succession as well as its chief beneficiary, had various motives for its role. King William III, inveterate foe of Louis XIV since 1688, was eager to make war on the Bourbons to save the balance of power and to protect his native Netherlands (he wrote to a Dutch official of his determination "to maneuver" the English people "gradually and carefully to the brink of war taking care that it remains unaware of what is happening"). The Whigs in Parliament were inclined toward hostilities for reasons of commerce, since England, like the Netherlands, already had a huge commitment to legal and illegal trade with Spanish America. They were aroused by the possibility of the wealth of the Spanish Main shifting to the control of French entrepreneurs, a possibility that seemed probability after Felipe V in late 1701 assigned the asiento (right to the slave trade) to the French. Daniel Defoe began his writing career at this time with a hysterical pamphlet predicting the ruin of English trade on the seven seas if a Bourbon were allowed to sit on the throne in Madrid. The English Tories, on the other hand, the party of the landed interests and more isolationist, were content to recognize Felipe V, but then they were stung to fury by Louis XIV's gratuitously insulting act of recognizing the Stuart pretender "James III" as England's ruler in September, 1701, at the deathbed of the deposed James II. Parliament soon voted William III subsidies to maintain an army and navy of 40,000 men each, perhaps one of the most successful investments that this body ever made and the near ruin of Felipe V. War was formally declared on Spain in May, 1702, two months after the death of William, who was succeeded by his sister-in-law Queen Anne (because the complete union of England and Scotland did not take place until 1707 under Queen Anne, it is proper to speak of the British, rather than the English, only after that date).

The War of the Spanish Succession was a somewhat tedious chronicle of marches, countermarches, maneuvers, and sieges by small professional armies. The first major fighting on Spanish soil since the reconquest now took place, but the war was also fought on several other fronts—in Belgium, in the Rhineland, in Italy, and in Portugal—and the fate of Felipe V depended to some degree on what happened in each theater.

Austrian victories threatening the French-Spanish position in northern Italy and a pro-Hapsburg insurrection in Naples caused Louis XIV to insist that Felipe V personally conduct additional Bourbon troops to that peninsula. Many Castilians criticized their king for departing the country in April, 1702, after the six-month royal honeymoon in Catalonia, but Felipe V took note of the fact that Felipe II had never shown his presence in the Netherlands during the Dutch Revolt, and he declared his resolve not to lose his Italian territories for the same reason. After being present at a victorious summer campaign, the young king made a ceremonial entry into Naples but found his reception far from enthusiastic. He passed into a state of deep depression, in additional measure owing to his first absence from his wife. Isolating himself in a gloomy palace, he found diversion only in playing games with an attendant entourage of freaks and in shooting birds out the windows. Yet when his tutor Louville slyly suggested a local liaison, Felipe's nature was genuinely scandalized. His general despondency was increased when he lost his luxuriant hair because of measles and thereafter had to wear a wig.

Meanwhile, Queen María Luisa journeyed to Saragossa, where she swore to uphold the *fueros* of Aragón in the name of her husband. Then in June, 1702, she made her first entry into Madrid, exciting applause as well as curiosity. Her entourage—the Princess of Ursins, her confessor, the ladies-in-waiting—were all French selected.

During the first years of the war the cause of Felipe V sustained several setbacks. The English Admiral Sir George Rooke, having failed to seize Cádiz, was later able to destroy a large part of the Spanish treasure fleet in a daring assault on Vigo Bay in October, 1702. That same month far to the north the French-Spanish army in Flanders lost Liège to an English-Dutch army under the Duke of Marlborough, who was to become the war's single most celebrated hero. Portugal joined the allies against the Bourbons in May, 1703, and in October Savoy changed sides, this treachery of Duke Victor Amadeus occurring notwithstanding his daughter's being Felipe's queen.

In the trail of these victories the potential anti-Bourbon party in Spain gained the needed focus of a leader on September 12, 1703, when the Archduke Charles was solemnly proclaimed in Vienna as King Carlos III of Spain and the Indies. His father, the Emperor Leopold I, had consistently refused to recognize Felipe V from the time of the death of Carlos II in 1700, but the maritime powers in turn declined to countenance any claim of Leopold to unite under himself the Austrian and Spanish inheritances. The powers eventually agreed to support a younger son's accession in Spain alone. Accordingly, that fall day the emperor, his elder son, Joseph, and Charles drove to the Favorita Palace outside Vienna and here the court heard Charles declared rightful King of Spain, at the same time as his father and brother renounced any prior claims. The Hapsburg family adopted a secret protocol, however, providing that, in default of male issue in the line of either Joseph or Charles, surviving male offspring of the other, and even female offspring, should succeed to both empires. In due course, most of the powers and lesser states of Europe, excluding France and Bavaria, recognized "Carlos III." The Pope, reluctant to offend any Catholic country, sent back unopened the letter from the emperor announcing his son's new eminence.

"Carlos III" and his family took leave of each other on September 19 with the same sort of mixed emotions that attended the departure of Philip of Anjou from France three years previously. His cavalcade in Spanish national colors made its way across Europe to England, where he was received by Queen Anne in London. "Carlos III" landed in Lisbon in March, 1704, and immediately surrounded himself with a court of the not inconsiderable number of Spanish grandees who had deserted to his cause. In Toledo, where she had been put in honorable confinement, the Dowager Queen Mariana told all who would listen that her dying husband, Carlos II, had verbally revoked his official will and named the Austrian his successor.

At eighteen "Carlos III" revealed himself to be not unlike his cousin and rival, Felipe V. A person attendant on Carlos' stay at Windsor described the Austrian thus:

> He had a gravity beyond his age, tempered with modesty. His behaviour was in all points so exact that there was not a circumstance in his whole deportment that was liable to censure. . . . He had the art of seeming well pleased with everything without so much as smiling once. He spoke but little and all he said was judicious and obliging.

Dignity, reserve, and a desire to please were both Carlos' and Felipe's, and also decided indolence. A minimum of education and a measure of common sense were shared by both. If moroseness was Felipe's idiosyncrasy, Carlos' was haughtiness and punctiliousness, a passion for ceremony that was both comical and exasperating to his English advisers. In looks, Carlos had the worst of it, being of medium height, somewhat heavy, and exaggeratedly Hapsburg in his jutting chin and drooping lip. "Carlos III" was as unmartial and uncommanding as his opposite in what was to be more a contest of arms than policy, but he was equally stubborn and tenacious in the assertion of his rights.

Bourbon France reacted strongly to the new Hapsburg pretension and sent large contingents of troops into Spain in February, 1704, to bolster the levies of Felipe V, who had returned from Italy and once in his wife's arms had recovered from his despairing lethargy. Louis XIV openhandedly sent twenty infantry battalions, six of cavalry, and two of dragoons to his grandson's support. In March Felipe V participated in a joint French-Spanish invasion of Portugal led by the Duke of Berwick (as a natural son of James II by Arabella Churchill, Marlborough's sister, he joined the French army and became a marshal). Although several towns were captured, they failed to take Lisbon, and the king returned to Madrid in July.

Marlborough achieved his most stunning victory at Blenheim in August, 1704, moving a British army from the lower Rhine area to join Prince Eugene in smashing the French and their Bavarian allies in the upper reaches of the Danube. The whole situation in Germany was reversed, the French threat to Vienna ended, and Bavaria knocked out of the war. The military might of Louis XIV had been decisively defeated for the first time. But for the repeated cautiousness of his Dutch allies, the brilliant English commander might have struck into France and threatened Paris itself.

Although the fate of Felipe V directly depended on the fate of the Rhine armies of his French protector, the event that same August that most distressed Spain was the loss of Gibraltar to the English. Admiral Rooke, after landing "Carlos III" at Lisbon with a sizable military force, had then sailed through the strait with the aim of mounting an attack on the French base at Toulon in cooperation with Austrian-Savoyard troops, a blow that Marlborough envisaged as even more decisive than his Blenheim campaign. The attack on Toulon came to naught, as did an attempted seizure of Barcelona, but on his return voyage to the strait Rooke was inspired by the idea of capturing Gibraltar, which was lightly held by Spanish troops and proved an easy victim of naval bombardment and assault by English marines. The commandant of Gibraltar surrendered to the Hapsburg, but Rooke took possession of the strongpoint in the name of Queen Anne, fulfilling an English ambition going back to the days of Cromwell. The French responded by assembling a French-Spanish fleet of ninety-six ships, but this was severely mauled by Rooke's squadron of sixty-eight later in August in the Battle of Málaga, the largest naval action of the war. After that France and Spain were entirely on the defensive in the Mediterranean and proved unable to dislodge the English from Gibraltar by repeated sieges from the land side. Felipe V was to say that the loss of Gibraltar was like "thorns in the feet," a sentiment still being echoed by General Franco.

During 1705 the opposing armies were largely stalemated in Germany and Italy, but in Spain there was a decisive turn of events when forces supporting "Carlos III" invaded the country from west and east. An English-Portuguese army under the Earl of Galway and the Marquis of Das Minas drove into Extremadura and besieged Badajoz. More dramatically a British fleet and army under the Earl of Peterborough bombarded Barcelona into submission on October 9. The Catalan citizenry now rose to massacre surviving Castilian soldiery. On November 7 the archduke made his solemn entry into the city, and delirious crowds cheered "Carlos III" and Peterborough as the two of them stood on a balcony throwing out handfuls of coins. During a great victory procession officials released flocks of birds to the sky to symbolize the birth of a new era under a Hapsburg ruler. All Catalonia showed its support for Carlos III as sovereign "Count of Barcelona," and irregular troops were raised in his support. Valencia fell to a Spanish force supporting the Hapsburg in December, and this month there were riots in cities of Aragón in resentment of the presence of a Bourbon-Castilian force. "Protect our *fueros* and leave no Frenchman alive," the mobs cried. When Felipe V with an army of 20,000 marched to recapture Barcelona in the spring of 1706, they met dogged resistance from the citizens behind their fortifications. The archduke showed himself an energetic leader and enhanced his popularity by announcing that he had had a vision of the Virgin supported by two angels blessing his cause. Just when the Bourbon troops had finally reduced the outworks and were on the point of capturing the city, an Anglo-Dutch squadron under Peterborough arrived, driving off a French fleet and landing 8,000 reinforcements. Felipe V was forced to raise the siege of Barcelona on May 10. Retreating westward, he found the road to Madrid cut and, abandoning his baggage, detoured miserably through the Pyrenees in order to reach Burgos. He arrived back in Madrid in June only to learn that his capital was in imminent jeopardy from another direction. The heartbroken king, who so easily lent himself to despair, talked of fleeing to America.

The English-Portuguese army moving eastward had taken advantage of the Barcelona diversion and captured Ciudad Rodrigo on May 26 and the university town of Salamanca on June 7. The Duke of Berwick, accompanied by Felipe V, retreated helplessly before their superior numbers and equipment without giving battle. The queen, the court, and the government officers left the capital on June 20. More grandees now defected to the cause of "Carlos III," who was proclaimed king when the allied forces entered Madrid on June 26. A touch of the past was evoked when the English commander Galway was entertained in nearby Toledo by the Dowager Queen Mariana, who celebrated the Hapsburg triumph at her palace in an unwonted blaze of candles. Elsewhere the English navy captured Cartagena, Alicante, and Majorca. Marlborough, having won a signal victory at Ramillies in May, projected a march to join Prince Eugene in Lombardy. Such a campaign was not necessary, for in this same disastrous year for the Bourbons, Louis XIV was forced by unceasing defeats to sign a truce with the emperor providing for the complete evacuation of Italy by the French. The Italian duchies were lost to Felipe V forever, to be regained by his sons, however.

After allied forces entered Saragossa on June 29, the four chief cities of Spain were held in the name of "Carlos III." Central Castile, as well as most of Aragón, Catalonia, and Valencia, had passed from the control of Felipe V, who, with his queen, was now reduced to living in an unpalatial house in Burgos surrounded by washing. The crown jewels had been sent for safekeeping to Paris, where there was talk in the salons of writing Felipe V off altogether. Louis XIV himself had opened peace negotiations with the Dutch, indicating that "Carlos III" could have Spain if his grandson were allowed to rule over some Italian territories. It appeared that Bourbon rule in Spain would last less than six years.

3. The Triumph of the New Dynasty

Felipe V survived the crisis of 1706 and kept his throne. His exertions on his own behalf counted for less than his stubborn insistence on his rights. Nor did he owe his fortune to his grandfather, for Louis XIV was more than once prepared to abandon him. What really saved the Bourbon cause in Spain was the determined loyalty of the Castilians to the king of their choice. In Castile the Hapsburg "Carlos III" was the foreign intruder. There was an old folk saying "Castile will never obey a king who enters by way of Aragón," and, indeed, it was the eastern Aragonese provinces that were the main source of Carlos' strength. In this sense, the War of the Spanish Succession was a civil war between the two parts of Spain that had been imperfectly united two centuries before by the Catholic monarchs.

The English-Portuguese soldiers occupying Madrid found themselves in general hated and in particular preyed upon by the most syphilitic women the community of prostitutes could find. Madrid youths shouted, "Long live Carlos III," but added under their breaths, "so long as he continues to throw money our way." Convoys from Portugal were attacked; couriers could not get through. Galway and Das Minas moved their forces east of

Madrid, but "Carlos III" delayed joining them with his Catalan army. The French took advantage of the allies' hesitation to slip more troops into the peninsula, and the Duke of Berwick's reinforced army forced the English-Portuguese to evacuate Madrid in October, 1706.

Queen María Luisa staged a triumphant entry into the capital at the end of the year. Her serene tenacity had done much to bolster her husband's spirit, and the sale of her jewels had paid his troops. Yet the queen was noble and realistic enough to write Paris: "One can clearly see that after God we owe the crown to the peoples." For her the return represented something of a personal vindication, and she took immediate steps to clear the court of the disloyal among the grandees, of the dowagers who insisted that she dress a century out of style, and of the dwarfs who, besides being unseemly, had spied on her in the past. Another woman of strong purpose, the Princess of Ursins, stayed on, more powerful than ever.

Felipe V and his queen greatly excited popular feelings in their favor by at last producing an heir, the Infante Luis, born on August 25, 1707. The houses of Madrid stayed illuminated without official order all through the crucial night, and there were rejoicings throughout Castile at the news of the first royal birth in Spain since 1661. The succession seemed assured, for the baby was "strong as a Turk," according to Ursins' report to Paris. The parents demurred about giving their son so French a name, but their doubts were removed by his being born on the day of St. Louis. Trumpeters across the battle line informed the Duke of Savoy that he was a grandfather, but they got no response. Felipe V, who usually hid his feelings completely, was observed cuddling the newborn child and murmuring over and over again, *"Mon fils, mon fils."* Two years later a Cortes officially acknowledged Luis de Borbón y Saboya as Prince of the Asturias. (The first Bourbon king's subsequent children automatically received the traditional titles of Infante or Infanta. Other persons of royal blood may be so designated by the sovereign.)

Meanwhile, in April, 1707, the Duke of Berwick defeated the allied forces of Galway in the Battle of Almansa, the most hard-fought engagement of the war. Paradoxically, the English-born Berwick commanded the triumphant French and Spanish troops, while Galway, who was of French origin, led the defeated English-Portuguese-German force (an Irish Catholic regiment fought for the Bourbon; French Huguenots fought for the Hapsburg). The victory was followed up by the recapture of Valencia and Saragossa. A month later Felipe V issued a stern decree depriving Aragón and Valencia of their Cortes and *fueros* as punishment for the disloyalty of these provinces. Probably the areas of Spain that had left the allegiance of the Bourbons had done so less because of enthusiasm for the cause of "Carlos III" than because of the bad condition of their defenses or their particular vulnerability to the English navy. Also, many rural and city risings directed themselves not so much against the Bourbons as against the rich. Nonetheless, the Bourbon king acted with a vengeance to subject Aragón and Valencia to the laws of Castile, a step not dared by even his strongest predecessors.

As the centralizing ambitions of Felipe V were revealed, resistance stiffened in Catalonia, the main area of Spain left to "Carlos III." The Hapsburg was careful to play up to local sensibilities, treating the Catalan Cortes with great deference, reducing the tax burdens on the people, and restricting his foreign troops from any display of their heretic religious rites. Residing in Barcelona, "Carlos III" never failed to observe local feast days; he rode about the city on horseback and made himself available to all petitioners. The Hapsburg proved less astute as a strategist, staying on the defensive. He was unable to prevent a Bourbon force in the summer of 1708 from cutting communications between Catalonia and his remaining Valencian ports, which were lost to him altogether by the end of the year. The defeats did not unnerve "Carlos III," who declared that he would "rather be buried under Barcelona's ruins than to yield." The Catalans admired his spirit, not his inactivity.

As if to underline his determination to stay in Spain, "Carlos III" brought a bride there in 1708. His choice was Elizabeth of Brunswick-Wolfenbüttel (her sister was to become in three years' time the miserable bride of the miserable Tsarevich Alexis of Russia, killed at the instance of his father, Peter the Great, in 1717). Elizabeth was a slender ash blonde with sparkling eyes and a rosy complexion. Her required conversion from Lutheranism to Catholicism had been accompanied by many tears, and her hopes of being allowed to take communion under both rites were rudely disappointed after she reached her new country. The marriage was performed at the seaport of Mataró. The phlegmatic Carlos wrote in his diary: "Rode to Mataró. Queen very beautiful. Quite content." Two days later he noted: "Queen night very sweet." The court at Barcelona found the new consort kindly and dignified. She received a lifelong facial scar, however, from the bite of a disrespectful Catalan black fly.

Outside the Spanish peninsula the year 1708 went badly for the Bourbons. The British navy seized the island of Minorca, which they held for the next seventy-five years as a vital all-weather base for operations in the western Mediterranean. In the Spanish Netherlands Marlborough displayed his lightning mobility and secured another signal victory in the Battle of Oudenaarde in July, after which the French were sent reeling back to their own frontiers. Marlborough proposed a daring strike directly at Paris, but his Austrian ally, Prince Eugene, insisted on the traditional city-by-city siege strategy. Lille, within France, fell to them in December.

A Louis XIV desperate to end the war initiated secret negotiations in 1709, offering to cease all support to Felipe V. The overconfident allies demanded large territorial concessions in the Rhine area and the removal of the pretender James III from France. These matters were negotiable, but the French king balked at the demand that he was to use French troops physically to expel his relative from Spain. Even the victorious Marlborough declared too late "were he in the place of the King of France he should venture the loss of his country sooner than be obliged to join his troops for the forcing of his grandson." The French nation rallied to their king when he now made an unprecedented public appeal for new sacrifices.

To placate the allies during 1709, Louis XIV did withdraw all the French troops in Spain except for small garrisons in the north. Even the French ambassador was recalled. Accusing the French of treachery, Spanish troops clashed with those of their departing allies. Unwilling to desert his followers, Felipe V wrote determinedly to his grandfather: "I shall never quit Spain save through death; I would rather prefer to perish fighting for it foot by foot at the head of my troops." The king was further incensed by a plot involving the Duke of Orléans, his cousin and for years his confidant as supreme French commander in Spain. Orléans was accused of courting popularity in Aragón and even of negotiating with the British with the aim of securing his own elevation to the Spanish throne. Felipe V let himself be persuaded that his cousin had contemplated having him poisoned, and despite all the efforts of Louis XIV to hush up the family quarrel, a feud between Felipe and Orléans became an important constant in European affairs for the next fifteen years. For his defiance, the king gained new esteem among the Spanish, who rejoiced at the seeming end of French influence at court.

By 1710 Louis XIV was now willing to subsidize the allies to the amount of 150,000 livres a month to dethrone Felipe V but the French still refused the use of their own troops and other exorbitant demands. The grandfather futilely demanded the grandson's abdication and tried to recall to France the Princess of Ursins, who, however, refused to desert her young royal protégés.

Thrown entirely on their own resources, Felipe V and his Spanish army failed the first tests, and disaster for the Bourbon cause seemed inevitable again. At the Battle of Almenara in southern Aragón on July 27, 1710, the allied army of the Austrian General Guido von Starhemberg and the British General James Stanhope carried the day. Felipe's force of 20,000 was even more severely defeated in a second battle on August 20 by the enemy's 23,000, mostly German, troops. On September 9 once again the Bourbon royal family and court evacuated Madrid. "Carlos III" entered the capital for the first time on September 28. The archduke attended the usual ceremonial service in the Church of the Atocha and took up residence in a palace outside the city, where he could enjoy the hunting that Felipe V had left off.

The Hapsburg triumph was again short-lived. The allied troops found Madrid half-empty and hostile, the populace aroused by the clergy over the discovery of numerous Anglican Bibles in the baggage of the English troops. Irregular forces loyal to Felipe V penetrated even to the suburbs. General Stanhope was forced to admit that "the country is our enemy and we are not masters in Castile of more ground than we can encamp on." Blocked in an endeavor to join a Portuguese army to the west, the allied army abandoned Madrid in November, retreating eastward toward Catalonia, as in 1706. Considerable credit in their discomfiture belonged to Louis XIV, who had relented of deserting his grandson and in August had sent him substantial French forces under the celebrated Marshal Vendôme. If "Carlos III" earlier had not ignored advice to march on Pamplona instead of Madrid, he would have been in a position to block the arrival of these reinforcements to his enemy.

On December 3, 1710, Felipe V reentered his capital and celebrated his Te Deum in the Atocha to the sound of cannon salvos. The outpouring of popular fervor was remarkable, the streets a blaze of flowers, decorative hangings, and so much silver it seemed as though the mines of the New World "had been bled dry." The haggard king, nearing twenty-seven, was apotheosized as Adonis; his queen, going to flesh and sickly, as Venus.

Marshal Vendôme did not let Felipe tarry at his devotions in Madrid but hurried him off with the French-Spanish army in pursuit of the enemy, which had split its forces. Unaware of Vendôme's proximity, Stanhope lingered at Brihuega, where his troops were surrounded and forced to capitulate on December 8 after the Bourbon army stormed the town. Moving back too late to help their allies, Starhemberg's Germans were caught at Villaviciosa the next day, and after a confused engagement retreated eastward. The night after these crucial victories that secured his throne forever, Felipe V complained to Vendôme that his bed had been left behind in the haste of the campaign. The French marshal replied grandly: "Your Majesty shall have the most splendid couch that ever a king has lain on," a pile of captured banners.

With "Carlos III" still defiant behind the fortifications of Barcelona and secure in the affections of all Catalonia the war on the peninsula might have seesawed back and forth indefinitely but for two events external to Spain. In early 1710 a Tory ministry had come to power in Britain, a ministry pledged to end the war and a ministry so unimpressed with Marlborough's recent victories as to dismiss him summarily from his command in late 1711. Even more consequential was the sudden death from smallpox of the

Holy Roman Emperor Joseph on April 17, 1711. Carlos' older brother, who had succeeded their father, Leopold I, as of 1705, had named Carlos the heir to the Hapsburg dominions in Central Europe. Now for the allies to continue supporting "Carlos III" in Spain would be tantamount to their favoring a revival of the all-encompassing empire of Charles V. The new head of the House of Hapsburg was too obstinate to give up any of his rights, refusing to leave Barcelona until September 27, when a British squadron convoyed him past lurking French warships to Genoa. Later in Frankfurt he was duly elected emperor as Charles VI, his Spanish titles being incorporated in the coronation instrument. He took up residence in Vienna in January, 1712.

The course of events was now also affected by a series of deaths and renunciations within the Bourbon family beginning with the demise of Felipe V's father, *Le Grand Dauphin*, in April, 1711. This was followed by the death of Felipe's older brother, the Duke of Burgundy, in February, 1712, and that of Burgundy's eldest son, the Duke of Brittany, in March. Thus Louis XIV, now seventy-two, lost three generations of his immediate heirs in less than a year. Bad luck and bad doctors were the probable causes, but some people chose to accuse the Duke of Orléans, the French king's nephew, of poison plots again. The French succession now rested on Burgundy's second son, a sickly two-year-old. At this juncture, to end British fears of a united Spain-France, Felipe V decided to renounce any claims to the French throne; his formal act to this effect on November 5, 1712, was confirmed by the Cortes of Castile. Louis XIV accepted this renunciation with reluctance, since he realized that France might need a king as experienced as Felipe, whose strong-minded wife was also a positive consideration. For his part, Felipe V was currently more dominated by feelings of gratitude to his supporters than by ambitions to succeed his grandfather. He declared that "nothing in the world will separate me from Spain and from the Spanish."

Peace negotiations had begun in earnest at Utrecht early in 1712 between the maritime powers on the one side and the French on the other. The emperor refused to stop fighting, but Prince Eugene's attempt to wage a campaign in the Rhine area without British support brought him severe defeats. Felipe V would have liked to pursue the war against Catalonia, as well as to seek some way of recapturing his Italian possessions, but there was no money and no more French arms. Hostilities were suspended on the peninsula in August, 1712.

The War of the Spanish Succession was brought to a close by the Treaty of Utrecht on April 11, 1713, or more accurately by a complex series of pacts among the powers extending to 1715. Felipe V lost all his nonpeninsular European possessions, the southern Netherlands (Belgium), Luxembourg, Milan, and Naples going to the emperor, Sicily to the Duke of Savoy. The dismemberment of Felipe's empire, the "seamless garment" that Carlos II labored so hard to save, was more complete than probably would have taken place at the latter's death in 1700 without the war. Felipe V did not recognize these losses, nor did the Emperor Charles VI recognize his rival as King of Spain.

In connection with the peace treaty, Felipe V as of May, 1713, decreed the applicability in Spain of the Salic Law, the French tradition that women cannot rule in their own right. Intended to ensure that no Hapsburg would ever sneak onto the Spanish throne through marriage, past or future, to a Spanish princess, the new statute confirmed by Cortes also had the effect of denying the possibility of a queen regnant in Spain, a principle contrary to Castilian practice in the past and one that would bring Spain untold grief in the next century.

The parts of the Utrecht settlement that Spain did consent to concerned its relations with Britain. Article Two of the treaty declared that never could "the kingdoms of Spain and France [be] united under the same dominion nor there be the same king of both monarchies." Felipe V made two painful territorial cessions to the British, Gibraltar and Minorca. Equally important, the British gained the *asiento,* or a thirty-year monopoly of importing black slaves into Spanish America. It was specified that the British South Sea Company could bring in 4,800 blacks each year (in the past this gruesome trade was carried on under conditions where one of three slaves survived to work in the mines or plantations). Moreover, the monopoly contained a provision that the British could send one ship of 500 tons each season for general trade with the Spanish colonies. Time proved that by secretly reloading this same ship the British had torn a huge rent in Spain's colonial system, a major result of the entire war. Such commercial privileges were specifically denied by the Treaty of Utrecht to Bourbon France, which additionally suffered the loss of Hudson's Bay, Acadia, and Newfoundland to the triumphant British.

For a while the whole peace settlement had been in jeopardy because of a whim of the Princess of Ursins. She had her eye on a tiny part of Luxembourg, not for itself but for the accompanying royal title that would enable her to live more grandly at the chateau she was building in France. Louis XIV had peremptorily to order Felipe V to quash his mentor's ambition.

One futile, British-inspired provision of the Treaty of Utrecht was a promise by Felipe V to grant an amnesty to the Catalans and to allow them the same privileges enjoyed by the Castilians. Catalonia, in actuality given the choice of unconditional submission to the Bourbon king or continued armed resistance, chose the latter course. Royal forces were compelled to invest Barcelona in the summer of 1713, but even after the troops of the emperor were withdrawn, a provisional government held out for several months against both military and naval assaults. Only after the most bitter house-to-house fighting did Barcelona capitulate on September 11, 1714. The Bourbons had their vengeance on the separatists: their military banners were burned in the square by the hangman; the surviving soldiers were sold into slavery; the six Catalan universities were closed; and the *fueros* were entirely abolished.

Within Spain the loss of the constitutional privileges of Catalonia, Aragón, and Valencia to the benefit of Castile was the main political result of the War of the Spanish Succession, apart from the fact of the survival of Felipe V and his new dynasty. A dozen years of fighting had harmed Spain relatively little. No appreciable population loss was sustained, and the economy, if anything, was stimulated. The drama of events, like the king's two flights from his capital, plus the presence of so many foreigners, with the French allies hated almost as much as the enemy troops, "may well have shaken Spain out of a stupor." Moreover, "the relatively mild impact of the war made it possible for a drastic reassessment of the priorities facing Spain . . . government finances, army reorganization, industrial advance, political unification." Reforms but hinted at during the war became the preoccupation of Felipe V and his successors in the following period, so that Bourbon Spain soon appeared to be as different from Hapsburg Spain as day from night, at least in the eyes of Bourbon apologists.

II.

The Melancholy King:
Felipe V (1700–1746)

1. The Schemes of Isabel Farnese and Cardinal Alberoni

T HE forty-six-year reign of Felipe V was the longest of modern Spanish history. The first part, taken up with the war to ensure his succession was a period when French influences were all-important. After 1714 the reign was dominated by the king's second wife, Isabel Farnese, and the Italian influences that accompanied her. It was a tedious era less noted for solid domestic accomplishments than for intense court intrigues and the rise and fall of favorites. Likewise, interminable wars and diplomatic about-faces produced few lasting results. Throughout, King Felipe V remained a remote colorless figure, not unpopular but remembered mainly for his seizures of melancholy and eccentricity. Yet, when all was done, Bourbon Spain had more than just edged into the eighteenth century; it was firmly on the way to catching up to Europe.

The birth of her fourth son, the Infante Fernando, in September, 1713, weakened the already delicate health of Queen María Luisa, Felipe V's Savoyard wife of thirteen years. She suffered from tuberculosis. After rallying briefly for a festive Christmas, the queen fell into a desperate condition. The leading physician of Paris was rushed to her bedside but to no avail, and the queen died in February with pious composure. Clearly she was worn out by the cares and anxieties of her political role, but it was also whispered that she was exhausted by the physical importunities of her oversexed husband, who was persuaded only with considerable difficulty to forsake his wife's bed the night before she died. On the day of María Luisa's funeral Felipe V went hunting as usual, pausing to watch the cortege moving slowly toward the Escorial. "Princes, are they human?" commented the Duke of Saint-Simon, the caustic and celebrated memoirist of the era of Louis XIV.

So completely needful of the domination of a woman, the king now fell under the direct influence of the Princess of Ursins. During the difficult last years of the War of the Succession and the negotiations at Utrecht, French influence in the Spanish court had been on the wane, and Spanish officials were in the fore. This development was reversed. The Spanish president of the Council of Castile was retired, and his functions were divided among five president-secretaries, suspiciously on the model of Louis XIV's ministries. The Inquisitor General Cardinal Giudice was dismissed, and devout Spaniards were shocked at the spectacle of the king and the Pope at bitter odds over the whole conduct of the Inquisition. The French financial expert Orry returned to Spain in 1713, becoming dominant in the conduct of state business in association with Ursins. For his sincere efforts to improve the system of tax collection, Orry became a hated figure whose life was threatened in anonymous graffiti. Stabbings of lesser French officials did take place. One secretly circulated cartoon of this time showed the lackluster king standing between a leering Ursins and Orry with the caption "This strumpet and this drunkard have corrupted this boy."

The worst of the rumors abroad was that Felipe V, having sufficient heirs already, was going to marry Ursins. The king's grandfather was particularly displeased with this prospect, and Madame de Maintenon was beside herself with envy that Ursins might gain the queenly title that had always eluded herself. In his bereavement Felipe had retired entirely from public view, taking up residence in the palace of the dukes of Medinaceli. Since this mansion was not large enough to accommodate more than a small retinue, the monks of a nearby monastery were turned out to provide Ursins with a suitable residence, and a covered gallery was then erected between the two buildings in indecent haste, the workmen being bribed to labor even on Sundays. Having gained herself the convenient post of governess to the royal children, Ursins became virtually the only person to see the king. Felipe's confessor eventually succeeded in having a private word with his sovereign and represented to him the ridiculousness of himself at thirty-one marrying a seventy-two-year-old. In one of his flashes of common sense, the king broke off the conversation with "Oh, no, certainly not that."

It was apparent that Felipe V would go over the brink of insanity if he were denied the pleasures of the marriage bed much longer. His distress took the form of cold sweats and violent headaches. Yet his extreme piety kept him from even considering a mistress. There were, of course, numerous candidates to be Felipe's consort. A Bavarian princess, eminently suitable dynastically, was rejected as too ugly, while a Portuguese princess appeared too headstrong. Another member of the House of Savoy reminded people of past treacheries, and the sister of the Duke of Bourbon was ruled out because of the growing undercurrent of francophobia. The choice, which proved fateful indeed, fell to Elizabeth Farnese, a princess of Parma. Almost as important for history was the man who proposed the Parma match, an adventurer with few equals, the Abbé Giulio Alberoni.

The man destined to throw Spain and Europe into turmoil for the next six years had been born in Piacenza, Italy, in 1645, the son of a poor gardener and a seamstress. Young Alberoni served as a bell ringer and clerk before his precociousness earned him a good clerical education, the post of tutor to a Roman aristocrat, and the distinction of canon in the church. His great ambition was to become a cardinal. The year 1703 found him attached to the Duke of Vendôme's French army in Spain, the abbé serving as an agent of the Duke of Parma, an Italian princeling whose domain was in the middle of the Bourbon-Hapsburg struggle in Italy. Cunning, insinuating, and above all resourceful, Alberoni came to meet generals and kings. His principal method of ingratiating himself was, strangely enough, through food. He purveyed Parmesan delicacies to his patrons and was not above seeing to the cooking himself, proving to be a master chef. Alberoni's voluminous correspondence back to Parma is an incredible catalogue of detailed orders for hams, cheeses, olives, and truffles. Delays or the shipment of less than choice items brought reproaches that Alberoni's carefully planned friendships at court were at stake. After 1710 Alberoni became virtually commissary general for the Spanish army, but he never forgot the personal touch of sausage and pasta diplomacy.

Delicacy of spirit was not a trait of Alberoni, who first recommended his Parma lady to the Princess of Ursins during the funeral of the late queen. Elizabeth Farnese was the niece and stepdaughter of the Duke of Parma, who was otherwise without heirs—a major consideration in her favor. She was also the niece of the Queen Dowager Mariana, then living in exile in Bayonne, and this relationship provided a touch of continuity with the Hapsburg past. For the benefit of Ursins, who fully intended to keep her ruling position in Spain, Alberoni stressed that Elizabeth was a simple country-bred girl, humble, tractable, and entirely domestic-minded. He implied that she did not know how to write, and he showed Ursins a miniature that portrayed Elizabeth so plain that the Frenchwoman suggested that it be retouched before reaching the king's eyes. In time Ursins heard stories of the princess' willfulness, but her courier was unable to halt the marriage by proxy of Felipe V and Elizabeth Farnese in the Cathedral of Parma on September 16, 1714. Henceforth she would be known as Isabel Farnese.

That December Queen Isabel made a leisurely progress across northern

Italy and southern France toward Spain, balking at a sea voyage just as her predecessor had done. She went sight-seeing in Genoa; she banqueted with the Prince of Monaco; and she had a long interview at Pau with her aunt, who was a great enemy of Ursins. At the frontier she refused to send home her Italian suite, as had been arranged, although she was persuaded to dismiss her handsome and overly familiar young chaplain. She was first greeted by her new subjects in Pamplona on December 11, the city outdoing itself with festivities and fireworks. Here also she first encountered Alberoni, who had hastened north; her initial distrust of the abbé was succeeded by every mark of "kindness and generosity," in his own words. It was the turn of the Princess of Ursins to greet her young sovereign at Jadraque. Isabel refused to advance more than partway down the stairs of her mansion when Ursins presented herself at eight o'clock in the evening. The two women embraced and were soon closeted in the bedroom. What was said can only be speculated upon. Perhaps Ursins was bold enough to chide the queen over her delay or over her appearance. Shortly, Isabel was at the door cursing and shouting to the guards Alberoni had stationed there, "Arrest this mad woman." She then made clear that she had been given every authority to act by the king, and forthwith Ursins, provided with only the court dress and jewels she was wearing, was packed into a coach and rushed across the wastes of deepest winter all the way to the frontier of France.

Ursins, whose services cannot be lightly faulted, was to earn only one curt letter of thanks from the King of Spain. Awaiting the pleasure of Louis XIV at a seaport near Bayonne, she wrote to Madame de Maintenon that she watched "the ocean which I see sometimes raging, at others calm. . . . So it is with courts." The princess found that she had too many enemies in France as well, so she fled to Rome, where her money from two royal pensions served her in good stead. She ended her days presiding resignedly but graciously over the impecunious court of the Stuart pretender, James III.

From her victory over Ursins Isabel Farnese proceeded to a complete triumph over the king, whom she married a second time in Guadalajara on the very snowy Christmas Day of 1714. The ceremony was performed by the Patriarch of the Indies in the palace of the dukes of Infantado. The royal couple first went to bed together late in the afternoon and then attended midnight mass. When the king emerged from the bedchamber the next morning, he was his new wife's "slave for life."

"The Court of Spain is totally different from what it was ten days ago," wrote the French chargé following the arrival of the king, queen, and Alberoni in Madrid. The French party loyal to the fallen Ursins was persecuted in every way, being replaced by Italians, including Parmesans, of course, but also large numbers of Neapolitans and other exiles from the king's "lost provinces." The reformer Orry took sudden flight to Paris and was replaced as chief minister by the recalled Cardinal Giudice. When the court moved to Aranjuez for Easter, Isabel was unchallenged in her influence. "The jealousy which the Queen's favors provoke is inevitable," crowed Alberoni, who also reported that she was "absolute mistress of the King."

If the queen dominated the king through the marriage bed, Alberoni in turn came to dominate the queen through his commissary. Imperious as she might be at such a young age, Isabel was completely inexperienced in politics and woefully educated, with little time and less inclination to improve herself through study. Alberoni wrote the Duke of Parma: "I recognize to my great grief that it bores her to talk of business." The abbé learned to gain the queen's confidence by ordering both her meals and her amusements. Soon he could report: "I'm succeeding better each day in accustoming Her Majesty to harness and to work hard at State Affairs. I try to bring them in the form of mincemeat, in order to spare her all possible fatigue." The abbé made himself indispensable to her daily existence, seeing to the purchase for her of horses or guns, to the staging of theater parties and banquets. He was to admit the following conversation: "I repeated to her that I was no longer the Minister of Parma but her nurse, and she mockingly replied that I was of an age to serve her as a mid-wife if need be. A brutal compliment," the favorite added.

Genuine midwives saw to the successful delivery of the queen of her first son, the Infante Carlos, in January, 1716. There had been apprehension about Isabel's health. The British ambassador anticipated "great changes" if she survived childbirth. Alberoni observed gleefully to his master in Parma: "If things go this way we shall have princes to people the world." Both predictions largely proved true. In the succeeding months Alberoni edged out Cardinal Giudice as chief minister and embarked on a striking program of reform and rearmament. His aim was none other than to provide thrones for the queen's children.

The perfect domestic turned prime minister, Alberoni proved to be a more drastic and dramatic reformer than the patient and precise Orry. He changed the coinage, abolished interior customs dues, and reduced the bureaucracy. He made efforts to revive trade with the colonies and to promote domestic industries of use for such commerce, establishing a linen factory at Guadalajara with skilled Dutch workers and a cloth factory at Veldemoro with English dyers. The new favorite reorganized the army into a force of 50,000 effectives, and he revived the iron and ship's stores industries, equipping new arsenals at Cádiz, El Ferrol, and Barcelona, which in turn supported a powerful new battle fleet.

Alberoni's measures inevitably aroused vested interests, and occasionally he despaired of his work: "I wonder whether I'll ever succeed in establishing a system or order and good government here. Everyone fights against it, and even if it were established I wonder if they won't destroy it by sheer ineptitude." His work did not go unappreciated abroad, however. The British minister wrote that no power on earth could resist Spain after a few more years of such advance. Alberoni himself had avowed: "Give me five years of peace and I will undertake to make Spain the most powerful monarchy in Europe." It turned out that his hand was forced after only two years.

Alberoni was little concerned to improve the well-being of the Spanish people but much determined to create the material basis for an aggressive foreign policy. Italy was to be the chief theater of Spanish Bourbon ambitions now and for the next forty years. For Alberoni there were the spiritual motivations of love for Parma and a desire to liberate all Italy from the Hapsburgs, who were hateful to himself and, as events proved, hateful to many Italians. For Isabel Farnese there were intensely selfish dynastic motivations. She wished to succeed to control of her native Parma and Piacenza, presently ruled by the childless Alexander Farnese, and she likewise had hereditary claims on the Tuscany of the House of Medici, which was dying out. These territories would be a far more exciting place for retirement than a Spanish nunnery or musty palace should her husband die early. If, on the other hand, Felipe V lived on and fathered many children by her, the Italian duchies would be suitable possessions for her sons, who otherwise faced every prospect of neglect in view of the existence of two infantes by the king's first wife. The single-mindedness with which Isabel was to pursue her Italian dreams has led many historians to blame her family egoism for all the sufferings of several wars. Actually, Isabel was not merely a grasping petty Italian princess, but through her Bavarian-Neuburg mother she was closely related to the ruling houses of Spain, Portugal, Austria, Poland, and the Teutonic Knights. The king's ambitions were also involved. Parma and Tuscany first of all represented a strategic wedge driven between the Hapsburg possessions in northern and southern Italy, territories lost by the Treaty of Utrecht that Felipe V had every wish to recover. Further, the domination of all Italy was a traditional Spanish priority, sanctified by Fernando the Catholic, who had seen that it was the key to Spain's being a first-rate power.

Spain's first moves to end the diplomatic isolation it found itself in after 1713 were not fruitful. Relations with France worsened considerably after the death of Louis XIV on September 1, 1715. His successor was his four-year-old great-grandson Louis XV, whose health was precarious. The nephew of Louis XIV, Philip, Duke of Orléans, had been named regent, and he quickly consolidated his control against all rivals. A debauchee and cynic of fifty-one, Orléans had once been a hero in the War of the Succession until he was forced to leave Spain under a cloud by a jealous Felipe V, who in following years grasped at every bit of gossip about his cousin's being a poisoner. Old hatreds were now intensified by Felipe V's conviction that he himself should be regent in France. Moreover, the Spanish king considered his claim as next successor to the French throne superior to Orléans' claim, despite the renunciations made before Utrecht. Many leading French legists had publically averred that such renunciations were null, and Felipe V eagerly agreed that he had overriding rights as an *"enfant de France."* The dreams of presiding at the Versailles of his youth were "the only things besides the marriage bed and a flushed woodcock that could raise him from his dark lethargy, put light in the vacant eye." There was even talk of Felipe's marching an army on Paris, but he was outmaneuvered by Orléans at every hand. The enmity of France was to make Alberoni's and Isabel's Italian policy much more difficult.

Alberoni turned to Britain, whom he granted an extremely generous commercial treaty in December, 1715, giving that country even further rights of trade in Spanish America. An intermediary in the negotiations was the Dutch minister in Madrid, Baron Ripperda, of whom much would be heard later in Spain. Friendship with Britain proved elusive, for King George I's German interests came first, and he signed an alliance with Hapsburg Austria in June, 1716.

The Emperor Charles VI still did not recognize the title of Felipe V, who in turn did not acknowledge the loss to him of former Spanish territories. Now there was talk of Austria's securing one of these territories, the island of Sicily awarded the Duke of Savoy in 1713, in exchange for another, the island of Sardinia, won for Austria by the British navy. Already aroused by this and other Austrian intrigues in the Mediterranean, Felipe V was provoked to rage by the high-handed arrest by Austrian officials in Lombardy of the new Spanish Inquisitor General during July, 1717. Alberoni was later to claim, against all evidence, that the Spanish sovereigns and the Duke of Parma pushed him into a war he did not want. He had at last won his cardinalate that very July, the college in Rome approving his elevation with one dissent—Cardinal Giudice. One thing that had recommended Alberoni to the Pope was his dispatching of six Spanish warships to aid the Venetians fighting the Turks. The resources of the emperor were also heavily committed to the same war with the Ottoman Empire. With Austria distracted, with Spain mobilized, it was a perfect opportunity for an expedition mounted at Barcelona to sail secretly against Sardinia in August. The whole island was subjugated by November.

The powers alternated threats against Spain with offers to mediate a general rearrangement of Mediterranean territories, including the eventual succession of Isabel's son to the duchies. Confident of his new power, Felipe V rejected any new "dictation," while the French envoy complained of "the whim of the Queen who won't hear any word but war." Alberoni still presented himself as a man of peace, all the while he energetically organized Spain for war. The man who could cook macaroni to perfection could also order vast armaments. Another armada was assembled in Barcelona, the greatest in Spanish history with 33,000 troops, 100 cannon, 22 battleships, and several hundred auxiliary vessels. It sailed on June 17, its destination kept secret from a universally hostile and apprehensive Europe. The descent was made on Palermo on July 1, the Sicilian nobility and militia flocked to the Spanish side, and the whole island was mastered within a few days.

Alberoni would have been content to hold Sicily as a negotiating piece, whereas the Duke of Parma advised an immediate drive against Naples. The whole situation was overturned on August 16, 1718, when Admiral George Byng with a powerful British squadron attacked the Spanish fleet without warning off Cape Passaro and destroyed most of its ships by sinking or capture. Later Byng aided the landing of Austrian troops which drove the Spanish back on Palermo. An angry and frustrated Alberoni reacted to the news: "The infamy of the English could not be blacker: the work and strivings of years rendered vain in the span of a moment."

Felipe V remained adamant against peace negotiations. Alberoni confided to the French ambassador that the king "will allow the four corners of Europe to be set ablaze unless some expedient can be found." The cardinal himself then undertook the blaze setting on a continental scale, employing every conceivable maneuver of double-dealing and subversion that even a cynical age was outraged. The ill success of Alberoni's endeavors should not obscure his sheer daring and imagination. To neutralize Austria, he tried to stir up Russia and Prussia against it, he did his best to thwart the conclusion of peace with the Turks, and he made promises to Savoy at Austria's expense. Then Alberoni's agents tried to persuade Sweden to invade England in support of the pretender. Britain replied by declaring war on Spain in December, 1718. The pamphleteer Defoe duly thundered that Spanish possession of Sicily meant the ruin of British commerce in the Mediterranean and that the Spanish navy must not be allowed "to grow to such an inordinate and monstrous pitch."

France declared war on Spain in the following January, 1719, the regent Orléans having been exasperated to fury by the numerous intrigues of Alberoni. The Spanish ambassador was discovered to be in secret negotiations with the eccentric and literary Duchess of Maine, who had had posters printed proclaiming the coming to power of her husband, the favorite bastard son of Louis XIV, with Felipe V to be his chief lieutenant. During subsequent intrigues against the regent, known as the "war of libels," Voltaire earned his first year of imprisonment in the Bastille.

Undaunted by the hostile combination facing Spain, Alberoni set out to carry war to his enemies. The pretender James III was spirited out of Rome and set up in residence at the Buen Retiro of Madrid. Of Spain's surviving fleet six battleships were assembled at Cádiz and sailed with 6,000 troops in early March with the aim of landing in western England to arouse supposed supporters of the Stuarts. Storms off Cape Finisterre forced this armament to retire, but a separate force of two frigates with 500 Irish Catholic troops successfully made a landing in Scotland. This little army received scant support from the Jacobites and was soon forced to surrender to the government of George I. Still another Spanish land-sea force was amassed at Corunna for the purpose of aiding Breton rebels against the regent, but it was blockaded by a British fleet. Alberoni had to observe wistfully: "Human schemes unaided by Providence are of little or no use. Of the plans I devised had but one of them been successful, it would have been enough to upset the enemy's designs."

Spain now paid directly for Alberoni's failed plotting. On April 21, 1719, it was invaded by a French army of 30,000 led by none other than the Duke of Berwick, half brother of the pretender and grandee of Spain for his triumph at Almansa in 1707. San Sebastián fell in August, and the Basque provinces were overrun. The French destroyed all of Alberoni's arsenals they entered, while the British navy effected a landing at Vigo and did the same there. Felipe V now abandoned his hunting to journey north with the queen and his heir in the vain hope of persuading French soldiers to desert to him as a grandson of Louis XIV. Alberoni, always resourceful, had fleur-de-lis sewn on the banners of the Spanish troops, but always cautious, he made sure that the king got lost when he set out personally to confront the French army. The queen rode about with a huge pair of pistolets on her saddle, dressed in a striking uniform *à la amazone* specially smuggled in from Paris. While Felipe tried to make clear that he was not fighting his nephew Louis XV but only the regent, Berwick was careful to advertise that he did not oppose the king but only his evil minister.

Alberoni fell from power with unexpected suddenness. On December 5, 1719, the king and queen departed the capital for a hunting sojourn at El Pardo, leaving behind an order stripping the favorite of all his Spanish offices and giving him eight days to quit Madrid and three weeks to be out of Spain. Forbidden to have an interview with the monarchs, the thunderstruck and embittered cardinal was hustled away through Catalonia, where he came close to being lynched. Then he simply disappeared, as agents of many countries searched for him. In 1721 Alberoni delighted the Romans by dramatically appearing from nowhere to take part in the election of a new Pope. He thereafter advanced rapidly as a papal administrator, founding a still-extant college for priests and advancing himself as a serious candidate to be Pope. Always protesting his good intentions when head of the Spanish government, Alberoni said unprintable things about his former sovereigns in private while securing a wide and sympathetic audience for his published memoirs, which included a plea for a sort of permanent league of nations. Numbering Walpole, Voltaire, and Frederick the Great among his admirers, when the cardinal died in 1752 at age eighty-eight, he could say with some truth that events had vindicated him.

Although variously characterized as a buffoon, an adventurer, and a statesman, Cardinal Alberoni in the opinion of most observers was made the scapegoat for disasters he was only partially responsible for. A British agent had got the ear of the Duke of Parma, who in turn secretly communicated with Felipe V to the effect that Spain could expect reasonable peace terms only if Alberoni were dismissed. Quite possibly Isabel Farnese defended her fellow Italian to the last, for in later years she spoke of recalling him. For all of Alberoni's deceitfulness and treachery, he was truly able and "the first minister who succeeded in raising Spain again from the slough of ignorant and impotent pride into which she had fallen to be an active force in the councils of Europe."

As for the war, it was concluded by the Treaty of The Hague of February 17, 1720, with Spain getting terms it might well have secured peacefully five years before. Felipe V once again renounced any claims to the French throne, and for the first time he recognized the loss of Flanders and the Italian provinces to the Hapsburgs. Sardinia was evacuated by Spanish forces and was awarded to the Duke of Savoy, along with the title King of Sardinia, while Austria gained Sicily in exchange. Ceasing to call himself "Carlos III," the emperor at last recognized Felipe V as king, and he and the other powers undertook to support the claims of Isabel Farnese's son Carlos to Parma, Piacenza, and Tuscany.

2. *Obsessions and Intrigues: The Lightning Reign of Luis I (1724)*

In the years after the fall of Alberoni the king's fits of depression began to border on insanity. Talk of his abdication was to assume dramatic, if brief, reality. The 1720's and 1730's also demonstrated the complete hold Isabel Farnese had both over her husband and the destinies of Spain.

THE SPANISH BOURBONS [58

Visiting Spain in 1721, the Duke of Saint-Simon found Felipe V sadly altered from the gravely handsome youth he remembered. His Hapsburg chin now stuck out grotesquely in an emaciated face. Hunchbacked, shrunken, stomach protruding, the king was so bowlegged that his feet fell all over themselves as he walked about hurriedly. When he talked at all, his voice was a drawl. The visitor was "confounded" to find the King "so foolish" in his appearance, Felipe wearing a ratty wig, a very worn brown serge suit, and a jumble of ribbons and orders that hid one another.

The king's physical condition was still sound, although he suffered from overindulgence in the hunt, at the table, and on the marriage bed. He was extremely prone to fits of what Alberoni had called "black melancholy," to the point that people despaired for his life or at least his sanity. Thwarted in his routine, as when he was sent off to Italy in 1702 or after the evacuation of Madrid in 1706, Felipe took refuge in nearly catatonic lethargy. In 1717, during the Mediterranean crisis, he suffered a complete mental breakdown. On this occasion he dementedly tore at his face in his sleep, woke up in pools of blood, and ran about with his sword crying "murder." Some secretions from his body caused his linen and bedclothes to have a phosphorescent glow, which the personal attention of the most pious nuns and the queen could not remove. This and many things played on Felipe's excessive superstition. Few kings were so limply dependent on their confessor as was the first Bourbon, who was wont to summon the priest at all hours. He gave the state of his soul complete precedence over the state of the state.

In his lucid moments, Felipe was kindly, generous, and merciful. The servants who knew him intimately loved him. The court which saw him at a distance begrudgingly admired his essential dignity. The officials who came in direct contact with him appreciated that he had both stubborn prejudices and sound judgments, when he was not being indolent and indecisive. Saint-Simon, so astonished at the preoccupations and sloppiness of the king in private, was equally impressed with his regal air in public, the grace and correctness of his speeches reminding him of Louis XIV. "He let flash his French heart without ceasing at the same time to show himself monarch of the Spanish."

The king's relationship with his wife was the talk of Europe. His grandaunt "Madame," close to Felipe in his youth, had these words to say about the adult:

> He loves his wife above all things, leaves all affairs to her, and never interferes in anything. He is very pious and believes he should be damned if he committed any matrimonial infidelity. But for his devotion he would be a libertine, for he is addicted to women, and it

is for this reason he is so fond of his wife . . . he is very easily led and for this reason the Queen won't lose sight of him.

Alberoni, in his memoirs, was more bitter and crude, writing that "Philip had only animal instinct, with which he perverted the Queen . . . he needed only a pre-dieu and the thighs of a woman."

The king's languor and attachment to his wife produced a situation where it could almost be said that Spain was ruled from "a bed of four and a half feet at most, of crimson damask, with four bed posts." Saint-Simon was witness to the scene of an almost recumbent king in his nightcap next to the queen sitting in her bedjacket doing embroidery, while state papers lay piled about among the balls of yarn on the bed and on an adjoining armchair. Here the chief ministers were received each morning.

When Felipe bestirred himself to attend entertainments or ceremonies, the queen never left his side, knowing how suggestible he was to anyone who had his ear. At official audiences she sat at his feet on a stool, coaching him with his responses, making up awkward gaps in conversation, and arranging the end of the interview when he showed signs of restlessness. She sat for hours with him in a hunting blind, waiting for the game to be driven past, and she was encouragingly nearby when Felipe played his nightly game of cards. Walking from one place to another, if the queen lagged a few steps behind, the king would stop and rejoin her. The longest she was ever out of his presence was for the half hour of her morning toilette. So dependent on each other from one moment to the next, neither of the royal couple was ever touched by a breath of scandal.

Etiquette dictated that Isabel Farnese could not govern Spain except at her husband's elbow, but no one questioned that she did so, sacrificing some of her exuberant nature to the deeply satisfying task of presiding over a royal court, however monotonous its routine. Impulsive, uneducated, she became through daily effort a fairly astute assessor of men and matters. Many Spaniards resented the extent of her influence, as well as the spontaneity of her character. In turn, she fully realized that she did not enjoy the popularity of her predecessor (on occasion street crowds yelled *"Viva la Saboyana"* when the Parmesan queen rode by). Once she avowed quite straightforwardly: "The Spanish do not like me, but I fully detest them also." Because of the hostility, she had no alternative but to cling to her eccentric husband and to associate with non-Spaniards, preferring not only her fellow Italians but all sorts of adventurous foreigners like Flemish from lost Flanders and Scots or Irish Jacobites. "An entourage of exiles is a sorry school of politics"—a fair criticism. High spirits and lack of self-consciousness, Italian rather than Spanish traits, saved Elizabeth from boredom and self-pity, and her maternal passion for her children's future gave her a strong hold on life. She could show a hot temper and on occasion cursed out ambassadors, but her underlying good humor and the king's gentleness dissolved the impact of most of her outbursts.

Court life became more circumspect as the king grew more crotchety and the queen more matronly. In the first years of their marriage, the adolescent bride had a taste for such recreations as organizing mock battles between her ladies and the king's attendant dwarfs and jesters, with confetti throwing giving way to wig pulling in the ensuing tumult. Sedate evenings at cards later became the rule, or an occasional entertainment. Lavish balls in the French manner were considered alien to Spanish tradition and contrary to propriety, particularly in view of the scandalous stories coming out of Regency France. Both the monarchs had an aversion to bullfights, so that this blood sport fell into complete disuse in Spain, and they shunned fiestas as much as possible.

With a view to isolating themselves further and with thoughts even of complete retirement, the royal couple in 1721 began the laying out of the vast palace and gardens of La Granja, also known as the royal site of San Ildefonso. The new residence was located fifty miles north of Madrid, well beyond the forbidding Escorial and on the other side of the Guadarrama Mountains that separate New and Old Castile. While on a hunting party, Felipe and Isabel had taken delight in the setting of a dairy farm (granja) belonging to a convent and purchased it. The surrounding beauty of snowy mountains and dense pine forests appealed to them more than to foreign ambassadors, who found it savage and inconveniently situated up impossible roads 1,200 meters above sea level. Picturesque Segovia was seven miles away, but La Granja was un-Spanish in tradition, barring the original farmroom that has been preserved amid palatial splendor. It was a blatant imitation of the Baroque symmetries and sculptural decorativeness of the Versailles Felipe remembered from his boyhood. Construction proceeded with scarcely a thought to cost, and accordingly, the expenses of the court were to triple under Felipe V from the days of Carlos II. Besides much imported Italian sculpture, the particular glory of La Granja was its twenty-six fountains, some of which could shoot 200 feet in the air, being fed from a tank high above on the mountains. Yet for all the cascading waters and gesturing statues the palace served at first only as a retreat for a brooding, praying king.

The court at San Ildefonso was stirred in January, 1722, by the announcement of a double marriage treaty with France. The Infanta María Ana Victoria, then three, was betrothed to King Louis XV, then eleven. To be educated in France, she was in effect exchanged at the frontier for the daughter of the Regent Orléans, Princess Louise Elizabeth, who was in due course married to the Prince of the Asturias, Luis, Felipe's eldest son by his first wife. A year later Orléans' second daughter arrived in Spain to become the fiancée of Don Carlos, the king's eldest son by Isabel Farnese. The motivations of the adult principals in these arrangements were complex and confused. The Spanish ruler openly sought to secure the regent's aid in his Italian projects. Privately, Felipe thought that the infanta at Versailles could further the claims of himself or his son to the French throne if Louis XV died prematurely. Likewise with an eye to the French throne, the regent thought he could influence his new son-in-law in his favor, as well as extend French influence in Spain generally. Most of these calculations came to naught. Orléans died in December, 1723, to the unseemly pleasure of Felipe V, who nonetheless acquiesced in the new regency in France of the Duke of Bourbon, his cousin.

Less than two months after Orléans' death, the world was astonished by the news from San Ildefonso that the forty-year-old Felipe V had voluntarily given up his crown. The instrument of abdication, dated January 10, 1724, declared: "Having considered maturely for the last five years the miseries of this life, owing to the infirmities, wars, and turmoil which God has sent me during the twenty three years of my reign, and seeing that my eldest son Luis . . . is married and of sufficient age, judgment, and ability to govern with justice . . . I have determined to abdicate all my States . . . to my said eldest son Luis." The document provided for the possible succession of Luis' brother, Fernando, and then the children of Isabel Farnese.

In their stupefaction at Felipe's act, people in Spain and abroad almost forgot that the great Carlos I in the sixteenth century had renounced his power in favor of retirement to a monastery, succumbing to a brooding melancholy. Observers at the time and historians later were insistent on finding ulterior motives for the new abdication. Felipe was alleged to have finally recoiled in disgust at the corruption of the Italians dominating the court, a claim for which there is no substantiation. He was supposedly convinced that the will of Carlos II was false and that he himself was a usurper, an unlikely conclusion after fighting the Hapsburgs for the crown for twelve years. A widely accepted explanation in European chancelleries was that the king's move was a sinister effort to remove legal scruples so as to put him that much closer to the throne of France. Popular sentiment in Madrid echoed this suspicion, as evidenced by the street poem to the effect: "Nobody escapes the world/ Nobody renounces in the name of God/ A king renounces so as to be two/ And a bishop so as to be Pope."

Actually, Felipe should have been taken at his word that religion rather than ambition was the reason. His life had always been a torment spiritually, with his confessor driven on more than one occasion to remind him that he was a king and not a monk. As alluded to in the abdication message, the king each year for five years had made a solemn vow to God to retire. Later Isabel Farnese confirmed in a conversation with an Italian ambassador that the royal couple had reached this decision during the Navarre campaign of 1719 and that she had taken similar vows at the side of her husband in the chapel of the Escorial. While there is reason to believe that the queen may have opposed taking the final step, she was powerless in this one instance to dissuade her tormented husband.

In a remarkably high-minded instruction to Luis and his queen, the retiring monarch adjured them to "render justice to all of your subjects, to the great and to the small, protecting the latter against the violence and extortions they were subject to." Specifically, "the vexations that the Indians suffer should be remedied." In general, "care for your people as much as you can and make up for what the hard times of my reign did not permit me to do." Finally, "be great Kings and at the same time great Saints." Felipe V therewith shut himself up in San Ildefonso, declaring somewhat ominously, "they can do what they want with my son but I will save my soul."

The people of Madrid turned out in the streets for days to cheer themselves hoarse at the prospect of the departure from the scene of the moody Felipe and the self-seeking Isabel. When Luis I appeared in the capital and was proclaimed king in the centuries-old manner on February 9, 1724, the mood was one of frenetic enthusiasm. All the grandees showed up for the hand-kissing ceremony, and every citizen was on hand to watch Luis go to the Church of the Atocha to give thanks. That Luis was young and Spanish-born obviously excited his new subjects. He responded to the acclamations with every sign of pleasure, and to symbolize his Spanishness as his first act, he reintroduced traditional Hapsburg etiquette at court. Promptly he was dubbed "the well-beloved," perhaps prematurely but scarcely too soon as events turned out.

Just over sixteen at the time of his accession, Don Luis was not unprepossessing in looks, and he bore himself with grace. He was tall, slender, and somewhat delicate of health. Blond like both parents, he had his long-deceased mother's gift of agreeableness, while he took after his father in his love of exercise, being adept at handball and bowling. The father and son rode and hunted together frequently. Another one of Luis' accomplishments and pleasures was dancing. His usual partner was perforce of protocol his stepmother, and Saint-Simon declared that they danced so beautifully together that if their station had permitted them to appear in a theater, the public would willingly have paid higher prices for tickets.

The new king's education had been neglected, prompting a French observer to call him "very ignorant," as well as "extremely timid and overly serious." The few early years when the Princess of Ursins was the royal governess had given him some Gallic veneer. Briefly, Cardinal Giudice had been his beloved tutor, only to be replaced by an Italian duke who was a better spy than teacher and who instilled in his charge little more than excessive piety and filial submissiveness. Much of the time Luis had been left in the care of valets, and he continued to be most at ease in the company of servants. Yet he was also very conscious of his family heritage, having as a boy written letters to the awesome Louis XIV, who was apprised of such things as his great-grandson's acquiring his first suit of man's clothes. Initiated partially into state affairs by his father when he was fourteen, Luis showed every sign of good intentions, but he also displayed timidity, indecisiveness, and indolence. "He resembles the King [meaning Felipe V] in many ways," Saint-Simon had observed a few years before Luis' accession, also noting that he was "very much a boy."

Luis I from the outset would probably have been a more self-assured ruler and more independent of his parents if his wife had been a source of support to him instead of being a distressing problem. As it was, he was once driven to write San Ildefonso: "I would prefer to be sent to the galleys than to live with a creature who observes no proprieties, who pleases me in nothing, and who does not think of anything except eating and appearing naked before her servants." He appended the remark that in some forty private conversations he had been able to have with his wife she had done nothing but laugh at him. The woman, rather girl, in question was Louise Elizabeth, Duchess of Montpensier, born in 1709 and thus twelve when she became Princess of the Asturias and fourteen when she became Queen of Spain. The fifth daughter of the Duke of Orléans, she had been reared in a household notorious for license, and all her sisters were already touched by scandal to some degree. Louise Elizabeth's woeful schooling was evident in the utterly ungrammatical letters she wrote back to Paris from Madrid. Yet she was smart enough to learn Spanish very quickly. "Madame" had already developed some very pronounced views on her grandchild even before she left: "One cannot say that Mademoiselle de Montpensier is ugly. She has pretty eyes, a fine white skin, a well-made nose, although a little thin, a very small mouth; for all that she is the most disagreeable person I have ever seen in my life; in all she does, when she speaks, when she eats, when she drinks, she is insufferable."

As for particulars of the idiosyncrasies of the new Queen of Spain, a historian has categorized them under three headings: "She had a strong penchant for water, for food, and for indecency." Water had some peculiar fascination for Luisa Isabel, her Spanish name. The least of her whims was to go walking in the rain with her skirts hiked up; the worst was her delight in turning on the trick fountains of San Ildefonso and drenching unsuspecting promenaders. Her mania for laundering her own clothes and even for washing the flagstones of her terrace, all in public view, once led her husband to talk of having her put away. All menial tasks seemed to interest the French princess, who once startled more than pleased her parents-in-law by presenting them with vegetables she had grown herself. The queen's eating habits were also offensive to Spaniards. Apart from the fact that she grew fat from gluttony, she ate with both hands, made disgusting noises, dined at improbable hours, deliberately let all her food get cold, doused everything with vinegar, and insisted on madly exotic dishes. In the course of her bizarre feasting she more than once let herself get drunk.

The gossip began immediately and increased with time about Luisa Isabel's indelicate behavior and indecency. One of her first public appearances had been for the purpose of bidding farewell to the French emissary who had brought her, none other than the Duke of Saint-Simon. She listened to his ceremonial effusions with no sign of attention and at the end did no more, and no less, than emit a loud belch. His stunned silence drew another room-shattering noise, and this was repeated as the Frenchman withdrew in confusion and as the courtiers tried to contain themselves. If some of the Princess of the Asturias' comportment was downright boorishness, some could be possibly excused as merely the frivolity of a very young girl, such as when she cut the skirt strings of her chief lady-in-waiting causing her great embarrassment in the full view of an assemblage. The most shocking single incident after Luisa Isabel became queen was the time she climbed a ladder to pick some fruit, found herself crying for help, and forthwith fell into the arms of a French officer, whom she later accused of insulting her. In an age when it was still held treasonable for a man even to touch female royalty, King Luis felt impelled to forbid the entirely innocent Frenchman ever to enter the palace again. The husband later dismissed several of his wife's ladies-in-waiting and maids on grounds of excessive intimacy with her. It had been brought to his attention that a favorite pastime of Luisa Isabel's was a game vulgarly called *broche-en-cul,* whereby she and her lady companions stripped naked, hobbled their arms and legs with sticks, and then butted each other about until someone was reduced to helpless recumbency on the floor. A Spanish commentator probably exaggerated when he used the word "obscene" in reference to this diversion. King Luis was prone to use the word "extravagances" when he drew up lists of complaints which he from time to time gave the queen. She would be penitent for a while, only to resume her caprices at the first opportunity.

The royal couple's estrangement may simply have reflected their difficulties in the marriage bed. They had not been allowed to sleep with each other for a full fourteen months after their wedding, much to the chagrin of Luis. The occasion of their first night together was recorded in the annals of the court: Queen Isabel supervised the undressing of the thirteen-year-old bride, King Felipe attended to his son, and then everyone ceremoniously saw to the pair's being brought together in the same bed. The whole court was on hand again the next morning, at which time "the prince had a gay air; the princess appeared flushed." The marriage may not have been really consummated for a long while, for there exist four letters from son to father pleading for very specific information about the sexual act (the scholar who reported finding these in the archives did not record their contents, for reasons of delicacy).

The "battles of the night" between the royal couple in Madrid, to use the expression of the French ambassador, were regularly brought to the attention of the ex-sovereigns beyond the mountains at San Ildefonso. Somewhat contemptuously called the "royal hermits" by the people of Madrid, Felipe V and Isabel Farnese had made a show of austerity, the one having disposed of his stables, the other appearing in simple dress, and the both managing with only sixty servants. They spent most of their days attending confession or mass, with occasional walks in the gardens or visits to neighboring religious shrines. Yet Isabel, in secret correspondence with the French ambassador, could not resist the temptation to interfere in the affairs of the young royal couple, having come completely to detest her daughter-in-law. Moreover, Felipe V's last act had been to appoint the members of his son's council, a group of nonentities who were accustomed to take orders from the principal secretary of state, a man named Grimaldi, whom Felipe insisted on keeping at his side. The resulting situation was described by the Venetian ambassador: "In every petty matter the oracle was consulted at San Ildefonso; it might be said that the royal title was in Madrid; its essence at San Ildefonso." After one particular instance where Luis reversed himself in deference to the wishes of his parents, Luisa Isabel as usual came right to the point and shouted in her husband's face, "You are not the king!"

Toward the end of July, 1724, Luis and Luisa Isabel effected a definite reconciliation, the king expressing his pleasure at his wife's complaisance by presenting her with a particularly valuable diamond. The young monarch also began to give more ear to the patriotic party at court who wished to withdraw him from the tutelage of the ex-sovereigns and who used as one means exposure of their sheer extravagance. Amid these hopeful signs for the future King Luis I suffered a fainting fit and had to leave mass on August 15. Within a few days his indisposition was diagnosed as smallpox. Felipe V, who had lost so many of his relatives to this scourge, refused to budge from San Ildefonso when it became known his son's condition was serious, while the infantes and many of the court made haste to remove themselves from the capital.

Always one to do the unexpected, Queen Luisa Isabel now insisted on staying at her husband's bedside, defying etiquette and risking contagion. Her solicitude and care were to no avail, and after the doctors admitted despair, the last resort was to bring to the king's room the bodies of two saints and holy images from churches near and far. Luis I died at 2:30 A.M. on August 31, 1724, just seven days after his seventeenth birthday, having reigned for considerably less than a year.

Inevitably, some court circles chose to believe that the "well-beloved" had been poisoned, most likely at the instigation of a stepmother ambitious for her own children. One rumor was that at the autopsy of the dead king the doctor in charge became ill and even burned his hands, so noxious were some of the organs examined. Present-day physicians who have studied the old medical records conclude that while Luis' doctors might have made some mistakes, like two bloodlettings, smallpox itself was sufficient cause of death. The foul-play theory also runs contrary to all the previous evidence of mutual respect and even affection between Luis and Isabel Farnese. The word "poison" did pass the stepmother's lips but in another context: resigned to the fact that her husband might let his second son, Don Fernando, succeed to the throne, she muttered that the Spaniards will "poison him with their false counsels and kill him just like the other."

As for Luisa Isabel, she did indeed catch smallpox but survived it without any disfigurement. The many who wished her the worst had only the satisfaction of seeing her eventually shipped back to France. Here she enjoyed all the honors due a Queen of Spain (still another woman who could sign herself *Yo la Reina*, Mariana, widow of Carlos II, lived on in Bayonne and later Guadalajara until 1740). Not without dignity at times and untouched by scandal with men, Luisa Isabel pursued with sublime indifference such of her eccentricities as laundering and gluttony. Badly brought up, always friendless at the Spanish court, and the victim of every spite from her parents-in-law, the wife of Luis I had never done a mean thing, if very few noble things. Yet the news of her death from dropsy in 1742 made the French court break out laughing.

Luis I had designated his father as his successor, but Felipe V had sworn to renounce the throne forever, and his act of abdication had provided that his second son, Fernando, was next in line. A regency for the ten-year-old prince, a situation favored by those of the nobility who dreamed of restoring the influence of their class, was considered unthinkable by Isabel Farnese, by leading members of the Council of Castile, and by the French ambassador, particularly in view of the storm clouds gathering in European diplomacy. The ever conscience-stricken king consulted theologians and the papal nuncio before he decided to resume the throne on September 7, 1724. There was a notable lack of enthusiasm in the country upon the reaccession of the gloomy, middle-aged monarch. The bitterness would undoubtedly have been overpowering if Spain had known that it was destined for a twenty-two-year déjà vu of meaningless wars over Italian real estate.

Spanish diplomacy underwent a complete reversal in the year 1725. For months a congress of European diplomats had been meeting at Cambrai in a futile effort to resolve outstanding disputes. The greatest problem was the refusal of the emperor to implement the earlier agreement to allow Don Carlos to succeed in Parma and Tuscany; rather the Hapsburg made moves to gain the areas for himself. In vain Spain sought the support of Britain and France. Then everything was thrown into confusion by the decision of the French regent, the Duke of Bourbon, to cancel the engagement of Louis XV to the Infanta María Ana Victoria. From the French point of view it was simply a matter of not being willing to wait for the seven-year-old princess to reach childbearing age when their young king was both virile and violent enough in his pursuit of hunting to jeopardize his health. Civil war faced France in the absence of a direct-line heir, and so Bourbon scanned a new list of one hundred eligible brides, including a daughter of the Prince of Wales (who refused to convert) and a daughter of Peter the Great (later Russia's passionate, lovable Empress Elizabeth). For Spain it was small satisfaction that Louis ended up making the strangest of French royal marriages on September 25, 1725, to the dowryless daughter of the obscure ex-King of Poland or that Bourbon was soon disgraced for his blunders. Thwarted in their French marriage design and deeply insulted, Felipe V and Isabel angrily demanded that all French personnel leave the country (the engagement of Don Carlos to Orléans' daughter was also canceled).

Alberoni had once toyed with the possibility of solving Spain's diplomatic frustrations by making a deal with the chief enemy, Austria, and this renewed prospect suddenly brought onto the scene one of the most extraordinary adventurers in history, the Baron Ripperda. He was sent on a secret mission to Vienna in the fall of 1724, a mission that could have easily been disavowed if events in France had turned out otherwise. A native of Holland but professedly of Castilian origin, Ripperda had served as a negotiator at Utrecht and then as Dutch envoy in Madrid. He went over to the service of Spain and became a protégé of Alberoni, who used him as manager of some of his new factories. Originally, Catholic, then Protestant in Holland, Ripperda ostentatiously reconverted in Spain and also ingratiated himself by the freehanded expenditure of his wife's wealth.

The commercial expert sent to Vienna proved to be fully as extravagant as Alberoni in pursuing diplomatic grand designs and double crosses on a European scale. And once again the sovereigns in Madrid were taken in by the exaggerated promises and fantasies. At the heart of the projects was the marriage of the Infante Carlos (aged eight) with the Archduchess María Teresa (aged seven), who was the sole heir of Charles VI, Holy Roman Emperor and once would-be King of Spain. Ripperda envisaged Carlos' eventual succession to all the Hapsburg lands in Central Europe and his succession in Spain as well, should the sickly Infante Fernando die. Felipe and Isabel were entranced at the idea of a new universal monarchy, as was the Pope, who was being converted by Cardinal Alberoni with a plan for a general crusade to reestablish Catholic supremacy in Europe. To Charles VI, not only did Ripperda hold out the prospect of Spanish aid against the Turks and the German Protestants, but he also dangled the bait of opening Spain and the Indies to the commercial endeavors of the emperor's pet Ostend and Trieste companies. France would be despoiled of its northern provinces in Austria's favor, while Spain would come by Roussillon, Navarre, Sardinia, Gibraltar, and Minorca. As usual Britain would be neutralized by supporting a restoration of the Stuarts.

Ripperda returned in triumph to Madrid in November, 1725, with a commercial treaty and a secret alliance with Austria. So excited was Felipe V by his seeming success that he allowed the first bullfights in twenty years and attended in person to ecstatic popular acclaim. Ripperda was made a grandee and a duke and given control of all the principal offices of the government. Once more the armories and naval arsenals of Spain bustled with activity, as a prelude to a repetition of the nightmare of 1718.

Even before Ripperda had returned to Spain, his boasts and indiscretions had alarmed the other powers and drove Britain, France, and Prussia to counter the Spanish-Austrian alliance with one of their own. British warships menaced Spain's coasts and the Indies. Moreover, the Austrian ambassador in Madrid revealed that his country had really committed itself to very little beyond friendship and favorable consideration of the marriage of the infante and the archduchess when they both were of age. Spain's treasury was soon depleted. Revolts broke out in the northern provinces. The historical script called for a scapegoat in this discrepancy of dreams and realities, and Ripperda was abruptly dismissed from all his posts in May, 1726. The king felt not unkindly toward the man and intended to pension him off, but Ripperda took fright at reports of his impending imprisonment and fled to the British embassy. Forcibly removed to a Spanish jail for two years, he secured his escape and eventually turned up in Morocco, where he pursued more adventures, converting to Islam, serving as prime minister to the Bey of Tunis, and at one point proclaiming himself King of Corsica.

Despite Ripperda's downfall, the pro-Austrian party remained ascendant at Madrid for a while longer. In a general reshuffling of officials the king's confessor was replaced by a Scots Jacobite, who, with the king's Irish Jacobite doctor, talked up the anti-British cause. The first Spanish ambassador arrived in Russia with the aim of gaining that emerging nation's aid against King George I. In February, 1727, without declaring war, Spanish forces began a futile five-month siege of Gibraltar. When no Austrian aid was forthcoming, a truce was signed in May. Nor would the Austrians give satisfaction relative to the future of Isabel's children in terms of archduchesses and Italian duchies. Accordingly, Felipe V once again allowed a complete reversal of policy, and by the Treaty of Seville of November, 1729, Spain gained from Britain and France new guarantees of support for the succession of Carlos in Parma and Tuscany. The inevitable price Spain paid for Isabel Farnese's ambitions was to forget the Gibraltar question and to favor the British over the Ostend Company in the American trade.

3. Palaces and Pieces of Italy

The Treaty of Seville, ending the diplomatic intrigues associated with Ripperda, was signed in that city because the Spanish court was there, and the court remained in the south of Spain for the next five years, trying as best it could to keep to itself the secret that Felipe V had gone almost completely insane. Without the stimulus of royal bounty, Madrid became "little more than a corpse," a description which often quite fitted the king.

Early in 1728 the king had suffered such a desperate mental and physical breakdown that no one expected him to recover. He was brought to his senses by the report of Louis XV's having smallpox and the renewed prospect of his own succession to the French throne. Troops were moved north, but the crisis blew over. In January, 1729, the king and queen traveled to Badajoz for the double marriage of the Infante Fernando and the Infanta María Ana Victoria with a princess and prince of Portugal. Later they moved to the Alcázar of Seville to witness the transferral of the remains of San Fernando to that city. There the news came of the birth of a dauphin in Paris, news that once and for all ended Felipe's grand dream, and he lapsed into the longest and darkest of his melancholies. Later a French envoy was to make a mot of the king's plight: "Since I have been in Spain I have seen him one year without his going to bed, one year without his getting up, and one year without his speaking."

For several long spells, one of which lasted six months, the king refused to leave his room or even to go more than a few steps from his bed. He rested for hours with fixed eyes, his mouth open and his tongue hanging out. Sometimes he would work his lips vigorously, but no sound would come forth. In these periods he would still not permit the queen to leave his presence or to talk to anyone out of his hearing. Each day in the late afternoon their two confessors would come and hear the monarchs aloud and simultaneously. The king did continue to eat prodigiously, causing him serious fits of indigestion. For weeks on end his only other activity was fishing in a basin that had been filled with fish and brought into the room.

Felipe went through phases when he refused to wash or shave or change his clothes. He would not let his nails be cut, and his toenails grew so long he complained that he could not walk. He wore his clothes to tatters and mended them himself when his valet pleaded inability. With the notion that he was to be poisoned by means of his shirt, the king started wearing his wife's bedclothes; an ambassador once interviewed him when he had on only a dirty blouse.

Some of the king's habits could be explained by his obsessions, although some peculiarities such as imagining himself to be a frog defied explanation. Going about in rags was a form of taking the vow of poverty. Pretending that he was a corpse or becoming catatonic were ways of not being king, to assuage Felipe's guilt feelings about resuming the crown despite his vows. Most of his manias had basis in religion, but on occasion Felipe reacted negatively to his faith, refusing the sacrament, ignoring his confessor.

Felipe kept talking about abdicating again. Once he smuggled a letter of renunciation to the council, but the queen managed to retrieve it in time. After that she denied him the possession of ink and paper.

Rarely did Felipe become actually violent toward others, although he might bite or scratch himself viciously. On one occasion he did pummel the foreign minister, and on another he struck out at Isabel Farnese. There were witnesses to a time when he cursed and reviled her at length, forcing her to beg forgiveness on her knees. Still, she could usually bring him around, even reduce him to tears, if she threatened to desert his bed.

In the third or fourth year of his mania Felipe became merely moody and crotchety. He led a routine life but kept strange hours, apparently confusing night and day. Dinner would be taken at 3 A.M., and he would retire at 5. Later his bedtime became 8 A.M., then 10. One bit of willfulness was having the palace windows shut during stifling summer days and wide open in the winter. Once the queen ventured to complain of the cold, and the irascible husband replied, "All right, let them close half the windows for my wife and leave the other half open for me." A tacit understanding arose between Felipe and Isabel that he would leave off his threats of abdication if she would abide such eccentricities.

A number of things combined eventually to bring Felipe out of his lethargy and imbecility. The queen and his councillors had long observed that major happenings abroad made the king lucid and active; now they learned to manufacture an atmosphere of crisis and military bustle. His threats of retirement largely ended when he heard the fate of old Victor Amadeus, King of Sardinia. Having hounded his eldest son to suicide, the Italian monarch abdicated in 1730 in favor of another son so that he could live with a mistress; the new king revenged his brother by throwing the father in prison, where he soon died. Still another factor in returning Felipe to normal was persuading him to move the court back to Madrid, with the attendant sojourns at La Granja and Aranjuez.

Building now became an obsession of the king and queen, as if to immortalize the achievements of the long reign. They further embellished San Ildefonso and its gardens, and when the old Alcázar in Madrid burned to the ground on Christmas Day of 1734, the royal couple had an opportunity to replace the gloomy palace they hated with something new and splendid. There arose on the west side of Madrid on a bluff overlooking the Manzanares River a huge granite edifice called the Oriente Palace that to this day is a worthy rival of Buckingham, or Schönbrunn, or the Winter Palace. The sovereigns employed the leading artists of Spain and Italy in its decoration, and Spanish ambassadors throughout Europe made their reputations in terms of the master paintings and canvases they sent back to the royal galleries.

One of Isabel's importations from abroad that had the most extraordinary effect on the king was the singer Carlo Farinelli, who stayed in Spain for many years after 1737, having already achieved the greatest fame in Rome, Vienna, and London. The thirty-two-year-old Neopolitan was a castrato with a voice range of eight octaves. One evening when Felipe had shut himself up in his room, Isabel had Farinelli sing an aria in an adjoining salon. These words drove the brooding monarch to tears:

> The sun so pale, the sky so troubled,
> Announce sorrow, presage death,
> All inspire me with remorse and horror.

Forthwith Felipe told Farinelli that he could refuse him nothing, and the well-coached visitor begged the king to shave, dress himself, and attend to state business. Farinelli sang the above aria and the same four others to the court every night for a total of more than four thousand times. Felipe's reform of his ways was not without some excesses. A British diplomat reported: "The King himself imitates Farinelli, sometimes air after air, and sometimes after the music is over, and throws himself in such freaks and howlings that all possible means are taken to prevent people from being witness to his follies."

If throughout the 1730's the atmosphere of the Spanish court was Italian, so too the aggrandizement of Isabel Farnese's children in Italy remained the cardinal aim of Spanish diplomacy. The first great success came in December, 1731, when Don Carlos with the blessing of all the powers was landed with 6,000 troops at Leghorn to take possession of the duchies of Parma and Piacenza following the death of the last Farnese duke. He made his state entry into Florence in March to be acknowledged as heir to Tuscany. Belated protests of the Pope and the emperor relative to their rights of ultimate feudal suzerainty did not dampen the enthusiastic welcome by the Italians for the gay and intelligent Bourbon prince. The years of lost wars and diplomatic disappointments were momentarily forgotten in a jubilant Madrid. Truly, "the persistence of one woman had reestablished Spanish influence in Italy and raised Spain once more to a leading place in the councils of the world."

Such was Europe's distrust of Spain's diplomatic morality that the gathering of a large armada at Alicante in the summer of 1732 produced much alarm. Would there be another invasion of Sicily? Gibraltar? Minorca? It turned out that the aim was simply the recapture of Oran on the North African coast, a stronghold lost to the Moors in 1708. The success of Spanish arms was due to the capability of the Spanish-born administrator José Patiño; ironically, Spain had been contested in North Africa by none other than Baron Ripperda.

The death of King Augustus II of Poland in February, 1733, plunged Europe into a general war that Spain was able to take advantage of. The Polish succession was disputed between Augustus III of Saxony, backed by Austria, Prussia, and Russia, and Stanislaus Leszczyński, the father-in-law of Louis XV, backed by France. At one point the ever-maternal Isabel Farnese proposed that one of her sons be elected as a compromise King of Poland. Failing this, her ambition turned to the remaining Austrian possessions in Italy. In November, 1733, Spain signed the Treaty of the Escorial with France, later known as the first of three *Pactes de Famille* (family pacts) between the two branches of the Bourbons. The two countries guaranteed each other's possessions, pledged mutual support of any future annexations, and declared all previous treaties void. War now broke out in central Europe and Lombardy.

France was to lose in Poland, but Spain gained in Italy. A Spanish force of 16,000, veterans of Oran, were landed at Genoa and joined troops of Don Carlos from the duchies. After permission was granted by the Pope to enter his territories, Carlos led his army across the Neapolitan frontier in March, 1734, entered Naples in April, and defeated an Austrian army decisively the next month. Sicily once again welcomed the Bourbons enthusiastically. Carlos was named King of the Two Sicilies in Palermo on

July 5, 1735, a second genuine triumph for Isabel Farnese's eldest, a man destined to be Spain's own greatest Bourbon king.

Despite the promises of the *Pacte de Famille*, France made a preliminary peace with Austria in October, 1735, without consulting Spain. In a complicated exchange of territories, Lorraine went as a consolation prize to Stanislaus Leszczyński with the provision that it revert to France upon his death. Duke Francis of Lorraine, who had married the Hapsburg heiress Maria Theresa, was compensated with Tuscany, while Parma and Piacenza, recently ruled by Don Carlos, went to the Hapsburgs. Furious at French treachery, Isabel Farnese was particularly upset to lose her native state and disappointed in not gaining more for her children, but Spain in 1738 had to accept necessity.

Incredible as it may seem, Spain found itself involved in a new war in October, 1739, the enemy being Britain. In English histories it is known as the War of Jenkins' Ear, after a British sea captain who displayed in a box to an enraged Parliament the ear he alleged was severed from his head by a high-handed Spanish coast guard officer in the West Indies. At issue were British abuse of their trading rights in Spanish America and Spanish overreaction to their smuggling. It was the first clear case of British public opinion, in the form of pamphleteers and public house orators, driving a reluctant government into hostilities, for a negotiated settlement was in the offing. Prime Minister Robert Walpole declared ruefully, "They now ring the bells; they will soon be wringing their hands."

Britain's leader opposed the war in large part because of his consciousness of Spain's new military and naval power. While the British navy did score some successes such as the capture and sack of the great isthmian entrepôt Portobello in November, 1739, an attempt to capture Cartagena of the Indies in 1740 failed miserably, after the governor of Spain's richest Caribbean port organized a heroic defense. In Spain itself the king rallied his senses, and the country rallied to him with great financial sacrifices. Embargoes and corsairs wrecked British trade, and once again Spain aided the Stuart pretender.

The War of Jenkins' Ear soon merged into a larger all-European conflict, the War of the Austrian Succession, which broke out after Emperor Charles VI died on October 20, 1740, having labored for decades through a Pragmatic Sanction to leave the entire Hapsburg inheritance to a woman, his only daughter, Maria Theresa, destined to be the most beloved of all her family. Despite having acceded to the Pragmatic Sanction, Felipe V at once laid claim to all the hereditary possessions of his old rival, claiming a dynastic right going back to an alleged dispensation of Charles V in the sixteenth century. Obviously, however, the real game was to secure more of Hapsburg Italy for the queen's offspring. Lombardy, Parma, and Tuscany combined, for example, would make a fine kingdom for the Infante Felipe.

Hostilities between the Spanish and Austrians opened in Italy in 1742. A Spanish army led by Don Felipe was landed in the north, but the King of Sardinia's decision to back the cause of Maria Theresa robbed Felipe of an early chance of victory. An army sent to his brother's aid by Don Carlos of the Two Sicilies had to be recalled after a British fleet sailed into the Bay of Naples in August and gave a one-hour ultimatum. Prospects seemed to improve when France joined Spain in a second *Pacte de Famille* in October, 1743, which was further cemented by the marriage of the Infanta María Teresa to the dauphin in December, 1744. The allies made plans to convey an army of 40,000 from Dunkirk to restore the Stuarts in Britain, but a joint French-Spanish fleet failed to win control of the seas after a sharp engagement with the British in February, 1744. ("Bonnie Prince Charlie" failed in his own attempt to win Scotland and England the next year, the famous "Forty-five.") In Italy Felipe briefly triumphed with French aid, driving a wedge between the Sardinian and Austrian armies so that he was able to capture his mother's beloved Parma and then to enter Milan itself in the fall of 1745. He was soon driven out, his armies crushed, after France once again betrayed the family compact and made a shabby deal with Sardinia in early 1746.

As usual, King Felipe V was alert and active in times of excitement, at this point taking more part in affairs than he had in decades. Then, in the midst of the military setbacks and the recriminations with France, the sixty-two-year-old monarch was suddenly dead on July 9, 1746, of a broken blood vessel, or of what is called apoplexy when talking of royalty.

Few in Spain regretted the passing of the first Bourbon king and the end of the influence of Queen Isabel Farnese. The country had been at war forty years of the forty-six-year reign, often for purposes which could raise little patriotic response. There was bitter resentment of the great favor that had been shown to foreigners at the court, first the French, later the Italians.

Yet the historian is struck by the many changes in Spanish affairs that began under Felipe V and were carried to glorious fruition under his sons. Undramatically, perhaps, Bourbon Spain had become vitally different from Hapsburg Spain, not only stronger but better governed, more soundly prosperous, and culturally more attuned to Europe.

The Bourbon monarchy was more absolute than its predecessors, more centralized, and more efficient. Only four perfunctory Cortes met during the reign. Even the nobility were disregarded as a political force, although their social-economic preeminence remained unchallenged. While flashy foreign favorites such as Alberoni and Ripperda seemed to loom large, their actual tenures were very short, and in the last two decades of the reign the king and queen relied almost entirely on a new class of Spanish-trained bureaucrats, generals, and diplomats who compared favorably with any country's. Institutionally, the cumbersome machinery of officers and councils, some of which went back to feudal times, began to give way to a modern system of secretary-ministers on the French model, ministers for foreign affairs, for war, for finance, and so forth. One of the greatest political changes was dictated by the way the Bourbons came to power, through the conquest and suppression of Aragón, Catalonia, and Valencia for their support of Carlos III. A captain general administered Barcelona now, not a viceroy. A unitary Castilianized Spain was at last a reality, although not an unmixed blessing or even a permanent fact.

Spain's economy grew with some purpose under Felipe V rather than languished in disorder. That is not to say, of course, that age-old inequities and oppressions ceased, nor were they even touched. Yet a more consistent and insistent application of mercantilist doctrines produced a greater prosperity for many. Alberoni's factory for woolens at Guadalajara was intended to end a shameful dependence on England for cloth, and a considerable cotton industry was stimulated by the prohibition of the import of foreign calicoes in 1718. Not since Fernando and Isabel was so much money and effort spent on creating a network of prime arteries, in this period a star of wagon roads from Madrid to key ports matching the governmental centralization in the capital. In an effort to revive economic relations with America, the sacred Seville-Cádiz monopoly of all trade with the Indies was first broken in 1728 when San Sebastián merchants were organized in a Caracas Company. Hindsight, however, suggests that Spain should have spent far more attention to America, less to Italy in this reign.

Spain under its first Bourbon king did not suddenly produce important philosophers, scientists, or artists—in the age of Voltaire, Linnaeus, and Hogarth. It did, however, produce one first-rate critic, Benito Feyjóo (1676–1764), a Benedictine monk and professor at the University of Oviedo whose very appreciation of how far culturally foreigners had progressed made him a passionate denouncer of Spain's torpor and backwardness. He "almost single-handedly kindled the flame that was to arouse Spain from the intellectual slumber" into which it had fallen. Feyjóo's essential message was that Spain needed fewer works of theology and more of science. His followers in the second half of the century were countless.

Feyjóo's skeptical spirit was a tonic for the newly founded Royal Academy of History of 1738, which set about to index the sources of Spain's past and to eliminate the fables. This was just one of numerous learned societies and educational institutions that came into being under Felipe V, such as the National Library, the Academy of Languages, and the Academy of Medicine and Surgery.

Dull when he was not insane, lazy, preoccupied with his sins, wife-dominated, Felipe V was a poor symbol for a new age. Yet the very coming of the Bourbon king to Spain "broke the gloomy spell of the House of Austria," in the words of Martin Hume, who aptly concluded about Felipe V: "Although the national renaissance of Spain coincides with his period, it received little impulse from him, except acquiescence and good intentions—which in the case of a monarch counts for much."

III.

The Enlightened Despots:
Fernando VI (1746–1759) and
Carlos III (1759–1788)

1. The Brief Glory and Insanity of Fernando VI

T HE Age of Enlightened Despotism is one of those familiar but
vaguely understood eras, like the Renaissance and the Industrial
Revolution, which it falls somewhere in between in the history
books. What historians mean by "enlightened" is not that all previous
periods were benighted but that Europe now experienced an intensified
skepticism, concern for knowledge, faith in science, and conviction that all
can be made well. "Despotism," a general term that could be applied to a
Caesar or to a Felipe II, signified in the new era that rulers like Louis XIV
or Peter the Great or Frederick the Great completely dedicated themselves
to their profession of statecraft and commanded perfected institutions to
secure their aims. In these senses, that they were aware of the best ideas of
their time and that they conscientiously worked hard at implementing
them, the sons of Felipe V were Spain's worthy contribution to the ranks of
the enlightened despots.

Spain's first Bourbon had had too many children, in that so much of the
nation's energy had been spent providing them with suitable estates. By his
first spouse, María Luisa of Savoy, the priapic Felipe V had four sons. The
eldest had actually graced the throne for several months in 1724, but the
phantom Luis I was less remembered than his all too human queen. As of
1746 the only survivor of the first marriage was the youngest son, now an
unassuming man of thirty-two, and he was duly proclaimed on August 10

King of Spain and the Indies as Fernando VI, reviving the name of the illustrious Catholic monarch of Spain's greatest age.

The Prince of the Asturias turned king, who had been bereft of his mother as an infant, had experienced not so much mistreatment during his youth as simple indifference from his stepmother, Isabel Farnese, whose every mark of warmth and concern went out to her own five children, all of whom soon enjoyed considerable distinction. Her eldest, Carlos, now thirty, had graduated from being the charming Duke of Parma to being the commanding King of the Two Sicilies. María Ana Victoria, twenty-eight, unsuccessfully betrothed to Louis XV, later wed the heir of Portugal and would eventually sit on that throne. Don Felipe, a Frenchified dandy of twenty-six, was destined to take over Parma from his brother and to found a long line of monarchs that some say have the best claim to Spain's throne today. María Teresa, succeeding in a sense where her sister failed, wed the French dauphin in 1745 but unfortunately died the next year, two weeks after her father. Then there was the nineteen-year-old Luis Antonio, called the Infante Cardinal, for he had enjoyed the primacy of Spain as Archbishop of Toledo since the age of eight, an honor he relinquished in 1754 in favor of the pleasures of the flesh, thanks to his indulgent half brother. Lastly, Isabel Farnese's sixteen-year-old María Antonia was as eligible a princess as existed in Europe and was soon to become the Queen of Victor Amadeus III of Sardinia.

The first true measure people got of Fernando VI was that he treated his assertive stepmother and truculent half brothers firmly but without bitterness. Isabel Farnese was allowed gracious retirement at San Ildefonso. The family's Italian policies were not abandoned, but Fernando drew a limit to Carlos' and Felipe's ambitions.

Fernando VI promised to be a good ruler but certainly not a great one. According to the French ambassador, "the new king has much piety, sweetness, goodwill, and justice; he is in no way acquainted with affairs in general or particular; he is not only timid but scrupulous." Singularly untrained for his role by education and isolated from administrative experience, he had the wisdom to recognize these facts. His lack of intellect, his tendency to indolence, and his ill health all counted against him, but he endeared himself to people for his tact, his kindness, and his ability to put affairs in the hands of able assistants.

The new king drew great strength from his Portuguese wife, Barbara of Braganza. Betrothed in 1729, Fernando had made a terrible face at the first sight of his bride-to-be, so unpretty was she, but the observer of this fact also reported that their union developed into "the most effusive and constant marital adhesion." According to an anonymous report, it caused one pain even to look at the queen, but such remarkable hideousness was evidently amply compensated for. The French ambassador reported that "the new Queen has much spirit, vivacity, and understanding. She thinks nobly and expresses herself gracefully. She is lofty but good and benevolent."

Soon not only the Madrid wits but the self-important envoys of Europe were whispering for all to hear that what had happened in 1746 was not that King Fernando had replaced King Felipe but that Queen Barbara had succeeded Queen Isabel. Given that the wife had greater strength of will than the husband, these rumors would have been meaningful only if the two monarchs were at some sort of cross-purposes. Childless, the royal couple had no dynastic ambitions. Bound together, by mutual ugliness perhaps, Fernando and Barbara shared a devotion to three things: to good music, the prosperity of Spain, and, above all, peace.

Contradictorily, Spain's navy was never stronger than under the pacifistic Fernando, but for the king his favorite fleet was known as the "squadron of the Tago," an assemblage of pleasure craft on the waterways near Aranjuez Palace thirty miles from Madrid and thus hundreds of miles from the sea. This was the Spanish equivalent of the musical barges that orchestrated Handel's *Water Music* for the delight of George II and his court on the waters of the Thames. After all, it was the 1740's, and Frederick the Great of Prussia was himself conducting chamber music concerts at Potsdam. Following a good day's hunting, the young but decorous Spanish court would retire to the riverside for a musical evening. The monarchs themselves relaxed on the *Royal* under a red velvet pavilion with silver trim and with baroquely turned columns as supports, fanciful cherubs bow and stern, and colorful banners streaming above. Among the fleet of fifteen boats were the "frigates" *San Fernando* and *Santa Barbara* and the xebecs *Orfeo* and *Tago*. There was a lesser ship in the form of a peacock and one in the shape of a deer. All these ships were manned by sizable gangs of oarsmen.

The eldest son of the celebrated Alessandro Scarlatti, Domenico Scarlatti (1685–1757), was the court music master, having earlier taught the queen as a princess in Lisbon. Also, the incomparable Farinelli stayed on in Spain, his talent and his influence remaining undiminished. Like Scarlatti, Farinelli enjoyed the most comfortable accommodations in the royal palaces and drove about in a coach with the royal arms. He was given a free hand in providing the backdrops for the royal entertainments and did much to remodel the Teatro Real, boasting that 150 horses could be used onstage in a grand spectacle. The Italian castrato is also credited with the invention of thunder and lightning machines for theatrical effects in the Italian operas he introduced into Spain. The esteem with which he was treated by two sets of sovereigns earned him the appellation "the prime minister," but politically he was almost entirely innocent, self-effacing, and disinterested. One must travel a few thousand miles to St. Petersburg to find an exact contemporary, Alexei Razumovsky, the lover of the Empress Elizabeth, whose devotion to art eclipsed any self-serving ambitions.

The harassing cares of state were not the métier of King Fernando VI, who yet earnestly wished others to make the country prosperous and enlightened. In this good intention the king was fully aided by a whole new generation of Spanish-trained administrators and statesmen who had gained their experience in the previous reign. There was no longer the *falta de cabezas* (lack of heads) that a reforming minister had complained of a century before during the Hapsburgs. Foreign affairs came to be the province of Don José Carvajal y Lancaster, a descendant of John of Gaunt and favorable to British interests. Carvajal was counterbalanced by the Marquis of Ensenada, dominant in the ministries of finance and war, who was noted for his French tastes as well as for his fierce Spanish patriotism. Intrigues were to abound among the rival foreign interests in Madrid, but the French ambassador observed with resignation: "King Fernando takes the reins on the most difficult occasion in a long time . . . the government of Spain had been French during the life of Louis XIV, Italian the rest of the reign of Felipe, now it is going to be Castilian and national."

The most pressing problem facing the ministers of Fernando VI was to bring to a close Spain's involvement in the War of the Austrian Succession and the related hostilities with Britain dating back to 1739. The fighting in Italy had seesawed inconclusively for years, but eventually the Infante Felipe, once the master of Parma and Milan, was forced to take refuge in France. Fortunately, brilliant French successes in Flanders more than made up for the fiascos in Italy when the peace terms were eventually settled at Aix-la-Chapelle on October 18, 1748, between France and Spain on the one side and Britain, Austria, the Netherlands, and Sardinia on the other. Queen Barbara's Portuguese connections had aided the initiation of peace feelers, whereas her mother-in-law at San Ildefonso had talked war to the last. For Spain, the main result of so much military clamor was that the Infante Felipe was confirmed as Prince of Parma and Piacenza. As for the commercial disputes outstanding with Britain in America, they were left in a state of deliberate indecision. No one was satisfied with the peace of 1748.

Peace after almost half a century of incessant war meant opportunities for internal improvements. Spain found in the Marquis of Ensenada a man capable, honest, energetic, and imaginative in all areas of endeavor, despite his penchant for intrigue and delight in ostentation. He initiated many public works including more trunk roads and the canalization of the Manzanares and Tagus rivers (in a celebrated contretemps of the seventeenth century, expressive of the ignorance and lethargy of Hapsburg Spain in its period of decline, a bishop had vetoed a project to connect these rivers, saying that if God had so intended, He would have done it himself). The languishing mines of both Spain and America were reopened by allowing the export of bullion, after providing for a royal share in the profits. Ensenada. made the first efforts in the direction of famine and unemployment relief. He abolished tax farming and proposed, without success, to eliminate the hateful taxes on food and to rely on a single tax on salt and external customs revenues.

With Fernando VI's blessing, Ensenada was instrumental in negotiating a historic Concordat with the Papacy in 1753. Papal relations with the Bourbons had been less than friendly during the War of the Spanish Succession, and since then, many other bitternesses had accumulated. A sharp conflict arose in 1747, when the Spanish index of forbidden books appeared with a title on it approved by the Roman index; it was less a question of who was more enlightened than of who had the final say, king or Pope. The new Concordat restored the royal absolutism in church affairs enjoyed by Carlos I and Felipe II and curbed the papal encroachments of the two intervening centuries: if two-thirds of church patronage was controlled by the Pope before the Concordat and one-third by the king, the situation was now reversed.

The king and Ensenada realized there was a new spirit abroad about religion, and they encouraged it. In the previous reign 728 auto-de-fés had occurred with 14,000 people receiving some form of punishment. Under Fernando VI such public spectacles ceased. A few investigations, a few reprimands, and a few nominal punishments—such was the new role of the Spanish Inquisition. Enlightenment did not dawn full bloom. In 1752 the old Hapsburg censorship laws were explicitly restated. The censors banned Montesquieu's monumental *Esprit des lois* in 1756 for its disrespectful passages about Spanish intolerance, but Spanish authors felt free to cite the Frenchman's other ideas.

"It is difficult to exaggerate the intellectual advances which Spain made during the short breathing time of peace" under Fernando. That venerable Voltaire of Spain, Feyjóo, became royal councillor through the efforts of Ensenada, and he dedicated the fourth volume of his great series of essays, *Cartas Eruditas y Curiosas* to the queen. Another luminary of the period was the first doctor of the king, Andrés Piquer, whose learning ranged from *Modern Logic* (1747) to the *Treatment of Fevers* (1751). Fernando VI encouraged the founding of three royal astronomical observatories, the planning of a botanical garden, the proliferation of learned academies, and the granting of generous subsidies to scholars for study in Spain and abroad. A student of Linnaeus' was encouraged to come to Spain, and he in turn sponsored botanical expeditions to the Americas.

A preposterous affair in the remote reaches of Spanish America led to the downfall of Ensenada, to whom Spain owed so much. British-Portuguese interests had proposed that Spain accept the Portuguese colony of Sacramento at the mouth of the Plate River in exchange for some upriver territory in Paraguay. This cession was violently opposed by local Spanish Jesuits, who got the ear of King Carlos of Sicily, and in turn Fernando VI's half brother began a secret correspondence with Ensenada, who became convinced that some dire plot was afoot to put Spain under British tutelage. To counter British influence at Madrid, Ensenada on his own started alliance negotiations with France and put the Spanish West Indies fleet on a war footing. Even Isabel Farnese became involved in Ensenada's scheming. When all the double-dealing was revealed, Fernando VI had no alternative but to dismiss his minister. The royal guard roused Ensenada from his bed on July 20, 1754, and he was retired to his estates with no questions asked about his considerable fortune. A recent British historian notes with pride that the exposure of Ensenada earned the British ambassador knighthood, whereas a recent French historian sees it differently: "In the interests of Spain he betrayed his master."

Ensenada's disgrace coincided with ominous rumbles of preparations for a new general European war. Since hostilities actually began in the North American wilderness with "Braddock's defeat" of 1755, the war is familiar to American students as the French and Indian War. In Europe it went by the name of the Seven Years' War (1756–1763), following the so-called Diplomatic Revolution, or a bizarre reversal of the usual lineup of the powers, with France and Austria fighting as allies against Britain and Prussia. Spain was assiduously courted by both the British and French, but Fernando VI was obstinate in his determination to remain at peace. Even propaganda that Britain and Prussia were Protestant villains failed to stir Catholic Spain. This unbreakable neutrality was really put to the test when the French navy seized the island of Minorca in May, 1756, from the British (this was the famous case in which Admiral Byng was shot on his quarterdeck for dereliction of duty). France now offered Spain its former island territory in return for belligerency, but the answer was still no. Britain in turn offered to cede Gibraltar itself if Spain should aid it in recovering Minorca, but again there was a refusal. Perhaps the most extravagantly futile offer, a French one, was to promote the Infante Felipe as future King of Poland. Incidentally, the years 1755 and 1756 were times of disastrous earthquakes in the Iberian Peninsula, when whole cities, notably Lisbon, were destroyed. In view of these new miseries on top of old oppressions, it would have taken a far different king from Fernando to plunge his country into new adventures.

It was a genuine tragedy for Spain that Queen Barbara died on August

27, 1758, after a lingering illness involving asthma and a blood disease. So close had the royal couple become that the loss of his wife drove Fernando VI to complete lunacy, the dementia suffered by the father becoming many times magnified in the son.

Having never considered any woman other than his wife, Fernando was thrown into a frenzy by suggestions that he remarry for the good of the state. Instead, he abandoned the capital and chose completely to isolate himself in the monastery of Villaviciosa, a property of his profligate half brother Don Luis and the very place where Juana the Mad had lived out her manias in the sixteenth century. Efforts to bring the king to reason were unavailing, and his condition grew clinically more distressing, about which we have the notebooks of Dr. Piquer himself for detailed evidence. Farinelli came to try the magic of his voice, but Fernando put his hands over his ears. For days the king would not speak or was in an incoherent torpor; at other times he screamed, threw things, and struck out at his entourage. Several times he tried to hang himself by means of knotted napkins or draperies; yet he was preoccupied with his murder and hid under the bed after the news of the famous assassination attempt of Robert François of Damiens on Louis XV. He would go without sleep for ten days on end, pacing his room for hours, and then for days he would refuse to leave his bed with the most unpleasant consequences. In the words of a contemporary, "he went to bed finally without wanting to get up, making in his bed all his feces which he threw at those who served him without discrimination." He died of a convulsive fit in the midst of his own excrement without the benefit of clergy on August 10, 1759.

The unpleasant circumstances of the passing of Fernando VI should not obscure the accomplishments of his reign, the intellectual upsurge, the first treasury surplus in memory, and peace, eleven years of peace. It was the wish of the deceased king and queen to be buried in the immense convent they had founded in Madrid, Las Salsas Reales (now the lawcourts). The simple inscription on his sepulcher reads: "Here lies the King of Spain, Fernando VI, a very good prince, who died without children but with a numerous progeny of paternal virtues."

2. The Apprenticeship of Carlos III

King Carlos III, the best of the Spanish Bourbons, was named successor by his half brother Fernando VI in 1759. Spanish-born, he had not set foot in his native land for almost thirty years. At age fifteen in 1731 he had knelt before his parents for their blessing, received the jeweled sword presented by Louis XIV to Felipe V on the eve of his departure for Spain, and then himself set out to rule over a new realm, in this case the Duchy of Parma. Three years later a letter from his mother announced his new destiny to be King of the Two Sicilies: "Go forth and win: the most beautiful crown in Italy awaits you." Win he did, and from 1735 to 1759 Carlos presided over the court of Naples (his younger brother Felipe became Duke of Parma).

The young Bourbon ruler set down among the Neapolitans and Sicilians brought to his task a passably liberal education, a good command of four languages, some training in the military sciences, and the drawing-room graces. Hunting seemed his only passion at first, but his habit of riding around the countryside without formality served to gain him early popularity. Southern Italy had known more successive cultures than perhaps any area of Europe, not the least of which were periods of Aragonese and later Spanish rule. Naples still treasured the memory of the fisherman Masaniello and the great revolt of 1646, while Sicily retained quite untouchable parliamentary, municipal, and feudal freedoms. Although the interlude of Austrian control at the beginning of the eighteenth century was generally a bad memory, there were still Hapsburg factionalists. It was a tough school of politics, but Carlos learned to apply himself to affairs, soon became virtually his own prime minister, and mastered the economy so thoroughly that he left a surplus in the treasury. Naples, with its half million inhabitants, its lazzaroni and equally bold hordes of prostitutes, its teeming slums, its gardens, its palaces, its boulevards, and its fantastic bay—all this seemed so timeless and unchangeable, yet Carlos even left his architectural mark on the metropolis. He embellished the huge reddish-pink Caserta Palace dominating the lower part of the city, establishing the national library there, as well as endowing the National Museum on the hill with the fabulous Farnese art collection given him by his mother. He was the founder of the San Carlo Opera House, the most grandiose in Europe for many years and the inspiration of Donizetti, Rossini, Bellini, and Verdi. Outside Naples Carlos created the great palace at Capodimonte with attendant porcelain and tapestry works.

It was as King of the Two Sicilies that Carlos sired a family of thirteen children. At twenty-two he married the thirteen-year-old Maria Amalia of Saxony, daughter of Augustus III, German elector and King of Poland. She was tall, fair, and blue-eyed, and she shared her husband's interest in the arts and outdoor pursuits. Unlike Carlos, Maria Amalia was utterly humorless and had an explosive temper, being known to slap her attendants on occasion. The placid king was completely devoted to his petulant wife. According to a British envoy, writing in 1753, they were the ugliest couple in the world, meaning no more, perhaps, than that the ravages of smallpox in their youths showed in their middle age.

The news of his accession to the throne of Spain reached Carlos III in Naples late in August, 1759, and he secluded himself for several days, less perhaps because of any grief for his tragic half brother, with whom he had had difficulties, than because of painful decisions that had to be made concerning his own family. He duly announced important dynastic arrangements to an assemblage of notables, Italian and Spanish. "The notorious imbecility of my royal first born," the Infante Felipe, made it necessary to disinherit this son altogether and to leave him in confinement in Naples. King Carlos then designated his second son and namesake Prince of the Asturias and eventual heir to Spain. Since "the spirit of the treaties concluded in this century proves that all Europe desires the separation of the Spanish power from that of Italy," the third son Fernando was to be left behind as the ruler of the Two Sicilies, and thus the jeweled sword passed from Louis XIV to Felipe V to Carlos III was now put in new hands. With the title Ferdinand I and a regency appointed by his father, the third son was to be founder of a separate royal dynasty. From now the world would know French Bourbons, Spanish Bourbons, Parma Bourbons, and Neapolitan Bourbons. These decisions made, Carlos and the rest of his family sailed off from Naples on October 6, 1759, to his own personal sorrow and probably to the genuine regret of his former subjects.

The ruler who had exchanged a small kingdom for a larger one landed at Barcelona October 17 and received an enthusiastic welcome from a city which half a century before had hailed so eagerly and supported so disastrously for itself his father's Hapsburg rival going by the same title of Carlos III. Carlos of Bourbon tactfully restored some of the liberties of Catalonia, and later he tarried respectfully in Aragón (also because the Prince of the Asturias had come down with measles). He did not reach Madrid until December 9, 1759, when he was greeted by the temporary regent, his mother, Isabel Farnese, whom he had not seen in decades. The entire royal family took up residence in the Buen Retiro, but Isabel soon retired to San Ildefonso, having been accorded every mark of respect by the new king and queen except being listened to politically. Carlos was slow to change his brother's ministers. Farinelli, however, was sent away, and Ensenada was recalled from disgrace, although given no power. Eventually, Carlos' trusted minister from Naples, the Marquis of Squillace, was given the key departments of finance and war. It was not until July 13, 1760, that Carlos III made formal entry into Madrid with the traditional celebration at the Church of the Atocha, followed a few days later by a perfunctory meeting of the Cortes to swear allegiance to him and his heir.

The queen soon regretted leaving Naples, "the city I carry in my heart." The Saxon princess complained of her new country's weather: "It rains, it blows, or when a good day comes around the heat is oppressive." She was not able to get fresh strawberries or other fruits as good as those in Italy, and she found Spanish women "the most ignorant creatures in the world."

On September 27, 1760, only a few months after the people of Madrid first saw her, Queen María Amalia was dead. She had suffered ill health since her arrival, and a bad fall from a horse hastened her end. The king was deeply affected by his loss and remained faithful to his wife's memory to his last day. He gave only passing consideration to remarriage and never engaged in any sort of dalliance. Some nights, he once revealed, he would walk about his apartments barefoot so as to cool any feelings of sensuality. This moral austerity, which in general he expected of others as well as of himself, was one of the first things Spaniards learned to respect in Carlos III.

In looks, Carlos was anything but handsome, having a huge pointed nose and a large drooping mouth set in an oddly triangular face creased by wrinkles. Princess Adélaïde of France refused to marry him after one look at his portrait. Otherwise, the king was an appealing person, having a genial air of confidence and robust good health, as befitted an outdoors man with temperate habits and simple tastes.

The king-huntsman was no novelty for Spaniards. In the case of Carlos III never a day went by when he was not out tramping the woods or riding the trails for two or three hours in the afternoon. Bad weather did not stop him, for as he pithily observed: "rain does not break bones." According to Casanova, Carlos' devotion to such exercise was in compensation for his sexual abstinence. In any case, the king took the greatest joy in his horses, and he fed his dogs himself. Once toward the end of his reign he totaled up his game book for the benefit of a visitor and concluded that he had shot 532 wolves and 5,323 foxes. Commenting on this toll of farm predators, the king said, "You see, my diversion is not useless to my country." Such a remark, together with the fact Carlos was in bed early and up early to busy himself with state affairs, was what distinguished him from his predecessors, who were all too often hunters and nothing else.

Hard work, which is a large part of the definition of an enlightened despot, had a special personal appeal to Carlos III, who wished to escape the fate of his two immediate Bourbon predecessors, victims of fantasy and madness. He astonished the Spanish from the first by his regular and long hours. The indolent rulers of the past became a memory, as Carlos methodically looked into and legislated everything. No genius, he was experienced with administration, entirely honest in his purposes, and dedicated to what he saw as justice. A man of great routine, he fulfilled all his public duties punctually and with the greatest dignity, in this reminding observers of his great-grandfather Louis XIV. Moreover, he expected hard work from others, on one occasion upbraiding the president of the Council of Castile with the words "Know that you do not come here to make pretty conversation; my desire is that you keep me informed of everything, that you see to it that affairs are taken care of promptly, whether major or minor; I also wish that if it is possible to bend justice that the poor get preference."

To conscientiousness Carlos III added complete assurance. Early in the king's reign a British envoy noted that he had "an uncommon command of himself on all occasions." The observer added this description of a genial autocrat: "He ever prefers carrying a point by gentle means and has the patience to repeat exhortations rather than to exert his authority even in trifles. Yet, with the greatest air of gentleness, he keeps his ministers and attendants in the utmost awe." Never for a moment did Carlos III forget that he was king, nor did anyone else.

In the first eight years of his reign Carlos III was responsible for two great misfortunes: a costly war with Britain and a violent popular uprising in Madrid. A lesser man would have been crushed by such disasters, but Carlos III recovered, learned, and turned events to Spain's profit.

Spain provoked Britain into declaring war on January 2, 1762. After more than a decade of peace so beneficial to the country, it now seemed madness to enter the Seven Years' War at a time when France was losing on every front. Not only had Britain's ally Frederick the Great of Prussia proved himself a military genius and master of central Europe, but also Britain itself, directed by the elder Pitt, had secured such fantastic victories in India and North America, as to crush France's overseas pretensions, seemingly forever. Perhaps the very extent to which France stood to be humbled, with the consequent change in the balance of power and with the Spanish empire exposed as the next victim, weighed on the mind of Carlos III, who may have overestimated Spain's strength and ability to redress the balance. Another motivation for the king was a simple desire to revenge that day in 1744 when a British fleet had threatened to bombard his Naples, forcing his surrender to terms. Unlike his recently deceased queen, the Spanish king was basically pro-French, or at least pro-Bourbon, and in August, 1761, he had put his signature to a third *Pacte de Famille*, providing for Spanish assistance to France if Britain would not let him mediate the war. In his offer to arbitrate between the belligerents, Carlos naïvely expected to throw in a bundle of Spanish grievances against Britain—ship seizures, colonial disputes, Gibraltar, and so forth. The ever-victorious Pitt wanted war, not talk, as early as 1761, but his colleagues temporized. At least the Spanish treasure fleet reached safety before hostilities began the next year.

Far from mounting any offensive action against the enemy, the Spanish empire soon suffered two staggering blows. In June, 1762, a large British fleet appeared off Cuba and landed troops to besiege Havana's Morro Castle, which held out valorously for forty-five days until an additional force arrived from New York. Havana surrendered on August 13 with the loss of twelve Spanish warships and stores worth millions. A month later across the globe another British squadron forced the surrender of Manila and levied a huge indemnity on the Spanish Philippines. Against these terrible losses Spain had the small satisfaction of forestalling a British descent on Buenos Aires and of capturing the nearby Portuguese colony of Sacramento. Carlos III ordered an invasion of Portugal itself, Britain's perpetual ally, with results rendered fruitless by the energetic counterattacks of a British officer of later fame, General John Burgoyne.

Carlos III should not have been surprised and angered that for the third time France ignored the *Pacte de Famille* and opened separate peace negotiations with Britain which culminated in the Treaty of Paris of February 10, 1763. Spain had no choice but to adhere. The British gain of Canada and India at the expense of France makes this treaty one of the most decisive in imperial history. For Spain, the net loss was considerable too. In order to regain Cuba and the Philippines, Carlos III had to accept the alienation of Minorca again and the cession of both North and South Florida to Britain. By way of some sort of compensation to its disillusioned ally, France handed over all Louisiana to Spain. The gift was not altogether a blessing, since determined resistance by the inhabitants of New Orleans and the Mississippi required a considerable Spanish expedition to assert its control in the later 1760's.

In so far as the Treaty of Paris of 1763 contained in it the seeds of the American Revolution of 1776, it held out for Spain the possibility of military revenge; but this was hardly apparent in the 1760's, and Carlos III turned to a program of recovery and reform at home. The chief bringer of new measures of enlightenment was the Sicilian-born Marquis of Squillace, a financial expert who was industrious but without political tact. The manner of man he was appeared in this description by a British envoy: "The Marquis Squilacci [*sic*] is not very bright. He is fond of business and never complains of having too much, notwithstanding the variety of departments that center on him." He also had a reputation for licentious living that offended many. Among the "foreign novelties" that Squillace introduced were such things as putting streetlights about Madrid. In a further effort to curb criminal elements in the capital the Sicilian next announced a ban on the huge round slouch hats and the nearly ground-length capes traditionally worn by Spanish men and traditionally useful, Squillace claimed, for the concealment of weapons. By this decree he produced one of the most violent popular risings that western Europe was to witness in the mid-eighteenth century.

Just as several decades previously Peter the Great of Russia sought visibly to westernize his countrymen by cutting off the long beards and sleeves of the boyars, Squillace proposed to bring Spanish men sartorially into the eighteenth century by having them wear the French-style tricorn hats and short capes. This was declared the standard for officials in January and for all males in the capital on March 10, 1766. The troubles began about 4 P.M. on March 23, Palm Sunday, when a handful of braggarts paraded before a barracks in their forbidden wide brims and trailing cloaks. Some overzealous soldiers took upon themselves to arrest a few of these and subject their clothes to some liberal shearing. As if by prearrangement, whistles and cries from the victims brought a mob of supporters running down the streets, and the soldiers were disarmed. Within minutes the entire center of the city was in an uproar with crowds crying, "Long live the king but death to Squillace." The new streetlights were the first targets for destruction, and then came the Sicilian's house, which was stormed and gutted, as were the residences of other foreign officials. Squillace and his family were absent from home and later escaped to the royal palace. Uncomprehending of the hatred he inspired, the reforming Sicilian told the king, "I deserve a statue."

The following day the reassembled mobs confronted a detachment of the Walloon Guards, an elite regiment of royal household troops recruited in Flanders. Subjected to a hail of stones, the soldiers panicked and fired on their tormentors, killing some. Before the Wallooners dispersed to their barracks, several of them had been seized by the Madrileños and murdered. Their mutilated bodies were dragged about, while their heads were held up on poles wearing Spanish hats. For the next day or two all efforts to subdue the frenzy by sending popular officials about were to no avail. Nothing would do but for the king himself to appear on the balcony of the palace and promise to meet the people's demands. Carlos III stood there gravely nodding his assent as a friar read out successive pledges to dismiss Squillace, to revoke the dress edict, to lower the prices of bread and other staples, and to grant a general amnesty.

The demands of the people revealed that things other than mere xenophobia were at issue. The arrival of accumulated bullion from America after the war had had an inflationary effect, and bad harvests over three years had raised food prices sharply. The fact that there were echoes of the Madrid riots in Barcelona, Saragossa, and cities of central Spain indicated that cheaper food was a prime factor. Yet no general assault took place against the rich, either secular or clerical. This circumstance led Carlos III and his advisers to suspect that the Squillace riots were not altogether spontaneous and that there were vested interests who manipulated the mob violence to discourage reform.

Hours after he made his concessions in public, Carlos III with the royal family departed from a little-used gate and rode to Aranjuez, thirty miles to the south, where the king stayed for the next several months. For three more days Madrid remained in the control of the rioters, who futilely demanded Carlos' return. Eventually, the king sent a message to the Council of Castile declaring that his health was gravely upset and that he would not consider return until the populace gave up their arms and resumed their occupations. He did see to Squillace's removal from the kingdom, assigning a detachment of troops to assure his safety, and eventually gave him new employment as ambassador to Venice. Madrid returned to normal, frustrated by the absence of the court.

Carlos now bore the added grief of the death of his mother, Isabel Farnese, at the age of seventy-three. Physically crippled at the end, so that she had to be supported by two women, the queen mother had never lost her taste for life or her sharp tongue. Opposing bitterly her son's flight from Madrid and his dismissal of Squillace, she had murmured to ambassadors who visited her at Aranjuez: "My son will fall into the same state as Felipe V; I will not live to see it but you will see it." Although this dark prediction never came true, during that summer of 1766 Carlos III did brood about removing the capital permanently from Madrid—Seville and Valencia were mentioned as alternatives—so surprised and distressed was he by the turn of events. When he did return in December, Madrid greeted him enthusiastically. The whole sequence of events can be pondered in contrast with those in Paris in 1789, when a genuinely cowardly and confused king let himself become prisoner of the citizens of his capital.

3. The Years of Reform

After the false starts, the remainder of the reign of Carlos III was characterized by unparalleled progress in domestic reform and unaccustomed victories abroad. Spanish rather than foreign officials held the limelight, not as favorites but simply as able administrators who had the confidence of the king.

The first of the notable reformers was the Count of Aranda who held the position of president of the council from 1766 to 1773. An Aragonese of distinguished noble family and considerable wealth, Aranda was a man of wide experience and cosmopolitan outlook. His firsthand study of the Prussian army of Frederick the Great had earlier influenced his activity as minister of war. A long residence in Paris found him the intellectual associate of Voltaire and the Encyclopedists, and he returned to Madrid to become the grand master of Spanish Freemasons. Somewhat homely in appearance, affable of manner, this man of the world was popular among the volatile Madrileños. Aranda immediately demonstrated both decisiveness and tact in dealing with the aftermath of the Squillace riots. He divided the capital into new police districts and took stern measures to expel vagrants. As for the new style of dress, he saw to its introduction gradually and piecemeal, beginning with court officials, later the members of the major guilds, and then lesser citizens. Pointedly, the public executioners and their assistants were kept attired in the villainous-looking round hats and long capes.

In this era the physical aspect of the capital changed markedly. The vast Oriente Palace was completed in the west, two of the great European artists of the day, Anton Raphael Mengs and Giovanni Battista Tiepolo, having worked on its decoration, particularly the paintings on the ceilings. Carlos III was also associated with other monumental buildings such as the Prado, the Customshouse, and the Alcalá Gateway, and during the reign the whole Paseo del Prado was laid out, to become the most fashionable promenade. A returned English writer commented on all the changes: "The appearance of Madrid is grand and lively; noble streets, good houses, and excellent pavements, as clean as it once was dirty."

The expulsion of the Jesuits from Spain in 1767 was the most sensational of Aranda's reforms. He meant to exact direct retribution for the great riots, after an extraordinary investigating committee found "the hand of a religious body" behind the recent disturbances. The king, devout as he was, could be easily aroused against any threat to his royal prerogatives, as he had already demonstrated as ruler of Naples. He was persuaded of specific acts of Jesuit disloyalty in recent events in Paraguay and Mexico, and he gave credence to reports that certain members of the Society of Jesus were plotting to replace him with his brother Luis. Aranda possibly concocted the tale that Jesuits were spreading the rumor that the king was an illegitimate son of Alberoni. The Jesuits found few defenders. Their monopoly of education was resented by the other clergy, many of whom were affected by Jansenist doctrines. The tacit alliance of Jesuits with the aristocracy, as their confessors and their tutors, was a source of envy and even hatred on the part of the bureaucracy and the masses. Already the Jesuits had been expelled from Portugal, accused of everything from commercial corruption to regicide. Likewise, France had found the order intolerably subversive of authority and a rival to royal power.

In Spain the expulsion was carried out with the utmost secrecy and efficiency, as well as with unintended cruelty. Sealed orders under the king's signature were sent out to be opened on March 31, 1767, in Madrid, a day later in the provinces. In the capital after the six colleges of the order had been surrounded simultaneously at midnight, their members were summoned to the refectories and in a matter of hours sent off in groups of ten in coaches to coastal ports, where ships were waiting for them. A letter of Carlos III commended the Spanish Jesuits to "the immediate, wise, and holy direction of his Holiness," but the unfortunates were left to suffer on shipboard for three months before they were reluctantly permitted to settle in the Papal States. Some 2,641 members of Loyola's Society of Jesus were thus expelled from Spain, with perhaps twice that number of novices affected. The victims offered no resistance and stirred no popular protest. Overseas another 2,267 Jesuits were arbitrarily uprooted, with even greater personal suffering. In the case of Mexico, for example, their going affected the operation of 103 missions and 23 colleges. The final chapter in this story took place on July 21, 1773, when a new Pope abolished the order altogether in the interests of the tranquillity of Christendom and of the dominions of the most Catholic king in particular.

The Inquisition in Spain made rumblings of protest when the Jesuits were expelled, initiating investigations regarding the religious reliability of Aranda and his assistants. The upshot, however, was a crackdown on the investigators, not on the men of enlightenment. In a hundred undramatic ways the Inquisition was curbed during the reign of Carlos III, losing, for example, its censorship powers. The public burning of an old woman as a heretic in 1780 was the last of the century. The tribunals were not abolished altogether, however, as Aranda and others probably wanted, and occasionally a sensational trial reminded citizens of a latent power. Having cut the Inquisition down to size, Carlos III could explain its preservation with the calm words "The Spaniards want it and it does not bother me."

Clearly, the church was on the defensive during the Bourbon eighteenth century, but the extent of its decline should not be exaggerated. Efforts to reduce the sheer number of clergy got nowhere, so that in 1788 Spain had 68,000 monks, 33,000 nuns, and 88,000 secular clergy, or a total of about 200,000 ecclesiastics in a population of 10,000,000, representing a percentage two or three times of that in France, for example. The tremendous wealth of the church continued to increase through the practice of mortmain.

Spain's educational system underwent a major overhaul under Aranda and other reformers, who sought to fill the gap left by the expulsion of the Jesuits and more generally to catch up to the rest of Europe, especially in the diffusion of scientific knowledge. In 1771, for example, the former Jesuit Colegio Imperial de Madrid became the Reales Estudios de San Isidro, with a new curriculum stressing experimental physics, logic, and the law of nature and nations, all to be taught "according to the lights given by modern authorities and without scholastic disputes." The king decreed that study of natural law was to be a prerequisite for a law career, at the same time cautioning students of the need for "subjecting the lights of our human reason to those of the Catholic religion." He sanctioned the extremely radical step of granting permission to the new institution to offer courses in philosophy and modern literature to the public at large.

A critical periodical press made its appearance in this era. The weekly *El Pensador* in the 1760's was typical of the new journalism, which attacked the foibles of the nobility and the ignorance of the clergy. In the 1780's the government's own Imprenta Real published a *Correo Literario de Europa* to keep the reading public abreast of the latest developments in science and letters. Despite frequent cases of censorship, on balance the government gave its approval to a huge volume of publications, including many key works of the foreign Enlightenment. For example, Beccaria's famous plea for penological reform was issued in translation in 1774 with a warning against taking him too literally. The great *Encyclopédie*, which had its troubles in France, was banned in 1759; but copies of it were available in Madrid, and lesser scientific encyclopedias were widely circulated. The contradictions of policy were well revealed in 1778, when the Inquisition condemned a man for corresponding with Voltaire and Rousseau. A royal councilloi who witnessed the proceedings broke down and confessed himself to being familiar with the works of the two mentioned, as well as those of Spinoza and Diderot. To gain pardon, he had to expose others with the same reading habits and promptly came up with the names of Aranda and two of his famous successors as head of the government, the counts of Floridablanca and Campomanes.

Campomanes was part of a strong current of original Spanish writing on the subject of economic reform. As an underofficial of the Council of Castile, he published a study calling for the promotion of greater employment in both industry and agriculture and for the encouragement of the middle class at the expense of the aristocracy. His radical work not only received a royal seal of approval but was sent officially to all bishops and top administrators.

Putting the new economic doctrines into practice, Carlos III and Aranda ordered dramatic new public works such as the Canal of Aragón, they inaugurated regular stagecoach service to the major cities, and they established a royal school of agriculture at Aranjuez. Through their efforts, Spain had its first census in 1786, before even Britain.

The government did much to revive old industries and to found new ones, using tariffs to discourage foreign competition. Despite frantic British protests, Carlos III sanctioned a complete ban on the import of foreign cottons in 1771, with the result that by the end of the century the Catalan textile industry was second only to that of the British Midlands.

Perhaps, nothing better illustrates the determination to break with

Spain's past than the following decree of Carlos III in 1770: "I order that nothing stand in the way of hidalgos supporting their families by engaging in a craft, in order to avoid the disadvantage of their being idle or badly occupied, and becoming a charge on society." Accordingly, thousands of people could keep their escutcheons of nobility and still be eligible for municipal office despite their pursuing such occupations as those of blacksmith, carpenter, or tailor.

An enlightened economic reformer, Carlos III was not, of course, a social revolutionist and did not seek to touch the fundamentals of society. Against the facts of stagecoaches and cotton factories, foreign visitors also noted the widespread misery of the lower orders, "the sight of poverty, or wretchedness, of rags in every street," in the words of an Englishman seeing Valencia in the 1770's.

The ministers of Carlos III achieved some of their greatest successes in the matter of making the Spanish overseas empire a viable common market area and source of strength to the home country. Early in the reign they allowed all parts of Spanish America to trade with one another, and in 1778 they made the great break with the past by permitting all parts of Spain to trade with all southern and central America (Mexico alone stayed a monopoly of Cádiz traders and Venezuela a monopoly of San Sebastián). These free-trade policies caused exports to the New World to increase fivefold, imports from there ninefold. The Spanish empire was no longer being run for the benefit of other countries.

The Banco de San Carlos founded in 1782 was a capstone of the new prosperity. Prevented by war from receiving the usual amounts of American bullion, the government resorted to issuing bonds to be guaranteed by this first national bank. When peace came, the bonds circulated at 12 percent over par.

Spain's regeneration in the mid-eighteenth century was not all the work of bureaucrats, although they played an indispensable role, as elsewhere in Europe. The spontaneous and private founding of so-called Societies of Friends of the Country (Sociedades de los Amigos del País) was one of the most striking developments of the period. The first such society appeared in the Basque country in 1765, Madrid gave a license to its Real Sociedad Económica ten years later, and the country had fifty-six of them by 1789. These organizations set out to stimulate local economies by conducting schools, establishing libraries, publishing technical works, and, above all, awarding prizes for outstanding inventions. Social distinctions were forgotten in widespread citizen cooperation to bring progress to the nation. The king himself patronized some of the societies, contributing prize money, and he was directly responsible for ending heated opposition to women membership in the Madrid group.

Historians have variously assessed the personal role of Carlos III in bringing the Enlightenment to Spain. Clearly, the king was "intellectually inferior to the other members of the club of absolute kings." He did not hobnob with Voltaire as Frederick the Great did; he did not write plays, dictionaries, and histories as Catherine the Great did; and unlike both, he did not advertise his acquaintance with the latest ideas by corresponding with his fellow greats. Carlos III was far more interested in hunting than reading or making smart conversation, although his interest in natural science and crafts was similar to the others (he learned to make boots and other articles with his own hands).

It is something of a paradox that Carlos III could be considered a great reformer at all, in view of his limited education, his conventional piety, and his almost obsessive attachment to routine. Yet these very things help explain the success of the changes, their general acceptance. A king who got out of his carriage to let a priest carrying the host ride while he walked behind with the other worshipers could not be accused of being too modern in his ideas. A king whose morality was unimpeachable could not be identified with radical, high-living foreigners. Carlos III saved himself from the serious difficulties some of his counterparts got into, notably Joseph II of Austria, by avoiding the doctrinaire approach and by not trying to do too much too fast.

The reforms under Carlos III were greater than in any other period in Spanish history and rival anything done in a like time in any other country. Perhaps, much more *should* have been done in the way of national regeneration. Whether more *could* have been done is debatable. The king was well aware of the Spaniards' resistance to change, once remarking that "they are like children who cry when their faces are washed." He saw his own main role as that of encouraging the efforts of others, including his own officials and local societies. His servants had long noted that the king was markedly attached to his old clothes, so that new suits had to be laid out for weeks ahead of time for him to get used to them. Similarly, with ministers like Aranda and later Floridablanca, the king liked familiar faces and, most important, was completely loyal to officials once they were in office. By choosing the best men as his agents, by backing them through anything, and by refusing to tolerate factions at court, Carlos III guaranteed steady, enlightened advance. Unfortunately, his successors, notably his son and the last king in this century, did not profit from the example of the fourth Bourbon.

4. The Taste of Victory

In 1776 Carlos III passed into his sixties. He still had the oddly appealing look and ways of a country gentleman. An English traveler wrote of the king at this time:

> His dress seldom varies from a long hat, grey Segovian frock, a buff waistcoat, a small dagger, black breeches, and worsted stockings; his pockets are always stuffed with knives, gloves, and shooting tackle. On gala days a fine suit is hung upon his shoulders, but as he has an eye to his afternoon sport, and is a great economist of his time, the black breeches are worn to all coats. I believe there are but three days in the whole year that he spends without going out shooting, and these are marked with the blackest mark in the calendar.

This description fits quite perfectly the familiar Goya portrait done of Carlos III a dozen years later: the bulging pockets are as noticeable as the blue cordon across the chest; the monarch holds a white glove in one hand and the muzzle of a rifle in the other; a hound is curled up asleep in the foreground while a landscape stretches away invitingly in the distance.

The king's daily schedule remained precise, and one could keep a calendar by his movements around the circuit of royal residences: El Pardo in January; Aranjuez for Easter; La Granja after July; El Escorial in October; and the season in Madrid beginning in December. Wherever he was, Carlos rose at 5:45, dressed himself, and prayed until 6:40, when his chamberlain and three doctors entered his room. After taking chocolate, he went to mass and visited his children, who were allowed to enter the royal study where the king worked on papers by himself from 8 to 11 A.M. Next, he gave interviews to ambassadors, according those of Naples and France precedence. At noon he dined in public, talking to various Spanish and foreign guests. In the heat of summer he then had a nap, but otherwise he went off hunting immediately, staying until nightfall. Further interviews with ministers or a game of cards preceded supper, which he took alone, and the king was always in bed by 11.

Aranda was dismissed from his post as president of the council in August, 1773, not because the king had lost any of his faith in reform but because of a diplomatic defeat. Back in 1770 Spain had tangled with Britain over the question of sovereignty in the Falkland Islands off Argentina. The governor of Buenos Aires used force to expel a British whaling station in the area; both sides prepared for war, but Spain had to back down when it became evident that France would not lend support. Another humiliation followed under the Marquis of Grimaldi, the foreign minister who tried to replace Aranda as the leading figure in the government. A large expedition was assembled in July, 1775, to punish the Dey of Algiers for his complicity in attacks by Moors on Spanish settlements in North Africa and for his connivance with the infamous "Barbary Pirates." Twenty thousand men landed near Algiers, only to be set upon by superior troops and forced to reembark with great losses of both men and equipment. The leader of this ill-starred adventure, an Irish-born general named Alexander O'Reilly, nearly lost his life on his return to an indignant Spain.

The timing of the Algiers disaster proved significant, coming just a few months after the revolt of the thirteen American colonies against British rule. When the destination of the Spanish expedition was still a secret, the brother of King George III predicted to the Spanish ambassador: "O'Reilly is going to take the Spanish fleet to his native land—I mean Ireland." The Spaniard replied that his Catholic Majesty was above taking such advantage of the "difficult situation" the British empire found itself in. This drew the cynical response: "So much the worse for his policy, for I can assure you that if Spain was in the position in which we are, we should not hesitate to invade Cuba or one of her other colonies." Indeed, international standards of morality of the day dictated hitting a traditional enemy when he was down, and Carlos III eventually used the American Revolution to Spain's advantage.

Grimaldi's failures as foreign minister led to his replacement, although as always Carlos III was slow to withdraw his confidence. In November 1776 Don José Moñino, recently created Count of Floridablanca, became the new head of the government. He had risen through the ranks of the bureaucracy, gaining experience as a fiscal of the Council of Castile and attracting the king's particular attention for his success as ambassador to the Holy See, during which time he persuaded the Pope to abolish the Jesuits. Unlike Aranda, Floridablanca was unaristocratic in his background, being the son of a notary in Murcia. Like his predecessor, however, Floridablanca was an enlightened legislator, enjoying a long term of office in which he used the royal power to the utmost to effect changes in the economy.

A treaty of friendship signed with Portugal in March, 1778, was the first significant success in foreign policy in a long time. A niece of Carlos III had just become queen of the neighboring country as Maria I. The treaty provided for a settlement of various colonial disputes by an exchange of territories, but Floridablanca's great coup was the neutralization of Britain's traditional ally at what would become a critical time.

At the beginning of 1778 France had thrown off the mask of nonbelligerence and signed an alliance with Britain's rebellious colonies. Burgoyne's surrender in the fall of 1777 and later the British evacuation of Philadelphia in June, 1778, suggested that now was the most favorable moment for taking revenge against Britain, a course which France urged on Spain. Aranda, currently ambassador in Paris, was vociferous for hostilities. Although Europe was amazed at the signs of British weakness and ineptitude, Carlos III and Floridablanca held back at first, remembering the defeats of the 1760's and taking to heart British representations that Spain's own empire was vulnerable if colonial revolts were encouraged. Then the king declared his desire to mediate the conflict, proposing to find some accommodation between Americans and British and between French and British, all the while hoping to make territorial gains for Spain itself. Adamant and without illusions about his fellow monarch's intentions, King George III wrote his prime minister as early as October, 1778: "I have no doubt next spring Spain will join France, but, if we keep her quiet until then, I trust the British navy will be in a state to cope with both nations." Its diplomacy rejected, Spain did declare war on Britain on June 16, 1779. A considerable patriotic response found expression in voluntary financial contributions to the royal treasury.

"Never, perhaps, has England been in more serious danger of invasion," admitted an English historian regarding the summer of 1779. A combined French-Spanish fleet paraded up and down the English Channel, seeking to engage a British squadron of half their size. More than 40,000 troops stood poised at Brest and Dunkirk, with transports ready to convoy them to the Portsmouth area, which was considered the key to Britain's maritime strength. Britain's genuine alarm was shown by orders sent from London for people in the coastal areas to prepare to drive their livestock inland and for harbor entrances to be blocked by sinking ships in them. The French-Spanish forces threw away their opportunity, however, being unduly frightened by their failure to eliminate any British warships other than one that they captured essentially by accident. Storms and sickness took their toll during the delays, and the fleets returned to Cádiz and Brest. The next year, 1780, the allies again controlled the English Channel, but again they failed to take full advantage of their unexpected success. Yet one ultimate effect of this activity was to prevent Britain from sending reinforcements to Lord Cornwallis, whose surrender in October, 1781, was a decisive event, brought about by a rare coordination of American, French, and Spanish land and sea forces on the far side of the Atlantic.

Dearer to the hearts of the king and of patriotic Spaniards than the chimera of invading England was the prospect of recapturing Gibraltar. From the very outset of hostilities the Spanish closely invested the British fortress by both land and sea, with the aim of starving the garrison into submission. Twice the British navy pulled off incredible feats of seamanship to run the entire gauntlet of French and Spanish naval bases, smash enemy squadrons in battle, and then revictual Gibraltar. With the Spanish navy at a peak of strength, with British admissions that ship for ship the enemy's ships were the better, and with all the logistical advantages to Spain, one must agree with present-day Spanish historians that there was a failure of leadership in the Spanish navy. The king must take some responsibility for the defeatism of his admirals, if not for their incompetence, and he was also overconfident that time was on Spain's side.

In this war Spain took its turn at attempting a deal with Britain behind the back of its French ally. At one point Britain's leaders seriously considered giving up Gibraltar in return for 2,000,000 pounds, Puerto Rico, and Spanish aid against the thirteen colonies. The news of these negotiations led the French to make greater efforts to help the Spanish, and beginning in July, 1781, a joint fleet and army successfully drove the British from the island of Minorca.

Overseas, additional victories came Spain's way. The admirals found the daring to capture two large British convoys near the Azores and bring back a large treasure to Cádiz. The governor of New Orleans showed great initiative first in subduing British outposts in the whole Mississippi area and then in capturing British Florida, beginning with the seizure of Mobile in March, 1780. Spanish and French squadrons had considerable success in the game of picking up West Indian islands until Admiral George Rodney redressed the naval balance by his victory at The Saints in April, 1782.

A final great attack on Gibraltar took place in September, 1782. In addition to bombardment of the rock from the land side, 20 huge, specially constructed floating batteries with 220 cannon attacked the harbor. These were a French inspiration, and King Carlos III gave them his full confidence. "It will soon be ours," he wrote. Within a matter of hours enemy fire destroyed the batteries, and for the third time a British fleet pierced the blockade the next month and relieved the fortress.

The War of American Independence ended with the Treaty of Versailles on September 3, 1783. The Americans, the French, and the Spanish all betrayed their allies at one time or another. King Carlos III held out stubbornly for Gibraltar, being willing to surrender other gains; but British public opinion would not hear of giving it up, and the government could say grandly that "Gibraltar being in possession of George III cannot be a subject of discussion." In the end Ambassador Aranda settled for Spain's keeping Minorca and Florida.

With only Jamaica (lost by the Hapsburgs in 1655) and Gibraltar (lost by the Bourbons in 1704) "unredeemed," Spain's world empire in 1783 stood at its greatest extent in history. Spain's military and naval forces were also at their best in terms of power and prestige in the final years of Carlos III. The recent war had probably stimulated the home economy more than it had hurt it.

One unwanted aspect of the war had been rumblings of discontent in the Spanish colonies. In Peru between 1780 and 1781 Tupac Amaru, a descendant of the Inca kings, led an anarchic Indian uprising that involved as many as 60,000 rebel soldiers before the Spanish governor suppressed it with the utmost severity (Tupac Amaru's body was mutilated and then pulled apart by teams of horses). In New Granada in 1781 occurred the so-called revolt of the *comuneros,* a foretaste of later struggles for independence. That Spain's government was somewhat helplessly concerned with the future of its colonies is indicated by a project of Aranda put forward in 1783 that Spanish America be divided into three large realms, each to be ruled by an infante, with Carlos III taking the title of emperor.

One difficulty with Aranda's proposal was that the royal family did not have a surplus of infantes, and the king had a low opinion of several of those available. Of Carlos III's brothers, Don Luis survived until 1785, having happily given up his cardinal's hat so as to marry a young mistress and to pursue no greater ambitions than clockmaking and bird watching at La Granja. The king was greatly saddened by the death of the man who was his favorite hunting companion. As for his children, the clinically imbecilic eldest son whom Carlos had disinherited in 1759 lived on in Naples until 1767, a prisoner in the hands of numerous chamberlains whose vigilance was not always perfect enough to keep the infante from such excesses as trying to assault sexually any woman who crossed his path. The second son and heir, Carlos, forty in 1788, was already known to his father as a complete dolt, while the monarch had nothing but shocked contempt for his wife, María Luisa, the Princess of the Asturias being an outrageous flirt. Fernando IV, King of the Two Sicilies, the third son, lived on to 1825 and sired a collection of children who were to be the laughingstock of Europe and the distress of Spain when they started intermarrying into the dynasty. The king's favorite child was Don Gabriel, his fourth son, a talented prince in his thirties with a considerable reputation as a classical scholar and musician. Possibly, Carlos III considered altering the succession in Gabriel's favor, only to be disappointed and overwhelmed with grief in early 1788 by the sudden deaths from smallpox of the infante, his attractive Portuguese wife, and their new baby. The youngest son, Antonio Pascal, a foolish young man of thirty-two, was destined to play a foolish role in the next reign.

Of daughters, Carlos III had a special kindliness toward the deformed María Josefa, who never married. Another infanta, María Luisa Antonia, had wed the Archduke Leopold of Tuscany, who later ruled as Holy

Roman Emperor. The king was satisfied at last to have a dynastic alliance with the Hapsburgs and to know that his relatives' possessions in Italy now and into the next century would be objects of defense rather than attack by Austria. The descendants of María Antonia included Napoleon's second wife and their son, as well as the royal houses of Saxony, Tuscany, and Brazil.

The bereavements and disappointments brought out the family melancholy in Carlos III, but never to the excess characteristic of his predecessors. In December, 1788, he changed his routine to go hunting at La Granja and caught a chill from which he never recovered. On his deathbed the king was typically resigned, calming the grieving Floridablanca with the words "Did you think I was going to live forever?" When the Patriarch of the Indies inquired if he forgave his enemies, the gentle old king answered: "It did not need this extremity for me to forgive them. They were forgiven in the moment of doing me injury." He breathed his last at 12:40 A.M. on December 14, after which his body was put in a catafalque which lay in state for a day. The next night the coffin was carried by torchlight between two lines of Spanish and Walloon guards with arms reversed on the road to the Escorial, where it was received by monks chanting the "Miserere" and was taken down to the place of decay while the soldiers fired three salvos and bells tolled. The captain of the guard cried out," "Señor, Señor, Señor," to be greeted with silence from the tomb, after which he broke his baton in accordance with tradition.

To say that Carlos III was and remained the most capable and best intentioned monarch of Spain since Felipe II is in a sense "small praise." "Among the enlightened despots of his own day, none was a more successful ruler." His unique greatness was simply that "he brought about, if only temporarily, a national revival in all spheres."

IV.
The Royal Cuckold:
Carlos IV (1788–1808)

1. The Earthly Trinity

DURING the period 1788 to 1808 Spain was ruled by three people: King Carlos IV, well intentioned but complaisant; his wife, María Luisa, a creature of extreme temperament and sensuality; and her lover, Manuel Godoy, an adventurer of more charm than ability. The queen herself referred to their strange relationship as the "earthly trinity," but the world chose to regard the things going on at the court of Spain as unholy and sordid. In normal times the relationship of the monarchs and their favorites might simply have provided material for gossip by the malicious or for intrigue by the ambitious or for sorrow by the thoughtful. Given in this era the outside shocks of the French Revolution and the rise of Napoleon, dynastic degeneration among the Spanish Bourbons was to become national catastrophe.

Carlos IV ascended the throne shortly after his fortieth birthday. During his youth first in Naples and later in Spain he had been exposed to first-rate tutors and professors, but he bore his education lightly. Although the father had taken steps to initiate the Prince of the Asturias into affairs of state, Carlos III could scarcely hide his contempt for his lethargic heir. The parental rejection led to a marked timidity in the son, who took refuge in mechanical piety and mental inactivity, all the while he and his wife sought physically to absent themselves and their small court from the great court.

The new king was well summed up as a "hale, good-humored, and obliging man." Vigorous and ruddy-complexioned like his father, Carlos IV was a more strapping type, fairly tall, broad-shouldered, and tending toward heaviness. He bore himself well. He had fairly regular features, with only hints of the family inheritance in his long nose, weak mouth, and protruding chin. Much in the look of Carlos IV reminded people of his contemporary, Louis XVI of France, for after all, both were not only Bourbons but also first cousins through their Saxon mothers. The portraits of both the Spaniard and the Frenchman show men of majesty and benevolence, while they also suggest a certain indecision and bewilderment.

Both these descendants of *le grand monarque* lacked his forcefulness and his sense of dedication to kingship as a craft. This generation of rulers seemed more like country gentlemen who valued their estates in terms of pleasures more than duties. Essentially kindly, mild-mannered, and with simple tastes, they were content, even eager to leave affairs to others.

There is no evidence that Carlos IV shared the feeblemindedness that disqualified his elder brother from the succession. Nor was he even slow-minded, giving indications of a good memory and ready understanding. Lazy-minded is probably the right word for a king who persisted in calling the ambassador of the United States the "minister of the colonies."

Carlos IV shared his father's delight in the outdoors but was one of those Spanish rulers who carried it to excess. Rain or shine, war or peace, grief or happiness the king hunted from 9 A.M. to 12 noon every day and then again from 2 to 5. Almost as if to advertise the extravagance of his passion for hunting, Carlos once ordered the gathering of 2,000 deer in a park and watched with delight as artillerymen fired cannon at them.

Hunting was not the king's only diversion. He was a connoisseur of the arts, and his faithful patronage of Goya is important. Evenings might find Carlos IV playing the violin in a palace quartet. But drawing room and art gallery were probably less congenial to this king than the stable and his carpentry shop, where he delighted in manual activity. Socially, the king's habits led to a kind of royal democracy where he was most relaxed bantering with or even trying wrestling holds on the servants. An ambassador from revolutionary France appeared almost shocked to report of the king: "He takes no account of distinctions of birth, and does not even notice them. . . . The Medinacelis, the Albuquerques, the Altamares, the Osimas, all these grandees who take such pride in their origins, mean no more to him than his grooms; he has the same way of speaking to anyone." The king had the same way of showing his affection for people, whether duke or valet—making fun of them and hitting them familiarly.

Probably the outstanding characteristic of Carlos IV was his abhorrence of scenes, a trait which he shared in full measure with the similarly weak-willed Nicholas II, last Tsar of Russia. "In a world which he dimly felt to be his enemy, he had reached the point of looking for nothing but tranquillity for himself. Anyone dispensing him from the need to take a decision himself was his friend. He would cheerfully give up anything if he would thereby avoid a flood of some one else's tears or even having to see a cross face." This spinelessness made Carlos IV the victim of the whims of his wife and her lover.

Queen María Luisa made her presence felt from the first hours of the reign when she received the foreign ambassadors in conjunction with her husband. Three years younger than Charles, she was his first cousin as the daughter of the Infante Felipe, the brother of Carlos III who had succeeded him as Prince of Parma. Also, through her mother she was a Bourbon descendant of Louis XIV. Betrothed to the Prince of the Asturias at thirteen, sent off to Spain the next year, María Luisa forgot the beginnings of a fine education and instead pondered the political influences wielded by her recent predecessors of like age, the consorts of Carlos II and Felipe V. Frivolity and imperiousness combined in her from adolescence. Her ambition had once found expression in a conversation with her slightly older brother. She said haughtily, "I shall finally be Queen of Spain whilst you will never be more than a little Duke of Parma." "Well," he replied, "the Duke of Parma will have the honor of slapping the Queen of Spain."

María Luisa's beauty as a young princess soon deserted her, but she never admitted the fact. Her vivacity made up in part for what nature increasingly denied her in looks, and she always wore the clothes of a woman much younger. The first Goya portraits of her show her in enormous hats with feathers and ribbons that were current Paris fashion. With auburn hair, great fixating eyes, and a sensuous mouth, she was the picture of the "passionate, unsatisfied woman bursting with ill-restrained desires." At the beginning of the reign the Russian ambassador had this unflattering impression of her:

> Many confinements, several illnesses, and what is, perhaps, the germ of a more or less hereditary disease have completely wrecked her. Her skin is greenish and the loss of several teeth, replaced by false ones, has given the coup de grâce to her outward appearance. The King himself has taken notice of it, and often tells her, jokingly it is true, that she is ugly and getting old.

Yet a decade and a half later the wife of a French marshal could report that "the Queen appeared to me to be still beautiful," despite her stoutness, her double chin, and "the look of a matron."

The stories of the queen's love affairs began when she was still Princess of the Asturias and have been greatly magnified by the turn of events and the passage of time. With her passive husband and her straitlaced father-in-law, quite possibly she was merely bored to death in her late adolescence and turned to love intrigues that may have been more platonic than the gossips would allow. The first men connected with her were handsome foreign and Spanish aristocrats at the court, and several in succession found themselves exiled to remote places by an outraged Carlos III. Perhaps, with the idea of attracting less attention, the princess turned to strapping young members of the royal guards, in whose number may be included Manuel Godoy's older brother Luis, also the victim of banishment. In these carryings-on the future queen developed ways of dissimulation which became second nature to her.

Foreign observers were more willing to talk of María Luisa's sensuality than later Spanish historians proved to be. Yet a respected Spanish scholar of recent times has contributed the tale of Padre Diego de Cádiz to substantiate her nymphomania. This Capuchin monk, a spellbinding preacher to great crowds, was called to the court of the Prince and Princess of the Asturias and received unusual signs of reverence from María Luisa. She wrote him letters relative to the cure of sicknesses and "especially from an ill which cannot disappear but for an evident miracle."

That the heir to the throne was oblivious to his wife's indiscretions seems incredible, but it was true nonetheless. Once Carlos III attempted to open his son's eyes to the reasons behind the banishments of his wife's friends. Fatuously, the younger man declared that a princess would never be unfaithful with a man of lower rank. "Carlos, what a complete fool you are" was the resigned reply. Having satisfied himself that he was doing his duty by his wife, Carlos simply did not want to trouble himself with scandal. This complaisance was expressed by the king many years later after he, his wife, and Godoy had been turned out of Spain, their relationships made an international sensation. The ever-genial Carlos asked the wife of the prefect of Marseilles how many children she had, and he affected surprise when she admitted to three. "Only three! Why, my Luisa has given me twelve. She is a good mother and a good wife. She has never given me the slightest anxiety."

The man who succeeded in making himself ruler of Spain by exploiting the lust and love of Queen María Luisa was Manuel Godoy, a guardsman sixteen years her junior. Born in 1767 in Badajoz, he was the third son of a local notable living in comfortable, if modest, circumstances. Godoy could claim noble origin on both sides of his family and scarcely deserved the epithet "sausage-maker" bestowed on him later by the Madrileños. His education at the hands of local schoolmasters was remarkably modern in its stress on natural science, history, and philosophy rather than devotional texts and the classics, but it was halted before he was eighteen, when Manuel was sent off to Madrid in his brother's footsteps to seek his fortune in the royal bodyguard. Lacking any sort of financial backing, the provincial gained entrée through his handsomeness and affability into circles socially and intellectually above him.

Godoy first came to the attention of the Princess of the Asturias about 1785. One story is that she happened to be watching him when he unconcernedly dropped a statue during a religious procession. Another legend is that he fell off his horse on the Segovia road while escorting the royal family back from La Granja to Madrid. He soon became the princess' lover, and his rise to fame and fortune after she became queen in 1788 can only be described as meteoric. By 1792 he had been named a grandee of the first class, a duke, and principal secretary of state. Later he was awarded the grandiloquent title Prince of the Peace, and it is as prince that the favorite comes down in history.

Godoy's looks were obviously his fortune. A contemporary described him early in his career as "tall, strongly made without corpulence, broad-shouldered, slightly bent, and very clear complexioned. The whiteness of his skin showed up the rosiness of his cheeks, a rosiness said by his enemies to be artificial but which was in fact certainly natural." The good complexion also set off Godoy's fine head of black hair. The man kept his physical attractiveness as he grew older. His virility and voluptuousness are indicated in the description of him at thirty-six by the wife of a British envoy: "a big strong corase man with a bright red complexion and a heavy sleepy sensual look."

The sheer insolence of Godoy's position probably added to his appeal. Basically agreeable and easygoing, he was also egotistical and put on airs as he amassed titles, wealth, and power. His efforts to pose as an intellectual were only half successful; his conversation was "precise but unsparkling"; his jokes were clumsy. But everyone conceded that Godoy was *listo*, a Spanish word meaning "sharp."

Godoy's "bedroom prowess" undoubtedly recommended him to the depraved queen. Their liaisons were regularized into the court routine, and love and politics became intermingled. At one o'clock in the afternoon Godoy attended the queen and king at dinner in his capacity as a gentleman of the Household. Then, he would retire for his own dinner to the office and bedroom he maintained under the royal apartments. Here he was "joined by the Queen, who, once the King has gone off hunting, arrives by a secret stair. It is in the course of these secret talks," wrote the Prussian ambassador, "that the Queen and Godoy decide what proposals to lay before the King." ,

As in the full classic story, not only was the husband duped by his wife, but the aging mistress was also taken advantage of by her lover. According to the French ambassador, J. M. Alguier, who was not above embroidering to keep Napoleon and Talleyrand amused back in Paris, Godoy got María Luisa "in such a corner" that he could treat her with scorn and insult. "She has often undergone acts of violence and brutality at his hands such as a drunken soldier would not permit himself with a prostitute." Such reports were exaggerations, but clearly Godoy was in a position to blackmail the queen. While fear of exposure and false pride may have induced María Luisa to keep up with Godoy, she also developed a genuine affection for him and increasing respect as well. In time María Luisa treated Godoy more as a spoiled son than as a lover, and she came to regard him as a political genius. However fickle and self-seeking Godoy might be, significantly he followed his royal mistress into exile when their scandalous world came tumbling down.

Both the queen and Godoy had other affairs, but he still maintained his ascendancy. Once the king asked Godoy in the queen's presence how it was that a certain guardsman named Mallo could afford new horses and fancy carriages. The favorite replied maliciously, "Sire, Mallo doesn't have a penny in the world, but everyone knows that he is kept by an old and ugly woman who robs her husband to pay him." Carlos laughed heartily and asked his wife what she thought, drawing the hesitant response "Oh, well, Carlos, you know how Manuel is always joking."

The favorite used his status to play the libertine on a grand scale, according to a Spanish contemporary, who described the usual scene in Godoy's palace as follows:

> The principal room was filled with a crowd in which the sexes were represented in almost equal proportions. As there was no difficulty about getting in, several women of doubtful reputation were to be found there, and even a prostitute or two—although these last only of the smartest. In addition, sad to relate, there were ladies present who, though as well-situated as they were well born, were just as ready to peddle their charms for the good grace of the all powerful Minister and sell their virtue for his favor; it even happened sometimes that mothers and husbands could be seen there trafficking in the chastity of their daughters and wives respectively.

This picture of systematic seduction is echoed, expanded, and transferred to the royal palace by the scandal-mongering Alguier, who said two or three hundred women might be in attendance on Godoy.

> A girl arriving with her mother always went in to the Minister without her. Those who went in came out again with heightened colour and rumpled dresses, which they would then smooth down in full view of everybody. . . . Every evening the same scene was enacted in the very palace itself, the Court looking on and the Queen's apartments being not twenty yards away; the latter would rage and scream and threaten—only in the end to admit herself beaten.

When Godoy was about thirty, he openly took one woman as his mistress. Her name was Josephina Tudo. The orphaned daughter of an officer, she first appeared as one of the petitioners to the great minister. Her youth, her lack of temperament, and her dark-haired lusciousness made her a complete contrast with the queen, who stormed and then made her a lady-in-waiting.

The favorite, whose ambition and self-esteem knew no limits, had once thought of taking as his wife Madame Royale, the daughter of Louis XVI. Shortly after he took up with "Pepita" Tudo, he did succeed in marrying into the Bourbon family itself, his bride being the Countess of Chinchón, a daughter of the morganatic marriage of Carlos III's brother Don Luis. The king and queen presided at the marriage ceremony in September, 1797, sponsoring their cousin and giving her a large dowry. María Luisa's motives in this matchmaking can be seen variously. Perhaps she was merely being maternal by making Godoy more respectable. Perhaps she was trying to distract him from Pepita Tudo, an attempt which failed, in any case, as the foreign ambassadors were quick to report to their capitals. Godoy had two children by his wife. The royal honors paid to his wife during her pregnancies and to the children at the time of their christenings were among the breaches of court etiquette that astonished people the most. Godoy also brazenly advertised that he was maintaining a *ménage à trois*, receiving guests at dinner with the princess sitting on his right, Pepita Tudo on his left.

Observers at the time and historians ever since have wondered how the king could remain oblivious to the special relationship of the queen and Godoy. The popular belief that the favorite was the real father of an infante and an infanta is among the other things mentioned in this report by Ambassador Alguier:

> The thing that must strike those most who watch Charles IV in the bosom of his Court is his blindness where the conduct of the Queen is concerned. He knows nothing, sees nothing, suspects nothing of the irregularities which have been going on for more than thirty years. Neither the warnings he has received in writing nor the intrigues going on all around him, nor the marks of favor lacking both pretext and precedent, nor the attentions which violate all usage and decency, nor even the existence of two children who bear, as is obvious to all, a striking resemblance to the Prince of the Peace—nothing has availed to open the King's eyes.

Alguier's explanation is that Carlos IV was too pure-minded to believe in adultery. (This explanation is usually given for the Empress Alexandra's refusal to believe the scandals about Rasputin.) The king's extraordinary credulity was certainly fostered by the queen's extraordinary experience at deceit. Moreover, as stated earlier, the king wanted tranquillity above all and may have been unconsciously relieved to have Godoy spell him in satisfying the demands of an insatiable wife. What is most important, however, is that Carlos IV became entirely reliant on Godoy's friendship and his willingness to offer him political tranquillity.

The king became so dependent on Godoy's daily companionship that there were rumors of a physical relationship between them, which appears preposterous even given Carlos' backslapping familiarity with men. To be credited at face value is this extraordinary confession of Carlos IV to Napoleon: "Every day, wet or fine, winter or summer I would go out after breakfast, and after hearing mass, go hunting up to one o'clock; immediately after dinner I would return to the hunting field and stay there until dusk. In the evening Manuel would never fail to tell me whether things were going well or ill, and I would go to bed to start again the next day." This post-hunting meeting of king and Godoy followed what was already described as the secret tête-à-tête of queen and Godoy, so that the minister would be giving his sovereign not only peace of mind but the queen's instructions as well. Other reports speak of the king's visiting Godoy mornings as the latter dressed, even helping him, or their taking walks together in the gardens of Aranjuez.

In recent times writers have sought to take at least some of the sex scandal out of the María Luisa-Godoy story. One has argued that María Luisa was only following a practice she had observed in the aristocracy of Madrid, that of keeping a *cortejo*, or attentive young man, with the benign indifference or even encouragement of the otherwise preoccupied husband. While such a practice may have been common in court circles, it could only scandalize the lower classes of Madrid and the provincials, all used to the chaste ways of the previous king. What actually went on between the queen and Godoy is probably less important than what people believed went on. The young poet Byron merely echoed common gossip in the first canto of *Childe Harold*:

> How carols now the lusty muleteer?
> Of love, romance, devotion in his lay,
> As whilome he was wont the leagues to cheer
> His quick bells wildly jingling on the way?
> Now, as he speeds, he chants 'Viva el Rey!'
> And checks his song to execrate Godoy,
> The royal wittol Charles and curse the day
> When first Spain's queen beheld the black-eyed boy,
> And gore-faced treason sprung from her
> Adulterate joy.

Byron chose to use the word "wittol" for Carlos IV, meaning a knowing cuckold.

Another interpretation of "the earthly trinity" is that Carlos IV and María Luisa deliberately sought to raise up a political adviser independent of the two court factions centering on Count Aranda of the aristocracy and Count Floridablanca of the bureaucracy. Godoy, "both energetic and flexible," was such a "person who would owe his position to them and on whom they could place their trust." This version of it all is essentially that presented in Godoy's own memoirs. Many of the letters preserved that the queen wrote her favorite were innocent of amatory content. "The King asks me to tell you," she wrote on one occasion, "how convinced he is of your friendship, loyalty, honesty, love, and respect for us, but especially for him." When she uses phrases like "you are our only friend," one is struck by the similarity to at least the political aspects of the Nicholas-Alexandra-Rasputin triangle.

Could all question of sexual scandal be left aside, the question would remain what political qualifications Godoy had to recommend him to such great distinctions and responsibilities. The evidence is that he was neither a fool nor a genius. Godoy's industriousness is attested by many Spanish and foreign contemporaries. One reported that "the Prince saw every paper and affixed a remark on the margin of every document," while another noted admiringly: "The Prince dispatches current affairs with great promptitude . . . his mind is altogether clear and balanced." A British observer went so far as to say "he seemed born for high position."

The test of events and later scholarship suggest that Godoy was in over his depth, that his limited education and talents were suited to smaller responsibilities or quieter times. He "was the crafty manipulator rather than the imaginative willful and self-assured dictator who let his decisions be shaped by prevailing conditions rather than by any long-range planning." He was a "toy of destiny and nothing more." In any event, his name and those of his royal sponsors were associated with utter disaster.

2. Goya, the Country, and the Other Spain

When Goya painted his dazzling and disturbing masterpiece "The Family of Carlos IV," he put himself at his easel into the background of the canvas, indicating great self-assurance on the face of it and, perhaps, some thought that the bizarre courtly group needed an intelligent, down-to-earth face as counterpoint. Goya belongs in the picture, for this critical age of Spanish history cannot be discussed apart from a man who is considered by many to be Spain's greatest artist, a man who must certainly be considered in the company of El Greco, Veláquez, and Picasso. Our idea today of the look of Carlos IV, María Luisa, and Godoy is almost entirely Goya's. Our visual perception of Spain's nonroyal problems and potentials at the turn of the eighteenth century is largely Goya's, too.

Francisco Goya was born on a small farm near Saragossa in Aragón in 1746, the last year of the reign of Felipe V. His family, of Basque origin, combined the traditions of craftsmen and of poor nobility. After a limited amount of schooling, he was apprenticed to a painter, who guided him in the copying of master prints. Stories of early signs of his genius and of his hell raising must be discounted. Even scholars are not sure of the first works attributed to him, which may include two unconventionally topical paintings, the "Squillace Riot" and "Carlos III Promulgating the Edict for the Expulsion of the Jesuits." Failing two artistic competitions in Madrid, Goya spent a profitable time studying in Italy and then returned to Saragossa to his first important commissions, the execution of religious frescoes for a local church.

Goya was in Madrid during most of the 1770's, working under the direction of the celebrated Mengs doing cartoons for the Royal Tapestry Factory. These were "rural and humorous" scenes, to use the words of the Prince of the Asturias, for whose dining room and bedroom in the El Pardo apartments the designs were intended. A letter of Goya expresses his pride and delight at showing some of his work to the royal family, after kissing their hands. There are aspects of the Baroque and Rococo in the tapestries, such as "Dance on the Bank of the River Manzanares," but their populace are traditional Spanish types, *majos* and *majas* (roughly "flashy dressers"), rather than Frenchified aristocrats. Importantly, Goya never succumbed to Neoclassicism, the precise and detached style of his greatest French contemporary, Jacques Louis David. Also, in this period Goya did his first etchings, which were studies in royal iconography in that he did spirited copies of Velázquez's paintings of the later Hapsburgs.

Following his unanimous election to the Academy of Art in 1780, Goya developed a great reputation as a portrait painter, doing canvases of Carlos III, numerous dukes and duchesses, and notably some of the more radical reformers like Gaspar Melchor de Jovellanos. The painter was just beginning to associate himself with the world of men of ideas when he was appointed one of the court painters in 1789 soon after the change of reigns. In this year Goya executed several official portraits of a bemedaled Carlos IV and a behatted María Luisa for the Academy of History and like institutions.

In 1792 while in the south of Spain, Goya suffered a serious illness, which left him deaf, like his near contemporary Beethoven, another genius who also spanned two eras. The nature of Goya's illness is a mystery.

Schizophrenia has been suggested, but this disorder is hardly consistent with an increasingly productive and versatile career dating to 1826. Syphilis is a frequent conjecture, but the supporting story that Goya's wife had only one surviving child in twenty pregnancies is untrue. A very recent theory is that Goya's unique ability to execute lifelike portraits after a few hours sitting exposed him to excessive amounts of lead from the white pigments he ground and used, causing fulminating lead encephalopathy. Whatever the cause, this crisis of health marked a tremendous transition in the artist's work, bringing out a darker side in him, such as is evident in his "Yard with Lunatics."

A second trip to Andalusia in 1797 resulted in Goya's stormy affair with the Duchess of Alba, Spain's richest woman, who had recently been exiled to her estates by a jealous Queen María Luisa. The legends of the antipathy of duchess and queen are many, of which the following at least fits in with the spirit of the times. To celebrate the completion of a new wing of her palace at San Cristóbal, the duchess invited the court to a gala, and the sovereigns were mollified by such attentions as a fireworks display at the climax of which the initials C for the king and L for the queen were written in the dark sky. Then, a G for Manuel Godoy appeared beside them, and there was consternation. Later the entire Alba palace burst into flames, the duchess having ordered the servants to set it on fire before the same revenge could be taken by her enemies. Other legends involving both the duchess and Goya concern the familiar paintings the "Naked Maja" and the "Clothed Maja," which she was supposed to have posed for but which were actually painted after her death, model unknown. Characteristically, Godoy, who must be credited with befriending Goya, added the "Naked Maja" to his extensive collection of provocative nudes, and interestingly, Goya had to answer for it when the work turned up in the hands of the Inquisition years later. As for the Duchess of Alba, there does exist the authentic and arresting portrait of her dressed in black as a *maja* pointing imperiously to the words "solo Goya" in the sand at her feet (owned by the Hispanic Society of New York).

His rejection as lover by the duchess, his illness, and also the troubles attendant on the ninth year of Spain's confrontation with the French Revolution, all were expressed in Goya's "Caprichos," a series of eighty satiric etchings begun in 1797 and published with official blessing in 1799 (minus two nasty caricatures of the duchess and queen). Called a "unique blend of dream and fantasy with social criticism," the "Caprichos" contain as subject matter foppish gallants, thieving ladies of easy virtue, pompous academics, suffering prisoners, and many witches and spirits of popular superstition. One striking drawing is of common people bearing aristocratic donkeys on their backs, but the artist did not spare criticism of the Spanish people's ignorance in the face of foreign enlightenment. As the author of the "Caprichos" Goya was to influence such romantic painters of the next century as Eugène Delacroix.

In 1799 Goya was appointed first court painter at a salary of 50,000 reales with a grant of 500 ducats for the maintenance of his carriage. The next year Goya made several trips to Aranjuez to do sketches from life of the Bourbons there and soon after produced the huge canvas known as "The Family of Carlos IV." This group portrait is arresting and disquieting as both art and psychology. The composition has little depth, but rather the random figures are "pinned like great insects to the neutral ground," suggesting "a closed world without escape and with just enough air to breathe." The assemblage is glittering in their medals, jewels, silks, and velvets, but they stand like puppets. "The faces are neither beautiful nor ugly, only 'real' which means terrifying in their intense reality." The straightforward characterization suggests degeneration.

The dominant, almost floodlit figure is that of Queen María Luisa, then forty-eight, who fixes the observer with a relentless gaze. Her face is wasted, her mouth agape, but her bosom almost seems to heave, and one can read into her brilliant eyes all one knows about her lusts. The figure of the king is slightly thrust forward, a George Washington type in white-wigged, stoutish dignity, a Louis XVI type in his benign bewilderment.

Other than the centrally placed monarchs, the group includes from left to right Bourbons of varying notoriety or colorlessness. The hard-looking Infante Don Carlos, aged twelve, was to be responsible for plunging Spain into three civil wars over the succession in the next century. His sixteen-year-old brother, the Prince of the Asturias, stands foremost in the picture, his posture ungainly, his look intense and moody; his destiny is to be the cruelest of the Bourbons as Fernando VII. In the background peers out the misshapen, befuddled face of the Infanta María Josefa, the deformed daughter of Carlos III. Next appears a young woman's figure with her face turned away: she was probably a Neapolitan Bourbon, Fernando's bride-to-be, whose looks were unknown in Spain. The most appealing personalities are the two delicate-looking children held by the queen on either side of her: the Infanta María Isabel, aged eleven, a future Queen of the Two Sicilies; and the Infante Francisco de Paula, six, father of a future King-Consort of Spain. These two children were commonly believed to have been fathered by Godoy.

Behind the king is his uncle the Infante Don Antonio, flabby, cunning-looking, but actually a silly-minded bigot. Next peeps out the bloated face only of Carlos IV's eldest daughter, the Infanta Carlota Joaquina, twenty-five and already Queen of Portugal. Hunchbacked as a result of a hunting accident, this infanta was described as a "riot of malformation" and disgusting hideousness, all of which did not prevent her from being even more brazenly oversexed than her mother. The tallest figure in the group is that of a cousin, Don Luis, Prince of Parma, blond and dazed-looking, dead in a few years at the age of thirty. Next to him, the last person portrayed is his wife, the Infanta María Luisa Josefa, who holds in her arms the infant Don Carlos Luis, briefly to reign as King of Etruria and lengthily to ponder it, dying only in 1883.

Much has been written to suggest that "The Family of Carlos IV" is some sort of caricature of the Bourbon family or at least some sort of devastating prediction. "It seems in this picture" that Goya "is making his own pitiless appraisal and behind the puppets decked in gold has an intuition of the final catastrophe." Yet the queen in one of her letters to Godoy pronounced it "the best of all paintings," and the other Bourbons who posed for Goya were all pleased. Nonetheless, this was the last Royal commission for Goya from the king and queen. A possible explanation is that the monarchs became increasingly upset by the background wall painting which partially frames María Luisa's head. A recent cleaning of this area of Goya's canvas reveals a scene of lechery, perhaps the Biblical story of Lot and his daughters, in which Goya could be saying something about Sodom and Gomorrah.

The missing figure in Goya's masterpiece is, of course, Godoy, who saw to it that the artist eventually paid him his due. In fact almost each time Godoy received a new medal there was a new portrait of him by some artist. In 1801 Goya did a huge canvas of the favorite on horseback, but this has been lost. What has survived is another portrait of that year, showing Godoy as a general on campaign with military banners, horses, and soldiers in the background. The self-satisfied, sensuous figure reclining back at a sharp angle again seems caricature, but there is no evidence that there was any displeasure.

After his royal patrons and Godoy were driven from Spain by Napoleon, Goya remained in Madrid. Before him were his renowned etchings "The Disasters of War," charges of collaboration with the enemy, and eventual exile under the returned Bourbons.

3. Spain and the French Revolution

In the next half year after the accession of Carlos IV occurred the inauguration of George Washington as President of the United States (April 30, 1789) and the first meeting of the Estates General of France (May 5). The juxtaposition of these events is significant, for the double impact of the American and French Revolutions proved to be the undoing of Spain and its empire.

Following the advice of his father and also the path of least resistance, Carlos IV kept the principal ministers in office, notably the Count of Floridablanca, who had dominated the government for thirteen years. How unlike so many royal sons who could not wait to change everything! The regime courted immediate popularity by an amnesty of prisoners, remission of taxes, and distribution of honors (Godoy's being made a colonel went unnoticed).

Serious food riots took place in Barcelona in early 1789. This event would have been readily forgotten but for the ominous news that began to come out of Paris, indicating that a great revolution was in full swing. The Spanish government successfully kept these reports out of the press—almost the only French item run in July was a notice about Louis XVI giving a cardinal his hat of office—but Madrid knew of the storming of the Bastille anyhow.

The administration reacted to the disturbing reports from Paris with a mixture of calm and caution. The king's coronation festivities proceeded as planned in September, 1789, with eight days of parades, receptions, fireworks, and bullfights in the Plaza Mayor. There were 65,000 visitors from outside the capital. The complete absence of political manifestations led the Prussian ambassador to conclude "the Spanish people are good, noble, and peaceable." A Cortes representing thirty-seven cities met and, with a reverence in complete contrast with the uproarious Estates General, swore allegiance to the king and the Prince of the Asturias. Under the presidency of Campomanes some discussion of substance took place in the Cortes, but the delegates appeared more interested in getting themselves better bullfight seats and in curbing bureaucratic changes than in challenging the system. From revolutionary Paris the Spanish ambassador observed: "None of the causes that could have been observed here for many years exist in our country where one finds religion, love for the King, devotion to the law, moderation in the administration, scrupulous respect for the privileges of each province and individual . . . and a thousand things the French lack." At first nothing happened to contradict such fatuous self-satisfaction.

In September, 1789, the government promulgated new censorship regulations to the effect that "all prints, papers, printed matter, manuscripts, boxes, fans, and any other object alluding to events in France" be sent from the customs ports directly to the secretary of state. The reference to "fans" might seem picky, but soon the Inquisition was turning up citizens possessing fans painted with representations of the fall of the Bastille or of the revolutionary hero Lafayette. Taking no chances, the Floridablanca regime ordered all nonresidents to leave Madrid, ostensibly to control postcoronation vagrants but actually to silence too talkative French visitors. Spaniards in France were requested not to write home about local developments.

The government got into a war crisis with Britain in 1789 over contested outposts in Nootka Sound (in the Vancouver area of Canada). With its usual ally, France, in such a state of turmoil Spain had little choice but to back down and pay an indemnity.

Spain eventually became so panicked over the French Revolution as to forget its own needs of change and progress. Parliamentary Britain did likewise, and at the other end of Europe Catherine the Great of Russia abandoned any pretense of liberalism and ended up banning some of her own political writings. As in Russia, the flourishing periodical press, one of the chief achievements of the previous era, was the first victim of the reaction in Spain. A decree of February, 1791, suppressed all private journals except the *Diario de Madrid*, which was forbidden to publish "verses or any political subject matter whatsoever." Some of the most liberal members of the government—notably Campomanes and Jovellanos —were exiled or imprisoned in 1790 and 1791. The hysteria intensified after an assassination attempt on Floridablanca, by a Frenchman it was true, but a person without clear motives or accomplices.

While Spain's intellectuals were being reduced to silence, the court gossiped about Godoy's promotion to adjutant general of the royal bodyguards in January, 1791, major general in February, lieutenant general in July. Queen María Luisa was declaring herself quite openly with these promotions and with gifts to her favorite like a carriage and six horses emblazoned with his monogram under the royal arms. Popular disgust found expression in such things as a dog appearing on the streets wearing a sign "I belong to Godoy. I fear nothing." The animal was imprisoned. "The grandees are furious, but they are at Godoy's feet," wrote the Prussian ambassador.

In June, 1791, Carlos IV's French cousins made their desperate attempt to escape abroad known as the "flight to Varennes." Louis XVI and his queen were hauled back to their capital in humiliation, the Parisians forbidden under dire penalties either to boo or cheer. In September the French king subscribed to the new constitution. The Floridablanca government reacted with a bravado that was soon to disappear from Spanish diplomacy, telling the National Assembly in Paris to be careful of the liberty and dignity of their king from whom the constitution had been "extorted" and further warning:

> It would be a great mistake to suppose that foreign powers have
> no right to take a hand in these events because they are the domestic
> concerns of France. War against France would accord no less with

the Law of Nations than one waged against criminals and rebels who usurp authority and make their own the goods of others.

In Spain itself Floridablanca announced dire restrictions on all foreigners, including a requirement that they swear a special oath to the king and Catholicism. Further immigration was discouraged, a complete reversal of the intentions of the previous reign and a contradictory and confused action since currently thousands of aristocratic and clerical refugees from the French Revolution were fleeing to Spain. Nonetheless, even these antirevolutionists, who had seen too much and knew too much, were tightly controlled as to where they could travel and settle.

Floridablanca was ousted as head of the government on February 28, 1792, having reduced the queen to tearful threats to go back to Parma by his insinuations about Godoy. Also, the king felt that minister's stiff notes to Paris were endangering the safety of Louis XVI more than helping him; a secret emissary from the French king had so informed him. Impatient to go hunting, Carlos IV signed an order for the dismissal of Floridablanca, who found a carriage waiting for him; the minister was eventually shut up in the fortress of Pamplona. His successor, incredibly, was his predecessor during the previous reign, the seventy-three-year-old Count of Aranda. The new government was variously seen as a revival of the power of the aristocratic party or as a fruit of the machinations of Godoy or as an admission that no single voice was to advise the irresolute king. Briefly, Aranda eased the censorship and the restrictions on foreigners.

In April, 1792, France went to war with Austria and Prussia in protest against their efforts to uphold the absolute prerogatives of France's own king. Rumors of treachery led to the storming of the Tuileries Palace in August, the imprisonment of Louis XVI, and his formal deposition on September 21, 1792. Moderate leaders such as Lafayette fled from the radicals in power, and the first wholesale massacre of the rich took place in September. Revolutionary fervor also enabled France that month to check the Austrian-Prussian invasion at the Battle of Valmy. Full of confidence, the new French National Convention in November issued a declaration that it "will accord fraternity and help to all peoples who shall desire to recover their liberty," meaning that the nations of Europe were being invited to overthrow their monarchies. A Spanish exile in Bayonne, a former pupil at the Reales Estudios, started publishing propaganda calling for a national uprising against tyranny and superstition. He got no signs of response.

Aranda having completely failed in his efforts to conciliate the French, a worried Carlos IV resorted to a desperate expedient and in effect replaced him with Godoy. The old man remained the nominal president of the council, but the twenty-five-year-old ex-guardsman was named principal secretary of state on November 15, 1792. His ostensible mission was to save Louis XVI from the guillotine, but it was whispered that the real reason for his elevation was the queen's desire to have him so preoccupied with state affairs that he would cease chasing after other women. According to a secretary of the French embassy, the period after the appointment of Godoy was the only moment when he felt the possibility of a revolution in Spain. The grandees were outraged at Godoy's sharing their rank, the intellectuals were frustrated by being out of power, and the masses were scandalized by the stories about the court. The smart set of Madrid turned to harassing the government by affecting French revolutionary ideas and modes. Many genuinely concerned Spaniards began to question the whole idea of royal despotism, if it was unenlightened and dominated by a favorite, as the best instrument for reform.

In fairness to Godoy, he was not uncourageous or reactionary, only incompetent to control events or to dominate the crosscurrents of opinion. In later years the favorite was to point with pride to such measures of his progressiveness as eleven new chairs of natural science in the universities, a ban on church burials as unsanitary, and the sending of missions to England to study industry. The censorship again was lightened, as evidenced by a newly authorized translation of Adam Smith's *Wealth of Nations* dedicated to Godoy.

Events in France forced issues in Spain. Louis XVI was put on trial in December, 1792. Godoy in the name of his own king made more strenuous efforts than any European to save the life of the French Bourbon king, offering Spain for his refuge and recognition of the French Republic in exchange. In spite of these representations, in part because of them, "Citizen Capet" was beheaded on January 21, 1793.

The news of the execution of Louis XVI reached Madrid nine days later. Carlos IV had allowed himself one private moment of recrimination against his cousin. A dozen years before at the time of the Spanish king's accession, the French king had jocularly demurred about sending him his respects, saying, "After all the poor man is a mere cipher, completely governed and hen-pecked by his wife." Now Carlos could mutter that "a gentleman so ready to find fault with others did not seem to have managed his own affairs so well." In public, however, the king and queen affected great shock at the fate of their fellow ruler, and the court and city went into deep mourning.

Ladies who wore French coiffures or dresses on the streets were liable to be shorn or stripped on the spot. The French ambassador was expelled on February 19, as war preparations proceeded apace, although Aranda and others still counseled neutrality. The National Convention in Paris, which had declared war on Britain and the Netherlands on February 1, resolved any dilemma by proclaiming hostilities with Spain on March 7. One of the revolutionary leaders aroused the Assembly with a disputable reference to 1700 and some questionable travel advice: "The Bourbons must disappear from a throne which they usurped with the blood of our ancestors. Let liberty be carried to the fairest clime and most magnanimous people of Europe."

Spain "took up arms against the Revolutionary invaders as no other people in Europe did at this time." Citizens made generous voluntary contributions to the treasury; grandees raised regiments at their own expense; and even the smugglers of the Pyrenees offered to devote themselves to military efforts. Godoy begged to be put in charge of a fighting force, but settled for a promotion to captain general. For the first time in well over a century the Spanish army took the military initiative against France and invaded Roussillon in April, 1793, besieging Perpignan and later capturing Hendaye to the west. On the other major war front the Austrians recaptured the southern Netherlands.

The triumphs of France's enemies in 1793 were short-lived after the nation was mobilized into action by the Committee of Public Safety. Robespierre and the extreme radicals in power began the famous Reign of Terror in July. Revolutionary armies drove the allies back across the Rhine in December, the same month the young General Bonaparte forced the British ignominiously to evacuate the foothold they had gained at Toulon. In the spring of 1794 the French pushed the Spanish back over the Pyrenees and invaded Catalonia. The traditionalist French commander looked to the annexation of the conquered province, but the political dreamer Robespierre talked of creating "sister republics." In the face of the volumes of revolutionary propaganda brought into northern Spain, the Spanish commander complained that "the French are waging war on us with pen and money more than with fire and sword." The surrender of San Sebastián to the French in July, 1794, produced shudders of alarm in a Madrid unsure whether military weakness or political subversion was involved.

As disillusionment with the war swept the court, Aranda raised the possibility of negotiations with France, but he concentrated his efforts on blaming Godoy for administrative inexperience. The favorite replied hotly that "it is true that I am only twenty-six years old but I work fourteen hours out of the twenty-four, sleep only four, and am continually at the service of the state." In March, 1794, the ever-hesitating Carlos IV asked Aranda to join Floridablanca in retirement, leaving Godoy without a major rival. That June Godoy exposed a plot on the part of lesser officials and lawyers to overthrow him and call a Cortes.

"Even the whores ask you about Robespierre," wrote a Madrid

clergyman in the summer of 1794, before the news that the dictator himself had ended up on the guillotine in July. Curiosity about what was going on in France was dominant, however, rather than sympathy with the Revolution. The Conspiracy of San Blas uncovered just before that saint's day in February, 1795, was an exception: a schoolmaster, a lawyer, and a doctor were involved in a pathetically private effort to collect arms and print propaganda in favor of a Spanish republic. Nonetheless, such conspiracies on top of the military defeats decided Godoy to make peace.

It says something for the chivalry and dynastic feeling of the Spanish court that in the peace negotiations with the new French Directory in 1795 their main concern was for the safety of the children of the executed Louis XVI, the dauphin and his sister. "Be assured," declared a Spanish envoy, "that if France gives us the choice between one of our frontier ports and these children we should prefer unhesitatingly them to it." The hapless "Louis XVII" died anyhow, and Spain made peace anyhow. The Treaty of Basle of July 22, 1795, provided for Spain's recovery of all recently lost territories except the Spanish half of the island of Santo Domingo. In the name of Carlos IV the Spanish negotiators agreed that certain pro-French conspirators be pardoned and French merchants allowed to return to Spain. The treaty was the beginning of the fatal subordination of monarchist Spain to republican France, although at the time it was hailed by the court as a great accomplishment. The king was lavish with medals and promotions, the most startling being the title Prince of the Peace given to Godoy. The fact that the favorite also was granted large estates in Granada and an income of 1,000,000 reales a year, making him one of the richest men in the country, was a much less bitter pill to swallow for the aristocracy than the fact of his unprecedented princely title putting him above all except the heir to the throne.

After shifting from war to peace with the French Republic, Godoy went one step further and made an alliance with the ex-enemy that many Spaniards persisted in regarding as the home of anarchy and the Antichrist. By the Treaty of San Ildefonso signed on August 18, 1796, Spain and France pledged to support each other militarily and navally against Great Britain. The favorite did not make clear what gains he had in view from switching enemies but merely asserted, with some truth, that "Great Britain has always gulled Spain." The French, whose General Bonaparte was winning stunning victories in Italy in the spring and summer of 1796, certainly looked like winners. Spain declared war on Britain on October 18, 1796, and immediately the combined Spanish and French naval strength forced Britain's young Admiral Nelson to abandon the Mediterranean altogether.

Those familiar with the outcomes of the three *Pactes de Famille* of 1733, 1743, and 1761 might have guessed that the renewed friendship of Spain and France would soon be racked by cross-purposes and treacheries. The French Directory was irritated by Godoy's clumsy intrigues to reconstitute a French monarchy in the person of the brother or cousin of Louis XVI or even of a Spanish infante. Spain was hesitant to join France in putting pressure on Britain's ally Portugal, since Carlos IV's own daughter was queen there. General Bonaparte in Italy paid scant respect to the sensibilities and territories of the Spanish king's other relations in Parma and Naples. And the influx of French visitors to Spain meant inevitably the dissemination of radical ideas, leading Godoy to say that "if the result of peace has been to introduce revolutionary ferment among us, we should have done better to go on with the war."

The war with Britain soon brought defeats. Admiral Nelson smartly defeated a French-Spanish squadron at Cape St. Vincent in February, 1797, and after that the British used their superiority to bombard Cádiz, to reassert control of the Mediterranean, and to capture Trinidad, one of Spain's prize Caribbean islands.

In the years 1797 and 1798 occurred many court intrigues and sharp changes in Godoy's fortunes. After marrying the Countess of Chinchón, the king's cousin, Godoy brazenly kept up with his mistress, Pepita Tudo. Thwarted in her intent to keep Godoy close to her, the queen found new favorites among the guards. In the face of his growing unpopularity Godoy tried a new political tack and in November, 1797, secured the appointment as minister of grace and justice of the relatively progressive Jovellanos, a man the queen hated for his austerity and his criticisms of her and the court. The liberals seemed to have regained control of affairs, but their gratitude to Godoy was minimal, and they joined representatives of the French Directory in bringing about Godoy's dismissal as First Secretary of State and chief of the royal bodyguards on March 28, 1798. The king was heartbroken to lose Godoy, declaring, "I shall be infinitely beholden to him the rest of my life." The queen, so ill-used by the favorite, was recaptivated by letters from him, some daringly allusive, such as "Manuel, who has given Your Majesty so many happy hours, will never cause you a moment's displeasure and will always remain the same loyal and grateful servant."

A few months after Godoy's giving up his offices, his successors at the head of the government were out, too. A mysterious illness, perhaps caused by poison, incapacitated Jovellanos and his chief associate in August, 1798, and later they were sent into exile. Although without portfolio, Godoy soon reasserted his complete power as favorite.

* * *

4. Godoy, Napoleon, and the Approach of Catastrophe

So far Spain's contacts with the French Revolution, now a decade old, had not been drastically consequential. The chief loss from the generally antirevolutionary policies pursued by the ministries of Carlos IV was the loss of momentum in the movement for internal reform, a loss of faith in the Enlightenment on the part of some, a loss of faith in the monarchy itself on the part of others. The reassertion of Godoy's control of affairs in 1798 and 1799 coincided with Napoleon's rise to supremacy in France. Dealing with Napoleon proved to be an entirely different and catastrophic thing for Godoy and the Bourbons.

The War of the First Coalition against France, which Spain had abandoned in 1795, came to a close in October, 1797, when Austria, the last of France's Continental enemies, admitted defeat in the Rhine area and Italy and signed peace terms. Only Britain fought on. France took advantage of its supremacy to occupy Rome and proclaim a Roman Republic in February, 1798, in defiance of the Pope. Napoleon Bonaparte, the ever-victorious general, now attempted a global strategy and embarked on his famous Egyptian campaign with the aim of striking as far as British India. The expedition sailed on May 19, 1799, effected a landing on July 1, and effortlessly defeated a Turkish-Egyptian force in the Battle of the Pyramids on July 21. Then the whole enterprise was cast into jeopardy by Admiral Nelson's smashing the French fleet in the Battle of the Nile on August 1. Spain and its navy stood aside in these events.

France's high-handed actions of the past and its present difficulties combined to bring about the War of the Second Coalition, the essential ingredient of which was a British-Russian alliance in December, 1798. Austria, Naples, Portugal, and the Ottoman Empire ranged themselves against the French Directory. Defeats soon followed the first triumphs of the allies, and by the end of 1799 the Second Coalition collapsed altogether, the Russians claiming betrayal by their British allies in operations in the Netherlands and by the Austrians in central Europe.

Against this background of French successes and the possibility of even greater successes, Napoleon overthrew the Directory on November 9, 1799, in the coup known as the 18th Brumaire. Having abandoned his army in Egypt but keeping the extent of the defeat there secret, Napoleon made himself First Consul, promising to end the corruption associated with the French republicans, all the while avoiding the revival of the old-regime oppressiveness associated with the French monarchists.

The news of Napoleon's coup was received with much satisfaction by the court in Madrid. Carlos IV, vastly relieved that Napoleon was counted a good Catholic, looked forward to the Frenchman's bringing peace to

Europe in general and security to the Italian Bourbons in particular. Godoy found satisfaction in the downfall of the Directory, which had been so instrumental in bringing about his own temporary eclipse. Queen María Luisa dreamed of Paris fashions. Napoleon was quick to mollify all with gifts, a special hunting gun to the king, a suit of armor to the favorite, and dresses to the queen "of the most dazzling kind such as an attractive brunette in her early twenties would select."

The Second Treaty of San Ildefonso of October 1, 1800, again proclaimed Franco-Spanish friendship and enmity to Britain. Also, Spain re-ceded Louisiana to France in return for Napoleon's promise to enlarge Parma, an instance of dynastic interests taking precedence over national interests that would have pleased Isabel Farnese. Napoleon sent his brother Lucien as ambassador to Madrid. The king was so taken by this Frenchman and his flattery as to present him with a pair of shoes made with his own hands. In his reports to Paris Lucien had good words for Godoy, who never ceased consolidating his power behind the scenes. "The number of Godoy's enemies shall not prevent me from saying that I have always found him agreeable, serviceable, sincere, and understanding; he is noble and gallant with the ladies, personally brave, and much better informed than his enemies admit." The two talked of a dynastic marriage, Bourbons and Bonapartes.

Once again France pressured Spain to attack Portugal, resulting in the War of the Oranges of May, 1801, so called for the orange branches the invading Spanish soldiers sent back to the queen. The Spanish monarchs were willing to undertake hostilities against one daughter, Queen Carlota of Portugal, to further with French aid the interests of another daughter in Parma, the Infanta María Luisa (shown with husband and baby in the Goya group portrait of this time). These latter Bourbons were given an enlarged kingdom of Etruria. The War of the Oranges was also the occasion for Goya's painting of a swaggering Godoy playing at soldier under the bombastic new title of Generalissimo of the Armies. The favorite wrote his royal mistress: "All is agitation, war-like bustle, and rousing fanfares, and all that, Madame, intoxicates the imagination. Let me never hear talk again of political intrigues—never, Madame, for the love of God . . . I want never to leave the colors. May Your Majesty deign to let me serve her with the sword for no shorter time than I have served her with the pen." The queen replied with less than regal language: "Do not expose yourself too much. . . . Do not take the field on that skittish horse of yours."

Godoy settled for a modicum of military glory in Portugal and made peace before any French troops arrived. The treaty ending the War of the Oranges on June 6, 1801, called for the cession of one town by Queen

Carlota and a bit of land in Guiana. Napoleon was furious at what he considered Godoy's treachery and had to be placated by a supplementary treaty providing for the closing of Portuguese ports to the British. Yet French initiative brought about the Peace of Amiens with Britain in March, 1802, and Spain was the loser to the extent of Trinidad.

In 1802, the first year all Europe had been at peace in a decade, the queen and Godoy lost one determined enemy and gained another. The mysterious death of the Duchess of Alba occurred in July, to be followed by talk of her being poisoned, by her perversely radical will leaving considerable property to her peasants, and by the sight of her enemies at court enjoying possession of some of her jewels and artworks. In September the court celebrated a double marriage treaty with the Bourbon court at Naples. María Isabel, the third daughter of Charles IV and María Luisa (by some accounts daughter of Godoy and María Luisa), was wed to Francis, the hereditary Prince of the Two Sicilies, and thus she was assured of the queenly rank already enjoyed by her sisters in Portugal and Etruria. In return, Fernando, Prince of the Asturias, was betrothed to his first cousin Maria Antonia of Naples. Considering Fernando's eligibility as heir to Spain, the latter arrangement was a great coup for Maria Antonia's mother, the masterful Queen Carolina, who was not above flattering Godoy to secure her ends. The wedding festivities, the balls and the bullfights, barely concealed underlying hatreds within the dynasty. Queen Carolina would refer to the Madrid royalty as a "family of cretins," while Queen María Luisa wrote to Godoy about "this rascally Court of Naples and this slut who fans the flames, my daughter in law." The new Princess of the Asturias did indeed work mightily to confirm in her husband his already deep antipathy to his mother and Godoy and their pro-French policies.

After barely a year of peace, France and Britain were at war again in May, 1803. Napoleon, to forestall the British navy, sold Louisiana to the United States on April 30, in blatant disregard of commitments not to give Spain's former possession to a third party. Yet the French demanded that Spain fulfill· its obligations under the Treaty of San Ildefonso to lend aid against Britain. Godoy demurred. The French ambassador in Madrid warned him that Napoleon had never been outwitted, least of all by a mere favorite. When Godoy persisted in maintaining Spanish neutrality, Napoleon resorted to sending a confidential message to Carlos IV revealing Godoy as an "intruding king," but this was intercepted by his wife and her favorite, who persuaded the witless monarch to return it to Paris unread. "The earthly trinity" persisted. About this time they were described as follows to Napoleon: the king was a benign nonentity who wore "threadbare" hunting clothes, the queen "could not take the plunge of growing old," and Godoy "had the air of a coachman."

In time Napoleon outmaneuvered Godoy, even resorting to threats of invasion. By a treaty of October, 1803, the price of Spain's staying neutral was set at its paying its ally 6,000,000 gold francs a month. A year later Spain went to war with Britain anyhow. The king's declaration of hostilities on December 12, 1804, was in part provoked by the British seizure of some of the American treasure fleet in October. The British saw advantages to having the Spanish empire out in the open as an enemy. In a grandiloquent reaction, Godoy caused more dismay than hope when he declared: "We will humiliate their intolerable pride . . . the tyrants of the seas shall die of rage before our eyes." It was the chimeric days of Alberoni and Ripperda all over again as Spain mobilized and built up its fleet. Godoy, whom the queen pronounced a far greater military genius than Napoleon, busied himself with projects for the recovery of Gibraltar and Jamaica, for a descent on Ireland, or for even an attack on India. Napoleon, who was thinking at this time of an invasion of Britain, humored the man he held in utmost contempt with gifts of fine watches and the cordon of the Legion of Honor.

Spain had aligned itself with France just at the time when a Third Coalition was being organized against that country, Austria and Russia joining Britain in January, 1805. Perhaps the least of the grievances of these two countries was umbrage that Napoleon had arrogated to himself the imperial title in the previous May. Usurper he might have been, but "Emperor" Napoleon was more than a match for the born emperors Francis I and Alexander I, whose armies he annihilated at the Battle of Austerlitz on December 2, 1805, perhaps the greatest of his military victories.

Spain's preoccupation at this time was the staggering naval defeat known as the Battle of Trafalgar of October 21, 1805, not the French triumph far away at Austerlitz. While Napoleon had temporarily abandoned any plan to invade England in favor of smashing his enemies in Central Europe, he still had prodded the admirals to break the British blockades of Toulon, Brest, Cartagena, El Ferrol, and Cádiz and to combine the French and Spanish fleets into a huge force that could contest the English Channel, the Mediterranean, and the Caribbean. The combination of fleets was indeed achieved, but then "the tyrants of the seas" under Admiral Nelson caught up with Admirals Pierre de Villeneuve and Federico de Gravina off Cape Trafalgar near Cádiz. In one of history's most famous and decisive naval engagements the twenty-seven British ships virtually annihilated the thirty-three battleships of the enemy. Spain lost eleven of its fifteen battleships involved in the engagement, including what was the largest warship in the world, *The Most Holy Trinity*, perhaps a portent for Carlos IV, María Luisa, and Godoy.

In the long view Trafalgar represented the final blow to Spain's pretensions to being a great naval power and the signal for the dissolution of the overseas empire which Spain could no longer defend. Independence was achieved by the Spanish American colonies only in the 1820's, but beginnings took place under Carlos IV and Godoy. For example, in April, 1806, the adventurer Francisco Miranda undertook the first of his four attempts to liberate Venezuela. A Creole who had seen military service under both the Spanish monarchy and the French Republic, Miranda accepted British gold and recruited his original force in New York. Also in 1806 the British made a naval descent on Buenos Aires, which was repulsed. The next year the British succeeded in capturing Montevideo but were thwarted in a new attack on Buenos Aires. In each case the British capitulation was effected not by any effort of Godoy in Spain, to whom appeals were made in vain, but by the energetic action of self-appointed leaders and local militia, all of which could not fail to stimulate Argentine patriotism.

Godoy's maneuvering became desperate as Spain's association with France against Britain proved increasingly costly. Some of Spain's distress was actually at the hands of its French allies themselves. In December, 1805, Napoleon found it to his advantage to proclaim his brother Joseph King of the Two Sicilies. As for the Bourbons, he simply proclaimed "the dynasty of Naples had ceased to reign." Carlos IV's brother took refuge in Sicily. The Spanish king was gravely upset by Napoleon's unexplained action, never suspecting that Godoy himself had helped bring it about by alleging to Paris all sorts of dark plots on the part of his enemy Queen Carolina of Naples.

Although the Princess of the Asturias, Queen Carolina's daughter, died in March, 1806, Godoy realized that the widowed Prince Fernando remained his implacable enemy. Accordingly, to prepare for the eventuality of the death of Carlos IV, the favorite set about to gain himself a "sovereign state," as he put it, or a place "to assure myself an existence which no violence can reach." He turned to secret negotiations with Napoleon, whose reputation for making and unmaking thrones was already considerable, and the French emperor encouraged Godoy in the belief that he might come to rule over all or part of Portugal.

Another wild tack in Godoy's policy followed upon news both of the British onslaught against Buenos Aires and of French-British negotiations behind Spain's back. The favorite now decided that the French alliance was ruinous for Spain, and he talked of an alliance with Britain and Russia, to be sealed by the marriage of an infante and a Russian grand duchess. On October 14, 1806, Godoy addressed a manifesto to the Spanish nation calling upon it to gird itself to meet the "enemy," without naming the enemy, which, nonetheless, everyone took to be France. This treachery was not forgotten by Napoleon, who that very same day had achieved another of his greatest victories, the complete rout of the vaunted Prussian army in the Battle of Jena. The ever-shifting Godoy promptly wrote to assure Napoleon of his "absolute devotion," calling him "the most perfect model of a hero that history has to show." These policy zigzags, resulting in no gain for Spain, made Godoy more unpopular than ever. To show their displeasure with public opinion, the king and queen moved the court from the Escorial to Aranjuez without the customary sojourn in Madrid.

Just when Godoy's diplomatic gestures were at their most frantic and futile, Napoleon was approaching the zenith of his power in Europe. With both Austria and Prussia knocked out of the fighting, France moved against Russia. The upshot was the truce signed at Tilsit, July 7–9, 1807, between Napoleon and Tsar Alexander I. Russia now became France's ally, joining Napoleon's grandiose Continental System, or the closing of all European ports with the aim of bringing Britain to its knees by economic means. Spain had already joined this blockade. Portugal delayed its adherence until too late. A French force of 20,000 under General Andoche Junot was welcomed into Spain in October, 1807, and within a month it had occupied all Portugal, forcing the royal family to flee to Brazil, fortunately with their treasure. By a secret treaty Napoleon and Godoy arranged for the partition of Portugal, with the south destined for Godoy as "hereditary Prince of Algarves" and the north pawned off as compensation for the Queen of Etruria, whom Napoleon had just unceremoniously ousted from Italy. The French army in Lisbon, however, made no move to implement the treaty as the months wore on.

The news of the arrest of the Prince of the Asturias on October 29, 1807, was the most sensational Madrid had known, even in these years of toppling thrones and raging wars. Godoy had inadvertently driven his greatest enemy at court into making a false move. With supreme effrontery the favorite had proposed that Fernando take as his second wife the sister of Godoy's wife. The rage of the heir to the throne knew no bounds, and he declared, "Let me rather stay widower all my life or turn myself into a monk than be brother-in-law of Manuel Godoy." The latter countered by having himself made commandant of the palace guards and used that position to effect the ouster of all of Fernando's advisers and household. In desperation, Fernando now made the nearly fatal mistake of writing to Napoleon. His letter of October 11 praised the emperor as the savior of Europe, sought his aid against "false and wicked people" at the Spanish court, and ended up begging the hand of one of Napoleon's relatives. Godoy's agents got their hands on this and other incriminating materials which were laid before the king. Carlos IV in turn wrote Napoleon telling of

Fernando's "appalling conspiracy," which involved thoughts of assassinating Godoy, of putting away the queen, and of dethroning him, the king. He confided to the French emperor that the Spanish throne should pass to one of Fernando's brothers. The same night of the king's letter to Paris a grim procession of Carlos IV, the chief ministers, soldiers, and masons with their tools passed through the Escorial Palace; they went to seize the Prince of the Asturias and to shut him up as a prisoner in his apartments, a move reminiscent of the chilling fate of Don Carlos, the demented son of Felipe II, in the year 1568.

There were many crosscurrents in this palace crisis, the details of which are not agreed upon to this day. Godoy left the embrace of a mistress in the capital to pursue complex intrigues at the Escorial. One disputed story is that Fernando had written some letters so incriminating that his mother hid them in her bosom to save his life. It is unfortunately consistent with what is known of the future Fernando that he had no compunctions about naming accomplices in his plottings or that the prince wrote a humble letter begging to "kiss the feet of His Majesty." The next day, November 5, the king was relieved to be able to go off on his hunting, having signed a royal decree forgiving the heir, all the while revealing humiliating details of the plot and promising further investigation. Madrid was in a great uproar, and peasants in the provinces were arming themselves in the cause of the prince, which was obviously the anti-Godoy cause.

Napoleon was key to the situation, not only because of his general power but also because of the appeals already made to him by all involved. In cold fury the emperor had threatened the worst if his name or that of the French ambassador was dragged into the proceedings against Fernando, whose safety he further guaranteed by direct representations in his favor, although he considered the heir a sniveling coward. That winter a stream of reports from the French ambassador and a special observer Napoleon sent to Spain appraised Paris of the general situation in Spain. The king was a fool and a weakling. The queen was a Messalina. Her "disgusting desires" had been used by Godoy first as a lover and then as a pimp. Napoleon then decided that the Spanish Bourbons must go.

V.
The Crisis of 1808–1814:
The Bourbons at
the Mercy of Napoleon

1. Uprisings and Dethronements

THE year 1808 was the most extraordinary in Spanish history in terms of the rapid unfolding of many events of untold future importance. Its only rival would be 1492, the year of the reign of Fernando and Isabel which saw the final reconquest of Granada from the Moors, the expulsion of the Jews, and the discovery of the New World. In 1808 Spaniards lived through a popular revolt causing the overthrow of Godoy, the abdication of Carlos IV in favor of Fernando VII, the dethronement and seizure of both rulers by Napoleon at the Bayonne Conference, French military occupation of the entire Iberian Peninsula, violent uprisings against the French in Madrid, the proclamation of Joseph Bonaparte as king, and finally the beginning of one of the greatest struggles for national liberation of modern times during which the term "guerrilla warfare" came into existence.

A commission of judges on January 23, 1808, acquitted "the accused of the Escorial" of plotting against the state for lack of evidence. Godoy's efforts to blacken the name of the heir to the throne essentially had backfired, for Fernando emerged more popular than ever and the rallying point for all those who hated the favorite.

The nation was moved to alarm when French troops seized the citadel of Pamplona by trickery on February 16, 1808, and then took Barcelona on February 29. Spain's ostensible allies against Portugal were acting like conquerors. Napoleon kept his intentions secret, however, causing Marshal

Joachim Murat, the French commander in chief in the peninsula, to complain that he "knew nothing of your plans," all the while he edged his troops closer to Madrid.

That winter the Spanish court moved from the Escorial to Aranjuez, again forgoing a stay in the capital. "The earthly trinity" behaved much as usual, except that they appeared tenser. Everyone soon knew that Godoy had slapped the queen in the face during a procession. When the king, walking ahead, stopped to ask what the noise was, the ever-compromised María Luisa covered up by saying she had dropped a book. The news of the approaching French armies produced consternation and panic. Godoy, proposing that the royal family imitate their Portuguese relatives and escape to America, made preparations for such a flight at Seville and Cádiz. Napoleon was at first pleased at the prospect of the Bourbons removing themselves from the scene, but then he decided the loss of Spanish America for possible use by France was unacceptable and ordered measures to seize the royal fugitives. No such flight took place, however, because Prince Fernando and his supporters opposed it in the council and Carlos IV could not make up his mind.

During the day and night of March 17 the grounds of the Aranjuez Palace were unusually crowded with people, courtiers, nobles and their retainers, and soldiers who had left the north at the approach of the French. Some of the aristocratic supporters of the Prince of the Asturias even mingled with the lower orders, passing out wine and cigars and indulging in revolutionary talk. The general mood of the people seemed festive, and Carlos IV was roundly cheered when he appeared on a balcony before dinner. At the meal Godoy talked gaily to his royal patrons while Fernando sulked. Then the favorite dined with the commandant of the Walloon Guards and retired to his own small house to make love to Pepita Tudo while his wife and children waited attendance in the next room. Just as the mistress was taking leave in her carriage late in the evening, an angry mob descended on Godoy's house and in a brief space of time stormed inside and ransacked everything. Godoy escaped with his life only by making his way to the attic and hiding under a pile of rugs. Outside, soldiers and civilians looted, got drunk, and congratulated themselves for preventing the flight of the court, for saving the heir to the throne, and for ending the power of the lecherous Godoy.

Early the next day the badly shaken king was persuaded to issue a decree which obliquely confirmed the revolution: "Desiring to command in person the Army and Navy, I relieve of his commands Don Manuel Godoy, Prince of the Peace, whom I allow to retire to whatever place he chooses." When all the royal family appeared in public later, they were greeted with wild enthusiasm. Although he had his people behind him, Carlos IV was still too timorous to expostulate with the French ambassador, to whom he granted an interview, and instead indulged in self-pity at the loss of his confidant.

Godoy suffocated under his pile of rugs all during March 18, giving himself up to a sentry stationed in his house at noon the next day. Taken away under heavy guard, he was spat upon, beaten, and bloodied by enraged bystanders along the route. Imprisoned in a stable, the once most powerful man in Spain was reduced to such a miserable state as to "melt a heart of stone," according to one of his captors. Here he was visited by the Prince of the Asturias, who told him that he forgave him personally but that the nation demanded his trial for monstrous crimes. Fernando had his first taste of vengeance. Groveling before his enemy, Godoy had the prescience to address Fernando as "Your Majesty." Indeed, that very day Carlos IV abdicated—"for my health's sake" and "in favor of my beloved son." A hysterical María Luisa had been unable to stay the action of her frightened and confused husband.

Then Carlos IV retracted his abdication on March 22, declaring that it had been forced on him. Craven, yet spiteful, he placed himself and his kingdom at the disposal of Napoleon in a letter sent to Murat. These actions attracted little notice on the day when the French commander and a brilliantly uniformed suite made their official entrance into Madrid at the head of thousands of French infantrymen, Hussars, and the very colorful corps of Mamelukes, native cavalry recruited during the course of Napoleon's Egyptian expedition. The populace of the capital turned out in great numbers to watch the strange parade, but their reaction was restrained, the people undecided whether the French had come as their deliverers from Godoy or as their oppressors. As for Godoy, King Fernando had maliciously ordered him escorted into Madrid that same day, but Murat forestalled this action which almost certainly would have resulted in a lynching.

What Murat was helpless to forestall was the state entry of Fernando himself into Madrid on March 24. The young king cut a haughty but inspiring figure on his white horse as he rode through the Atocha Gate followed by a small escort, including a carriage with his younger brother Carlos and his conniving uncle Antonio. If the French had received a polite reception, the new arrivals were greeted with mad fervor, booming guns, pealing bells, and fireworks. Weeping, laughing crowds accompanied Fernando down the road covered with flowers and capes to the royal palace, where he took up official residence. With an eye to the dark future and dissipated hopes, a Spanish historian wrote: "Never was a monarch able to enjoy a more magnificent, nor a more simple triumph, nor did one ever contract a more sacred obligation to reciprocate in all earnestness the disinterested love of such loyal subjects."

The first actions of Fernando VII were conciliatory. He tried to placate Murat, who would not recognize him, by sending as a gift to the French nation the sword taken from Francis I in 1525 after he was captured by Charles V in the Battle of Pavia. As for his parents and Godoy, the new king was willing to let them retire to an independent sovereignty in the Balearic Islands, a proposal Carlos IV might have accepted but for the stormy opposition of his wife. Fernando ordered the release of such political prisoners as Jovellanos and the repeal of the harshest recent police measures. So popular was the young monarch that official bodies within days were begging to commission his portrait; thanks to this, Fernando granted Goya two sittings on March 28, the only encounters between two men who became increasingly antipathetic. Certain measures the new regime took, such as suspending the previously authorized sale of some church property, suggested that Fernando already "looked to reaction rather than reform for support," but before the king's degree of enlightenment could be put to the test, Napoleon took charge of events.

Napoleon kept Spain, its royal family, and even his own subordinates guessing for more than a month. His train of thought was privately revealed as early as March 27 in an abrupt letter he sent his brother Louis, whom he had made King of the Netherlands two years previously: "The King of Spain has just abdicated; the Prince of the Peace has been put in prison. I have resolved to put a French prince on the throne of Spain. The climate of Holland does not agree with you. I am thinking of you for the throne of Spain. Answer me 'yes' or 'no.' " Upon Louis' huffy refusal, Napoleon wrote a similar message to his brother Jerome, King of Westphalia, on April 10. This same day the emperor dispatched a message to Murat in Madrid urging him to prepare for street fighting and advising him to use the strongest hand against the Spanish people, whom apparently Napoleon did not altogether trust to accept his dispositions peacefully. Meanwhile, Napoleon had sent invitations, which were really veiled orders, for Fernando VII, Carlos IV, the queen, and Godoy to come to Bayonne to confer with him.

Fernando VII started his journey north on April 10, having named a governing junta in Madrid headed by his uncle Antonio. He encountered touching effusions of patriotic support in every town he passed, but he also met French troops everywhere. Hesitating at Vitoria, Fernando was put somewhat at ease by the assurance of the French agent A.J.M.R. Savary that "I will let myself be beheaded if the Emperor has not recognized Your Majesty as King of Spain and the Indies a quarter of an hour after your arrival at Bayonne." The local populace cut the traces of the king's carriage, but Fernando passed on anyhow on the advice of his tutor, Juan Escoiquiz, who with badly mistaken erudition cried, *"Jacta est alla,"* when they crossed the Bidassoa into France. Fernando would not see Spain again for six years. Cordial and noncommittal at a dinner meeting in Bayonne on April 21, Napoleon left it to Savary to inform a shocked Escoiquiz that Fernando must renounce the throne. The emperor took time to inform his foreign minister, Talleyrand, that "the tragedy . . . is in its fifth act" and that Fernando was a complete coward who "eats four times a day and has no ideas on anything." Secret messages, however, got through to the young Spanish king at the end of the month, saying that, in effect, the Spanish nation would resist foreign dictation to the last drop of its blood.

Godoy was next to arrive in Bayonne on April 26, and again Napoleon was a friendly host. When Carlos IV and María Luisa reached the French city on April 30, they were treated to cannon salutes. After the elder Bourbons had paid their respects to Napoleon and voiced their parental grievances to him, there was a confrontation of all the principals at which hand kissing would normally be in order. Carlos IV cut off his youngest son, Don Carlos, with an abrupt "good day" and then turned on Fernando with the words "Have you not brought sorrow enough on my white hairs? Be off. I do not want to see more of you." Thereupon Carlos and María Luisa fell into the arms of Manuel Godoy with every sign of affection. The setting for this reunion was the chateau in Bayonne where the widow of Carlos II had spent thirty of her years. Having observed the whole family, Napoleon wrote to Talleyrand that Fernando was "very stupid, very wicked," that King Carlos is "a nice man," and that "the Queen has her heart and her past on her face."

Napoleon liked to have things in writing. On May 2 he came into possession of a letter from Carlos IV castigating his son as unfit to rule. On May 4 he and Godoy had drawn up a kind of treaty whereby Carlos IV handed over to the emperor or his nominee all dominion over Spain and its empire in return for guarantees of income and estates in France. The older Bourbon was true to his ancestors only in insisting that the empire be kept intact and undilutedly Catholic. Godoy saw to inserting a provision that his own property be restored to him. They had only to force Fernando VII to renounce his rights. This decision was being pressed on him by his wrathful parents and a scornful Napoleon on the afternoon of May 5, when the first news arrived of a great anti-French insurrection in Madrid.

Despite the disquieting reports from Bayonne, the city had remained tranquil under the control of Murat's troops. The peoples' feelings of national humiliation boiled over, however, when they learned that Napoleon had ordered all remaining members of the Bourbon family to be escorted to France. These included Fernando's uncle Antonio, his sister the ex-Queen of Etruria, and his youngest brother, the Infante Francisco de Paula. When carriages were made ready the morning of May 2 and their intended royal occupants appeared at the palace gates, an assembled throng raised great shouts of protest. Additional French troops sent to the scene were greeted with shots, and they in turn fired on the crowds. By noon French artillery was using grapeshot indiscriminately. Murat, heeding Napoleon's advice, made a great show of force as the day wore on, moving large numbers of cavalry and infantry into the city with great precision. They were met with frenzied opposition from the Madrileños, largely the poorer people. The rich locked their doors, and the Spanish garrison, except for individual heroes, stayed in their quarters. "Balconies, windows, garrets, and roofs vomited stones, flints, bricks, and tiles, torn out with bare hands, kettles of boiling water, tables, benches, tubs, dismantled furniture, and anything that might strike, wound, mangle, or kill." Orderlies murdered French soldiers in the hospitals. Most memorable were the attacks of women with knives against the horses of the Mameluke cavalry; this was the specific scene depicted by Goya in one of his greatest paintings called simply "Dos de Mayo," the date which patriotic Spaniards have ever since commemorated as the beginning of a heroic struggle for national liberation.

By 2 P.M. on May 2 the French had the situation largely under control and that night began the bloody reprisals. Anyone caught with weapons was hauled before a firing squad. These executions were also later immortalized by Goya in his matching canvas in the Prado the "Tres de Mayo," showing nameless victims with convulsively outstretched arms falling before the volleys of French rifles. These paintings that might be considered just patriotic propaganda are widely hailed today as a landmark of modern art for their treatment of contemporary themes with the utmost passion and with technical innovations. In the course of the whole confrontation perhaps 400 Spaniards died. Murat, who decidedly under-stated French losses at 31, was to boast that "yesterday's affair delivers Spain to the Emperor." A Spanish official replied with greater foresight: "You should say that it places Spain beyond his reach forever."

Madrid's outburst understandably enraged Napoleon at the time of his final and decisive interview with the Bourbon royalty at Bayonne. It also provoked Carlos IV to denounce Fernando again to his face: "The blood of my subjects has been shed and the blood of the soldiers of my great friend Napoleon! You are in part responsible for their slaughter." As for Queen María Luisa, she muttered things about having the recalcitrant son guillotined. "What a mother. She horrified me," wrote Napoleon. The emperor departed after an ultimatum to Fernando: "If between now and midnight, you do not recognize your father as your lawful king and do not so inform Madrid, you will be treated by me as a rebel." The young monarch of less than six weeks gave in. The resistance of even a brave man might well have broken down in the face of the knowledge that in 1804

Napoleon had not hesitated to execute Duke of Enghien, a Bourbon claimant to the French throne. On May 6 Fernando recognized the superiority of his father's title to his own and thereby enabled Carlos IV to ratify the document handing Spain over to Napoleon.

Deposing the Spanish Bourbon dynasty was one of the most high-handed actions of Napoleon's career and one of the most fateful. With a kind of injured innocence Napoleon wrote to a confidant: "Yes, I know what I am doing is not right, but why don't they declare war on me? . . . And why did they come?" Years later, after he had time to think it all over on St. Helena, Napoleon persisted in blaming the events at Bayonne on Bourbon family intrigues rather than Bonaparte family ambitions.

Spanish civil, military, and ecclesiastical officialdom appeared to accept without question the change of regime. During early May Murat in the royal palace received a steady stream of public and private men of importance come to pay respect and offer allegiance. The Cardinal Archbishop of Toledo, for example, a cousin of the ex-kings, was servile in his expressions of support. After all, had not Fernando himself in a manifesto from Bordeaux warned that "rivers of blood" would flow if there were resistance to the "wise decisions" of Napoleon?

When Napoleon wrote to Joseph Bonaparte in Naples on May 11, he delivered what was more an ultimatum than a request: "King Carlos has ceded me all his rights to the crown of Spain. The Prince of the Asturias had renounced, beforehand, his pretended title of king. The nation, through the organ of the Council of Castile, asks me for a king. It is to you I have destined the crown. Spain is not the kingdom of Naples. . . . It has immense revenues and the possession of all the Americas. You will receive this letter the 19th; you will leave the 20th." Hours after receipt of this letter on May 21 Joseph departed for his new destiny, telling neither his wife nor his mistress of his intentions. While the dutiful brother was still on the road, Napoleon issued a stirring proclamation to Joseph's kingdom-to-be: "Spaniards, after a long agony your nation was perishing. I have seen your ills. I shall remedy them." On the practical side, the emperor ordered frigates and troops to be sent from Spanish ports to secure the support of Mexico, Venezuela, and Argentina.

The very day of Napoleon's proclamation less grandiloquent but equally serious proclamations began to come out of Spain itself, like the declaration of the "Junta of Oviedo" that it had "reassumed sovereignty" until such a time as Fernando VII could be restored to his legitimate throne. The bells pealed, mobs seized the arsenals in the name of the junta, and the Asturians prepared to fight the foreigner just as Pelayo had defied the Moslem tide back in 723. To which Spanish town goes the honor of initiating the war of national liberation, is a disputed question, but clearly within the space of a week at the end of May all areas not directly under French occupation were up in arms under juntas that were formed when established local authorities hesitated. Valencia and Cartagena rose on May 23, Saragossa touched off all Aragón on May 24, and Seville followed on May 26. The failure of the authorities in various localities to pay special honor to San Fernando Day, May 30, confirmed people's worst fears about the fate of Fernando VII, whose rescue and restoration now became the rallying cry of the nation.

The French began to get some inkling of the fierce struggle that had been touched off when their army in Barcelona tried to break out of that city on June 4 and was driven back with heavy losses. Far to the south Cádiz fell into rebel hands, and on June 14 the French naval squadron there was bombarded into surrender. To the west a French army of 6,000 tried to recapture Saragossa on June 15 only to meet frenzied resistance, not so much from Spanish soldiers as from crudely armed civilians. Before the enemy gave up the siege, they had killed half the populace of the city and left only fifty houses standing. This was the first and one of the greatest stories of heroic resistance that would sustain patriotic hearts over the next six years of horror.

Joseph Bonaparte arrived in Bayonne on June 7, 1808, having been proclaimed King of Spain and the Indies by the Council of Castile the day before. In his first proclamation to Spain "Don José Primero" pledged himself to work for the "happiness of the generous people whom Providence has entrusted to our care" and above all to see to "the integrity and independence of the Kingdom," suggesting right from the start that the older Bonaparte regarded himself as something other than the mere lieutenant of the younger. Nonetheless, Napoleon was the one who had taken the initiative in calling a Spanish constitutional convention in Bayonne on June 15. Most of the delegates were appointed rather than elected, and only 91 of 150 eventually signed their country's first written constitution, which was as enlightened as the French one of the time and equally innocuous. On July 9 King Joseph crossed the frontier into Spain with a brilliant convoy of one hundred carriages escorted by French hussars to guard against "bandits."

The disturbing reports of Spanish resistance soon took on the character of grim reality in Joseph's mind. From Vitoria he wrote Napoleon: "If Your Majesty does not have a Continental war you should consider seriously sending Spain many troops and funds." From Burgos on July 18 came the message: "It seems that nobody has wanted to tell the exact truth to Your Majesty. . . . I am not frightened by my position, but it is a unique situation in history. I do not have one single partisan here." Napoleon was not moved by his brother's despair. In a letter on July 19 he pointedly reminded Joseph that the first Bourbon, Felipe V, had had to conquer his kingdom, and then he blithely counseled: "Have courage and be gay and never doubt of complete success." The next six years of Spanish history were to be a kind of triangular interplay among the well-intentioned, diffident Joseph, the ever-imperious Napoleon, and the generally hostile but divided Spanish nation.

2. The Bonaparte Intruder King, José I (Joseph Bonaparte) (1808–1814)

When King José I entered Madrid for the first time on July 8, 1808, he was greeted by artillery salvos, smart salutes from the lines of French troops in the streets, and almost total silence on the part of the populace. Even when he ordered the first bullfights to be held in many years, ordinary citizens stayed hostile. The magistrates and many of the high nobility duly came to swear allegiance, and a considerable number of the intellectuals were enthusiastic in their support. The new king was able to muster a Court largely thanks to these *afrancescados,* the Francophile or at least French-thinking element who regarded the Bourbon past as corrupt and benighted and who looked to future progress on the model of Spain's neighbor to the north. For the majority of Spaniards, however, Joseph was and remained *el rey intruso,* the intruder king.

Joseph was more than just a Frenchman: he was a Bonaparte, a member of a mysterious and fascinating clan. He had been born in 1768, making him eighteen months older than Napoleon. A special lifelong intimacy developed between these two of the Bonaparte brothers, as well as marked differences between them at an early age. When they ranged the countryside together, Joseph saw natural beauty, Napoleon saw battlefields; when they bade each other farewells, Joseph was tearful, Napoleon controlled. The younger brother never changed his opinion expressed in the 1780's that the elder had a "light spirit" disqualifying him for a military career. All the Bonapartes, however, had what was considered a Corsican spirit, including self-confidence, an ability to adopt to circumstances, a belief in fate more than in God, and a sense of family. Their destinies were European. Joseph, like the others, was educated in France, but he had to return to Corsica at age eighteen following the death of his spendthrift, visionary father to become head of the family of four brothers and three sisters. He took up the management of the business affairs of his beautiful, uneducated mother, and ever after this brother's special ability was financial, "the craft and sullen art of saving well."

The exigencies of Corsican politics forced the whole family in 1793 to take refuge in France, where they accommodated themselves to the changing currents of the Revolution. In 1794 Joseph married into bourgeois wealth; his bride was named Julie Clary. Napoleon's rise as a general aided his brother's fortunes, so that following the former's famous victories in Italy in 1797, Joseph was playing a complementary role in diplomatic posts in Parma and Rome. He returned to France to manage Napoleon's newfound riches, taking the opportunity to buy himself and Julie a chateau in Louis XIII style at Mortefontaine, forty kilometers from Paris. From here and from his *hôtel* in Paris, Joseph consciously built up a Bonaparte mystique in public opinion, and he was an extremely influential force behind Napoleon's coup d'état of 1799. In the ensuing years, often working behind the scenes but enjoying the reputation of being the one man who would talk frankly with Napoleon, the eldest Bonaparte negotiated important treaties with the United States, Austria, and the Papacy.

In January, 1806, Napoleon typically ordered his brother to take over the army invading southern Italy, giving him forty hours, and Joseph typically obeyed, his eventual reward being the crown of the kingdom of Naples. Here during the next two years was performed the dress rehearsal of the drama of the kingmaker and the puppet-with-a-conscience that later took place in Spain. When Joseph set out to win the hearts of the Neapolitans by presenting their statue of San Gennaro with a jeweled collar, Napoleon chided him that confiscations and executions were more appropriate. Joseph came to rely strongly on French officials and a French army of 40,000, but he also embarked on a program of reforms, curbing feudalism, tapping church wealth, and promoting education. Despite two assassination attempts, Joseph could consider himself successful and popular, like the Bourbon Carlos III who had graduated from this kingdom to that of Spain in 1759. Joseph was even more reluctant than his predecessor to leave, despite Napoleon's too-eager persuasion to the effect that "at Madrid you are in France; Naples is at the end of the world." The first letter "José I" wrote the emperor after his cold reception in Madrid in July, 1808, said, "I have not been received by the inhabitants of this town as I was by the Neapolitans."

When Joseph arrived in Spain, he was just forty years old. Considerably taller than Napoleon, he had the most regular features of all the Bonapartes—small but pleasant eyes, a straight nose, and a well-shaped mouth. People noticed his expressive hands, his distinctive bearing, and a kind of melancholy in his look. The new king was obviously well educated and cultivated. Ten years before, he had written a novel, and he frequently demonstrated his predilection for reading aloud the French classics. Lacking were the extraordinary intelligence and perception of Napoleon, as well as his brother's capacity and taste for hard work. In fact, Joseph had something of the Bourbon in him, a tendency to indolence and indecision alternating with brief moments of stubbornness and assertiveness.

"What struck contemporaries most was his kindness," according to a recent assessment of King Joseph. The adjectives describing him that come to mind are largely un-Napoleonic—placid, imperturbable, charming, amiable, reasonable, soft-spoken. To his Spanish supporters he remained generous and faithful forever.

One side of Joseph was the man of gentle manners and simple tastes. A week before he left for Spain he could write his mistress in Naples with all sincerity: "I prefer the private life into which I was born to that of Kings." A contradictory side of him was the man of great vanity and flights of ambition. He developed a penchant for uniforms and an obsession with etiquette. Disdaining at first the French title of imperial prince, Joseph came to insist on keeping it despite his newer dignity and on keeping his right of succession to the French throne (shades of Felipe V!). Napoleon once quipped that Joseph was so conscious of his family position that he really regarded his brother the emperor as a usurper. When the matter of his Spanish titles came up, Joseph wanted the full ancient claims including Burgundy and Milan, but Napoleon held him to "Don José Napoleon, by Grace of God and the Constitution of the State, King of Spain and the Indies." The new ruler could not wait to sign his first proclamation *"Yo el Rey"* in the manner of Carlos I. Such pretensions, as well as a desire to please and help Napoleon, served to keep Joseph on the Spanish throne in spite of his own diffidence and his subjects' recalcitrance.

Among Joseph's motivations was a feeling of mission in Spain, the mission of replacing feudal holdovers and superstition with modern ways and ideas. He looked upon the resistance to his rule not as patriotic but as reactionary. His upholding of the banner of enlightenment is what earned him the support of many of the radical intellectuals, but it unfortunately was also the source of most of his difficulties with Napoleon.

About seven months into his reign, Joseph wrote off to Napoleon, whom he called "Sire," "I am King of Spain only by force of your arms. I could become it through the love of the Spaniards, but for that it is necessary that I govern in my own manner." The emperor's reply to "Your Majesty" was true to form: "You won't be successful in Spain except with vigor and energy. This talk of goodwill and clemency won't come to anything." This irreconcilable conflict of philosopher-king with pragmatist-militarist was to be expressed many times. Two years on the throne, Joseph still fretted to his wife: "It must not be expected of me to govern Spain solely for the good of France. . . . In Spain I have duties which my conscience dictates to me." One can juxtapose to these words this frank outburst by Napoleon: "The

King must be French. Spain must be French. It is for France I conquered Spain. . . . I have only one passion, one mistress, France. I sleep with her." Napoleon did not want things for Spain; he wanted things from Spain, supplies and, above all, money. Once summoning every bit of irony and contempt in his voice, Napoleon said of Joseph: "He wants to be loved by the Spaniards."

A lesser source of friction between Napoleon and Joseph was the latter's pleasure-loving ways. The French emperor once dismissed his brother as "a king who is always with the women playing hide-and-seek or blindman's bluff," considering such activities perhaps more reprehensible than bed-room escapades. Probably, Joseph's apologists protested too much when they emphasized that he never neglected state duties, even though "he had a particular penchant for the opposite sex." In any case, Joseph had numerous affairs during all phases of his career. One of the lasting loves of his life was the Duchess of Atri in Naples, by whom he had a child. Often after getting a woman pregnant, Joseph would find it convenient to go off on an inspection trip, but in the case of the duchess he did not make a break and kept up a lively correspondence with her after he was posted to Spain, where he soon began relationships with a voluptuous ballerina and a complaisant countess. Only rarely did the genial libertine encounter a refusal or a comeuppance such as the story of his taking an interest in the spouse of one of his generals during a boating party and his asking the husband, "If the king made court to your wife, what would you do?" "I would kill him, sire," was the retort, which Joseph found lacking in good humor.

Joseph's wife, Julie, showed him the utter devotion of never being jealous or reproachful. "The best creature who could exist," was Napoleon's description of his sister-in-law, who compensated with sweetness and intelligence for her lack of figure or prettiness. The couple's two daughters, Zenaïde and Charlotte, spent part of their childhood in Naples but never came to Madrid, nor did their mother, a Queen of Spain with whom Spaniards had no more acquaintance than with Queen Mary, the Tudor wife of Felipe II. People whispered that Joseph's womanizing was the reason for keeping his wife in Paris and Mortefontaine. A more judicious explanation for Julie's not coming is as follows: "If her departures were put off each time, it was because the situation was dangerous in Madrid itself, or because the king was on the point of abandoning his shaky throne, or because he had need that his wife intervene for him with the emperor."

Oddly, King Joseph's genuine promiscuity caused less comment from suspicious, fault-finding Spaniards than did his false reputation for drunk-enness and excess as a gambler. "Pepe Botellas," or "Joe Bottles," became, perhaps, the most common sobriquet for the intruder king. The cartoons and graffiti that were the work of the underground always pictured him as a drinker or a cardplayer. Such was the ill fame of a king who was nothing more than a genial gourmet, a connoisseur of wines, and a devotee of a nightly round of games of twenty-one.

On August 1, 1808, ten days after his first arrival in Madrid, King Joseph was forced to evacuate the city. The French slowly retreated north and made a stand on the Ebro River. Taking up residence in a noble's house in Vitoria, Joseph typically alternated strategy sessions with pleasure. His effort to seduce the governess brought him the greater prize of her mistress, a marquise, with whom he carried on for years. Impulsively, he bought the house itself for 300,000 francs, declaring that this action showed his determination never to leave Spain.

Joseph's reign had got off to a bad start as a result of a stunning defeat of French arms. An army had been sent south to subdue Andalusia, but it soon found itself in difficulties with regular and irregular Spanish troops hastily organized by the juntas. Confidently, Murat in Madrid refused reinforcements, telling his subordinate general "the first cannon shot you fire into that rabble will give back forever tranquillity to Andalusia and, I dare say, to Spain." Quite the contrary happened, and at Bailén on July 22, 1808, the French force of 17,365 ignominiously surrendered, having already lost 2,000 men. The capitulation of one of Napoleon's armies was unheard of, and France's enemies all over Europe took heart from the achievement of an ill-led force of raw recruits. Many of King Joseph's collaborators deserted his cause at this time. Later that year Napoleon rather hysterically berated one of the French officers responsible for Bailén, blaming his cowardice and incompetence for a defeat that could change the "destiny of the world." The emperor, however, did not despair altogether. "The past is always without remedy," he said, looking for some counterstroke. From Paris, nonetheless, he could not prevent Spanish armies from reentering Madrid in August, nor could he stay the abandonment of the siege of Saragossa that month, following the defeat of a renewed French assault in ferocious house-to-house, room-to-room fighting such as the world had never seen.

A new element entered the Spanish picture on the day Joseph abandoned Madrid, when a British force of several thousand troops were landed in Portugal under the command of General Arthur Wellesley, better known by his later title the Duke of Wellington. The British government had toyed with a project to send this force to stir up revolution in Spanish America, but they decided that harassing Napoleon closer to home held advantages over overseas adventures. Wellington's victory over Marshal Junot's forces at the Battle of Vimeiro on August 21 assured the continued, ultimately decisive presence of British land forces. For the first time, perhaps,

Wellington demonstrated that steady infantry in a "thin red line" could defeat the vaunted shock tactics of French troops advancing in columns. Unfortunately but not untypically, the British government replaced Wellington with a senior but less daring commander who neglected the opportunity to smash the French army in Portugal altogether and, instead, by a truce convention allowed it to be evacuated on British ships back to France.

The British successes galvanized the will of the Spanish resistance, which was headed by a Supreme Central Junta, meeting first at Aranjuez on September 25. Among its prominent leaders was the eighty-year-old Floridablanca, who died in a few months; the radical reformer Jovellanos, who had refused a post in King Joseph's ministry; and the poet Manuel José Quintana, who was a superb propagandist. Governing provisionally in the name of Fernando VII, the *Suprema* was not too successful in uniting the activities of the existing local juntas, nor did it really satisfy the demands of the increasingly restless Spanish American colonies. Its plan to encircle King Joseph's army north of the Ebro came to naught; instead of 500,000 troops, it raised only 130,000, which was about the number of rifles the British could supply and did so promptly. Yet the fact that the Supreme Junta was even able to survive the next few months was "nothing short of a miracle."

On November 4, 1808, Napoleon himself arrived in Spain and took command of some 200,000 French troops. He soon made clear his ruthless approach to the situation. At an interview he had with some Spanish clergy the emperor declared simply, "Messieurs Monks, if you try to interfere with my military affairs I promise you I shall have your ears cut off." The French army defeated the Spanish outside Burgos on November 10, stormed into the old cathedral town, and subjected it to an atrocious day of sacking and carnage. By December 2, the third anniversary of the Battle of Austerlitz, Napoleon was at the gates of Madrid. Despite brave talk of the capital imitating the heroic resistance of Saragossa, Napoleon's threat that all military personnel found in the city would be shot caused Madrid to capitulate on December 4.

Napoleon the irresistible general turned into Napoleon the overriding legislator on the day of Madrid's surrender. With a stroke of a pen he decreed the elimination of feudal rents in Spain, the reduction of the number of religious houses by two-thirds, and the complete abolition of the Inquisition. His proclamation of December 7 blamed all of Spain's troubles on "perfidious men" and British interference, and he held out the watchwords "national regeneration" and "liberal constitution." Piqued for not being consulted by Napoleon in these gestures, King Joseph in residence at El Pardo Palace asked to abdicate, but his brother ignored him.

Displaying some regard for Spanish sensibilities, Napoleon did not make a conqueror's entry into Madrid, and, in fact, he visited the capital for only one day and then briefly. In company with Joseph and a small suite, he inspected the immense Oriente Palace. Pausing to rest his hand on a carved lion on the marble balustrade of the grand staircase, Napoleon said soothingly, "My brother, you are better lodged than I." Later the emperor looked intently at a portrait of Felipe II. That December 23 occurred a formal oath taking to King Joseph by 30,000 heads of families in Madrid, including the painter Goya. These Madrileños were obviously relieved that they were to be ruled by the well-intentioned Joseph rather than by his whirlwind brother.

One further victory convinced Napoleon that he could depart from Spain with confidence to meet a new war threat from Austria and to counter intrigues by his supposedly devoted lieutenants in Paris, Foreign Minister Talleyrand and Police Chief Fouché. The British army in Portugal under Sir John Moore had invaded northwest Spain in October. Napoleon met the danger by rushing an army of 80,000 across the Guadarrama pass in the dead of winter, and then left it to Marshal Nicolas Soult to defeat the enemy in the Battle of Corunna on January 16, 1809, a battle which cost Moore his life and led to the British evacuation of the peninsula altogether for a brief period. The next day Napoleon set off for the Tuileries, having promised King Joseph to return to Spain when possible.

Relieved to a degree to be rid of his demanding brother, King Joseph made his second formal entry into Madrid on January 22, 1809. He and his splendid retinue took the time-hallowed route through the Atocha Gate down to Puerta del Sol past the Prado, receiving this time warm applause from a fair number of spectators. Later in a speech at the Church of San Isidro the Bonaparte king extolled Spanish national independence, citizen rights, and the Catholic faith. He spoke in his newly learned Castilian, ordering soon after that this language be spoken at court to the exclusion of French. By October of that year Joseph was hearing *"Viva el rey"* on every side when he appeared in the streets. His pardoning of two deserters from running the gauntlet was the occasion for great popular rejoicing, while the news that France had smashed Austria for the third time in fifteen years decided many Madrileños to reconcile themselves to what seemed the new order of things in Europe.

As Joseph entered the second year of his reign in the summer of 1809, he was in a position to initiate an extensive program of reforms. He went his brother one better in terminating all feudal rights and all religious orders. Church lands were put up for sale to private individuals, as were the properties of known members of the resistance. The Bonaparte king established a stock exchange and numerous schools, including one for girls.

He divided Spain into thirty-eight departments on the best French model of centralized government. He brought progress in city planning, notably the building of covered sewers, and organized market areas. For leaving a permanent mark on Madrid with the laying out of many small squares, King Joseph added *El rey plazuelas* to his other nicknames.

At moments King Joseph believed he had gained the popularity he so assiduously courted. He visited Madrid's churches tirelessly and received the blessings of hundreds of priests. When he rode in the Campo de Casa every afternoon, he was greeted by aristocratic ladies in their carriages. Delegations of peasants from the country came to offer fealty, and writers and scholars graced the king's gala dinner parties. Joseph frequently received ovations at the theater, which he enjoyed attending, and he wisely had inscribed on the royal box a motto which tried to capture the spirit of it all: "Live content, my Lord, reign and forgive." The intruder king encountered many discouraging signs, too, however, such as the animation which seemed to come over the crowds after the news of British victories or after reports that guerrillas had dared in the night to raid as far as the Atocha Gate. The following anecdote well illustrated the king's perplexing position. He once received one of his Spanish aides accompanied by his young son dressed in the uniform of a court page (there is a comparable little Goya portrait, incidentally). The king, whose Spanish never quite freed itself of Italian forms, made conversation by asking why the lad wore such a grand dagger: *"¿E per que tienes tu questa spada?"* *"Para matar franceses."* ("To kill Frenchmen") was the child's unabashed reply.

During 1809 French armies gained control of virtually all Spain. In the north Saragossa fell on February 20 after another siege, and two Spanish armies nearby were defeated. To the west a British army under Wellington, who had landed in Portugal again in April and invaded Spain in July, was checked at the Battle of Talavera on July 28, a drawn battle the Englishman called "the hardest fight of modern times." While the French-Spanish side had been hampered by disagreements between King Joseph and Marshal Soult, Wellington developed a great mistrust for the Spanish troops under his command and chose to retreat back to Portugal in August. Then the southern armies of the *Suprema* were all but wiped out ten miles south of Aranjuez in the Battle of Ocaña on November 12, which cost 10,000 Spanish casualties and 26,000 prisoners. King Joseph rode into the midst of this debacle, begging French soldiers to spare the lives of the "poor Spaniards" who "will one day be your companions in arms."

A self-assured King Joseph with a veteran army of 50,000 crossed the Sierra Morena in January, 1810. Within a few days Córdoba, Granada, and Málaga gave in without resistance. Then fell the great prize, Seville, after the Supreme Junta hastily left for Cádiz. The Bonaparte monarch entered

Seville on February 1 and took up residence in the Alcázar, where he daily received expressions of support from throngs of notables. A Te Deum was sung in the great mosque-cathedral, at which time the French army received back its standards lost at Bailén. The king made a fervid appeal: "Spaniards, rally around me. Let from this day begin for the nation an era of glory and well-being." Joseph should have dallied less in the gardens of the Alcázar and moved swiftly to capture Cádiz, the last center of Spanish resistance, a spark that would keep alive a flame that would become a fire. That the Cádiz insurgents refused even to negotiate went hardly noticed by King Joseph, who triumphantly wrote off to a friend: "The crossing of the Sierra Morena . . . has been followed by successes greater than I could hope for. All towns have sent me delegates and since I have been here the inhabitants have given me more proofs of adhesion than I ever received in the Kingdom of Naples."

Joseph's optimism was dissipated by a single action of his brother. On February 10, 1810, Napoleon decreed that Catalonia, Aragón, Navarre, and Vizcaya would be detached from Joseph's rule and administered directly by French generals. He gave considerations of military expense for robbing Spain of its territories north of the Ebro in clear contradiction of promises made at the time of the Bayonne Conference. For its provocative effect on Spanish nationalism this step has been called "one of the errors of the emperor which would have the worst consequences." Still involved in the pacification of the south, Joseph rejected advice that he abdicate and instead sought to reverse Napoleon's decision. He wrote his wife hopefully from Seville, where he stayed to participate in Holy Week: "The way I have been received surpasses all idea, and if they would let me act freely, this country would soon be happy and tranquil." On his return to Madrid on May 15 he still received a joyous welcome from the population. Then, in July, came the news that Napoleon was willing to drive his brother Louis from the throne of Holland for interfering with France's military and economic exactions. The news that Napoleon was already treating the north of Spain to the same harsh measures led Joseph to predict to his wife on August 21 that Spain would soon be a "blazing furnace" unless the French stopped. Julie Bonaparte, although quite sick, was apparently pursuing the possibility of her husband's retiring from his impossible task, for her letter of August 22, which crossed his, spoke of a two-hour interview with Napoleon. "I asked him as a favor to let you live in whatever part of France he chose to name. He replied that you were a king and you would die a king." Thus, Joseph found himself in the hopeless crossfire of Napoleon's willfulness and Spanish patriotic sensibilities. By October 9 he wrote Paris: "Opinion today has entirely turned against me."

* * *

3. The War of Liberation

In the fall of 1810, when King Joseph Bonaparte was beginning to despair of his lonely task, the Spanish nation was confronted by four loosely related events, each of which was to have a tremendous impact on its future. Spanish America began to revolt against the mother country. The battered British army on the peninsula escaped annihilation by retreating to an impregnable position in Portugal. Guerrilla resistance to French occupation flared up with greater intensity, and an unprecedented free Cortes met in Cádiz to draft a constitution for the liberated Spain of the future.

The general crisis of 1808 and succeeding years produced new strains in Spain's overseas empire. The government of King Joseph was simply unable to defy British naval power and to assert its pretensions in the Americas, and the conservative governors and notables there lackadaisically acted in the name of the exiled Fernando VII, sending off the annual treasure shipments to the Supreme Junta in Cádiz. The lessening of control by the homeland, however, had its result. As early as May, 1810, a provisional junta proclaimed itself in Argentina after ousting an unpopular viceroy, and although they at first paid lip service to legal ties with Spain, they never allowed the full restoration of the authority of the home country. The Hidalgo Revolt in Mexico on September 16, 1810, was more dramatic, a movement of Creoles, mestizos, and Indians led by an eloquent priest with an explicit program of national independence and social reform. Miguel Hidalgo's ill-organized horde of 80,000 supporters captured Guadalajara and threatened Mexico City itself before a small disciplined "royalist" force defeated them in the Battle of the Calderón Bridge on January 11, 1811, later capturing and executing their leader. Mexico's liberation was thus momentarily defeated, but there and elsewhere outbreaks of unrest continued.

By the fall of 1810 Britain had committed 25,000 redcoats to the war in the Iberian Peninsula, and in addition, Wellington commanded about 24,000 Portuguese troops. Napoleon, for his part, had increased his investment of French troops in the area to the huge total of 350,000. Not surprisingly, the emperor thought in terms of his generals disposing of the enemy in one powerful stroke. Marshal André Masséna, moving westward from Madrid, was able to eliminate one of the few remaining regular Spanish armies and to defeat Wellington in battle, forcing him to retreat toward Lisbon. There Wellington revealed his ace in the hole, the "lines of Tôrres Vedras," or two concentric rings of forts, blockhouses, and earthworks that he had for a year carefully been building twenty miles from the Portuguese capital. When the French arrived, their first feint at this perfect defense position was stopped dead. Truly, "when the French turned back from Monte Agra on October 14, 1810, the tide of French conquest in Europe turned also."

British historians call the fighting in Spain after 1808 the Peninsular War, and until recently most of them blithely insisted that Wellington won almost completely by his own efforts. The Spanish speak of the War of National Independence, and they claim with justice that Spanish patriots deserve a huge share of the credit for defeating the French. When Wellington made his stand at the line of Tôrres Vedras, for example, Spanish guerrillas disrupted and delayed Masséna's advance for two months.

By the fall of 1810 regular Spanish armies had ceased fighting except for the garrisons of Cádiz, Valencia, and a few other ports. Unorganized warfare, however, was developing apace. The Supreme Junta had expressly authorized a *corso terrestre,* or fighting by individuals or groups in the name of Fernando VII, with explicit provision that such activists be given aid by local authorities and be allowed to maintain themselves by claiming rewards and distributing booty. Observers gave the name "guerrilla war" to what seemed a new phenomenon in nineteenth-century Europe. Some of the guerrilla bands that sprang up to fight the French were led by regular army officers while others deliberately shunned traditional ranks and discipline. Some resistance fighters were motivated by lofty patriotism; others were driven to vengeance by personal experience with rape, plunder, and desecration on the part of the foreigners; and still others came to the struggle through criminal intent such as smuggling.

The number of guerrilla fighters never reached over 50,000, but they tied down enemy forces six times that. The whole struggle probably cost the French 180,000 casualties to 25,000 Spanish, a far different proportion than would occur in conventional warfare. Rarely did the guerrillas attempt pitched battles, and only against equal forces. Using hit-and-run tactics devastatingly, they created a situation whereby a courier to France needed an escort of 50 men, a convoy from France the protection of 500 soldiers. The French commanders made the mistake, in Napoleon's eyes, of trying to hold down large areas with garrisons instead of using flying columns and terror tactics. Another difficulty for the French was that they could not find any spies, whereas almost every Spaniard seemed willing to be eyes and ears for the guerrillas and for the British.

Napoleon had been blinded by what he knew of the weakness of the Bourbon court, the laughable disorganization of its army, and the crying social injustices beyond. He made the "fatal mistake" of expecting to find Spain "an inanimate corpse," according to Karl Marx. Or in the words of a

Swiss recruit who was sent to Spain: "We believed, and Europe believed it too, that we had only to march to Madrid to complete the subjugation of Spain. . . . The wars we had hitherto carried on had accustomed us to see in a nation only its military forces and to count for nothing the spirit which animates its citizens."

The French reacted to Spanish resistance with a mounting level of atrocities, which the Spanish often matched in kind. To French commanders the Spanish freedom fighters were simply bandits to be hanged or shot or worse. The gruesome chronicle of torture, mutilation, and execution has been imprinted visually on the world's mind by the artist Goya, whose series of etchings called the "Disasters of War" rank prominently in an already versatile oeuvre. Goya lived in Madrid during what was essentially a civil war, but he was never an active collaborator with the regime of King Joseph. He did some portraits of French generals, perhaps a canvas of the Bonaparte ruler himself, but he also traveled to Saragossa after the heroic defeat of the siege of 1808, and in 1811 he tried to escape to free Spain altogether, only to be brought back by the pleas of his family under threat of the loss of all their property. Goya's "Disasters of War," with their stupefying realism, are more a horrified protest at man's inhumanity in general than outright anti-French propaganda.

While Spain's War of Liberation was heroic, it was also traumatic and full of portents for the future of the Bourbon monarchy. The springing up of city juntas confirmed earlier tendencies toward separatism. The prominence of self-appointed resistance leaders has led one Spanish writer to say that the war was "the great academy of bossism," and military figures received undue political importance.

The social composition of the Spanish national movement against the French was remarkable and unsettling. The Bourbon family in effect abdicated leadership in 1808, the nobility were largely neutral, and many of the most progressive intellectuals supported King Joseph. Essentially, the resistance was taken up by the middle and lower classes. "Everything was rotten in Spain except the hearts of the poorer people." The resistance appeared to be unaristocratic, unenlightened, and unquestioning in its acceptance of faith and tradition. As such, the whole movement appeared reactionary, and indeed, was so regarded by liberal supporters of King Joseph, one of whom was to declare that "the nation . . . fought with its characteristic stubbornness against its own happiness."

What saved free Spain in 1810 from simply trying to turn the clock back to the despotic, church-ridden, socially oppressive past was the activity of the Cortes, which opened in Cádiz on September 24. At first free Spain had been directed by the Supreme Junta, which later gave way to a regency. In turn public opinion prodded this body into calling a representative assembly. Because so much of the country was under French occupation, many of the delegates to the Cortes were appointed rather than elected. These circumstances favored the liberal organizers of the Cortes, although the ensuing body of 184 members with one-third clergy and one-sixth nobility can scarcely be called a radical assemblage. Unquestionably, Cádiz itself was the most progressive-minded city in all Spain, having developed a substantial commercial class and having been exposed to the influence of a large colony of British traders and of numerous French naval personnel between 1795 and 1808.

The unusual and historic Cortes sat in the city's Church of San Felipe Neri (which today is so covered with commemorative plaques that the Franco government simply cannot hide this symbol of a more enlightened past). Conducting their sessions in a quasi-religious atmosphere, the delegates deliberated under a huge portrait of Fernando VII, but from the first the Cortes asserted that they, rather than the sanctified crown, were the repository of national sovereignty. They passed a resolution that they would not recognize treaties signed by the king under duress (at a time when the exiled Bourbon was seeking to marry a Bonaparte).

The Cortes of 1810 felt impelled to take radical actions not only because of unleashed public opinion in the streets of Cádiz but also because of the competitive example of the regime of King Joseph, which had simply decreed reforms. Painfully the liberal majority pushed through such enactments as the abolition of torture, the elimination of guilds, the abolition of seignorial rights, the institution of a progressive tax, and the limitation of censorship to religious matters. They also saw the need to legislate the end of oppressions and tributes in Spanish America, particularly with respect to the Indians, but they offered too little, too late.

The most memorable and also the most controversial achievement of the Cortes was the so-called Constitution of 1812, which, although it was legally in operation only a few random years, remained the touchstone of Spanish politics all through the nineteenth century, as well as a model for other countries the world over. Debated article by article over a period of six months, the constitution was signed by all 184 members of the Cortes on March 18 in a deceptive mood of national unity. The next day the regents and delegates swore an oath to it, as Cádiz's cannon boomed in its honor and in honor of the fourth anniversary of the accession of Fernando VII. Ironically, the cannon of the French besieging Cádiz also fired salutes, for it was the saint's day of King Joseph.

The Constitution of 1812, which scarcely seems radical today, was considered extremely advanced in view of Spain's previous political backwardness, and as such, most historians are tempted to call it unworkable. (Karl Marx, however, called it "adopted to the needs of modern society.") The break with the past was far from complete; for example, one article declared that Catholicism was "the only true faith" and "forbids the practice of any other." Yet, with so little recent experience with truly representative government, Spain was now given a powerful unicameral legislature elected on the basis of residential male suffrage. Equality before the law and taxation based on ability to pay were two other wrenching departures from the historic social equilibrium. A conservative, exaggerating the potential new rights of the Spanish masses, declared that the Constitution meant "to take the dregs from the bottom of the glass and to put them on top."

The main part of the Constitution of 1812 that was to provoke decades of controversy and bloodshed was the matter of the prerogatives of the king. The hotly debated Article Three as originally drafted stated that "Sovereignty resides essentially in the Nation, and to this latter consequently belongs the right to establish its fundamental laws and to adopt the form of government best suited to its needs." College students today required to distinguish the underlying political theory of Hobbes against that of Locke would profit by considering the pragmatic positions Spanish conservatives and liberals took on the two clauses of this article. In effect, both Hobbesians and Lockians accepted the first proposition that there is an original social contract whereby the people establish a government or kingdom (the vote was 128 to 24). The Hobbesians triumphed in securing the elimination of the second clause, thereby saying that once primary sovereignty is given to the king, it cannot be recovered by the people (the vote was 87 to 63). Having thus given the king something just short of divine right stature, the Constitution rather contradictorily restricted his exercise of the executive power, providing for the Cortes' overriding a royal veto and for legislative assent to the king's leaving the kingdom, to his entering into alliances or treaties, and even to his marriage.

The deliberations of the Cortes of Cádiz had a kind of heroic unreality as long as the military situation in Spain, and indeed in Europe, was unresolved. During 1811 the war was essentially stalemated on the peninsula. Wellington, having masterfully kept his army intact behind the lines of Tôrres Vedras, drove the French into Spain in March. Failing to capture Badajoz, the British army again retreated on Portugal.

King Joseph slipped off to visit Paris on May 15, 1811. Despite his brother's threats to have him arrested at the frontier, Joseph insisted on having an interview with Napoleon, and after the latter recovered from his rage at seeing Joseph in a Spanish uniform, he made him generous promises to increase French subsidies and to decrease French exactions. When the Spanish monarch returned to Madrid on July 15, he was greeted by a triumphal arch and noisy crowds. For another period in his reign the intruder king happily acknowledged applause at *corridas* and felt safe to mingle with his subjects on the Paseo. Despite his current affair with a French businessman's wife, Joseph asked Julie to join him in Madrid, but Napoleon held this up, as he did his Paris promises.

The year 1812 was a nightmare for Napoleon's empire while King Joseph floundered on the sidelines. Wellington was able to capture Ciudad Rodrigo on January 19. Although British troops sacked the town horribly, the British commander was rewarded with an earldom by his own country and the status of duke and grandee by the Spanish. The situation in Spain was now drastically changed by the withdrawal of more than 100,000 French troops to take part in Napoleon's projected invasion of Russia. King Joseph's first reaction to these developments was to try to free himself altogether from reliance on his brother and to create an independent Spain sanctified by a national congress including representatives of the resistance. The Cortes of Cádiz, having just published their Constitution, brusquely rejected all overtures. Then Joseph once again accepted his obligations to his brother after Napoleon named him his supreme military commander in Spain on March 16. The course of events might have been entirely different if Napoleon in 1808 had given Joseph similar authority over the self-willed and self-serving French commanders. Ever-vacillating, Joseph also considered abdicating his responsibilities, as was revealed after guerrillas ambushed Joseph's private secretary on April 9 and published his confidential papers.

Wellington, moving his 45,000 troops eastward, encountered the main French army of equal size at Salamanca, and here he succeeded in winning one of his greatest victories on July 22. After this disaster the French were in full retreat, and King Joseph had no choice but to abandon Madrid on August 12, 1812. He got small satisfaction from recalling that Felipe V had also twice been ousted from his capital. Wellington made his triumphal entry into the Spanish capital soon afterward, reporting that "I am among people mad with joy," a somewhat equivocal statement from a man who distrusted crowds. The Cádiz Cortes, which he also distrusted, made him generalissimo of all the forces in Spain, and London rang bells for its new hero. Goya now had a chance to paint his famous portraits of Wellington, the more familiar today for one having been stolen from the National Gallery of London in 1962. One legend is that Goya had to be restrained from shooting his distinguished sitter after Wellington made deprecatory remarks about Goya's work. In any case, Wellington tarried too long in Madrid and almost threw away his victories.

Just when King Joseph was being driven from Madrid, Napoleon and his grand army of 600,000 were 2,000 miles away on the point of entering the great fortress city of Smolensk astride the road to Moscow. Spain and

Russia, being at opposite ends of the continent, are rarely treated in conjunction historically, but in truth many parallels exist between these two king-ridden, noble-ridden, priest-ridden countries at once so backward, yet called into prominence in European affairs. Napoleon, on the eve of his invasion of Russia, conversationally asked an envoy of the tsar how so religious-minded a nation could hope to resist him. "How about Spain, Sire?" was the telling reply. Indeed, most historians would rate Napoleon's attempted subjugation of Spain and of Russia as his two greatest errors. In his own reflections at St. Helena Napoleon said "the unfortunate Spanish war was a real sore, the original cause of all France's misfortunes." As for Russia, the central chapter of Napoleon's downfall is a well-known story: his hard-won victory at Borodino, September 7, the only time the Russians made a stand; his entry into Moscow followed by the firing of the city and the continued refusal of the tsar to make peace; and finally the horrible retreat beginning October 22 in the face of winter and Russian guerrillas. A mere 100,000 crossed back over the Russian frontier on December 13.

In another change of the fortunes of the conflict in Spain, King Joseph was able to reenter Madrid on November 2, 1812, Soult's army coming up from Andalusia had been able to effect a junction with the king's army of the center, and the combined force swept through the capital, crossed the Guadarrama Mountains, and tried to revenge the earlier defeat at Salamanca by trapping Wellington in the same place. With 70,000 troops to the enemy's 90,000 Wellington admitted that he was lucky to escape in a rainstorm. While a bitterly disappointed Joseph returned to the Oriente Palace that December, a jauntily confident Wellington let himself be feted in London and Cádiz. The latter city had the most gala party in its history in honor of the British "grandee," after soldiers with bayonets cleared out the largest building in town, the poorhouse. Wellington deigned to address the Cádiz Cortes in Spanish, but he soon decided that the Spanish liberals had sealed their doom and that of their Constitution by making the drastic break with the past of voting the abolition of the Inquisition on January 22, 1813.

The French had to be defeated first before left and right in free Spain could go for each other's throats. In February, 1813, another large part of the French army was recalled across the Pyrenees to fight for Napoleon against the invading Russians and reawakening Prussians in central Germany. For a few remaining weeks King Joseph maintained an almost carefree front in Madrid, showing himself frequently in public, but then on March 17, 1813, he left the capital for the last time with a huge baggage train, a force of French and loyal Spanish troops, and thousands of terrified afrancescados. Wellington moved east and north rapidly in an effort to cut him off. After taking Valladolid and Burgos without difficulty, the British caught up with Joseph at Vitoria, where the ever-romantic King had resumed his affair with the marquise of Montehermosa.

Failing to find out that he was outnumbered by Wellington 80,000 to 65,000, Joseph with ridiculous confidence saw fit to erect stands in the streets for spectators of the battle, which took place on June 21, 1813, and soon turned into a complete rout of the French. The king literally had to escape from his carriage by the door of one side when the Tenth British Hussars charged up with pistols blazing on the other. Joseph's silver *pot de chambre* was a captured prize that has been used as a champagne cup in the regimental mess of the Tenth Hussars ever since. In fact, "the farewell plunder of the whole of Spain" was that day strewn on the road at Vitoria, the British capturing not only 151 cannon and the French army payroll of several millions but also numerous state documents, all of Joseph's letters, and his tremendous art collection including works of Velázquez, Van Dyke, and Rubens (the Spanish in the end let Wellington keep the paintings but protested bitterly Joseph's removal of the Spanish royal jewels to Paris, including the diamond "La Peregrina," which Elizabeth Taylor acquired in 1969). The plunder was too tempting for the British soldiers, and these "scum of the earth"—Wellington's exasperated words—missed the opportunity to cut King Joseph off from the road to Pamplona and eventual refuge in France with 12,000 of his supporters. Yet the Battle of Vitoria was one of the most triumphant of Wellington's career, earning him the rank of field marshal and causing Beethoven to compose the piece *Wellington's Victory*. Austria now threw its decisive weight in against Napoleon.

A month after Vitoria the "Count of Survilliers" was back in residence at Mortefontaine. Napoleon, fearing intrigues by his brother, ordered the Paris police chief to arrest Joseph if he visited Paris even incognito, but Joseph came and went anyhow to attend the theater and visit the Marquise of Montehermosa, now in residence in the French capital. Meanwhile, Wellington stormed San Sebastián in August, 1813, and crossed the French frontier on October 7, about ten days before Napoleon suffered his overwhelming defeat by the allies at the Battle of Leipzig. Fantastic rumors were abroad that the British commander had converted to Catholicism and was on the point of declaring himself King of Spain, but actually he was just busy investing Bayonne. Overseas José Morelos declared Mexico independent in November 1813 and Simón Bolívar made himself dictator in Caracas.

Without ever formally abdicating his title of King of Spain, Joseph Bonaparte performed his last services for his brother as a Frenchman, being named lieutenant general in charge of the defense of Paris in January, 1814. (Napoleon trusted Joseph less in the bedroom, briefly putting credence in reports that he had used his position to seduce the empress, the Hapsburg-

Bourbon archduchess whom Napoleon made his second wife in 1810.) Under the blows of the allied invaders Paris surrendered on March 31, and Napoleon abdicated for the first time on April 13, leaving to rule over the island of Elba. Joseph escaped to Switzerland on April 15, where he soon after received a delegation of his Spanish supporters who wanted nothing but to bid farewell to him as a "good Spaniard." On May 2 Louis XVIII entered Paris, having promised a constitutional charter under the restored French monarchy. A month earlier his Bourbon cousin Fernando VII had ridden into Madrid to frenzied cries of *"Viva el rey"* and *"abajo la constitución."*

VI.
The Worst King:
Fernando VII (1814–1833)

1. Royal and Semiroyal Exiles

A REPUBLIC-ADMIRING Spaniard might have rejoiced that on New
Year's Day, 1814, no monarchs remained on Spanish soil. No fewer
than three kings had sat on the throne in the course of 1808—Carlos IV, Fernando VII, and José I, not to mention the uncrowned ruler,
Manuel Godoy. All these men were still alive in 1814, and each had his
supporters. Their lives in exile, of considerable personal interest, were of
some import for Spain's future.

Joseph Bonaparte, having intended to settle down on a comfortable
estate in Switzerland with his wife, returned to France during Napoleon's
Hundred Days, and simply as "Prince Joseph" he headed the Paris
government during the Waterloo campaign. After the defeat and Napoleon's second abdication, he made his way to Rochefort, where he purchased
an American brig. Joseph proposed to let Napoleon escape to America in
his place, but the ex-emperor refused to be a fugitive in disguise and thus
condemned himself to dreary exile at St. Helena. The elder brother, using
his incognito as Count of Survilliers, evaded British navy searches and
reached New York City in August, 1815. The forty-seven-year-old ex-king
was soon recognized on Broadway by a former officer of his guards, who
knelt, kissed his hands, and cried, "Your Majesty, here!" The notoriety of
the foreign guest prevented his getting an interview with President Madison,
but his prominence served to enable him as a noncitizen to buy a town
house in Philadelphia at 260 South Ninth Street (today bearing a
commemorative plaque) and an estate at Point Breeze in Bordentown, New
Jersey. Never at a loss for money, Joseph also speculated in land tracts near

Watertown, New York, where his interest is perpetuated in the name Lake Bonaparte.

Point Breeze on the Delaware River was Joseph's particular delight, and here he brought his library, paintings, and furniture from Europe. The local people were delighted in turn by the jobs the new squire provided as he spent openhandedly on roads, bridges, and a much-enlarged mansion, following a fire. He also kept in readiness a barge with sixteen rowers to convey friends from Philadelphia. When Joseph tried to introduce ballet into his evening entertainments, his lady American guests were so shocked as to retire, but people were sufficiently sophisticated and Joseph sufficiently discreet to permit him several amorous affairs involving a number of illegitimate children. His wife, Julie, never joined him in America because of business matters and her ill health, but Joseph was visited by his daughters, Charlotte and Zenaïde, the latter the year after she married a son of Lucien Bonaparte.

Joseph had little to do with Napoleon on St. Helena, except to pay some of his bills. The ever-political Napoleon once commented perceptively about his brother: "If I were in his place, I would make myself a great empire of all Spanish America, but you will see that he will become a bourgeois American and spend his fortune making gardens." In 1816 some French refugees in Texas actually plotted to have Joseph proclaimed "King of Mexico," but he said no to any proposals to involve himself in Spanish affairs again. Joseph did take an interest in the Bonapartist cause in France, however, particularly after Napoleon's death in 1821. When Lafayette made his triumphal return to the United States in 1826, Joseph vainly tried to enlist his support for Napoleon's son, and again in 1830, when the Bourbons were overthrown in Paris, the squire of Bordentown futilely asserted his nephew's rights, with the expectation of himself serving as regent. The "Napoleon II" in question expired miserably in an Austrian prison, and soon after, the younger Lucien Bonaparte died, ending any possibility of Joseph's daughter becoming Empress of France. Twice in this period, 1832 and 1836, Joseph visited London, each time showing himself hostile to the independent ambitions of his other nephew, Louis Napoleon, the future Napoleon III, for to the end Joseph considered himself head of the clan.

In 1841 Joseph finally won permission to live in Florence, where he joined his wife after a separation of twenty-six years. He lived unpretentiously in the Italian city until his death in 1844 at age seventy-six. Now buried in the Invalides near Napoleon, the onetime José Primero and his memory are little commemorated in Spain. The Paris *Herald Tribune* in 1963 carried an item about a 24,000-square-foot lot in Bordentown, ending "if no descendant of Joseph Bonaparte is found to claim the land, it will go to Ocean Spray"—that is, the cranberry company.

While Joseph Bonaparte was living in bourgeois comfort in Bordentown and dabbling in an occasional political intrigue, his Bourbon predecessor, Carlos IV, was residing in a palace in Rome and indulging in little more than bygone royal ceremonial. Having "thrown a kingdom out the window" at the Bayonne Conference of 1808—with perhaps the main aim of spiting his son—Carlos IV took little further interest in Spanish politics.

From Bayonne the Spanish monarchs had traveled north, staying briefly in Bordeaux, where the queen found some trunks with gowns of the Empress Josephine and promptly amused herself by trying them all on. Their first permanent place of exile was a lodge at Compiègne, Napoleon reserving the main palace for his own use. Here Carlos and María Luisa presided over a court of about 200 people, including their youngest son, Francisco de Paula, and their daughter the ex-Queen of Etruria. Not only did Godoy join the ménage, but so did his brother, his mistress, Pepita Tudo, her two sons by him, her mother, and two aunts. The king soon complained that the hunting at Compiègne was uninteresting, and he vainly begged Napoleon to fulfill his promise to let him establish himself at the old and grand Bourbon property of Chambord. Godoy fretted at the cramped quarters and talked of living in Paris, a move which would have had Napoleon's approval since he rated the Prince of the Peace "a quite unimportant person."

Discomfited by the northern French climate, Carlos IV moved his entourage to Marseilles in September, 1808, and he lived there until 1812, first in a house in the center of the city and later on an estate outside, where the hunting was still frustratingly bad. Citizens of Marseilles hissed Godoy on the streets, but as a Bourbon, Carlos enjoyed expressions of sympathy and occasional cheers from many Frenchmen, to which he responded with paternal grace and handouts. The largesse was in short supply after Napoleon in 1809 cut the exiled king's maintenance from 500,000 to 200,000 francs. The queen had to sell jewels and dismiss servants. Still "the earthly trinity" tried to maintain the same sort of routine with which they had unsettled Madrid at the turn of the century: the king's morning walk with Godoy; the king puttering, receiving, and banqueting; and the king's early retirement, leaving Godoy with the queen and the ladies. The three were unmoved by two halfhearted attempts by members of their court to arrange their escape from France to a British warship.

In July, 1812, this Spanish court in exile was allowed to move to Rome. The temporary residence for assorted Bourbons and Godoys was the splendid Borghese Palace. At sixty-four the king was too gouty to enjoy hunting and he turned to collecting wristwatches. His majordomo, for example, had to wear six timepieces in his sash and could not announce dinner until each one had chimed. The queen, full of complaints, still found pleasure in extravagantly current fashions. Godoy, more voluptuous than ever, relived memories by putting on his old uniforms, while María Luisa would purr "how handsome he is." Events in the world outside were merely inconveniences. When Joseph Bonaparte and the French were driven from Spain in 1813 and 1814, Carlos IV made no effort to reclaim his throne or to contest the restoration of Fernando VII. For his part, Fernando did make futile representations to the Pope to separate Godoy from the ex-sovereigns. The son and also "cousin" Louis XVIII of France reluctantly paid the debts run up by the royal ménage, which was now living in the Barberini Palace. Since Fernando harbored fears that his father might retract his abdication once again and that Godoy was capable of any maneuver, he planted many of his agents in the staff at the Barberini, with the result that Carlos IV's treasured tranquillity was frequently disturbed by intrigues and recriminations.

The Roman exiles were thrown into further turmoil in 1818, when Carlos IV left by himself to visit the court of his brother Fernando IV at Naples on the occasion of the marriage of his son Francisco de Paula to a Neapolitan princess. The ex-king was entranced by the land of his birth and was apparently relieved to be rid of his wife and Godoy for the first time in decades. He was at last made to see his undignified position as husband by his brother and was roused to such fury that he refused to return to Rome, except for one brief visit.

Accordingly, the king was absent when María Luisa died on January 2, 1819, from a lung condition. Godoy, however, was loyal to his patron and shared the last hours after her confession until her "passionate soul, now serene and purified, parted from the soiled body, which had been so long her folly." Twenty-one cardinals attended her magnificent obsequies in the Church of Santa Maria Maggiore. Carlos IV wrote "Friend Manuel" with dignified sorrow from Naples to request that he live with his children "at some distance off," softening this with the observation that the move "will not prevent you from coming to see me as often as you want." Then, on January 19, Carlos IV was dead too, a victim of fever and gout. His brother paid him the strangely appropriate compliment of not interrupting his hunting to be present at the deathbed. The bodies of Spain's fifth Bourbon king and his consort were later buried in the Escorial at the command of Fernando VII, who was careful to demand also the return of all their valuables.

His royal protectors dead, Godoy found himself in his early fifties a down-and-out has-been, as well as something of a political pariah. His earlier hope to have his marriage annulled so that he could wed Pepita Tudo had been thwarted by the concerted opposition of Fernando VII and Carlos IV, whose agents had also combined to force him to renounce a legacy from María Luisa. The rumored riches that Godoy had spirited out of Spain proved nonexistent. His Bourbon wife, the Countess of Chinchón, had taken refuge in Toledo and refused to communicate with him since that fateful year 1808. Only her death in 1828 permitted Godoy at last to make Pepita Tudo his wife. In 1830 Godoy was in such straitened circumstances that he bowed to pressure from Fernando VII to give up his title Prince of the Peace in return for money, enough money so that he bought a small estate near Rome to which the Pope appended a ducal title.

Whatever his title, Godoy was snubbed by Roman society, and presently he decided to try his fortunes in Paris, taking rooms at Number 59b Boulevard Beaumarchais. There Pepita Tudo endeavored to establish a smart salon but succeeded in entertaining only the most mediocre collection of Frenchmen and foreigners, while the many Spanish refugees in the capital demonstrated open hatred for Godoy. The wife came to dislike the husband too, and in 1833 she abandoned him to live out her days in Madrid with her remaining family.

The Neapolitan Bourbon Cristina, who became regent of Spain in 1833, may well have been Godoy's granddaughter by Queen María Luisa, but the link did him no good. All he had was a small pension from King Louis Philippe, who remembered Godoy's kindnesses to French exiles. Accordingly, the ex-favorite took the last resort of the dishonorable and discredited and published his *Memoirs* in 1836–1837. The four volumes of rambling and self-serving apology and conceit were received with mild curiosity in both France and Spain. Few people on the boulevards, however, knew that the familiar figure in white whiskers with the sensual eyes had once ruled Spain.

His final years brought Godoy no vindication but some improvement of his circumstances. Godoy's lawyers persuaded the government of his putative great-granddaughter Queen Isabel II in the 1840's to restore to him his properties in Spain, his titles as duke and captain general, and his right to live in Madrid. Then his legitimate daughter decided to give him a large annual income. Nearly eighty, Godoy chose to remain in Paris, living in sumptuous quarters at 20 rue de la Michodière. He died in 1851, the year Joseph Bonaparte's nephew made himself dictator of France.

Godoy's genes and titles have been perpetuated to the present. His surviving daughter by his Bourbon wife married the Italian Prince Ruspoli, by whom she had two sons. Four generations of their descendants have succeeded, with about twenty-five of them alive today, including a fifth Duke of Alcudia.

Fernando, the prince Godoy had succeeded in cheating of the Spanish throne in 1808, spent the next six years as a prisoner of Napoleon. It was in the name of this unseen Fernando VII that the War of Independence was fought. Whereas Spaniards regarded Carlos IV as a cuckolded old fool, his wife as a shameless hussy, Godoy as an unspeakable monster, and Joseph Bonaparte as a drunken upstart, they chose to call Fernando *el deseado,* the desired or the longed-for one. They had little inkling of the true nature of their absentee idol.

Born in 1785, so that he was approaching the age of thirty during his confinement, the Prince of the Asturias was already wasted in appearance and warped in mind. His youth had been a long and terrible trial, putting up with the tyranny of his mother, the threats of disinheritance by his father, and the plottings of Godoy. His held-in rage was greatest with respect to the favorite, whom he loathed but whom he had to treat with fawning respect by parental command. When the heir had shown any mind of his own, he was deprived of his friends, and he was constantly spied on. Many people believed that his wife had been poisoned, perhaps at the instigation of the queen, who had once called the Princess of the Asturias "that slut from the court of Naples." Then came the heady days when Fernando was acclaimed king and first tasted vengeance at Godoy's expense. There followed his terrifying confrontation with Napoleon, his forced renunciation, and the new humiliation of exile. It is small wonder that suspiciousness and deceit became second nature to Fernando.

The years had taken their toll of Fernando's looks. In Goya's family portrait of 1800 he appeared an ungainly and brooding but not unattractive youth, while his official portrait as king in 1808 shows him with a kind of fierce dignity. His mother dismissed him as "ugly," and his mother-in-law chose to call him "hideous to look at," as well as "utterly dull." At thirty he was tubby, bloated, and distinctly unhandsome, with a low forehead, an outsize nose, a twisted mouth like his mother's, and an undershot jaw.

Fernando definitely possessed intelligence, albeit more in the order of craftiness than intellectuality. His tutor and longtime confidant Escoiquiz had tried to guide him through the best learning of the day, as well as through the intrigues of the court. As an adult, however, Fernando took refuge in a narrow-minded piety and a mistrust of persons with superior knowledge. Some of his associates in exile were aristocrats, men of limited ideas, but many of his intimates were servants. This predilection for lowborn company and coarse humor was a lifelong thing, as was the absence of real friendships and loyalties.

Spaniards were sadly deluding themselves to believe that Fernando spent his exile in France defying Napoleon, plotting his own escape, and pondering the welfare of his subjects. The truth was that he existed in comfortable indolence on Talleyrand's estate at Valençay, together with his silly-minded uncle Antonio and his sullen younger brother Don Carlos. "All one could say about them during these five years is that they lived," wrote the French statesman, who was astonished at the docility of his charges and also somewhat piqued that he could not stir in them any great interest in his fine library. Occasionally, the Bourbon princes did take down a book, but they read them only after Uncle Antonio had busied himself removing any offensive illustrations. More often the brothers passed the days taking promenades in the garden or playing cards and billiards. Fernando also joined his uncle in embroidering a robe for a statue of the Virgin in a nearby shrine. By French standards they all spent an excessive amount of time in prayer. Fernando was subject to a minimum of constraint, and Napoleon wrote at St. Helena "the fact is that he was scarcely guarded at Valençay and that he did not want to escape."

Fernando defied his French hosts only in the matter of his sex life. Napoleon had confided to Talleyrand: "If the Prince of the Asturias were to become attached to some pretty woman whom we were sure of, it would be no disadvantage, for it would give us another means of watching him." All attempts to seduce the Spaniard failed.

Remarriage, however, was on Fernando's mind. His intended was none other than the niece of Napoleon, the national enemy. Fernando had not seen the woman in question but was motivated sheerly by a desire to ingratiate himself with his captor, whom he asked to adopt him as a son. In connection with this marriage hope, there exists an incredibly abject letter of Fernando to King Joseph in Madrid begging him to intervene with his brother. The Bourbon, who once had the prerogative to confer the Order of the Golden Fleece, meekly asked the Bonaparte to make him a member of a new royal order initiated by Joseph. He closed his letter to the usurper of his throne with the words "I desire to prove to Your Majesty the sincerity of my feelings and my confidence in You. The devoted brother of Your Catholic Majesty. Fernando."

Le Moniteur in Paris published many such submissive messages from Fernando: congratulations to Joseph on his assuming the Spanish throne, to Napoleon on his remarriage, and to both on the occasion of French victories in Spain, as well as elsewhere. The supporters of "the desired one" in Spain could only argue that *Le Moniteur* indulged in forgeries and deceptions. They would have been better informed if they knew that Fernando revealed to his French jailors the name of an Irish count who earnestly had plotted the prince's escape to Spain.

Isolated and watched, did Fernando know of the heroic battles and skirmishes fought in his name? Did he know of the juntas, the regency, and the Cortes of 1810 trying to regenerate and modernize the Spanish nation? The answer is yes. Fernando's liberal-minded French doctor and his wife made several trips to Spain during the period in question and would not have failed to talk of what was going on. There is no evidence that Fernando made any secret efforts to encourage his supporters. Given that the prince had the fate of the Duke of Enghien to make him discreet, his complete silence and inactivity must in large measure be put down to cowardice and apathy.

Fernando's release from confinement at Valençay came about not because of any efforts of his but because of Napoleon's desperate situation in 1813 as Russian-Prussian-Austrian armies closed in on France from the north while Wellington's British-Spanish force drove up from the Pyrenees. First occurred a backstairs intrigue, one last effort to link Bourbon and Bonaparte fortunes: Julie Bonaparte proposed to Napoleon that her husband, Joseph, renounce the Spanish throne on condition that their twelve-year-old daughter Zenaïde marry the twenty-nine-year-old Fernando. Napoleon decided to deal with Fernando more directly, and accordingly, in a letter of November 12 he proposed to recognize the prince as king and to withdraw all French troops from Spain, but only if the British got out also. Napoleon's transparent motive was to free French forces for fighting elsewhere, but he sought to convince Fernando that the British in Spain represented a threat to throne, religion, and social order. Always cunning, if not honest, Fernando first protested his nation's debt to the British and his unwillingness to sign anything without consulting the regency. Then, on December 11, hopeful of gaining immediate release, Fernando subscribed with Napoleon to the Treaty of Valençay, which included Napoleon's above-mentioned proposals and a royal promise not to persecute the *afrancescados* still in Spain. He was permitted to send a confidant to Madrid to seek the regency's ratification of the agreement. This mission failed because the famous Cortes resolution of 1811 expressly forbade acceptance of any treaty signed by the king under duress.

As events transpired, with the Napoleonic empire collapsing all around, Fernando received his unconditional freedom on March 7, 1814. Less than three weeks later the "longed-for one" crossed into Spain.

2. "Long Live Our Chains"

In 1814 Spain was in shambles, materially wrecked and spiritually confused. Exactly one century earlier the country had emerged from the War of the Succession, which, like the recent War of Independence, had been fought the length and breadth of the peninsula between rival groups of Spaniards aided by rival foreign forces. The former war, however, had been limited in ferocity, fought by professionals, and almost untouched by ideology so that in 1714 the Bourbons settled down to rule a Spain that was as prosperous as, if not more than so, at the beginning of hostilities. In contrast, the War of Independence had been a war without quarter, a total war, and a fanatical crusade. The restored Bourbons in 1814 found a nation with many of its cities sacked or bombarded into rubble, its countryside depopulated, its highways at the mercy of bandits, its trade and industry paralyzed, and its empire slipped from the control of the home country. That year governmental revenue covered barely half of expenses, the swollen army went unpaid, and the salaries of all officials were in arrears. Particularly damaging was the stoppage of American bullion shipments, which ordinarily accounted for a quarter of the treasury's income.

In 1714 Spain had prospects and the Bourbons had ambitions for the country as a world power of the first rank. In 1814 nation and dynasty could only resign themselves to being third-rate—unless the empire were recovered. Failing to repossess its overseas might, Spain became a nation "capable only of making war on itself." With the major exception of the War of 1898 forced on Spain by the United States, Spain has not fought any foreign wars since 1814 but civil war has been endemic (1820–1823, 1834–1839, 1873–1875, and 1936–1939 are the most important manifestations, but one should also take into account scores of coups and assassinations). The sorry legacy of the War of Independence was a division of the nation into an irreconcilable left and right, and the working out of this conflict produced a series of wild zigzags from the restoration of Fernando VII to Franco.

What divided Spain in 1814, and in truth has ever since, was the Constitution of 1812 with its limitations on royal power, its assertion of popular sovereignty, and its guarantees of freedom of expression. Closely related to the Constitution were the other major works of the Cortes: the curbs on feudal privileges and the limitations on the church, notably the abolition of the Inquisition. The proponents of these changes called themselves Liberals, and they dubbed their opponents Serviles, servile in their willingness to submit to a revived royal absolutism with its attendant restoration of feudal and clerical power.

One may try to sound impartially critical about this basic political split, as, for example, in this statement by a recent historian: "The traditionalists [Serviles] seemed to remove themselves from modern reality; the liberals appeared to want to cut Spain's roots with the past." Such words conceal fighting issues and raise the problem of terminology. The Serviles of 1814 considered themselves traditionalists or "conservatives" in the dictionary sense in that they wanted to conserve a pre-1812 Spain. Their opponents labeled them reactionaries for wishing to turn the clock back on the achievements of the Cortes. This conservative tradition moves down through the Carlists of the 1830's, the Conservative Party of the 1880's, and the Falange of the 1930's. Its supporters were consistently drawn from the large landowners, the higher clergy, and the top army officers. The Liberals of 1814 considered themselves moderates, constitutionalists, and "liberals" in the dictionary sense of wishing a limited amount of change. Their enemies labeled them radicals for using 1812 as a starting point. This liberal tradition likewise takes on different names at different periods, and its base of support remained constant—the middle class of the cities, the intellectuals, and lower-ranking army officers.

The rival fortunes of liberals and conservatives at the polls, and all too often on the battlefield, depended on the attitude of the masses, who were often branded by right and left alike as fickle, superstitious, and ignorant. In 1814 the actions of the masses overwhelmingly supported the party of king and church. One frequent explanation is that the millions of peasants and workers craved only economic normality and did not understand the new institutions projected by the Cortes, being particularly suspicious after the war of anything that smacked of foreign innovation. Observers have often said that the masses tended meekly to follow the opinions of the priests. What has not been well argued until recently is that in 1814 there was no "radical" party in the dictionary sense of a group willing to overturn the whole system for the benefit of the people at the bottom. The liberals of the day, albeit considered extremists by their enemies, were actually quite reluctant to touch property rights. While the Cortes appeared to be approaching radical economic legislation when it authorized the sale of communal village lands and the abolition of the guilds, actually the rich were the ones who bought up these lands, and the rich also benefited from a surplus labor force unprotected by the job security once given by the guilds. Accordingly, the masses may well have turned away in disgust or apathy from the reformers who were so clumsy or so fearful about helping them. Or, put in another way, "a social and economic reform pushed through regardless of opposition might have counterbalanced adhesion to king and church."

Given the fact that both conservatives and liberals in 1814 had passed from the point of heated debate in the Cortes to arming themselves for a future showdown, Spain in its crisis seemed in great need of a king who was firm, forthright, honest, and reasonable—a Carlos III, perhaps. Sadly, Fernando VII was none of these things.

All over Europe the year 1814 was one of "restoration" after twenty years of revolutionary turmoil and war. In some countries, like France, the old dynasties came back but with new constitutions in their hands. Elsewhere the restored rulers indulged in complete reaction, an extreme case being the Italian prince who made his courtiers not only dress as they had in 1792 but also resume their ranks of that year. In no country was the drama of conflict between old and new so theatrical as in Spain.

The Constituent Cortes of 1810 dissolved itself in October, 1813. It was superseded by a regularly elected Cortes, which met first in Cádiz but after January, 1814, sat in Madrid, just as the capital was making the first preparations to receive back its royal martyr and hero. The membership of the new Cortes was distinctly more conservative than the old, but nonetheless, a large majority felt so self-important as to vote on February 2 detailed instructions regarding the manner of the king's return. Fernando was not to be obeyed until he had sworn to the Constitution, he was not to be accompanied by any foreigners or troops, and he was not to deviate from a specified itinerary once he had entered Spain. A greater man than Fernando might well have found this intolerably presumptuous.

Fernando seemed to be in a conciliatory mood. On March 10, three days after his release by the French, he sent a letter to Madrid that was only mildly equivocal: "The reestablishment of the Cortes of which the Regency has appraised me as well as anything else done during my absence that is beneficial to the kingdom will receive my approval as being in accord with my Royal intentions." During his journey to the frontier the king discussed the Constitution of 1812 with a British general and commented that it had "many good" as well as "inadmissible things," adding, "however, if my refusal to swear to it could cause bloodshed I will swear to it tomorrow." He entered Spain on March 24 at Gerona and that day wrote the Regency of "my desire to do everything in my power which will benefit my subjects."

The reception Fernando received in various towns of Catalonia and then in its capital, Barcelona, was one of "indescribable enthusiasm." The excited crowds were, however, shouting slogans such as "Long Live the Absolute King," "Long Live the Inquisition," "Down with Liberty," and even "Long Live Our Chains." The impression this popular sentiment made on Fernando was readily worked upon by his entourage, ultraconservatives to the man, including his brother Carlos, his uncle Antonio, his tutor Escoiquiz, and various dukes and bishops. These persons persuaded the king to visit Saragossa on April 6, although it was not on his prescribed route. During the king's stay General José de Palafox, the leader of the heroic resistance of the Aragonese capital against the French, was the only man the king heard speak in favor of his unconditional acceptance of the Constitution. A critical development came on April 12, when the king was nearing Valencia: he was given a manifesto signed by sixty-nine conservative deputies of the Cortes, men later to be known as *las Persas* because they started their address with the observation that it was customary in ancient Persia for five days of complete anarchy to take place before a new king succeeded his predecessor. By analogy, they argued that Spain had just undergone its orgy of experiment and that now it should return to the old ways. The Persians repudiated the Cortes as unrepresentative and the Constitution as unworkable, saying that "absolute monarchy . . . is the work of reason and intelligence." They drew the line only against "arbitrary monarchy," favoring a traditional or feudal type of Cortes to help the king achieve justice.

The next moment of drama occurred on April 16, when the King encountered at Puzol the president of the regency, this dignitary being his cousin the Cardinal Archbishop of Toledo. The latter's mission was to present the Constitution for swearing to, before he paid any reverence to the king. The two men faced each other in a moment of embarrassment. Glaring, Fernando held out his hand and snarled peremptorily, "Kiss!" The regent complied and then was coldly dismissed. In Valencia itself the king again drew warm welcoming crowds, probably stirred up by the earlier arrival of the infantes Carlos and Antonio, and it was here that Don Francisco Elío, a captain general who had been a hero of the War of Independence, grabbed a flag and made an impromptu speech which ended up with the declaration that "the blood which remains in all Spanish soldiers will be spilled to preserve for you the Throne with the plenitude of rights which nature granted you." This action was the first pronunciamiento, the first time of a long series when Spanish generals have set themselves against the civil power. The mood of the street people was similar to that of General Elío, for they promptly set about smashing a tablet marking "Plaza of the Constitution" and replaced it with "Plaza of Fernando VII."

In Madrid the sentiment was still constitutionalist. On May 2 a new meeting place for the Cortes was dedicated in a monastery building remodeled by the efforts of many ordinary citizens working side by side with laborers paid by the rich. On the façade were statues to Religion, Fatherland, and Liberty. Guns, bells, processions, and a Te Deum marked the sixth anniversary of the *Dos de Mayo*.

Two days later in the Declaration of Valencia Fernando VII abruptly and emphatically repudiated all the work of the Cortes as inspired by a subversive minority imitating the French Revolution. The decree read: "It is my royal will . . . to declare that Constitution and those decrees nil and of no value or effect, now or ever, as if such acts had never taken place." All persons continuing to support the Constitution either vocally or in writing were declared guilty of *lèse majesté* and subject to the death penalty. The only concessions by the king were a statement that "I detest and abhor despotism" and a promise to convoke a traditional type of Cortes. The next day, May 5, the king left for Madrid.

In an act that was a "masterstroke of treachery" on the night of May

10–11 the captain general of Castile arrested scores of liberals in and about Madrid. His victims included two regents, members of the Cortes who had not signed the manifesto of *las Persas,* and known constitutionalists both in and out of officialdom. He ordered the arrests before the king's declaration was promulgated in the capital May 11. The posting of the royal decree sent crowds rampaging through the streets to the familiar cries of "Long live the absolute king." They vandalized the Cortes building, erased inscriptions honoring the Constitution or even the nation, and attacked citizens who refused to bow to portraits of the king. When Fernando himself entered the city on March 13, "it was not rejoicing, it was not jubilation, it was a frenzy that his appearance inspired after six years of absence and slavery. The populace, which had gone out the distance of more than four leagues from the city, enthusiastically took control of his coach, persons of all classes pulling it until the arrival at the palace." The enthusiasm was slightly less unanimous than for the king's triumphal reception in 1808 after the fall of Godoy, a time before deep political division existed.

Fernando's return was the signal for the most thoroughgoing reaction, a reaction that went beyond reversing the recent reforms of the Cortes to nullifying some of the gains made under the enlightened kings of the eighteenth century. Fernando restored the Inquisition in full force, taking a personal interest in its prisons and trials. He allowed the Jesuits to come back and ordered all ecclesiastical and feudal properties that had been sold since 1808 returned to their original owners with no compensation to the interim purchasers. The latter act reinstated the seignorial rights of the nobles over 25,000 villages. Despite the king's earlier promise, he decreed the expropriation and perpetual banishment of 12,000 *afrancesados.* The new regime banned foreign books and canceled freedom of the press. Within a brief time only two newspapers were left in Madrid, so supervised and limited in their political content that a British visitor reported that he could find in them only weather reports and "accounts of miracles wrought by different Virgins, lives of holy friars and sainted nuns, romances of marvelous conversions, libels against Jews, heretics, and Freemasons, and histories of apparitions."

The nations of Europe, themselves on a distinctly antiliberal course, were nonetheless shocked by the arbitrary excesses of the regime of Fernando VII. The newly made Duke of Wellington arrived in Madrid eleven days after the king and reported that the reaction was "highly impolitic but it is liked by the people at large." Probably he remonstrated with Fernando about the arrests, involving some persons instrumental in his own victorious campaigns in Spain, but the British conservative was more concerned to caution some fellow generals against resisting the king and precipitating civil war. King Fernando's cousin Louis XVIII was more open in showing his disgust with the outrages in Spain. When Napoleon staged his "Hundred Days" comeback after March, 1815, the French Bourbon refused Fernando's proffered aid, even ordering a contingent of Spanish troops back across the frontier. Disdain on the part of the powers about the treatment of Spanish liberals combined with the diplomatic incompetence of Fernando to render Spain an unheeded voice at the Congress of Vienna ending in June, 1815. The five great powers at Vienna put back the pieces of the world to their mutual satisfaction, while Spain got the merest scraps—the tiny Italian duchy of Lucca for the King's sister, promises about Parma after Napoleon's consort, now ruling there, died.

Europe's scorn did not stay Fernando from further cruelties. He continued to persecute suspected liberals in every way, employing informers, house searches, the revived use of torture, venal judges, and farcical trials. When eventually the king's own courts balked at the lack of evidence of specific wrongdoing and at the arbitrary procedures, the king intervened personally in fifty unsettled cases and by decree in December, 1815, sentenced the prisoners either to death or to imprisonment in the unspeakable African penal colonies (two future prime ministers were so exiled).

The number of victims of the reaction was in the hundreds only, a smaller number than were to suffer from a new white terror in Spain a decade later. Recent scholarship has shown that what seemed pure vengeance on the king's part was also a matter of not enough jobs to go around so that the more junior officers and officials lost their posts for economic rather than political reasons. In a period of desperate financial retrenchment, the king naturally used his patronage for the benefit of his supporters of 1808 and of 1814, with the result that many of the heroes of the War of Independence found themselves pushed out. "There were simply too many victors to enjoy the spoils" (an explanation which also helps explain the Stalin purges of the 1930's or the McCarthy-era housecleaning of the 1950's).

"The poor generals are left to plant cabbages"; so wrote a contemporary regarding the dearth of official jobs. Many army leaders, led less by restlessness than by ideological conviction, resorted to insurrectionary action against the tyrannical Ferdinand VII. Francisco Espoz y Mina, a small landowner turned guerrilla leader in Navarre, tried to reassemble his army and seize Pamplona as early as the fall of 1814. He escaped to France to await better days. Porlier, a midshipman who rose to the rank of general during the War of Independence, seized Corunna in September, 1815, and proclaimed the Constitution of 1812. The revolt in this seaport city, typically liberal, was suppressed by forces from the neighboring cathedral city of Santiago, typically clerical and reactionary. Other wartime leaders tried to raise Catalonia in 1817 and Valencia in 1819. In the capital occurred the "Conspiracy of the Triangle," a plot to assassinate Fernando involving a secret society of Freemasons. According to its enemies, Freemasonry was the source of most of the troubles of the day, an assertion that is true insofar as that many of the liberals who found the abuses by the king intolerable were members of lodges. The strength of their convictions is illustrated by the story of a Freemason prisoner who feigned a willingness to reveal important secrets to the king in a personal interview and then made use of his opportunity to lecture Fernando and to exhort him to join the society.

The post-restoration years were not uniformly oppressive and negative, for the king was too unstable and devious to pursue a consistent policy. Amid great popular rejoicings and expressions of optimism from liberals Fernando remarried in September, 1816. He and his brother Don Carlos married Portuguese princesses who were sisters. The new Queen Isabel succeeded in lifting the gloom from the court, distracted the king from his worst associates, and put in words for political moderation. Soon afterward the military courts-martial were disbanded, and a hated police chief dismissed. In December, 1816, Fernando appointed an avowed liberal named Martín de Garay as minister of finances. The government's economic situation was critical, with expenditures half again as much as revenues. The new minister had no recourse but to lay new taxes on the king's chief supporters: the landed rich and the clergy.

The breathing spell was of short duration. In September, 1818, Garay and two fellow ministers were roused from their beds in the middle of the night and sent into exile. The beneficent influence of Queen Isabel ended with her death in January, 1819.

Disturbing ministers in their repose was very much Fernando's way of ruling. Men who thought they had the king's trust were often abruptly disillusioned when they found themselves posted to oblivion in the provinces. There was the instance of the minister of justice who was awakened early in the morning to find the king personally going through the papers on the man's writing table. There were five ministerial posts; some thirty men occupied them in the years 1814–1820.

Equally influential in the king's policy-making as his ministry was his counterministry, or camarilla, an informal group of men he frequently consorted with over cigars and dirty stories. This "buffoon parliament," as it was characterized by the liberal and the prudish alike, consisted of unrespectable and irresponsible types ranging from ex-bullfighters to palace servants. Fernando obviously preferred their company, their flattery, and their uncomplicated reactions when laws were being considered or love affairs gossiped about. Yet, painfully aware of his father's folly in having a favorite, Fernando never let himself be dominated by any individual, never mixed the personnel of ministry and camarilla, and never failed to treat all the members of each with a sneering contempt. Fernando's geniality with ordinary people, even if mixed with bad temper and sarcasm, gave him a kind of popularity with the masses as against the aristocracy or the intelligentsia.

3. The Loss of the Empire in the Americas

Spain itself might well have borne with Fernando's brutal incompetence for an extended period in view of the general longing for tranquillity. The colonies were not so inert, however, and their movement toward cutting all political and financial ties with Madrid led Fernando to mobilize the Spanish army for the purpose of repressive action overseas. This futile undertaking produced in turn a new revolution in Spain.

It would be unfair to assess to Fernando VII the major share of the responsibility for the loss of Spanish America even though this momentous development occurred essentially during his reign. Historians agree that the problem was one of "centuries of slighting, humbling, and wronging" the colonies so that it was only strange "that the monarchical fervor, the affection towards the mother country, remained in force as long as it did." Hapsburgs and Bourbons alike not only oppressed the native Indian and half-breed populations in every way but also rendered the millions of Spanish settlers second-class citizens by giving the most important government offices and economic privileges to Spaniards sent out from the home country. The resentment caused by this discriminatory policy was aggravated by three outside factors: the age-old desire of British commercial interests for the colonies to deal with them directly; the same kind of pressure from merchants of the new United States, itself an example of the benefits of national independence; and most recently the ideals of liberty and popular will coming out of revolutionary France.

The first major stirrings of revolt in Spanish America were the Tupac Amaru Indian uprising in Peru in the 1780's, Miranda's filibusters in Venezuela in 1806, and the discomfiture of British invaders and Spanish viceroys alike in Argentina during 1806 and 1807. The political restlessness already evident before the brief triumph of Fernando VII in Spain in 1808 was much intensified during the six years of the War of Independence when the king was a prisoner of Napoleon. Only minimal sentiment in favor of Joseph Bonaparte existed in the colonies, but by 1814 every colony with the exception of Peru had made some sort of break with the traditional control of the home country in the form of ousting viceroys, establishing juntas, or even holding congresses, all the while professing allegiance to Fernando VII and the Supreme Junta or Cortes ruling in his name.

Restored to power, Fernando did everything to make the colonial situation even worse. The example of his tyrannical regime in Spain itself could not fail to alarm those Spanish Americans who had already succeeded in gaining some measure of local freedom. In other areas where royalist rule was reasserted the populace was exposed to the perfidy of the king and his administrators, who forgot promises of amnesty and reform and reverted as soon as possible to the old methods of police terror, Inquisitional snooping, and economic exploitation. Fernando was also guilty of throwing away chances to settle for half a loaf when more and more parts of Spanish America opted for separation: he refused sincere requests from both Mexico and Peru to let them be ruled by their own Bourbon princes. Finally, Fernando can be blamed personally, but so can liberal and conservative politicians in Spain alike, for having "failed altogether to grasp the magnitude of the task involved in a military subjection of so vast a continent." Or, in the words of the American traveler Michael Quinn, the king was "delirious" to think that he could reconquer Spanish America "with a handful of discontented soldiers."

The Bourbon cause in the New World still seemed salvageable in 1814. A belated revolt in Peru that year, a revolt of colonials and Indians, was crushed by local royalist forces, and, oddly, this relatively inaccessible area in the center of the southern continent remained loyal the longest thereafter. Likewise, a local royalist force drove Simón Bolívar and his partisans of independence from Venezuela in 1814 after ferocious fighting and gruesome atrocities particularly by the Llanero Indian tribes whose aid was enlisted by the Spanish authorities. The next year a force of 14,000 veteran Spanish soldiers arrived on the northern coast. Commanded by Pablo Morillo, another wartime success story of a lieutenant become captain general, this expedition had been ominously beset by desertions and near mutinies, but once landed, it swept all before it, capturing Bogotá in 1816 and pacifying all of New Granada (Colombia). Bolívar fled to Jamaica, returning soon after to keep alive the spark of revolt.

In Mexico, too, the royalists triumphed once reinforcements arrived from the home country. Following the crushing of the Hidalgo Revolt of 1811, José Morelos, another priest, had put together an insurrectionary army in 1813 and threatened Mexico City. He was defeated and executed in December, 1815. A temperate viceroy kept this second major part of Spanish America loyal for the next six years. In 1817 a watchful local naval commander defeated in Mexican waters a filibustering expedition including British and North American volunteers led by the nephew of the Spanish *guerrillero* Mina.

In a large degree the lack of a Spanish naval presence enabled Argentina far to the south to continue its defiance of Spanish control, the only area to do so at this point. The cities of the Río de la Plata, or Plate River, were able to build up a superior fighting fleet of their own, which under American and British officers not only defended their estuary but eventually carried out operations against the Spanish in the Pacific. Although a formal declaration of independence for the provinces of the Río de la Plata did not come until July, 1816, the Argentines had earlier begun to carry their antiroyalist politics to other provinces. In the case of Paraguay, the invading Argentines were defeated, but the end result was Paraguay itself declaring independence. In June, 1814, the Argentines captured Montevideo, eliminating the last Spanish stronghold and last hope in the area, but once again an independent nation, Uruguay, was the upshot.

Next the Argentines spread the flames of revolt across the Andes into Chile. An army led by José de San Martín won the Battle of Chacabuco in February, 1817, taking 4,000 Spanish prisoners and liberating Santiago. In April, 1818, he defeated a royalist army sent down from Peru in the Battle of Maipú. The demoralization of the Spanish troops was shown by the figures of 2,000 killed and 3,000 taken prisoner. Independent Chile likewise developed an effective navy.

If San Martín was the hero of the south of the continent, Bolívar was the liberator of the north. In 1818 he moved from his island fortress to seize the entire basin of the Orinoco River. The fierce Llanero Indians, whom the Spanish paid off with ingratitude, deserted to the side of independence. General Morillo and his Spanish veterans were still able to win most of the pitched battles in Venezuela, but then Bolívar moved his army westward across the Andes into New Granada. There in August, 1819, his ragged forces won a signal victory at the Boyacá River and entered Bogotá. Soon after Bolívar was proclaimed president of Greater Colombia, symbolizing that much of the northern part of the continent had been freed.

By 1820 only Peru and Mexico remained of Spain's continental American possessions. Yet King Fernando and his ministers were still convinced they could reconquer, although they faced the nearly unsolvable dilemma of Spain's budget being unbalanced because of the loss of the colonies and of Spain's military efforts being inadequate because of the bankruptcy. They had lost precious funds already by buying eight battleships from the reactionary Tsar Alexander I which turned out to be completely unseaworthy. Nonetheless, by determined action they assembled an army of 20,000 men in Cádiz, whose sailing was just a matter of time as transports were painfully collected. Local dissensions in Argentina made the prospects of a successful descent in this area more favorable than at any previous time in a decade. The army never sailed, however.

The complete demoralization of this Spanish army destined for overseas was in striking contrast with the old spirit of the conquistadores, who seemed to brook no obstacles and no fears. One adverse factor was the presence in Cádiz's hospitals of hundreds of casualties of Morillo's earlier campaigns, men horribly wounded, emaciated, and fever-ridden. Despite the fact that the press was controlled, scare stories crept into its pages about the dangers of fighting tigers and alligators, as well as the barbaric South Americans. Then the government failed to alleviate professional army complaints of bad supplies, wretched barracks, and low pay or no pay. Freethinking officers bridled at having to say the rosary daily in formation. Many of the rank and file were being kept beyond the terms of their enlistment. Almost inevitably the army reached the conclusion that the real enemy was not overseas but the tyrant at home who had created the problem overseas and was sending them there to solve it. An abortive coup occurred in Cádiz as early as July, 1819; the real thing followed the next year.

4. A Second Round of Revolution and Reaction

Spain's first army pronunciamiento for liberal ends was the call to revolt on January 1, 1820, by Colonel Rafael del Riego, commander of the Asturias battalion stationed near Cádiz. Riego chose to proclaim the Constitution of 1812, without consulting his fellow conspirators, perhaps, "just to give their rebellion an honest appearance." He succeeded in capturing some of the senior army officers in the area but was thwarted in an effort to seize the city of Cádiz itself. Riego then set out with about 1,500 men on a march across southern Spain, hoping to gain recruits but actually suffering from desertions. In a further bid for popular support the rebel leader on February 1 proclaimed the end of tithe payments and a 50 percent tax cut. By early March he was reduced to a force of some 45 men miserably encamped outside Córdoba.

Even though Riego failed to raise Andalusia, his actions provoked revolt elsewhere. Corunna came out in favor of the Constitution of 1812 in late February, followed by Saragossa and Barcelona. Mina reappeared to lead the Navarrese. Revolutionary juntas sprang up in various towns as in 1808. A newly appointed commander betrayed the king by leading a mutiny of troops at Ocaña, forty miles from the capital. Everywhere disaffected army officers were the catalyst of the insurrections. The populace at large was discontent over inequities in taxation, judicial corruption, and governmental partiality in employment. Wellington reporting to London was partially accurate when he said that the people had lost confidence in the government but were indifferent to the Constitution of 1812. Symbolically, the Constitition of 1812 was a convenient rallying cry for all anticonservatives, not only in Spain but also in Portugal and Italy, which had similar revolutions in 1820. In fact, 1820 was a year of alarm for much of the European Establishment: within a month of Riego's pronunciamiento had occurred the assassination of the French heir, the Duke of Berri, and the Cato Street Conspiracy in England, a plot to kill the entire Tory Cabinet.

The Madrid government remained always a step behind the revolutionary tide. On March 3 it announced that local authorities were being invited to suggest reforms. On March 5 it declared that a Cortes would be summoned and on March 6 that they would meet as soon as possible (Fernando had hitherto not kept his promise of 1814). Still the crowds surged around the streets forcing citizens to kneel to the book of the Constitution which was paraded about on an equal footing with the host. A large demonstration outside the royal palace on March 7 finally brought the king out on a balcony to bow his consent to the restoration of the famous charter. Fernando took a formal oath to the document on March 9 before a large assemblage. The patronizing announcement of this in the *Gaceta* ran: "The wishes of the people and of the army having come to my notice, I have heard their prayers and like a tender father have granted that which my children considered conducive to their happiness. I have sworn to observe the Constitution for which you were sighing, and shall ever be its stoutest prop. Let us step out boldly, I at your head, along the constitutional path." The supremely hypocritical monarch, who had once abased himself before his parents and later cringed before Napoleon, endured still another great moment of humiliation.

In the capital Fernando assented to the creation of a Provisional Junta to supervise the government until the Cortes met. It was headed by his old enemy of 1814, the Bourbon cardinal. The king also assented to the formation of a new ministry composed of men Fernando sardonically labeled his "jailbirds," since several of them, including their chief, Agustín Argüelles, had spent the years of reaction in the penal colonies. During the tenure of the Provisional Junta the swing of the pendulum in favor of a liberal program was complete. The regime released political prisoners and invited the *afrancesados* back to Spain. Some seventy of the *Persas* of 1814 lost their titles and jobs, being confined to nunneries ostensibly for their own protection. The Jesuits faced expulsion again. The liberal government declared the Inquisition abolished once more and permitted a mob to smash into its headquarters, where they found only one deranged prisoner and more wine kegs than torture machines. A national militia was reestablished. Soldiers of the army learned by a decree of June, 1820, that they could disobey anticonstitutionalist officers. Bishops and priests were charged to propagandize in favor of the Constitution in the seminaries and from the pulpits, a bitterly resented and widely resisted order. A free press reappeared, a spate of journals ranging from the idealistic to the scurrilous.

The Cortes met in July 9, 1820, a body dominated by the men hounded out of public life in 1814. The king's opening address, written for him, declared that "his most ardent longings have been fulfilled." Hours earlier his palace camarilla had been plotting his escape from the capital. The Cortes, however, was more than willing to take Fernando at face value; in a euphoric mood it voted to erect a statue of the king holding the Constitution and to give him the title Fernando the Great. In the way of serious legislation the Cortes enacted a lasting division of Spain into fifty-two provincial units, and it put into effect a modern and humane penal code after consulting by letter with the eminent British philosopher of utilitarianism Jeremy Bentham. When the Cortes took up additional difficult problems such as church property and seignorial rights, the debates became prolonged and often bitter because the liberals provided to be at odds among themselves as well as with the conservatives.

By the late summer of 1820 the liberals had split into two factions, the *Moderados* (moderates) and the *Exaltados* (exalteds or radicals). The *Moderados* were satisfied with the achievements so far and sought now social peace and an accommodation with king and church. They were called traitors to the revolution and secret conservatives by the *Exaltados,* who wanted sweeping economic changes and further curbs on royal and clerical power. In their enemies' eyes the *Exaltados* were secret republicans and anarchists. The split was in part generational, pitting the reformers of 1814 against the younger insurrectionists of 1820. Antagonism between the factions increased when the ministry for economic reasons sought to disband a large part of the army, the chief source of strength for the *Exaltados,* to say nothing about jobs. Riego, now a general, lent his prestige to the *Exaltado* party, staged a triumphal entry into Madrid in August, 1820, and later acknowledged an ovation at the theater by leading the singing of the revolutionary anthem. The song, which has come down as the "Hymn of Riego," was full of democratic and anticlerical sentiment ("If the priests and monks knew/ The thrashing they were in for/ They would join the chorus singing/ Liberty, Liberty, Liberty"). Even this became too mild for *Exaltado* hotheads, who took the chanting the more vulgar "Traga-la" ("Swallow it," meaning the revolution). The nervous government posted Riego away from Madrid and made an attempt to crack down on extremist orators and political clubs.

The split in the ranks of the liberals could only give satisfaction to the conservative, or traditionalist, party in and out of the Cortes. Manifestations of extreme right-wing feeling were soon forthcoming after the initial shock of the beginning of the year. A bishop founded the Society of the Exterminating Angel to fulfill privately the work of the Inquisition and to propagandize against the Constitution. Royalist guerrilla bands took to the field.

The king too tried to exploit *Moderado-Exaltado* differences in every devious way, but he found united opposition to his efforts to reassert royal authority. Even though the Constitution expressly granted him a temporary veto, he was forced to approve immediately a law expropriating certain monasteries. He retired in anger to the Escorial in November, and while there, he used his appointive power, also constitutionally unchallengeable, to replace a liberal captain general of Castile with a reactionary one. Madrid was instantly in an uproar, and the ministry compelled the king to return to the capital and hear threatening crowds boo him as he smiled uncomfortably on the familiar balcony. For the first time, perhaps, Spaniards showed disrespect to the person of their monarch. The ministry allowed the radical clubs to reopen and made Riego captain general of Aragón.

It now became more fashionable for the crowds assembled nightly before the Oriente Palace to yell insults at the king than to cheer the Constitution. Citizens threw stones at Fernando's carriage and were involved in a bloody clash with the royal guard. When the king opened a new session of the Cortes in March, 1821, he duly read the high-sounding message prepared for him and then added on his own a diatribe against the ministry for permitting such outrages. The ministry resigned, to be replaced by a new group of moderates faced with the same problems of reconciling demands for law and order with demands for meaningful social reforms.

Elections for a new Cortes showed major gains for the *Exaltado* radicals, who capitalized in part on the fact that the former Cortes members were ineligible for reelection. More important, underlying social discontent was beginning to find expression at the polls. The peasants had been recently hurt by falling prices and city workers by unemployment (they resorted, like their contemporary Luddites in England, to smashing laborsaving textile machines). The new Cortes was the first with no bishops in it and few men of rank; it elected Riego president of the assembly and declared his "Hymn" the national anthem.

The king's reaction to the *Exaltado* majority in the Cortes was to name in March, 1822, a new ministry composed of *Moderados* and headed by Francisco Martínez de la Rosa, another "jailbird" whom Fernando also dubbed "little Rose the sweet stuff maker." The well-meaning ministry found its task impossible in the face of the hostility of the Cortes, which was so touchy about its incorruptibility as to make it a crime for one of its members to enter a ministerial office. Martínez tried to resign several times, only to be refused by the king. Fernando was already begging Russia and France to intervene in Spain, and he needed chaos in the government to support his pleas.

The next crisis came on July 1, 1822, when four of the six battalions of royal guards marched out of Madrid and took up a menacing posture at El Pardo Palace. Suspecting a royal plot, the ministry again tried to resign, but the ministers were forcibly confined in their offices by the king. In this complicated affair the *Exaltados* out of office accused the ministry of a plot to change the Constitution in the king's favor. When the royal guards both at El Pardo and in Madrid tried to overpower the city on July 6, they were defeated and disarmed by line regiments, militia, and volunteers led by Riego and Evaristo San Miguel.

Now the king was compelled to name a more radical government headed by San Miguel. A great banquet took place in Madrid to celebrate the defeat of the reactionaries. Taking power on July 10, 1822, the new regime was known as the all-Masonic ministry or the Ministry of the Seven Patriots, according to people's political biases. Like its predecessors, the ministry was ground down by its middle position between a conniving king and vociferous critics on the left. On the one hand, they forbade Fernando to leave the capital on the grounds that at San Ildefonso he was surrounded by reactionary plotters. On the other hand, the ministry felt obliged to persecute agitators making such demands as that the king be put on trial for treason or that Spain declare war on a hostile Bourbon France. In an effort to silence extremists on both sides, they revived rigid censorship, so that the American observer Michael Quinn noted with surprise and dismay that "in perhaps no capital of Europe was freedom of opinion less tolerated at this time than in Madrid." Meanwhile, organized into the Apostolic Army of the Faith, royalists seized La Seo de Urgel near the French border and proclaimed a regency, claiming that the king was a prisoner of the radicals, an idea Fernando did nothing to discourage in his secret appeals to his fellow European monarchs.

Spain was not left to work out its own turmoil, for Fernando's pleas found response and Europe decided to intervene to uphold monarchy against revolution. "Europe" at this time meant the Holy Alliance of Tsar Alexander and Metternich, the Holy Alliance so infamously dedicated to the maintenance of the status quo everywhere that in recent years the Chinese Communists have revived it as a convenient label for their enemies. Although considering himself above membership in the Holy Alliance, the Pope was closely associated with its policies and in the case of Spain had been thundering against the Constitution of 1812 since its inception. Indeed, of all the countries in the world only the United States had shown any sign of approval of the new regime in Madrid. (Some European oppositionists, of course, were favorable to the Spanish revolution. The poet Shelley wrote an "Ode to Liberty," hailing a "glorious people" for "scattering contagious fire into the sky.")

The Holy Alliance had already authorized a successful armed intervention by Austria against newly established constitutional governments in Naples and Piedmont. A congress at Verona debated the Spanish situation in October, 1822, and after rejecting the tsar's offer somehow to march a Russian army into Spain, the powers gave France the mandate to act against its Bourbon neighbor. The British alone, in the person of Foreign Minister George Canning, protested such intervention in the affairs of another country, but even Canning could not conceal his distaste for the Spanish *Exaltados,* and Wellington at Verona dropped elaborate hints on just how a military occupation of Spain should proceed.

Accordingly, on January 6, 1823, the Russian, Austrian, and Prussian ambassadors gave identical notes to the Spanish foreign minister to the effect that Spain must restore its king to his rights or face the consequences. Ten days later the envoys demanded their passports. On January 25 King Louis XVIII told the French Chamber of Deputies that "a hundred thousand soldiers under the command of the Duke of Angoulême were about to march, invoking God and St. Louis, to save the throne to the descendants of Henry IV and to bring that fine kingdom into agreement with Europe." Like Britain, France had had some reservations about such an intervention, but doubts were cast aside in the face of pressure from French holders of Spanish bonds, of fears of Louis XVIII for his own throne, and of hopes that a glorious military campaign would make the French army more pro-Bourbon and less pro-Bonaparte.

The imminent French invasion led to a theatrical reconciliation of *Moderados* and *Exaltados* in Madrid and much patriotic oratory. The Cortes approved a huge war loan and a larger army. Royalist guerrillas, however, prepared to welcome the invaders and intensified their own activity. One of their forces defeated governmental troops in a pitched battle at Brihuega in January, 1823, thereafter throwing the capital into a panic.

The Cortes authorized the government to move to Seville, and on March 20 it forced Fernando VII to accompany them on its flight from the capital, after he had balked in every way, from fomenting mutinies to pleading ill health. The king was told with the kind of humor he himself employed that the southern climate could not fail to improve his health. Fernando began jotting down lists of the names of his tormentors.

The Duke of Angoulême's superbly equipped army of 100,000 crossed into Spain on April 17, 1823. Their march south was a promenade. The French avoided very carefully any sort of provocations of the populace that might have started another 1808. They were greeted as liberators in many areas. Halfhearted or treacherous commanders of the Spanish government forces offered little resistance, except the *guerrillero* Mina in Catalonia whose hit-and-run tactics, carried even into France itself, showed what a determined resistance might have done. The Guadarrama passes uncontested, the French forces entered Madrid at the end of May. Their royalist Spanish allies, supporting the regency in Fernando's name, formed a so-called Apostolic Ministry, declared all laws since 1820 void, and started purging constitutionalists.

By June 15, 1823, there were two regencies in Fernando's name, for when the liberal government had to abandon Seville for Cádiz, they took the king with them by force. The Constitution of 1812 provided for a regency if the monarch was incapacitated, and the ministry decided that Fernando's refusal to escape from the approaching French indicated his temporary incapacity. The Duke of Angoulême's forces appeared before Cádiz on August 16 and fought the one bloody battle of the year on August 31, when they stormed the defense outwork known as the Trocadero (commemorated to this day in the Paris landmark). The siege of Cádiz lasted two months. The refugee government was not able to repeat 1810 and agreed to surrender after they lost any conviction that they represented the nation defending its king against his enemies. At the end the garrison and populace of Cádiz angrily took matters in their own hands and forced Fernando VII to promise an amnesty, "complete and absolute oblivion" of the past, before he was allowed to sally forth and greet the French duke. So occurred Fernando's second "liberation" from part of his people.

The remainder of the reign of Fernando VII, the period 1823–1833, was a more horrible reprise of the reaction of 1814–1820. He instantly broke his promise of amnesty by calling for the deaths of the men who had voted for his temporary deposition. What was further in store was evident from his decree forbidding constitutionalist officials and generals to come within five miles of the route of the king's return to Madrid. Once again the capital greeted "the desired one" joyously, despite the fact that there were 112 executions in eighteen days. Riego was one of the most prominent persons who suffered the death penalty; despite his unseemly pleas for forgiveness, he was dragged to the center of Madrid in a coal cart, hanged, and his quartered body exposed to ignominy.

This period became known as *la década funesta,* or as the years of Calomarde, after the minister of justice who made himself the perfect instrument of the King's malace. One could find little amusement in the fact of Tadeo Calomarde's lowborn origin or his several flirtations with liberalism when this frightful official saw to it that the mere possession of a portrait of Riego or being caught in the act of defacing a royalist inscription brought the death penalty. A disgusted Duke of Angoulême and subsequent French representatives vigorously protested the new reign of terror. Calomarde's ostensible concession was an amnesty law of May, 1824, which turned out to be so full of loopholes that it provided for the killing of hundreds more. When the moderate royalist Zea Bermúdez protested the "fierce and hideous vengeance" that was taking place, Calomarde declared his determination "to stamp out from Spanish soil the last and faintest trace of the idea that sovereignty can reside elsewhere than in the royal person." To such an end he closed all the universities. With his usual cruel humor the king then solemnly announced the opening of a school of bullfighting in Seville. In the general purge after 1823 an estimated 44,000 people suffered imprisonment, 20,000 exile, and 100,000 loss of their posts.

Once again Spanish liberals, usually army leaders, resorted to armed attempts against tyranny. A seaborne descent on Tarifa took place in 1824 and one on Alicante in 1826. The July Revolution of 1830 in Paris was the signal for 20,000 Spanish exiles in France and England to mount incursions across the Pyrenees. The ineffable Mina reappeared as the chief leader but drew little response. In 1831 Spanish exiles from Gibraltar were tricked by agents of the king and the governor of Málaga into effecting a landing in that area: fifty-two men were slaughtered mercilessly. That same year in the north of Spain the government had a seamstress executed for embroidering on a banner "Law, Liberty, Equality."

A novelty in the last decade of Fernando's reign and an indication of the intensity of the political malaise of Spain was extremist activity by rightists also, people who in effect were saying that the king was not despotic enough. In response to French pressure, Fernando had not countenanced the restoration of the Inquisition in 1823 and had disbanded the cruder forms of judicial terror. These policies hardly justified accusations from the Society of the Exterminating Angel and similar reactionary groups that the king was an ingrate, a secret constitutionalist, or a prisoner of the Freemasons. In 1825 an actual armed revolt occurred under the banner of putting the archconservative Don Carlos on the throne and extirpating all liberals. Two years later much of Catalonia was in open unrest with rightist juntas formed and thirty battalions of rebels under arms. It required a personal tour of the area by Fernando to convince royalist and clerical fanatics that he was not a captive of Madrid radicals. With impartial cruelty, the king subsequently authorized many executions, some to hush up people who could implicate in the rightist plottings important generals and officials like Calomarde. The simultaneous hanging and shooting of some of the victims was a bizarre invention to satisfy both civil and military justice.

After two decades of the reign of Fernando VII, with its incredible level of interval violence, materially Spain had made no progress and spiritually it had refused to enter the nineteenth century. Under the more or less enlightened Bourbons of the previous century Spain had shown definite signs of catching up to the rest of Europe in all respects. After 1814 Spain was revealed as a classic case of a backward country where confused leadership and mismanaged resources combined to produce stalemate. One is hard put to point out any gains made under Fernando: the opening of the Prado galleries to the public was one step forward that one hopes does not delude present-day tourists about the general nature of the period. (Actually, Ferdinand's predecessors were responsible for the quality of the collections in the Prado and his second wife, Isabel of Braganza, took the initiative in establishing the museum based on them.)

While foreign travelers at the time might still find a modicum of bygone culture in Madrid itself, they were astonished to tour a supposedly civilized country and encounter the worst possible roads, the most wretched inns, and the most pervasive banditry. For example, the American poet Henry Wadsworth Longfellow, who visited Spain in the late 1820's, made these observations: "The whole country is overrun with robbers. Every village in La Mancha has its tale to tell of atrocities committed in its neighborhood. At night in the capacious inn-kitchens my fellow travellers would huddle together and talk of the dangers we would pass through on the morrow and converse for hours in that mysterious undertone which always fills the mind with phantoms." Benjamin Disraeli, visiting Andalusia somewhat later, claimed that bandits would shoot any traveler who had less than $16 on him. Much could be blamed on the devastation of the Napoleonic Wars, but little economic recovery occurred thereafter. True to the familiar story of the backward country, Spain did incur foreign indebtedness running into the billions of reales; the liberal politicians of the 1820–1823 interval, finding loans more popular than taxes, bear a large share of the blame.

The liberal interlude with all its uncertainties was also the final fatal period in Spain's relations with its overseas empire. Mexico declared its independence in February, 1821, first as a constitutional monarchy willing to accept a Bourbon ruler, even a fugitive Fernando VII. The Creole General Agustín de Iturbide, who for ten years had proven his royalist loyalties against all insurrectionaries, ended up proclaiming himself Emperor Agustín I in May, 1822, but after his reign of less than a year Mexico became a republic. Resisting coercion from the Mexicans, the United Provinces of Central America declared their independence in July, 1823 (at one point, rather than submit to Iturbide, San Salvador had proposed joining the United States). Meanwhile, on the southern continent Bolívar had liberated Venezuela in June, 1821, and Ecuador a year later, both countries being united at first in Greater Colombia. Pushing northward from Chile, San Martín proclaimed the independence of Peru in July, 1821, but royalists retook Lima twice in the next years, and San Martín and Bolívar nearly clashed in the area. In the final battle of Ayacucho in December, 1824, the marked superiority of the Spanish royalists in numbers and artillery over their enemies proved less important, as usual, than their demoralization and lack of leadership.

At a moment when reaction seemed triumphant in Spain and Europe, the celebrated Monroe Doctrine of December, 1823, was a warning to Fernando VII and the Holy Alliance not to try to reestablish Spanish influence in the Americas. The restoration of such a hegemony was more than unlikely in view of Spain's bankruptcy, the disposition of the British navy, and the mood of the Spanish Americans. Accordingly, when Fernando VII died in 1833, his once-proud title of King of the Indies meant nothing more than that the Spanish flag still waved over Cuba, Puerto Rico, and the Philippines.

Depending on the politics of the historian, Fernando VII has been evaluated as a monstrous reactionary and alternately as a heroic defender of tradition. According to the weight one assigns in history to the individual as against society, the king can be personally blamed for a disastrous reign or he can be termed "only an instrument in the hands of his people," the latter being the view of Jean-Louis Jacquet, a recent French historian of the Bourbons. Some case can indeed be made that Fernando did respond to the mood of the mob and also the advice of his fellow monarchs, but to say this is not to exonerate him. Gerald Brenan, concerned with the psychological interpretation of Spain, concludes that this monarch had all the defects of his people and none of their virtues. Clearly, his cruelty, his arrogance, and his bigotry stand out, even if one does not consider them necessarily Spanish traits. In psychological terms, it is easy to see how the degradations and frustrations of the king's earlier years might have produced the deceits and vengeances of later on. Yet it is difficult to sympathize with a ruler who started as a martyr and repaid goodwill by becoming a tyrant, a ruler who did this not only in 1814 but a second time in 1823. The conclusion that is true about Fernando VII is what was said about the reign of his younger contemporary Tsar Nicholas I: "It was all a terrible mistake."

VII.
The Crisis of 1833–1839:
The Dynasty Split

1. *The Succession Problem and the Last Years of Fernando VII*

THE evil influence of Fernando VII in Spanish affairs did not cease with his death but in the matter of the succession to the throne has continued to this day. The worst of the Bourbons was the last undisputed king. Since 1833 a dynastic conflict between the line of Fernando's daughter Isabel and that of his brother Carlos has burdened the nation with three open civil wars, as well as bitterly divided and significantly weakened the power of the monarchy's natural supporters at every critical juncture of Spanish history.

Fernando VII, it was whispered, was a Bluebeard, each of whose first three wives sickened and died after a few years of contact with him. The original bride of 1802, María Antonia of Naples, was vivacious, cultivated, and a good influence on her husband, sharing his loathing of the Godoy-dominated court of his parents. Admittedly delicate and consumptive, she died in 1806 under suspicious circumstances, having left no children. After ten years of ostensible continence, Fernando then married Isabel of Braganza, who, like her predecessor, was a first cousin. Isabel had some liberalizing effect on a dark period of his reign but was remembered otherwise only for her passion for needlework. Without surviving children, Queen Isabel died in 1819. The third wife of Fernando was María Amalia of Saxony, who was far less successful than her predecessors in curbing her husband's coarse and brutal ways and no more successful in producing an heir to the throne. Gentle and saintly or insipid and religion-ridden, according to one's lights, María Amalia composed poems to her husband

and hymns to the Virgin in the critical 1820's as unfulfilled revolution gave way to relentless dynastic intrigue.

As long as Fernando remained childless, which situation applied in 1814 or 1820 or 1829, his brother Don Carlos was the natural heir to the Spanish throne. For traditionalists this prospect was supremely satisfactory, for, according to a familiar cliché of the day, Don Carlos was more royalist than the king and more Catholic than the Pope. In Goya's "Family" of 1800 Don Carlos appeared as a sullen pre-teen-ager, and he was remembered for being alone of his family to defy Napoleon in 1808, refusing to surrender his rights of succession with the words "I would rather die than live without honor." He shared the humiliating and uncertain years of exile in France with Fernando, and he remained by preference entirely friendly and loyal to his older brother.

In looks and temperament the brothers were remarkably different. Don Carlos was the taller, with less exaggerated Bourbon features and with deepset eyes contrasting with Fernando's popeyed look. The younger brother was extremely pious and moral, dignified and severe, frank and honorable in all his dealings, and politically somewhat naïve and diffident in contrast with the lecherous, sarcastic, and unscrupulous king. Don Carlos' admirers found him sublime; his enemies considered him at best a blockhead, at worst a devil.

What Don Carlos lacked in energy and decisiveness was amply compensated for by his wife, Doña María Francisca of Braganza, whom he had married in 1816 on the same day Fernando had married her Portuguese sister. Francisca was arrogance and ambition personified, a formidable woman single-minded in her determination to see her husband sitting on the throne and the succession going to the eldest of her three strapping sons.

The king had another brother, Don Francisco de Paula, born in 1794 six years after Don Carlos. The pretty little boy holding the queen's hand in the Goya group, Francisco was widely believed to be the son of Godoy. He bore "an almost indecent likeness to the Prince of the Peace." On grounds of bastardy he was excluded from the royal succession by the Cortes of 1810, but there is one good reason to believe that he really was legitimate: in 1817 both Godoy and ex-Queen María Luisa had tried to promote a marriage between this infante and Godoy's avowed daughter by the Countess of Chinchón. Short, red-haired, and unprepossessing in looks, Francisco had few talents but attracted notice by his reputation for being a liberal or a kind of Spanish Louis Philippe (it is tempting to make an extended comparison of the king, Don Carlos, and Don Francisco with Louis XVIII, Charles X, and Louis Philippe). This liberalism found expression in Francisco's becoming a Freemason in 1825 and eventually holding top office in that society. He joined at a time when Don Carlos had insisted on King Fernando's keeping on the books a law making such membership a capital offense.

Francisco de Paula's influence on affairs came to be almost entirely a result of the forcefulness of his wife, Doña Carlota of Naples, whom he had married in 1819. So involved were the marriages between the courts of Madrid and Naples that Carlota's father was Francisco's uncle and her mother his sister. A Junoesque type, blond, tall, and massive, Carlota was "a huge fat frightful woman" and "the veriest scold in Madrid," capable of swearing like a carter. However rough-talking, Carlota was in a Cinderella position at the court, since her husband was only fifth in the line of succession. In particular, Doña Carlota resented the airs and snubs of Don Carlos' wife, Francisca. A vicious enmity between the two women sprang up after an incident during the festivities attendant on King Fernando's meeting the Duke of Angoulême outside Cádiz in 1823: Carlota appeared dressed in plain traveling clothes on Francisca's assurance that she and the queen were doing likewise, only to find the other ladies resplendent in their best jewels and finery. To her frustrations the redoubtable Carlota was to apply the greatest abilities at meddling and intrigue, which were more than once to change the course of Spanish history.

The lines of battle were already well drawn between the conservative Don Carlos and Doña Francisca on the one hand and the liberal Don Francisco and Doña Carlota on the other when King Fernando's third wife, María Amalia, died in May, 1829. As always, there were rumors that she had been poisoned, her darkish complexion while she lay in state being cited as evidence. Despite his being prematurely worn out and crippled with gout at forty-four, the libertine king announced his intention to remarry as soon as possible, leaving the preliminary searchings for a bride to his ministers and his two sisters-in-law. "No more rosaries!" the middle-aged roué did say, indicating his distaste for overly pious German princesses. Within an unseemly brief time of the queen's death, Doña Carlota showed Fernando a ravishing portrait of her own Neapolitan sister Cristina and registered her first great triumph when the delighted king consented to marry her. With her sister on the throne, Doña Carlota would replace Doña Francisca as second lady of the land.

Predictably, there were strong objections to the king's choice of bride from the quarter of Doña Francisca, who spread tales that Cristina was a granddaughter of Godoy, that she was a shameless flirt who already had a child, and that any princess still unmarried at twenty-three must be undesirable. As for the first matter, Cristina was the daughter of Fernando's sister the Infanta Isabel, who was deemed by some to be Godoy's child (her ever-spiteful mother-in-law, Queen Carolina, called her "this epileptic bastard"). The Cortes of 1810, however, did not question Isabel's legitimacy as it did with her brother Don Francisco. Of all people the king would have been the last to have anything to do with a Godoy. There was foundation for the charge that Cristina was a "royal coquette," the words used by the future Lord Malmesbury who reported after a visit to Naples that several men had been jailed for behaving too intimately with the princess. Malmesbury noted his surprise on being presented to Cristina that she did not cast down her eyes demurely but "she stopped and took hold of one of the buttons of my uniform to see, so she said, the inscription on it, the Queen indignantly calling her to come on." Rather than being offended, Fernando was pleased to hear that Cristina was both highly sexed and seductive, and if she had borne a child, it spoke well of her fecundity. As for the fact that Cristina was unmarried at twenty-three, it was explained simply by her determination to settle for nothing less than a queenly crown. That Cristina was the king's niece and sister-in-law did not bother him or anyone else.

On September 24, 1829, Fernando asked for Cristina's hand, and she soon after set forth across Italy and France toward her new country. In Rome she received the Pope's blessing (and dispensation to marry her uncle); in Turin she met the future King Victor Emmanuel; and in Grenoble she met the future King Louis Philippe (married to her aunt), as well as was taken in hand there by sister Carlota. From the Spanish frontier she was escorted south by Don Carlos, an irony, since he was to become her mortal enemy. The people of Barcelona enthusiastically turned out to admire Cristina's entrancing beauty, particularly her blond hair and blue eyes, and people were soon talking of her kind and tolerant ways, about such things as her dancing with nonaristocrats or her showing concern that soldiers of the guard were not wearing warm cloaks in the cold. After Cristina made her formal entry into Madrid wearing a robe of brilliant Neapolitan blue, liberals took to displaying the color as a kind of emblem. She arrived at Aranjuez on December 8 and captivated the king during dinner the next day. The marriage took place at the Church of the Atocha on December 12. A new gaiety soon pervaded the gloomy and sanctimonious court, with balls taking precedence over religious ceremonials to the distress of Don Carlos and Doña Francisca and to the satisfaction of their younger counterparts.

The new queen had been brought up by parents who thought that princesses should excel at dancing and riding rather than reading. She made up with shrewdness, however, her lack of education, and she mastered Spanish court politics with great rapidity. The king could not refuse her anything. Her present influence over him and her future importance became dramatically evident when heralds in Madrid plazas on March 29, 1830, startled people with the announcement of a royal Pragmatic Sanction providing the succession of Cristina's children to the throne even if they were female. Soon afterward the court made it known that the queen was pregnant, and in June the prospects of Don Carlos were doubly thwarted by Fernando's drawing up a will giving the crown to the unborn child. Ironically, no one prayed harder than the liberals that the tyrant king have an heir.

The question of the right of a woman to succeed to the Spanish throne, the question which to this day has split the Bourbon dynasty, has a complicated history but no definite answer. In medieval Castile daughters of kings without sons succeeded, rather than their uncles or male cousins, and this tradition was specifically acknowledged in the law code of Alfonso X in the thirteenth century. The accession of Isabel the Catholic in 1479 is a clear instance, and her daughter by Fernando V, Juana the Mad, was accepted in 1516 as queen in the Aragonese provinces as well.

In 1700 the first Bourbon came to the throne through both the principle of inheritance in the female line and the royal will of Carlos II naming his heir. Not until 1713 was the woman-excluding Salic Law extended to Spain by Felipe V, who was intent on pleasing a war-torn nation and Europe by ensuring that the Spanish throne could not be united with Bourbon France or Hapsburg Austria through the marriage of an infanta. Ironically, Felipe put into effect a French royal practice largely at the insistence of Britain, where reigning queens were a familiar tradition. The Salic Law was duly sanctioned by a Cortes, as was its abrogation in 1789 at the behest of Carlos IV. Why Carlos IV, with two living sons, reinstated female succession is something of a mystery. One explanation is that he was indulging in the old dream of the union of Spain and Portugal, which could occur if his daughter Carlota, potentially queen of the neighboring state, survived her brothers. Another conceivable factor was the king's aversion to the Neapolitan Bourbons and the possibility of their succeeding to the Spanish inheritance. It is also not clear why the Cortes action of 1789 was kept secret at the time. What was done by Fernando's Pragmatic Sanction of 1829 was simply to publicize the earlier action.

By protesting the Pragmatic Sanction, which Don Carlos and his successors have done insistently, these self-styled traditionalists have been opposing the more ancient usage of Spain in favor of the relative novelty of the Salic Law. The Carlist position, however, cannot be dismissed so easily as unreasonable. The king's brother argued that he was born in 1788 under the newer dispensation and that his given divine right of succession could not be taken away from him by the Cortes' action of a year later. He pleaded ignorance of the changed law until its publication in 1829, by which time it had surely lapsed, he argued. Averring his complete loyalty to the king and refusing to countenance any plotting in his own name, Don

Carlos publicly expressed his determination to assert his rights when the time came. His hopes to enlist support from the ultraconservative French King Charles X were abruptly ended by the July Revolution of 1830, which brought the Orléanist line of Louis Philippe onto the French throne and the principle of an elective rather than divine right monarchy into men's consciousness. (The supporters of the deposed Charles X and his descendants were henceforth known as the Legitimists in contrast with the Orléanists, who were also overthrown at a later juncture. Thus, two lines of French Bourbons existed.)

On October 10, 1830, about ten months from her wedding day, Queen Cristina gave birth. The king was foremost in the expectant assemblage in the antechamber of the lying-in room. When an attendant appeared with the baby on a silver platter, in accordance with age-old custom, Fernando could not restrain himself and hissed loudly, "What is it?" "A robust infanta, Your Majesty," was the reply. Fernando was visibly shaken, while his entourage had their private feelings of disappointment or relief. Three days later the *Gaceta* announced the royal intention to give the baby the title Princess of the Asturias, "in order that she may be accepted as the hereditary and legitimate successor to the throne, unless God should be pleased to grant me a male heir." The tiny heiress was duly christened María Isabel Luisa, with the preferred name Isabel linking her to Spain's greatest queen.

A few months later Queen Cristina was pregnant again and was delivered on January 30, 1832. Again hopes rose and fell with the coming of the Infanta Luisa into the world.

In the summer of 1832 the court moved as usual from Aranjuez to La Granja, although the humidity and high altitude of San Ildefonso were bad for the king's worsening health. His gout severely aggravated, Fernando suffered a seizure on the night of September 13–14, and his condition was so critical that he was given the last sacraments. The barracks at La Granja was considered pro-Carlist, and liberal businessmen in Madrid began to send their money out of the country. The queen, who tirelessly nursed her husband, summoned the leading minister Calomarde and asked his advice on how to avoid civil war. His first proposal, which the king accepted, was that Cristina be named regent and Don Carlos her chief counselor. Rather ingenuously the king's brother replied that his "lack of instruction and talent" prevented him from taking what would be a subordinate role to the queen's, and he also refused any secret deal involving a future marriage of his eldest son to the baby Isabel. On the night of September 17 the distraught queen was persuaded that Spain's only salvation lay in the repudiation of the Pragmatic Sanction. Her resistance was broken down by the insistent arguments of Calomarde, Doña Francisca, the king's confessor, the Bishop of León, and, surprisingly, the Neapolitan ambassador. The next day Calomarde convinced the king, the minister treacherously concealing evidence of public support for the queen, because he had secretly gone over to the Carlist party. Fernando signed the repudiation of his daughter's rights at 6 P.M., specifying that it be kept seal unbroken in the hands of the president of the Council of Castile until the time of the king's death.

These tense events took place in the absence of Doña Carlota, who was sojourning with her husband Don Francisco, on their estates near Seville. She might never have known of the king's secret disinheritance of her niece but for the fact that the Carlists could not keep quiet about their triumph. On hearing the news, the royal virago saw to it that her carriage made the 400-mile journey to La Granja in forty hours. She stormed into the palace cursing. Without any authority other than her terrifying personality Carlota summoned the president of the Council of Castile, took the king's repudiation from his hands, and tore up the document before his face—a dramatic legend that is not accepted by some historians. Next, she berated her sister the queen for her weakness and stupidity, summoning up such Neapolitan street terms as *Sciocca, Pazza,* and *regina de galleria.* Carlota's final victim was Calomarde, whom she reviled at length as mean and treacherous before giving him a resounding slap in the face. This slap too is considered a legend by some, but the last Bourbon, Alfonso XIII, used to take delight in showing visitors the corner of the desk at which it supposedly took place. Carlota's slap is also famous for Calomarde's gallant reply. The lowborn minister knew his manners and his classics when he murmured the title of a Calderón play, *"Los Manos Blancos No Ofenden."*

Whatever the myths, Fernando did indeed repudiate his repudiation. In a public statement on December 31 he revealed that there had been a "horrible plot" as "disloyal and deceiving men surrounded my bed" resulting in the "decree torn from me in the suffering of my illness." Calomarde was promptly sent into exile in the provinces, but fearing worse to come, he escaped across the frontier disguised as a monk.

Queen Cristina was named regent October 6 during the remainder of her husband's illness, and in the ensuing months Spain was once again treated to an abrupt swing of the political pendulum. The enlightened conservative Zea Bermúdez was recalled from the ambassadorship in London to replace Calomarde as prime minister. The government announced the reopening of the universities and freedom of the press, followed by an amnesty for some 10,000 prisoners and exiles. The seemingly progressive-minded queen was instantly the toast of liberal politicians and also of the capital's intellectual and artistic community, for she showed a lively interest in their activities, sponsoring Italian opera and lending her name to the foundation of a

Conservatory of Music. She gave a painting of "Cupid and Psyche" executed by her own hand to the Academy of San Fernando.

Even the callous and cynical king, after a seemingly miraculous recovery, was impressed with the signs of Cristina's popularity when he was able to make the return journey to Madrid that winter. The Carlists took another view of this political honeymoon since many of them lost their positions in the government and army or retired in ominous disgust as did the Bishop of León. Even some contemporary historians of the era comment darkly that not the queen but Doña Carlota and the Masonic lodges had become the real rulers of the country.

After the uncovering of conspiracies in favor of his brother in several cities, Fernando on March 16, 1833, "authorized" Don Carlos to accompany his sister-in-law the Princess of Beira back to Portugal, following her visit to Madrid for the occasion of the marriage of her son to a younger sister of Cristina. This announcement was in effect a command for Don Carlos to leave, and typically he obeyed. He was destined not to see Spain again for a year, Madrid never. The king, however, had made a mistake in sending his brother to a country where he had many supporters and, with a perverse historical coincidence, to a country where the drama of a reigning female being opposed on the battlefield by a legitimist uncle was already being acted out.

Precedent required that the title of a Prince of the Asturias be confirmed by a Cortes (Don Carlos never enjoyed the title, much less confirmation). Accordingly, King Fernando summoned a Cortes on June 20, 1833, the only Cortes of his reign he freely assented to, a traditional assemblage of privileged clerics, grandees, and burghers. It met at the Church of San Gerónimo and, like its predecessor of 1789, confirmed the abrogation of the Salic Law. Then the dignitaries personally swore allegiance to the Infanta Isabel as Princess of the Asturias. In her first public ceremonial the two-and-a-half-year-old infanta failed to appreciate the splendor of the occasion or the dignity of the hundreds of men who kissed her hand, and she cried a lot. Don Francisco led the number of grandees who swore; Don Carlos was the absent leader of those who refused and stayed away.

Relations between the newly fulfilled Fernando and the newly confounded Carlos continued at first to be cordial. The king wrote affectionately to Portugal asking his brother to explain his reasons for failing to swear to Isabel. The stilted but candid reply was that Don Carlos would not surrender "rights which God gave me when he willed my birth, and only God can take them away from me by granting you a son, which I much desire, possibly even more than you." Considering Carlos' presence in Portugal provocative, Fernando sent a message on May 6 that he was dispatching the warship *Loyalty* to convey his brother to the Papal States, which, he said, corresponded more to Carlos' predilections than strife-ridden Portugal. Carlos responded that he found Portugal peaceful; later he temporized, saying he would obey "my lord and king," but he ended up moving to the summer camp of the Portuguese pretender. Now Fernando wrote angrily of "cunning subterfuges."

Then, on September 29, 1833, King Fernando was dead of a violent fit of apoplexy. Coarse, but an astute political observer, the king had once commented: "Spain is a bottle of beer and I am the cork: when that comes out, all the liquid inside will escape, God knows in what direction." Like Louis XV's *"après moi le déluge,"* the prediction is remembered because it came true.

The official proclamation of the new ruler came a month after the king's death. The standard-bearer of the kingdom, the four kings at arms, grandees, generals, and lancers of the guard rode in colorful procession amid noisy crowds from the Ayuntamiento (town hall) to the Oriente Palace, where Queen Cristina appeared on the balcony with her child cradled in her arms. The senior king at arms unfurled the royal standard and then shouted, "Castile, Castile, Castile for Queen Doña Isabel II." Then he and his colleagues showered coins on the spectators.

A few months later the Duke of Wellington in London had occasion to comment on King Fernando's death to a friend. His words were: "To bequeath a civil war to one's country! One may love a woman very well but one should not quite incur a civil war for her sake. The fact is that when an old man falls in love with a young woman there is no saying what may be the consequences."

2. Doña Cristina Versus Don Carlos

The will of Fernando VII provided that his widow, Doña María Cristina, rule as regent for their two-year-old daughter. Twenty-seven years old, tall and curvaceous, the queen regent brought to her task beauty and vivacity, a limited intellect, common sense, a taste for pleasure combined with piety, and above all a stubborn determination to enjoy for herself and her children the full measure of royal material prerogatives, if not necessarily all royal political prerogatives. She had few confidants, losing eventually the support of her sister Doña Carlota, but all the while she had to cope with a dreary succession of ministers and generals acting in her name. With courage and resilience Cristina hung on as mistress of the royal palace for eight years and played a considerable role in Spain's affairs for that much longer.

The queen regent was fortunate in the critical beginning weeks for inheriting a picked set of loyal officials headed by the prime minister, Zea Bermúdez, a firm and incorruptible conservative. At his direction, her cautious first manifesto of October 4 declared: "I will maintain scrupulously the form and fundamental laws of the monarchy, admitting none of the dangerous innovations of which we already know the cost. The best form of government for a country is that to which it is accustomed." Franco could have avowed as much. There was no mention of a Cortes. A further amnesty was forthcoming, however, permitting liberal leaders of the 1820 era to return. These and younger leftist politicians were not going to be satisfied with Zea Bermúdez's enlightened despotism. The conservative banner having been preempted by Don Carlos, the queen regent was destined to become both the promoter and victim of liberalism.

At Coimbra in Portugal Don Carlos was informed by a Spanish official that Fernando was dead and that he should dutifully fulfill his brother's order to proceed to the Papal States. "Now I am the King," was Carlos' unhesitating reply. Grand or naïve, he acted as if his rights to the throne would not be questioned and in his first royal manifesto he confirmed Zea Bermúdez as *his* prime minister. If Carlos was reluctant to take precipitate action in his cause, his supporters were not. Six days after Fernando's death, October 3, the postmaster of Talavera in Castile, Manuel González rejected the orders he was receiving from Madrid and on his own authority proclaimed "Carlos V" the true ruler of Spain. This call happened to receive little local support, and González and his adherents were easily captured and executed. But elsewhere in Spain other manifestations for Don Carlos intensified into open revolt after the senior male Bourbon issued a call to arms on November 4. Don Carlos acted, never hastily, after he digested an October 17 decree of the Madrid regime declaring him an outlaw and his properties forfeit. So financially pressed was the pretender at this time in his wanderings about Portugal that his wife and sister-in-law were forced to sell their jewels. These haughty but determined ladies set the type for his manifestos with their own hands and did their own cooking. The pretender hoped that a personal appearance might win over the Spanish army stationed at the frontier, but its commander, although personally sympathetic, warned Don Carlos that he would be seized by the troops who were loyal to the queen regent. The same commander later tried to capture Don Carlos in a raid across the Portuguese border. He failed, but he was able to boast that Don Carlos' precipitate escape had left him without a change of linen.

While the would-be Spanish Bolingbroke remained in Portugal, his partisans went wild in Spain. The right-wing *guerrillero* the priest Merino, whom the left-wing *guerrillero* Mina had chased about in 1821, emerged to lead a Carlist army at Logroño, on the border of Castile and the northern provinces. The three Basque provinces by vote of their traditional parliaments went Carlist, as did Navarre. What really gave potency to the movement, however, was the leadership of a Basque *guerrillero* of tested fame, Tomás Zumalacárregui.

During the Napoleonic Wars Zumalacárregui had risen from cadet to captain. For leading royalist volunteers in 1823 he was rewarded with the governorship of El Ferrol, but later he was forced to relinquish his post for being a reactionary. This decidedly old-school man was elected commander in chief of the Navarre Carlists in October, 1833, and, when disunified command proved costly, his leadership was accepted by the three Basque provinces as well. In three months time Zumalacárregui put together a sternly disciplined and surprisingly well-equipped army of 8,000 men; in a year he commanded 35,000. An opponent in admiration of Zumalacárregui's training abilities once said, "That man could make soldiers of trees if he had no other materials." The Carlist commander saw to the regular financing of his force by levying taxes in the name of "Carlos V," by confiscating the goods of liberals, by collecting customs at the French frontier, and by soliciting contributions throughout Europe from sympathetic kings and known conservatives. The bullnecked, taciturn Zumalacárregui was soon known to readers of illustrated journals all over the world, pictured always wearing the goatskin cloak and red beret of the ordinary peasants who served Carlism, often on the strength of their faith in "Uncle Tómas."

The First Carlist War, which lasted six years, was a civil war fought ostensibly over the question of female succession but fought actually over conservative versus liberal ideology, with an added element of sectional conflict. The juridical question of the validity of the Salic Law or of the Pragmatic Sanction was really a pretext, masking the basic cleavage of Spaniards into believers in absolutism and believers in constitutionalism. The civil war was a renewal of the dramatic clashes of 1814 and 1820. Nor did the personalities matter. In the words of a Spanish historian: "If Don Carlos had embraced the principle of revolution and Doña María Cristina those of pure monarchical tradition, the liberals would have invoked the *legitimidad agnaticia* of the Bourbons and in the mountains of Navarre they would have defended—and not for the first time—the right of succession of women."

The ideological issues are well stated by the historian Gabriel Jackson:

> Underlying the dynastic quarrel was the deeper question of the role of the Spanish monarchy. Should it welcome the growth of capitalism, centralize and standardize its governing methods, permit a certain degree of liberty of the press and the universities, and avail

itself of the accumulated wealth of the Church—all of which things had occurred in France? Or should the monarchy reaffirm the exclusively Catholic, predominantly agrarian and decentralized character of traditional Spain.

In general terms, the Cristinos, as supporters of the queen regent came to be called, embraced most city people, most townspeople, the business community, the intellectuals, the liberals, the radicals, the anticlericals, the Freemasons, and the majority of the officers of the regular army. The influence in the enemy camp of Freemason politicians and generals was exaggerated by the Carlists, who in contrast enjoyed the open or secret loyalty of virtually all the regular and secular clergy. Otherwise, the Carlists included some army officers, a generous sprinkling of aristocrats, and in terms of numbers many yeoman peasants from the north. The Carlists were to be castigated as being "comprised entirely of thieves and assassins," by George Borrow, the English Bible salesman whose memoirs of his Spanish travels in this era are as fascinating as they are prejudiced. Borrow's extreme judgment has some foundation in fact in that many seedy adventurers, robbers, and smugglers found Carlist military activity to their convenience. ("It is a Carlist invention that a pure bandit can claim for himself the name of *guerrillero,*" wrote Karl Marx.) Even the conservative Sir Charles Petrie admits that the Carlists "attracted to their colors both the best and the worst elements in the population."

In the course of the war Carlist forces traversed every province of Spain, but they held no area for longer than a few weeks except the Basque provinces and Navarre. Here the Carlists drew on the sectionalist feelings of the agrarian population, their attachment to their special parliaments, their tax privileges, and their other centuries-old *fueros.* To this day much of Carlism is fear and resentment on the part of non-Castilians of the centralizing tendencies of the civil and military authorities in Madrid. Accordingly, in geographical terms the Carlist War represented a kind of secession of the fifth of Spain lying north of the Ebro. The social-ideological dimension of the struggle, however, dictated that Cristino forces remained in isolated control of Bilbao, San Sebastián, Pamplona, and most of the other urban concentrations in the area.

The first months of the fighting were desultory. A Cristino column had to battle all the way to join up with the defenders of Bilbao. General Zumalacárregui was eventually driven back into the mountain valleys of Navarre, where his men knew every footpath and could count on succor at every outlying farm. Avoiding pitched battles, the Carlist forces had a maddening capacity to melt away into thin air; the men went home "to change their shirts" only to reassemble with lightning discipline where least expected. The government's effort to blockade the enemy with lines of forts also failed to deter Zumalacárregui from raiding where he chose. The Cristino commander in frustration turned to terror tactics, threatening death to all Carlists caught with arms and dire treatment of their sympathizers, including women. For their part the Carlists were known for such atrocities as capturing and torturing the members of town councils so as to gain funds and information. "No-quarter" battles became the rule, both sides shooting all prisoners as well as the wounded.

The brutal fighting in the north had been going on for only three months when Madrid society had something more titillating to talk about, the queen regent's special relationship with a Agustín Fernando Muñoz y Sánchez, a former corporal of the guard who suddenly boasted the unusual title of gentleman of the royal bedchamber. The attachment probably began soon after King Fernando's death, although some claim before. According to one story, Muñoz first came to Cristina's attention when her carriage had an accident during a winter journey to La Granja over the Guadarrama Pass. The royal vehicle skidded into a farm wagon, and Cristina's arm was cut by broken glass. Muñoz bandaged the wound with his handkerchief. Another version has him romantically kissing her own bloody discard. Within a few days during a stroll in the palace park the Queen Regent managed to dismiss all her attendants except Muñoz and promptly declared her love for him. It was not surprising that the hot-blooded, lighthearted widow wanted to have an affair, but it was startling that she chose to marry her lover secretly two days after Christmas that same year of 1833. There was difficulty finding a discreet priest. One claim is that the papal nuncio gave special powers to Muñoz's village curate. A counter story is that one of Muñoz's friends officiated, having no other status than being the possessor of a hunting license. The four witnesses to the ceremony were sent away from the capital afterward.

It was no mystery why the young sensual Cristina would be attracted to Muñoz, an Andalusian of exceeding handsomeness. His features were truly classical, his pale complexion in striking contrast with his dark mustache, arched eyebrows, and full hair. Particularly exciting were Muñoz's large, dark, languid eyes. He was broad-shouldered, tall, and slim, in sum "a very noble looking man," in the view of the American traveler Alexander Slidell Mackenzie. The corporal's background was more modest than noble, his father of hidalgo lineage having been reduced to running a tobacco shop. Unlike that other royal favorite of recent memory, Godoy, the new husband of the queen regent gave himself few airs and, outside the bedroom, always appeared to defer to Cristina in the manner of a humble subject, calling her *mi ama* (my mistress). Muñoz also was wiser than Godoy in eschewing any political role, although his business speculations on the basis of tips from ministers of finance were eventually to prove embarrassing for the dynasty.

Courtiers started calling Muñoz "Fernando VIII" behind his back when they noticed that he was wearing the late king's tiepins, and Madrileños generally observed that the man was Cristina's inseparable companion on her carriage rides. The press was forbidden to mention any relationship. As for why Cristina chose to marry rather than just keep a paramour as her mother and grandmother had done, this was explained by her sincere attachment to the teachings of the church. The marriage was not publicly avowed for eleven years, however, because the convolutions of male supremacist feeling and monarchical convention would have forced Cristina to cease being regent and guardian of her children if she owned to having a husband. Yet the union was an open secret. The Carlists thundered about deposing the "royal whore," while the liberals used their knowledge to blackmail Cristina into accepting even policies that offended her piety.

Madrid politicians and the generals alike agreed that little spirit could be aroused for the war against Don Carlos if the lovelorn queen regent continued the semi-absolutist ministry of Zea Bermúdez. In January, 1834, Cristina consented to replace him with Francisco Martínez de la Rosa, the *Moderado* "jailbird" whom Fernando was forced to put up with as prime minister in 1822. Martínez captured popular interest by promising a Cortes, and on April 10, 1834, the regime promulgated an Estatuto Real detailing the constitutional arrangements. It fell decidedly short of the document of 1812 by making no mention of popular sovereignty. Instead of a single Cortes, there was to be a bicameral legislature, with a House of Notables— aristocratic, clerical, or royally nominated—as a conservative counterweight to a House of Proctors, elected indirectly on the basis of property qualifications. The lower house had no power over the ministry, its own dissolution, or what subjects it could discuss. The new Constitution was recognized as a weak copy of the charter Louis XVIII gave France in 1814. Imitating the French was also a criticism of the hit play written by the versatile prime minister, *La Conjuración de Venecia*, which opened five days later in a Madrid theater. The artistic sensibilities of Martínez further found expression in the loving specifics he composed regarding the costumes of members of the House of Notables—"ducal mantle, broad sleeves of turquoise velvet, tunic of gold with lace cuffs reaching well below the knee, white silk stockings."

It was, indeed, the "Romantic" age of poet-politician, but the liberals were not lulled into any complacency. Just as in 1820, the politicians split into two groups, which now emerged under the names of *Moderados* and *Progresistas*. The latter radicals wanted nothing less than the Constitution of 1812, being unsatisfied, in the words of a satirist, with "Chambers mildly representative, Tyrants tinged with democracy." Nor could the Estatuto Real please the Carlists, who believed in no constitution at all.

Before *Moderados* and *Progresistas* could probe their animosities, there were new developments in the Carlist War, developments of international scope. Embracing the general cause of constitutionalism, a Quadruple Alliance of Britain, France, Spain, and Portugal came into being on April 22, 1834: its aim was to expel the two pretenders on the Iberian Peninsula, Dom Miguel and Don Carlos. For their part the British pledged to blockade the Carlist coast on the Bay of Biscay and later took extraordinary legal action to allow the radical Anglo-Irishman George de Lacy Evans to recruit a foreign legion to fight in Spain. As for France, whose representative for the signing of the alliance happened to be the eighty-year-old Talleyrand, its promises to keep supplies to the Carlists from crossing the French frontier would have been a decisive contribution to their defeat, but the execution of this policy was haphazard to the point of being farcical. The Quadruple Alliance enjoyed the moral support of the United States and the Scandinavian countries, while the eastern autocracies sympathized strongly but unhelpfully with Don Carlos. Lord Palmerston, the British foreign secretary, had written: "I should like to see Metternich's face when he reads our treaty." The leader of the Holy Alliance duly reacted in writing, altogether humorlessly, that the Spain of the three-year-old Isabel II was "revolution incarnate in its most dangerous form." The Italian states, including the Naples of the queen regent's brother, agreed with Metternich, in particular opposing the principle of female succession. The Netherlands was concerned with Don Carlos' selling them the Philippines.

Interestingly, the five Rothschild brothers were initially divided in their Spanish policies. Nathan in London afforded the Cristino government a loan, while Salomon in Vienna and James in Weimar sought not to antagonize Metternich. In the end, the members of the House of Rothschild emerged in control of the Almadén mercury mines and, to prove their neutrality, engineered at great profit to themselves a drastic fall of Spanish bonds on the stock exchange.

While the British government was the main prop of the Quadruple Alliance and hundreds of Englishmen fought for Queen Cristina, some private individuals of conservative convictions fought on the other side, one of the bizarre instances being a young Irish aristocrat who used his yacht to seize Málaga briefly in the name of Don Carlos (this zeal helped make him Bishop of Dublin later on but had the opposite effect when he was considered for Archbishop of Canterbury).

Queen Maria's Portuguese armies were heartened by the Quadruple Alliance to corner Dom Miguel and force him to recognize his niece and agree to his perpetual banishment in return for a pension. At this juncture Don Carlos might have battled his way into Spain with several hundred of his supporters and whatever Portuguese legitimists cared to join the fighting there, but he took the circuitous route via England, arriving on a British warship at Portsmouth June 16. Accompanying him were his wife, their three sons, and his sister-in-law and future wife, the Princess of Beira, and her family. He was immediately confronted by a British foreign officer, who presented the pretender with a convention of capitulation and a promise of a far more lavish bounty than Dom Miguel's. "Carlos V" huffily refused to cede what he considered his God-given rights or to restrain his adherents. When the Spanish ambassador sought an interview, Don Carlos demurred with the words "I have no ambassador at the Court of London." The embarrassed and divided British government accorded its royal guest some honors, but when he engaged a house in London, he was closely watched, virtually quarantined.

The British police were taken in by a subterfuge of their august guest. Don Carlos dyed his hair and shaved his mustache, his friends supplied forged Mexican papers, and the pretender made the Channel crossing to Dieppe on July 2. Leaving Paris, Don Carlos was so well disguised that when he stared out of his carriage at his cousin Louis Philippe, the French king merely bowed in gracious appreciation. The French police turned out to be not so innocent, not only in this Carlist escapade but in similar ones over the next few decades. With their certain connivance and with the help of French legitimists Don Carlos made his way to the Spanish frontier, which he crossed on July 9. He had left the country as the king's brother; he returned as the claimant of his niece's throne.

Once arrived at the frontier village of Elizondo, Don Carlos proceeded to act the king in every conceivable way. He appointed Zumalacárregui lieutenant general and commander in chief of his forces. He named a ministry and conferred honors and titles on a whole coterie of court officials. Soon afterward the "royal capital" was moved to Oñate, a pleasant provincial town where as much ceremonial as possible was carried on in its one mansion, its commodious cathedral, and its ample plaza, where, for example, a military band played patriotic songs and operatic pieces when Carlos took his dinner. Missing from the scene was Don Carlos' truly regal and forceful wife, Doña Francisca, whose ill health compelled her to remain in England. She died soon afterward in September, 1834. That month Don Carlos happened to be in Guernica to swear to the *fueros* of the Basque provinces at the site of a historic oak tree.

The presence of their absolutist monarch in their midst produced a high pitch of enthusiasm in the Basque and Navarrese villages which celebrated with Te Deums, fiestas, and military reviews. Some foreign observers were not so impressed with the royal newcomer. One wrote that he was "disgusted" with Don Carlos' pretensions and unrealistic behavior, which included such bizarre whimsies as insisting that an altar be erected in the line of fire during a battle. The pretender himself avoided military action. The ever-critical George Borrow characterized Don Carlos' whole perform-ance as "imbecility, cowardice, and cruelty." Yet "Carlos V" seemed secure in his dignity and popular appeal, even if, when Cristino forces got too close, he had to be conveyed about the mountain fastnesses on the famous surefooted *el burro del rey*.

The people of Madrid reacted with alarm to Don Carlos' rumored successes in the north and with hysteria to the presently raging cholera epidemic. The priests of the capital declared that the plague was God's visitation for the errors of liberalism, while the anticlericals maintained that the clergy were poisoning the wells to prove their point. The result on July 17, 1834—which just as well might have been July 17, 1934—was a mob descent on Madrid's religious establishments and the murder of a few score priests. There followed the execution of one person for theft, but none of the ringleaders of the violence was punished. The message the Carlists chose to receive was that queen and constitution spelled the eventual wiping out of the faith.

A week later the Cortes provided for in the Estatuto Real had its first sitting. Many of its members were uncertain of their politics, but all were convinced of the need to ask the ministry embarrassing questions about its war policies and its economic intentions. The delegates had also been witness to the obligatory public appearance of the queen regent at the opening ceremonies. Despite a profusion of petticoats, Cristina was obviously pregnant. That spring and fall Cristina moved restlessly from one to another of the royal palaces outside the capital, avoiding being seen as much as avoiding the cholera. Eventually, after she had gone into complete seclusion at El Pardo, she gave birth to a daughter November 17. That night her and Muñoz's baby was carried off discreetly from the palace in a closed carriage, to be taken care of by the widow of a court functionary living in Segovia. Later, when the court was in residence at La Granja to enjoy the hunting, Cristina and Muñoz would nightly journey to Quitanares, where the nurse brought the infant. People remarked upon the lavish appoint-ments of the nurse and the guards on the roads. Almost exactly a year later the queen regent had a second daughter.

The Carlist War was at a stalemate by the end of 1834. North of the Ebro River the Cristinos managed to hold onto only Bilbao, San Sebastián, and Pamplona. With the one side frustratingly unable to subdue the countryside and the other helplessly unequipped to capture cities, the level of mutual cruelty intensified to the point of becoming an international scandal. The

British government sent its representative, Edward Granville Eliot to negotiate with both camps, and the ensuing Eliot Convention of April 27, 1835, pledged the generals to respect at least hospitals and prisoners. These negotiations produced an uproar in the Cortes, where the *Progresistas* accused the *Moderado* government of using Eliot to reach some general accommodation with the Carlists. They also expressed fears that the Martínez de la Rosa ministry was seeking an alliance with France, whose troops, ostensibly to be used against the Carlists, might repeat the counterrevolutionary invasion of 1823. The ministry lost a vote of confidence, and the whole stormy session ended with the queen regent's proroguing the Cortes on May 29. Martínez resigned a week later, and another liberal with credentials from a bygone era was made prime minister with the thankless task of placating the radicals in Madrid while fighting the reactionaries in the north. The government put the nation even more hopelessly in debt; Spanish bonds sold for a fraction of par on the Paris and London markets.

The completeness of the military deadlock was revealed in the summer of 1835 at great cost to both sides. General Baldomero Espartero, the commander of Bilbao, tried to break out and resume land contact with the main Madrid armies. He was thrown back with a loss of 2,000 troops. Spurred by this victory, the Carlists decided to abandon their successful guerrilla tactics and to attempt a conventional military siege of Bilbao. The motivation of the Carlist council was financial and political: they needed Spain's third largest seaport to impress the international money market and to gain for themselves recognition as genuine belligerents by Austria, Prussia, and Russia. General Zumalacárregui was opposed to the strategy, having already resigned once as Carlist commander in chief in protest over the unmilitary sychophants and incompetents who increasingly seemed to have Don Carlos' ear. He was commanded to do his duty and lead the attack on Bilbao, although his forces could muster only eight antique cannon against Espartero's forty pieces of artillery. In the course of bitter fighting, Zumalacárregui was struck in the leg by a stray bullet, an incompetent doctor let the wound become infected, and suddenly the best of the Carlist leaders was dead. Don Carlos was not fully aware of the seriousness of this event. To a historian using hindsight "it was the turning point of the Carlist fortunes; with Zumalacárregui all unity of plan and authority were lost." Yet the Carlists enjoyed other highpoints, while several times the Madrid regime appeared on the brink of collapse.

The Carlists were forced to abandon the siege of Bilbao on June 24. During their retreat they were caught up with and severely defeated by the main Cristino army at Mendigorría July 16. In the midst of the most intense fighting that day, which cost the Carlists 2,000 men, Don Carlos was observed sitting quietly in the village munching on a loaf of bread. He barely escaped the scene a few hours later. It was the first major Cristino victory, but it was not followed up.

3. The First Defeat of the Carlists

Throughout 1835, the year in which Don Carlos turned fifty, the stiff-necked Spanish-born grandson of Carlos III was compelled to make the best of a poky itinerant court in the wilds of Navarre. Not yet thirty, Doña Cristina, Neapolitan-born, the widow of a king, and the wife of a corporal, presided grandly over the Oriente Palace, La Granja, and Aranjuez. These Bourbon protagonists occasionally negotiated with each other in secret, all the while their supporters fought to the death. Both were symbols more than leaders and were frequently at the mercy of factions within their own parties.

"Strange infatuation when men will spill their blood and money for so miserable an object." British observers were generally critical of the haughty, obstinate, yet uninspiring man who styled himself Carlos V. One castigated the pretender as "an imbecile with whom nothing was to be done, bigoted and perverse, and in the hands of men as narrow-minded as himself, a coward too, and without a spark of energy and talent." Such opinions were conditioned by the political prejudices of the writers. Yet the Duke of Wellington, no disparager of kings or conservatism, once spoke of "a sort of cretinism" in the case of Don Carlos and another time dismissed him "as one of the silliest devils I ever knew." The onetime liberator of Spain was convinced that Don Carlos' character prevented his cause from winning. Liberal historians, to whom Carlism seems an unviable proposition, are nonetheless amazed that so many fought so fiercely in its name, regardless of the leader in question. A parallel exists between Carlism and Jacobinism in eighteenth-century Britain: the Stuart pretenders seemed feckless as leaders compared to the dedication of their followers.

A visit to Don Carlos' remote court was a must for curious foreign travelers in Spain in the 1830's, and not all of them found him a villain. One Englishman conceded that "his dark eyes gave expression to his face; and the sweetness of his voice and the gentleness of his manners surprised you into loving him, whatever were your opinions of his political rights." Other foreigners were impressed with the would-be king's candor and honesty. His Spanish supporters, of course, found Don Carlos' dignity, reserve, and taste for ceremony truly regal, and his ostentatious piety entranced churchmen.

Never comfortable in a uniform, Don Carlos would happily have left military matters altogether to others—call this cowardice or a wise assessment of his own talents. Yet he was the ultimate voice of decision in the war making, and he hurt his cause badly by his irresolution and his inability to judge men. The pretender's indecisiveness was proverbial. After hours of argument in council for this or that action he would break discussion off with *vemos* (we will see). Several historians have noted that each of Don Carlos' formidable two wives were the "true masculine types" in the branch of the dynasty which denied female rights. Unfortunately, Don Carlos was a widower in the critical years 1834–1838. As for advisers, Don Carlos all too readily listened to pretentious aristocrats and sanctimonious priests who often disparaged his most successful generals for being too rough-and-ready. Perhaps the best measure of Don Carlos' willingness to listen to crazed and impractical fanatics was his decree of August, 1835, naming Our Lady of the Sorrows generalissimo of his armies.

The Isabel II whose title "Carlos V" contested was still an unknown quantity as a toddler of five, but her mother, Cristina, was a determined, full-blooded woman who stirred men's hearts, even if she could not control their actions in behalf of her cause. Eventually the cares of her office took some toll of the queen regent's looks, but she remained a beautiful woman—chestnut hair, white skin, rosy cheeks, a nicely curved mouth, and ears so exquisite as to provoke Slidell Mackenzie to remark on this feature of a woman's body for the first time in his life. Unlike her sisters, Cristina did not let herself get too fat, just pleasingly fleshy. At a palace ball in the 1830's Cristina was described as "very handsome and beaming with goodness as she always does." A less flattering view conceded that the Neapolitan princess "has acquired gravity and self-possession" but added "there is nothing about her to suggest a royal personage."

A gracious hostess and an addict of the polka, Cristina was also a wife and a mother. It is going too far to call her "a perfect wife and a good mother," the view of one biographer of her daughter. Certainly, Cristina's relationship with her husband Muñoz was essentially a noble one in spirit. She craved a kind of moral sanctity, together with bourgeois respectability and homey pleasures, while she had to keep their private life secret and to treat him as a servant in public. There were rumors of Cristina's having affairs with handsome new men she encountered, but the fact is she stayed with the imperturbable and understanding Andalusian the rest of her life. An English diarist, explaining Muñoz's place in his wife's affections, wrote that "as he never attempted to check a passing indiscretion, he always remained master of the field." The queen regent's imposing older sister, Doña Carlota, was offended by Muñoz's humble origins and tried to create a scandal where there was none, going so far as to propose that she herself should replace Cristina as regent and guardian. The growing enmity led to the removal of Carlota and her husband to France.

As for Cristina's suitability as a mother, Queen Victoria once wrote that her contemporary "wasted her time in frivolous amusements and neglected her children sadly," referring to the child queen as "poor little Isabel." Other evidence suggests that the regent was full of devotion and concern for her children, both royal and common, but was too indulgent of them, so that Isabel did indeed grow up to be spoiled and capricious to an extreme.

Cristina's strong inclination to relax with her husband and children led her to prefer living in the outlying palaces, and this fact weakened her influence on affairs in Madrid. The regent was destined to reign more than she ruled, a well-intentioned but limited woman who enjoyed being bowed to in public and endured being browbeaten in council.

With no end of the war in sight, with anarchy sweeping the cities away from the front, and with the mood of the Cortes increasingly critical, the queen regent had no choice but to approve the formation of a truly radical ministry on September 15, 1835. It was headed by the supremely self-confident Juan Álvarez Mendizábal, whose Basque name was taken by some to be Jewish. A business speculator and financial wizard, Mendizábal had spent many years in London as an exile and later as ambassador, becoming so English-minded that he was dubbed "John and a half." With mesmeric oratory, the new prime minister promised all things to all men, including being able to defeat the Carlists without imposing new taxes or invoking French intervention. A measure toward accomplishing this was the institution of obligatory military service for all between eighteen and forty: 100,000 men were added to the army and funds also came to the treasury, thanks to a typically "liberal" provision that men of property could buy exemption from service.

Mendizábal also spoke confidently of settling church-state difficulties but soon revealed his intention of making the Catholic Establishment not a beneficiary but the main victim of his policies. In the government's extreme financial plight the wealth of the church was a tempting prize and anticlericalism an easy way of stirring popular support. The first step was to expel the Jesuits for the third and final time, confiscating their properties. Eventually Mendizábal was emboldened to order the expropriation of all religious orders except those involved in teaching, nursing, and missionary activity. These official measures provoked a considerable unofficial echo in the way of mobs desecrating churches and lynching priests, to the horror of the queen regent and the law-minded. Yet for all that respectable people might decry attacks on the church, these same people profited the most from the sale of church lands and properties. Thousands of provincial landowners and members of the middle class in the capital and elsewhere became inalterably committed to supporting a liberal regime, as against a Carlist or even a conservative government, because of their involvement in these land purchases. Mendizábal's financial expedients produced one of the major economic revolutions of modern Spanish history in terms of the amount of property exchanging hands. For the prime minister, steeped in British liberal economics, his policy was conceived of not only as short-term money raising but also as a long-term effort to involve large groups of Spaniards in the untraditional pursuit of moneymaking. Nor was church property the only target; this revolution by statute saw laws permitting the sale of the common lands of the villages and the breaking up of entailed estates. Two major criticisms can be made of these laws. The poor, as well as the small peasants, benefited not at all from the land sales; such was the level of social consciousness among even radicals of this day that only one member of the Cortes suggested that they should. And the government budget benefited far less than did the speculators; within a year official Spain was just as broke as before.

The fourth year of the Carlist War brought little change except an escalation of atrocities. In Aragón a heightened amount of guerrilla activity occurred in association with the rise to prominence of the Carlist leader Ramón Cabrera, an ex-seminarist who before he was thirty became a master of surprise tactics and also a systematic practitioner of terror. Stories were soon appearing in the Madrid press of the "Tiger of the Maestrazgo" and his cruelty—his taking hostages, his holding villages for ransom, and his using prisoners for bayonet and lance practice, including even Cristino soldiers who were duped into enlisting on his side. As reprisal, the Cristino General Nogueras in February, 1836, had Cabrera's mother executed without even the family and religious amenities accorded a common criminal. He claimed, unjustifiably, that the woman was involved in a plot to seize the city of Tortosa, and far from being ashamed of his deed, Nogueras publicly promised to shoot Cabrera's sisters in due course and to kill five relations of Carlist soldiers for every Cristino prisoner who was a victim of Cabrera. The Carlist general replied by having four innocents shot, including a nineteen-year-old girl who was so obviously in love with her captor, the Carlist leader, that the news of their marriage was more anticipated than that of her death. According to one estimate, Cabrera was directly responsible for 180 cold-blooded killings before his mother's execution and 730 afterward. His subordinates, who merited less publicity, were guilty of even more outrages, and certain Carlist bands, subject to no discipline and little more than outlaws, were the most vicious. The government's record was hardly better: after mobs were stirred up by false rumors in Barcelona, the authorities did not prevent them from massacring all the Carlists in the city's prisons, 107 men.

When the Cortes met in March, 1836, they were already aroused by Mendizábal's dictatorial ways and unkept promises of victory. In April the prime minister had to fight a duel with a former associate who had accused him of malversation in office. A month later he was removed from his position by the queen regent who was tired of his insulting manner of treating her (he once felt her bodice to see if she was pregnant), distressed by his anticlerical laws, and alarmed by his attempts to discredit the conservative generals who were the mainstays of her power. When a new prime minister also could not deal with the fractious Cortes, Cristina consented to its dissolution in May. *Progresistas* started riots all over Spain.

A telling measure of the nearly complete breakdown of the Spanish government by the summer of 1836 was the accomplishment of the Carlist General Miguel Gómez in leading a force of 2,700 men on a six-month foray that took them 2,500 miles north, west, and south of Madrid. At one time he took Santiago; later he held Córdoba. The Cristino generals appeared incapable of halting this wild adventure, even though Gómez marched with a wagon train containing the booty of a score of provinces. Eventually General Ramón Narváez caught up with the Carlist force, but a mutiny in his own army prevented him from annihilating it, and General Gómez regained the Carlist lines with more men than he had had at the start. Yet such irrational intrigue prevailed in Don Carlos' camp that Gómez was soon after arrested for not doing more.

The news of such Carlist successes produced a revolution from the left. Radical juntas sprang up in the major cities, just as in 1820. Queen Cristina and the court were at La Granja, where the local garrison soon caught the revolutionary fervor. The ensuing events of the night of August 12 have been pictured by radicals as heroic scenes of citizen soldiers debating constitutions and singing the "Hymn of Riego" as they marched on the royal apartments. Conservative detractors of the same incident say that the soldiers were drunk, that each man had received two ounces of gold from the Masons, and that their officers had conveniently absented themselves in the capital ostensibly to see a new production of Donizetti. In any case, a delegation of soldiers headed by a Sergeant Gómez forced the queen regent to grant them an interview. Three hours of heated discussion followed with the sergeant matching wits with the ex-corporal's wife on such subjects as the meaning of liberty. The soldiers outside became more menacing and raucous, making some choice comments about Cristina's love life, and in the end the queen regent, weary but admirably self-controlled, as well as realistic, signed a three-line decree putting the Constitution of 1812 into effect for the third time. George Borrow reported that the soldiers had already bound, gagged, and leveled guns at Muñoz, and the British ambassador wrote that if Cristina had not signed, "she and her children would have been massacred beyond a doubt." Uncomprehending that there were limitations to her sanctity, the six-year-old Queen Isabel was to cry out, "Mama, why don't you shoot the cannon?"

After vainly offering bribes to the mutineers at La Granja and then rejecting a show of force as too dangerous for the royal ladies there, the ministry in Madrid confirmed officially the queen regent's concessions. The royal family had the degrading experience of being escorted back to the capital by their captors. Muñoz later returned more discreetly and ceased to appear with Cristina in public.

In retrospect, the period immediately after the August Revolution of 1836 seemed the best opportunity for Don Carlos to take over Spain, not so much by military conquest as by political persuasion. Humiliated and angry at the politicians, the queen regent asked her brother Ferdinand II of the Two Sicilies to mediate the dynastic quarrel, again proposing the solution of a marriage of Isabel II with Don Carlos' son. The pretender stubbornly would not negotiate until the legitimacy of his own title was acknowledged. Meanwhile, in Madrid a new radical ministry resumed actions against the church, menaced the rich in general, and suspended payment of the external debt. The *Progresistas* controlling the Cortes threatened to proscribe all *Moderados*, many of whom had already fled the country. Here was Don Carlos' chance to rally moderate as well as conservative elements of Spanish society and perhaps even to gain the support of the British and French, but the pretender refused to be conciliatory and continued to insist on ruling the country on his own autocratic and clerical terms. When the Madrid radicals came up with a surprisingly unradical Constitution on April 27, 1837—a compromise between the doctrinaire document of 1812 and the royalist grant of 1834—the *Moderados* were won back to the anti-Carlist side.

Having thrown away better political and military chances the year before, Don Carlos in the spring of 1837 decided to issue the call for a great invasion beyond the Ebro to Madrid. "Success is not in doubt," he proclaimed, "just one effort and Spain is free." The Carlists assembled a force of 12,000 infantry and 1,700 cavalry under the command of the pretender's nephew, the twenty-seven-year-old Don Sebastián. He defeated the Cristinos handily in two battles in June and joined up near Tortosa with the guerrilla army of Cabrera, who, as the Carlists' one really successful commander, should have been given supreme command but was not. The "royal expedition" south was more than a military campaign; it was an expedition of Don Carlos with his whole entourage, expectant court officials, foreign ambassadors and observers, and most prominently great numbers of discontented clergy who were "like the people of Israel on the march to the promised land." On August 9 the Carlists captured La Granja. On September 12 Don Carlos was at Arganda, just ten miles from Madrid, while Cabrera's troops actually attacked the capital's Retiro Gardens. The queen regent could hear the guns and watched skirmishing through a telescope from the roof of the Oriente Palace.

The pretender made plans for a general levee to be held in his honor in Madrid on September 13 and issued a pompous manifesto to the citizens declaring that "the hour has come when the conquering arm of the invincible Don Carlos would break the yoke of a handful of ambitious cowards steeped in the most horrible crimes." Belatedly, he promised that "the Prince of the Asturias [his son] will occupy the throne of Spain which his father cedes to him; the daughter of Ferdinand VII will be his wife; and the august widow will return to Italy to enjoy that which is hers by right." The gates of Madrid remained shut, however, and there was not the hoped-for rising by a Carlist fifth column (an anachronistic term but an appropriate one, for Franco's associate, General Emilio Mola, used it in the same circumstances almost exactly 100 years later). The queen regent, now opposed to any compromise with her brother-in-law, knew that Espartero's army, hurrying to her aid, would fight loyally. When Don Sebastián and Cabrera both urged storming the walls, Don Carlos remained ensconced in prayer. He had a genuine horror of bloodshed. Finally, he ordered the drums to roll, not in advance but in retirement, after he had spent one day in sight of Madrid. The retreat became something of a rout with only 4,000 Carlists recrossing the Ebro on October 24.

Following his defeat before Madrid, Don Carlos listened to the worst of his advisers and imprisoned the best of his generals on charges of treason. Then a series of defeats led him to reverse himself and to restore to command some of the disgraced men, notably the relatively liberal General Rafael Maroto. The change in Don Carlos' mood may have been less conviction than preoccupation with connubial matters, for in October, 1838, he remarried, his bride being the Princess of Beira, his sister-in-law and the mother of Don Sebastián. She had arrived via France at the little court, which was now in Estella, and the strong-mindedness of this second Carlist queen brought a momentary burst of enthusiasm for the cause, succeeded unfortunately by a renewed play of factions.

While the Carlists floundered, the Cristinos also gave themselves over to internal dissensions, the power struggle of politicians in Madrid now being succeeded by a rivalry of generals. General Espartero, although associated with the radicals, gained further prestige for his drastic measures to restore discipline in the army of the north (he once waited three months to surround and decimate by lot a unit that had murdered its own commander). Espartero's greatest rival and later the darling of the conservatives was General Narváez, another war hero who had recently trained a new army in the south-center. It became a question of which commander got more funds and more attention. A series of pronunciamientos and counterpronunciamientos by the two convulsed the country throughout the fall of 1837, with Narváez losing out eventually and fleeing.

The end of the First Carlist War came about after Espartero, now all-powerful, opened negotiations with his former comrade-in-arms Maroto, ostensibly over an exchange of prisoners but actually over all issues. The Carlist general was also forced to counter enemies in his own camp, on one occasion having four recalcitrant generals shot in the back and on another browbeating Don Carlos himself. Maroto did not succeed in getting the pretender to take a more conciliatory political stance, and he drew only a benign smile when he suggested that the northern provinces were too exhausted to go on fighting. The news that Maroto was negotiating with Espartero on his own produced one more tragicomic incident, Don Carlos personally haranguing his assembled battalions and getting not so much as one cheer. A last-minute plot to seize and execute Maroto failed. On August 31 Maroto and his staff rode into Espartero's camp at Vergara, where the two generals embraced each other theatrically and touched off a joyous fraternization of Cristinos and Carlists.

The crux of the so-called Embrace of Vergara was Espartero's promise that the Carlist officers would not just enjoy amnesty but would be confirmed in all their grades, decorations, and salaries. According to rumor, the queen regent's government had to pay out an additional 30,000,000 reales in bribes, but Cristina was known to have sighed, fervently, if inelegantly, "I would give my shirt" to end the cruel and costly fighting. Despite the fact that the nation was bankrupt, the agreement to ensure the Carlists their jobs meant that Spain was doomed to have the highest proportion of officers in its army of any country, one to every six or seven soldiers. Otherwise in 1839 the government made rather vague promises to respect the *fueros* of the Basques and Navarrese, which in time lost most of them but not all. Don Carlos was accorded the rank and prerogatives of an infante, but nothing was said of any dynastic marriage arrangements.

Don Carlos had little alternative but to retire to France, which he did on September 14, 1839, accompanied by the Princess of Beira, her sons, and several thousand of his red beret followers. He issued a parting curse against "the infamous traitor and treachery that had sold for foreign gold and recognition of military rank, God, the King, the Country, and the Fueros," indicating succinctly the scope of Carlist aims and also their order of precedence. The devout and unbending man was now confined by the French government in Bourges.

The day the pretender crossed the frontier General Cabrera's force fighting in his name captured 2,000 Cristinos, and for months afterward he terrorized the countryside from his stronghold at Morella. As late as March, 1840, Cabrera almost took Saragossa by surprise, but Espartero's overwhelming concentration of men against him at last forced the Tiger of the Maestrazgo to enter France on June 2, 1840. Thousands more Carlists joined their leader in exile, but numbers preferred suicide or, in the case of two Aragonese soldier friends, fought each other to the death with bayonets, a reminder of the fanaticism that characterized the whole Carlist movement (they successfully skewered each other, according to a contemporary print). Cabrera was involved in later Carlist adventures.

The "Six Years' War" may have cost Spain as much as 140,000 men and 21 billion reales, a tremendous sacrifice for a backward country not recovered from the Napoleonic and Latin American wars. The issue of the right of Isabel II to occupy the throne was temporarily resolved, but the family quarrel continued with intensity, a personalized reflection of the underlying ideological divisions wracking the country. The Carlists had lost the war largely because they "proved in the long run madder and more foolish than their adversaries." The anti-Carlist side won despite mutinies, pronunciamientos, hatred between *Moderados* and *Progresistas*, and constant manifestations of disrespect for the throne. These afflictions, particularly the political meddling by generals, unfortunately continued to dominate the politics of Spain as it passed from the Cristino into the Isabeline era.

VIII.
The Scandalous Queen: Isabel II (1833–1868)

---

1. The Overthrow of the Regency

THE reign of Queen Isabel II (1833–1868) corresponds in time with the early and middle era of Queen Victoria (1837–1901). Like Britain, Spain now entered the age of railroads and gaslights, frock coats and crinolines, and middle-class comforts and middle-class morality.

The Isabeline and Victorian courts, however, could hardly have been more different. The British sovereign came to the throne almost because of the fact that she was a woman, for several historians aver that British public opinion would have preferred a republic to another dirty-old-man son of George III. Queen Victoria, of course, ruled the more serenely as her name became the more identified with virtue and propriety. In contrast, the Spanish monarch's being female almost cost her her throne from the start. Her life was outrageous, her rule was tumultuous, and she was deposed for being a nymphomaniac. Unwittingly, Victoria had a hand in Isabel's fate, and oddly, the two Queens were always cordially disposed toward each other.

While on the subject of Spanish and English queens, it may be noted that the Spanish form of the name is definitely "Isabel." The English seem to prefer the more romantic-sounding Isabella. Actually, the Spanish render Elizabeth as Isabel, so that readers of Madrid picture magazines featuring royalty have to think twice when they see Isabel II (meaning the current English queen). Although never much of a student, Isabel II of Spain was duly impressed with her great fifteenth-century predecessor and imitated her in signing her name Ysabel.

Isabel was not quite nine when Don Carlos gave up his effort to deprive her of her crown. Though the Carlist War had come near the royal palace only once, she must have had some fantasies about her uncle, for once she reacted with complete terror on being told that she was to greet a Don Carlos, who turned out to be another relative by that name of her mother's family. She had also lived through the terrible night of the mutiny of August, 1836. Nonetheless, Isabel emerged basically a happy and affectionate youngster, winning and confiding, but more than a little capricious and spoiled. Reading did not interest her at all, nor did sewing, only pets and toys. She was so lazy that it took four women an hour to get her into her clothes, and her table manners were deplorable. One of the queen's biographers gets around the fact of her being an indolent and willful child by saying that "the little Isabel was a symbol of her country's heart both in its warmth and lack of discipline."

Still ruling in Isabel's name was her mother, the Queen Regent Cristina, who had seen her wide royal prerogatives embodied in the Constitution of 1834 considerably reduced by that of 1837. If not the would-be absolutist that her enemy Don Carlos was, Cristina was conservative and clerical in her sympathies and in her choice of court officials. The choice of ministers was, of course, dictated more by events, as *Moderados* and *Progresistas* struggled for advantage in periodic elections of the Cortes. In January, 1840, the country had returned a strongly *Moderado* Cortes amid protests from their opponents that the ministry had rigged the voting. The new conservative majority set out to ensure even more control of the electoral machinery in the future by passing the Law of Municipalities, whereby the crown would receive the right to name Spain's mayors from among councillors elected by property owners. The *Progresistas* stood to lose their grip on many municipal councils.

Regent, ministry, and Cortes did not constitute the power structure at this point, however, for very much to be taken into account was Spain's most successful general, Baldomero Espartero, whom a grateful Cristina had named Duke of the Victory even before the Embrace of Vergara. Son of a cart driver, hero of three wars, and profiteer from same, Espartero chose to be a political enigma for a while. He influenced ministries but did not take power himself. He hobnobbed with *Progresistas* at the same time he was earning the *Moderados'* respect as a strict disciplinarian. Brave, frank, and vastly popular, Espartero was also vain, indecisive, and essentially ignorant. Such was his reputation for self-indulgence that a speaker in the British House of Lords suggested that Spain's man of the hour "wore out more sheets than shoe leather."

The queen regent and Espartero finally clashed openly in the summer of 1840. Having given birth to still another child by her secret husband, Muñoz, Cristina left Madrid for the north on June 12. One of her intentions was to conduct this infant to the frontier so that servants could then take her to join in Paris the four other Muñoz children whose existence was not public knowledge in Spain. Also, she sought to bring the child queen for a cure at the baths of Las Caldas in Catalonia: Isabel had great difficulties with her complexion, suffering all her life from ichthyosis. Near Lérida the queen regent had an interview with Espartero, who now revealed his *Progresista* leanings by telling her to get rid of the *Moderados* and all their works, the ministry, the Cortes, and the Municipalities Law. He still refused to take power himself, but the general encouraged radical demonstrations in his behalf, as when he entered Barcelona in triumph on July 13 two weeks after Cristina's merely correct reception there. Piqued, the queen regent signed the Law of Municipalities the following day. In the ensuing weeks mob violence swirled around the royal residence in Barcelona, Espartero's troops appearing helpless to contain it. Cristina went on to Valencia on August 22, hoping to get the backing of the troops of the more conservative General Leopoldo O'Dónnell, but the people of this city too chanted only *Progresista* slogans. A junta was formed in Madrid on September 1 to resist the Law of Municipalities. It was the most revolutionary situation in Spain since 1820. Espartero's letters to Cristina became demanding to the point of insolence. After he staged his hero's entrance into Valencia on October 8, Cristina seemingly capitulated, agreeing in an interview to a ministry of the general's choice.

At the swearing in of the new *Progresista* ministry on October 12, 1840, Cristina made the astonishing announcement that she was abdicating, renouncing the regency. Refusing to recant her past actions, as the new regime wanted, or to abandon her courtiers, Cristina asked that a manifesto be published explaining her act in terms that would serve to make her out as a martyr. The ministry not only demurred but confronted her with its knowledge of her marriage to Muñoz, which was unconstitutional and incompatible with her being regent. She blushed with fright, muttering, "That is not certain," (meaning the "priest" *did* have only a hunting license?). At length a compromise message to the nation was agreed on that blamed neither Muñoz nor the *Progresistas* for the regent's departure but rather "the present state of the nation and the delicate nature of my health and my inability to yield to the exigencies of some of the terms." Cristina, who felt deserted and betrayed by Espartero, got in a famous last word to him when she declared, "I have made you a Count and a Duke but I could not make you a gentleman." She sailed for Marseilles on October 17 after a tearful departure from her two royal children. Passing through Montpellier on her way to Paris, she caught a glimpse from her window of the Carlist General Cabrera, another refugee because of Espartero.

The ten-year-old Queen Isabel II left Valencia on October 20 and made a ceremonial entry into Madrid on October 29, General Espartero riding at the side of her carriage. Dances, parades, fireworks, and military reviews did not distract Isabel from the bitter knowledge that she had been forcibly separated from her mother.

General Espartero, the carter's son, was to be dictator of Spain for the next three years. He did not technically become regent for the young queen until so named by the Cortes on March 19, 1841, after a tremendous wrangle over whether he should be associated with two or four other regents or none at all. By threatening his retirement, Espartero eventually won what he wanted, but his increasing petulance caused disenchantment in many of his nominal supporters. Little was accomplished in this *Progresista* interlude from 1840 to 1843. Opposition mounted from many quarters, however, the queen mother Cristina in Paris being the chief intriguer, her sister Carlota providing a counterplot, Don Carlos having his day, and Narváez and other conservative generals waiting in the wings. All the while Isabel grew up.

At first Isabel was allowed to cling to her beloved old governess, the Marquise of Santa Cruz, but eventually the woman was dismissed by Espartero on suspicion that she was a go-between between the queen and her mother in exile. People personally uncorrupted by the court and unfamiliar to Isabel were put in charge of her, people chosen strictly for their political and private virtues. The new governess, or *aya,* was the kindly but staunchly *Progresista* Countess of Mina, widow of the famous *guerrillero.* Later the austere Marquise of Begida, known as the "republican marquise," was named *camarera mayor* (principal lady-in-waiting). For chief tutor, or *ayo,* the queen came to know the brilliant Salustiano Olózaga. Other teachers included the Romantic poet Manuel José Quintana and the liberal prime minister of a bygone era, Agustín Argüelles, known as the Puritan. Such a humorless lot could easily be made fun of, and Isabel was secretly encouraged to do so by such of the old aristocracy as she was in contact with, but she came to resent that she was more watched than served, more instructed than loved. That such men as Argüelles and Quintana deliberately neglected Isabel's education, as she was to charge much later, is very hard to believe.

One consolation for Isabel was the companionship of the Infanta Luisa, her sister two years younger than she. The two girls, approaching their teens, appeared young for their age, entirely light-headed, but with a certain precociousness. The Countess of Mina summed up their very modest educational attainments as follows: "They can read and write and know a little arithmetic; they pronounce French well, speak it, translate it, and write it; can conjugate a verb, know a little music, and geography." To this she added sadly: "But lack of attention and interest is a grave inconvenience with which we have to struggle all the time." What distracted Isabel in this period may only be surmised, but probably it was not yet men or even clothes. It is known from an inventory of 1844 that the Queen of Spain possessed only twelve day dresses, twelve nightgowns, assorted undergarments, and thirty-six towels.

Her giddily maturing daughter in the care of strangers, the Queen Mother Cristina in France unceasingly plotted her own return to Spain. After less than a month in exile, she had issued a manifesto declaring that she had left the country only to avoid another civil war and being "condemned to read a new martyrology of the loyalty of Spain." Plaintively, she said, "She who has been your Queen asks of you nothing more than that you should love her daughters and respect her memory." Later she challenged the Espartero regime more directly, avowing that she was still queen regent. The Madrid government felt compelled to publish these messages in the *Gaceta*, along with hastily composed rebuttals.

Cristina's role as a wronged refugee was played from strength and comfort. Having been careful all her life to defer to her uncle King Louis Philippe, she got herself established in comfortable apartments in the Palais Royale and was virtually a daily guest at dinner in the Tuileries. Louis Philippe was openhanded in his support of her intrigues across the Spanish frontier. He and his chief minister, François Guizot, found her less-than-reactionary conservatism much to their taste and to their needs in France itself. Also, Cristina deliberately made a kind of pilgrimage to Pope Gregory XVI, traveling to Rome to deliver an "act of repentence" for the anticlerical legislation enacted during her regency and receiving in return all necessary dispensations for her marriage to Muñoz. Her brother Ferdinand II of the Two Sicilies even forgave her now, begging her presence in his capital. She returned to Paris, however, and to a very congenial and luxurious life with Muñoz and their several children, three more being born in the French capital. How much money the queen mother had brought out of Spain was the subject of impassioned accusations at the time and of later controversy among historians. Certainly, she took considerable jewelry and valuables with her from Valencia, and quite possibly she had previously provided against a rainy day by making foreign investments. She was able to purchase a town house on the rue de Courcelles and to buy Malmaison, the Empress Josephine's old residence, for 500,000 francs. Funds were not lacking to reward her supporters in Spain and even to pay a few agents to watch Don Carlos living in comparative penury in Bourges.

Cristina's sister Carlota proved to be not an ally but another person to be watched and countered. Don Francisco and his wife had been living in Paris since 1838, but Cristina's arrival there saw no reconciliation, only renewed recriminations against the Muñoz marriage and Carlota's mounting jealousy of her sister's success with Louis Philippe. The fearsomely spoken Carlota had failed miserably in the delicate business of promoting a marriage between her daughter, another Isabel, and the French king's second son, the Duke of Nemours. This defeat had been followed by disgrace when Carlota's prized princess eloped with a ne'er-do-well Russian aristocrat, Count Gurowski. Doña Carlota, however, had a greater prize in mind: the marriage of her son Francisco de Asís to Isabel II, Queen of Spain. Her sister reacted to this project very coldly.

Frustrated in her Paris intrigues, Doña Carlota decided to seek her ends in Spain itself. Since her return would embarrass a friendly government, France sought to impede it, at least openly. She and Don Francisco had to make their way south by separate routes, the husband eventually getting into his homeland by the kind of mountain pass route Don Carlos had used. Carlota's carriage was stopped by French guards at the frontier. She stormed out, saying, "I will not be held back by this new outrage. Let us walk." Whether it was her quivering bulk or the fact that she was the king's niece, no one dared stop her.

Once in Madrid, Carlota made every effort to influence her niece, the queen, but the Espartero government saw to it that she was kept away from the palace. The virago then took to waylaying Isabel on promenades, but this too was stopped. When a spokesman for Espartero tried to reason with Carlota, she resorted to kicking him. In this one matter Espartero and Cristina in Paris were unwittingly in league. The queen mother managed to smuggle a letter to her daughter in a book of Parisian fashion plates. Her message ran: "My sister Carlota is a real mischief-maker, there has been no conspiracy in which she hasn't taken part, no intrigue but she has been at the bottom of it, no act of my government which she has not fought. Don't trust that woman." Yet in the end Carlota succeeded in planting a history-making seed: she got a flattering portrait of her son Francisco into Isabel's hands, and the queen took to cherishing it in a little treasure box. Forced to retire to her Andalusian estates and be quiet, the grand Carlota was fated to die prematurely, succumbing to measles in January, 1844, before her scheming bore fruit.

New defiances of the dictator Espartero from Cristina in Paris brought intensified responses in Spain. In a manifesto of July 19, 1841, the ex-queen regent asserted her natural and legal rights to be at the side of her daughter. To show sympathy to her claim, numbers of the aristocracy left the Madrid court. The generals reacted more forcefully, beginning with O'Dónnell's trying to raise the garrison of Pamplona in September, 1841. Demonstrations took place in Saragossa, Vitoria, and Bilbao, where the plotters hoped to be able to kidnap Isabel. Narváez, working from Gibraltar, tried to stir up Andalusia. Don Carlos from Bourges futilely urged his followers to eschew support of these royalist manifestations in favor of the wrong royalty.

The most dramatic Cristinist attempt to change the regime occurred in Madrid on October 7, 1841, that "awful night" as described by Isabel's governess, the Countess of Mina. Three hundred soldiers of the Regiment of the Princes led by the General Manuel de la Concha marched on the massive Oriente Palace intent on seizing the queen. Although Concha was unable to gain the support of the bodyguards, his men easily entered the palace courtyards and then headed for the grand staircase, the one about which Napoleon had once complimented his brother King Joseph. Only a score of the Corps of Halberdiers, decorative oldsters like the English Beefeaters, were on guard, but these started shooting determinedly from windows and balustrades. Isabel, her sister, her governess, and a few attendants were awakened by the sounds of guns being fired, windows being broken, and doors being smashed. They huddled together in fright seemingly for hours, the worst of it being that they had no idea what was going on, whether the attackers were rescuers or murderers. At midnight one of the chief plotters, the young General Diego de León appeared on the scene but without reinforcements. Hours later the rebels were surrounded by troops and militia loyal to Espartero. León was among those captured and shot. So great was Espartero's fear that a similar attempt might succeed later that his government considered sending Queen Isabel to Cuba for safekeeping.

The ex-Regent Cristina in Paris cried at the news of León's execution. Espartero's ambassador in Paris, Olózaga, whom she treated with grand disdain, succeeded only in getting her denial of complicity in the plot, not a disavowal of its aims. Later, when the Spanish government demanded that France expel Cristina for further plotting, Guizot blandly parried: "We cannot refuse hospitality to the niece of the King." Soon afterward Spain made a futile protest that the French consul in Barcelona was blatantly stirring up revolution.

Espartero, whose reputation had been hurt by his dilatoriness in acting against León in Madrid, betook himself personally to the north to restore order. His decree of October 29, 1841, brought about the almost complete suppression of the Basque *fueros*. A year later he confronted an even more menacing situation in Barcelona, which rose in revolt against its captain general. Radical leaders were demanding Espartero's resignation, a more democratic constitution, and the queen's marriage to a Spanish prince. Another major factor was the fear of Catalan business interests that the pro-British Espartero was about to sign a commercial treaty with Britain that would render Catalan textiles uncompetitive. Finally, in what was one of the first really socialist manifestations in all Europe, workers with demands against property took the lead in the movement. The revolt would undoubtedly have collapsed from lack of momentum, but Espartero refused all compromise and treated a horrified nation to the spectacle of his bombarding Barcelona into submission from December 2 to December 4. The long-term effect of these actions was to convince Spain's outlying provinces, which were the richer ones, that monarchs and centralizing bureaucrats in Madrid spelled their ruin.

Progresistas and *Moderados* alike were now outraged at the high-handed Espartero. The Cortes refused to accept a new ministry named by the dictator. The military then moved to center stage. After the signal of an insurrection in Málaga on May 23, General Francisco Serrano and Colonel Juan Prim took over Barcelona, and Generals Concha and Narváez landed at Valencia, to begin a march on Madrid. Henceforth, right through Franco, Spanish revolutions and counterrevolutions tended to begin in the extremities. A kind of sham battle between Esparterist troops and those of Narváez took place at Torrejón de Ardos on July 20, followed by a theatrical fraternization and Narváez's entry into a delirious Madrid on July 23. Serrano and Prim received their Roman-style triumphs the next day. Espartero, moving southward, threatened to bombard Seville into obedience and finally fled the country on a British warship. The seemingly universal hatred of him was to prove a deceptive and passing thing, and like his conservative counterpart, Narváez, he bided his time in a Britain always hospitable to exiles.

The generals of the 1843 revolution rewarded themselves and their officers with a blanket promotion of one rank. Ordinary soldiers also learned the benefits of mutiny by gaining a two-year remission of service. At least the oversized army was reduced.

Although General Narváez was to be virtually a new dictator for more than a decade after 1843, jealousy of him at the outset precluded his being named regent. Since the queen was but one year short of the legal majority of fourteen, it was found expedient to declare her already of age. Officials announced this decision, taken by a Cortes, at a grand assembly in the palace, after which Isabel II acknowledged saluting troops and cheering crowds from the traditional balcony. Narváez was at her side, as were her sister Luisa, her uncle Francisco de Paula, and his son Francisco de Asís. Later the queen took an oath to the Constitution which included the strangely abnegatory words "If I fail to fulfill this my vow in whole or in part, I must not be obeyed, and all that I have done contrary to it shall be null and void." For the girl ruler the most pleasant part of her new status was the return of her old governess, the Marquise of Santa Cruz.

Descriptions of Isabel at thirteen vary with the beholder but not too much. Martin Haverty, an English "wanderer" in Spain who observed her and her sister at the Cortes, wrote of the queen's appearance:

> She is by no means as beautiful as the Infanta, but is much fairer; her figure also is good, and her neck and arms worthy of a sculptor's study; and she seemed already to have sprung into womanhood [a patently wrong observation, as will be seen]. She was robed in white satin, waved with flowers of delicate tints, and wore a diadem of silver richly spangled with diamonds.

As for her deportment, the witness was quite critical:

> The manner in which she acknowledged the salutations of the peers was neither graceful nor courteous; and in general the abruptness and impatience displayed in her movements contrast strongly with the natural grace of the young Infanta.

Another Englishman, Martin Hume, both traveler and serious historian, was less impressed with Isabel's looks but more with her bearing:

> At this period she was a stoutly built, very precocious girl with full cheeks, a snub nose, and thick sensuous lips, incredibly ignorant, but with a great deal of natural shrewdness; in manner somewhat bluff, jovial, and outspoken, partaking of her father's malicious jocosity and her mother's frank fascination. . . . With no steadying sense of responsibility whatsoever, she had yet a high notion of queenly dignity, and a noble carriage, which frequently invested acts of thoughtless levity with an appearance of magnanimous condescension.

Hume also lays a basis of exoneration for the queen's subsequent political frivolity and opportunism:

> She had seen fine words and high professions cloaking mean deeds; she had seen bloodshed, tyranny, cruelty, and rapine masquerading under the garb of liberty; her mother an idol one day and a fugitive the next; Espartero a hero and a hunted traitor within a month, and it is no wonder that her belief in truth, honor, and patriotism was already wavering at an age when most girls believe no evil.

Isabel's reign, her being at least nominally on her own, began with an alarmingly capricious incident. The prime minister was Salustiano de Olózaga, whose varied career included being a young revolutionary under the death sentence, then orator in the Cortes, tutor to the Queen, and ambassador to Paris. A radical tolerated for expediency by Narváez, Olózaga was confronted with a conservative majority in the Cortes and sought to give himself some political leverage by obtaining a decree of dissolution of the Cortes from Isabel. She granted this on the night of November 28, but talked to by her entourage, she made the charge the next day that the prime minister had manhandled her into doing it.

> Olózaga insisted, and I again refused to sign the decree. I rose and turned to the door which is at the left of my desk. Olózaga placed himself in front of me and bolted that door. I turned to the opposite door, and Olózaga again came before me and bolted that door also. He caught hold of my dress and obliged me to sit down. He seized my hand and forced me to sign. After that he left, and I withdrew to my apartments.

That this improbable story was the invention of the willful young queen is suggested by the testimony of her attendants in an anteroom that they heard nothing extraordinary but did see Isabel give the departing Olózaga a box of candy for his daughter. Also, the doors had no locks. Dismissed and impeached despite his denials, Olózaga fled the country disguised in the classic way as a monk.

Isabel, unparented and having her own way, took to eating and drinking to excess, aggravating her skin condition. She was expected to grant audiences to everyone, and she did so, mixing girlish innocence with flirtatiousness. Once she was found playing hide-and-seek with one of the ministers in her private apartments. The British prime minister felt obliged to intone in writing that Isabel's mother in Paris might well worry about "the violation of her daughter in her own palace."

The next prime minister of Spain was the political adventurer Luis González Bravo, who as a young pamphleteer in the 1830's had called the queen regent a "royal prostitute." Ironically, he became the instrument of Cristina's return to Spain. Despite loud protests from radicals about Cristina's having despoiled the treasury, González Bravo restored her pensions and even the arrears. He arranged that the ex-regent's secret marriage be publicly acknowledged and Muñoz created grandee and Duke of Rianzáres. Cristina's having still another child delayed her departure from Paris. Her progress to Aranjuez, where she arrived on March 22, 1844, was greeted with popular jubilation. Queen Isabel had earlier said to Santa Cruz, "Do what you want, but no one can stop me when I see Mama's coach from running to meet her." Only when told that the scene of the family's reuniting would be immortalized by artists did she consent to act with more dignity, but still the meeting was warmly affectionate.

General Narváez himself was prime minister when Cristina made a ceremonial entry into Madrid through the Atocha Gate on October 10, 1844. He was in this office sporadically until his death in 1868, also operating behind the scenes and enduring periods of exile. He was the conservative mainstay of Isabel's reign, always ready when needed, leading Cristina to murmur once on his recall, "Ramón, you know very well you are indispensable." An Andalusian whose impetuous courage brought him fame in the army, Narváez married well (a cousin of the Empress Josephine) and lived in a sumptuous palace in Madrid. His passion for women and gambling, it was said, kept him from sleeping long enough to stay in power. As a politician, or as the statesman he considered himself, he was remembered for his hard look and fierce temper, his hatred of the press, and his seeking conspiracies everywhere. He was always trying to read the faces of the palace servants, whom he had the police check and watch incessantly. Asked when desperately ill if he forgave everyone, the irascible general was to say, "My enemies? I have none. I have had them all shot."

In the first year of Narváez's power, between the Revolution of 1843 and the return of Cristina, there were 214 political executions. The new Cortes meeting in the fall of 1844 had only one opposition member. The regime was strong enough to balance the budget for the first time in decades and to initiate a lasting tax reform, replacing 100 different levies with 5. Radicals bitterly but futilely opposed the reliance on indirect taxes (the abolition or reinstatement of the octroi, or surcharge on the cost of articles of consumption, was henceforth the test of whether a regime was liberal or conservative). Also, the regime enacted a new Constitution on May 23, 1845, a document closely resembling the royalist Statuto of 1834. Unlike the radical Constitution of 1812 or the similar one of 1837, the new charter did not include a provision for the Cortes' approval of the monarch's marriage. While the Constitution proved hardly more long-lived than its predecessors, Narváez's establishment of the Civil Guard (Guardia Civil) endowed Spain with a lasting institution, which to this day is the darling of supporters of law and order and the bane of dissenters. All in all, if the claim is accepted that the country needed a decade of peace and prosperity after one of war and turmoil, it essentially got it with the repressive Narváez regime. And for many there were more interesting things to talk about than politics—like the matter of the queen's marriage.

Isabel was at that age. Puberty had not come, however, and she was taken first to Barcelona and then to San Sebastián in the expectation that sea bathing would hasten the event. Each day thousands of Basques would gather in the latter city to see their young sovereign emerge at 1 P.M. from her special pavilion on the beach. The hoped-for physical change did not occur while she was there, but two sons of the French king did appear.

2. The Disastrous Marriage

Force a hot-blooded, hedonistic young woman to marry an effeminate, fussy young man, and it usually means domestic trouble. For the Bourbons it meant dynastic tragedy. For Spain it meant revolution. For Europe it meant wars.

The "Affair of the Spanish Marriages," as it is known in European diplomatic history, stemmed from the fact that Spain had a very marriageable queen, as well as an eligible infanta. The early 1840's were still an era when dynastic alliances supplemented power politics. Accordingly, Queen Victoria and Palmerston, King Louis Philippe and Guizot, King Leopold of the Belgians, Metternich, and other outsiders busied themselves with selecting the appropriate husbands as intently as did the Queen Mother Cristina and her sister-rival, Doña Carlota (regardless of whether either lady was in or out of Spain), and Generals Espartero and Narváez (whichever happened to be in power). There were open negotiations and secret deals, agreements made and betrayals revealed, leading candidates confounded and obscure claimants pushed forward, and sudden deaths and other strange turns of events. Much bitterness was engendered at the time, and British, French, and Spanish historians have wrangled over it ever since. When all was said and done, the real tragedy was that so little account was taken of the needs of the central figure, the headstrong Queen Isabel II.

In mid-nineteenth-century Europe there were scores of princes for the Spanish royal house to choose from, but certain prejudices greatly reduced the number of genuine possibilities. It was essential that a king consort of Spain be a Catholic-born prince or at least a convert. For example, as early as 1838 Queen Cristina had discussed with the British ambassador the possibility of a match with the House of Hanover, only to be told that it was inconceivable that any of its members would change his faith. A Hohenzollern prince would present, perhaps, the same religious difficulties but not so, of course, a Hapsburg. Both Prussian and Austrian princes were out of consideration, however, because their countries had recently supported the Carlist cause. A Portuguese connection for their offspring was always a favorite project of Spanish Hapsburg and Bourbon kings alike. Espartero and Spanish liberals looked quite favorably on Dom Pedro, the son of Queen Maria, as a husband for Isabel, but their dream of a unified Iberian Peninsula was anathema to the Portuguese and to their British protectors.

A French marriage for Isabel was the dearest wish of Queen Cristina, who not only was Louis Philippe's niece but also was greatly in his debt for the pension he paid her when she was a refugee and for the support he gave that facilitated her return to Spain. These ties precluded any thought of a link with the French Legitimist line in exile. Of the several sons of the Orléans-line king, the third, the Duke of Aumale (born 1822), and the fourth, the Duke of Montpensier (born 1824), were considered the most suitable for Isabel. Aumale had already made a reputation for himself as a military commander in Algeria, causing Narváez to exclaim to the French ambassador on one occasion: "Let me govern three years with one of the sons of your king, and I will make Spain a great power." The British reaction to a French prince sitting on the throne of Spain was entirely hostile, just as if 1844 were 1700 or 1808. "*We* could *never* allow that," wrote Queen Victoria succinctly and with her usual underlinings.

Just as Cristina and Louis Philippe thought Bourbon-Orléans, Queen Victoria and her husband Prince Albert thought Saxe-Coburg. The candidate they had in view and promoted vigorously was their cousin Prince Leopold of Saxe-Coburg-Gotha (born 1824). That the prince in question personally abhorred the idea of marrying Isabel was forgotten in the diplomatic maneuverings, which were pursued most avidly by Leopold's uncle King Leopold of Belgium, who was in the early stages of peopling thrones from Bulgaria to Mexico. Too many Saxe-Coburgs around were just what made Leopold's candidacy utterly unacceptable to France, which was already surrounded by them in Britain, Belgium, and Portugal.

Since their cooperative ventures of 1830 in putting that very King Leopold on his throne and of 1834 in expelling the Iberian pretenders, Britain and France tended to act in concert as the "liberal powers." In the tradition of this *entente cordiale,* Queen Victoria and Prince Albert sailed to Normandy in their new yacht *Victoria and Albert* for a meeting with King Louis Philippe and Queen Marie Amalie. Much of the serious negotiations during the four days of festivities at the Chateau d'Eu were carried on by the respective foreign ministers, Lord Aberdeen and Guizot, but at one crucial moment on a walk after breakfast Louis Philippe paused as if to rest and then made a final plea to his royal guests for the candidacy of his son Aumale. Politely rebuffed, he in turn insisted that Queen Victoria drop the candidacy of Prince Leopold. All subsequently agreed that the Hapsburgs should be excluded from consideration and further that a suitable husband for Isabel II must be found among the descendants of Felipe V. The British indicated their willingness for the Infanta Luisa to marry the Duke of Montpensier but, very importantly, made this conditional on Isabel's marrying first and having children.

There were four male descendants of Felipe V of appropriate age and singleness. The leading name was Carlos Luis, Count of Montemolín (born 1818), the eldest son of the pretender Don Carlos and thus Isabel's first cousin. Then came the two sons of Don Francisco and Doña Carlota,

KING FERDINAND AND QUEEN ISABELLA.
[Fac-simile of an exceedingly rare contemporary print.]

(THE BETTMANN ARCHIVE, INC.)

(NEWARK PUBLIC LIBRARY)

Fernando of Aragón and Isabel of Castile, who descended from the first petty Christian kings of the eighth century, united all Spain in the fifteenth century and launched a great empire in the New World.

The misshapen, imbecilic Carlos II (1665–1700) was the last successor of the great Hapsburg monarchs Carlos I and Felipe II of the sixteenth century. His reign left Spain in desperate straits of military weakness and economic collapse.

Louis XIV of France in the grand salon of Versailles Palace presents his grandson Philip of Anjou as king of Spain. The claims of the Bourbon Felipe V were contested by the Hapsburg "Carlos III" in the War of the Spanish Succession (1700–1714).

(NEW YORK PUBLIC LIBRARY)

(NEWARK)   (NEWARK)

(Left) Felipe V (1700–1746), portrayed as a young man by Rignaud, reigned longer than any of his successors. His rule was remembered for constant wars and the king's attacks of madness.

(Right) In a short reign Fernando VI (1746–1759) brought his country peace and enlightened reforms. He succumbed to madness because of grief over the death of his wife.

(Left) Isabel Farnese, the Italian second wife of Felipe V, dominated her eccentric husband and squandered Spain's resources winning thrones for her children in Parma and the Two Sicilies.

(Right) The greatest of the Bourbon monarchs, Carlos III (1759–1788), restored Spain to the front rank of European nations. Although devoted to hunting, as indicated in this portrait by Goya, the king was a hardworking administrator.

(THE BETTMANN ARCHIVE, INC.)   (NEW YORK PUBLIC LIBRARY)

THE NEW DYNASTY BUILDS NEW PALACES

The Oriente Palace on the west side of Madrid was begun under Felipe V and finished under Carlos III. Napoleon remarked on the grandeur of its appointments. In his study in the north wing Alfonso XIII made the decision to leave the country in 1931.

(NEW YORK PUBLIC LIBRARY)

La Granja Palace, also known as the royal *sitio* of San Ildefonso, was intended as an imitation of the Versailles Felipe V knew in his youth. The Baroque buildings, surrounded by fountains, are nestled in the mountain forests north of Madrid.

(NEW YORK PUBLIC LIBRARY)

The palaces at Aranjuez contain many richly decorated apartments such as these. This other summer retreat of the Bourbons lies to the south of the capital on the river Manzanares, where the Spanish monarchs maintained a fleet of pleasure craft.

(NEW YORK PUBLIC LIBRARY)

(Left) The insolently handsome guardsman Manuel Godoy was the lover of Queen Maria Luisa and confidant of King Carlos IV (1788–1808), the rulers pictured in Goya's celebrated "Family" (see book jacket). The favorite's bumbling policies brought French occupation of the country.

(Right) Joseph Bonaparte was imposed on Spain as King José I (1808–1814) by his younger brother Napoleon. His well-meaning rule failed in the face of a national war of liberation.

Goya captured all the horrors of the French occupation and the Spanish resistance in a series of paintings and etchings. This large canvas in the Prado commemorates the 1808 uprising in Madrid against Napoleon's troops, which included the colorful Mameluke cavalry from Egypt.

(THE BETTMANN ARCHIVE, INC.)   (NEW YORK PUBLIC LIBRARY)

(Left) The subject of another Goya portrait, the embittered Fernando VII (1808) (1814–1833), was restored after Napoleon's downfall. His reign, a nightmare of repression, was marked by the loss of the Spanish-American colonies.

(Right) The Neapolitan-born Christina, fourth wife of Fernando VII, was regent for her daughter Isabel from 1833 to 1841. The right of women to rule in Spain was disputed by an uncle, Don Carlos, and the Carlists plunged the country into three civil wars in the next forty years.

Right- and left-wing extremists subjected Spain to innumerable military coups, insurrections, and revolutions in the nineteenth century. This lithograph depicts the burning of the ex-regent's palace in 1854.

(NEW YORK PUBLIC LIBRARY)

(THE BETTMANN ARCHIVE, INC.)   (NEWARK)

(Left) The exigencies of European dynastic politics forced the sensual Isabel II (1833–1868) to marry her effeminate cousin Francisco de Asís. After many scandals, all the Bourbons were driven from the country by a military revolt.

(Right) Ex-Queen Isabel II lived on to 1904, using her Palacio de Castilla in Paris as a base for all manner of intrigues.

———

In 1870 Spain tried a new dynasty in the person of Amadeo I of Savoy. The Italian king's brave entrance into Madrid was followed by political frustration and his abdication in 1873.

(NEWARK)

(THE BETTMANN ARCHIVE, INC.)   (NEWARK)

(Left) The generals brought back the dynasty in 1874 in the person of Isabel's son Alfonso XII (1874–1885). The scrupulously constitutional king was a victim of tuberculosis at an early age.

(Right) The Austrian-born regent María Cristina brought Spain through the disastrous Spanish-American War of 1898. She is shown here with the boy Alfonso XIII, who was king from the moment of his birth in 1886.

––––––––

(Left) Alfonso XIII (1886–1931) married Queen Victoria's granddaughter, who became popularly known as Queen Ena. Their marriage was made tragic by assassination attempts and by hemophilia in their children.

(Right) A royal playboy but an active ruler, Alfonso XIII faced many crises, including military interference in politics and socialist agitation. Pictured here with a prime minister who was assassinated just before World War I, the king eventually resorted to a dictatorship in the 1920's. He was ousted by revolution in 1931.

(NEWARK)   (NEWARK)

TODAY'S SPANISH
ROYALTY FACE
THE FUTURE

Don Juan Carlos was educate
in Spain following an agreemen
between his father, Don Juan
and dictator Franco. The
prince's arrival in Madrid i
1955 was the occasion for
royalist demonstration.

(NEW YORK PUBLIC LIBRARY)

The young pretender lights tł
old pretender's cigarette at
bachelor party before the fo
mer's marriage to Princess S
fia of Greece. In 1969 Franc
designated Juan Carlos as h
successor, but Don Juan, tł
third son of Alfonso XIII, h
not given up his own heredita
claim to the throne.

(WIDE WORLD PHOTOS)

The Francos were recent
linked by marriage to the Bou
bons. The dictator's gran
daughter María del Carm
Martínez in March, 1972, m;
ried Alfonso Jaime, son of D
Juan's older brother Don Jain
Pictured at the wedding a
nouncement are Mrs. Fran¢
the bride; the groom; Fran¢
the groom's mother, Emma
ela of Dampierre; Princess So
Prince Don Juan Carlos; a
the bride's father, Cristó
Martínez-Bordiu.

(WIDE WORLD PHOTOS)

Francisco de Asís, Duke of Cádiz (born 1822) and Enrique, Duke of Seville (born 1823), likewise first cousins to the queen. Also to be considered was the Neapolitan Bourbon the Count of Trapani (born 1827), Cristina's brother and thus a young uncle of Isabel.

The marriage of Isabel II to Carlos Luis, alternately considered by both sides during the recent Carlist War, still had much to recommend it by way of permanently ending the dynastic split and thereby reducing the possibilities for future civil strife. Of course, the Duke of the Victory, Espartero, was bitterly opposed to the project during his regency, and his British friends were adamantly anti-Carlist. Yet King Louis Philippe was favorable to such a match, having been in the early 1840's both host to Cristina in Paris and polite jailor to Don Carlos and his family in Bourges. Metternich in Vienna was entranced with the idea and contributed the dubious historical analogy of the joint sovereignty of Fernando and Isabel in the fifteenth century. The envoy sent by the Austrian chancellor to Bourges, however, found Don Carlos unwilling to discuss either the marriage or his own abdication in his son's favor.

Eventually, second thoughts prevailed in the Carlist camp, for on May 18, 1845, "Carlos V" abdicated in favor of "Carlos VI." In his manifesto explaining his act, Don Carlos never swerved from the conviction that he was the King of Spain by right, but he pleaded a desire to forget politics and pursue domestic tranquillity. The son's reply was typically traditionalist in its words about submitting to the "sovereign will" of the father and taking up the "duty" of ruling. What was new, however, was the appeal to the Spanish nation composed by the English-educated young man, for it hinted vaguely about the desirability of constitutional institutions and modern ways of thinking. This unexpected liberalism was not strong enough to prevent Basque villages from celebrating the accession of "Carlos VI" or to attract much notice in the rest of Spain. When a Madrid pamphleteer did send up a trial balloon proposal that Carlos Luis be husband and consort to Isabel in the manner of Prince Albert of England, there was the immediate rejoinder from Carlist circles that their man was king already and would rule as one. In the end, legalisms about legitimacy mattered less, perhaps, than the fact that Carlos Luis was cross-eyed. After inspecting her cousin's picture, Isabel II announced quite firmly: "I will not marry a man with a squint."

This escapade was not the last Spain would know of the twenty-eight-year-old pretender, described at the time as "a little insignificant man." Unfortunately lacking either his father's presence or his mother's assertiveness, Carlos Luis would succeed only in bringing moments of comedy to the Carlist cause during his "reign" lasting to 1861.

A kind of compromise on the male-female succession issue and on that of consortship would be achieved by selecting as the queen's husband hers and Carlos Luis' first cousin Francisco de Asís. Indeed, the young man's parents had assiduously promoted this match practically since the day of Isabel's birth. They were not above such ploys as pushing him, now a colonel of a regiment, to dance with the queen at every opportunity. Whereas Don Francisco de Paula's involvement in liberal and Masonic circles both helped and hindered his cause, Doña Carlota's intrigues in their son's favor—her attempts to cajole Louis Philippe in Paris and to browbeat her niece in Madrid—had thoroughly alienated Cristina from her sister and all her works. The unexpected death of Carlota in 1844 shortly before Cristina's return to Spain removed some of the family bitterness. The son, however, presented other problems. Francisco de Asís, army officer or no, was decidedly effeminate. His calling his aunt ironically "Madame Muñoz" did not endear him to her. "What can be hoped of a husband who is really a cretin?" wrote the British ambassador, who also spoke of Francisco's "utter imbecility."

In the spring and summer of 1845 most of the principals came around to the feeling that the perfect candidate was the queen's young Neapolitan uncle, the Count of Trapani. Queen Cristina represented him to her daughter as tall, good-looking, and skillful at riding. Louis Philippe was also delighted with the prospect of putting one of his close kinsmen on a throne. The British raised no objections. Metternich pressured the court of Naples to recognize Isabel's title as queen at last and to send an embassy offering the hand of their prince. An uproar against Trapani went up in the Spanish press, however. The Neapolitan Bourbons were held in popular contempt for many reasons, including their past support of Carlism. The young man in question was described as ugly, unprepossessing, and possibly not heterosexual. Worst of all in the minds of Spanish anticlericals, Trapani was currently a student at a Jesuit college in Rome. Cynically, and also futilely, Louis Philippe observed: "But the way to make him popular in Spain will be to make him run away from the College and give out that he will have nothing to do with the Jesuits." Narváez alone probably had the power to manipulate Spanish public opinion into acceptance of the Jesuit-educated Neapolitan, and the general swallowed his distaste for the unsoldierly prince and vigorously pushed his candidacy, only to be temporarily out of power at the crucial time.

If opposition from the left killed the chances of the Count of Trapani, rightists eventually vetoed the candidacy of the Duke of Seville. There was a general flurry of interest in late 1845 that the younger of the sons of Don Francisco de Paula and Doña Carlota possessed the virility and force of character seemingly lacking in Francisco de Asís. A dashing naval commander, Enrique had attracted the favorable notice of the queen, but then from the very deck of his warship stationed in the Bay of Biscay he issued a political manifesto in April, 1846, a manifesto supporting the aspirations of some people in open insurrection in Galicia. Hotheaded was the word for Enrique's action if it was merely a spontaneous gesture; miscalculated was the word if he thought that rallying the *Progresistas* to his cause would help him. Narváez declared that the infante's views were incompatible with monarchy, and Cristina persuaded the queen that she had been insulted by her cousin and should banish him, which she did. In exile Enrique became the darling of Espartero and of English liberals. More important, Louis Philippe described the too independent-minded prince as a "repugnant little monster," and the new British ambassador at Madrid, Henry Bulwer, conceded that he was "wild and unmanageable."

"La reine est nubile depuis deux heures," the French ambassador, Charles Bresson, almost breathlessly informed his government on March 1, 1846. Isabel's coming into puberty was, indeed, an event of international importance, and everyone prepared for a rush of developments. Bulwer, whose personally bitter rivalry with Bresson was a factor causing difficulties all along, told his government that the queen insisted on being "married somehow and to someone immediately." In Paris Guizot confided to an English visitor: "You don't know what these Spanish and Sicilian princesses are like. They have the devil in their bodies. It is always said that if we don't make haste, the heir will arrive before the bridegroom."

Unquestionably, Queen Isabel was in fine fettle in these days when she was the center of so much attention. The American ambassador in Madrid at this time was Washington Irving. He had no cause for diplomatic intrigues like his European counterparts, but he took care to write down his impressions of the Spanish court, such as this description of a gala evening of dancing at the palace:

> There were blunders in the quadrille which set the little queen laughing. . . . She was at times absolutely convulsed with laughter, and throughout the evening showed a merriment that was quite contagious. I have never seen her in such a joyous mood, having chiefly seen her on ceremonious occasions, and had no idea that she had so much *fun* in her disposition. She danced with various members of the Diplomatic Corps; and about four in the morning, when she was asked if she could venture upon another dance, "Oh, yes!" she said; "I could dance eight more if necessary." The Queen Mother, however, got her away between four and five.

Events now moved so fast that letters and dispatches among the principals crossed one another, and even the recriminations could not keep pace. Having given up on the Duke of Aumale, Don Carlos Luis, Don

Francisco de Asís, Don Enrique, and the Count of Trapani, the queen mother showed a new strong interest in Prince Leopold of Saxe-Coburg-Gotha and went so far as to write his father on May 2, 1846. Acting largely on his own, the British ambassador, Bulwer, was assiduous in representing Leopold to her as tall, handsome, pleasing in manner, and moderate in his political views. That spring Leopold happened to travel through Spain on his way to visit his royal brother in Portugal. Despite the fact that the prince deliberately avoided being received by the court at Madrid, the French were suspicious that some plot was going on contrary to their interests.

It was the French ambassador Bresson's turn, acting independently of Paris, to revive the candidacy of Don Francisco de Asís, coupling this with the bait of a simultaneous marriage of the Infanta Luisa to the Duke of Montpensier, all despite the Eu agreements of 1843, which had been renewed in 1845. The queen mother still reacted with great distaste to her nephew. In one of her interviews with Bresson, she asked, "To be sure, you have seen him, you have heard him: his hips, his movements, his sweet little voice. Is it not a little disturbing, a little strange?" When Bresson remained silent, Cristina exclaimed: "And at twenty he hasn't had any adventures!" Suavely, the Frenchman argued that Don Francisco's diffident and moral ways reflected his devotion to the queen and his humble hopes about his future. Such discussions continued into the summer, Cristina weakening. Her husband, Muñoz, was particularly impressed with the prospect of a French royal marriage for his younger stepdaughter, and exchanging visits with Bresson at the opera July 13, he told him of his certainty about the deal.

The negotiations were still too halting and open in options for one to accept the claim that "a dark scheme" was entered into by Cristina and the French in the summer of 1846. Yet this is the point of view of the influential British historian of Spain W. G. Clarke. His full charge goes:

> It was believed that Isabel's union with her effeminate and feeble cousin precluded all chance of succession and that the throne of Spain would fall to the children of her sister. That so wicked an agreement should have been entered into by a mother and abetted by a statesman of the highest position seems well nigh incredible. . . . Isabel's happiness weighed as nothing against the advance of the Orléans family. Her scandalous life is partially excused by her mother's fiendish betrayal.

As the French groped, more than schemed, toward a solution favorable to themselves, so did the British. The fall of the Tory government on July 6, 1846, brought the Whig Palmerston into the Foreign Office, a man famous for his high-handed and assertive policies. The anti-British historian Pierre de Luz sees this change as "one of the great events in the history of the world" for its effects of ending British-French cooperation on the Spanish Marriages and other questions. After two weeks in office Palmerston sent a memorandum to Bulwer in Madrid advancing Prince Leopold as the leading contender, putting in a good word for Don Enrique, and gratuitously denouncing the Spanish *Moderados* in power. It was "one of the most reckless letters ever penned by a Foreign Secretary." The French, to whom Palmerston quite offhandedly showed his dispatch, took alarm and were now in a position to say that it was the British, not they, who were about to violate the Eu accords. Queen Mother Cristina became convinced that Don Enrique was going to take over Spain with the aid of the British navy ("The English and the revolution menace us"), and she went along completely with Bresson's plans.

For the first time now Don Francisco de Asís entered the drama personally, knowing that he was the fatted calf in Bresson's mind, possibly in his aunt's. From his army post on July 13 he wrote a letter to Don Carlos Luis strongly urging that the Carlist pretender wed Isabel. Francisco ended by stating his willingness to do his duty in these words: "But if your marriage becomes impossible . . . I believe that my conscience (I do not speak of my interest, for a throne holds nothing seductive) orders me imperiously not to expose Spain to a new conflict." In this message can be read several things: a secret conviction that Carlos Luis had the best claim to the throne; genuine and noble scruples about exposing Spain to civil war; and a misogynist's reluctance to marry Isabel. Urged on by Cabrera and other Carlist fire-eaters, Carlos Luis did not deign to reply to his cousin's letter, apparently believing that the whole Spanish prize would fall into his lap. Having tried to salve his personal and political conscience, Don Francisco had no alternative but to obey his father's orders and to make his presence visible at the court.

On August 9 Muñoz informed Bresson not only that he expected Francisco to come to Madrid in a week but also that the ladies' hesitations about the marriage would be overcome. Cristina was possibly persuaded that she was doing the right thing by her daughter marrying her to a passive husband, since the queen's health caused worry that a pregnancy might be harmful. Isabel herself now proved the final obstacle.

In a light-headed moment the young queen had once said that she would be happy to marry Francisco if he were a man. With him now thrust at her at court, she reacted coquettishly and peevishly to his timorous advances. Less than impressed with his newly sprouting mustache and deepened voice, she told him: "When I fall in love with you, I'll let you know." Her skin condition had cleared up considerably, so that she was feeling fully desirable and she was jealous of the prospect of her sister marrying the manly Montpensier. When she realized that the possibility of her marrying Francisco had become a probability, she hysterically threatened abdication, retirement to a nunnery, or running off with someone in the manner of her cousin Isabel. The mysterious religious figure Sor Patrocinio, whose influence over both Cristina and her sister was much talked of in anticlerical circles, may have played a major role in convincing Isabel, and Francisco too, that refusal meant civil war and the destruction of the faith. Also, the queen mother made it plain that if Isabel did not marry her cousin, then any other marriage would be postponed a long time. On August 28 the queen emerged crying from a long conference with her mother and Muñoz, and it was suspected that the final decision had been made. Not until September 4 did King Louis Philippe give up the possibility of disavowing his ambassador's efforts, resigning himself to the end of the *entente cordiale.* A major consideration on the part of the "Bourgeois King" was the desire to see his son come into the Infanta Luisa's inheritance. The forthcoming simultaneous marriages of queen and infanta were announced to the Cortes on September 14.

Queen Victoria found the news from Spain "infamous," particularly since her first formal notification of the French triumph was a letter from Queen Marie Amalie with homey solicitations about Victoria's health and a "by the way" about the Duke of Montpensier's approaching happiness with the infanta. The British monarch fumed about Guizot's being "shabbily dishonest," and she wondered if she could ever deal with Louis Philippe again. She wrote King Leopold on September 14: "The little Queen I pity so much for the poor child dislikes her cousin, and she is said to have consented against her will." Palmerston, equally frustrated and powerless, wrote Bulwer telling him to make determined but discreet efforts to rally *Moderados, Progresistas,* and even Carlists in a "great national effort to free the country of French domination." In Ghent the exiled Enrique, Duke of Seville, issued a message of protest that his brother Francisco had broken a personal pact that they should marry both sisters or not at all. From Bourges Carlos Luis sent a manifesto to his Spanish supporters to "rise and rally round the standard of your lawful prince." The Carlist headed for Britain, however, not the Spanish frontier, and only the brief seizure of Cervera in the name of "Carlos VI" marked this new appeal for armed strife.

Born of such controversy as to be ill-fated almost inevitably, the double marriage of the queen with the Duke of Cádiz and the infanta with the Duke of Montpensier took place with due ceremony on the queen's sixteenth birthday, October 10, 1846. Isabel was splendid in white and diamonds but notably plump. Francisco, according to a malicious observer, looked like a girl in his general's uniform. Both cried at the conclusion of the ceremony. The tall, supercilious Montpensier cut a truly kingly figure, and Doña Luisa carried the day for sheer loveliness.

As for the infanta's wedding night, the story was told that she was so frightened that she hid a lady-in-waiting behind her bed for moral support and that Montpensier had firmly to assert his rights to privacy. Little is known of the first bedroom encounter of Isabel and Francisco except for her celebrated later reminiscence: "What shall I say of a man who on his wedding night wore more lace than I?"

Ten days of festivities in Madrid followed the wedding, a grand round of fireworks, bullfights, Te Deums, and banquets. The Plaza Mayor boasted fountains of wine and of milk on one occasion. The entire garrison was dined in style, and 9,000,000 duros were distributed to the poor. Afterward the royal couple set off for a honeymoon in Aranjuez. Their carriage broke down on the way, forcing them to spend several hours in a hayloft. When they arrived late at the country palace, no one expected them, and they had to make their own beds. More important, within a few months Francisco was living by himself and Isabel was in the embrace of the first of a long series of lovers.

"In fact, the Spanish Marriages from beginning to end spell horror." The most triumphant smile on the wedding day had been Bresson's; the French ambassador for family reasons cut his throat a year later. Louis Philippe derived scant advantage from his dynastic diplomacy, for within two years he had lost his own throne and found himself taking a ship to England disguised as "Mr. Smith." One of Isabel's former ladies-in-waiting was next to grace Marie Amalie's throne as the Empress Eugénie, but the deposition of the outrageously immoral Isabel in 1868 started the train of events that brought about the overthrow of Eugénie's husband, Napoleon III. That is to say, the Spanish Marriages led into the Franco-Prussian War, which many consider a primary cause of World War I, and so on and on.

3. Royal Escapades

Many historians have written about nineteenth-century Spain concentrating on the frequent change of ministries, the corrupt elections to the Cortes, financial scandals, and other serious matters without paying much heed to the loves and frustrations of Queen Isabel II and her consort, Don Francisco. Other writers have dwelled on the outrageous court intrigues without any real accounting of the bewildering political changes of the day. Actually, there was a fascinating interplay between the caprices of the dynasty and the general movement of the nation.

Central to the whole drama of Isabel II is the nature of her husband, Francisco de Asís. Was he homosexual or just a gentle type? Could he father her children and did he? What were his ambitions? The answers are not always certain. The eldest son of the ineffectual Francisco de Paula and the domineering Doña Carlota was born in 1824. If one is tempted to blame the parents for their child's marked delicacy and diffidence, one has also to account for his younger brother Enrique, sturdy to the point of truculence. Francisco's upbringing as an infante was not unusual except that during his family's exile in Paris he was able to attend the Lycée Henri IV. Afterward he pursued an army career, serving in various garrison towns in Spain and attaining the command of a regiment prior to the time of his marriage in 1846. The new king consort's mannerisms, once known only to his fellow officers and at court, now came to the public's attention and he was promptly nicknamed Paquita, roughly Franny. He was of slight build, spoke in a high voice with much inflection, and moved about like a "mechanical doll." According to gossip, Francisco was unduly devoted to perfumes, jewels, and fine fabrics. He took many baths in an era when men did not (it has been argued seriously that Spaniards have had a habitual aversion to baths as a reaction against Moslem and Jewish cleanliness). He also liked to rise in the very early hours of the morning to go out and paint delicate little landscapes. Those with a knowledge of Bourbon dynastic history recalled that "Monsieur," Louis XIV's brother, was decidedly effeminate, about the only other well-known case in the family.

The bachelor scholar was probably the right career for Francisco, who was urbanely elegant in half a dozen languages and genuinely erudite about history and literature. He was distracted, formal, and overprecise. His greatest admiration was for things English: only English clothes were "fit to cover a gentleman," he would say, and only English servants were sufficiently unobtrusive and efficient to wait on one.

In looks Francisco was neither handsome nor unpleasing. His pictures are hardly different from those of scores of mustachioed, dark-haired, pale-faced Spanish gentlemen of the day. Alleged by some to be a grandson of Manuel Godoy, Francisco had none of the swarthy sensuality of this royal favorite. To the contrary, he was so unmistakably Bourbon that one of his children later declared that "in features he might well" be taken as the "Brother" of Queen Isabel. He had a clear forehead, a normally sculpted mouth, and a rounded chin. In his eyes one can, perhaps, detect an expression of reserve, of self-absorption, and even a kind of fright.

Francisco's aunt and now mother-in-law, Cristina, not only had commented on his mincing ways but had also expressed dismay at his not having had affairs. Later the royal doctor was to testify with conviction that the king was not impotent. The queen's first lover, however, told the British ambassador that he was certain that Francisco was incapable of sexual relations with his wife because Isabel was still a virgin long after her wedding night. If Francisco practiced homosexuality actively, he was fairly discreet about it. Nonetheless, eyebrows were raised at his "inseparable companionship" in the 1840's with a Don Antonio de Meneres, for whom Francisco obtained the title Duque de Baños (*baños,* meaning baths, seemed a whimsical title). Once on a visit by himself to the French court, Francisco caused endless titters by blurting out, even before greeting his hosts, *"Où est Lambert?",* the person in question being his well-favored valet of many years before.

Frustrated as a husband, Francisco was also destined to be thwarted in his efforts to play a political role. His title King was entirely ceremonial. The queen would not even allow him to attend cabinet meetings, much less relinquish any of her royal prerogatives to her consort. Accordingly, Francisco was condemned to trying to influence affairs by intrigues, at which he proved persistent but not very adept. Probably Francisco would have made a capable monarch, having a very lively intelligence, being a good conversationalist, and enjoying an easy acquaintanceship with politicians, businessmen, and intellectuals alike. In contrast with his wife, he could be hardworking and persevering in his aims. His ideas tended toward absolutism, even Carlism, in effect. Yet this very conservatism, plus Francisco's military status, his dutiful piety, and his avoidance of open scandal, made him an appealing figure to many Spaniards, who were unaware of or indifferent to his personal idiosyncrasies. Francisco was not allowed to exercise his royal qualities but was asked to do just what he could not do—satisfy an abnormally demanding bed partner.

If Don Francisco's sexual nature remains somewhat mysterious, Doña Isabel was unquestionably a nymphomaniac. She was on the order of a Catherine the Great. Even if she probably failed to equal the Russian monarch in sheer numbers of lovers, the Spanish queen rivaled her in their variety—a soldier, a composer, a singer, a dentist, and so forth. Spanish historians are still guarded to the point of being prudish about Isabel's private life, but not so the non-Spanish. A clear accusation but an interesting exercise in delicacy is this quotation from a British writer: "It is believed that she suffered from a trouble that made normal standards of morality almost impossible for her, and, in any case, had not her marriage placed a woman of her temperament in an almost intolerable position?" A French historian comes more to the point, explaining Isabel's oversexed nature and her lack of guilt about it in terms of heredity. "The daughter of an uncle and a cousin, Isabel descended twice from María Luisa, a known nymphomaniac, one time from her father, the libertine Fernando VII, and on the other side from her maternal grandmother, María Isabel, who loved love and beatings." Moreover, in reference to the royal ichthyosis, "Isabel was, before all, a sick person in whom sexual love was excited by eczemal itch."

While Isabel's nymphomania can be explained in terms of heredity and physiology, it was also a lifelong protest and vengeance against the inhuman marriage arranged for her by others. All Europe was at fault for marrying the exuberant queen to her mousy husband. Their relationship was extremely complex since they were forced to go through the motions of being a wedded pair. Gloating that the marriage he had opposed was in difficulty from the start, Ambassador Bulwer used a fine choice of words when he reported to London: "The young Queen did not dislike her husband so much as she disregarded, and, in a certain sense, despised him."

Isabel was a woman of many passions besides sex. Eating was one of her greatest delights, with her taste running toward the heavy dishes of the national cuisine and the richer French ones. As a result, she gradually became enormously fat, even grotesque in her later years. While she was still a young woman, her portraits show her somewhat puffy-looking, but she was attractively proportioned, and had beautiful features, especially her delicate rosy complexion and her lively, searching eyes that could both seduce and intimidate. Her plumpness was all vivaciousness, not languor.

In her late teens Isabel gave full reign to her high spirits. Only her mother dared cross her in her pursuit of fun and excitement, and Cristina was often absent in Paris. The queen could party all night and every night. She delighted in the company of high society, enjoying gossip and contributing her own considerable wit. She loved ballroom dancing and could also throw herself into the spirit of a street fiesta. Her husband hated both. She loved riding. Some of her escapades came close to causing real trouble. During a foray to a *barrio* carnival the police had to intervene between the royal party in disguise and local celebrators. Another time, after a late-night visit to the Countess of Montijo and her daughter Eugénie, the future empress, Isabel and her friends galloped gaily back toward Madrid, passed a sentry post, and were shot at by the guards. If such adventures disturbed the queen's ministers, so did her whimsical hours, with meals every day served at different times and with officials kept waiting for hours to conduct state business. Often Isabel did not retire until 5 A.M. and got up at 3 P.M.

For all her thoughtlessness Isabel was noble of mind and heart. She wanted to do right as ruler, even if she could not help at times giving herself over to uncontrolled laughter during Cabinet meetings. She tried to please everyone, as was evidenced by her lifelong efforts to effect a reconciliation with the Carlists. Her good nature prevented her from harboring hatred or rancor. Also, for all her frivolity, Isabel could be truly regal. One of her intimates later summed up her sovereign as follows: "She was as a woman more a woman and as a lady more a lady than any I have ever known." Imposing herself, the Empress Eugénie once remarked on Isabel's *"très grand air."*

Whether it was more a virtue or a weakness, Isabel was always remembered for her extreme generosity. In the course of her twenty-five years of active reign, she reputedly gave away something like 100,000,000 pesetas in presents and alms. Down-and-out aristocrats and unlucky politicians of all parties could count on her openhandedness, as could old servants, artists, and, above all, religious people. The cliché that this woman had no idea of the value of money is confirmed by the story that once the queen's steward set out 2,000 five-peseta pieces on a palace table to show her what some extravagant gesture would cost her; she settled for 20 pieces. Another anecdote concerns an incident during the celebration of Holy Tuesday when the sovereign traditionally washes the feet of several unfortunates. During the proceedings one of the queen's jewels fell onto a beggar's plate. "Keep it; it is fate which gave it to you," was her instant reaction.

Isabel's love affairs and her dilatoriness about state business made her a victim of factions and adventurers, so that she was a well-meaning but essentially incapable ruler. Her extreme piety—be it guilt, tradition, or conviction—gave undue influence at court to fanatical religious personalities of whom the most notorious was Sor Patricinio, who could display very convincing-looking stigmata on her hands, so long as she was not under a doctor's care. Radicals came to attribute all the queen's mistakes to the influence of this person, whereas Isabel herself in reminiscence averred indignantly: "I declare before God and men that she never meddled in the affairs of governments and politics." All her life Isabel considered the protection of the church to be her most sacred duty, and probably she could see nothing political in her subservience to the clericals. A paradox of the queen's situation was that "as she became more and more religious, she became less and less moral," with the result that the most sanctimonious court in Europe was also the most scandalous.

The queen's first lover was known as "General Beautiful," for Francisco Serrano was reputedly the handsomest man in Spain. Born in Cádiz, Serrano had shown both courage and brilliance in the field and was a lieutenant general by the time he was thirty-three. The man was destined to play a major political role in Spain over the next thirty years, bringing with him a kind of vague liberalism and more ambition and vanity than sense and resolution. Not politics, however, but simply the general's good looks, his soldierly ardor, and his courtly ways—all the things that her husband lacked—first attracted the queen to him. Within weeks after her marriage in

1846 their relationship came to public notice, especially after such incidents as when Serrano sat through an entire performance of the opera with his opera glasses fixed on the queen. After it became obvious that Isabel and Serrano were sleeping together, Francisco de Asís indignantly moved into quarters well separated from his wife's bedroom. The situation was a fine opportunity for the British ambassador to meddle with a view to winning the second round of the Spanish Marriages imbroglio: if the Queen had a child by the general, the Montpensiers and the French party would be confounded.

In these early months of his marriage Francisco was floundering in all his efforts to define his status. Inevitably, the king in name only surrounded himself with a group of self-seeking courtiers, mostly reactionary and clerical, who seconded his ambitions to do more than just spend his newly voted civil list of 5,500,000 reales. This palace camarilla at one point discussed seriously a project to pick a private quarrel with Serrano and to arrange for his being shot down. The plot came to naught, but Francisco made clear his determination to be self-avenging guardian of his wife's morals as well as a political force.

As the hostility between the royal couple became a scandal, the prime minister intervened in the form of posting General Serrano to Navarre. The queen's lover went only as far as Aranjuez, and when the ministry undertook to discipline him, Isabel exercised her prerogative of dismissing it. The queen herself left the capital for the summer residence on May 6. Shortly before her departure an attempt was made on her life, a crazed lawyer-journalist shooting at her from such close range that her face and clothes were burned. No accomplices were uncovered, although there were wild rumors about plots involving Don Francisco or the Montpensiers. Isabel, laughing at danger as always, spared the man's life. While her husband pouted at El Pardo, Isabel spent a leisurely summer with Serrano at Aranjuez, with many boating parties on the river, the queen possessing a far more decorative and sumptuous rowing launch than the one used by her forebear Fernando VI exactly a century before. Excursions to neighboring royal sites may have seen Isabel and Serrano talking of love in the very same gardens where Cristina and Muñoz had pledged their devotion. The queen mother, however, did not appreciate the parallel. Although soon after her daughter's marriage she had stormed at Francisco as an unfit husband, she never countenanced unsanctified intercourse for herself or for Isabel. Helpless to make the queen behave morally or even decorously, Cristina left for Paris in a bad humor. Once there, she relented, writing Isabel a long letter blaming herself for all the difficulties.

By the late summer of 1847 Isabel was obviously pregnant but seemingly unconcerned. The minister of the interior drove to El Pardo to try to persuade Don Francisco to make a show of being with his wife. The hapless consort received him amiably and replied at length:

> I understand what you mean but an outrage has been committed against my marital dignity. That is monstrous since I ask for so little. I know that Isabel does not love me. I forgive her for that as our marriage took place for reasons of state. There was no mutual affection. I always tried to save appearances, never wanted a final rupture, but Isabelita has less delicacy than I. . . . The presence of a favorite would not have been disagreeable to me if conventions had been observed. But they should not have insulted me. Serrano must disappear. He had spoken rudely of me. I am not going to stand for that. Serrano! Do you know who he is? An abortive Godoy. The real one, in order to make himself loved by my great-grandmother, had made himself agreeable to Carlos IV.

(Godoy might otherwise have been on Don Francisco's mind, for in this same year Isabel's government restored to him, then living in Paris, his confiscated fortune, which he enjoyed until his death four years later.) Doña Isabel, without making any attempt to dismiss her lover, did announce in the press on August 16 that "she is disposed to join her august husband from this moment." Pettishly, in seeming triumph, Francisco stated, "That is fine. We will return to the discussion within four months." By then, he calculated, the public would know that he and the queen had been separated for more than nine months. Told of this scheming, Isabel replied calmly that her husband could not scare her.

Both the queen, now in Aranjuez, and the queen mother, still in Paris, decided that the strong hand of Narváez was again required. The conservative general returned on August 27 from his ambassadorship in France pledged to "kick out Bulwer and have Serrano shot." He got nowhere at first with either royalty or politicians, and instead, a ministry was formed, headed by the Marquis of Salamanca, the leading stock-market speculator of the day. Not the least of Salamanca's aims was to use the government to recoup his personal financial reverses, and he also sought to protect investments he had promoted for the queen, Muñoz, and Narváez. He had a remarkable number of other intrigues in hand as well. He tried to placate British opinion and money by naming General Espartero a senator and granting amnesty to the Carlists. He sent secret proposals to "Carlos VI" regarding a marriage between him and Isabel, if an annulment of the earlier union could be received from Rome. The Pope, who had made clear his outrage at Isabel's conduct, was to be mollified by negotiating a favorable concordat. Salamanca also set out to please General Serrano by making him a captain general in Madrid, all the while he promoted a rival for the queen's affections and with considerable success. Isabel's new lover was an opera singer named Mirall, who found favor for his beauty, his voice, and his build.

Salamanca's term of office was sensational for its bravado, but it lasted only a month. On October 4, 1847, General Narváez presented himself alone in the council of ministers and announced, "Gentlemen, by royal order you have been relieved of your functions." Somehow he had persuaded the queen that a general housecleaning was in order and that he should be given a free hand "to seize the stick and strike hard," his own words. Within days everything changed. Narváez effected a reconciliation between Doña Isabel and Don Francisco, and he recalled Cristina from Paris so that she could no longer plot and could lend some respectability to her daughter's court. The singer Mirall was sent away, and so was General Serrano, who was bought off with the captain generalcy of Granada. Probably Serrano was disgusted with the queen's fickleness, and she was also tired of him. Nonetheless, the end of her first great affair distressed her: "This night Her Majesty was emotionally upset and one could see signs on her face of her having cried." At the end of the year she suffered a miscarriage.

Narváez's direct exercise of power from October, 1847, to January, 1851, earned his regime the name of the Grand Ministry. He put competent officials in office and made efforts to balance the budget and to expose the shady dealings of Salamanca and his friends, but the queen's prodigality largely defeated the first and her protection of Salamanca the second. Nonetheless, Narváez's firmness in this period spared Spain the cataclysmic upheavals that overtook almost all European countries. The year 1848 opened with a revolution in the kingdom of Naples against Isabel's uncle Ferdinand II, who had earned the nickname of Bomba for his willingness to bombard his own subjects into submission. In February Louis Philippe was overthrown in favor of a second French Republic. His daughter-in-law, Isabel's sister Luisa, had a harrowing escape from the Tuileries to haven in England, later moving to Spain with her husband Montpensier. Mobs humiliated the King of Prussia in Berlin. Metternich fled Vienna. Republics were born violently in Budapest, Venice, and, most disturbingly for the Spanish government, in Rome. At the end of the year Narváez sent Spanish troops to the aid of the Pope; they earned many medals for a minimum of fighting, in large part because the French reserved to themselves the role of the Pope's saviors. Virtually all these revolutions were in the name of a constitution and citizen liberties, which Spain already enjoyed in some measure. One exception to this rule that Isabel might well have pondered were the events in Munich, where the Bavarian King Ludwig I was driven from his throne by conservative and clerical rioters scandalized by his affair with the dancer Lola Montes, who, incidentally, claimed to be Spanish born.

Spain witnessed some violence in 1848, provoked by both the left and right. In March the ordinarily elegant parade of vehicles and promenaders in the Paseo del Prado was turned into mad chaos by rioters, the queen's carriage returning to the Oriente Palace with difficulty. In May two battalions of the Regiment of Spain took over the Plaza Mayor and surrendered only after three hours of assault by Narváez's troops. Executions and deportations followed, but the most sensational casualty of these events was the British ambassador, Bulwer, who was handed his passports in June, 1848, together with a thirty-one-page memorandum detailing his crimes such as giving false news, corrupting officials, and encouraging revolutionaries. According to one legend, Narváez dismissed Bulwer with a kick in the pants.

That same month the Carlist hero General Cabrera slipped across the frontier and within a short time was leading an army of 10,000 Basques, Aragonese, and Catalan rebels. Actually, Carlist guerrillas had been operating in the north since October, 1846, when "Carlos VI" denounced his cousin's marriage. Cabrera stated his intention this time to employ humanitarian tactics, but the apathy of the people to his cause and the success of the government in encouraging desertions led him to revive terrorism. Madrid newspapers featured with horror the story of a priest who tried to assassinate the Carlist leader being forced to eat his own poison. Later the Carlists decided that the presence of the Count of Montemolín would generate support—unlike Don Carlos, the son was an unknown quantity to the people—but the French police prevented his crossing the frontier and forced him to return to England. In April, 1849, Cabrera abandoned the struggle once again, thus ending what was called the Second Carlist War. (The Tiger of the Maestrazgo eventually mellowed about Spanish politics after he moved to London and at age forty-three married a twenty-three-year-old Englishwoman who was worth 25,000 pounds a year and who forbade him to smoke in her presence.)

Farce now overtook the Carlist cause. The pretender in England resumed his courtship of Miss Adeline de Horsey, daughter of Spencer Horsey de Horsey and a lively, beautiful adventuress who became consumed with the desire to be Queen of Spain. The Count de Montemolín's parents and advisers were adamant against such a match, but the love-stricken Carlos Luis persisted and finally resorted to signing in secret an "abdication" in favor of his brother. He thereafter took his fiancée on a walk on the shores of Lake Windemere, and the following conversation took place. "Dear one, for you I have abandoned my throne." "Your crown, what are you saying?" "Yes, I have abdicated. Now I will marry you. Come to my arms,

Countess." "Imbecile!" She subsequently broke off the engagement in May, 1849, later marrying the Earl of Cardigan, the hero of the Charge of the Light Brigade. As for the Count of Montemolín, he briefly considered suicide but ended up crawling back to his father, Don Carlos, now the Count of Molina, who was living with royal honors in Trieste as a favored guest of the Hapsburgs. The prodigal was made to recant his abdication, and the next year he pleased his family by marrying a Bourbon, Carolina of Naples, who was also Cristina's sister. The second son of Don Carlos, Juan Carlos, who had refused his brother's offer of the throne, was currently traveling about Europe without his estranged wife, the Princess of Modena. The third son, Fernando, still lived with his parents in Trieste. Of all of them, the stepmother, the Princess of Beira, did the most to keep alive the fires of Carlism, having strongly abetted Cabrera in his recent attempt.

Madrid was astonished on October 19, 1849, to read that Prime Minister Narváez, so recently victorious over both radicals and traditionalists, had been ousted by a cabal of Francisco de Asís' courtier henchmen, who proceeded to form a ministry of nobodies. By persistent intrigues the queen's husband had become governor of the royal palace. Ostensibly living on good terms with Isabel, Francisco privately declared, "If one day is formed a ministry under my influence, there will hang from the queen's balcony all those who have been her lovers." The person who had the most to be frightened about was the current paramour, a successful general, the Marquis of Bedmar. He and the queen were known to have late tête-à-tête suppers at Lhardy, the best French restaurant in Madrid. His fears were groundless, for the very next day the *Gaceta* announced that Narváez had resumed control, packing off Francisco's "Lightning Ministry" so that they could "rest from the fatigues of office." The whole thing was more ridiculous than threatening. Narváez spanked Don Francisco by having him closely watched and deprived of his lucrative post as intendant of the royal patrimony. After stormy scenes with the queen, the general secured the retirement of the Marquis of Bedmar on grounds that he was an offense to the court. Once again the stigmatized hand of Sor Patrocinio was traced to Francisco's childish action and to Isabel's acquiescence in it, and the nun was returned to her convent in Badajoz.

Court and country had several months of tranquillity until July 12, 1850, when the ceremonial cannon boomed out the news of the birth of an infante to the queen. The likely paternity of the child had been much speculated about, even Queen Victoria taking note of it. The Marquis of Bedmar was the popular guess, but the consort Francisco upset expectations this time by doing nothing to show his displeasure, rather taking pains to appear with the queen in public both before and after the delivery. Clearly, whatever political status Francisco enjoyed depended on his claim to be father of the heir. Since many feared that Isabel might not survive childbirth, Francisco tried beforehand to assume the presiding chair at the council of ministers, but in this effort he was blocked by Narváez, a contretemps which made the two everlasting enemies.

The new royal infant, apparently healthy and scheduled to be christened Fernando, was dead within an hour of his birth. Rumors flew that he had been strangled. Without any evidence people suspected the Montpensiers. The Infanta Luisa had given birth in the fall of 1848 to a daughter, who now remained the heiress presumptive. The estrangement of the queen and her sister dated from this tragedy, with the former showing a patent concern about keeping the latter away from her succeeding children. As for Francisco, he mysteriously commissioned a portrait of the dead infante.

Narváez, whose control of the political situation seemed so secure, was forced to flee the kingdom in January, 1851, because of a revolt among his own conservative supporters and also because of wavering whims of the old and young queens. Cristina wanted the Muñoz children created infantes; Narváez would just as soon that she and her family left him in peace by returning to Paris. Isabel, so recently furious with the minister for his dismissal of her lover, was now to exclaim: "But, Mama, what do you want me to do without Ramón?" "Choose between him and me," replied the mother who owed the general so much. Narváez was the one to go, departing with the defiant words: "I am not beaten yet. I thank God that he has given me a head and a heart and luck."

Narváez's successor as prime minister was Juan Bravo-Murillo, a former minister of finance who had broken with his chief because of the general's refusal to pare down army expenditures. The first predominantly civilian ministry in recent memory took office, and people also noted that the prime minister did not feel obliged to be in constant attendance on the queen, as when she went to the opera. The government courageously faced the financial situation, declaring Spain virtually bankrupt and retiring the debt at 50 percent of value. British and other foreign creditors were shocked, but rather than collapse as predicted, Spanish industry and trade flourished with the restoration of financial confidence. People hailed the conclusion of a Concordat with the Papacy on March 16, 1851, as another major accomplishment of the Bravo-Murillo regime. Church-state relations had been embittered by the confiscations of the 1830's, which the Pope now guardedly recognized, and the church in return gained state-guaranteed maintenance of the clergy, complete clerical control of censorship and education, and the restoration of three religious orders. The Concordat, cherished by the queen, was regarded as a complete surrender to the Pope by radicals and as not enough of a surrender by the Carlists.

At peace with the Holy Father, the queen was rewarded with the successful delivery of a child on December 2, 1851. It was an infanta, who was duly christened Isabel and for the next six years was considered heiress to the throne. The queen could hardly let her baby out of her sight. Gossips immediately named the child La Aranuela after the Count of Arana, Isabel's current lover, but Don Francisco had presented her as his daughter on the traditional silver salver. A ninety-four-year-old duke was among the witnesses of this ceremony, and to him the king consort said, "You who have known four reigns, look at this Princess of the Asturias, who could be your sovereign."

Don Francisco's musing about the accession of the infanta almost came true, for Queen Isabel was nearly killed by an assassin on February 2, 1852. She was scheduled to go in great pomp to the Church of the Atocha to give thanks for her child and present her to the patron saint of Madrid. Wearing a crimson mantle and a green velvet gown decorated in gold with the lions and towers of Castile, Isabel was walking down the grand corridor of the palace when a priest slipped through the halberdiers. By appearance he wanted to present a petition, and the monarch signaled for him to advance, only for the man to plunge a stiletto into her chest. Her stays and the gold trim prevented the wound from being fatal, but the queen fainted after murmuring, "My child, care for my child." The crowding around of the attendants did threaten the infanta's safety, but a quick-thinking colonel held the baby over his head, earning himself the rank of marquis for his action. The assassin was a Franciscan priest, a sixty-year-old Raskolnikov type involved in mysticism, political radicalism, and hypochondria. Defiant after his crime, regretting that he had not thought to poison the dagger, he denied being part of any plot, nor was any evidence of one ever brought forward. Yet the French ambassador wrote that society believed "it is the king who wanted to have the queen assassinated"—for reasons of political power. Despite Isabel's intercession for his life, the assassin was taken to his execution tied to a burro and dressed in a bloody robe; he was garroted; his body was burned; and his ashes were scattered—the last such auto-da-fé proceeding in Spain.

When Isabel did appear again to give thanks at the Atocha on February 2, the crowds roared their goodwill and elation. The queen was more than forgiven for her scandals; her monarchy seemed one of the strongest in Europe.

4. Railroads and Revolutions

A mark of unfolding national prosperity, the building of Spain's first railroads in the 1850's was also accompanied by financial frauds, in which the royal family had their hand. Prosperity did not still the fractiousness of the extreme right and the extreme left, and after two decades of violent swings of the political pendulum a full-scale revolution brought the monarchy crashing down.

Actually Barcelona, always ahead of the rest of the country, built Spain's first railroad in 1848, but more publicity attended the queen's opening of a line from Madrid to Aranjuez on February 9, 1851. The 36-kilometer run, which took two hours, ended in 100 meters of solid silver track and a grand staircase to the royal station. Soon Isabel II had her personal railway car, more sumptuous than even Queen Victoria's: the main salon, hung with sky blue satin and velvet, contained four huge armchairs grouped around a table encrusted with topazes and emeralds. This pandering to Isabel's taste for luxury was a touch of the financier and ex-Prime Minister Salamanca, who sold the Aranjuez line to the state for 60,000,000 reales.

By 1860 the northern trunk line had been completed to the French frontier. Railroad building had its opponents, including some who simply feared innovation, some who feared to facilitate a new French invasion, and many who were outraged by the fantastic corruption involved. During the building of the line north, landowners received a great windfall from the treasury if the tracks crossed their properties, and accordingly, speculators saw to it that the line took a wildly circuitous route, including swings onto three holdings in the vicinity of Madrid belonging to the queen herself.

When the Cortes in 1853 challenged the scandalous railroad contracts, Queen Isabel angrily prorogued it and dismissed the ministry for failing to protect the name of the dynasty. Another ministry fell after it could not halt new exposures of financial skulduggery involving the queen mother. In the general crisis Madrid began to expect the coming of a right-wing dictator, since both the queen and her husband were attracted to authoritarian methods. Neighboring France, which contributed much of the capital for Spanish railroads, also at this time offered a political example; in 1851 the president of the Second French Republic, Louis Napoleon, made himself dictator and the next year revived the French empire (this was five years after the death in Florence of Joseph Bonaparte, his uncle and the onetime king of Spain). Spain, however, did not go rightward at this time but leftward.

The revolution which finally came in the summer of 1854 was, perhaps, an inevitable reaction to ten years of rule by the conservatives. The fact that the people were enjoying markedly good times did not make them less critical of corruption and inefficiency. One of the chief objects of popular wrath was the Queen Mother Cristina, who was labeled *la ladrona* (the thief). Regarding her speculative activities, the French ambassador reported that "there is not a single industrial negotiation in which she or the Duke of

Rianzáres [her husband] don't take part." Queen Isabel, for her part, had lost her recent popularity not so much for financial dishonesty as for sexual misbehavior. What the underground Spanish papers were saying in lurid detail about their monarch was merely echoed by the lofty London *Times* on July 25, 1854, when it declared Isabel "guilty of high treason against the cause of virtue and morality."

As usual with Spain's modern revolutions, the one of 1854 began with a pronunciamiento. The call to arms came from General O'Dónnell, whose turn it was, the wits said. The queen responded by riding back from La Granja in such splendid style that she overawed Madrid, but she was dissuaded from going to face down the mutineers in person. The minister of war rallied a loyal force, and as in 1843, a mock battle followed, with both sides claiming victory. O'Dónnell was joined at Aranjuez by General Serrano, and they issued a joint manifesto calling for constitutional reforms and a national militia to oversee them. Various cities rose in their support, and barricades went up in Madrid. At the bullfights the crowds sang the "Hymn of Riego." Eventually the people of the capital gave themselves over to rioting and arson, the objects of their hatred being the houses of the newly rich (unlike 1834, when the monasteries were the targets). They set fire to the mansions of two recent prime ministers, and then they sacked the palace of Queen Cristina, who fled to the royal palace and later offered her house as a national charity. The current prime minister felt that the situation was so out of hand that Queen Isabel should leave by rail with such loyal soldiers as remained, but she demurred after hearing the French ambassador declare, "Sovereigns who abandon their palaces in revolutionary days never return to them."

Persuaded of the need of a truly dramatic concession to the revolutionaries, Isabel signed a letter recalling that great idol of the masses in 1840, General Espartero. (According to Karl Marx, Espartero "like Mahomet waited for the revolutionary mountain to come to him.") Before returning to Madrid, the general made clear that he must have his own way, insisting on a complete purge of the royal household and the use of national militia as palace guards. "Never has anyone talked to me like this," cried Isabel II after Espartero's envoy berated her at length about her private life. She threatened to abdicate but ended up not only accepting Espartero's demands but also issuing a manifesto of apology to the nation on July 26, an admission of her having been misled by bad advisers and having made grave mistakes. The queen decided to humiliate herself, after being a virtual prisoner in her palace for weeks, in order to protect her daughter's rights and to stop talk of the throne being offered to her sister Luisa.

All Madrid turned out to witness General Espartero's triumphant return July 28, 1854. The popular hero rode about amid decorated balconies and showers of flowers standing in a carriage and waving his sword. People sang to the tune of "La donna e mobile" the words *Muera Cristina, muera la ladrona, viva Espartero*. The following day a somewhat disgruntled O'Dónnell, the man who had started the revolution, enjoyed a more restrained welcome, which was climaxed by the two generals embracing in public. Espartero became prime minister; O'Dónnell settled for minister of war. Over the next two years took place a silent struggle between these two consuls, Espartero being a *Progresista*, O'Dónnell a *Moderado*.

The man-in-the-street revolutionary of 1854 wanted one thing above all, vengeance on Queen Cristina even to the point of putting her on trial. Espartero and O'Dónnell agreed to the sequestration of such of the ex-regent's property as she had not had removed to France, and they found it expedient to promise that Cristina would not be allowed to escape "not by day, not by night, not furtively." For her part, Cristina grandly declined any furtive French leave, saying, "I shall depart the country as a Queen or I shall not leave it." Queen Isabel firmly resisted any further harassment of her mother and then authorized her immediate departure with a suitable escort of "my noble army." On the morning of August 28, Isabel, looking disheveled and in tears, waited on Cristina in the latter's bedroom. Francisco de Asís and Rianzáres could barely part the two women. The two generals joined the royalty in a procession down the grand staircase to the main courtyard, where a two-horse carriage and two squadrons of cavalry waited to take the queen mother's party to Portugal. In time Cristina resumed residence in Malmaison, enjoying the friendship of Napoleon III just as she had that of Louis Philippe, despite the continuing revelations of her financial chicanery coming out of Spain. Told that a friendly party at court was seeking her return, Cristina authorized a press release: "Queen Cristina does not expect to return in triumph to her old palace in Madrid. Tired of ingratitude, she intends to remain absent from the country where her immense services have been so ill repaid."

The renewed separation of royal mother and daughter was again the occasion of intrigues involving the rival branches of the dynasty. The original pretender, Don Carlos, died at age sixty-seven on March 10, 1855. He was buried in the Cathedral of San Giusto in Trieste dressed as a Spanish captain general. The inscription on his tomb reads "Carlos V Hispaniarum Rex—in prosperis modestus, in adversis constans." Meanwhile, the diplomatic corps in Madrid was being treated to the spectacle of Queen Isabel openly complaining of her treatment by the left-wing regime and threatening to abdicate. Her husband, Don Francisco de Asís, put two and two together and opened secret negotiations with the second pretender, the Count of Montemolín. He proposed that he and Isabel abdicate and that Montemolín succeed to the throne as "Carlos VI" and as an absolutist.

In time would occur a marriage between their daughter, the three-year-old Isabel, and Montemolín's son, as yet unborn, with this son automatically succeeding to the throne at age twenty-five. Francisco always seemed to regard himself as a usurper and occasionally made Isabel feel the same way about herself. Montemolín could not agree more, but their scheme came to naught in the face of Cristina's spirited opposition from Paris and the fact of the conservatives' return to power in Spain, removing much of the political appeal of a Carlist solution.

The queen and Espartero had clashed over his sponsorship of a bill to sell church property. At a midnight meeting of the council in February, 1855, the never-gentlemanly general at one point shouted at Isabel II, "Let's go. You're crazy." Later she signed the act in tears, writing a secret letter of apology to the Pope. When Espartero initiated a new purge of court personnel, the king consort was manhandled as he tried to resist at the main door of his wing of the palace. Also, Sor Patrocinio was placed in confinement and her "stigmata" cured medically. A year later the more moderate General O'Dónnell managed to maneuver Espartero out of power, and he crushed a radical insurrection in the latter's favor, General Serrano playing a leading role in the suppression, which involved the bombardment of the poorer sections of Madrid. While Queen Isabel and O'Dónnell were in agreement on certain policies, such as lifting the sequestration of the queen mother's property, the prime minister was unwilling to undo all the reforms associated with the Revolution of 1854. The queen, who had earlier murmured to O'Dónnell, "You will not abandon me," was the one to abandon the other at the first opportunity, naming in October, 1856, as head of the government General Narváez, the one man the queen felt totally secure with. Out went the recent anticlerical laws, and back came the food taxes.

While presiding over another conservative interlude in Spanish politics, Narváez and his firm hand served to get the royal family over a crisis involving a new pregnancy of the queen. Since late 1856 Isabel had been having an affair with a handsome Valencian named Antonio Puig Moltó. Although an officer in the engineers corps, Puig Moltó was not as dashing as his predecessors in the queen's affections; rather he was extremely young, sandy haired, gentle-mannered, and delicate of health. Many people believed that he was responsible for Isabel's baby, but some observers suggested that a young American dental assistant named McKeon was the father. Whatever the rival claims, few gossips were willing to credit Don Francisco de Asís for his wife's condition, and the king consort confirmed suspicions by showing every sign of jealousy and distress. On one occasion, knowing that another man was in the queen's apartments, Francisco tried to storm in for a confrontation. He was accompanied by the minister of war, who killed an aide of Narváez guarding the queen's door, only to be cut down himself by Narváez's own sword (the press reported the two men as victims of an epidemic that seemed to claim no other lives). The wronged husband turned from boudoir maneuvers to serious political intrigues, talking in secret of having himself named regent. The French ambassador thought he had some idea of what was going on in the royal family when he reported:

> In the first rank of those who wish to overthrow the queen is King Francisco de Asís, her husband. . . . The new pregnancy of the queen has reanimated, if possible, the vengeful instincts of the king: after deplorable scenes with the threat of the most scandalous revelations he has already obtained from his wife a kind of moral abdication and now he proceeds with resolve to his object directed by some members of the clergy, fanatic and known adherents of the Carlist party.

In the end Don Francisco swallowed his pride and presented on the silver salver the infante delivered on November 28, 1857. The male child was the first Prince of the Asturias born in the nineteenth century, an event strengthening Queen Isabel's popularity and her position against the Carlists. After the traditional grand procession of the leading grandees and clerics through the palace, the infant was christened Alfonso Francisco de Asís Pío Juan María Gregorio Pelayo de Borbón y Borbón (the Pío was for the child's godfather, Pope Pius IX, whereas Pelayo commemorated Spain's eighth-century first king). Less reverently, street people nicknamed the baby the Puigmultejo.

The decade after the birth of the heir was prosperous and tranquil, at least on the surface. Control of the government peacefully alternated between Generals Narváez and O'Dónnell. The queen's preference for Narváez as a dancing partner once caused O'Dónnell's resignation, but she also prompted the former to leave office by saying, "You like the institution of monarchy but O'Dónnell likes me." The more conservative Narváez identified himself with police tactics, such as in the case of the bloody repression of peasant protesters in Andalusia in 1857, but the liberal O'Dónnell, if less harsh in his use of the Civil Guard, did nothing more than the other to alleviate the conditions of the masses. Both men resorted to the despicable policy of diverting popular attention to overseas military ventures. For the first time since Fernando VII Spain tried to play the great power.

Madrid newspapers headlined the name Saigon for the first time in the summer of 1858. Spanish soldiers intervened in Indochina after the murder of a missionary bishop, but France sent more and better provisioned troops and brought off the fateful annexation of three new colonial provinces. More success attended a Spanish campaign against Morocco the next year, following a border incident. O'Dónnell personally led an expedition of 40,000 men and fourteen warships (ten of them steam vessels) and captured Tetuán on February 6, 1860. During the subsequent public thanksgivings in Madrid the queen walked barefoot in a procession as a penitent while at her side O'Dónnell bore a taper as well as the new title of Duke of Tetuán.

With much of the Spanish army committed in Morocco, the Carlists made a new attempt to seize power but achieved only a new farce. The second pretender, the Count of Montemolín, was already a balding forty-year-old. While so far he had made only one futile attempt to join his followers in Spain, he never ceased producing propaganda and bribes from his stepmother's palace in Trieste. Now an opportunity presented itself in the offer of the ambitious young captain general of the Balearic Islands, Jaime Ortega, to lead an invasion of the mainland with a force of 3,500. In view of Don Francisco's recent intrigues with the Carlists, the plotters had hopes of a rising in Madrid and the ready abdication of Queen Isabel. Ortega duly effected a landing on the Valencian coast and he confidently ordered a special train to Madrid. When he revealed his intentions to his men, however, and called on them to cheer "Carlos VI," the soldiers responded by cheering for the queen. Warned by Napoleon III, the Spanish government was prepared for the situation, easily overpowered Ortega, and had him summarily executed. An even more zestful triumph was the capture of the Count de Montemolín and his brother Fernando, these unmilitary princes having accompanied the expedition and lamely gone into hiding. "Carlos VI" wrote an abject letter to his cousin Isabel II begging her leave to "enjoy in peace the seclusion of home." Her government exacted a price for his return to Trieste: formal renunciation of claims to the throne by himself and Fernando. Since Montemolín's rights were supposed to be divinely given, his craven abandoning of them hurt the legitimatist cause not only in Spain but throughout Europe.

Carlist circles were further dismayed that summer when Montemolín's second brother, Don Juan Carlos, took up the claim to the throne, an action he had eschewed in 1849 during the crisis of his brother's first abdication over Miss de Horsey. The new pretender had long offended his family by his perverse opinions, his abandonment of his wife, and his meanderings about Europe in unseemly company. Their annoyance turned to rage when they read the accession manifesto of "Juan III" which promised to pursue his cause without resort to arms and to offer Spain "national prosperity in harmony with the light and progress of the age." This pledge to be enlightened in the manner of his "upstart" contemporaries Napoleon III and Victor Emmanuel II was antithetical to the whole Carlist tradition. Indeed, "a nineteenth century progressive was hardly the man to breathe new life into a sixteenth century crusade."

Released from Spain and lectured by his stepmother, the Count of Montemolín repudiated his abdication on June 15, 1860. The Carlists now afforded two rival pretenders since Don Juan stayed in the game. Tragedy soon resolved the whole situation—namely, the strange death of the Count de Montemolín on January 13, 1861, preceded by that of his brother and followed by that of his wife. Don Fernando was stricken in Styria, and his two relatives died in Trieste after accompanying his corpse there. Officials gave the cause as "fever," but many people suspected poisoning. Don Juan Carlos now "reigned" without rival, but the Princess of Beira had no use for this stepson and was busy grooming his eldest male offspring to be "Carlos VII."

Carlist intrigues not backed by force were no worry to the queen's government, which continued to deploy its military and naval resources in overseas endeavors. In March, 1861, Spain undertook the reoccupation of Santo Domingo, and in November it joined France and Britain in an armed intervention in Mexico. Although Spain had finally acknowledged Mexican independence in 1836, the reimbursement to Spanish citizens of 8,500,000 pesos remained in dispute. The current radical government of President Benito Juárez was adamant against paying. The United States, of course, was at this time involved in its Civil War. O'Dónnell in a moment of bluster saw fit to tell the British ambassador, "If Mexico doesn't accept, we will make war on it and we will make war on the United States if necessary." As in Indochina, Spain soon found its military efforts completely overshadowed by the actions of France. Queen Isabel dreamed of putting a Bourbon prince on a Mexican throne, but Napoleon III ignored his ally's pretensions and sponsored the disastrously tragic rule of the Hapsburg Emperor Maximilian and his consort, the Saxe-Coburg princess Carlota. During the Mexican adventure, which took many lives and gained less money than it cost, Generals Serrano and Prim made heroes of themselves and gained many expressions of the queen's admiration. Both were to betray the monarchy within the decade.

Still another display of O'Dónnell's diplomatic bravado involved Spain in a war with Peru and Chile in January, 1866. For once Spain's navy was successful in mounting a blockade and winning a sharp engagement at Callao. What these actions gained beyond prestige was soon forgotten.

Queen Isabel's popularity appeared enhanced by the victories overseas and the deceptive quiet at home. In the course of 1862 she embarked on a grand tour of the country, enjoying a warm welcome in Catalonia, so often the center of revolution, and ending with a joyous reception in the chief cities of Andalusia. The University of Granada presented her with a gold replica of the crown of Isabel I. During the tour Francisco de Asís fulfilled his role as consort with imperturbable dignity, and it was the first time the populace had a view of the five-year-old heir, Alfonso, as well as the ten-year-old infanta, Isabel. Three additional infantas were born in the early 1860's, arousing goodwill toward the dynasty in some, indifference in others, and the usual gossip about their paternity.

The queen threw away all tranquillity in 1864, when she took a new lover of dubious background but definite pretensions, a man named Carlos Marfori. Born in Cádiz in 1818 the son of an Italian pastry cook, Marfori had dabbled at being an entertainer before entering an army career. His military attainments gained him little respect from the army hierarchy, but his marriage to a cousin of Narváez, which that general at first opposed, eventually brought him preference, the post of civil governor of Madrid, and the eye of the queen. People were surprised that Isabel, known for her taste in good-looking young soldiers, would turn to this middle-aged and obese, albeit flamboyant and sensual type of man, whose thick lips, heavy jaw, and swarthy complexion caused whispers that he was of Moorish origin. Many at court found it distasteful that the swaggering, unmannerly Marfori with his pointed mustache acted as if he wanted all the world to know that he was the queen's lover. Most dangerously for the dynasty, Marfori, unlike his predecessors, chose to meddle in politics, assuming official positions not only in the royal household but in the ministerial government as well. With Marfori around, observers in Madrid began to notice a marked hostility of the populace to the queen when she traveled in and out of the capital and a renewed restlessness of the politicians and generals.

However preoccupied with sensual pleasures and however indolent about state duties, Isabel was concerned to the point of hysteria about one subject, the position of the church. In the year 1861 occurred the proclamation of a united Italy under the King of Sardinia, Victor Emmanuel II, in defiance of the wishes of the Pope and at the expense of much papal territory. The other major victims of Italian national unification were the Neapolitan Bourbons, Isabel's cousins losing forever the throne founded in their dynasty by Carlos III. Don Francisco and the clerical faction at court had favored armed intervention by Spain early in the situation, but O'Dónnell recognized that the military costs would be far greater than fighting Moors or Vietnamese, and he declined a proposal of Napoleon III that Spain "reoccupy the position belonging to it in the European concert." The Spain of Isabel II was not destined to attempt the aggressive Italian policies of her eighteenth-century ancestor Isabel Farnese. Nonetheless, the Spanish government remained the only major one to refuse recognition to the kingdom of Italy, at the insistence of the queen, until O'Dónnell, embarking on his third ministry in June, 1865, found it politically expedient to defy the Pope and acknowledge the king. This development was accompanied by many tearful scenes involving the queen, the resignation of her confessor, and a renewed persecution of Sor Patrocinio. The estrangement of Isabel from her moderate supporters grew inevitably.

An interesting sidelight of this Italian situation was that in 1865 King Victor Emmanuel ordered his second son, Amadeus, to take his summer vacation in Spain in order to improve relations between the dynasties. Amadeus threw himself into sightseeing and partying through all the famous cities of Andalusia, on September 3 reaching Madrid, where he took rooms at the Hotel de Paris on the Puerta del Sol. His obvious enjoyment of a bullfight immediately endeared the prince to the populace. He was also an enthusiastic observer of a military review and mock battle, at which time he met Spain's leading generals. Ironically, in view of later events, General Serrano bade good-bye to Amadeus with the words "We hope Your Highness has had a pleasant trip and will return to Spain soon." On September 7 Amadeus reached San Sebastián and at the Palacio de Marros in Zarauz knelt and kissed the hand of Queen Isabel, who found him a "handsome fellow." Don Francisco talked to him amiably in Italian about Italian literature until his wife cut him off impatiently. At a gala banquet Amadeus had eyes for everyone except the bright-eyed, pig-tailed, plumpish Infanta Isabel, whose hand in marriage he reportedly had come to seek. "See you soon" were the careless last words of Queen Isabel, who was preoccupied with preparing for a state visit the next day of Napoleon III and the Empress Eugénie, her former lady-in-waiting and dear friend. As San Sebastián festooned itself for the French, the Italian prince departed unnoticed. He was destined to return in eight years not as the infanta's husband but as Spain's elected king.

"Poor Isabel! A throne which seemed so solid!" These words were uttered by the same Empress Eugénie, who was soon to lose her own throne. The first event in the series that led to the toppling of the Spanish monarchy was a pronunciamiento by General Prim before two regiments in Aranjuez in January, 1866. His attempt was completely abortive, and Prim escaped to Portugal, where he encouraged other conspirators in Madrid to subvert the garrison there. In due course a mutiny occurred in July at the San Gil barracks, led by sergeants in the tradition of the La Granja uprising of 1854. Preparing countermeasures, O'Dónnell told Serrano, "Today it is necessary to die for the queen," but Serrano replied confidently, "No, General, today is a matter of conquering for the fatherland" (this from the one of the two men who had actually been Isabel's lover). The government succeeded in suppressing the San Gil rising and executed seventy of the rebels, making them martyrs, but many conspirators were left at large.

The next year was free of insurrection, but the antiregime forces went far in perfecting their organization and broadening their support. A large number of Spanish exiles met in Belgium and by the Ostend Pact of June, 1867, pledged themselves to the overthrow of the queen and the summoning of a constituent assembly to decide the future form of the Spanish state. By agreeing to refrain from proclaiming a republic immediately, Spanish democrats and socialists, who were short on supporters but long on oratory, were able to ally themselves with the less radical *Progresistas* and still less radical *Moderados*. All these groups were united in their disgust with the reactionary, clerical palace camarilla which favored ministries so incompetent, so corrupt, and so disrespectful of constitutional liberties. The politicians were willing to appeal to the vanity of promotion-hungry generals, to the lingering fantasies of the Carlists, and to the masses' discontent over taxes and land policies and their resentment over their numbers being sacrificed in incomprehensible overseas ventures. In sum, Spain contained many combustibles.

Queen Isabel appeared largely oblivious that her immorality was an additional rallying cry for the opposition. In January, 1868, she joyously received from the Pope a dispensation for her private sins and a "Rose of Gold" for her outward services to the church. The Pontiff's gesture was made "to attest and declare publicly and solemnly and with a perpetual monument of the love which from the bottom of our heart we profess for you, as much for your eminent merits before Us, the Church, and before the Holy Apostolic See, as for the other virtues which adorn you." The latter phrase could not have failed to produce sardonic hilarity. Death now claimed the queen's two mainstays, O'Dónnell in November, 1867, and Narváez in April, 1868.

In the summer of 1867 the government summarily deported General Serrano to the Canary Islands because it feared that he was going over to the opposition. Soon afterward the court was startled to learn that the Duke of Montpensier, his wife, and family had also been sent into exile. The queen was not unhappy to be parted from her sister who had seen fit to come up from Seville and give her long lectures on the subject of her lover Marfori. The husband had been in secret correspondence with both Generals Prim and Serrano, and he contributed 3,000,000 reales to the finances of the opposition. Montpensier had a vision of his wife, Luisa, replacing Isabel as queen with himself as the real voice behind the throne; but Serrano had regentlike ambitions for himself, and Prim also betrayed his benefactor, to his everlasting hatred, by negotiating with agents of Napoleon III. Sojourning in Vichy and Lyons in early August, 1868, Prim received assurances that the French emperor would be neutral toward the imminent Spanish revolution if Prim gave assurances that the Spanish revolutionists would not support the Orléans Bourbons (the Montpensiers' daughter Maria Francisca had just recently married her cousin, namesake and son of Louis Philippe, who was the very monarch Napoleon III had superseded on the French throne). Meanwhile, the captain of the ship taking the Montpensiers into exile offered to sail to the Canaries to pick up General Serrano, but the duke decided otherwise and landed in Lisbon on August 3.

Plottings became true revolution on September 18, 1868, when the commandant at Cádiz, Admiral Juan Topete, issued a pronunciamiento that prompted insurrectionary juntas to be formed in cities all over Spain. The bluff, uncomplicated admiral was ready to proclaim Queen Luisa, and "had Montpensier been in the country at the time the revolution might have been his." Topete decided to wait for a constituent assembly, being persuaded by General Prim, who appeared on the scene. Prim had booked second-class passage from England to India and then surreptitiously taken ship from Gibraltar to Cádiz. Soon afterward General Serrano arrived from the Canaries. The group agreed to issue a vague manifesto in favor of "Spain with honor," rebuffing again overtures from the Duke of Montpensier and allowing the crowds to chant "Death to all the Bourbons." Prim sailed off to raise the seaboard cities, and Serrano marched north with an army.

After the court had spent the customary sojourns at La Granja and the Escorial, Queen Isabel left by rail for San Sebastián on September 17. Both her husband and her lover were in tow. The first reports about Prim, Topete, and Montpensier did not appear to upset the queen. Perhaps she thought that it was just 1854 again, meaning that she would merely have to make Prim prime minister and accept a new Constitution. She also expected to get material and moral support from Napoleon III who was taking his vacation at nearby Biarritz, but her imperial counterpart declined any meeting (French money interests involved in Spanish railroads were pro-opposition, among other factors). Upon the news of the Cádiz revolt, she did name a new prime minister, the brave and not illiberal General de la Concha (coincidentally, the queen invested him in a hotel room on the famous crescent-shaped Paseo de la Concha in San Sebastián).

Concha left for Madrid and later wired Isabel that she should proceed without delay to the capital but without Marfori "who would be badly received by the populace, having formed part of the dismissed cabinet." Although Isabel reacted to this demand with petulant annoyance, Marfori offered to go into exile. The queen, keeping her lover at her side, actually boarded a train for the south when they got reports of disruptions on the rail line. In the course of many anguished discussions in San Sebastián, Francisco de Asís offered his dubious services as negotiator, and some talked of Isabel's abdication in favor of the ten-year-old Alfonso. The perceptive Marfori observed that a monarch of Spain can relinquish the throne "to rest like Charles V [Carlos I] but not in the face of insurrection." Deciding to wait on events, Isabel took the precaution of sending for her 42,000,000 reales' worth of jewelry.

The rebel army of General Francisco Serrano and the royalist force of General Manuel Pavía met at Alcolea near Córdoba on September 28, 1868. Bloodier than the similar half-spirited encounters of 1843 and 1854, the battle was a definite victory for Serrano.

The court at San Sebastián learned of the defeat that night, and Isabel once again faced painful decisions. She was able to wire the Pope, in essence, "Shall I abdicate?" and received the reply "No." The following day, September 29, she chose to board a train for France. The queen was crying as she leaned on the arm of her bewildered husband, her lover and her family trailing behind. The Prince of the Asturias, dressed in blue velvet with a lace collar, looked especially woebegone. At the frontier she declared, "I thought I had more roots in this land," and a few days later at Pau she denounced "the insane presumption of a few men." In Madrid a provisional government proclaimed the deposition of the entire house of Bourbon.

Queen Isabel II had not abdicated legally, nor had she really been dethroned by force. Rather, she had simply given up for personal reasons. Unlike other times when Isabel risked death to keep her throne, "in 1868 she preferred to lose her crown rather than be separated from Marfori." The new element in the picture was that she had "a man who understood her, a man who satisfied her, a man who perhaps saw in her another thing than Queen of Spain." This interpretation relates plausibly to the situation faced by Edward VIII almost seventy years later. Yet if the British monarch's decision to stay with the person he loved had no serious political repercussions, Isabel's removal of herself from Spain caused her country five years of turmoil and brought Europe a very consequential war.

In evaluating the reign of Isabel II, some historians have stressed the revival of national prosperity, the greatest since the days of Carlos III, as measured by such statistics as the amount of gold in circulation—450,000 pesetas in 1833, 7,700,000 in 1845, and 100,000,000 in 1865. Perhaps the queen had very little responsibility for these economic gains, but if so, her will was also not all that decisive in the forty different ministries, one civil war, two mass revolutions, eighteen major pronunciamientos, two royal assassination attempts, and several bungled colonial ventures in the course of her reign. While Isabel fell far short of being a dedicated ruler, she received ambiguous and inadequate help and tutelage from her famous five generals—Espartero, Narváez, O'Dónnell, Serrano, and Prim—who "considered themselves saviors of something that nobody knew what it was." In sum, the reign "so full of incident lacked any greatness."

No historian can say for sure if Isabel's nymphomania offended large numbers of her subjects or simply made her more human in their eyes. The radical novelist Benito Pérez Galdós' assertion that "never was a queen more loved" stands in contradiction to the disastrous denouement of her reign. Regal, passionate, generous, religious, and incompetent are the sure words we are left with for Isabel II.

IX.
The Crisis of 1868–1874:
The Monarchy in Doubt

1. The Search for a New King

IN the century before 1868 Spain endured seemingly more than its share of vicissitudes: the enlightened reforms of Carlos III gave way to the selfish vagaries of Carlos IV, María Luisa, and Godoy; the national upsurge of 1808 was followed by the devastating struggle with Napoleon; the high hopes of the Constitution of 1812 were wrecked in the absolutist reaction of Fernando VII; the liberal promise of 1820 was reversed in 1823; and then came the dynastic civil war, the pronunciamientos, and the dizzying fluctuations of the Isabeline era. The departure of Isabel II ushered in seven years of more turmoil and hard choices for the nation. The Bourbons watched and waited when first Spain searched for a new king, then tried out another dynasty, and finally experimented without a monarch at all.

The day after she left Spain Queen Isabel II was received at the railroad station in Biarritz by the French imperial family. Napoleon III, hypocritical about his secret acquiescence in the Revolution of 1868, accorded the queen full royal honors. The Empress Eugénie wrote later of her astonishment that Isabel had completely recovered her composure and "remained cheerful and insouciant, as if no distressing event had taken place." The prince imperial and the Infante Alfonso, each aged about eleven, felt the drama of the day and fell into a tearful embrace.

On October 3 Isabel took up temporary residence in the small castle of Pau that had been the birthplace of Henry IV, her ancestor going back eight generations. She was accompanied by her large family and an entourage including Sor Patrocinio and Marfori. From Pau the queen issued a defiant manifesto to Spain, but aside from a handful of grandees who sent offers of men and money, few people were willing to do much to restore her to the throne. In November Isabel left for Paris, where she bought the commodious palace of a ruined Russian gambler on the rue du Roi de Rome (later rue Kléber—the building, which overlooks the Arc de Triomphe, is now the Hôtel Majestic). The mansion, renamed the Palace de Castilla and ostentatiously decorated with the royal arms, was to be an outpost of Spanish monarchism for the next thirty-six years. One small consolation for Isabel was that down the Champs-Elysées was her mother Cristina's mansion; the younger Bourbons, to their surprise, got to meet their Muñoz relatives for the first time.

In Spain, General Serrano made his triumphant entry into the capital on October 3, and later Admiral Topete and General Prim arrived, the last stirring the most passionate enthusiasm among the populace, who were even ready to credit him, not Serrano, with the victory over the royalists at Alcolea. Serrano, however, became president of a provisional government, and Prim contented himself with the ministry of war. The political situation in the ensuing period was the more stable for the fact that the moderate Serrano and the radical Prim did not clash openly, although their servants in neighboring palaces seemingly made every effort to create difficulties between them.

The new government promptly decreed all the things that revolutionary regimes had accomplished in 1820, 1841, and 1854. They suspended reactionary laws and enacted anticlerical measures; they provided for freedom of the press and scheduled a Cortes, to be elected by universal suffrage. Even though arms were distributed to all comers, disorders were at a minimum. In various cities juntas did take it upon themselves to abolish all taxes, and crowds demolished statues of the queen and burned her pictures in public. Streets named for Serrano or Prim replaced those once commemorating royalty. The revolution in its first heady days was known as *El Glorioso*, and Alexandre Dumas, visiting Barcelona, felt moved to tears at the signs and prospects of the "universal republic of brothers" (much the same reaction as George Orwell in the same city in 1936).

That same October 3, the day of Isabel's arrival in Pau and Serrano's welcome in Madrid, an important event occurred in Paris: the abdication of Don Juan in favor of his son the Count of Madrid. This action by the unstable maverick pretender made it possible for all Carlists to unite in support of the energetic, attractive twenty-year-old who took the title Carlos VII. His supporters expected that this third-generation Carlist would appeal to Spanish monarchists as a Bourbon uncompromised by association with Queen Isabel. Three weeks later the young claimant wrote to the courts of Europe of his intentions; "If God and the course of events place me on the throne of Spain I shall try to reconcile loyally the useful institutions of our epoch with the indispensable ones of the past, leaving to the Cortes, freely elected, the great and difficult burden of giving my country a constitution, which, I hope, will be both definitive and Spanish." To this message the various monarchs replied noncommittally through their chancelleries, except for the Pope, who wrote a warm response in his own hand, and the Disraeli ministry in Britain, which replied with disdain approaching discourtesy.

Don Carlos' relatively moderate political stance produced some snorts from Carlist traditionalists, who, nonetheless, proposed to bring about his rule in Spain by promoting armed uprisings in Catalonia, Navarre, and the Basque provinces. Such Old Carlists were successfully countered by a group of New Carlists, sometimes called neo-Catholics, who wanted to organize an electoral movement and to carry through their program in the forthcoming Cortes. Led by the politician Candido Nocedal, they mounted an effective propaganda campaign in Spain, publishing in the next few years some eighty-three newspapers, fourteen reviews, and fifteen satirical journals, as well as circulating pamphlets in the tens of thousands. These efforts were financed by the contributions of legitimist well-wishers in both France and Spain, by the 200,000 francs lent Don Carlos by his rich uncle the Duke of Modena, and by the proceeds of pawning the jewels of his winsome and ambitious wife, "Queen" Margarita.

In the fall of 1868 the principals involved made a genuine and dramatic effort to end the thirty-five-year-old split in the Spanish Bourbon dynasty. Queen Isabel invited the Count of Madrid to visit her in her Paris residence, but her cousin declined to compromise his position by showing such deference. In turn, she could not bring herself as Queen of Spain to call on the house of a pretender. They then arranged to meet as if by chance on the rue de la Grande Armée. Don Carlos took the arm of Doña Isabel, and Don Francisco took that of Doña Margarita, and the four of them sauntered off unnoticed by the other promenaders. At this meeting Isabel proposed that Carlos recognize her as queen, that she designate him infante and captain general, and that they all work for the restoration of the monarchy. The pretender demurred, pleading his obligation to his supporters. During a later arranged meeting in the Bois de Boulogne, Carlos countered with the proposition that Isabel recognize him as king, that he educate her son Alfonso in Spain, and that the rival claims of the two men to the throne be left for a decision at a later date. Isabel did not agree to this, but she did promise to contribute money to the Carlist press. Later the queen was to say with a sigh, "Carlism is synonymous with gentlemanliness," and a certain goodwill between the two sides replaced the old bitterness, even if no concrete agreements were ever reached.

The fate of Spain was not, of course, the plaything of its various royal exiles. The general historian of Spain might well see less long-range significance in the activities of Don Carlos than in the arrival in Spain in the fall of 1868 of an emissary of the great European anarchist leader Mikhail Bakunin. Without money and without knowing a word of Spanish, this agent helped kindle a mass movement involving thousands in the course of a few months. The next year the International established a Spanish Section, and Marx and Engels took a renewed interest in Spanish affairs (having already written incisive analyses of such events as the Revolution of 1854). A major expression of radical social discontent occurred early in 1869 in the form of insurrections in the cities of Cádiz, Málaga, and Saragossa, risings prompted by labor disputes and the government's efforts to disarm the obstreperous militia. The government provoked further riots by decreeing the conscription of 25,000 men for reinforcements to Cuba to put down a serious nationalist revolt there (the Cuban insurrection, lasting from 1868 to 1878, prefigured the struggle for independence culminating in the Spanish-American War of 1898). One of the high hopes of the Revolution of 1868 fostered by many politicians was that conscription was a thing of the past. Forced to employ repression and conscription, the government hurried to undercut socialist and republican propaganda by giving the country a constitution and finding it a king.

Great numbers of people turned out for the elections early in 1869, and the resulting Constituent Cortes, considered by some the most brilliant assemblage of Spaniards ever held, met for the first time on February 11. The vast majority of deputies were Liberals (a new name for the old *Progresistas*), but there were some seventy Radicals (at this time, anti-monarchists) and twenty Carlists. The Cortes spent much time debating such questions as the desirability of an upper house, the separation of church and state, and the permanent expulsion of the Bourbons. Observers claimed that these discussions sold fewer newspapers than the revelation that most of the royal treasure was missing. On May 21 the Cortes decided definitely that the monarchical form of government would be continued and on June 1 promulgated an entire new constitution. The document was very close to the Constitution of 1812 in its limitations of royal prerogatives. A new provision allowed for religious toleration, causing many priests to oppose it. On June 15 the Cortes elected Serrano regent, as the law provided. The temporary ruler used the title of Highness, but in terms of real power Serrano lived in a "golden cage," according to the republican Emilio Castelar. Prim, now prime minister, enjoyed more executive authority, but since all political attention was focused on the matter of finding a permanent monarch, the Prim regime of some eighteen months "may be summed up as being happy in having no history."

As recently as 1846 the Spanish people and the courts of Europe had gone through the excitement and worry of finding a man to sit on the throne in Madrid. Then it was a matter of choosing a consort, but even so, the final choice was disastrous. Now Spain was seeking a real king who perhaps would found a new dynasty. To the usual criteria of the ruler being Catholic, personable, and capable of having heirs, the mood of the country in 1868 dictated in addition that he be ostensibly liberal. "Looking for a democratic king is like looking for an atheist in heaven," Prim admitted later, after he had begun the traditional procedure of paging through the *Almanach de Gotha* for suitable candidates. Another difficulty was that the throne of Spain was currently looked upon as a dubious prize by many princes who were aware of what the past promised for the future in the way of ever-changing ministries, Carlist pretenders, and other problems. European royalty had very much on their minds the recent tragic fate in Mexico of the Emperor Maximilian, a case of the most well-intentioned and high-minded of princes assuming a crown in 1863 only to be shot by his own people in 1867.

The search for a Spanish monarch ranged far indeed. Agents of Prim approached the brother of the Danish King Christian IX, who refused to become Catholic, and the heir to Sweden, who felt he had better prospects at home. A Jewish financier at one point promoted Grand Duke Constantine of Russia. A considerable part of the dominant *Progresista* party in Spain was willing to seek a nonroyal king—namely, the venerable popular hero General Espartero, living in retirement in Logroño. The regent of 1841 and the dictator of 1854 was touched by the petitions with numerous signatures begging him to be crowned "Baldomero I," but he refused, pleading old age, ill health, and the absence of children.

Seven royal candidates were prominently discussed in 1869 and 1870. Their partisans distributed thousands of pictures of each, usually dressed as a Spanish captain general or in coronation robes. Although the Bourbons were legally disbarred from the contest, one natural choice was Alfonso, the eleven-year-old son of Isabel and presumably of Don Francisco de Asís. His accession would entail the alarming prospect of a protracted regency. Such would not be the case with his Carlist counterpart, the twenty-one-year-old Duke of Madrid, but the Carlist cause was distasteful to many. Still within the Spanish dynasty were two other candidacies: the forty-four-year-old, French-born Duke of Montpensier, who as the Infanta Luisa's husband had been looking about with an eye to the throne for two decades; and Enrique, the forty-six-year-old Duke of Seville and younger brother of Don Francisco, whose reputation for radicalism, which ruined his chances in 1846, was more of an asset now. Among foreign princes, a favorite choice from the beginning was Ferdinand of Saxe-Coburg, a fifty-five-year-old widower who, as ex-consort in Portugal, had earned respect for his progressive views. Perhaps, the best known to historians of all the names was Leopold of Hohenzollern-Sigmaringen, a thirty-eight-year-old cousin of the King of Prussia, a Catholic, and a liberal. Finally, many of the *Progresistas,* who insisted on a non-Bourbon king, favored the Duke of Genoa, the forty-one-year-old cousin of Italy's forthrightly constitutional and anticlerical King Victor Emmanuel. The rise and fall of these seven candidacies produced not a few dramas.

Many Spaniards would have been excited to know that Don Carlos set foot on Spanish soil for the first time in July, 1869. An overenthusiastic supporter had persuaded him that his mere presence would deliver the city of Figueras into Carlist hands and be the signal for a general rising in his favor. Everything went wrong, and the pretender did no more than cross over an isolated stretch of frontier, fire six shots into the air with his revolver, and then return to the safety of France. Carlist hopes still ran high, however, particularly since their greatest military hero, Cabrera, had decided to abandon his life of retirement in England and become their commander in chief. Mellowed by his knowledge of British politics, the sixty-two-year-old "Tiger" regarded the Carlist guerrilla activity already taking place in Spain as premature and his new sovereign's recent escapade as foolhardy. After the old man openly disagreed with him at an interview, Don Carlos confided to friends that "the day my cause triumphs, my first charge will be to shoot Cabrera." Cabrera resigned forthwith, a seeming triumph for Carlist fire-eaters urged on, as always, by the Princess of Beira. Later "Carlos VII" told his supporters that he was personally taking military command, making the announcement amid cries of *"Viva el Rey"* at a meeting in Vevey, Switzerland in April, 1870, which brought together eighty-nine Carlists—grandees, generals, and representatives of local juntas. Nonetheless, this group voted to concentrate on propaganda activity.

While the Carlists were busy wrangling among themselves, the candidacy of the Duke of Genoa for king held people's attention, only to be terminated abruptly. Originally in 1869 Prim had sent an ambassador to ask about the possibility of getting Victor Emmanuel's second son, Amadeus, Duke of Aosta, but the Italian king put him off by suggesting instead his cousin, then a sixteen-year-old student at Harrow. The ambassador found the young Genoa "gentle," meaning that the duke would need a long internship as ruler. When his prospects became generally known, Napoleon III saw fit to write Genoa's mother: "Madame, if your son is King of Spain, pray for him." An alarmed parent begged Victor Emmanuel to spare her only son, and on January 2 the king announced that he would not force his cousin to accept.

A fatal duel between two candidates for the Spanish throne was the sensational news of March 12, 1870. One protagonist was Antoine, Duke of Montpensier, brother-in-law of Queen Isabel since the Affair of the Spanish Marriages but increasingly suspect by her and many as a Machiavellian intriguer. Tall, commanding, the French duke remained the soul of sophistication as he entered middle age, dutifully attending the masses his wife insisted on but limiting them to twenty minutes. He had turned the Infanta Luisa's vast estates in Andalusia into profitable farm enterprises, and he had made her palace of San Telmo in Seville a center of clever conversation and liberalism. After Montpensier's money had helped finance the Revolution of 1868, his claim to the throne was viewed very favorably by Serrano, Topete, and other moderates, but Prim and Napoleon III were unalterably hostile to this Orléanist Bourbon. Montpensier's dueling opponent was his wife's cousin and the queen's brother-in-law Enrique, Duke of Seville, who had retired from his naval career but had never ceased to air his radical views. He had been married morganatically to a lady named Elena de Castelvi y Shelly, but in 1870 he was a widower (the marriage produced well over a hundred descendants, including the fifth Duke of Seville, who married a German princess in 1973). Newspapers controlled by Enrique began to vilify Montpensier and his ambitions, at one time referring to him as a "puffed up French pastry cook." A challenge followed, and the mortal encounter took place in Madrid. Each of the royal enemies fired three shots, Enrique being fatally wounded by the last round. A memorial inscription subsequently put on Enrique's house referred to him as the "only honest Bourbon," and his supporters vowed to do anything to keep Montpensier off the throne. The winner of the duel was forced to pay a sizable indemnity to his victim's family and to be banished for one year. Montpensier tried unsuccessfully from abroad to run in two constituencies for the Cortes, and then, abandoning his own candidacy, he proposed to sponsor that of his nephew Alfonso, an offer which Queen Isabel contemptuously refused.

Spain's search for a king seemed to be over on June 19, 1870, when Leopold of Hohenzollern accepted Prim's offer of the throne. Son of the governor of Prussian Westphalia, Leopold was the brother of Prince (later King) Charles of Rumania, who had been elected to his throne in 1866 and was ruling successfully. The candidate was known to be very rich, learned, affable, and liberal in his political views, and he already knew Portuguese, thanks to his charming wife, Antonia, an infanta of Portugal. Earlier Leopold had declined the honor, saying he would accept the Spanish crown only upon orders of his king, Wilhelm I, who initially refused to pressure his cousin. Historians are generally agreed that the Prussian Chancellor Otto von Bismarck spent months in intrigues, probably with the aim of provoking a war with France, before persuading the Prussian prince and king to agree to seek the Madrid throne. They made the condition that Leopold be elected by a large majority of the Cortes. Leopold's new enthusiasm for the job was mercilessly caricatured by many Spanish, who, finding the name Hohenzollern hard to pronounce, enjoyed calling him *Olé, olé, si me elegen* ("Hurrah, hurrah, if only they elect me"). Incredibly, because of misunderstandings, the Cortes prorogued themselves before any vote. When news of the Prussian maneuvers leaked out to the newspapers, members of the French Chamber of Deputies started making speeches threatening war on July 6, and Leopold's father withdrew his son's candidacy on July 11. The French were understandably hysterical about the prospect of having a Prussian ruler on each side of them.

Interest in the Prussian candidacy was diverted by the announcement in Paris on June 25, 1870, that Queen Isabel II had abdicated in favor of her twelve-year-old son Alfonso. She had difficulty making her decision, having declared on the road to exile, "I am still Queen of Spain, and I will never abdicate." The conservative politicians who formed her entourage kept encouraging her to hope for a military coup in her favor, but the insinuations of many of these about Isabel's "human weaknesses" alienated them from her one by one. Moreover, Don Francisco had renewed his threats of exposing Isabel's private life; rather than go through a lawsuit, the queen's lawyers eventually arranged a generous financial settlement on the husband that enabled him to retire apart from her to a small house in Paris together with his friend Antonio Meneres. Later Isabel came around to the idea that she would abdicate if and after the Cortes chose Alfonso as king. The Marquis of Miraflores persuaded her that such an action "would be a direct attack on the honor of Your Majesty, a consecration of the right of the revolution which dethroned her, the converting of the hereditary monarchy into an elective one" (this same principle has motivated the current pretender, Don Juan, to oppose Franco's designation of his son Don Juan Carlos as his successor). Subsequently the queen's most sage and self-sacrificing adviser, the Duke of Sesto, got her to abdicate unconditionally. Marfori was opposed to the end.

The proclamation of "Alfonso XII" was sympathetically received by many of the courts of Europe, but it caused little stir in Spain. Everyone's attention was soon fixed on the coming Franco-Prussian War, a direct consequence of Isabel's deposition and an indirect result of her marriage twenty-four years earlier. In the celebrated Ems Telegram of July 13, a communication from the Prussian king to his chancellor slyly edited and released to the press by Bismarck, Wilhelm appeared to have insultingly dismissed the French ambassador when the latter pressed that monarch to declare Prussia's everlasting commitment not to support a Hohenzollern for the throne of Spain. As Bismarck foresaw, the "Gallic bull" duly responded to the "red flag" by declaring war on July 19. The Prussian army swept into France, but Prussian diplomacy was unsuccessful in inducing Spain to invade its neighbor from the south with 30,000 men.

Alfonso waiting in Paris for the call that did not come, Don Carlos in a like situation in Switzerland, the Duke of Genoa having refused, Leopold of Hohenzollern forgotten, Enrique dead, Montpensier disgraced, there remained the candidacy of Prince Ferdinand of Portugal, and it too ended with a definite no on August 14, 1870. Ferdinand, aside from looking suspiciously on his potential position in Spain as a "cage of fetters," was determined to marry a low born singer. Even when the Prim government made great concessions with regard to both wife and politics, the prince abruptly declared his intention to seek a life of ease.

After Napoleon III, defeated decisively by the Prussians at the Battle of Sedan on September 4, had abdicated, the Parisians enthusiastically proclaimed the Third French Republic. The new regime, calling itself the Government of National Defense, in desperation called on Spain to aid it with 80,000 troops, offering to support Prim if he proclaimed himself president of a fellow Spanish republic. However anti-Bourbon, the general remained a monarchist. France's discomfiture in the fall of 1870 also caused it to withdraw its garrison in Rome, and King Victor Emmanuel of Italy took advantage of the development to seize the Eternal City and make it his capital, confining the Pope to the Vatican.

"At last we have a king," exclaimed Prim, who was hunting near Toledo. The pressure of events in France and Italy, more than Spain's need, drove Victor Emmanuel to direct his son Amadeus to wire his conditional acceptance of the Spanish throne on October 13, 1870. The Italian king's seizure of Rome had angered Catholic opinion and Catholic courts, who now even talked of a restoration of the Neapolitan Bourbons. Moreover, the existing republic in France and the prospect of one in Spain could not fail to intensify republican sentiment in Italy. All these threats to Victor Emmanuel's own throne would be countered by having Amadeus king in Madrid. The Spanish ambassador further preyed on the Italian monarch's conscience by expressing alarm about the cause of monarchy in Europe generally and by the likelihood of anarchy in Spain specifically if some king were not offered to that country before the Cortes reassembled on October 31.

The selection of the Duke of Aosta was not entirely a surprise, although earlier refusals had turned attention away from the court of Italy. The young prince was known to be personable, forthright, and progressive. He had distinguished himself in the military, and he had an estimable wife, who had just had a son. Above all, Amadeus shared the liberal and anticlerical reputation of his father. Back in the summer of 1870, when his candidacy had been promoted by Britain and France, Amadeus had told Victor Emmanuel that he had a "secret repulsion" to leave Italy and to take on "political strife" in Spain. Now he accepted because of filial, patriotic, and humanitarian duty. His telegram to Prim mentioned his hopes to "unite the friends of liberty, of order, and of constitutional rule," and ended with the promise "I will accept the Crown if the vote of the Cortes proves to me that it is the will of the Spanish nation."

Prim formally announced Amadeus' bid on November 3 and scheduled the vote for November 16. The Carlists protested loudly. They were seconded from the other extreme by the republicans, whose spokesman, Castelar, most eloquently echoed the traditionalists' doubts about the whole idea of an elected monarch: "Kings can come from a temple but not from an assembly; they can descend from a cloud, from a mystery, but not from an electoral urn." In the ensuing balloting Amadeus received 191 votes, a republic 63, Montpensier 27, Espartero 8, Alfonso 2, the Infanta Luisa 1, and blank ballots 19. Having hoped for 200 or more votes, Amadeus settled for less, and his Spanish career started under the stigma of being "King of the 191."

Don Carlos denounced the election in manifestos, and so did Queen Isabel, who smarted from the irony that the son of the man to whom she tried to refuse recognition as King of Italy was about to sit on her own throne. Because of the turmoil in Paris, the heads of the rival branches of the Bourbon dynasty were living quite near each other on the shores of Lake Geneva.

2. King Amadeo I (1871–1873)

Amadeus of Savoy was not the first modern King of Spain to speak Castilian with a strong accent. He was preceded sixty-three years before by Joseph Bonaparte, who was very like the monarch of 1871 in his elegance, good intentions, and futility. Imposed by force of French troops, José I had been widely execrated as *el rey intruso* and *Pepe Botellas*. Spain's first elected ruler, Amadeo I, was accorded the sobriquet *el rey caballero* by friend and foe alike. Unfortunately, while he had few foes, Amadeo had even fewer friends, and he was to depart his adopted country in as much frustration as, if less ignominy than, Napoleon's brother.

Spanish newspaper readers duly learned that "Don Amadeo is of tall figure, elegantly slender, majestic; his look is energetic and expressive and his gestures reveal grace, finesse, and an uncommon dignity." Thoroughly regal-looking for public purposes, the young monarch revealed himself to have a "languid and fascinating" mien in private. Time was to show that

Amadeo was the most accessible and courteous of kings, that he was unique in meaning exactly what he said, and also that he was deficient in both will and intellect.

Born in 1845, Amadeo was the second son of the bluff heir to the kingdom of Sardinia, Victor Emmanuel, and of his Hapsburg cousin, Maria Adelaide. "How he looks like Charles Albert!" his grandmother had said of Amadeo, who even as a child had the slight melancholy of his visionary grandfather, a king forced to abdicate in 1849. The world of ideas, however, attracted the energetic young prince far less than outdoor life and military posturing. Exposed to the finest Italian professors, Amadeo did not even appreciably lose his Piedmontese accent.

From an early age Amadeo faced royal responsibilities. In 1860 he and his older brother, Humberto, preceded their father to Florence, which became the first capital of a united Italy. At eighteen Amadeo was offered the throne of anarchic Greece, but his father said the new Italy needed all its dynasty. Summers the prince traveled extensively—to Turkey, to Scandinavia, and significantly to Spain in 1865, on which occasion he had impressed Queen Isabel with his good looks and good manners. When the Prussian-Italian War with Austria broke out in 1866, Amadeo persuaded his father to let him fight in the front lines, and he was promptly wounded leading a foolhardy charge against an enemy-occupied farmhouse.

Amadeo married in May, 1867, after courting almost as an impossible lark the wealthiest and most beautiful young woman among the Piedmontese aristocracy, Maria Victoria de la Cisterna, known as the Rose of Turin. The young lovers first honeymooned in Paris, where the International Exposition was in progress. During the visit Amadeo fondled the six-month-old Leticia, cousin of Napoleon III, who was destined to be the Italian's second wife. At Windsor the couple made a good impression on Queen Victoria, and her government later looked favorably on his candidacy for the throne of Spain. Returned to Italy, Amadeo assumed the duties of vice admiral of the navy, visiting the chief ports of the new kingdom and in 1869 making a ceremonial journey to the Holy Land and Egypt. Of these untaxing tours, a lady-in-waiting was to remark, "Rather than belong to the court, it seems we formed a group of traveling comedians." María Victoria murmured happily, "I wish to be a true sailor's wife." When their first son, Manuel Filiberto, was born in 1869, they little expected that in two years he would exchange his title of Duke of Padua for that of Prince of the Asturias.

Amadeo's lack of cultivation was amply compensated for in his wife. María Victoria had been born in 1847 in Paris, where her father, one of the richest men in Italy, was in exile for his outspoken liberalism. The father had married a French woman in a double wedding ceremony with the

Prince of Monaco. French was the language spoken between mother and daughter, and María Victoria came to know six other languages as well. When the family resumed residence in their Turin palace, María Victoria received the best possible education in the arts and sciences. She also had a profoundly religious sensibility, once writing a young friend: "I hope God will send many heavy crosses for me to bear." Her mother, who let the daughter out of her sight only to go to church, made the telling pronouncement that "María will marry a royal prince or become a religious."

One of the first Spanish officials to encounter María Victoria was unstinted in his admiration for her:

> She has a face with features that are pronounced and beautifully correct; the brilliance of her eyes is special and also her penetrating glance; her voice is soft and affectionate, and her conversation instructive and agreeable; and her presence inspires not just the most profound respect but the most genuine sympathy. Although everyone had heard praise of her fine qualities, the reality surpassed our expectations and all left taken with her who was to be Queen of Spain.

The departure of the new monarchs for Spain was attended by every sort of bad omen. Italian society affected shock at the lack of style of the members of the Spanish commission, headed by the radical leader Manuel Ruiz Zorrilla, that had come to acknowledge Amadeo. At 10 A.M. on December 4 in the throne room of the Pitti Palace Amadeo read his acceptance speech in Italian with a trembling voice, as his father looked on in great content. Zorrilla led the cries of *Viva el Rey*. The politician declared publicly, "I am royalist about this king," pledging his earnest support, but privately Zorrilla remarked, "The new king is a child with a beard." Soon after anonymous assassination threats against the royal couple began to arrive, and then a mysterious message from the Regent Serrano advising the postponement of their departure. Bravely, Amadeo announced his desire to disembark at Barcelona, where a yellow fever epidemic was raging, but deeply upset by his encounter with the Spanish politicians, he confided to an army friend that "I am going to accomplish an impossible mission." María Victoria alternately tried to buoy her husband's spirits and to hold back her tears of apprehension, admitting that she thought of Marie Antoinette. Some Italian newspapers cruelly referred to their departing prince as Maximilian II. Leaving Turin on December 25 and for the first time wearing the uniform of a captain general, Amadeo stood smoking all the way to Spezia. There he said good-bye to his brother Humberto as the royal standard was run up on the Spanish warship *Numancia*.

After a stormy crossing from Italy Amadeo's ship put in at Cartagena on December 30. Strangely, there were no salutes and no pilot at first. When the pilot did come aboard, he brought the staggering news of the assassination three days before of General Prim, Amadeo's most influential supporter. Later Amadeo received Admiral Topete, who had opposed his election and who now advised him to remain on his ship. With typical bravado, Amadeo insisted on touring the port, and his regal amiability soon drew *vivas* from the curious population. The king's entry into Madrid, planned for New Year's Day, was postponed to occur after Prim's funeral.

General Prim was ambushed the night of December 27 on his way to the ministry of war, his carriage being attacked by several gunmen on both sides of the Calle de Turco. Despite previous attempts and a warning at this time, Prim took his usual route, having boasted that the bullet had not been made that would kill him. His wounds failed to heal because of a liver condition, and Prim died on December 30. Historians have heatedly debated about the responsibility for the crucial killing, variously accusing the republicans, the Isabelists, the Carlists, the Duke of Montpensier, and the Regent Serrano. The most recent study of the crime by a Spanish historian reaches this conclusion:

> Of the case it is clear, with absolute security, that the executor of the assassination was [José] Paul y Angulo [a republican deputy disappointed in his efforts to be appointed ambassador in London, where he had financial interests], in connivance with José María Pastor, chief of the bodyguard of the Duke de la Torre [Serrano], that the assassins together with Paul y Angulo and the same Pastor were convicts of low class, to some of whom were promised escape from their sentences, and that the money to buy them came from the pocket of Soles y Compugano, aide of the Duke de Montpensier.

In any case, with the loss of Amadeo's chief advocate, "the monarchy of Savoy was born dead."

After a brief sojourn at Aranjuez, Amadeo traveled by train to Madrid, arriving at 1:15 P.M. on January 2. At the station Serrano counseled him that since Prim's assassins were still at large the king should discreetly take a carriage to the Oriente Palace. Amadeo replied, *"Avanti! A caballo!"* and, dismissing Serrano's offer to be at his side, insisted on riding twenty paces ahead of the entourage of generals and squadrons of cavalry. Few decorations were to be seen along the snowy streets, but the bystanders in the freezing cold became increasingly animated as Amadeo made his serenely poised progress through the city. First the king went to pray at the Church of the Atocha, and after passing through the Paseo del Prado, he made a majestic appearance at the Cortes building, where he swore on the Gospel to the Constitution of 1869. At the ministry of war he paid a courtesy call on the widow of General Prim, who mysteriously replied to his expressed determination to track down her husband's murderers: "Then Your Majesty won't have to go far to find them." At the palace Amadeo received the notables of the land and later went out on the balcony to cry *Viva España* to the crowd below. He had to order the palace servants to remove from sight numerous personal possessions of Queen Isabel. When the next morning the new king ordered breakfast for 8 A.M., he was informed that it could not be ready before the hour of 11, as in the previous reign, and he had to ride over to the Café de Paris to get something to eat.

María Victoria and the children did not join Amadeo until March 17, 1871. Just before she left Turin, she had received an anonymous letter informing her that her husband was conducting amorous escapades with various ladies in Madrid. After a serious illness, described officially as a high fever but more likely a nervous breakdown, she came by ship to Alicante to be embraced by Amadeo and showered with flowers by enthusiastic crowds.

When Amadeo became king, Serrano ceased to be regent and instead became prime minister of a "government of conciliation." A new Cortes met on April 3, more radical than the previous one. Eighty of the 191 deputies who had voted the crown for Amadeo were not returned by their constituencies. After much noisy but insubstantial maneuvering for advantage between the Radicals and Liberals, Serrano resigned and Zorrilla, the Radical leader, became prime minister on July 24. The ministerial crisis delayed the king's departure for the usual royal sojourn at La Granja until July 27: poison-pen letters to María Victoria, who had gone earlier, alleged that Amadeo was dallying amorously with the "Lady of the Balcony" who had a house on the Castellana where she enjoyed nightly visits from the king. The royal family vacationed decorously, the children reveling in the gardens and fountains of the palace, the queen immersed in her reading, and the king pursuing the hunt with all the fervor of many generations of Spanish kings. During this first summer the monarchs were present at the opening of the first Madrid tramline—from the Puerta del Sol to the Calle de Salamanca.

King Amadeo, who had seen little of Spain except during his private tour of the southern provinces in 1865, resolved to show his presence in the eastern and northern areas. Despite tearful scenes with María Victoria, he refused for reasons of safety to let her accompany him, departing on September 2 and subsequently visiting Valencia, Barcelona, and Saragossa. Although many people turned out to inspect their new monarch, their attitude was reserved and continued to be so even after the old popular hero

Espartero gave the visiting king his blessing. On one occasion a republican mayor of a town lectured Amadeo to the effect that while the people would refrain from assassinating him they would prefer to have him as a democratically elected president. The royal tour was adjudged a failure when Amadeo returned to Madrid. Meanwhile, the queen's carriage had been involved in a nasty mob scene in the Puerta del Sol. María Victoria tended thereafter to distrust the Radicals and was relieved when Zorrilla was ousted as prime minister by the efforts of the Liberal Práxides Sagasta, who, after a stopgap government, succeeded in putting himself in power on December 21. For his part, the king was somewhat uncomfortable with Sagasta, who had earlier demanded that Amadeo part with a mistress he had brought from Italy. Actually, both monarchs went out of their way to conceal their personal prejudices, instituting Wednesday-evening dinners at the palace to which politicians of all shades of opinion were invited. Often as not the Liberals and Radicals forgot their manners and heatedly argued in the royal presence. Amadeo, looking serene, tried to steer the conversation to frivolous topics. María Victoria, equally amiable, proved more attentive to, and informed about, what was being said.

By New Year's 1872 Amadeo realized that he had not made himself a popular king. The monarch was more resented than hated. His being a foreigner—"King Macaroni"—was inevitably the focus for critics, who took exception to his dress, his eating habits, or his halting Spanish. Once after making a patriotic farewell to troops leaving for Cuba, Amadeo confessed to Admiral Topete that he would sooner join the fighting than speak Castilian. The language barrier was used by officials as an excuse to circumvent the king's desires. Many of the clergy fomented hostility to the king, muttering about the past, not his past, but his family's, specifically the fact that the king's father had despoiled the Pope and stood excommunicated.

A measure of the insecurity of Amadeo's position was his nearly complete rejection by the Spanish aristocracy. According to an Italian newspaper, only 2 of 82 Spanish dukes acknowledged the Savoyard king (20 of 753 marquis, 30 of 546 counts, 10 of 76 viscounts). Futilely, Amadeo created about eighty titles in two years. Many of the nobility were Carlists, some of whom ostentatiously displayed their preference by wearing a daisy (commemorating the name of Don Carlos' Queen Margarita). The numerous Alfonsists pointedly gave fancy-dress balls featuring modes from the previous reign or even gowns with the Bourbon fleur-de-lis. The Savoy monarchs constantly encountered signs of disrespect, such as members of a prestigious club refusing to uncover their heads, citizens neglecting to rise and give the pregnant queen a seat in the public gardens, wellborn women dressing in whores' mantillas during royal promenades on the Paseo, and street boys yelling uninhibited and unprotested insults. Once María Victoria sighed that "everyone can shout and demonstrate except us."

On balance the king's unassuming ways probably drew more derision than admiration. Lovers of the grand style affected amazement that the royal family lived cozily and austerely in only three small apartments in the Oriente, where they had a superb view of the Casa de Campo (Queen Isabel, so informed in Paris, exclaimed, "Poor children. They can't even move about"). Amadeo made a point of being frequently out among his people. Even though the traditional trumpets might announce his post-lunch departure from the palace, he rode with only a single attendant in red livery following him fifty paces behind. The king toured thus through the streets of his capital looking at the shops and staring back at the people, with an "almost infantile expression." He bought his Virginia cigars himself, he might appear at the theater unannounced, and he took his wife for ice cream at the Café Suisse just like any substantial citizen. Some people undoubtedly were impressed with Amadeo's bravery, and others looked favorably on his democratic handshakes (one small-town official so honored once blurted out in delight, "We are all grandees of Spain"). Yet others recalled that the bourgeois ways of King Louis Philippe did not help him in the long run. A noted Spanish historian argued that Amadeo made himself unpopular precisely because of his lack of the "defects" of the national character symbolized by the arrogant and malicious Fernando VII.

Probably Amadeo's extramarital adventures caused more titillation than shock. Everyone knew of the "Lady on the Balcony" on the Castellana. A contretemps occurred when one of the king's aides had to bribe and threaten her to recover the royal love letters. Amadeo's visits to the theater had as one aim the meeting of attractive actresses, and late in his reign he was linked to the wife of the correspondent of the London *Times*. Like his father, Victor Emmanuel, who ended up marrying his mistress, Amadeo considered his private life his own affair.

María Victoria, who earned some sympathy as a neglected wife, did nothing to discredit the queenly image expected of her, except, perhaps, being too intelligent. At the beginning of the reign she endured a difficult brouhaha over who was to be her chief lady-in-waiting. After the widow Prim accepted and declined, her great rival, the wife of Serrano, did likewise. The widow O'Dónnell eventually took the post, almost completing the round of the wives of Spain's mid-nineteenth-century generals. Generally popular and wholly in keeping with the queen's nature was her habit of going daily to one or another of the capital's churches, where she would sit with the congregation. Charity being the traditional preserve of the consort, María Victoria was exceptional in her generosity and disbursed on a regular annual basis millions of pesetas. The money came in part from the state treasury but also from the monarchs' private fortune. The queen's chief pride was her asylum for the children of Madrid's laundresses; this foundation, before its physical destruction in 1936, was embellished by María Victoria's successors, who received unjustified credit for its inspiration.

Society was divided over the queen's clothes, some preferring the bejeweled and fabric-rich style of Isabel II, others sympathizing with the young successor's taste in blue or velvet gowns, simple white hats, a few pearls, and the novelty of furs. Nor was María Victoria's intellectuality completely appreciated. She was a studied patron of writers and artists, many of them obscure. She could write confidently to a friend that "I feel admiration for Velázquez, but my favorite painter is Murillo with his virgins and children. I believe that Goya, without doubt, is the one who has best captured the Spanish spirit." At her dinner parties the queen impressed even scientists with her knowledge and awareness, but the ignorant exaggerated her attainments to include Arabic and astronomy.

Snubbed by the aristocracy, the young monarchs were unsuccessful in mollifying the politicians. "Shorten the table," commanded King Amadeo with false unconcern when it appeared that the leaders of the Radical Party were all going to boycott the weekly Wednesday political dinner. After the Cortes passed a Radical-sponsored vote of censure of him, the Liberal Sagasta had simply held new elections, which he won easily. The king expressed concern that the elections might be rigged, drawing this equivocal assurance from Sagasta: "Your Majesty need not worry. The elections will be altogether as honest as they can be in Spain."

When the king opened the new session of the Cortes on April 17, he tried to ignore the fact that many of the delegates from the northern provinces were absent. The reason was that the Third Carlist War had broken out. Although the Carlists had successfully lodged a small party in the Cortes, Don Carlos decided that the parliamentary route to power would be too long and that his followers would lose heart. Accordingly, he issued a manifesto on April 14 calling for a "general uprising" on the twenty-first. On May 2 "Carlos VII" himself and his brother Alfonso Carlos crossed over the frontier into Navarre, thanks to the outrageous ineptitude, amounting to connivance, of the French police. He had come, he said, "to encourage the brave, to hearten the lukewarm, and to strike terror into the hearts of traitors." In "Carlos VII," Carlism now had a "Bonnie Prince Charlie": the twenty-four-year-old grandson of the unprepossessing original Don Carlos was handsome, well built, and commanding in expression with his full, square-cut beard. His cause was also enhanced by the fact that he was seeking to oust not a fellow Bourbon but a foreign king. The contest had at least two ironies: Amadeo and Don Carlos had played together as boys in Modena, and during the First Carlist War Amadeo's grandfather Charles Albert had consistently supported the cause of the Salic Law, by which he himself had come to his throne.

Once again the Carlist effort proved more farcical than dangerous. No towns rose in support of the pretender, and his supporters were forced to plunder because of lack of supplies. Leadership was lacking also. At the village of Oroquieta Don Carlos with 4,000 men was literally caught napping by a smaller government force, which succeeded in killing 40 Carlists and capturing a few hundred. Don Carlos never fired a shot and fortunately had a swift horse to take him back over the frontier four days after he had come. General Serrano, sent north by the government on May 24, negotiated a generous amnesty for the Carlist soldiers—unwisely, for Don Carlos repudiated it and sent his brother to Catalonia to stir up further guerrilla activity.

The Liberal Sagasta was ousted on May 22, charged with misappropriation of state funds for electoral purposes. His natural replacement, Zorrilla, unaccountably refused the prime ministership, and the king then turned again to Serrano, naming him prime minister. In the face of a mounting press campaign insulting to the royal family, Serrano proposed the suppression of constitutional guarantees. Vacillating but doggedly constitutionalist in his convictions, Amadeo declared, *"Yo contrario,"* at a crucial meeting of the Council of Ministers and accepted Serrano's resignation on June 12. The ministry had lasted less than three weeks.

The longest and the final ministry of the reign came to power the next day, when Zorrilla was persuaded by his followers to become prime minister. Queen María Victoria, already prejudiced against the Radicals, had had a few personal run-ins with Zorrilla, one over an unauthorized trip, another over an interview she had with Serrano. Zorrilla purged her personal household as punishment. The king, for all his goodwill toward the politicians who spoke an alien language too fast, came to realize that Zorrilla's choice of words was somewhat vulgar and that his fist pounding on the table was definitely overbearing.

Zorrilla had held office a month when an assassination attempt against the monarchs occurred on July 18. Despite warnings that a plot was afoot, Amadeo insisted on taking his wife for their usual walk and ice cream in the Retiro Gardens. Coming back on the Calle Arenal, the royal carriage ran into a fusillade of bullets, which miraculously caused no injuries. Amadeo jumped up and shouted, "Here is the King. Fire at him, not at the others." In the excitement the king never spoke better Spanish, and he coolly inspected the scene of the crime the following day, while a huge demonstration of loyalty took place in the Puerta del Sol, the greatest moment of popularity of the House of Savoy. In August Amadeo toured the northern provinces and was moved by his cordial welcome in these Carlist-infested areas. When the new Cortes met on September 15, the monarchs were well received by the delegates, but many newspapers continued to vilify the royalty.

The marital difficulties of the royal couple combined with politics to produce the final crisis. Amadeo continued to excuse himself nightly after dinner to pursue his philandering. He finally succeeded in having an affair with a woman in high society (she later explained her disloyalty to the Bourbons by saying that her motives for submitting to the king were subtly political and that she was prepared to play Judith). María Victoria took to keeping vigil on her husband's nocturnal goings and returns. Sentries reported that they must be seeing Bourbon ghosts watching from the palace windows. Aside from personal hurt, the queen was alarmed for Amadeo's safety. Her forbearance gave way at last, and on December 4 she told Zorrilla that she was leaving Spain, no matter what. Failing to mollify the queen, the prime minister informed her that if she departed, it would be without her children. This threat calmed María Victoria, and she was distracted by the pleasure of seeing her eldest son receive the coat of arms of the Prince of the Asturias on December 8.

Large-scale rioting broke out in Madrid on December 11, 1872. Republican slogans were to the fore, and the anarchists too were testing their power, having just held their first congress at Córdoba. One source of popular fury was Zorrilla's failure to keep his promise to abolish conscription: the exigencies of the fighting with both the Carlists and the Cubans forced the government to announce a levy of 40,000. Although the government easily reestablished order, King Victor Emmanuel wrote his son advising him to turn again to the strong hand of General Serrano, but Serrano told Amadeo he could offer him no support as long as the Radicals were not suppressed in some way. Next the king had a shattering crisis with the Radical ministry. The royal couple's third son, the Infante Luis Amadeo, was born on January 29, and for his baptism the king decided to dispense with traditional Bourbon ceremonial and keep it a simple family affair. Zorrilla promptly threw his greatest table-thumping spectacle, claiming that his ministers had been insulted by being excluded from the baptism. The Radical leaders were placated by giving them commemorative medals, which they accepted and the Conservatives refused. Amadeo ordered the distribution of 4,000,000 reales to charity on the occasion of the royal birth, but no bishop came forth to perform the baptism, which was done by the queen's confessor.

King Amadeo I first announced his intention to abdicate in a private interview with Zorrilla on February 8. The ultimate crisis turned on an event remote from his reign: during the Sergeants' Revolt of 1866 officers of the artillery corps were killed at the instigation of an officer who subsequently was appointed by the Radical ministry to successive captain generalcies, only to have his subordinates refuse to serve under him. A delegation of artillery officers subsequently waited on King Amadeo and proposed a drastic change in the constitution in the direction of absolutism. The king protested his liberalism. Soon afterward, however, Amadeo was confronted by the ministry's purging the artillery corps and calling a vote of confidence in the Cortes, all against his express wishes. Consulting with Liberal leaders, the king found that they had little trust in him, all the while they advocated measures which he felt would bring much bloodshed. Accordingly, Amadeo told Zorrilla of his determination to depart.

Aware of the crisis, people in Madrid had started arming themselves, and Zorrilla vehemently protested the king's abdication as handing the country over to anarchy. The queen had the final word in making up the king's mind, telling Zorrilla contemptuously that he confused democracy with the "rabble." At an agitated final meeting of the Council of Ministers on the morning of February 11 Amadeo announced, "I can do nothing in the face of the indifference of some, the irradicable enmity of others, and the impotence of the few who are truly faithful to me." He also noted sadly that he had sacrificed much of his personal fortune and his royal rights in Italy. Court officials prepared a manifesto of abdication in which Amadeo said he might successfully have led the country against a foreign enemy, "but all who with sword, pen, and word aggravate the evils of the nation are Spaniards." The Cortes received Amadeo's message without stir and declared officially its intention in the future of offering him not the crown again but "the dignity of a citizen in the bosom of a people independent and free."

No crowds assembled and virtually nobody came to say good-bye when the ex-monarchs left the Oriente Palace at 6 A.M. on February 12. María Victoria was so sick that she had to be carried. Their train to Portugal had only one first-class coach, without heat or dining facilities, and Amadeo had to buy his wife sausage soup in a station canteen. Crossing the frontier, he said, "Thank God, at last we can live in peace."

In a few years María Victoria died of tuberculosis, a forgotten royal figure although she had been "one of the most generous, cultivated, and beautiful queens Spain ever had." Shortly afterward Amadeo married his young niece Leticia. They lived as Italian royalty performing ceremonial duties. When he died at age forty-five in 1890, unable to go on living without being a king, according to his doctor, Amadeo's last words were *"Avanti, avanti."*

Amadeo's youngest son, once an infante of Spain, lived to become a famous North Pole explorer. The successors of Amadeo's firstborn have recently acquired royal pretensions: ex-King Humberto II of Italy (voted out in 1946) in November, 1971, announced his intention to disinherit his only son for marrying without his approval and to transfer the rights of succession to a remote cousin, Amadeus of Aosta, born in 1943 and the great-grandson of the Savoyard King of Spain.

3. The First Spanish Republic

Having dethroned a bad monarch in 1868, Spain spent two years looking for a good one, who was then suffered to rule for only two years. At this juncture the country was to try two years without any king; the result was a degree of anarchy unusual even for Spain. There were now three sets of displaced Spanish royalty, of whom only the House of Savoy was indifferent to the prospect of regaining the crown. The Alfonsists mainly waited for their prince to come of age, while the Carlists persistently sought to establish themselves in Madrid by force of arms.

General Prim had once told the leading Republican politician Castelar: "If it were not easy to make a king, it will be even more difficult to make a republic in a country where there are no republicans." Nonetheless, by a vote of 258 to 32 at 3 P.M. on February 11, 1873, the combined Senate and Chamber of Deputies voted to make Spain a republic. Legalists ever after argued that the Cortes action was improper, since the Constitution of 1869 made no provision for changing the nature of the state and expressly forbade the two houses to sit as one body. The Radicals, heirs of the *Progresistas*, who were the overwhelming majority of the deputies and who, despite their name, were now monarchists by conviction, supported the republic as an interim expedient, knowing full well that the royal houses of Europe would be hesitant about finding Spain another king. The noisy Republican minority, some of whom had threatened to leave the Cortes session as corpses if they did not have their way, was the only party with a definite national program, and as always, France set itself as a potent example, Spain's neighbor having been a republic for two years.

Eschewing "President" or "regent," the Cortes used the noncommittal term "Chief of the Executive Power" to designate the new head of state, a politician named Estanislao Figueras. His regime began with the finest ideals and promises: popular sovereignty, complete civil liberties, general amnesty, and the abolition of conscription. The Republicans soon forced the Radicals out of the original coalition ministry, and the Cortes disbanded in late March, 1873. The Radicals tried on April 23 to regain power by assembling sympathetic army units in Madrid's bullring, but

General Pavía, captain general of New Castile, refused to lend them the support they counted on and the populace of Madrid showed themselves overwhelmingly hostile to "enemies of the Republic." General Serrano now fled the country. New elections in May returned almost all Republicans, who in the Cortes on June 8 went further than before and voted by 210 votes to 2 that Spain was a "Federal Republic." They projected a decentralized nation of seventeen states. Figueras mysteriously disappeared, to be replaced as Chief of the Executive Power by the self-effacing, idealistic Francisco Pi y Margall, a chief architect of the new order of things but a man no more capable than his predecessor of restraining the country's headlong rush to complete social disorder and civil war.

The Carlists proceeded to plunge northern Spain into chaos, going far beyond their insurrectionary activities against King Amadeo. The choice they could offer now was the clear one of monarchy versus republic. Moreover, the decided anticlerical bent of the Republicans in Madrid provoked a renewed religious fanaticism among Carlist supporters (foreign observers noted with some amazement that officers and men in Carlist formations daily said their rosaries together). Out came thousands of hidden rifles, and once again the mountains echoed to the cry *Dios, Patria, Rey*. In February, 1873, Don Carlos' brilliant new commander, Antonio Dorregaray, arrived on the scene, a forty-five-year-old who had served in the First Carlist War and subsequently gained distinction in the army. By late spring Dorregaray had enlisted 50,000 men in his forces, supplying them with modern arms obtained through smuggling and outside financial aid. He decisively overcame the initial effort of the government to defeat him at Eraul (earning him the title of Marquis of Eraul from Don Carlos, who assumed this royal prerogative).

As in the First Carlist War, the rebels had to confine their activities to the open countryside. Lacking artillery, they could not capture or hold the northern cities, whose populations were anti-Carlist in sympathy anyhow. As before, the Carlists were reduced by frustration and need to a war of reprisal and plunder, blackmailing towns into giving up treasure, burning the houses of suspected republicans or of too liberal priests, and massacring prisoners. Traditionalist fanatics made wanton attacks on railroads and telegraphs. The antiquarianism of the Carlists' methods and ideas shocked European newspaper readers.

Don Carlos put some restraint on Carlist atrocities after he himself arrived in Navarre on July 16. Forgetting the humiliation of Oroquieta the year before, thousands of peasants flocked to get a glimpse of the attractive and majestic prince. Don Carlos knew what was expected of him and proceeded to Guernica, where he swore under the historic oak to the *fueros* of the Basque provinces, many of whose people now rejoined his cause. The pretender was accompanied by his queen, Margarita, who threw herself into organizing hospitals to serve combatants of both sides (grateful republican wounded reportedly sighed *"Viva la Reina"* at the sight of her). Other Bourbon royalty soon enlisted in the promising crusade, including the two sons of the Duke of Seville (Montpensier's victim) and the dashing Count of Caserta, son of the last King of the Two Sicilies. Even Don Carlos' father, Don Juan, showed up; the eccentric ex-pretender came with his own invention of collapsible rubber boats for building bridges, a secret weapon that appears not to have been used.

The Carlists won their first major town on August 24, capturing Estella, of hallowed memory from the First War, and the second city of Navarre. Here in a small house on the Plaza de Fueros Don Carlos set up his court. He appointed a ministry, but he surrounded himself mainly with fighting men, showing himself to be quite different from his grandfather by keeping etiquette and ceremonial to the minimum. Only a handful of grandees were in attendance and just one bishop so that the civilian-military antagonism that poisoned the bygone campaign was largely absent. Soon the pretender boasted possession of arsenals, a mint, a university, a war college, and a small railroad.

About the time the Carlists established themselves triumphantly at Estella, the Alfonsists at the Palacio de Castilla in Paris were quietly celebrating a success of their own, an agreement by various generals and politicians who supported the rights of Queen Isabel's fifteen-year-old son to put their cause entirely in the hands of the master Madrid parliamentarian Antonio Cánovas del Castillo. "There is only one man in Spain capable of putting Alfonso on the throne and consolidating the monarchy—that man is Cánovas," so the Duke of Sesto advised the mother and son, who duly gave him full powers on August 22. Arrived in Paris, Cánovas was grateful to find his would-be monarch to be understanding, sensible, and resolute—the most intelligent prince in Europe, he said. He was annoyed that Isabel and Marfori would not let him see Alfonso alone, and he faced all manner of intrigues by old courtiers. On two occasions Marfori nearly persuaded Isabel to renounce her abdication and to return to Spain in the manner of Don Carlos, but although living apart, Don Francisco de Asís managed to put in a decisive voice in support of his son. Cánovas was even able to persuade Queen Isabel to live more decorously and economically in order to improve both the image and finances of the monarchists. As for Cánovas' program of action, he represented a definite shift from the hope of imposing Alfonso on Spain by some general's pronunciamiento (Isabel was quite amazed that Serrano did not proclaim him when Amadeo abdicated). "I would not like it if the restoration of the legitimate monarchy was due to a coup d'état," declared the farsighted statesman, who set about building a big movement of public opinion in Alfonso's favor. In effect, while Carlists fought in the hills and villages, the Alfonsists propagandized in the cafés and salons of Madrid and other big cities.

The republican government was failing both politically and militarily. In less than a year four successive commanders were sent out from the capital to pacify the north, and each failed miserably. Demoralization of the government forces was apparent. After all, had not the politicians promised the end of conscription? Mutinies were frequent, as were murders of officers. The garrisons of Barcelona and Pamplona on separate occasions flatly refused to march out to fight the Carlists.

Unable to deal with the danger from the right, the republic simultaneously faced a great upheaval from the left. In the summer of 1873 all but one of the major cities of southern Spain rose in revolt. In this so-called Cantonalist Insurrection the Madrid bureaucracy and the propertied classes were the enemy. Cities such as Valencia, Granada, and Málaga proclaimed themselves completely independent cantons, like the city-states of old, and revolutionary juntas proceeded to do such things as socialize wealth, tax only the rich, regulate wages, and mint their own money. Cádiz declared itself a free port. Anticlerical fanatics in Seville proposed to turn the cathedral into a café. The most prolonged and violent uprising was in Cartagena, where irregular troops raised the red flag over the citadel and seized all the public buildings, after which the six warships in the harbor mutinied. Acting as the Canton of Murcia, the rebels tried to use their warships to persuade other coastal cities to revolt or to levy exactions on them, resorting to bombardment on occasion. In turn, British, French, German, and United States warships on the Mediterranean station were forced to constitute themselves a peace-keeping force outside Cartagena, interfering with both the mutinous ships and those of the Spanish government.

The Cantonalist Insurrections were blamed on the socialists and anarchists by the republican press of the day and by many later historians, who exaggerated mob excesses, just as for 1820 or for 1936. Genuine grievances of the masses counted for more than the small amount of left-wing propaganda circulating. The socialists' Karl Marx in London was actually confused by the events in Spain, which seemed to be favoring the aims of his chief enemy in the International, Mikhail Bakunin. Far from subverting Spain with huge amounts of "red gold," the anarchist leader could not raise enough money even to go to Spain himself. Their enemies also accused the Cantonalists of playing into the hands of the Carlists, and vice versa, in the interests of disorder. In isolated fact, a Carlist group did publish a fake anarchist newspaper calling for a "bloodbath" against the rich.

The Cantonalists within each city were often bitterly divided in their aims, and the complete refusal of the rebel cities to cooperate with each other made the government's task of repression easier. Some cities were bombarded into submission, but General Pavía had to storm Seville, encountering street barricades and buildings set on fire with gasoline. The Canton of Murcia held out until January, 1874, at one point even seeing fit to declare war on Germany. A naval blockade and a siege by 7,000 soldiers were required to defeat Cartagena's defenders, 2,500 of whom went into exile in North Africa sailing off on the *Numancia* (the same ship that had brought King Amadeo to Spain).

Emilio Castelar, the fourth Chief of the Executive Power in the course of several months, took office on September 8, 1873. Resolute, able, a centralist rather than a federalist republican, Castelar gained absolute civil and military powers from the Cortes, which was adjourned until New Year's. His dictatorship was no more successful than the previous ministries. Leftists blamed him for relying too much on the regular army, while rightists blamed him for not restoring military discipline. Nationalists blamed him for a humiliating backdown to President Grant when Spain's repressive actions in Cuba aroused the ire of the United States. The government's great effort to crush the Carlists was bloodily defeated in November, in a battle where Don Carlos horrified his generals by exposing himself to enemy fire.

On January 2, 1874, a military coup by General Pavía overthrew Castelar. Meeting that day, the Cortes not only had refused to renew Castelar's extraordinary powers but voted no confidence in him 120 to 100. Then the captain general sent a message giving the deputies five minutes to empty the chamber. Too late Castelar's opponents offered to support him. Soldiers cleared the chamber after a few scuffles and revolver shots in the air. Pavía was not seeking power himself. A meeting of moderate party leaders decided to make Serrano president and to have a coalition ministry of the Radicals, Alfonsists, and Liberals. In this seeming demise of the Spanish Republic, Serrano's mission was not to make new constitutional arrangements but rather to meet the grave new threat from the Carlists, which overshadowed everything else for almost all 1874.

The previous Christmas Day Don Carlos had been solemnly annointed "King of the Basques." He boasted at this time that he could march about all northern Spain as easily as if he had already been crowned in Madrid. In January the Carlists surrounded Bilbao. Tolosa fell to them in February and became their new headquarters. Money and arms were relatively plentiful. Most of the Carlist generals now favored a quick general movement on Madrid, keeping in mind that the Serrano regime was untried and that the Alfonsists might attempt a restoration by coup. Don Carlos decided, however, to make the fatal mistake of 1835 all over again, to besiege and capture Bilbao, which seemed an easy victory and afforded a port with all its advantages for getting supplies and for provoking international recognition of the Carlist belligerency. Although cut off from the sea and dominated by Carlist entrenchments on the heights, Bilbao with a few thousand defenders managed to hold out against ten times that number of Carlists, until General Serrano himself came to its rescue. On April 28, 1874, Serrano succeeded in turning the lines of the besiegers, and his subordinate, General José Gutiérrez de la Concha, entered Bilbao on May 2.

The Carlists retired from Bilbao in good order, and not until July did the government attempt to strike at their stronghold at Estella. Again in the shadow of the Montejura from June 25 to 27 the Carlists won a stunning victory. General Concha was killed by a stray bullet, depriving Serrano of one of his best generals and ending a hope of the Alfonsists that Concha would proclaim their prince. Don Carlos celebrated his greatest victory with almost feudal pomp, riding into Estella on a white horse. He would have done better to pursue the enemy and to curb the revengefulness of his commanders, who ordered fifteen enemy prisoners shot for alleged crimes against Carlist properties. Among the victims was a German captain. Such an outrage offended Bismarck, and Germany now led the European powers in extending recognition to the Serrano government.

Don Carlos held his ground in Spain for another year. On the first anniversary of his arrival, July 16, he issued a manifesto reaffirming his party's faith in traditional institutions but adding that they must be in harmony with the spirit of the modern age. This appeal to moderate public opinion did not prove successful, and the Carlists' military efforts likewise failed, all at a time when victory seemed close. With the main armies confronting each other in Navarre, a force under Don Alfonso Carlos from Catalonia was able to reach within eighty miles of Madrid, capturing the city of Cuenca. Having surrendered on honorable terms, Cuenca was then treated to an orgy of killing and looting by the Carlists, unrestrained, perhaps actively encouraged, by Don Alfonso Carlos and his wife. Had discipline been maintained, the force might have pushed on to Madrid, but disorderly retreat followed instead, and soon after the pretender's brother returned to France in a pique.

Yet, as of the summer of 1874, Don Carlos still had reasons for optimism. His army numbered 100,000 effectives. Arrayed against them in the war zones were 150,000 men, while the republic faced the additional burden of maintaining 50,000 men in the peaceful provinces and 75,0000 fighting the Cuban insurrectionists.

The rest of 1874 was quiet politically and militarily until the salons and cafés were set buzzing by the publication of the "Sandhurst Manifesto" on

December 1. The Infante Alfonso, then a cadet at the British military school, had come of age on November 24. His classmates and instructors celebrated his seventeenth birthday with toasts to "Alfonso XII," and an avalanche of greetings arrived by mail from Spain. The manifesto, showing the hand of Cánovas, spoke tactfully of Spain's recent turmoil and called for a "hereditary and constitutional monarchy" having "flexibility." People were struck by the closing words: "Be whatever my fate decrees, I will not cease to be a good Spaniard, nor, as all my forebears, a good Catholic, nor, as a man of this century, a genuine liberal."

The inevitable pronunciamiento occurred after President Serrano had gone north early in December to deal personally with renewed Carlist guerrilla activity, leaving the military men free to intrigue. In the early hours of December 29, 1874, a General Arsenio Martínez de Campos drew up a few hundred troops in the square of the town of Sagunto, near Valencia, and delivered a moving speech, ending with "*Viva Alfonso XII.*" The soldiers responded with enthusiasm, dreams of promotion overcoming any scruples about their having sworn allegiance to the republic. By nightfall they had gained the support of the chief general in the area and another 10,000 men. Martínez de Campos had wired to Cánovas in Madrid: "When you receive this, we will have initiated the movement in favor of Don Alfonso." The parliamentarian was annoyed at what he considered to be a premature coup, but honorably he refused to go into hiding and suffered arrest when the government became aware of events. Within a few hours more than 10,000 goodwill cards were sent by people to Cánovas' place of confinement. On the morning of December 30 the minister of war toured the barracks of the capital only to find the troops solidly for the Bourbon prince. After radicals talked of arming the civilian populace in defense of the republic, the captain general of Castile, General Fernando Primo de Rivera, took over the capital's streets. A hero of the recent siege of Bilbao and a personal friend of Martínez de Campos, General Primo de Rivera was the uncle and great-uncle respectively of two of Spain's most famous rightist politicians in the next century. In vain, Prime Minister Sagasta exchanged hysterical telegrams with President Serrano. Gaining his freedom, Cánovas declared himself prime minister on December 31, acting in the name of Alfonso XII and more precisely claiming authorization to do so by his August, 1873, understanding with Queen Isabel and her son.

An army pronunciamiento in 1868 had overthrown the Bourbons, and an army pronunciamiento at the end of 1874 brought them back. Both actions were, of course, unconstitutional, but they appeared to have widespread support in the country, which received the revolutions by telegraph, as it were.

Don Alfonso had come down to London with the other Sandhurst cadets at the end of their first term on December 23, 1874, and was on his way to spend his vacation with his family. The young foreigner with just one aide had difficulty procuring a bed at the Charing Cross Hotel, eventually paying two guineas in advance for a room on the third floor. After a rough crossing of the Channel, the prince in his red uniform was met at the Paris station on the afternoon of December 30 by Queen Isabel and his sisters. Although he found in the Palacio de Castilla much mail for him from Spain, his family pressed him to get ready for the theater. While changing, he was handed an envelope with writing in a woman's hand saying *"urgente."* On the card inside, with a mysterious letterhead of *X* and *P* crossed, were the words in French: "Sir, Your Majesty has been proclaimed king yesterday afternoon by the Spanish army." Alfonso put the note away and without saying a word went off to the Gaîeté Theater, where his sisters found much amusement in the play *La Poule aux Oeufs d'Or* while he watched the door of his box apprehensively. Back at the Palacio de Castilla, Alfonso was confronted by his excited mother, who had just been told of General Martínez de Campos' "madness" in issuing the monarchist pronuncia-miento. The son replied serenely, "I already know the news, and I have decided to leave for Spain whatever happens," and then went to bed. Arising late in the morning, he went to his mother who rendered him the gracious reverence due a King of Spain. Scenes of family hugging and kissing followed. Later hundreds of well-wishers arrived, for all of whom protocol and even past bitternesses were forgotten. Alfonso alone remained pensive. "But, Alfonso, why so serious?" the queen cried. "Because I would like to make myself a great name in history."

X.

The Constitutional Monarchs:
Alfonso XII (1874–1885) and
the Regent María Cristina (1885–1902)

---

1. The Restoration of the Bourbons

THE restoration of the Bourbons in 1874 was to give Spain almost two decades of tranquillity after seven of constant turmoil. The relative public calm and prosperity were not directly the personal achievement of the new King Alfonso XII; more important were the general craving for order, the flexible constitutional arrangements, and the self-restraint of Spanish politicians and generals. Yet in Alfonso the country enjoyed a ruler who was altogether good-natured, intelligent, and noble-minded—a worthy counterpart of any of the monarchs of his era.

The parentage of Alfonso XII raised questions on the grounds of both legitimacy and inbreeding. His birth to Queen Isabel in 1857 produced widespread rejoicing and also widespread snickering over the possibility that the father was not the king consort, Don Francisco de Asís, but Puig Moltó, the engineers' lieutenant who was currently the queen's lover. The debate whether or not Alfonso was Bourbon or Puigmoltejo gave way in time to inconclusve speculation on whom he resembled when grown. In facial features Alfonso was certainly closer to the unprepossessing Don Francisco than to the extraordinarily handsome Puig Moltó. On the other hand, the infante had a predisposition to consumption, the cause of the lieutenant's death. During the several years when Republicanism and Carlism ran high in Spain a strong undercurrent of innuendo existed about his legitimacy, largely to be forgotten when he became king. As for Alfonso's general heredity, the facts are quite astonishing, the more so for historians not having dwelled on them: his officially recognized parents were cousins, as were his grandparents and his great-grandparents. All eight great-grandparents and twelve of sixteen great-great-grandparents were descendants of Louis XIV. Such interbreeding among the Spanish, French, Neapolitan, and Parma Bourbons was hardly less pronounced than the intermarriages of Spanish and Austrian Hapsburgs that had culminated in the disastrously deformed and unstable Carlos II. Yet hereditary disabilities apparently have not bothered the recent Spanish Bourbons until British Queen Victoria's hemophilia entered the picture.

Alfonso's first eleven years, spent in Spain as Prince of the Asturias, were an unpromising beginning, a case of overprotection and undereducation. Given his mother's unfortunate experience with her firstborn son and given the new infante's susceptibility to colds and respiratory infections, not surprisingly the gentlemen governors were charged above all with watching Alfonso's health. "He woke up at midnight, sneezed, and blew his nose" was a typical entry in the official log kept for the anxious Isabel, or "last night he did not sneeze more than once." His bowel movements were a subject of constant concern, second only to his performance of his religious duties, for Queen Isabel insisted that her child be subjected to an intensity and duration of religious instruction that, as one observer noted, would have qualified him to sit on the Council of Trent. The candid confidence of a playmate of the infante to his father is revealing: "Alfonso does not know anything. He is taught nothing but religion and drilling. After the religious lesson, which was very dull, Alfonso was given a spear and a sword and he waved them about." Next to religious persons, military figures predominated in Alfonso's upbringing, and he retained a lifelong interest in soldiering, which fortunately was not so exaggerated as in the contemporary Russian and German rulers. As a child, Alfonso started with a plain soldier's uniform and gained his sergeant's stripes after behaving well at a public reception. Shortly thereafter occurred the Sergeants' Revolt of 1866 and the attendant executions, causing the prince to throw a fit of tears that he could not perish at the side of his fellow rankers—an omen, perhaps, of democratic humility.

Oversolicitous of her son in many ways, Queen Isabel was chiefly at fault for his haphazard training. He appeared to have inherited from her his seductive dark eyes and winning smile. While Alfonso had a slightly melancholy air about him that reminded people of Don Francisco, the father had shown little concern for any of his children's rearing, and he and the son were never close.

Alfonso was a slight, bright-eyed, and somber boy of eleven when Queen Isabel was ousted from Spain in 1868. What was disaster for his family was beneficial for broadening the heir's horizons. Living with his mother in the

Palacio de Castilla in Paris, Alfonso almost ceased to see his father, but in the Duke of Sesto he had a high-minded father figure. From him came the prince's first bicycle and roller skates. He frequently went horseback riding in the Bois de Boulogne with two young Spanish aristocrats and visited all the tourist attractions of the French capital. Enrolled in the Collège Stanislaus, where he pursued a broad curriculum of humanities and sciences, the young Bourbon proved himself more than the equal of his fellows, largely because of his phenomenal memory.

Early in 1870 Alfonso visited Rome incognito as the Count of Covadonga, but he was received with royal honors by the Pope, from whose hands he received his first communion (this gesture and the salutations sent Alfonso by virtually all of Spain's church hierarchy were significant slaps at the Carlists and recognitions of Isabel's religiosity). Then, coming home from an excursion on that August day in 1870, the son was gravely informed by his mother of her abdication. "Alfonso, give Pepe [the Duke of Sesto] your hand, for he has succeeded in making you king." Thereafter Alfonso nurtured a sense of high destiny. When the Franco-Prussian War broke out the same month, Alfonso was jealous that his college friend the prince imperial went off to fight while he and his sisters were taken by his alarmed parent to summer at the Norman fishing village of Hougatte. After the Battle of Sedan and the fall of Napoleon III, Isabel loaded herself and her family into a train for Geneva, where Alfonso went to a public class in physics at the insistence of a new no-nonsense tutor. The family returned to the Palacio de Castilla following the peace and the bloody Paris Commune (people had eaten Alfonso's pets, and his favorite Tuileries gardens were in ruins). The summer of 1871 and the next he spent at Deauville, meeting there the imaginative young writer Jules Verne.

The Duke of Sesto considered it wise to remove Alfonso altogether from the suffocating atmosphere of the court in exile—the frivolities of the mother, the bickerings with the absent father, and the mere presence of the lover Marfori, whom the son loathed. Accordingly, Alfonso was sent off to Catholic Austria in February, 1872, to become a student at the Theresanium in Vienna. He stayed briefly at the Favorita Palace, where the Hapsburg Archduke Charles had laid down his challenge to the throne of Alfonso's ancestor, Felipe V, in 1703, and he made a very favorable impression on the dean of conservative rulers, the Emperor Francis Joseph. With a staff including the Duke of Sesto and other Spanish gentlemen and the companionship of numerous archdukes, Alfonso eagerly threw himself into hunting, touring, and adding German to his good command of French and English. The director of the Theresanium reported to Isabel that "His Highness has passed a brilliant public examination . . . he is a good

Catholic, his conduct in all aspects has been exemplary . . . he is leaving fortified, grown, and in good health."

On his return to Paris in 1873, Alfonso found that all the talk was of the abdication of King Amadeo, the difficulties of the Spanish Republic, and the renewed hopes of the Bourbons. His new mentor became Cánovas de Castillo, who had to steer him past Marfori's intrigues and, in fact, did everything possible to disassociate Alfonso from the unseemly past and present of his family. England was already familiar to the prince, who had toured there in 1873, hobnobbing with his old friend the prince imperial and the slightly disreputable Prince of Wales. Now Alfonso was enrolled at the Royal Military College of Sandhurst, taking up residence in September, 1874, in a small cottage with four servants and rented furniture. When the seventeen-year-old cadet submitted a modest budget to his mother, he did not feel free to request his own horse, but Isabel gave him one anyhow. Cabrera, of all people, sent over pheasants and game for Alfonso's table, the Carlist leader living nearby and having changed his politics so far as to recognize the title of the young prince. Alfonso took readily to the cadet's life of study and exercise, spending weekends at various noble or royal houses.

Alfonso's becoming seventeen was closely followed in December, 1874, by his joyous reunion in Paris with his family and the exciting news that he had been hailed as king in Spain. No longer a gangling youth, Alfonso was now a slightly built, fine-featured young man with a deep voice, the beginnings of a beard, and a great maturity of manner. "If he had been a little taller, he would have qualified as a good-looking devil," wrote a contemporary. His movements were graceful, and his look could only be described as seductive. His natural charm captivated all, causing absolute worship by his sisters. The circumstances of Alfonso's life in exile had taught him simple ways, directness of manner, and disregard of flattery. He had known adversity and had received the education of an ordinary good student.

When Alfonso XII set off to claim his throne, he knew that a rival king was already in Spain, his twenty-six-year-old cousin, who still held court in Estella and directed the military efforts of thousands of followers. Having never met but always acutely aware of each other, the two Bourbon princes were conceivably mutually jealous, each admiring the other's reputed strengths. Don Carlos was the more handsome, majestic, and commanding; Don Alfonso the more educated, clever, and purposeful.

On the eve of his departure for Spain, Alfonso had to contend with misguided intrigues within his immediate family. The Duke of Montpensier had hurried to Paris to give his nephew a banquet, but he was firmly

rebuffed in his aspirations to play regent. Also, Queen Isabel had high
hopes to return to Spain, but she was tactfully dissuaded by Cánovas, who
wrote her: "Your Majesty is a historical epoch, and what the country needs
now is a different reign, a different epoch from the previous one. When the
reign has actually taken on all its true character and the new epoch is
completely defined, that will be when Your Majesty can and should come."
Attending the opening of the new opera house on January 5, 1875, Alfonso
drew cheers from the audience, and the next day he left Paris, amid his
mother's tears, royal salutes, and the excited attention of the press.

At Marseilles Alfonso boarded *Las Naves de Tolosa*. He wore the Order
of the Golden Fleece and the insignia of the four great military orders on
his captain general's uniform, which had arrived from a Madrid seamstress
at the last moment. His ship received the salutes of Barcelona on January 9,
and the first person he greeted on board was the general who had
proclaimed him, Martínez de Campos. Later he wired his mother: "The
reception which Barcelona has given me exceeds my hopes, exceeds your
desires." Now on the *Numancia*, he proceeded to Valencia, where during
two days of joyous fiesta he repeated in speeches his pledge to be "King of
all Spaniards." Then a special train took him to Aranjuez.

The delirious reception of Alfonso XII in Madrid on January 12, 1875,
recalled similar royal restorations. Charles II of England in 1660, however
cynical about the fickleness of crowds, was received with such jubilation
that he could only wonder why he had not returned earlier. Fernando VII
of Spain in 1814 found the popular expectations so hysterical that he could
do anything. The outpouring of enthusiasm for Alfonso in 1875 certainly
far exceeded that for King Amadeo almost exactly four years previously,
although the ceremonial format was the same. A signal gun at 11:30 A.M.
announced the king's arrival at the train station, and throughout the capital
the troops drew up in formation and the citizens placed finishing touches on
the triumphal arches and the houses draped in red and yellow bunting.
After greeting Prime Minister Cánovas, Alfonso mounted his white horse,
Segundo, and rode out into the clear, cold day. A witness described the rest
of the triumphant parade:

> In this manner, managing the horse with such adroitness and
> aplomb as if he wished to show that with his energetic character,
> despite his years, he knew how to grasp the reins of government,
> with his face to the right and saluting without cease, with a noble
> and gracious smile, followed by a staff more bright and splendid
> than had been seen in a long time; escorted by units of cavalry and
> infantry, his passage celebrated with hurrahs, acclaims, blessings,
> and tears . . . with every instant verses, flowers, and doves being

thrown from the balconies, receiving homages and gifts, hearing the hallowed notes of the "Royal March," there is lacking means to describe their gratitude and happiness, in this manner the king traversed the Atocha road, entered under a canopy into the basilica, heard with concentration the Te Deum, visited the sepulchers of Concha, Palafox, and Castaños, continued the length of the Prado, saluted with respect the Dos de Mayo obelisk, entered the street of the Alcala. . . .

A spectacular review of the troops at the palace ended the exhilarating occasion.

"The wine has been poured," said Cánovas of the restoration. "Now we must taste it." A few days later he declared, "I am enthusiastic about the king. We understand each other. . . . Those who were ministers of his mother can appreciate the difference, for this reign there will not be camarillas or favorites, and if the country knows enough to elect a worthy parliament, it will exercise its sovereignty without hindrance." For the next ten years the young king and the parliamentarian three times his age were to have an affectionate, harmonious, and fruitful collaboration that reminds historians of Wilhelm and Bismarck, Victor Emmanuel and Cavour. No Cortes sat during 1875, but the restoration was marked by a minimum of reprisal or vindictiveness, unlike 1814, for example. The reestablishment of clerical domination in the schools and the elimination of civil marriages were immediate indicative changes.

Alfonso spent only four days in Madrid. He presided at the council, he attended a gala at the Teatro Español and he opened the assembly hall of the university, on the last occasion misplacing the speech Cánovas had prepared for him but impressing all with his extemporaneous eloquence. He also impressed the top generals with his military acumen at a briefing on the Third Carlist War the day before he set off for the front. The king knew that his personal future hung in the balance and that the nature of the new political regime could not be established until peace was achieved. He felt that his presence was necessary to inspire the army despite the mild objections of Cánovas.

The spirit of the Carlists was inevitably sapped now that their enemies fought to the cry of *Viva el Rey.* In vain Don Carlos announced that his rival was "King of the Revolution." Alfonso spoke of the changed circumstances of the war in his manifesto to the Basques and Navarrese on January 23: "If you are fighting in the cause of royalism, I am the representative of the dynasty to which your fathers swore faith. If you are fighting for the Catholic faith, I am a Catholic and will right the wrongs done to the Church. . . . You yourselves love liberty: you cannot deprive

Spaniards of it. . . . Before beginning battle, I offer you peace." The young monarch's reckless courage nearly resulted in his being captured in a skirmish, while his good sense in sending the royal chefs back to Madrid served to earn him the soldiers' esteem. Alfonso was present at the successful raising of the siege of Pamplona on February 7. When a subsequent government attack on Estella miscarried, his advisers decided that the royal presence would be a hindrance to an upcoming war of attrition, and the king returned to Madrid.

Alfonso regained his capital only to be faced with more unseemly family intrigues. The government felt that Queen Isabel's immediate return would be embarrassing, but it welcomed the coming of Alfonso's sisters. "The more royal heads where the crown could be placed immediately, the less risk for the principal one, that is, His Majesty, the king," was Cánovas' observation. Alfonso installed the recently widowed Infanta Isabel as hostess at the Oriente Palace. Piqued into an incredible breach of trust with her son, Queen Isabel turned to the Carlists, at first flaunting an intimacy with Princess Margarita. Then she went so far as to begin a correspondence with the pretender himself, accepting his portrait with profuse thanks. The pretender in his letters was insistent on his rights, all the while professing magnanimity: "I am the legitimate King of Spain, and as such I open my arms to press to my heart my dear cousin the Infante Alfonso." The bait that Don Carlos held out to the woman of forty-five, who was frustrated for being ignored, was her return to Spain. He wrote on May 25: "I reign in the beautiful provinces of the north. . . . If you wish to go to Lequeitio or Zarauz . . . you could occupy the same palaces which you then inhabited, since I don't think it possible that the sailors of your son in that area would continue to bombard these ports." After hesitations and renewed negatives from Madrid, Isabel replied on July 3: "If my son doesn't call me, I will have done my duty and I will accept the affectionate offer of my noble cousin Carlos." The misguided plottings proved pointless in the face of developments in the war, but the Madrid government did stop Isabel's pension.

Don Carlos could not replace the leadership lost to his cause with the defections of Cabrera and Don Alfonso Carlos. His forces suffered so many defeats that the government allowed King Alfonso to resume nominal command. On February 9, 1876, General Primo de Rivera finally captured Estella. The government forces were simply too strong and his followers too short of everything except bravery, so that Don Carlos had no choice but to flee once again to France, with almost 10,000 supporters. He crossed the frontier over the bridge at Arnequi as his ever present trumpeters sounded the "Royal Anthem." "Volveré" (I shall return) was his defiant prediction, but history dictated not only that the Third Carlist War was over but also that no similar armed attempts would take place in the future. The French police this time hustled the pretender to England, where he was hissed by crowds and shunned by society led by the Prince of Wales. Meanwhile, Alfonso XII received a roaring reception in Madrid on March 20 that exceeded even his reception fourteen months previously, and he ever after carried the sobriquet *el rey pacificador.*

The regime now forgave Queen Isabel her aberrations and allowed her to return to Spain on July 29, 1876. The crowds at the railway stations were enthusiastic as she rode south, and she cried to hear the *vivas.* Cánovas warily let her go no farther than the Escorial at first and then saw to her establishment in the ancient Moorish Álcazar of Seville. A seeming reconciliation of the queen mother took place with the Montpensiers, who also returned to enjoy their Andalusian properties. The degree of religious pomp at the Álcazar court provoked one local official to complain, "Spain has returned to the Middle Ages." Later, when Isabel tried to interfere in national religious affairs, the king had to silence his mother, just as he once pointedly censured a mayor for forcing Catholic baptism on the children of Protestants.

The rivalries within the dynasty resolved, it was time to make a general political settlement. Accordingly, the regime promulgated a new constitution on July 2, 1876. The document was the personal work of Cánovas, a cultivated, honest, but too cynical statesman. "I have come to galvanize the political corpse of Spain," he said. A compromise between the "royalist" one of 1845 and the "republican" one of 1869, the Constitution of 1876 was ostensibly progressive and workably vague on touchy questions. It provided for a bicameral Cortes elected by limited suffrage and empowered to approve all legislation. The ministry was responsible to the Cortes, and any action of the king had to be countersigned by a minister. The king retained considerable power in making appointments and granting titles and honors. The Constitution embodied civil liberties and virtually complete freedom of the press.

What made the Constitution of 1876 ultimately self-defeating was that it concealed Cánovas' determined intention that no genuinely free elections take place under it, and none did occur until after its demise in 1931. The ministry absolutely controlled the appointment of governors and mayors, who in turn manipulated the lists of voters to produce the desired results, so that at times in the future the official press would announce election figures even before the voting had taken place. On the local level in rural areas the voting was controlled by the *caciques,* or feudal bosses, whose traditional origins did not justify the fact of their notorious corruption and strong-arm methods in the late nineteenth century.

That the elections were entirely crooked did not mean one party government but the deliberate rotation of Conservative and Liberal ministries under Cánovas and Sagasta. In the course of the next twenty years either of these two men held the office of prime minister continuously but for three short intervals. Cánovas, wise enough to realize that in the past the denial of power to the Liberals had been the cause of repeated appeals to violence, was willing to share the spoils of office with them. The understanding between Cánovas and Sagasta colored the whole restoration. The Republicans were the common enemy, a few of whom were occasionally let into the Cortes as window dressing. Between Liberals and Conservatives the differences were not great, the former being more anticlerical and business-oriented, the latter showing greater concern for agriculture and social welfare. Entirely devoted to being a constitutional monarch, King Alfonso XII was aware of the farcical nature of the two-party system but accepted it with helpless resignation. Once asked by his sister if a new ministry would be better than that of the other party, he replied, "No. It makes no difference. They are the same dog with different collars."

Cánovas' extraconstitutional arrangements meant the systematic exclusion of the lower orders from political power. He and the king probably hoped that genuine democracy would evolve, but the architect of the restoration felt that the upper classes must first be trained for political responsibility by encouraging them to prosper in business enterprise. "If we can get the privileged classes to work, that is the whole problem," he once declared.

To Cánovas' grand design of controlled elections and encouragement of moneymaking was added his absolute insistence that the army stay out of politics. Much of the military's role in the recent events of 1868–1874 had been discreditable, to say nothing of its repeated interference earlier in the century. Now promotions from the ranks largely ceased (as against the careers of Espartero, O'Dónnell, and Prim), and the close comradeship of officers and men, which many foreign observers had remarked in Spain in previous times, became a thing of the past. An officer's taking an interest in public affairs was discouraged. In time the Spanish army became a kind of closed corporation, as the church had already become and the business class was becoming. That class antagonisms were to intensify to the point of great violence by the turn of the century is of small wonder. The price Spain paid for a decade or two of tranquillity under Cánovas' arrangements was to be exceedingly high.

As for the king, he had a high sense of his responsibilities as a constitutional monarch and a determination to stay on his throne. "I never fear a revolution," he once said. "I am determined never to go into exile, and I will never cross the Bidassoa with my head on my shoulders. I will die in Spain."

Just before promulgating the Constitution of 1876, the Cortes decided on a financial settlement for the various Bourbons. It set the yearly maintenance of the king at 7,000,000 pesetas; his designated successor, Prince or Princess of the Asturias, received 500,000; each infante, whether sons of the king or of the Prince of the Asturias, 250,000; each infanta, 150,000; Isabel II, 750,000; Francisco de Asís, 300,000; María Cristina, 250,000.

2. Royal Romances and Royal Tragedies

The first years revealed King Alfonso XII to be a dedicated ruler. Admired by many as *el rey pacificador,* he was loved by some as *el rey romántico.*

A methodical person, Alfonso pursued a businesslike routine that was in marked contrast with the disorganized ways of Queen Isabel. He rose early to put in long hours on state affairs, and in the afternoons he exercised vigorously. The king had dinner at seven thirty in an era when society ate at ten or eleven. The unconventional hours reflected the king's impatience with tradition and ceremony. Some of his first actions made clear that the palace etiquette of his mother's day was unwanted. He ended the practice of kissing the royal hand and dispensed with the official and four guards who accompanied each dish from the royal kitchen (also, Alfonso did not *tutear,* or "thou," everyone, just close friends). In matters of protocol Alfonso's court was far less stuffy than the short-lived court of his cousin and rival at Estella, but the king avoided the complete informality of his immediate royal predecessor in the Oriente, King Amadeo. Much of Alfonso's time was devoted to receiving mayors and laying foundation stones, functions he handled with the greatest dignity tempered with affability.

Perhaps in simple reaction to the brief years of the democratic monarchy and republic, elegance and style returned to Madrid social circles under the restoration. Dandies appeared on the boulevards, and people entertained at elaborate parties. The young king fitted in well with the new splendor, being both clothes-conscious and devoted to dancing. He presided serenely over such dazzling occasions as the opening of the Teatro Real on October 4, 1877, at which seats cost thirty reals. Elena Sanz sang captivatingly, and her charms were not lost on Alfonso, as time would prove.

A more than conventional patron of the theater, Alfonso also was an avid reader, and he frequently found time to spend literary evenings, taking delight in reading Romantic poetry aloud to a set of close friends in a gay, almost bohemian atmosphere. The king turned his hand occasionally to writing for the amusement of his circle. One of his stories was a mock-serious account of a hunt in which fifty-one shots were expended to fell three deer. Another published effort was called *Memorias Autobiográficas de Don Paco*, which concerned a black mongrel dog well known and well loved by many in Madrid. The tale duly recorded Paco's attendance at Forno's Café, his appearances at opening nights at the theater, his promenades in the Retiro Gardens, and his accidental death at a bullfight.

Alfonso's fine sense of humor was recorded in many other ways. Once he smilingly brought on surprise and indignation at an evening gathering by reading a recent speech in the Cortes by a Republican deputy which lambasted the monarchy in general and himself in particular. He enjoyed telling of the time when, riding with a small-town mayor, he could not make conversation because of the steady *vivas* of the street boys. His apologetic complaint to the local worthy drew the startled response that if the mayor had known His Majesty had wanted to talk, he would not have paid the cheerers so much. One day when the Duke of Sesto unaccountably failed to be on hand for the king's arising, Alfonso gravely kneeled down and peered into the cupboard under the bed where the chamber pot was kept, announcing that "Pepe" was not to be found. Another anecdote told of the young monarch concerned a colonel of considerable youth whose hair had turned white. At a reception the man had explained to Alfonso's fascination that during service in the Philippines he had been swimming across a river when his leg had been seized by an alligator, and, escaping with his life, he found his hair turned snowy. Some time after their first encounter Alfonso recognized the colonel again despite the fact that his hair was now dyed black. "Were you bitten by an alligator again?" was the king's opening remark.

A young bachelor, Alfonso liked his nocturnal outings, enjoying the company of some of his young friends of Paris days and sometimes suffering that of the Duke of Sesto. Like King Amadeo, Alfonso considered his private life not the public's business, and he was hardly more discreet about it. On at least one post-midnight occasion startled street people were asked to give the royal party directions back to the Oriente.

Alfonso's high spirits and love of sport provoked one minor crisis with the prime minister. The king's friends proposed to throw a rodeo, and he looked forward to joining in all the action. Cánovas' wise, if pompous, reaction was "I will lead the king to his death in front of an army fighting the enemy or defending the crown from the revolution. Then he would fall with glory, but I will not consent that he suffer harm to his person from a cow's kick or a bull goring him." The king was in a bad humor for a few days, then admitted with resignation, "He is hard with me, but it is because he truly loves me."

Every private and public reason existed for the king to get married, his having celebrated his twentieth birthday in November, 1877. Cánovas had been canvassing the courts of Europe in the usual manner. Princess Beatrice of England, he learned, would not change her religion for the privilege of becoming Queen of Spain (her daughter would do exactly otherwise at another juncture of history). The search was pointless, however, since Alfonso had already made up his mind. He once told his sister the Infanta Paz: "There are two things upon which I will never give way, though it cost me my crown. I will not suppress religious liberty and I will never marry against my will." The king's choice was his seventeen-year-old cousin Mercedes de Montpensier, with whom he had fallen in love in his days of exile in Paris and with whom he had been corresponding secretly ever since. She was the fifth daughter of Queen Isabel's quietly dignified sister Luisa and Louis Philippe's son, the brilliant and conniving Duke of Montpensier.

Alfonso's romance faced difficulties. In a letter of September 13, 1877, his sister Paz noted: "I have just come back from a long drive with Alfonso. . . . The poor boy is awfully in love with our cousin Mercedes, but it seems both the government and Mamma are against the idea of such a marriage." Deputies made excited speeches in the Cortes that Spain was repeating the marital nightmare of 1846 and that Montpensier sought to be a power behind the throne. Montpensier's past intrigues with republicans and even his success at running his estates were among other things held against him. Queen Isabel, who had been publicly reconciled with her sister and brother-in-law for some time, reverted to her earlier suspicions of them. Moreover, she still nursed her own persistent dream for a dynasty that would effect a reconciliation with the Carlists by having her son marry Don Carlos' sister. In view of her own sad experience, it is strange that she opposed his obvious love match. Violent family scenes took place. On September 15 Paz reported: "Yesterday Alfonso told me he intended to speak seriously with Mamma about his marriage and that he won't leave here until an understanding is come to. In the afternoon Mamma's eyes were red, and I could see she had been crying; but Alfonso told me in the evening that all was arranged." Queen Isabel's tears expressed anger as well as sorrow, for shortly afterward she returned to the Palacio de Castilla in Paris, doubly indignant that her daughters would not come with her. Early in December the Duke of Sesto went to Seville to ask Mercedes' hand formally, and on the twenty-sixth the Montpensiers were the pleased hosts at a lavish engagement ball for the royal couple at their Palace of San Telmo.

The wedding was celebrated in Madrid on January 23, 1878, with a pomp the Spanish capital had not seen in decades. The king ordered a special railroad spur built to the palace at Aranjuez so that the queen-to-be could embark there in a splendidly decorated coach. From the station to the Church of the Atocha a dazzling procession took place with colorfully uniformed troops and the nobility riding in specially ordered "mail coaches" with sidemen and trumpeters in profusion. An unusual concourse of Spanish royalty was on hand for the occasion, including, besides the king, his three sisters and the various Montpensiers, the couple's mutual grandmother Doña María Cristina, a white-haired seventy-one but still strikingly beautiful, and the king's father, Don Francisco, full of high-voiced self-importance on his first return to Spain in nine years. Queen Isabel was absent. The festivities lasted for five days with the usual round of balls, bullfights, and popular fiestas. Electricity was a novelty in Madrid this year, almost as if introduced for the occasion, and the royal couple inaugurated the Hipódromo de Castellana in a brilliant ceremony.

Alfonso's wedding had not been affected by the death of King Victor Emmanuel II of Italy on January 9, the king having little regard for the sovereign who sought to supplant the Spanish Bourbons with the House of Savoy in the person of his son. Interestingly, Alfonso's predecessor, King Amadeo, encountered Queen Isabel at the Paris Exposition that May, and the two ex-rulers found each other congenial and joked together about "my ministers." The death of Pope Pius IX on February 7 was, on the other hand, a distressing thing for Alfonso and his new bride, for the Pontiff's warm friendship and support had helped significantly in the restoration and in the defeat of the Carlists. The sad news from Rome was soon counterbalanced by the joyful intelligence from Havana that the Cuban Insurrection had been seemingly settled by a truce agreement, which was announced at the opening of the Cortes on February 17.

The newly married couple quickly captured the imagination of the people because of their youthful freshness, their decorousness, and their obvious attachment to each other. One vignette of the happy pair given by the Infanta Paz concerns their receiving the exotic Annamite embassy in the throne room of the Oriente. The Asian visitors made three low obeisances, all the while holding and staring fixedly at an ivory portrait of their own king, and then chanted a long speech in singsong. "Alfonso and Mercedes did not dare look at each other for fear of an explosion."

Of Mercedes, her other sister-in-law, Eulalia, wrote in her memoirs: "She was a real beauty. Her large dark eyes, shadowed by sweeping lashes, her hair of the true Andalusian black, her mouth and delicate complexion made her a real prototype of lovely Spanish womanhood, so delicate and distinguished." Further, according to the infanta, "my brother and his wife were idyllically happy in their married life, and their happiness was reflected in all around them." The idyll was incredibly short-lived.

The Montpensiers were notoriously plagued by ill health in their children, the malicious even calling this part of their "curse." The queen's sister was suffering acutely from tuberculosis since the beginning of the year, and her illness was ostensibly the reason the royal couple did not go to the Paris Exposition. In May rumors spread that Queen Mercedes herself was sick with a severe gastric illness. She journeyed to Aranjuez in the hope that the fresh air would be beneficial but returned to the capital soon afterward to avail herself of more doctors. By June 18 she was suffering a high fever and received the last sacraments on the twenty-fourth, hearing from her bed at the same time cannon salvoes in celebration of her eighteenth birthday. Alfonso and his aunt never left the bedside, while the palace was a crowded chaos of hurrying clerics, kneeling generals, and dignitaries catching naps on couches. Troops outside had difficulty controlling excited crowds, for all the places of public accommodation in Madrid had closed as a sign of respect. Mercedes died at noon on the twenty-sixth. "Against this horrible sarcasm of destiny protested everyone, the palace world, the upper and lower classes of Madrid, and the entire people of Spain," wrote the novelist Benito Pérez Galdós. As cannon boomed funereally, Mercedes was the first queen whose coffin was taken to the Escorial by train.

Two months later the ex-Queen Regent Cristina died in France. Her lover and husband of forty years, Muñoz, had predeceased her by five years. The king's grandmother was not buried with her second husband, however. Her body was brought back to the Escorial to lie next to that of Fernando VII, of dim memory, indeed. One of her last sentiments was: "Tell my Alfonso he must console himself and make Spain flourish." Queen Mercedes, not being the mother of a Spanish sovereign, was not accorded a place in the Escorial's burial place of the kings. Alfonso, his grief overwhelming, had first proposed to build a cathedral in her memory on the Calle Mayor near the palace, a Spanish Taj Mahal to cost millions of reales. Later a white tomb was made for her in a side chapel of the Escorial.

In the first months the king's anguish was pitiable, and many felt he never recovered from the loss of his first love. He spent hours on end at the tomb of Mercedes, avoided all gatherings except necessary state functions, and even gave up his horseback riding. Eventually Alfonso emerged from his ordeal noticeably more flippant and cynical in his conversation, mechanical and heedless in his pursuit of pleasure.

Perhaps the inheritance of his grandfather Fernando VII drove the bereaved Alfonso XII to become a libertine. Perhaps his sensuality was excited by the disease which was beginning to ravage his lungs. In any case, the king had no difficulty meeting attractive women, for, aside from his own inviting looks and manners, many observers attested that society women were outrageously forward with their favors, doing anything to get into the palace. One general, for example, took advantage of an interview with the king to present him with a handkerchief made by his daughter and thereafter was emboldened to bring the daughter, who this time offered some homemade slippers of great ugliness. That the daughter was the real offering filled Alfonso with disgust.

The king's taste ran to divas. One of his first great affairs was with Elena Sanz, who, according to Pérez Galdós, was not only a perfect Amneris in *Aida* but a "woman as good as bread, all passion, generosity, tenderness." After a rags-to-riches career in Spain that culminated in tours of European and American capitals, she found herself in Paris in 1873 calling on Queen Isabel and the Duke of Sesto, her sponsors in the past. The Queen persuaded the forty-year-old voluptuous beauty to visit Alfonso at the Theresanium in Vienna, and the sixteen-year-old student was duly awestruck. Later she at first resisted seduction by the young admirer now turned king and widower, but eventually she gave up her singing career and established herself near the palace in a mansion. She bore Alfonso two sons, Alfonso and Fernando. When the king remarried, Elena discreetly left for Paris, where Isabel greeted her with the greatest affection as her "daughter-in-law before God."

On March 25, 1878, the first public appearance of Alfonso XII in Madrid since the death of Queen Mercedes was marred by an assassination attempt on the Calle Mayor. His assailant, who shot at him twice, was a deranged twenty-two-year-old barrelmaker, whose final diary entry that day was: "I have little time to live since Alfonso is coming in an hour and afterward they will condemn me to death." Execution was indeed the fate of the assassin, at Cánovas' insistence over Alfonso's objections. The day after the attempt Alfonso and the Infanta Isabel drove to the Atocha, where they were received with the greatest fervor. The king's popularity was evident elsewhere in the country, when he opened the direct railroad line to Portugal at Badajoz in February, 1879, and when he welcomed Crown Prince Rudolph of Austria-Hungary to Barcelona in May. The populace was impressed particularly with Alfonso's disregard for his own safety.

Death seemed to hover about the young king. In April his sister-in-law María Cristina died in Seville. Alfonso was once again beside himself with grief, apparently having had intentions of marrying this other Montpensier daughter. In August the family suffered the loss of the eighteen-year-old Infanta Pilar, who, attending a rural fiesta in Guipúzcoa, had succumbed within thirty-six hours to an attack of consumption, a disease Alfonso shared with her but kept secret. "Everyone loved Pilar best of all," wrote the Infanta Paz, who believed that her sister died heartbroken because of the loss of her beloved Louis Napoleon, prince imperial, killed fighting with the British army against the Zulus in South Africa.

The need for a direct heir to the throne made Alfonso's remarriage essential, and he yielded to the importunities of his ministers, almost indifferently letting them debate about the eligibles. Cánovas favored Sophia of Belgium, but fortunately she was too young at fourteen, being destined to help drive her husband, Crown Prince Rudolph, the Hapsburg, to suicide at Mayerling. The choice fell to María Cristina of Austria, the twenty-one-year-old daughter of the Archduke Charles Ferdinand and cousin to the Emperor Francis Joseph. She was the king's relative in the fourth degree, the connection going back to the marriage of a daughter of Carlos III to the later Emperor Leopold II. Alfonso remembered her from his student days when her parents had entertained him warmly. She, for her part, had been infatuated with Alfonso and, upon learning of his marriage to Mercedes, resigned herself to becoming abbess of a wealthy Prague order called the Noble Dames of Moravia. The prospective match was known to Alfonso's family in early June, 1879, but not until August 22 did the King, traveling incognito as the Count of Covadonga, depart for the Gascon beach resort of Arcachon, near Bordeaux, to ask for María Cristina's hand. The king was a woebegone figure, his arm in a sling from a carriage overturning (an aide had to write his love letters to Elena Sanz for him). Under a picture of Queen Mercedes the future queen said what was on both their minds: "Señor, my great desire is to make myself like her, but I do not dare believe that I could ever replace her." After several days' visit, having gained the parental consent, Alfonso was to write his sisters, teasingly to be sure: "What is too bad is that while the mother pleases me more, I have to marry the daughter."

After renouncing her rights in Austria-Hungary, María Cristina left for her new country on November 17, stopping to pay her respects to Queen Isabel. The still-scandalous woman of forty-eight found her future daughter-in-law starchy, but she could not have been more pleased at the prestige of an alliance with the most ancient, conservative, and Catholic Hapsburgs. The bride traveled by train into Spain and was greeted by Alfonso on November 24. While staying at El Pardo, the always correct María Cristina had occasion to tell the president of the Cortes: "I ask that from today you consider me a Spaniard, for my sole duty is to love Spain and to make for the happiness of the king in the modest sphere of the home." She had no premonition that she would be fated to rule Spain for seventeen years.

The day of the wedding, November 29, 1879, was bright and mild after two weeks of rain. María Cristina began dressing at eight fifteen. Cannon salutes marked Alfonso's departure to receive her at ten thirty. Then followed the familiar parades and ceremonies of a Spanish royal wedding, with the great novelty that this time the procession of the carriages of royalty and aristocracy had an elaborate historical aura. Each coach was accompanied by footmen and soldiers of a different epoch (the spectacle was so unusual that it is commemorated in a series of sixty-four little engravings of each grouping, the most expensive single purchase a tourist can make in the bookshop of the Oriente Palace). During the ensuing five days of festivities, the royal couple inaugurated the great dining room in the palace, replacing the dazzling hall of columns as a site for banquets since Alfonso had the memory of the latter being used for Mercedes' funeral.

A month after the wedding a baker fired two shots at the monarchs while they were driving near the palace but succeeded only in grazing the king's head. The queen's self-possession at the time after an impulsive embrace of her husband earned her popular acclaim, as did her many acts of charity and piety. Society sensed, however, that this was a marriage of convenience, quite unlike the previous one. Alfonso's sense of humor was not altogether appreciated by María Cristina, and at least once, when she whispered to him for help with a reply to somebody in Spanish, he gave her the wrong words.

The royal couple's first child was born on September 11, 1880, a girl to the great disappointment of the king, who knew his health was not good. The infanta was christened Mercedes at the suggestion of the queen. With an ill grace unusual for him, Alfonso tried to minimize the ceremonies in honor of the birth, perhaps not unwisely, for the baptism, with the child in the arms of Queen Isabel, was spoiled by the primate and the patriarch of the Indies, who nearly struck each other with their religious insignia over some matter of precedence. The Conservative Prime Minister Cánovas, with economies in mind, persuaded the royal couple to forgo investing Mercedes with the honors of Princess of the Asturias, an action reversed by the Liberal Sagasta the next year. Another infanta, María Teresa, was born on November 12, 1881.

While María Cristina showed every sign of having fallen in love with her husband, Alfonso soon became bored with the woman he married for reasons of state. The wife was not particularly attractive—she was so nearsighted that she almost always wore glasses, she had the hanging lower lip of the Hapsburgs, and she was stiff-necked in her ways. The king resumed his extramarital affairs, finding himself another diva, this one's forte being *Les Huguenots*. The king's nocturnal absences and his wandering eye went not unnoticed by the queen, who resorted futilely to tears, to rages against courtiers suspected of abetting her husband's trysts, and to threats to return to Vienna.

The king's restlessness may well have been aggravated by the absence of the sternly paternal Cánovas from the prime ministership. The Liberal Party had long accused the Conservative leader of being dictatorial, and the wrath of popular manifestations against him sometimes spilled over against the king. Alfonso refused his signature to a proposal giving Cánovas even more power, and Cánovas resigned, saying later that he faked the whole crisis in order to give the Liberals a taste of power and thus to give the monarchy "two feet"—that is, to make the other party pro-dynasty.

Sagasta, whom the king found too unctuously respectful, headed an effective Liberal ministry which pursued some reform but also found itself in the unwelcome role of repressor. The government, having legalized trade unions, grew alarmed when major strikes took place in both city and countryside and when both socialists and anarchists started organizing politically. The police discovered, or more likely manufactured, evidence of a formidable secret society called the *Mano Negra* (Black Hand) whose aim was to murder all landowners. The Liberal regime, by authorizing 8 executions and 300 jailings, drove the anarchists underground again. "Social troubles are nothing new," wrote the king, showing that his liberalism had its limitations.

Both Sagasta and Cánovas supported a foreign policy for Spain that leaned away from the French Republic and favored the Triple Alliance of Germany, Austria, and Italy. A commercial treaty with Germany early in 1883 signified the alignment. The king "earned his salary," to use his own expression, in the area of diplomacy, making a tour of European capitals later that year. He received a warm welcome from his wife's Hapsburg relatives in Vienna, where he enjoyed visiting his old school. In Berlin Bismarck pulled out all the stops to make his reception impressive. On one occasion in Germany Alfonso wore the uniform of honorary colonel in a Prussian Uhlan regiment, and even before he subsequently reached France, he learned that French patriotism had been aroused by his action. Nonetheless, the king proceeded to Paris on September 29, 1883, only to be confronted by persistently booing crowds. When his advisers urged him to leave immediately on the royal train, Alfonso refused to be upset and completed his state visit with aplomb. Spanish patriotism in turn was brought to fever pitch by the news from Paris, and the king received the wildest possible ovation back in Madrid.

After the king's return from his European tour, Cánovas regained power in January, 1884. Society was more interested in parties than politics. One of the great galas of the decade was a period costume ball at the palace of the Duke of Fernán Núñez in February at which the host appeared as Felipe II and Queen María Cristina came dressed as an eighteenth-century lady.

The king's health became a major topic of conversation. At the end of July, 1884, when Alfonso went off to take the waters at Beteler, all Spain knew that he was seriously sick. His intimates despaired over his emaciated looks, his sunken eyes, his listlessness, and his voice that broke from coughing.

The reports of the precariousness of the king's health and the fact that he had only two very young daughters as heirs stirred intrigues within the dynasty and gave hopes to the republicans. Alfonso's uncle, the Duke of Montpensier, once again renewed the maneuverings that as far back as the 1840's had earned him the reputation of being Machiavellian. One project of his was for a marriage of the king's sister Eulalia to his son Antonio. Another was to ingratiate himself with the Carlists.

As for Don Carlos himself, he pursued his old dreams and added some new ones. In 1881 the pretender had been expelled from France for attending a royalist mass at St.-Germain-des-Prés against the orders of the government. He took up residence in Venice, which he had known fondly as a boy. His palace became the center of renewed propaganda and conspiracy. "Queen Margarita" did not join her husband but, long annoyed at his philandering, took advantage of the uprooting to establish herself on an estate at Viareggio. The couple decorously exchanged visits twice yearly. Don Carlos' political pretensions were extended upon the death of the Legitimist French pretender, the Count of Chambord, at Frohsdorf on August 24, 1883. The French Orléanists now hoped that all French monarchists would rally around their pretender, the Count of Paris, who was married to Montpensier's daughter Maria Francisca. The Countess of Chambord, however, took charge of her husband's funeral and stubbornly insisted that the male Carlists, being descendants of Louis XIV, be given precedence before the Count of Paris. Henceforth, Don Carlos considered himself rightful King of France as well as of Spain. The Pope, however, once again dispelled hopes of Don Carlos' sitting on the Spanish throne by a letter to the priesthood telling them not to support him in any way.

Alfonso XII lived out his final days with grace and heroism. Earthquakes devastated much of Andalusia in early 1885, and the king promptly toured the area. At Málaga people were entranced to see the king toast his own sardines in the manner of the humble. That July came the dismal news of a serious outbreak of cholera at Aranjuez. Knowing that Cánovas would forbid his presence there, Alfonso furtively left with a single aide for the Atocha station, bought two ordinary tickets, and bantered with a man gaping at him in amazement from an adjoining train until he left for the stricken city. There the king visited the houses of the sick to offer sympathy and money. He told officials, "You will understand that after the so many most pleasant days I've passed in the *sitio* [royal residence], enjoying its enchantments, today, when the people, the garrison, and my servants suffer the ravages of this cruel epidemic, it is only right that I come to show how much I lament their misfortune and to offer my consolation." Once again the king's return to Madrid was the occasion for a tumultuous popular outburst, the crowds insisting on pulling his carriage themselves.

Alfonso was further taxed in September, 1885, by the outbreak of a crisis with Germany over the Caroline Islands in the Pacific Ocean. A German gunboat had run up the German flag over Yap Island when the Spanish authorities tried to interfere with a German factory there. The press fanned popular outrage in Madrid, and the German legation was stormed. The king's calm and that of others led to the dispute's being mediated by the Pope, with the islands eventually going to Germany in return for a handsome payment to Spain.

The court was heartened to learn that Queen María Cristina was pregnant again, but the king had the sad presentiment that he would not live to see a son, having once expressed wistful envy at the sight of a workman carrying his little boy. The royal family moved to El Pardo in late October, 1885, hoping that the country air would prolong Alfonso's life. Not until November 24 did the government admit publicly the desperateness of the king's condition, although Cánovas had known the worst since July. On that day the king went for a carriage ride with his aunt Montpensier, and later, sitting in an armchair, he talked affectionately to María Cristina and all his family, including Queen Isabel, who had come from Paris. His mother confidently left him to go to the opera, where she was stunned to receive news that the king was sinking. The ever-contentious Isabel vented her hatred of her daughter-in-law by saying, "My son is dying and they let him die like a dog." Priests gave the last sacraments to Alfonso at 8 A.M. on November 25, and he was dead within the hour. In Paris, Don Francisco "cried like a child" when he heard of the death of his son.

The day after the death of Alfonso XII occurred the passing of General Serrano, once the "General Beautiful" of the young Queen Isabel, revolutionist and regent in 1868, sulky politician under King Amadeo, and strong man president in the last year of the republic. In his dying delirium Serrano had cried, "Give me my sword. The king is dying, and I must be at his side." The political impotence of this last of the great king-making generals of the nineteenth century and the elimination of the military from government was one of the accomplishments of the brief reign of Alfonso XII. Not profound or dramatic in his impact on Spanish affairs, the eighth Bourbon monarch with his grace, bravery, and political delicacy had given the country a welcome breathing spell, and his death was widely and sincerely regretted.

3. The Regency of Virtue

The death of Alfonso XII left Spain in the same predicament it faced fifty-two years before when Queen María Cristina of Naples became regent for the three-year-old Isabel and the female succession was promptly challenged by Don Carlos. Now in 1885 the mother was María Cristina of Austria, the daughter was the five-year-old Infanta Mercedes, and the antagonist was Don Carlos' grandson styling himself "Carlos VII." Some differences in the situation were that Spain had enjoyed constitutional government in the interval and that Carlism was discredited by three atrocity-ridden, costly, and futile civil wars. Even more important was the fact that the present María Cristina was pregnant, so that people were called upon to swear allegiance to the "heir of Alfonso XII," perhaps a boy.

The twenty-seven-year-old regent met the ordeal of her husband's funeral with unaffected grief and assumed her new political responsibilities with regal self-control. Her position was strengthened by the prompt recognition of an appreciative Pope and of the major European countries headed by the court of her Hapsburg relatives in Austria-Hungary. Most Spanish politicians rallied to María Cristina's support, although some Republicans muttered threats and the Carlists made the expected protests.

More difficult for the regent to contend with were plottings involving the immediate royal family, both those residing in Madrid and those abroad. One party at court felt that Alfonso's eldest sister, Doña Isabel, had a better claim to the regency, but this infanta did nothing to bear out the ambition she was accused of having (the most malicious press reports attributed the death of Queen Mercedes to her). Also, an ultra-clerical faction saw possible profit in reviving the claims of Queen Isabel, arguing that her abdication in 1870 was never official. As usual, the ex-sovereign was foolishly irresolute in her stance, regarding María Cristina as a foreign upstart and not wanting to play second fiddle to anyone "not then, not before, not later." The politicians dreaded a return of Isabelism, and the government felt obliged to demand her return to Paris, later even pleading with the Pope to make representations to her. The backers of the regent asked the Duke of Montpensier to stay in Paris, but he returned to his Spanish estates and pursued his customary maneuverings. Still another relative, the Duke of Seville, son and namesake of the Enrique of 1846 and 1868 notoriety, forced a palace interview in which he tried to browbeat María Cristina. This Bourbon earned exile for his seditious remarks, and he fled to France to issue a republican manifesto (earlier he had fought for the Carlists).

It is small wonder that not knowing whom she could count on, María Cristina took refuge in a protective reserve and chilliness. These characteristics were perhaps hers by nature as well. The controlled and reticent Hapsburg with her large set jaw and her frozen looks had long since been contrasted unfavorably by people with the unaffected and captivatingly beautiful first wife of the late king. María Cristina gained the nickname of Doña Virtudes, meant as a compliment by some, a sneer by others.

The new queen regent could be compared to many women sovereigns. Her namesake and the great-grandmother of her children she resembled in her regality, stylishness, and willpower. But unlike that María Cristina or her daughter Isabel, she did not at all project the image of obese self-indulgence, being slender-waisted and erect. Of course, María Cristina found entirely alien the irregular hours and exuberant permissiveness of the court of Isabel, and in turn the ex-queen disliked her daughter-in-law as a kind of living reprobation. Which of Spain's three nineteenth-century women rulers was the most pious would be a futile argument: all were excessively devoted to the church, María Cristina of Austria, perhaps, being less ostentatious about it but just as influential in her clerical impact on politics (one critic of the regent's religiosity has questioned her having horseshoes hanging over virtually every door of the summer palace).

Among foreign queens of the day, María Cristina was not unlike Queen Victoria, who was her senior by forty years but, nonetheless, her admiring visitor in the 1890's (on this first visit of a reigning British monarch to Spain, Victoria found the tea served her undrinkable). More a contemporary of the Spanish ruler was the Russian empress, Marie of Denmark, fated in time to be known as a grande dames' grande dame, but in this era known for her radiance and party giving. María Cristina was altogether unlike her relative the Empress Elizabeth of Austria, so celebrated for her delight in culture and travel that she became known as a kind of royal bohemian. The regent's love of the arts and letters was, however, unusually intense. Some Spaniards were put off by her erudition, but she pursued these pleasures in the bosom of her family.

In politics, Regent María Cristina kept to the scrupulous constitutional path charted by her husband, never for a moment indulging in the whims and wiles of her female predecessors. She was tactful, high-minded, and conscientious in the performance of her duties, showing a steady good faith that earned her the full confidence of the politicians. According to a relative, she deliberately tried to appear naïve before the men she dealt with, concealing her considerable insight. While she was capable of expressing indignation at the country's stagnation, as much as any drawing-room matron might, she gave no indication that she had any intention of changing the system she found.

The day of Alfonso XII's death Sagasta replaced Cánovas as prime minister, the two men having conferred two days before in the park of El Pardo, neither getting out of his carriage. Although sure of his majority, Cánovas saw the desirability of handing power over to the Liberals at a time when radical elements would try to exploit the crisis accompanying the change of rulers. In office, Sagasta duly relaxed political controls, and he was duly faced with serious uprisings in favor of the republic, one in January in Cartagena, where the rebels seized the castle temporarily, and one in September in Madrid, where rioters briefly gained control of the main streets and railroad station. Civilians were mainly involved in both cases, but army units mutinied too, indicating that the separation of the military from politics was not an accomplished fact. The regent intervened personally to prevent executions, an action which earned her immediate popularity. After the usual rigged elections held in April, 1886, Sagasta and a "Long Parliament" stayed in power for the next five years, to the dismay of Conservative spoils seekers.

Just as in the old storybooks or movies, the cannon of the Campo de Casa would fire a twenty-one-gun salute if the queen gave birth to a boy baby, whereas fifteen booms sufficed for a girl. The crowds near the palace in Madrid waited with unconcealed excitement when the Regent María Cristina was delivered on May 17, 1886. Trolleys all over the city stopped when the cannon started. Upon the sixteenth salvo the people went wild, the tension over, the bets decided, and their hopes fulfilled. Sagasta had the pleasant duty to present the infant on a silver salver to the palace invitees, and he announced with relief and awe, "We have just about the smallest quantity of King we could possibly have." Years later the subject of such curiosity and rejoicing confided to a questioner, "Some historians maintain that I remained perfectly quiet on seeing Sagasta, but that when Cánovas del Castillo came near me I began to cry. If this is true, it is what we can term an outstanding example of childish liberalism." The phenomenon of a born king, in the strict sense of one given allegiance while still in his mother's womb, had occurred in Western history only once before, in 1316, the person being John I of France, who lived only five days.

On the occasion of the baptism a few days later the regent ordered the palace galleries opened for the public to watch the infant being carried by his *ama,* the Duchess of Medina de los Tôrres, in a procession of the grandees of the realm past 200 halberdiers dressed in mid-nineteenth-century tricorns and knee breeches with long coats of red, blue, and silver. The primate and papal nuncio officiating, the child was christened Alfonso León Fernando Santiago María Isidro Pascual Anton. His family debated over his simple reign name, rejecting Felipe VI or Fernando VIII as smacking of absolutism and also rejecting the historian Cánovas' pet idea of Carlos V as sounding Carlist. Despite his dead father's having expressed misgivings about the unlucky number, María Cristina's wifely sentiment prevailed and Alfonso XIII came into history (she could also argue that the current Pope, her strong supporter, Leo XIII, was not an unlucky figure).

As coin collectors and stamp collectors well know, in the 1880's and 1890's currency and postage with likenesses of Alfonso XIII as a baby, as a toddler, as a boy, and so on appeared in profusion. The charming story is recounted in the memoirs of Princess Bibesco, a member of Rumanian royalty, that as a little girl summering in Biarritz she and her playmates heard of the child monarch beyond the mountains to the south and saw impressive engraved evidence of his existence. They decided that such a monarchy was a paradise where grown-ups were sent to bed early and every day was celebrated as a birthday. Pledging secret allegiance to the "King of the children," they awaited his arrival from San Sebastián to "liberate" them. Sore was their disappointment a few years later to learn that Alfonso's mother had him studying eleven hours a day.

The queen regent at first deemed it good to expose her son in public at frequent intervals, to delight his subjects and to counter shyness on his part. Before he was one year old, Alfonso was present at the opening of the Cortes. At age two, all dressed in white lace with a feathered cap, he was taken to the Barcelona Exhibition, and he performed little bows to the eager throngs at each railroad stop on the way. Later María Cristina allowed him to mingle with 12,000 schoolchildren at a party at the palace. But after a visit to Seville Alfonso contracted a severe case of typhus, and the queen regent became fearful for his health. The mistaken opinion of the day held that he could be hereditarily prone to tuberculosis because of his father. In 1890, aged five, Alfonso had a nearly fatal illness, wrongly diagnosed as meningitis. Unconscious, without pulse and his heart almost stopped, he was pulled through by a doctor after twelve precarious days. Queen Isabel, who was on hand during a permitted visit, wrote to her daughter of the family's "terrible fright." Later she reported "the little King is again so nice and lively, very quick and intelligent. I must confess he enchants me with his artless prattle. . . . It is a miracle that he is alive." During this crisis ex-King Amadeo wrote Queen Isabel of his concern, and observers noted that leaders of all political factions in the country crowded to the palace to offer their congratulations on Alfonso's recovery. His death might well have meant turmoil.

One result of the fears for Alfonso's life was that the northern military-naval outpost of San Sebastián became a resort city, for María Cristina was convinced that the sea air was healthful, and she started to spend long summers there. So averse to travel that the spring-summer palaces at La Granja and Aranjuez fell into disuse, the regent had built the red-tiled, rambling, semirustic palace of Miramar on a promontory overlooking the "concha" beach of San Sebastián (a few hundred yards from the hotel where Alfonso's grandmother made her decision to quit the country in 1868). Here the royal youth learned to swim and to boat and gained a lifelong devotion to, and confidence in, outdoor sports. His mother made this assessment of the boy:

> He is good, but so eager, so turbulent, so eager for liberty. He envies the fisher children on the shore. Perhaps he is right to do so after all. He is not proud, but he wishes to look dignified, and when I scold him—which I never do in the presence of any other person— he keeps back his tears. I believe he will do. I have worked so much towards making him worthy of Spain as towards making Spain worthy of her beautiful self.

Whatever else the complete emphasis on bodily care in his boyhood may have done, Alfonso enjoyed remarkable powers of physical resistance most of his life.

Family relationships in the household of María Cristina were strong and binding, the very opposite of the alternately smothering and indifferent ways of Queen Isabel. The regent herself admitted that she doted on the infantas Mercedes and Teresa and on Alfonso, declaring that she found more excitement in "their little histories of their day's doings than I do in all the affairs of state."

At age seven Alfonso was no longer allowed to be the "wild pony" that Princess Bibesco once admired. The women of his entourage gave way to men, and he embarked on serious schooling. Up at seven thirty, then breakfast, then a long walk, he was studying by nine. His first lessons were in French or English, and in time the king became an accomplished linguist. At ten he went to the palace riding school and was encouraged to be the horseman his father had been. Daily lessons in sciences or geography followed. At one he had lunch with one of his tutors and then more lessons until tea with his family at five. Even more studies preceded dinner at eight, his mother keeping her husband's un-Spanish hours. After prayers, bed by ten was the rule. Historians have given differing assessments of the last Spanish king's education, ranging from the view that it was excessively clerical and reactionary to that it was the best of any Spanish monarch's in generations. His aunt Pilar, stressing the liberality of Alfonso's upbringing, noted that once, upon finding a tutor reluctant to discuss Fernando VII and Isabel II, the young king prodded: "Do not hesitate. These matters belong to history and I must know the truth." Many years later Alfonso himself, addressing a school, boasted of his "why" asking capacity when young, saying, "I have been the companion of the child questioners of Spain." Critic and admirer alike agree that the boy king took to soldiering with the greatest relish. Alfonso also sought out the company of grooms when young and later found convivial association with the cadets of the various armed services. At best he gained a sort of insouciance and bonhomie, at worst an excessive respect for the military. When he was fifteen, he was caught trying on the armor of Charles V; he outgrew it, at least physically. A university education for Alfonso, a wish of his mother, was deemed impractical by the politicians.

Readers of slick magazine biographies of current young royalty would find familiar the anecdotes told to give some idea of the young Alfonso's character: stories of the child's too haughty recognition of his own importance and of his being put in his place, stories of his crying fits followed by tear-dried exercises in royal dignity, and stories of flattery being countered with precocious humor. Of the many tales about Alfonso XIII as a boy, perhaps the most appealing concerned the time he was punished by being locked in his room. When his screaming and banging were to no avail, he ran to a window on the main courtyard and yelled *"Viva la Republica."*

The six-year-long ministry of Sagasta following the change of reign was relatively uneventful. In 1890 the prime minister achieved a democratic reform he had once opposed as too risky—universal suffrage for males twenty-five or over with established residency. The measure was hotly debated the year before, with Cánovas in determined opposition, but the Regent María Cristina gave royal assent. Within six months Sagasta resigned as head of the government, his Cabinet split on the question of free trade versus protectionism. Once again Cánovas became prime minister, himself wisely pledged not to reverse events, the regent graciously neutral. The first elections under the new law took place in 1891, and the Conservative leader proved himself capable of securing his majority in the time-honored way. Many of the newly enfranchised failed to vote. The republicans showed unexpected strength in Madrid and the big cities, but Cánovas did not panic, as a successor was to do in 1931. After two and a half years of power, he was again succeeded by Sagasta.

The orderly transfer of power between Conservatives and Liberals ill concealed growing social tensions and the despair of the leftist parties at the farcical electoral process. The first of an epidemic of bombings occurred in 1891. While the Spanish socialists tried to organize workers, the anarchists resorted to "propaganda by deed." Moreover, a rash of explosions in Catalonia reflected the sudden upsurge of separatist sentiments there. The police responded to the outrages with outrages, forcing an admitted British conservative to say that they behaved like "wild beasts." Assassinations provoked brutal executions, which in turn provoked more assassinations.

A violent fracas in Madrid in 1895 between journalists and officers over the "honor of the army" produced a governmental crisis that toppled Sagasta and brought Cánovas to power once more. This time he lent himself all too willingly to the politics of repression. On August 9, 1897, the Conservative statesman was assassinated at Santa Águeda where he was taking a cure. His assailant was a young Italian anarchist outraged by reports of police brutality. Actually, the wave of major assassinations was worldwide in this era, President Sadi Carnot of France falling victim in 1894 followed by the Empress Elizabeth of Austria in 1898, King Humberto of Italy in 1900, and President William McKinley in 1901. The loss of Cánovas to Spain, a man so responsible for the restoration of 1874 and its cynical underpinnings, spelled the end of an era. Late in his life the Conservative leader had taken a young wife, and his newly found aggressiveness and intractability may have been designed to impress her. In the period just before his death Cánovas, the former conciliator in the 1885 war crisis with Germany, had become the most jingoistic patriot in the worsening situation with the United States over Cuba.

4. The Spanish-American War and National Soul-Searching

The twelve-year-old King Alfonso XIII liked to play with his soldiers and toy warships in the palace parks and ponds until the disasters that befell Spain's armed forces in 1898 discouraged him from such pastimes. After the Spanish-American War a national soul-searching revealed that the Bourbon nineteenth century had left Spain woefully behind the rest of the world and that the future was alarmingly uncertain. The royal family offered picturesque personalities but few leaders.

Cuba experienced several insurrections against Spanish rule in the nineteenth century, causing friction between Spain and the United States. It was the familiar colonial story of captains general being entirely arbitrary, of the best jobs going to Spaniards, not Cubans, and the economy being run for the benefit of the home country. The ten-year revolt of 1868 occurred at a time when Spain itself was experiencing a chaotic series of regimes, and then and later no reform of the Cuban situation came from Madrid. When a new struggle for independence began in 1894, Prime Minister Cánovas sent to Cuba General Valeriano Weyler, already known as "the butcher," who, applying the policies of scorched earth and concentration camps, caused 200,000 deaths among the rebels and the innocent. President Grover

Cleveland offered to mediate, but as the regent wrote to a friend, "this would hurt the national feeling of the Spaniards and I would *never* accept it." The warmongering "yellow press" in the United States was fully matched in Spain, where the newspapers so concentrated on the atrocities allegedly committed by the Cubans that people assaulted peace talkers in the streets.

Conciliatory moves by the Spanish government, such as the recall of General Weyler, were set to naught by the blowing up of the battleship *Maine* in Havana Harbor on February 15, 1898, at the cost of 270 lives, an act which the United States unfairly attributed to the Spanish naval authorities, so demonstrably incompetent otherwise. Historians have debated at length such questions as whether idealism or imperialism drove President McKinley and Congress to declare war on Spain in April. Without a doubt, the regent and the Spanish government had to accept hostilities since giving in to the United States would have invited revolution at home. The Carlists were already clamoring noisily about the national honor.

Spain proved to be "about as ill prepared as a country could be" for the war, although many European observers at the time underestimated the United States with a regular army much smaller than its enemy's and a navy only about equal in size on paper. Both before and after the outbreak of war, the Regent María Cristina appealed to the European powers for help, receiving sympathy only from the Pope and Emperor Francis Joseph. The first decisive action took place far away in the Philippines on May 1, when Admiral George Dewey totally destroyed the Spanish fleet in Manila Bay. A new fleet sent out from Spain reached the Red Sea before reports of forthcoming American operations in Spanish waters forced it to return. Manila surrendered to an American land force on August 13 after a mere show of resistance, the captain general being relieved to let in the Americans before Emilio Aguinaldo's Philippine guerrillas took over. The east coast of the United States had its turn to be panicked in May, when a fleet under Pascual Cervera, Spain's best admiral, sailed across the Atlantic, but Cervera's destination was Cuba and his fate was to be bottled up in Santiago Harbor and later destroyed in another completely one-sided naval engagement. Lack of leadership and of modern equipment, rather than lack of Spanish bravery, explain these disasters.

Before the end of July the regent's government began peace negotiations and on December 10 signed the final Treaty of Paris, whereby Spain lost the Philippines, Cuba, and Puerto Rico (the last, with more local self-government than Cuba, had shown little inclination to be freed).

A war so brief and so disastrous naturally raised a cry in Spain for scapegoats. People blamed and denounced the regent as much as the politicians in power, but María Cristina bore herself with her usual calm and reserve, confiding only to her sister-in-law, "I hardly ever laugh now and can think only of sad things." The Carlist leader in the Cortes thundered, "Unhappy is the country which is governed by women and children," and the government reacted with considerable alarm to the possibility of a new Carlist insurrection in the north. The country was too exhausted, however, for another civil war, and in responsible quarters a mood of sober self-assessment set in. The "generation of 1898" came to designate an upsurge by Spanish intellectuals whose critical writings about their own country briefly brought Spanish letters to a par with the best of Europe. In a sense, imperial defeat was a blessing for Spain in focusing attention on its internal affairs, even if the hard choices necessary were not taken in the long run.

Despite the new railroads and factories, the electric lights and the smart shops on Madrid's transformed Avenida or Barcelona's Rambla, statistics showed that Spain remained exceedingly backward. Of the thirteen countries of western-central Europe Spain was the last in percentage of city dwellers. Spain's trade was proportionately less, its farms more unproductive, and its factories smaller than its counterparts'.

The strong momentum of economic progress Spain enjoyed under enlightened Bourbons in the eighteenth century largely ceased after the beginning of the nineteenth, in part because of a series of incompetent rulers but more directly because of incessant, desperate, and inglorious wars, at home and overseas. The treasury was perpetually bankrupt. About two-thirds of the budget went to nonproductive expenditures, such as the debt, the army, and the police. Money was lacking for social reform, even when the politicians agreed on measures. A Factory Act passed in March, 1900, limiting child and female labor but providing little enforcement, was "the sum total of social legislation" in the era.

Spain presented a mixed picture in its political institutions at the turn of the century. Absolutism seemed a thing of the past, the nobility were unobtrusive in government, and with broad civil liberties and universal suffrage the country was ahead of many European nations. Great drawbacks in the constitutional system, however, were local bossim (the *caciques*) and the rigged elections, which systematically excluded from the Cortes all but a handful of Socialists and a small number of Republicans, regardless of the popular appeal of these parties. Millions of Spaniards ignored the political process altogether and turned to the anarchists, who helped bring off the country's first general strike in Barcelona in January, 1902. Barcelona was also the center of revived Catalan separatism, essentially a movement of the prosperous businessmen of this area, which the Madrid-controlled police combated with such bizarre methods as encouraging gangster bombings.

Despite Cánovas' efforts the over-officered army maintained its singular place in the Spanish state, causing the politicians to be constantly afraid of a new pronunciamento. Universal conscription was maintained, although the country had no enemies and virtually no empire. The lower classes were well aware that 200,000 of their number had died, largely from disease and neglect, in the decade of repression in Cuba.

Finally, the "generation of 1898" pondered unhappily the special position of the Spanish church. The anticlerical 1830's were long past. The price Spain paid for the lavish piety of Queen Isabel and the Regent María Cristina and for the Pope's blessing of the Alfonsist Bourbons was the church's stranglehold on education and its ownership of perhaps one-third of the capital wealth of the country. The church might gain in power, but many workers no longer believed in miracle-working images and resented the priests as much as the rich (it has been said that *everybody* in Spain follows the church, half with a candle and half with a club).

Leftists were not the only people who talked of drastic solutions to Spain's problems. On the extreme right the Carlists talked revolution, too. For them church and army were not problems, but places where they recruited support. The extent of Carlist preparations for a fourth great rising after the defeat of 1898 both amazed and frightened the government, which declared martial law in the northern provinces and seized vast quantities of arms and propaganda, including coins and stamps honoring "Carlos VII." The pretender himself, however, failed the cause; a determined man might well have ousted María Cristina as regent and relegated the adolescent Alfonso XIII to being a mere infante.

Following his prolonged effort on actual Spanish soil to win the throne during the republic and early years of Alfonso XII, the still-youthful Don Carlos had first retired to Paris and then joined the Russian army in time to fight in the Turkish War. Thereafter, never at a loss for funds, he traveled extensively and in the grandest manner, touring every continent and making two trips to the United States. An admiring Italian prince once called the pretender "the king of the gentlemen and the gentleman of the kings." After he was expelled from France in 1881, he made his base the stately Palazzo Loredan on Venice's Grand Canal. He was away on his travels when his father, Don Juan, died in Brighton in November, 1887, but he saw to it that this "maligned, superseded, and ignored" member of the Carlist line was entombed in Trieste Cathedral under the inscription in Latin "Juan III, King of Spain."

Don Carlos' wife, Princess Margarita, from whom he was separated, died at Viareggio in 1893, and he promptly remarried a woman twelve years his junior, the Princess Berta de Rohan, who claimed ancient Breton royalty but was counted part of the Hapsburg family. Whereas the first wife had countered Don Carlos' tendencies to pompousness and display, Princess Berta treated her husband with the most insinuating deference. Her wiles and her indifference to the Carlist cause were the despair of Melgar, the pretender's longtime secretary and later biographer. At the critical juncture in Carlist fortunes following the Spanish-American War, a go-between arranged a secret meeting between "the butcher" General Weyler and Don Carlos to be held at sea off the port of Ostend. The general wished to meet Don Carlos alone to discuss a possible coup d'état, but Princess Berta insisted on coming, and rebuffed, she persuaded her husband abruptly to return to Venice. Carlist circles fumed that their hero, just turned fifty, seemed to prefer his home life to military action. Melgar resigned, after twenty years' service, protesting the princess' grand housecleaning of most of the Carlist archives.

In one of his art-*cum*-travelogue descriptions, this of Venice at the turn of the century, Sacheverell Sitwell offers a striking vignette of this Bourbon in exile:

> The floating ease of an afternoon spent in a gondola was enlivened, of a sudden, by much noise and stir coming from the water-gate of a near-by palace, the Palazzo Loredan. The iron gates were thrown open, a wooden gangway was put down, and an immensely tall old man with a square white beard, dressed, if I remember right, in black, but wearing, certainly, an immense black sombrero, came down the steps, and, leaning on the arm of a little black page, crossed the plank into a waiting gondola. The negro page followed him and stood in the bows of the boat, while six gondoliers in magnificent liveries lifted their painted oars, in stripes of red and yellow, and in an instant the gondola slid from the shadows into the sunlight and was gone. To our enquiries, we were told that this was the Pretender to the Throne of Spain. It was, in fact, the embarcation of Don Carlos.

Almost any visitor to Venice could catch a glimpse of the Spanish claimant and his soignée wife: they were habitués of the Café Florian on the Piazza San Marco, always accompanied by their boarhounds and a retinue. When Alfonso XIII came of age in 1902, Don Carlos made the usual gesture of asserting his own better rights to the throne and even set off for Spain, offering no fuss when he was turned back by the French police. "Carlos VII" died on June 17, 1908, grand to the end in his pretensions, serene in his inaction.

Don Carlos left four daughters and one son, all by his first wife. Born in 1870, that strange year when Spain was searching for a king, Don Jaime was educated at a small college in London and at the Austrian military academy. He reflected his mother's cosmopolitan tastes, and partly to correct this, he was encouraged to visit his father's "realm," crossing into Spain in 1894 under a transparent incognito. The Spanish government wisely refused to show concern, and the newspapers merely reacted with curiosity or ridicule to Don Jaime's visiting Carlist shrines in the northern provinces and his being photographed in front of Madrid's Oriente Palace. On his return to Venice, Don Jaime had several disagreements with his stepmother, who blocked a marriage alliance of his desiring and once even accused the son to the father of harboring lusts for herself. He then sought to establish himself elsewhere, having shown little interest in Carlism and disdaining even to speak fluent Spanish. An earlier attempt by Don Jaime to enter the Austrian army had been rebuffed when Emperor Francis Joseph wrote: "I have no wish to see the Austrian uniform on the son of a prince who dares lay claim to the throne of Spain, which my niece, María Cristina, occupies with such dignity." In 1896 Don Jaime was accepted into the Russian army, earning commendations for service in the Boxer Rebellion of 1900 and the Russo-Japanese War of 1904–1905. He returned from the Far East to take up residence in the Chateau de Frohsdorf, which his family inherited from the Count of Chambord. The life of Paris captivated the bachelor prince more than Spanish castles in the air when he became head of the Carlist clan on his father's death in 1908. He was kept to the traditionalist mark, however, by his uncle Don Alfonso Carlos, the bloodthirsty commander of 1874, still very much alive but, unfortunately for the cause, childless.

Aside from the Carlist father, son, and uncle, Alfonso XIII was the only male Spanish Bourbon alive when he began his active rule in 1902. At seventeen he became patriarch of a considerable family of women, including a grandmother, a mother, three aunts, two sisters, and assorted cousins.

Gradually the mid-nineteenth-century relics passed on. Don Francisco de Asís lived until a few weeks before the start of his grandson's rule. The ex-king consort had exchanged his modest villa in Épinay for a mansion when the restoration brought him a larger income. While insisting on royal ceremonial on the part of his friends and servants, Don Francisco pursued a quiet existence of reading history, composing music, collecting pictures, and traveling, especially in England. The slight, elegantly turned-out old man could be encountered on occasion on the Bois de Boulogne walking his poodles, who were all named for his wife's lovers. On family birthdays he and Queen Isabel exchanged visits, their initial courtesies often giving way to recriminations as if they were two rival generals fighting past battles. When he died on April 17, 1902, she and his family were absent from the scene at his express wish. His living past eighty was unusual for a Bourbon. His daughter Eulalia was somewhat bitter in her memory of him: "The small slender man with his beautiful hands and soft voice stirred no chord of feeling in our hearts . . . he vanished into the shadow of death, leaving me only the faint memory of his hands that had never caressed me, and the sound of his voice which, gentle as it was, had never uttered a single word of endearment." Eulalia's older sister, Paz, however, had slightly fonder reminiscences of her father, such as his taking her shopping in Paris, her being unable to choose anything she liked, and his later sending her a brooch with a donkey made of diamonds.

Queen Isabel outlived her husband by only two years. Officially only Countess of Toledo since 1875, she had a country estate at Fontenay-Tresigny but preferred to entertain in lavish style at the Palacio de Castilla in Paris. Visitors came and went by the hundreds, including sentimentally loyal grandees, generals and conspirators of all sorts, local social climbers, and presidents of France. She also took some delight in reading cheap novels, but an observer noted that only two books were on display: the *Bible* and *Don Quixote*.

Isabel's fatness had become legendary, and she never made any effort to control her eating. When still in her fifties, she took great pleasure in giving masked balls and seemed oblivious to the fact that no costume could conceal her huge bulk. Once when she was being presented to the Pope, she knelt and could not get up again. Eventually, Isabel was too enormous to go walking or riding, and she ceased her visits to Madrid, which usually had been politically embarrassing. At a distance the ex-queen was coarse-looking, ugly, and porcine, but she retained her wit, animation, and charm, with her clear eyes alternately seductive or imperious. Queen Victoria, visited by her at Windsor in the 1890's, was impressed.

Even in her old age Isabel managed to keep a breath of scandal about her. Her lover Marfori died, but soon afterward visitors became aware of the constant presence in the Palacio de Castilla of Haltmann, a Hungarian Jew of uncertain background. A little, mustachioed man, Haltmann was a caricature of Isabel's former paramours, and his odd manner of servility combined with authority upset many of the older courtiers. Queen Regent María Cristina, visiting Paris, carefully telephoned in advance to assure herself that Haltmann would not be there. Some people were certain he was a lover; others came away convinced that he was just a disinterested administrator of Isabel's financial affairs. He lived away from the palace, but almost daily he was the last person to see the ex-queen, who still kept her very late hours. Her disorderly habits began to take their toll on Isabel's health, and she suffered from arthritis. She fell victim to influenza and aggravated her condition by insisting on welcoming and saying good-bye in the cold to a visitor, the ex-Empress Eugénie. Death came to the seventy-three-year-old on April 9, 1904, in the presence of her surviving daughters Isabel, Paz, and Eulalia.

Another grand old royal figure, the Duke of Montpensier, had succumbed to apoplexy in 1890 on his Andalusian estate at Sanlúcar de Barrameda. The king's great-uncle had been hovering covetously around the throne for half a century, but his lordly sophistication had not served to gain him control of it. His mousy wife, Isabel's sister the Infanta Luisa, lived to 1897, entirely caught up in religious devotions (Pope Leo XIII endured for a while her habit of bringing him a sackful of religious objects to be blessed one by one and then decided to bless all at once). Of the many Montpensier children, several had died early from consumptive diseases, including the short-lived Queen Mercedes. Their daughter María's marriage to the Count of Paris relinked the family to the line of Orléanist French monarchs, while their son Antoine's marriage to his cousin Eulalia was also typically Ptolemaic, proving to be exceedingly unhappy but fruitful of heirs to the Montpensier fortune.

The Infanta Isabel, eldest daughter and namesake of the late sovereign, was a beloved feature of Madrid life right down to the fall of the dynasty in 1931. In 1868, not quite seventeen, she had submitted to an arranged marriage with the Count of Girgenti, son of the last King of Naples. Her husband, an epileptic, shot himself while staying at a hotel in Lucerne in 1871. As a widow, Isabel was never touched by anything resembling scandal, unlike her mother, whom she otherwise resembled in her obesity, generosity, and amiability. Her unaffected good humor was evident when a journalist likened Isabel in her palace to a pearl in an oyster shell. "Here is one who will not dare call me the snub-nosed one," replied the infanta, alluding to her popular nickname of La Chata. Street carnivals were one setting in which Isabel liked to show herself, but she was also a serious patron of music, never missing a concert, never turning away a serious performer or a composer in need. For a few years Isabel acted as hostess for her brother, Alfonso XII, and afterward she pursued ceremonial royal duties with indefatigable and winning dignity. "The dynasty comes first," she insisted to her sisters. "You must be an Infanta first and a woman afterwards." Decidedly conservative in her views, Isabel's family consciousness made her a uniquely valuable asset to the Spanish Bourbons over three reigns. Her nephew's wife was to describe Isabel as "the one I loved most."

The Infanta Paz was less known to the Spanish public than her older and younger sisters. In 1883, at twenty, she married Prince Ludwig Ferdinand of Bavaria, her first cousin, and went off to preside over Schloss

Nymphenburg near Munich. Her husband was a dedicated doctor, while she wrote poetry all her life. The modest, cultivated couple were special favorites of Bavaria's romantic, unbalanced King Ludwig II, who, before his mysterious death in 1888, exchanged verses with his Spanish relative and delighted in showing her and her husband some of his extravagant castles never open to anyone else.

Queen Isabel's youngest daughter, the Infanta Eulalia, wrote several sensational books on royalty that embarrassed her nephew the king, and she perhaps deserves a book herself as a madcap princess extraordinary. She was named after Spain's second-century saint who shrilly denounced the Roman emperor and other false gods in the marketplace and for her trouble had her breasts removed by red-hot pincers. A tomboyish and precocious girl, the infanta early railed against ignorant clerical teachers and fawning courtiers. Eulalia developed into a considerable beauty, the greatest probably in three centuries of the Spanish dynasty. Tall, slender, graceful, always well turned out, "she was very elegant," in the recollection of her nephew's wife. She was also a studied flirt as a young woman, remarking later that the "calf's eyes" approach of young officers at court was usually followed by their declarations of willingness to die for her. "I did not want to see their blood, but their brains, and either they had none or did not consider it necessary to use them in conversation with a princess."

After the years of exile in Paris, Eulalia had returned to Madrid to be the happy child confidante of her brother Alfonso XII and then of the much-admired Queen Mercedes. She disapproved of the straitlaced María Cristina, and she broke off an engagement to an Austrian archduke when she realized that she would be doomed in Vienna to an even stronger dose of Hapsburg etiquette. A woman of Eulalia's rebellious temperament was naturally attracted to the cultivated Duke of Montpensier, and she fell in with his plan that she marry his son Antoine. Although soon disillusioned with her fiancé, who turned out to be both dull and effeminate, she failed in efforts to break off the engagement, being told that the marriage was essential to assure the succession to the throne. The wedding in March, 1886, took place in mourning because of the recent death of her beloved brother, King Alfonso XII.

In the 1890's Eulalia played the infanta with growing ennui and cynicism. The number of Te Deums she listened to, she wrote, would have deafened the ears of heaven, and she laid more cornerstones than there seemed physical space to erect buildings on. In 1893 she was somehow chosen over her decorous sister Isabel to represent Spain and dynasty in the New World. When she disembarked in Havana unwittingly wearing an ensemble in Cuban revolutionary colors, Eulalia caused first shock, then delight, but her cordial reception did not give her any illusions about the rottenness of the colonial administration and the prospect that "Cuba was gone." Her tour of the United States in connection with the Columbian Exposition of 1893 was also a huge personal success, although "nothing had happened to change my belief that my public life as a Royal Personage was a busy futility."

Her brother's son securely on the throne, the older Montpensier dead, and her own sons grown, Eulalia separated from her husband. "We had never quarreled," she explained. "I should say we were never sufficiently interested in each other to quarrel." Following a few years in Paris until the death of her mother, Eulalia bought a house on the Norman coast near where she had spent summers as a child. "Here I can say, and do, and think, and write what I please." Travel was very much to the liking of this feminist rebel, who numbered the tsar, the kaiser, Oswald Spengler, and Gabriele d'Annunzio among her acquaintances. Her first published exposure of royalty was a scandal in 1911.

The less-than-sacrosanct position of Spanish royalty at the turn of the century was revealed by the riots which greeted the marriage of Alfonso XIII's eldest sister, the Infanta Mercedes, to Prince Charles of Bourbon, the son of the pretender to the throne of Naples. The bridegroom's being of dethroned royalty was not the sore point but the fact that he had been one of the more successful enemy generals in the Third Carlist War of the 1870's. Heavy formations of troops guarded the Oriente Palace during the wedding, and Mercedes' giving birth to a son in 1901 caused a minimum of popular rejoicing, although the infant was officially heir to the throne until the king himself sired children. Mercedes died in childbirth in 1903. Thereafter her husband, now the Infante Carlos, married Princess Louise of France, and one of their children, Doña Mercedes, became the wife of Don Juan, the pretender to the throne since 1941.

XI.
The Playboy Politician:
Alfonso XIII (1886) (1902–1931)

---

1. Bombs and Bridal Bouquets

KING even before he was born in 1886, Alfonso XIII came of age and assumed his royal responsibilities on May 17, 1902. His father had felt that a thirteenth Alfonso would be unlucky. Unlucky he was, in some measure a victim of events, but Spain's ninth Bourbon monarch did much to bring about his own downfall, after a reign lasting longer than any but that of the first Bourbon.

Alfonso had been baptized with a long string of titles: "King of Spain, Castile, León, Aragón, the Two Sicilies, Jerusalem, Navarre, Granada, Toledo, Valencia, Majorca, Minorca, Jaen, Algarve, Algeciras, Gibraltar, the Canary Islands, East and West Indies, India, and the Oceanic Continent, Archduke of Austria, Duke of Burgundy, Brabant, and Milan, Count of Hapsburg, Flanders, the Tyrol, and Barcelona, Lord of Biscay and Molina, Catholic Majesty."

These historical relics sounded even more hollow in 1902 after Spain's losses in the recent war with the United States. The old formula "by Grace of God" had been dropped, for Spain's monarch was a constitutional ruler. At 2 P.M. that May afternoon Alfonso in a clear firm voice declared before the Cortes: "I swear to God on the Holy Gospels to observe the Constitution and the laws. If I do this, may God reward me; if not, may He call me to account." For the first time the king appeared out of his cadet's uniform, being dressed as a captain general. Prime Minister Sagasta acknowledged in the name of the Cortes Alfonso's oath, which in time would prove to be an embarrassment to the king.

Spanish monarchs do not have coronation ceremonies. For one thing, the

318

crown jewels were lost during the Napoleonic era. The small crown and scepter displayed during the swearing in were the personal possessions of the dynasty. Queen María Cristina, who that day relinquished her powers as regent, was accorded the honor of a chair of state next to the king's, and later his first decree was to give her precedence over all Spanish royalty, even successors to the throne (for years Alfonso found it difficult to walk in front of his mother). Leaving the Cortes building, son and mother rode in a splendid procession through the streets of Madrid. The atmosphere of general jubilation was marred only by a man's breaking out of the crowd and throwing something in the royal carriage. The missle turned out to be not a bomb but a petition of a deranged person to marry the Infanta María Teresa, the king's sister. At the Oriente Palace the new king received the special envoys of thirty countries, according to Jabez Curry, the American sent by President Theodore Roosevelt, the special courtesy of being greeted first after only the papal nuncio.

On the first day of his personal rule, Alfonso pointedly insisted on meeting with the Council of Ministers. The expected idle formality turned into a slightly ominous crisis. The young king spoke of his monarchical rights being infringed by the government's decision to close down some military establishments for economic reasons. The ministers listened to Alfonso's assertions without protest. Years later the Liberal leader the Count of Romanones was to muse: "Ah, if the day had not been so hot, perhaps, the fate of the Constitution would have been different from what it is." In succeeding months Alfonso showed a certain capriciousness in keeping the ministers waiting for him. What really began to alarm the politicians, however, was the king's display of royal willfulness of a sort unknown in the days of his father and mother. In the fall a miners' strike in Bilbao threatened much violence until the captain general of the area accepted the workers' demands, despite contrary instructions from the ministry. The king openly congratulated the officer and made clear his support of the military as against the civilians in government. Soon afterward Alfonso caused the fall of a Cabinet by interfering in the choice of chief of staff of the army.

"He will do" had been the proud maternal assessment of the young Alfonso. Whatever the future might say about the king's political abilities, it was manifest from the beginning that he was a handsome figure and an engaging personality. His Spartan upbringing had endowed him with robust health and a strong physique. Taller than average, he was well fleshed and muscular, all the while having the appearance of being fine-boned and slender. He had large hands with long, tapered fingers. An admiring biographer described him as "a supreme elegance of strong male outlines."

Not handsome in a classical sense, Alfonso was striking-looking, his face harmonious, his features prominent but not exaggerated. In him were evenly combined the Bourbon and the Hapsburg for the first time since Felipe V. Observers attributed to the Bourbon paternal side the broad forehead, the small but lively brown eyes, and the curved mouth, as well as good humor and vivacity of character. From his Hapsburg mother he inherited a slightly jutting chin and a delicate bone structure, together with a certain dignity and elegance of bearing. Fine-complexioned, the king wore his full and smooth dark hair with a part exactly in the middle, reminding one not so much of bygone dynasts as of Rudolph Valentino. Alfonso was meticulous about his appearance, buying most of his clothes in England. He preferred dark suits in light fabrics, white shirts with high collars, gray ties, and black shoes. "For many years he dressed divinely" was his wife's fond reminiscence. An Italian journalist paid him the compliment of saying that he looked "consummately royal" even in sports clothes.

The young king's exceptional charm was soon widely known. With his animated face went a pleasing intensity of manner. The Rumanian princess who as a child had lionized the boy king was later captivated by him as a man, writing: "I see in his eyes that singular brilliancy, that intense ray which leads one to believe there is a fête going on in his mind, a sort of mental illumination . . . the strongest impression is one of personality . . . so vividly himself." A Russian grand duke in exile was to take particular note of Alfonso's spontaneous and natural smile:

> When Alfonso XIII smiled, I have never seen a face as capable as his of so rapidly changing expression. All monarchs are adroit at the art of smiling, but in Alfonso XIII this faculty acquired the virtue of magic. A second ago he was "all jawbone" and brought to mind the semblance of a maternal forebear, a ruler of the Holy Roman Empire; he was a Hapsburg. The smile changed him once more into a son of his father, a Bourbon.

The ready grin shows up in so many photographs of the king that often he seems to be mugging at the camera, giving him an almost comic appearance which does not at all accord with people's firsthand impression of him.

Few monarchs of his day were so little pompous as Alfonso, according to handwriting experts. Capable of great solemnity, he also had the common touch, and in this respect, he was the ideal Spanish hidalgo, proud, yet amiable, capable of inspiring both respect and affection, above either affectation or vulgarity. Some court officials felt that the new king was too extroverted, taking umbrage at his habit of speaking to anyone on hand after some public ceremonial. One overzealous aide once felt obliged to warn a construction foreman beforehand: "If His Majesty speaks to you, pretend you're dumb." These same court officials were blamed by democratically minded critics for steering the king to talk only with sportsmen and aristocrats, even if he were visiting, say, a university.

Even as a young man Alfonso had a deep voice, which was well modulated and a trifle nasal; he spoke with the lightness and quickness of intonation of a Madrileño. He would have made a good orator and regretted that his constitutional position gave him little opportunity to express himself in public. As a conversationalist he was superb.

Alfonso made known his wish that he be able to chat informally with ambassadors after the public presentation of their credentials. Early in Alfonso's reign the new British ambassador presented himself with full etiquette, after which he fell absolutely flat as he retreated from the throne. The king never twitched a muscle until the man had left the room and then doubled up in helpless laughter—behavior which served to endear him forever to the ambassador concerned. Stories of Alfonso's irrepressible humor are numerous. Before his marriage the young king liked to slip out of the palace at nights for incognito revelry, at which times the guards were instructed to desist from any sign of recognition. Once a new guardsman presented arms, causing Alfonso to tell him confidentially, "Tomorrow at the guard mounting you will see the King and then you will not mistake me for him again. . . . You see, the King always wears a uniform or has a guard." People relished the occasion when a dignitary from South America rhapsodically observed that in Bogotá every *cuadra* had its poets and scholars. In Columbian idiom *cuadra* meant city block, whereas in Spain it stood for stable. The king solemnly nodded at the man's assertion, observing mildly that the typical Madrid *cuadra* had only mules and asses. Alfonso's humor leaned heavily to irony, which Edward VII was once told was unfair for a monarch, something the Spaniard's wife reminded him of on occasion. He also had a taste for high jinks, on occasion climbing atop palace statues and once riding into a cousin's bedroom on horseback.

Alfonso's way of life was simple and his routine methodical. He never slept later than 7 A.M. His bedroom in the Oriente, which tourists may view today exactly as it was, down to the last photograph, was as Spartan as a student's room, with an iron bed, a mirrored armoire, one armchair, a small table and straight chairs, and virtually bare walls. In the small adjoining bathroom the king habitually read the daily newspapers for about an hour, making notations on them so that he could question the ministers later in the morning. He put in several hours daily on official business. Meals were unelaborate, Alfonso being strictly a meat and potatoes man, or "very carnivorous," in his wife's words.

Conscientious in his duties, Alfonso was at heart an outdoors man, who tirelessly pursued a wide range of sports, such as riding, gymnastics, fencing, swimming, and tennis. As a huntsman, he was entirely in both the Bourbon and Hapsburg traditions. His abilities with a shotgun were to earn him the admiration of his British relatives, and once a British groom was to observe that if Alfonso was as able a ruler as he was a judge of horses, he must be able indeed. Later in his career the king became so identified with fast cars and polo playing that the playboy image was easily attached to him.

Active, affable, magnetic, Alfonso was entirely sure of himself. The only male in a family of females, the king since childhood had been treated with such flattery and deference that a kind of imperiousness came naturally to him. His aunt Isabel was particularly guilty of solving all family problems by saying, "The King wishes it." Lacking the skepticism and tolerance of his father, lacking the indolence of his Bourbon ancestors, Alfonso had a cynicism and impatience about him that some would call Hapsburg traits.

The king was intelligent, earnest, quick-witted to the point of being precocious, but not intellectual. He read little. His interest in art was limited to such things as Wild West films, and his interest in music was confined to military marches. The twentieth-century renaissance in Spanish arts and letters that was to produce a Picasso, a Lorca, and a De Falla found no support from the royal palace.

According to an official profile of Alfonso, "he has an extreme affection for military drill, being devoted to everything that has to do with the organization and administration of the Army and Navy." What might have been just a reassurance to patriots actually expressed the fact that Alfonso was a man happiest in a barracks atmosphere, a man who surrounded himself with generals, and a man who fantasized of martial glory. Anglophile in many of his tastes, Alfonso did not profit from the comfortably civilian image of his future mentor and close relative Edward VII of Britain. Rather he took after such contemporary monarchs of ill memory as Tsar Nicholas II and Kaiser Wilhelm II. Neither weak-willed like the former nor bombastic like the latter, Alfonso was nonetheless their equal as a militarist to the depth of his being, with his predilections for uniforms, spit and polish, and parades.

The kaiser happened to be the Spanish king's first state visitor. A question of protocol arose whether Wilhelm's actual accession in 1888 gave him more seniority than Alfonso's birth in 1886 and rule in 1902. Nonetheless, with the Moroccan crisis between Germany and France at the center of European diplomacy and with several eligible German princesses to promote in the mind of the eligible Spaniard, Wilhelm II made the first gesture, arriving with his yacht and a small fleet at Vigo Bay in March, 1904. The kaiser found his young counterpart "very sympathetic," but

Alfonso was noncommittal at the time about his guest and in October acquiesced when his government made a deal with France to partition Morocco without any consideration of German interests.

Having spent his first three years acquainting himself with his own kingdom, at age nineteen Alfonso set out on a round of foreign travels. First he visited Paris in May, 1905, at pains to counteract any idea he was pro-German. His reception by the French turned from warmth to adulation after an assassination attempt by anarchists, who were never caught. He was riding back from the Opéra with President Émile Loubet when a bomb exploded next to their carriage at the rues de Rivoli and Rohan. Alfonso displayed the utmost courage, standing up to stop the crowds from panicking and reassuring his host with the words "Be calm. It is nothing. It is a firecracker such as kids in Spain explode to amuse themselves." Later the king spoke of his "baptism of fire." He would coolly dismiss this and several subsequent assassination attempts over the years as "risks of the trade." He insisted that the full schedule of his Paris visit be continued, earnestly performing such pieties as visiting the baptismal font of Felipe V at Versailles. His youthful exuberance and spontaneity also endeared him to the crowds, finding expression in such gestures as kissing a market girl, which the press hailed "as if he had given the kiss on the cheeks of Paris." Society was impressed, too. Princess Bibesco's sister wrote: "The word chic seems to have been invented for him."

When Alfonso went to visit England in early June, King Edward VII arranged that he take the long passage from Cherbourg to Portsmouth so that the British could display the might of their Channel fleet. After being received by his sixty-four-year-old counterpart at Victoria Station, Alfonso plunged into the usual routine of a state visitor: a banquet at Guildhall, military reviews, hunts in Scotland, and a soiree in the Blue Salon of Buckingham Palace at which Caruso and Melba performed. It soon became evident to all that the real object of Alfonso's visit was matrimonial. His heart's desire was supposed to be the king's niece, Princess Patricia of Connaught, whose looks had impressed him first in photographs and now again in constant social encounters. Only subsequently did people learn that the Englishwoman had deep reservations about changing her religion and was already involved romantically with another.

Speculation about the king's marital intentions increased that summer when he journeyed from San Sebastián to the French castle at Pau, once a property of his ancestor Henry IV and currently of the Countess of Paris, matriarch of the French Orléanists and sometime sponsor of the Carlists. The king's interest here was supposedly in Princess Louise of Orléans, his cousin as a granddaughter of the Montpensiers.

In November Alfonso returned the kaiser's visit and spent several days in

Berlin, lending himself to Wilhelm's penchant for exchanging national uniforms. All was not cordiality, however. Alfonso defied etiquette by returning to the palace in ordinary cabs and by speaking in Spanish at a banquet after the kaiser spoke in German instead of the mutually agreed-on French. In a comical incident the zealous Berlin police arrested "three Spanish anarchists" who turned out to be pacifists from the United States. The press was mostly concerned, however, that the Spanish king was seen frequently with Princess Maria Antonia of Mecklenburg-Schwerin. He was reportedly looking lovelorn at the opera.

Public interest in Alfonso's bride-to-be was so intense that the newspaper *ABC* in September, 1905, published the pictures of eight possible candidates and solicited votes on "who will be the future Queen of Spain." The tabulation of results was as follows:

> Olga of Cumberland, 21, niece of Edward VII—2,165 votes
> Victoria of Prussia, 13, daughter of Wilhelm II—12,901
> Wiltrude of Bavaria, 21, granddaughter of the Prince Regent of
> Bavaria—2,814
> Patricia of Connaught, 19, niece of Edward VII—13,719
> Maria Antonia of Mecklenburg-Schwerin, 21—7,040
> Beatrice of Saxe-Coburg, 21, niece of Edward VII—4,903
> Victoria Eugenia of Battenberg, 18, niece of Edward VII—18,427
> Louise of Orléans, 23, of the Montpensiers—10,675

The young king relished the attention his personal affairs excited. That fall he named a sailing yacht *Queen X*, and he would greet his valet in the morning with a cheerful "Who have the press married me to this morning?" The journalists' imaginations ranged far indeed: a Berlin newspaper, for example, carried a cartoon of "Princess" Alice Roosevelt, the President's daughter, with the caption "Alfonso of Spain wishes to marry? I am not unwilling. Both our names begin with 'A' so we can both use the same handkerchiefs."

Actually, the readers of *ABC* were quite perceptive, for Alfonso had long before made up his mind in favor of Princess Victoria Eugenia of Battenberg. The ministers knew, for her photograph was on his desk, and Romanones described his sovereign as "hopelessly in love." In the reminiscence of the queen herself, she was greatly distressed to learn that Alfonso's first notice of her at a party in England had been the question "And who is the girl with hair that is almost white?" since she feared he thought her an albino. The king's opening question to her was whether she collected postcards, and thereafter he sent them to her assiduously. For her part, Victoria Eugenia was romantic about all things Spanish because of the influence of her godmother, the Empress Eugénie, once lady-in-waiting to Queen Isabel. Her only other suitor of note had been Grand Duke Boris, perhaps the most loutish of the Romanovs.

Still, before any official announcement, Alfonso visited his bride-to-be in Biarritz in January, 1906 and she called on him at his mother's house in San Sebastián. In the latter city she converted to Catholicism on March 7, swearing at her "rebaptism" that "with a sincere heart . . . I detest and abhor all error, heresy, and sect contrary to the word of the Catholic, Apostolic, and Roman Church." Public protests took place in Britain over her having to change her religion, but Edward VII ruled that as a Battenberg she did not come under the restrictions of the Royal Marriages Act. He was generally favorable to the match but may also have told his niece that if things went wrong "don't come whining back here." The engagement was announced in London and Madrid on March 9, the Spanish prime minister afterward informing the Cortes of Alfonso's obeying "the impulses of his heart" and "his duties towards the Spanish people." The king made an incognito trip to England again in April and May, during which time he received his first golf lesson from Victoria Eugenia or Ena, as the press now called her. In the course of a visit to Windsor Alfonso stood before a portrait of Felipe II's tragic Tudor bride "Bloody Mary" and amused his entourage by declaring "if the princess whom I am going to marry looked like her, I would have indeed avoided asking for her hand." Journalists turned historians made much of the fact that this would be the first Spanish-English royal involvement since Felipe and Mary, noting the later farce of Prince Charles' courtship of Felipe IV's sister in 1624 and also earlier dynastic links such as that of Eleanor of Castile and Edward I, Constance of Castile and John of Gaunt, and Catherine of Aragón and Henry VIII.

The wedding was set for May 31. Ena crossed the frontier at Irún on May 25, and Alfonso accompanied her on the train that brought her to a specially built station at El Pardo, where her first gesture was to curtsy to the Spanish flag. The English princess' brothers dressed in kilts caused some stir, but a far greater sensation was the escapade of an English-born hoaxer who earlier had passed himself off as Ena's brother and had been received by the Infanta Isabel and the Archbishop of Toledo, as well as had dunned numerous grandees. A grand concourse of real royalty came for the occasion: the Prince of Wales and his wife (the future King George V and Queen Mary); the Archduke Francis Ferdinand without his wife (he was touchy about her lack of precedence because of her morganatic status); the Grand Duke Michael (tsar for a day in 1917); the Duke of Aosta (son of the onetime King Amadeo of Spain); and princes of Prussia, Belgium, Portugal,

Sweden, and Greece. Madrid hotel and hostel prices soared because of the influx of visitors; most of the titled notables stayed with grandees.

The wedding day was fine and sunny. By 6 A.M. crowds lined the streets which were profusely decorated with balcony hangings, festooned flags of both countries, pictures of the royal couple, and triumphal arches. At 8:30 the king arrived in his sixty-horsepower Panhard 50 to convey his bride to the ministry of war, where she dressed, wearing for the occasion the veil of Queen Isabel II. Alfonso later awaited her at the Church of San Gerónimo, arriving at 10:40 and becoming increasingly agitated when the bridal party was half an hour late. Actually Ena's delay was caused by the prime minister's tardiness in reaching her, but the king was thinking of the anonymous message with a photograph of a man received the night before saying that plotters intended to stop the marriage by murder if necessary. Police experts from five countries had been on hand to investigate such things, and the church had been thoroughly searched. In due course the queen-to-be arrived, and the marriage was celebrated in a "very fine" service with "splendid singing" lasting two hours, according to the Prince of Wales.

Nineteen state carriages and twenty-two owned by grandees were assembled for the procession from the church to the Oriente Palace. The last four were those of the Prince of Wales, the Queen Mother María Cristina with the bride's mother, Princess Beatrice, King Alfonso and Queen Ena, and finally an empty "carriage of respect." The church service over, the royal vehicle traversed the usual ceremonial route through cheering citizenry until it came to a stop opposite Number 88 Calle Mayor, just a few hundred yards from its destination. Ena, whose mutual language with her husband was still French, asked Alfonso why they had halted and the king replied, "Probably because of some delay caused by those alighting at the palace." The rain of bouquets around them caused Alfonso to exclaim, "I forbade the throwing of flowers." Then he reassured her by adding, "Now there is no longer any danger." He had not told his bride of the assassination threat. Before she could say, "What danger?" they were overwhelmed by a tremendous flash and deafening explosion caused by a bomb concealed in a bouquet that fell close to the right of the carriage. Their senses recorded screams, the smell of charred flesh, and dense black smoke. Alfonso's first reaction was that the queen was dead since she had thrown back her head and closed her eyes, her veil and stockings covered with broken glass and blood, the blood of a footman it turned out. Once assured that Ena was unhurt, Alfonso leaned out his window to ask what had happened. Informed that the carriage could not proceed because of the dead and wounded horses, he had the presence of mind to order: "Open the doors, bring the carriage of respect, and tell the Queen Mother and Princess

Beatrice we are all right." The bystanders indulged in "frantic cheering," according to the Prince of Wales, as the king helped the queen into the new vehicle and then commanded, "Slowly, very slowly to the palace."

Again in the words of the Prince of Wales, "Naturally on their return both Alfonso and Ena broke down, no wonder after such an awful experience. Eventually, we had lunch about 3. I proposed their healths, not easy after the emotions aroused by this terrible affair." Officials later determined that 23 persons had been killed and 108 wounded. Aside from casualties among the carriage attendants, aristocrats suffered more severely than middle-class spectators, for they occupied the lower balcony spaces at the scene of the explosion. The whole bombing incident was amply photographed.

The British royal visitor was mainly correct in reporting that "the swine that threw the bomb was a syphilitic pervert of the name of Matteo Morral, who managed to effect his escape but who committed suicide a day or two later in order to avoid arrest." Subsequent police investigation revealed that Morral had attended the Escuela Moderna in Barcelona run by Francisco Ferrar, who was long suspected by the police as an advocate of anarchism and free love. No plot was ever proved, but Ferrar was a celebrated victim of police terrorism three years later. Five days before the assassination attempt a man and his son observed a person cutting letters into the trunk of a tree in the Retiro Gardens. After the man who presumably was Morral departed they found that he had written: "Alfonso XIII will be executed the day of his marriage." The police had no way of knowing that he was the same person who had rented a room with a balcony at Number 88 Calle Mayor for 25 pesetas a day. Asked to share his balcony on the wedding day, Morral had politely refused, saying that friends were coming. He claimed he had a weakness for flowers, receiving daily bouquets, and on the fatal day he pleaded a stomachache, putting up a "do not disturb" sign. He walked out of the hotel after the bombing, was hidden by friends in a town outside the capital, and met his end only after killing a police officer who had seen one of the pictures circulated of him.

The wedding tragedy shocked the world, causing untold harm to Restoration Spain's image, to say nothing of implanting a certain reserve about her new country in the mind of the queen. Every effort was made to allay immediate hysteria. The immensely popular Infanta Isabel drove through the streets of Madrid hours after the bombing, and the next day Alfonso and Ena themselves toured in his Panhard without escort, the king taking only the precaution of having four fresh tires installed to avoid any possibility of a seeming explosion from a flat tire. He canceled the ball scheduled for the wedding but allowed a reception to be held for 7,000. The wedding cake, a British novelty introduced to Spain for the occasion, weighed 300 kilos. Numerous private balls took place, as well as gala opera parties and outdoor events, for one of which were assembled 128 automobiles and 2 balloons. During a royal *corrida*, at which Manolete, among others, fought, the king offered this advice to his foreign bride: "For God's sake don't show anything on your face, either fright or disgust, for every eye is turned on you." Like most Englishwomen, Ena was later to confess that she loathed bullfights, but she learned to be unflappable at them, watching the proceedings with binoculars the glasses of which had been painted black.

The royal honeymoon was spent at La Granja. The couple daily watched the changing of the guard and visited the stables. Once Alfonso organized a steeplechase, at which he showed off quite brazenly his own riding prowess. Another time on a brief return visit to Madrid, Alfonso did the driving, with the chauffeur in the back seat, and he set a record to the capital, averaging 100 kilometers an hour. Ena appeared to enjoy everything, although Spanish food made her sick for a few days (she never quite got to like Spanish cooking except gazpacho, which was a huge favorite).

The new queen was destined to become a matriarch of a reflourished dynasty, living to see the baptism of her great grandson and enjoying the esteem of many Spaniards until her death in 1968 ("Ena" also seems to be a favorite with crossword puzzle makers). Born at Balmoral Castle in 1887, Victoria Eugenia was the thirty-second grandchild of Queen Victoria and, in her own recollection, had so many first cousins as to need no other playmates. Her mother, Princess Beatrice, as the youngest child of Victoria, never ceased her attendance on her mother, so that Ena learned discipline, punctuality, and decorum at her grandmother's six-thirty dinners. Her father, Prince Henry of Battenberg (great-grandfather of today's Prince Philip), was an army officer who died in 1896 during fighting in what is now Ghana. His daughter remembered a postcard from him praising the beauties of Seville. Reared with her three brothers, Ena outgrew a certain tomboyishness but retained an openness of manner and a delight in exercise.

To her new Spanish subjects Ena appeared a "picture book English princess," with "the corn-colored hair, the sky blue eyes, and the milk and roses complexion." Her sheer loveliness excited crowds to murmurs, and her stylishness won over society. Like her husband, she was painstaking in her dress. Lady Lucie Duff-Gordon wrote of her: "I can think of no one who possesses the 'clothes sense' to a greater degree than the Queen of Spain. Had she been born into another position she would have made a fortune as a 'grande couturière.' "

Visiting Ena in the 1920's, Grand Duchess Marie of Russia declared that "she was by far the most human representative of her kind in spite of the long period of years spent at the stiffest court in Europe. She achieved a perfect balance between ease and simplicity on the one side and the obligations of her rank on the other."

Her position at the Spanish court was lonely and difficult at first. Alfonso remained very attached to his mother, who wore mourning for forty-four years and liked to have the palace lights extinguished by ten thirty. While María Cristina professed love and admiration for her daughter-in-law, she remained distant and slightly disapproving. Long afterward in an interview Ena was to murmur, "Twenty-four years we lived together!" As queen, Ena found that she inherited ladies-in-waiting, some of whom went back to the 1850's (the Duchess of Fernán Núñez had served four monarchs). With time and patience Ena introduced innovations in the royal routine, such as English-style afternoon teas and shorter court dresses. Her habit of smoking shocked some, and her husband had to request her to refrain in public places. The Spanish language was a trial for her, in part because she was given no teacher and found herself learning it from the servants. She achieved the ability to understand a conversation in half a year, according to her reminiscence, but not the ability to start one for three times that long.

Once asked if she had ever been consulted about Spanish political matters, Queen Ena instantly replied, "No, no, never," adding only that she might reveal to her husband in private her "feminine intuition" about public personalities. Wife of one who was ultimately considered a tragically misguided king, Ena was never even obliquely accused of being a Marie Henrietta, a Marie Antoinette, or an Alexandra. The public accepted her as simply the gracious sponsor of charities, her most memorable good works being Madrid's first Red Cross Hospital, Spain's first school of nursing, and the League Against Cancer and Tuberculosis. More than her husband, Ena was a patron of the arts, frequently being seen at the Teatro Real and at concerts (she was such a devotee of the opera that a special phone brought the music to her apartment in the palace). She shared with Alfonso a passion for such activities as golf, riding, and water sports (when she went swimming at San Sebastián, she dispensed with the long, loose-fitting garments of the 1890's in favor of a form-fitting suit, but nonetheless, two policemen in uniform accompanied her, right up to their necks in the waves). Trout fishing was a particular delight of the queen.

Unlike the Empress Alexandra in any political sense, Queen Ena shared with her cousin the misfortune of being a carrier of hemophilia, and the happy royal honeymooners of 1906 were doomed to become worried and eventually embittered parents. King Alfonso had been warned of the danger before his wedding, but with the same bravado he showed about assassination he took the risk to marry the one he loved. The worst fears were confirmed after the birth of Alfonso, the Prince of the Asturias, on

May 10, 1907, who was diagnosed as a hemophiliac almost from the beginning. Medical science was still hazy about the nature of the disease, causing Ena to believe mistakenly that a German great-great-grandfather was the source of it whereas current scholarship views Queen Victoria as the begetter. Ena's grandmother, mother, and aunt were the female carriers of the defective X chromosome, but the victims were males.

Victoria's son Prince Leopold died in 1884 at thirty-one from a minor fall; Empress Alexandra's brother Frederick died in 1873 at three and the new Russian tsarevich, Alexis, was plagued by the disease throughout his short life. As in the case of the tsarevich, the condition of the heir to the Spanish throne was kept as secret as possible, and the public was lulled by the many photographs appearing of a sturdy, smiling, and strikingly blond young Alfonso.

More distress was in store when the second son, Jaime, was born in 1908, a deaf-mute. Two healthy daughters, Beatriz and María Cristina, were delivered in 1909 and 1911 and then in 1913 the Infante Juan, of entirely sound physique, as attested by the fact that he is still pretender to the throne. A male child, born dead in 1910, was probably a hemophiliac, and the royal couple's last son, Gonzalo, who was born in 1914, was a sufferer.

2. Political Instability and World War

Shortly before the birth of the Prince of the Asturias in 1907 Spain's most celebrated writer of the day, Benito Pérez Galdós, publicly announced that he had become a Republican, speaking of a "national asphyxiation" for which he blamed the monarchy. In actuality, Spain's political crisis, particularly the ministerial instability, was in large part a result of the weakness of its leading political parties. Yet, even Alfonso's Liberal admirer Romanones conceded the dire effects of the penchant for intrigue of a king "who seemed to enjoy changing frequently the persons to whom, more or less completely, he gave his confidence." Unquestionably, Alfonso XIII let his personal feelings obtrude in politics: unlike his immediate predecessors, he openly promoted his friends for posts in the army and church hierarchies, and occasionally his preferences and prejudices made and unmade prime ministers.

In the first four years of Alfonso's personal rule, there were fourteen ministerial crises and eight different heads of government. The Conservatives had been floundering in search of a leader since the assassination of Cánovas in 1897. With the death of Sagasta in January, 1903, the other chief upholder of the restoration of 1875 was gone too, and the Liberals fell into contentious disarray. In the long periods when negotiations were being conducted to form a new ministry, the king was not only the one source of stability but also the chief decision-maker. Given Alfonso's natural pride and imperiousness, he came to exaggerate his political abilities.

Critics of the king were to charge that he had inherited a strain of political frivolity from his great-great-grandmother María Luisa of the disastrous Godoy era. Tenuous genetics are involved in such an assertion, and to say that the king temperamentally lacked the patience and restraint to be a constitutional monarch is equally dubious. Alfonso suffered fools badly, but he did suffer them for most of his reign. Even later enemies of the monarchy concede that while Alfonso enjoyed using his power, he had no intention at first of deliberately bypassing or discrediting the parliamentary regime. At the time of his marriage, he hailed the Cortes with apparent sincerity and spoke of the need for "constant and intimate cooperation between Parliament and the Royal Power." Alfonso's new British relatives certainly encouraged him on the strictly constitutional path.

Neither the unintellectual monarch nor the traditional politicians could face up to the root of Spain's troubles: the crying oppression of the rural and urban masses. Peasant uprisings, in part anarchist-led, occurred with increasing regularity, to be grimly repressed by the Guardia Civil. Yet the Cortes never seriously considered land reform. Major strikes and industrial disturbances were a relatively new phenomenon. Yet the Cortes did not undertake extensive factory legislation for another decade. The rigged elections effectively kept radicals out of both the Cortes and local bodies. Only by discovering the government's system of marking the ballots of safe voters did two Socialists get themselves elected to the Madrid municipal council in 1905.

The Spanish army, smarting from its defeat in 1898 and rarely apolitical, was the cause of a governmental crisis in 1906. Garrison officers in Barcelona sacked two newspapers that published cartoons considered slurs on the army. In the ensuing confrontation between military and civilian power, the king remained reasonably neutral, but he was pleased when a Liberal ministry passed a law making offensive attacks on the army a matter for military rather than civilian courts.

Food riots and growing violence in Barcelona led to the coming to power of a Conservative ministry headed by Antonio Maura, which lasted an unusually long time, from January, 1907, to October, 1909. The Liberals, deprived of the patronage of alternation in office, threatened to become republicans if this "joke" continued. Maura, who promised a grand program of reform, was remembered for little except repressiveness as the bombings continued. In 1908 an explosive was thrown at the king in Barcelona. He had earlier rejected warnings, saying, "I am King of the whole of Spain. When I am afraid to visit any part of my kingdom, then it is time for me to abdicate."

Spain's growing reputation as a land of anarchist outrages made it difficult to improve its international prestige, a matter of particular interest to the king. Edward VII steadfastly refused to reciprocate with a state visit to Madrid, and a Foreign Office spokesman in London went so far as to declare that any royal meeting was out of the question "until the Spanish Government have introduced a more efficient service of police, which will probably be never." Because of Alfonso's threats to cease visiting London and because of the danger of putting him under the influence of the kaiser, the British contrived the expedient of having an exchange of shipboard visits at Cartagena in April, 1907, Edward VII coming with the *Victoria and Albert* while Alfonso showed off his *Giralda*. In October all was cordiality when the king and queen spent time in London and Paris. A year later they paid a state visit to Budapest. The queen mother was shocked to hear that Ena refused to kiss Emperor Francis Joseph's hand with the explanation that she did not do so for her royal English uncle. This was the last state visit made by the Spanish monarchs until after the First World War.

In the era when the great European empires were lined up in the Triple Alliance of Germany, Austria, and Italy and the Triple Entente of Britain, France, and Russia, Spain ranked as a third-rate power and was courted by the others only because of its having a territorial beachhead in Morocco, which was one of the few remaining prizes left in the scramble for colonies. Spain's efforts to turn the Moroccan situation to its profit resulted only in a bloody upheaval at home.

The Spanish army with typical ineptitude had let an expeditionary force be ambushed by the Moroccans outside Melilla. The aim of this military thrust had been to protect some new iron mines, popularly believed to be owned by the Jesuits but actually a concession acquired by the Liberal leader Romanones. The war office now called up the reserves in Catalonia, despite the fact that since 1898 popular antipathy was strong against imperial ventures in which the conscripted working class suffered the most. The departure of these troops from the railway station was the signal for a city-wide uprising in Barcelona in July, 1909, known as Tragic Week. Mobs controlled the city for days, burning more than fifty religious institutions. The repression required the shooting of almost 200 people. Much of the initial violence was caused by the gangster groups the Madrid government had once encouraged; but these eventually deserted the fray, and leadership of the masses passed to the fledgling Anarchist and Socialist parties, which called a general strike in Catalonia for July 26 and in all Spain for August 2. The popularity of the extremists was expressed by their subsequent electoral gains, including a seat in the Cortes for the Socialist leader Pablo Iglesias.

The ferocious measures of repression eventually discredited the Conservative Maura government, particularly after an uproar of international scope occurred when the regime sanctioned the arrest, court-martial, and immediate shooting on October 13 of Francisco Ferrar. The celebrated director of the Escuela Moderna, admittedly a profligate, and the associate of the 1906 assassin Morral, Ferrar was charged on very dubious evidence, with inciting the recent rioting. The king failed to stay Ferrar's execution, but a week later he engineered Maura's resignation in favor of a Liberal ministry. Alfonso still considered himself a "liberal," and he declared that he was accessible to all political groups, even Republicans. Probably the Spanish king was warned against embracing reaction at the funeral of Edward VII in May, 1910, by the more enlightened of the members of the last great assemblage of European kings and emperors. The permanent overthrow of the monarchy in Portugal in October of that same year was also a sobering event.

Since the beginning of 1910 a new political strong man had emerged in Spain in the person of José Canalejas, a scholar, a Radical turned Liberal, and an engaging personality who won wide confidence, including that of King Alfonso. While contemplating broad reforms to allay the unrest of the masses, Canalejas confined himself at first to curbing the church, making it live up to the Concordat of 1851 and closing down unauthorized convents and monasteries (the so-called Padlock Law of December, 1910). Clerical interests reacted hysterically, parading in the streets with sacred relics usually brought out in times of national disaster. The Pope hinted that he might favor the Carlist pretenders in the future. The king nonetheless stood by his prime minister, although he intervened to temper the anticlerical legislation and took steps to demonstrate his piety in public.

Canalejas in turn fell into the role of repressor. Once an opponent of conscription, he used the draft to break a railroad strike in September, 1912. He succeeded in closing down the anarchist press, but one of the members of this party had the last word when he killed Canalejas with two shots on November 12, 1912, after the prime minister had stopped to look in a bookshop on the Puerto del Sol. Alfonso broke precedent by attending the funeral, even though the murderer was still at large. Afterward he named Romanones as the new Liberal prime minister, and he made new gestures of royal conciliation to the left.

Five months after the murder of Canalejas, on April 3, 1913, there was a new attempt on the life of the king. This time he was returning on horseback down the Calle de Alcalá, after having reviewed the annual swearing in of recruits on the Paseo de Castellana. In the king's own words:

I saw a man coming at me armed with a revolver. He fired and I rode at him. When he was quite close, he tried to seize my bridle as he fired a second time, the flash singeing my glove, while the ball grazed my horse. I immediately wheeled "Atalun", who knocked the man over with his shoulder; at that instant a policeman sprang on him; his third shot was fired from the ground and whistled overhead.

After dismounting to make sure that his horse was not seriously injured, Alfonso regained his saddle, stood, and shouted to the bystanders, "Señores, it is nothing. Viva España!" Later the king remarked that his polo-playing experience served him well on this occasion. He commuted the death sentence of the assassin, an epileptic anarchist from Barcelona who said he was avenging Ferrar.

Spain's attention was diverted from its internal problems by the outbreak of World War I. On August 7, 1914, the government declared the country's neutrality, an action later unanimously endorsed by the Cortes, and Spain subsequently never came close to being drawn into the conflict. While the king did reassure the French privately that they could strip the Pyrenees of troops, the possibility of Spain's entering into the war on the side of the Allies was not actively canvassed by the Allies, who feared that Spain would demand imperial compensations. Germany, some claim, made informal offers of Gibraltar, Tangier, and Portugal if Spain would fight on the side of the Central Powers.

Both the court and the country were divided in their sympathies toward the belligerents. The Queen Mother Cristina had kinsmen archdukes fighting for Austria, while Queen Ena's brother Maurice served in the British army and was killed in the trenches. The royal ladies managed to stay on cordial terms by restraining their feelings and never discussing the war. As for the king, he remained an enigma and appeared uncommitted to either side. Some observers like Vicente Blasco-Ibáñez were sure he was pro-Central Powers, having in the past expressed an admiration for the Kaiser and an affection for Emperor Francis Joseph. Yet the British ambassador was certain that Alfonso, as a devotee of Paris and London, secretly favored the Allies. The king once did drop the remark, unworthy of him but not untypical, that "there is no one who wants to fight but the canaille and myself." In truth, the masses, as well as radical and socialist politicians, were strongly in favor of the Allies. So too were the leading industrialists of Barcelona and Bilbao, but the middle classes at large were credited with being anti-French—ever since 1808. The landowners, the clergy, and the army tended to sympathize with Catholic Austria and authoritarian Germany. The Carlists in their press also supported the Central Powers, but their titular leader, Don Jaime, was outspokenly pro-French.

Spain's efforts to mitigate the unnecessary barbarities and sufferings caused by the war were admirable indeed, and in this activity Alfonso XIII played his finest role. A letter from a Frenchwoman to the king inquiring after the fate of her prisoner-of-war husband elicited a reply in the royal hand and initiated an organized campaign to help all POW's by collecting information about them, facilitating their correspondence, and furthering their welfare in detention. What began as the work of the king's private secretary soon required a staff of forty people, everything at the royal expense. The first POW released as a hardship case through Alfonso's intervention was a young Frenchman named Maurice Chevalier. The king also promoted relief for civilians in war zones. Besides these essentially charitable activities, Alfonso constantly appealed diplomatically or personally to the belligerent governments, protesting atrocities and deploring reprisal policies. He is credited with saving several persons from execution, and possibly, if he could have contacted the kaiser directly, he would have stayed the death of Nurse Edith Cavell.

Spain profited greatly in a material sense for its neutrality in World War I, being a source of food, textiles, and other supplies, especially to the Allies. Money poured into the country, almost as if the sixteenth-century era of flowing New World bullion had returned. The gold reserves in the Bank of Spain rose from 567,000,000 pesetas in 1914 to 2.2. billion in 1918. The new prosperity affected wide sectors of the population, but it was not matched by any accretion of political and social stability. Instead of the nation's being strengthened, according to Brenan, each class and institution merely gained added strength to fight the others.

Spain's wartime problems boiled over in 1917. Early in the year the government surmounted a crisis after Germany's declaration of unrestricted submarine warfare. A public outcry occurred over the loss of tens of thousands of tons of Spanish shipping, especially over one particularly shocking sinking off Cartagena, but Spain did not follow the lead of the United States, which entered the war in April. Another major international event of this time, the Russian Revolution, attracted attention in the country only among leftist circles. Yet given the similar backwardness of their institutions, Spain might well have gone the way of Russia if it had been involved in military sacrifices.

The first troubles came from an unexpected quarter, the Spanish army, supposedly the chief proponents of law and order. Not only had wartime inflation stimulated unionization of workers making wage demands, but also doctors, civil servants, and even priests had taken to organizing associations. Now army officers formed so-called Juntas de Defensa to press for better salaries as well as for commendable professional reforms. They then started using their power to bully the civilian government, helping to cause the fall of Romanones Liberal ministry in April. In June a group of officers in Barcelona sacked a newspaper office in an incident similar to that of 1906; they were publicly commended by the juntas and two captains general.

Some hoped briefly in the summer of 1917 that the protesting army men might align themselves with reform rather than reaction. The so-called Renovation Movement suddenly swept the country, a movement articulated by radical politicians and funded by big business. Its aim was to end the system of local bossism and rigged elections by rewriting the Constitution. The government did everything to obstruct the reformers, and the king turned a deaf ear to their program, the last serious effort to revitalize the system until the overthrow of the monarchy. The Renovation Movement suffered almost complete collapse when its leadership was compromised by association with a general strike that broke out in August. The government had mishandled a strike of the Northern Railroad Workers, and the socialist trade unions (UGT) called a national stoppage. During the suppression troops used machine guns against crowds of workers, leaving 70 dead and 1,000 wounded and taking 2,000 prisoners. Any idea that the army juntas might join forces with the unions was dispelled.

The helplessness of the civilian politicians was further demonstrated in early 1918, when a paralyzing telegraph strike caused another ministry to fall. In this crisis Alfonso XIII intervened strenuously, alternately citing the possibility of a military dictatorship and threatening to abdicate if the Liberals and Conservatives did not back a "government of conciliation"— that is, a coalition. Eventually, he named the Conservative Maura as prime minister, and the king personally allotted the other ministries among a group that included four ex-prime ministers. The new regime achieved some respite from the national unrest by such measures as releasing the socialist strike leaders from prison. The membership of the UGT quadrupled.

Maura was once again driven from office in November, 1918, leaving Spain without a ministry at the time of the Armistice ending World War I. The nation was too self-preoccupied and the politicians too mutually distrustful for Spain to play any important part at the Versailles Peace Conference, to the bitter disappointment of the king. Hollow-sounding, indeed, were his words to a conference of 7,000 mayors assembled to congratulate him on his relief efforts: "I have immense faith in the future of Spain. If she was great in the days of Charles V, she will be greater still in the not far distant future."

During the first postwar year, 1919, the level of violence in Spain mounted to unprecedented heights. Barcelona, as so often, was the main trouble spot, with the so-called war of the gangsters raging month after month. Whereas once the Madrid government had abetted the unions and encouraged gangsters to attack the Catalan businessmen associated with the movement for autonomy, now the military authorities and big business sponsored gunmen who killed the organizers of the new anarcho-syndicalist unions, the CNT, and the workers often replied in kind. A strike at the Canadiense electrical company in February, 1919, a strike which could have been settled but for the machinations of the authorities, developed into a two-week work stoppage in Barcelona. The strikers were peaceful and disciplined, but the military governor resorted to arrests, martial law, and conscription. When the civil governor protested and proposed concilia- tion, his military opposite simply put him on a train to Madrid. To the dismay of moderate opinion, King Alfonso XIII personally intervened, defiantly making the military governor civil governor as well and authoriz- ing him to undertake the harshest measures of repression.

During this chaotic struggle of groups and institutions, prime ministers came and went in rapid succession. The new British ambassador wrote to London that the situation was becoming critical. His report was an able summary of Spain's many problems:

> If I had to paint an impressionist picture of Spain in 1920, I would take a large canvas and produce on it a stage in a state of chaotic welter on which various politicians would prominently figure, pulling strong in different directions and to no purpose across a background of strikes, bombs, and outrage, of apparent general discontent, of committees of military officers springing suddenly into the fore- ground and retiring as rapidly for no apparent reason, of railway companies carrying on systematic sabotage against themselves in order to force the Government and the country into raising rates, of banks and profiteers indulging in wild speculation in foreign exchanges, undermining all the advantages obtained by her policy of neutrality during the Great War, of regionalism in an extreme form increasing in certain provinces and on the other hand extreme centralization clinging to floating straws of hope of maintaining itself, all awaiting the advent of some wise strong man to emerge on the stage to haul these tragi-comedians into their right place and allow the play to proceed to the benefit and content of the public in the play-house.

The assassination of the Conservative Eduardo Dato on March 8, 1921, was the third killing of a prime minister in a score of years. Three persons in a motorcycle with a sidecar opened up fire on him when he was crossing Madrid's Plaza de Independencia on his way home from the Cortes. Leftists spoke of a necessary reprisal for the officially sponsored terrorism in Barcelona. Rightists claimed that Dato's reform program scared extremists.

For his part, the king indicated he thought little of the prospects of reform from any source. A speech he made in Córdoba in May included these ominous words:

> I am not an absolute monarch. . . . Responsibility has been conferred on Parliament, and it is a severe thing to say, but it is the bold truth, that Parliament is not living up to its duties, and many schemes presented to it which would be of great benefit to the country do not make headway. . . . I have been King for nineteen years, and I have never criticized the Constitution. I know my ground, and I know what I may say. And because I know this and in view of the state of things I have described, I feel the necessity for the Provinces to support a movement in support of the King, and then in Parliament the welfare of the nation, and not political interests, will triumph.

Within three years the Constitution was dead and at the hand of Alfonso XIII.

3. The Resort to Dictatorship

The 1920's were to be the "Roaring 1920's" for Spain too, by the lights, of course, of a small minority, the aristocracy and the newly rich from the war. The playboy king and his horsey English queen dominated the society and sports pages. As in virtually all the Western world, thought of social reform languished, except among a few intellectuals, of whom Spain had an outstanding share. The condition of the masses grew worse or at least more glaringly disparate from that of the smart set. Because Spain was one of the first countries to resort to dictatorship, Alfonso XIII was able to enjoy something of a rest from politics, only to find when it was all over that he had lost his job.

The king and queen resumed their annual trips abroad in 1919. Their reception in Paris was enthusiastic, where the memory of their wartime relief activities was fresh. In London Alfonso flashed his old humor to admiring crowds, on one occasion leaning out his cab window to say, "I see you have recognized my ugly nose." The Spanish monarch was jauntily confident at a time when Europe's royalty was in disarray, the kaiser chopping wood at Doorn, the Austrian emperor languishing on Madeira, and the Russians murdered in Siberia. The tsar's cousin Marie recalled Alfonso expansively comforting her: "I want to tell you how much I have felt for you all. I am not like so many of the others who turn their backs on you when anything happens." He drove to her down-and-out London apartment and was completely at ease, "gesticulating, laughing, full of vitality, sympathetic." Later, during a Paris meeting, she found Queen Ena more reserved and thoughtful, reporting her wistful exclamation: "And who, after all, can tell, Marie? In a very few years I might join you here."

Spain's royalty made Biarritz in the 1920's "a paradise for the social climber." The king and queen spent long summers in nearby San Sebastián, living in the queen mother's sprawling tile-roofed beach castle Miramar. Many days they would motor to Biarritz, mingling informally with the promenaders and shoppers, visiting the casino, and attending balls and parties. The road between the Spanish and French resorts became a kind of racetrack for the aristocracy.

Alfonso himself was the most dedicated automobile lover of all. Speed fascinated him, and he delighted in setting new records if, for example, he had to leave Miramar to attend some function at Madrid's Oriente Palace. The police in a small town outside the capital once had seven speeders in jail on a single night, each claiming to be the king driving incognito. Reminiscing of this era, the queen confessed: "It was terrible. The things we did. I don't know how we came out alive." A prime minister futilely tried to remind his sovereign that his fame would not rest on his abilities as a chauffeur but on his performance of his royal duties. The politicians did dissuade Alfonso from becoming an active aviator, but he had not missed the chance to go up in the dirigible *España* in 1913.

Polo was another pastime which Alfonso pursued recklessly. One attraction of Biarritz was its facilities for polo, but several grandees obliged the king by constructing fields and stables near San Sebastián, as well as laying out golf courses for the queen. During one polo match Alfonso's horse stumbled in a hole and the king was badly thrown. He was unconscious for a full twenty minutes, and some feared permanent damage to his brain. The royal sportsman laughed it off, telling Bibesco on another occasion that he enjoyed swatting the polo balls which he carefully named after politicians he disliked.

Winston Churchill, an acquaintance of Alfonso in the 1920's, wrote admiringly of him that "the long years of ceremonial, the cares of state, the perils which beset him have left untouched that fountain of almost boyish merriment and jollity." Other observers were less impressed with the chosen image of a king who was "a perpetual young man," in the words of Blasco-Ibáñez. Now in his thirties, Alfonso was still the dapper playboy, "the most elegant" of his royal relatives in the estimation of the slightly younger Prince of Wales (Edward, the future Duke of Windsor). With his straight dark mustache, which he enjoyed fondling, the king was still exceptionally handsome or at least distinguished-looking. His health was excellent, despite his tendency to smoke great numbers of cigarettes.

In the older Alfonso restlessness and cynicism had begun to replace exuberance and affability. His widow, when asked when the king was most content, replied, "I would say the first fourteen years. Afterward Spanish men always become more gloomy. I don't know why things don't amuse them as when they're younger. The king, as a young man, was like castanets of happiness." Once in the 1920's the wife had observed, "He tires of everything. Some day he will tire even of me." The royal couple were growing apart. She remained ever wary of Spain, remembering all the violence beginning with the near tragedy of her wedding day. His mercurial Latin personality clashed with her English composure, although she was hardly as staid as her mother-in-law. In time, other women came into the king's life, so that even reticent monarchist biographers of Alfonso are forced to allow that he was "not a model husband."

The difficulties between Alfonso and Ena were aggravated by recriminations over their children. The Prince of the Asturias, Don Alfonso, thirteen in 1920, suffered greatly from his hemophilia, often being too weak to move and spending long periods confined to bed. He was beginning to show signs of emotional instability, for he nurtured resentments, particularly against his mother, for his affliction. The public, insofar as it was aware of the heir's condition, was not universally sympathetic; some people even believed rumors that each day the royal family sacrificed a young soldier to provide blood for Alfonso.

The second son, Don Jaime, was of a remarkably sunny disposition, almost pathetically so in light of his deafness and near inability to speak. The youngest, Don Gonzalo, showed marked precociousness but required the attention of doctors and nurses as much as his eldest brother. Only Don Juan and the two daughters were free of physical disabilities. The sickliness of so many of the royal children was particularly exasperating to the father, who was wont to lecture them on the virtues of the outdoor life, exercise, and confrontation of danger.

Not surprisingly, the queen saw more of the family than the king. Ena was not the sort of mother to leave the rearing of her children to nurses and governesses. Every morning she was on hand to plan the children's studies and schedule for the day. She enjoyed taking them on excursions to Charlie Chaplin movies or to donkey rides in the Zarzuela. When Madrid's "Ice Palace" opened in the early 1920's, the royal children were among its first delighted visitors, but the press of curious crowds discouraged the queen from repeating the visit. As for the father, the infantes and infantas saw him for perfunctory "good mornings" and then for slightly longer companionship at tea. Don Juan was later loyally to affirm that Alfonso was a good father, but in fact, the man-about-town and political manipulator was often too preoccupied to be close to his children.

The young Bourbons had their moments of fun, sometimes at their father's expense. Don Juan recalled a time in San Sebastián when the king wished to sail a small boat around the harbor and inspect the warships there without their being alerted to his presence. His plan was ruined when Don Juan and his brother broke out with the "Royal Anthem" on their toy musical instruments, and the nearby ships one by one started firing salutes and turning out their own ship's orchestras.

Aside from his immediate family, Alfonso XIII played patriarch to numerous members of his dynasty in the 1920's. His aunt Paz, for example, was driven from Munich by the revolutions in Germany after the war, and she and her doctor husband were given accommodations and responsibilities in Spain. The Infanta Eulalia, the king's youngest aunt, presented an entirely different sort of a problem—literary scandal. In 1911 the king had tried all sorts of cajolery and threats to prevent her from publishing her memoirs with their revelations about the follies of royalty. She published anyhow, and the family recriminations went on for years. Encountering her at a party in Paris in 1921, the genial Alfonso could only say, "Aunt Eulalia, let's make peace. We're both making fools of ourselves."

The king's Carlist rivals provided him with few worries in the 1920's since the head of the clan, Don Jaime, was more interested in nightclubs than in preparations for dynastic civil war. The fifty-year-old Bourbon prince still commanded fanatic loyalty as rightful occupant of the throne in some circles, as Alfonso once learned in a startling way. A cousin of the pretender was in the Spanish capital to visit a sick son, and Alfonso kindly thought to ring her on the phone. "Who is this?" she asked. "It is the King," said Alfonso. "Oh, Jaime, what are you doing in Madrid?"

In the summer of 1921 Alfonso XIII had much to be preoccupied with besides his family. His dream of military glory in Morocco was rendered a nightmare by the Riffs. On July 23 the king was in Burgos to assist at an unusually theatrical patriotic ceremony, the transference of the remains of the eleventh-century national hero El Cid to a grandiose tomb in the cathedral. Alfonso used the occasion to make a flamboyant speech about Spain's past power and prestige, and he then tried to arouse his listeners with the words "Spain is great enough still to realize her destiny; and apart from what Spain is on the Peninsula, and with what belongs to us on the other side of the Strait, we have enough to figure among the first nations of Europe." The king had hoped to be able that day to announce a striking military success in Morocco. Instead, the reports began to circulate of the disaster at Anual, one of the greatest colonial debacles of modern times.

Spain's interest in Morocco, which predates the Bourbon dynasty, received new impetus in 1909 after an agreement with France to divide the whole area between them. The Spanish sphere, smaller than the French protectorate to the south, presented difficulties because of its mountainous terrain and its uncivilized inhabitants, the fierce Riff tribesmen. After establishing a stronghold at Melilla, the Spanish undertook a gradual political penetration of the area, developing roads, farms, schools, and iron mines. With the Riffs seemingly cowed, in 1921 General Silvestre undertook a dramatic surge forward by marching a large column forty miles from Melilla to Alhucemas. On the very day of the king's Burgos speech, July 23, the Spanish were ambushed at Anual by a smaller Riff force under their redoubtable leader Abd-el-Krim. Few Spanish soldiers escaped: 10,000 were killed and 4,000 captured with all their equipment. Silvestre committed suicide. A short while later a Spanish fort was overwhelmed at the cost of hundreds more casualties and prisoners, with officers displayed in chains to be held for ransom. The Riffs then attacked Melilla itself, which barely held out.

Shock and dismay over the Anual disaster turned to an unprecedented public outcry against the army leadership, reaching right up to the king himself. The press with some difficulty established the facts about the poor preparations made for Silvestre's expedition and the collapse of discipline during the fighting. Newspaper stories revealed that many officers were absent from their commands at the time of the ambush and, what was worse, that some officers had been guilty of supplementing their pay by selling arms to the enemy. Moreover, deeper criticisms were leveled at an army which consumed half the state budget and needed 25,000 officers for its 200,000 men. Yet the army managed to hamper all official investigations of the situation by a commission of the Cortes and to block a definitive report. Two more prime ministers lost office because of the scandal. The army juntas of 1917 were revived and threatened the politicians. Alfonso XIII appeared more worried about upholding army morale than in preserving civilian control. In addition, the king was personally compromised in the Anual operation. He had promoted the pugnacious Silvestre to his command and prodded him to achieve a striking victory. "Do as I tell you and pay no attention to the Minister of War, who is an imbecile" was one royal telegram reportedly sent to Melilla. The left claimed that Alfonso's plan was to end the parliamentary regime as soon as victory was announced.

The search for the truth about Anual, or at least scapegoats, preoccupied the country for two years. Meanwhile, rightists took note of Mussolini's "March on Rome" and his designation as premier by the Italian king on October 29, 1922. "From tomorrow," *il Duce* had declared, "Italy will not only have a Ministry but a Government." Spain's ever-changing ministries floundered on. The "war of the gangsters" continued in Catalonia, marked by such outrages as the assassination of the CNT leader and the murder of the Cardinal Archbishop of Saragossa as reprisal.

The stage set, the seemingly inevitable military coup took place on September 13, 1923, after General Miguel Primo de Rivera used a riot in Barcelona as an excuse to proclaim material law and sent wires to the other captains general advising them to do likewise. When the ministry in power called for Primo's dismissal, he countered with a manifesto urging the ministry's dismissal and took the train to Madrid. Ten days earlier two generals had warned the king of the need for, and the likelihood of, such a military take-over, and Alfonso had advised the ministry to reach some accommodation "with the generals."

Alfonso XIII was sojourning at San Sebastián. On September 13 he had a polo match with an American team, saying later, "It was a hard game and I was pretty tired after it." He was called urgently to the phone, and the prime minister told him of the mutiny of the Barcelona garrison. The king said in effect, "I told you so," and told him to check the other garrisons. That night there was a dance at the Miramar, and the king took time off from the festivities only to accept the resignation of one minister who felt he was unpopular with the army. After Alfonso had retired, the prime minister phoned again at 1 A.M. with more bad news. The king replied, "You have got into the trouble and it is for you to get out of it. What do you propose to do?" When the prime minister inquired about the king's intentions, especially when he was coming to Madrid, Alfonso said, "I don't know," sharply and hung up. Shortly thereafter the king was awakened by a call from General Primo de Rivera, who said, "Your Majesty, I have revolted with the garrison of Barcelona to the cry of 'Viva el Rey and Viva España.' I place myself and the troops at Your Majesty's disposal. The ministry must go out the window, but we are loyal to Your Majesty." Alfonso turned to an aide and mused, "Am I awake? Am I dreaming? Am I mad? I don't understand a revolution which places itself at the disposal of the King. What does it all mean?" Then, he informed Primo that he was too tired to think and retired again for four hours. In the early morning he called the Madrid commandant, adjuring him to keep order and to jail the ministers if necessary for their safety. A breakneck drive to Madrid was followed by a conference between Alfonso and the prime minister, at which the latter was induced to resign his post rather than be dismissed. Later the king summoned Primo de Rivera and appointed him prime minister. The general responded by saying that his military associates could not deal with the Cortes and that "We must govern by Royal Decree."

Having endured twenty-one ministries over as many years time, Alfonso XIII now had to accommodate himself to a lengthy "dictatorship." General

Primo had simplistic political ideas: to him all the "professional politicians" were bad, being "responsible for the wrongs and misfortunes which began in 1898." The crucial moment for constitutional government came on November 11, 1923, when the presidents of the Senate and Chamber of Deputies waited on the king to remind him that according to Article 32 of the Constitution it was his duty to convene a Cortes within three months of its dissolution. This provision had been scrupulously observed since 1876. Whether out of fear of Primo or sympathy with him, Alfonso XIII refused to take action, thereby breaking his coronation oath. Not allowing a Cortes to be called was a mistake on Primo's part, for he might well have gained an overwhelming endorsement.

The new dictator had been born in 1870 into the landowning aristocracy of southwestern Andalusia. His upbringing was much influenced by his uncle, General Fernando Primo de Rivera, military hero of the Restoration of 1874 and twice governor of the Philippines, who earned the title Marquis of Estella and passed it to his nephew. At age twenty-three the younger Primo had been decorated for bravery in a Moroccan campaign (it was rumored that he also shot and killed his commanding officer for trafficking with the enemy, the only Spanish casualty listed for that year). Wounded again in Morocco in 1911, the general was eventually rewarded by being made governor of Cádiz. In 1919 he was captain general of Madrid but lost this post because of political indiscretions. Later as captain general of Catalonia he made his coup of 1923.

Little in Primo's education or training prepared him to run the Spanish government, but he went at his task with supreme confidence. He held ideas on all subjects and legislated accordingly. He was "very amateurish" in the evaluation of the British foreign secretary, who conceded, however, that Primo was "more serious and reasonable than I expected." The general's first moves were to institute a tight censorship, deport outspoken politicians, and harass the traditional political parties out of existence. The regime forbade strikes and undertook a particularly harsh crackdown in Catalonia, where it stifled the workers' agitation and silenced the autonomy movement by such measures as banning the use of the Catalan language (even Catalan songs and dances were forbidden). Centralization in Madrid reached a new peak under the Andalusian general. All was not oppressive and unenlightened. The institution of compulsory arbitration boards, for example, curbed some of the excesses of business as well as restrained labor. Primo even gave an ear to socialist proposals and extended a strange toleration to the Socialist Party, of all organizations, seeing it as a counterweight to the anarchist underground. By undertaking a massive program of public works, he went far to solving the unemployment problem.

To say whether or not the dictatorship was widely popular would be impossible, but unquestionably Primo's personal habits caused widespread amusement, if not admiration. He was the soul of simplicity, wearing the cheapest clothes and even letting out suits as he became progressively fatter from overeating. He still sat at his usual window table at his club, and when he frequented the theater, he joined the crowd in the stalls. One evening in a playhouse he inadvertently lit a cigar, and being reminded that smoking was forbidden, the genial dictator jumped up and announced, "Tonight everyone may smoke." He liked to sit in the cafés until 4 A.M. Often he would then reel home to issue communiqués and proclamations that were published the next day and repudiated the day after. Primo's more impulsive pronouncements, obviously made under the influence of liquor, became treasured mementos for a public bored with the censorship.

If Primo's disorderly day-to-day habits made life difficult for responsible Spanish officials, even worse was his custom of disappearing for long periods to some country retreat where he surrounded himself with roistering friends, both men and women, and kept the phone off the hook. A popular couplet of the 1920's ran: *"Naipes, mujeres, y la botella/ Son el blasón del Marqués de Estella"* (Cards, women, and the bottle are the escutcheon of the Marquis of Estella).

Spain's polo-playing king may have looked down on the vulgar antics of the dictator, but Alfonso XIII was in no position to dispense with Primo, if indeed he wanted to. Relations between the two men were correct, never cordial. The king had every reason to fear that the dictator and the army could take away his throne. Supporters of the dictator carefully planted rumors that Primo was considering passing the crown to the Infante Alfonso, who had turned sixteen (the legal age) just before the coup of 1923, or, if this prince and his brother Jaime were barred by their physical disabilities, to the thirteen-year-old Don Juan, in which case Primo would exercise a regency. While perhaps resenting his ignominious position, in the early years of the dictatorship Alfonso XIII made the adjustment of sharing the limelight, even to playing second fiddle to the general. In the later years Primo came to rely more on the wisdom of the king, who was experienced enough in politics to be the dean of Europe's monarchs. Any picture of a politically frustrated Alfonso must be drastically modified if one bears in mind the view of the politician and royal biographer, Miguel Maura, that the 1920's represented a "healthful and happy vacation" for the king.

Alfonso's basic approval of Primo's regime was made plain in an interview he granted a French journalist in April, 1925. He immediately insisted that in no country were the police "less a nuisance" than in Spain, although there was now assurance that people would not be robbed in the streets or shaken down or killed. The king noted that, unlike Prohibition-bound New York, Madrid allowed drinking and, in fact, "you can cry, howl, or sing until four in the morning if that pleases you." He later felt induced to burst out: "But damn it all, you've got to pay for it. Primo has made us break the Constitution and that is serious." Yet the king declared his conviction that the immediate restoration of the Constitution would mean a return to "crimes and strikes." He felt that the regime was accepted by all but a few thousand intellectuals. The charge of lack of democracy he countered with the question "This peaceful acceptance, this perfect tranquility, which you can observe everywhere, is that not a plebiscite which the nation gives every day tacitly in favor of the dictatorship?" Whatever private reservations Alfonso might have had about Primo, he allowed the monarchy to become entirely identified with the dictatorship, to his ultimate great cost.

The king told his French interviewer that the alternative to the dictatorship in Spain was a Soviet regime, as in Russia, a lesson he said was initially learned by Mussolini's Italy. His knowledge of the Italian regime was firsthand, for in November, 1923, he and Primo had visited Rome, traveling to Spezia on the battleship *Jaime I*, with the cruiser *Alfonso XIII* as escort, and thence by train. In the Italian capital planes dropped flowers on a grand parade in which Alfonso and King Victor Emmanuel III rode in the first carriage, their queens and heirs in the second, and Primo and Mussolini in the third. On one occasion Alfonso introduced Primo with the words "This is my Mussolini." The Spanish king was perhaps just being flippant or egotistical. His nervousness about the new situation was indicated by a strangely non sequitur speech he made to Pope Pius XI which included the words "If like another Urban II in defense of the persecuted faith you start a new crusade against the enemies of our holy religion, Spain and her King will never desert the place of honor." Exactly what crusade Alfonso had in mind was not clear, and the Pontiff's response was noncommital. The king's rhetoric had a curiously reactionary, Carlist ring to it.

Unlike the posturing *Duce*, Primo de Rivera was able to gain genuine military glory in the 1920's. Faced with a new Riff outbreak in the summer of 1924, the Spanish dictator personally directed a withdrawal to the coastal strongholds—a brave and sensible move. Abd-el-Krim then made the mistake of striking at the French in Algeria. The Spanish, still smarting from the Anual disaster, could take some satisfaction from seeing the French increasing their forces by 50 percent and sending over two marshals, one of them Pétain. The French requested joint military action at a conference in Madrid in July, 1925, and the September Primo de Rivera commanded the landing of 8,000 soldiers at Alhucemas Bay. The hazardous operation came off well, Primo admitting his good luck as well as careful planning, and Abd-el-Krim was put to flight. The next year a Spanish army under General José Sanjurjo joined the French in an encircling campaign that resulted in the Riff leader's surrender in May, unfortunately for Spanish pride, to the French. The pacification of Morocco was completed by 1929. The cost since 1911 had been close to $1 billion. To Primo's credit, he sought no new worlds to conquer but gingerly began cutting back military appropriations.

Having avenged Spain's "honor" in Morocco, Primo de Rivera pronounced the end of the dictatorship on December 3, 1925. He was merely playacting, for the general immediately had himself named prime minister of a new Cabinet in which generals predominated. If Primo had really retired at this point, he would have earned himself a hero's status, but instead he put his popularity to further tests. A plebiscite held in September, 1926, registered 6,000,000 votes in his favor, with no negative votes counted.

The plebiscite for Primo was organized by the Unión Patriótica, an organization formed in 1926 to supplant the traditional political parties. This group was also responsible for calling a consultative assembly on May 31, 1927, a body quite unlike the Cortes in view of its representation by professions and its complete powerlessness. It all smacked of Mussolini's corporate state, and people criticized the king for presiding at the opening convocation. Yet Primo was no Mussolini, and Fascism was not Spain's fate in the 1920's. The Unión Patriótica was treated as a joke by all but a few place seekers. The middle classes stood aside from it, and it was never more than a feeble imitation of the massed marchers and entrenched bureaucracy of Fascist Italy. Failing, really disdaining, to develop a mass movement in his name, Primo also eschewed an ultranationalist, expansionist foreign policy, the other hallmark of fascism.

Dearer to Primo's heart than chanting rallies were solid public constructions. His six years were the greatest era since Carlos III's in the eighteenth century for the building of roads. Schools, hospitals, irrigation works, electricity networks, and state hotels proliferated, and for the first time substantial amounts of money were spent on historical restorations. Spain's growth and superficial prosperity were celebrated in the great exhibitions at Barcelona and Seville in 1929. Many visitors considered the larger Barcelona exhibition the most beautiful world's fair architecturally to date. The Seville exhibition stressed the Spanish heritage of South and Central America, for both Primo and King Alfonso were enamored of a kind of cultural Hispanism, with a few political fantasies thrown in. The king opened the two exhibitions and was visibly pleased at the warm ovations the royal party received.

One public work that Alfonso XIII wished particularly to identify himself with was the building of a new university city on the outskirts of Madrid. He laid the foundation stone in 1927 on the twenty-fifth anniversary of his reign. The *ciudad universitaria* was to be Alfonso's Escorial, and it was designed in that style. Ironically, however, the dictatorship was driven by mounting student agitation to close the University of Madrid for eighteen months. Primo's policies toward the intellectual community had been consistently clumsy. The severe censorship came at a time when Spain was still experiencing a literary renaissance, and the intellectuals resented such practices as police eavesdropping on conversations and opening letters. Even the censors could not stop the uproar of protest when Primo, seeking clerical support, authorized Jesuit and Augustinian colleges to issue degrees. He hastily withdrew this decree, as he did so many others. Another time the dictator himself accepted an honorary degree from the University of Madrid, and the students promptly held a counterceremony in which a donkey was academically honored.

Far more serious than the student rioting for Primo's future were the first signs that he was losing the support of the army. In January, 1929, a unit of the traditionally obstreperous artillery corps seized the barracks of the Civil Guard in Ciudad Real and cut the railroad line. This action drew echoes in Valladolid and Segovia. The crisis was serious enough for the king to countenance the proclamation of martial law. The other army garrisons supported the dictator at this time, but the subsequent execution of some of the mutineers, the first such executions under Primo, alienated many of the military caste.

The year 1929 was also that of the great worldwide crash. The Depression hit Spain earlier and harder than most countries. The public works program involved overspending, and the cost of the Barcelona and Seville exhibitions was out of proportion to Spain's financial resources. Under Primo the national debt had risen 40 percent. Now the peseta plummeted on the international exchange markets. In the wake of the collapsed prosperity came charges of mismanagement and corruption among friends of the dictator and even among members of the royal family.

Primo's fall from power was not all that sudden. In the words of Brenan, "the last two years were a *corrida* in which students, ex-politicians, Liberal journalists, generals—anyone who wished to figure in the lime-light—took up his *banderillas* and challenged the Dictator, while an apathetic crowd looked on." The ease with which Spaniards turned against their military-heroes-become-politicians was already well demonstrated in the nineteenth century. In the case of Primo, as people tightened their belts, his high living ceased to be amusing and seemed undignified and selfish.

Aware of his declining prestige, Primo in early 1930 sent a circular to the captains general asking for expressions of confidence. Those that replied did not commit themselves. More important, Alfonso XIII was infuriated by Primo's action, which he learned of only from the newspapers, since it bypassed the royal channels of authority. The monarch demanded the dictator's resignation and received it on January 28. The discouraged, increasingly ill general was the first to acknowledge his mistake and went into voluntary exile after issuing one last theatrical communiqué that ended "and now for a little rest after 2326 days of continuous uneasiness, responsibility, and labor." He died that March 16 in a small Paris hotel on the rue de Bac, having alternated his last days between visits to churches and whorehouses.

Primo de Rivera's remains were brought back to Madrid for a hero's funeral as "*el Salvador de España.*" In the eyes of his admirers he was associated with law and order, public works, and an unaccustomed measure of international prestige for the nation. His opponents, while decrying the paternalism and repressiveness of his regime, acknowledged Primo's personal honesty and good intentions. He was one of the first, one of the most colorful, and perhaps the most humanly attractive of all the dictators. Rather than model himself on Mussolini, he was more a modern-day Moorish caliph.

Alfonso XIII, always agile, never generous, absented himself from Primo's funeral. If the king hoped to disassociate himself from the dictatorship, he did not succeed but rather earned contempt for disloyalty ("Primo's enemies blamed the sovereign for the Dictator's rise; his friends for the Dictator's fall."). People recalled a treacherous Bourbon king of a century before and dubbed Alfonso "King Fernando Seven and a Half."

Observers linked the king's error in ignoring Primo's funeral to a more general failing of his political touch following the loss of his mother, whose wisdom had been a check on his impetuosity. The former regent died of angina pectoris on February 28, 1929. The commotion her death caused in the palace persuaded the royal children that "the revolution" was at hand, an indication that fears for the future of the monarchy were already being voiced. Alfonso was more moved by his mother's passing than anyone recalled ever seeing him. He collapsed sobbing in his office when her cortege moved up the Calle de Bailén on its way to the Escorial. He was to give way to tears again two years hence when he looked at María Cristina's portrait for the last time before he left Spain.

XII.
The Crisis of 1931–1939:
The Dynasty Overthrown

1. The Downfall of Alfonso XIII

WHEN King Alfonso accepted General Primo's resignation in January, 1930, a political vacuum existed in Spain. One possibility would have been the establishment of a royal dictatorship replacing Primo's, a regime of the sort that King Alexander had introduced in Yugoslavia a year earlier (he was later assassinated in Marseilles in October, 1934). For Spain, royal dictatorship would have been essentially a Carlist solution, and Alfonso rejected it, either from conviction or from a feeling of powerlessness. The army no longer trusted him, nor did the old politicians who came back into prominence. Outwardly confident, the king maneuvered fitfully and blundered himself eventually into exile.

General Dámaso Berenguer succeeded Primo as prime minister. A colorless, well-intentioned professional soldier, he had been high commissioner in Morocco and thus in some degree shared the blame for the Anual disaster, a fact that his opponents exploited. His regime, which all regarded as a stopgap, was known as the *"dicta-blanda"* in contrast with the previous *"dicta-dura"* (a play on the Spanish words for bland and hard). Berenguer decreed an amnesty and the easing of censorship, and he dismantled Primo's system of political patronage and control.

The general's main mission was to prepare for the holding of elections, but he and the king let themselves be persuaded by Romanones and Manuel Prieto, former prime ministers and leading lights of the moribund Liberal and Conservative parties, to delay the voting for more than a year. Instead of the traditional monarchist parties reviving in the interval, groups on the left monopolized public attention. Even prominent rightists returning from exile disassociated themselves from Alfonso. The leading intellectual José Ortega y Gasset, created a sensation with an article which, Cato-like, declared: *"Delenda est monarquia."* Republicans, socialists, and Catalan separatists used the relative new freedom to join in August in the Pact of San Sebastián for the overthrow of the Bourbons. Ironically, the vacationing subversives plotted in the summer resort the king had done so much to make fashionable. The police chief, General Emilio Mola, knew of these activities but was apathetic about them, for, as he later admitted, he considered the monarchy a lost cause. He did not act even when the oppositionists agreed on the membership of a Revolutionary Committee, which was, in effect, a shadow government and was received as such with acclaim at public debates and at bullfights (without variation the same men actually took over the ministries in 1931).

Alfonso XIII showed no more alarm at the situation than to quip, "I am no longer in fashion now." He granted an interview to Miguel Maura, son of the turn-of-the-century Conservative prime minister, and he heard with equanimity the young politician's declaration that he was becoming a republican so as not to leave the field open to leftist extremists. "While I live, the monarchy runs no danger," Alfonso announced in reply, but he could not resist another joke and added with a smile: *"Après moi le déluge."* The king was jauntily at ease and pleased with his reception when in June, 1930, he visited the new military academy at Saragossa and was shown around by its first director, General Francisco Franco. Following the successful military repression of a strike in Madrid, Berenguer announced: "The Army is entirely loyal, and political revolution is impossible."

That he could not count on the army was abruptly made clear to the king the following month when the garrison at Jaca mutinied in the name of the republic. The insurgents killed six officials and used priests as shields before they were subdued. Alfonso was so enraged that he opposed any trial for the ringleaders, two captains, and he subsequently insisted on their immediate execution after their trial. Creating these martyrs was Alfonso's "worst mistake." The police now arrested Maura and the other members of the Revolutionary Committee, confining them in the Model Prison, where they were given great leeway to propagandize beyond the walls.

On December 16 occurred a new crisis, both alarming and bizarre. Major Ramón Franco, the general's brother, flew over Madrid with a squadron of planes which scattered leaflets threatening to bomb the capital if the garrison would not support a republic. An aviation hero for a pioneer flight across the South Atlantic, the younger Franco had wanted to drop explosives on the royal palace. Alfonso watched the whole performance from the roof of the Oriente. The government's reaction, approved by the king, was to disband the entire Spanish flying corps as a unit with distinctive uniforms, adding that many more men to the roster of its enemies.

General Berenguer resigned on February 15, 1931, to be replaced as prime minister by the even more innocuous Admiral Juan Bautísta Aznar, with a Cabinet that included his predecessor and an uninspired collection of old politicians like Romanones. Too late King Alfonso sent out feelers to prominent leftists, even ones in exile and in prison, but when one such leader found Alfonso personally prejudiced against many of the best minds in the country, he left the interview muttering, "With this man it is impossible to do anything."

Floundering as he was, Alfonso XIII gained a false sense of security from the triumphant reception given Queen Ena on her return from England on February 16. Cheering crowds greeted the queen at every stop on her train trip from Irún, and in Madrid at the railroad station and before the palace the royal family heard thunderous shouts of "Long live the monarchy" and "Down with the republic." "I thought I was the most popular human being in Spain," declared the queen later, adding, "How could a nation change its sympathies so abruptly?" The reason for the queen's visit to the land of her birth was that her seventy-five-year-old mother had fallen in Kensington Palace and broken her arm. In mid-March Alfonso airily slipped off for a short visit to London, ostensibly to congratulate his mother-in-law on her recovery.

The long-awaited elections were held peaceably on Sunday, April 12, 1931. The voting was for municipal councillors, since the old politicians had persuaded Alfonso that by first controlling the municipal bosses they could control subsequent elections to the Cortes (shades of the clash between the Queen Regent Christina and Espartero in 1841). To the surprise of all, even the republicans, the first returns were overwhelmingly antimonarchist. About twice as many people voted as normally. When all the votes were in, a majority of councillors around the country were monarchists, but forty-six of fifty provincial capitals went republican. Madrid elected almost all republicans, as did Barcelona, where the regime paid the price of its suppression of Catalan aspirations for autonomy. A shocked Alfonso said of the elections, "I had the impression of calling on an old friend and finding him dead."

Monday, April 13, was generally quiet in the capital. Prime Minister Aznar, who had read a novel during the election returns, was agitated enough to tell a press conference, "What more crisis do you want than that of a country which went to bed a monarchist and woke up a republican?" The government seemed hypnotized into inaction. The war minister, General Berenguer, exchanged messages with the captains general about keeping law and order, and ominously neither he nor the military mentioned the king. Alfonso himself contacted General Sanjurjo, head of the 28,000 Civil Guard, and received discouraging replies about the loyalty of this national police force. Here was another key security official who was lukewarm about the royal regime, like General Mola, the Madrid police chief, who unconcernedly went to the theater that night. At 11 P.M., that is, during the theater hour, the first great crowds assembled in the Puerta del Sol to demand Alfonso's abdication, but they dispersed at 2 A.M. The anxious king was on the phone constantly but went to bed assured of support from many quarters. The Infanta Beatriz, a cousin by marriage of the king, told her husband, "Go home, get your pistols and a toothbrush and pajamas; you are a great strong man and the King may need your help." Meanwhile, at a meeting in the bar of the Ritz Hotel a group of royalist intellectuals decided to advise Alfonso to leave the country temporarily.

In the early morning of April 14 Alfonso XIII told ministerial callers that he had agreed that he should absent himself from Spain until the Cortes elections gave a definitive mandate on the future of the monarchy. The Count of Romanones, apparently obsessed with the fate of the Romanovs in Russia, did much to panic Alfonso into leaving immediately. Via Dr. Gregorio Marañon, physician to the king and high society, Romanones was informed that Niceto Alcalá Zamora y Torres, once his private secretary and now head of the Revolutionary Committee, felt that civil war was hourly imminent and that Alfonso must depart Spain "before sundown." The exact interplay of actions by Maranon, Romanones, General Sanjurjo, and other major participants in the fall of the monarchy are debated to this day, with accusations of treachery cropping up from all quarters. In any event, the last session of the royalist Cabinet took place at 5 P.M. on April 14, during the course of which one minister argued passionately for military resistance and General Berenguer said he would take the king's orders. Alfonso ended the meeting with a dignified announcement: "On taking leave of you and preparing myself to leave, perhaps forever, from this house where I was born, I can say only one thing, for it is my only thought and my only desire, 'Long Live Spain.'" Having been informed that the republic had been proclaimed in Barcelona and elsewhere, the king lit a cigarette and went to the window to ponder a red flag flying over the ministry of communications.

Alfonso's decision to leave quietly and quickly was later hailed as a generous effort to avoid civil war. It was "an act of humanity and of the *gentleman* who knew how to lose." The king's detractors were less impressed with the nobility of his motives, pointing out that the king knew he could count on few swords and little treasure in his behalf. The grandees as a class were silent, fearing a desperate social revolution if the political overturn were thwarted.

Unlike Tsar Nicholas II fourteen years previously, Alfonso XIII did not abdicate but just suspended his rule. He did not hand over the monarchy to his heir, since like the Russian royal family, he had to take into account the problem of hemophilia. Some courtiers talked of a regency by Queen Ena for one of the sons, but they were told it was politically impossible. The king's farewell manifesto had both prodigal-son and dog-in-the-manger qualities about it. The Republican government refused to allow its publication, but Spaniards learned of it from foreign newspapers. Alfonso said,

> The elections held on Sunday have revealed to me that I no longer hold the love of my people, but my conscience tells me that this attitude will not be permanent, because I have always striven to serve Spain with the utmost devotion to the public interest even in the most critical times. A King may make some mistakes, and without doubt I have some times done so, but I know that our country has always shown herself generous towards the faults of others committed without malice.

The message continued:

> I renounce no single one of my rights which, rather than being mine, are an accumulated legacy of history, for the guardianship of which I shall one day have to render strict account.

Here was a kind of divine right or Carlist stance, but Alfonso also acknowledged that Spain was the "sole mistress of her destinies." He thus set the stage for Spain to be a monarchy without a king.

At 5 P.M. on April 14 King Alfonso told Queen Ena he was leaving the capital at 8. They had dinner alone and in near silence in the small room where they usually took tea. She was amazed at his indifference to packing any of their possessions, and she decided herself to stay that night. The king, later accused of ungallantly abandoning his wife and children, had reasons for haste and heartfelt assurances from several ministers that his family was in no danger. He made brief and dignified farewells to the palace halberdiers and to an assemblage of weeping servants. The only moment when the king displayed any trace of emotion was a pause on the grand staircase beneath the portrait of his mother, a thoughtful look and a quick salute. On the terrace outside Alfonso got into a car, together with a cousin, a duke, and the minister of marine. He declined this time to drive himself. They sped off via the Toledo Bridge, a second car following with a valet and the luggage. Posters were just beginning to appear on the streets of Madrid proclaiming the Second Spanish Republic with Alcalá Zamora its provisional president.

The revolutionary leader had forbidden Alfonso to take the familiar journey to San Sebastián and then France for fear of popular demonstrations in favor of the monarchy in the northern provinces. Instead, the chosen destination was the naval city of Cartagena in the southeast, which he reached at 4:30 A.M. Alfonso was able to phone the Oriente Palace to reassure the queen. A marine guard paid the king the usual honors, but when he boarded the cruiser *Príncipe Alfonso*, the captain of the ship refused to raise the royal standard and did not even allow the departing sovereign to listen to the radio on the day-long voyage. Upon his disembarkation on French soil at Marseilles, Alfonso broke into tears, a loss of control he had allowed himself only once before, at the time of his mother's death. "Excuse me, General," he told his companion, "for I am abandoning that which I love most in the world."

Queen Ena spent the last night in the bedroom of her youngest daughter. The people who remained in the Oriente had some apprehensions, since the crowds outside, generally good-natured, did egg on a few rowdies in their efforts to climb onto the balconies and to smash a truck against one of the gates. News dealers shouted insulting headlines hour after hour. In the early morning the queen heard mass and supervised the packing of a few favorite mementos and valuables, including Queen María Cristina's jewels. The tourist visiting the Oriente today is happily amazed at the sheer number of family photographs and other personal belongings that were left. During her farewell to the staff Queen Ena murmured to a lady-in-waiting, "Take care of my Red Cross." Since they were told it was dangerous to go to the main railroad station, the queen's party planned to drive by a secret gate to catch a train at the Escorial. At 8 A.M. a chauffeur carried out the Infante Alfonso, twenty-four, who was suffering from severe hematoma, received as a result of shooting birds with a shotgun from an airplane a few days before. His dog, Peluzon, joined him in the first car. Two other automobiles contained the infantes Jaime and Gonzalo with their tutors. The last car followed with the queen and her daughters Beatriz and Cristina. No representative of the British embassy was on hand for the departure, just one British officer in a private capacity to pay his respects to the queen, his fellow countryman.

The queen's leaving was supposed to be as unobtrusive as possible, but in the Casa del Campo west of the capital, and still in sight of the great abandoned white palace, a large group of well-wishers was waiting. Ena got out of her car and held an impromptu court seated on a large rock. The photographs of this moment show a portly woman dressed in a dark suit with furs and a cloche hat. The scene was described by the Infante Pilar in these words:

> Queen Victoria Eugenia had held many Courts in the Palace on the horizon, received foreign Sovereigns, being the central figure in many splendid and sumptuous ceremonials. At not one of them had she been more queenly, more royally self-controlled, more splendidly a woman than on this sun-drenched morning with a rock for her throne, the high blue sky for her canopy, and the unfailing love of a few of her truest friends and servants as her only solace and support.

The queen displayed no rancor, although she did say, "I thought I had done well." Later, waiting at the Escorial station, she made a point of telling everyone, "My husband has not abdicated; he has signed nothing," but when an aristocratic lady said, *"Hasta la vista,"* to her, Ena replied, "Those who leave now are not going to return." The train that took her away bore the royal arms and was driven by the Duke of Saragossa.

The downfall of Alfonso XIII occurred so quickly that his next to youngest son, Don Juan, was still at naval cadet school in Cádiz. The director had him summoned from class and put on Torpedo Boat Number 16, which arrived at dawn on April 15 at Gibraltar. The Spanish warship did not run up the flag of the republic until after the personable young man had landed amid cheers of *Viva el Infante*. Resourceful and modest, Don Juan put up at a hotel, but the British commandant, who by coincidence had said good-bye in 1874 to Alfonso XII at Sandhurst, insisted on granting him royal honors and later arranged his reunion with his family in Paris.

"The monarchy was slain by its own hands, not by ours," wrote Miguel Maura, speaking for the Second Republic that was proclaimed on the day of King Alfonso's flight. The 1931 overthrow was indeed partly self-inflicted, but "slain" was too strong a word, as events have proved, for a dynasty which has always tenaciously clung to its rights and is destined to be restored again. The parallels are strong with the two other times the Bourbons found themselves rudely ousted from Spain. The deposition of 1808, ostensibly at the hands of Napoleon, was actually blundered into by Carlos IV and María Luisa. If their heir, Fernando VII, then too abdicated under duress, the nation chose to see him an unwilling victim and to uphold his rights for the future. Like her grandson, Queen Isabel II refused to abdicate after she paid the price of her indiscretions and fled the country in 1868, and her stubbornness paved the way for the restoration of 1874.

How much Alfonso XIII was to blame for his downfall is naturally a central point of debate in the more than twenty biographies that have appeared since. At issue are both political prejudices about the monarchy and historiographical convictions about how much a leader can control events. The conservative writer Sir Charles Petrie, for example, concludes that "the times were out of joint" as far as Alfonso was concerned, but "very few monarchs could have done better, and the vast majority would have done a great deal worse." Petrie concedes that like most Bourbons, Alfonso was most successful at the beginning of his reign and gradually lost his "old self-confidence and sureness of touch," but he insists that the politicians, not the king, blocked Spain's progress and were to blame for the ultimate debacle. Gerard Brenan advances the completely contrary view, seeing Alfonso as not the thwarted but as the thwarter of needed social changes. "Whether from love of power, instability of character, or sheer ignorance of social conditions in his country, he regularly and unfailingly wrecked" reform programs. Brenan and other liberal historians judge Alfonso as essentially a reactionary intriguer, while Petrie and his like emphasize his good intentions and patriotism.

One can speculate on what sort of a king might have survived the storms of Spanish politics in the first three decades of this century. He should have been scrupulously constitutional, all the while encouraging the elimination of rigged elections and bossism. He should never have imposed his personality in the matter of ministerial changes. He should have disassociated himself from the army as much as possible. He should have identified himself with the best minds of the country. He should have avoided any playboy image amid mass misery. Alfonso XIII failed on all counts.

2. The Second Republic and Monarchist Intrigues

The Second Spanish Republic, proclaimed in the streets of Madrid even as King Alfonso pondered his decision to leave, was born amid expressions of hope for the future and of bitterness about the past. A crowd toppled the statue of Isabel II in a square near the royal palace. As in 1868, a deliberate change in national symbols took place, with audiences singing the "Hymn of Riego" instead of the "Royal Anthem" and towns all over the country replacing Plazas de Alfonso XIII with Plazas de la República. Avowed monarchists simply kept quiet, while the press indulged in scandalmongering about former royalty, producing more noise than substance.

The new regime existed precariously from 1931 until General Franco began the Civil War in 1936. It was longer lived than the First Republic of 1873–1874, although like its predecessor, it harbored powerful enemies on both the extreme right and extreme left. The daily headlines alternated between proclamations of ambitious, controversial reforms and reports of outrages by fascists or anarchists. Occasionally, there was news of the social doings of the deposed Bourbons, of monarchist plottings, and of renewed recriminations between the Alfonsist and Carlist branches of the dynasty.

King Alfonso XIII and various members of the royal family were reunited in Paris at the Hôtel Meurice. The first days of exile were especially saddened by the death of the Infanta Isabel on April 22, 1931. The king's seventy-nine-year-old aunt had been too ill to leave Madrid at the onset of the revolution. "Let them come if they want. They can't do more than kill me," she said. Actually, the infanta was personally so popular that the crowds treated her palace on the Calle de Quintana with special respect, and the Republican government offered to let her stay in Spain undisturbed. She refused and left the country, dutiful to the last to the dynasty she had served with grace, if without political insight.

The republican press published exaggerated stories to the effect that King Alfonso had anticipated his exile and invested a fortune abroad. While scarcely one of the world's richest men, as some claimed, the former monarch was never at a loss for funds. Besides maintaining a spacious apartment at the Hôtel Meurice, he bought a large villa near Fontainebleau. Within a short time of his taking up residence there, he was elected honorary president of the nearby American golf club. He also gave attention to the careers of his children, such as placing Don Gonzalo in the University of Louvain. He personally conducted Don Juan to England and saw to his enrollment in the Royal Naval College at Sandwich. In England, as well as in France, King Alfonso received demonstrations of sympathy, people still remembering his wartime relief activities.

Shortly after their removal from Spain Queen Ena indicated her desire to be separated from her husband. He complied with her wishes, giving her the villa at Fontainebleau. Aside from basic personality differences, an accumulated resentment of past infidelities and her distaste for Parisian night life provoked her to make the break after twenty-five years of marriage. Alfonso's indiscretions, with the rumor that a divorce was in prospect, hurt him politically.

Inevitably, the former king was importuned to give his reactions to the situation in Spain, past and present. He first expressed himself publicly in an interview with a correspondent of *ABC*, an avowedly monarchist newspaper in Madrid, then as today. Alfonso was anything but defiant or inflammatory, declaring, "Monarchists who wish to follow my advice will not only refrain from placing obstacles in the Government's path but will support it in all patriotic enterprises. . . . High above the formal ideas of republic or monarchy stands Spain." With regard to his overthrow, he repeated the theme of wishing to avoid civil war: "I declined the offers made to me to remain and rule by force." Wistfully, he then averred: "I have not hesitated to leave Spain, making for her the greatest sacrifice of my life, when I understood that Spain no longer loved me. It would be very sad if I did not hope that, one day, history will do me justice." Without being provocative, Alfonso still expected to be recalled to Spain, just as his grandmother had six decades previously.

Before long, manifestations in Alfonso's favor took place in Spain itself. The Cardinal Primate of Toledo circulated a pastoral letter praising the king and chiding the people for remaining indifferent. The government succeeded in getting the Pope to allow the archbishop's expulsion. Shortly afterward, on May 31, 1931, a violent confrontation of monarchists and supporters of the republic occurred in Madrid. A group of army officers and aristocrats met at a house on the Calle de Alcalá to talk of founding a monarchist club. In response to the loud strains of the "Royal Anthem" played on a phonograph coming from the windows, two latecomers in a taxi shouted, "Long live the monarchy," as they arrived, to which their driver responded with "Long live the republic." They struck him, and within a brief while the assembled bystanders were persuaded that the driver was dead. An outburst of car burning followed, and then a march on *ABC* and the destruction of its printing plant. The next day masses of rioters razed the main Jesuit church in the center of the city and other religious institutions. Other cities echoed the violence as people struck out at clerics and suspected monarchists indiscriminately. Right-wingers sensationalized these events into a great orgy of sacrilege and lawlessness, while a sober analysis concludes that 6 of Madrid's 150 cloisters were destroyed. The government, which hesitated too long to send in the Civil Guard so hated from the old days, ended up blaming the monarchists and suspending *ABC*.

Persecution encouraged monarchists in Spain to raise their heads politically. Among other things, aristocrats resented the republic's official abolition of titles and such unofficial harassment as mailmen refusing to deliver letters with titles in the address. Monarchist candidates, however, did very poorly in the elections on June 28, 1931, for the Constituent Cortes, which were won overwhelmingly by a Republican-Socialist coalition. Avowed supporters of King Alfonso gained only about fifteen seats, while Carlist candidates did somewhat better with almost twenty.

Carlist monarchists had the advantage over the Alfonsists in that they did not have to waste their energies explaining and apologizing for the actions of a deposed sovereign. Their candidate for the throne was the sixty-year-old Don Jaime, who, signing himself "Jaime III," had waited only a week after his cousin's overthrow to issue a manifesto on April 23 calling on all antirepublican Spaniards to rally to his banner. In due course, Navarrese and Basque peasants started oiling their guns, and aristocrats with lesser titles of nobility began to walk taller (the Alfonsists tended to be richer).

In actual fact, the Carlists had a very untypical leader in the person of Don Jaime. He could only be called a disappointment to the cause, if one compared him to his ostentatiously regal and militaristic, indeed simplistic, father, the "Carlos VII" for whom thousands died in the Third Carlist War of 1873–1876. Although the son's military credentials were considerable, as a veteran of the Russian army in two wars, he had retired in 1909 to the life of a gentleman, alternating his time between the Bourbon chateau at Frohsdorf and an elegant apartment in Paris on the Avenue Hoche. He had never married, lending credence to the suspicion that he aspired to end the vendetta within the Spanish Bourbon dynasty with his death. Widely read, progressive in his ideas, he was "the antithesis of cheap romanticism" and "too modern a man for so archaic a cause" as Carlism. Yet he was unwilling to relinquish his status as titular head of the movement and allowed traditionalists to propagandize in his name.

If Don Jaime was a diffident Carlist, his followers were only too ready to mouth the slogans about God, Fatherland, and King that showed them to be spiritually back in the seventeenth century. One evocation of their dream of old-time royal absolutism is the following retort of the Carlist leader in the Cortes, the tall, commanding, and cynical Count of Rodezno, who, when asked by a friend who would be prime minister if a Carlist king were put on the throne. "You or one of these gentlemen," he said, "it is only a matter of secretaries." "What would you do?" "I? I should stay with the king and we should talk of the chase."

In October, 1931, Spanish royalists were variously astonished, excited, and alarmed to learn that ex-King Alfonso had called on the Carlist pretender at the Avenue Hoche on September 29 and that Don Jaime paid a return visit to Fontainebleau a day later. People recalled the similar meetings between Queen Isabel and Don Carlos in the Bois de Boulogne in 1870, which produced a near reconciliation of the rival branches of the dynasty. The first press communiqué about the meetings was noncommital:

> Don Jaime and Don Alfonso of Bourbon have just concluded a double interview with the object of affirming the unity of their ancient house and to tighten the bonds between the two branches of the family of Bourbon of which they are each the respective chiefs. They have been separated solely for political reasons not by personal disaffections; the two princes, united in their common love of Spain, have decided to establish between them relations of fraternal amnesty so as to work for the salvation of Spain.

Newspapers promptly indulged in intense speculation that some serious agreement had been made, such as Alfonso's recognizing Jaime as head of the family in return for the latter's giving his blessing to the former and his children as heirs to the throne. Carlist circles immediately denied that there could be any such compromise of their Salic Law principles, but their conviction that no deal had been made was weak.

Possibly on the very eve of the day of a dramatic announcement, Don Jaime suddenly died on October 2, shortly after returning from a drive. Carlist sympathizers in Spain draped their balconies in black and consulted their genealogies to see who their new leader would be. The title was promptly assumed by the deceased pretender's uncle, Don Alfonso Carlos, a man in his eighties and childless. The new claimant was very much cut in the typical Carlist mold, however, and was remembered for his military exploits in the Third Carlist War. Grand, arrogant, entirely uncompromising in his absolutist-clerical beliefs, Don Alfonso Carlos had been living in various castles in Austria, where he displayed the royal arms of both Spain and France, and when he traveled about in a carriage, he was escorted by four horsemen in livery. After consulting with his principal supporters, Don Alfonso Carlos issued a manifesto from Milan asserting his God-given rights to the Spanish throne. It had a "splendidly anachronistic" ring to it. He also repudiated plans for Carlist groups to cooperate with the Alfonsists in local politics. He did hold out to "my beloved cousin Alfonso," a man who had been an acknowledged king for forty-five years, the prospect of being the pretender's heir, but only if he upheld the "traditional regime."

While Alfonsists and Carlists aired their dynastic disputes, mainly in the safety of exile, the Constituent Cortes in Madrid on November 12, 1931, approved a committee report condemning Alfonso XIII for high treason and confiscating the royal properties. If the former king returned to Spain, he would be liable to life imprisonment or to death if he continued in his "acts of rebellion." The indictment accused Alfonso of acting unconstitutionally, of conspiring to bring about the dictatorship of 1923, of encouraging "administrative immorality," and of indulging in "*lèse-majesté*" toward the people. Only the Count of Romanones eloquently protested, challenging the Cortes to prove specific acts of wrongdoing. One effect of this "rancorous and needless act of persecution," in the words of *ABC* (again suspended and fined as a result), was to make Alfonso abandon his lofty political posture. He no longer discouraged his followers from insurrectionary plans. In December, 1931, the first issue of a blatantly antirepublican journal *Acción Española* appeared, and secret efforts were initiated to subvert the officers corps.

Also in December the Cortes promulgated a new, highly progressive Constitution for what was called a "Republic of workers of all categories." Alcalá Zamora now took up the former royal duties and conducted palace ceremonials as president, while the more radical Manuel Azaña succeeded him as prime minister. The Cortes set about legislating drastic social reforms, adopting various measures that aroused the ire of clericalist opinion such as civil divorce, secularization of education, and restrictions on religious orders. The regular army faced a reduction from sixteen to eight divisions, the abolition of captains general, and the retirement of two-thirds of the officers (at full pay). The regime projected equally thoroughgoing agrarian reforms, including confiscation of large estates, and drafted a statute granting Catalonia considerable autonomy, with its own parliament, tax powers, and flag.

Monarchists of both camps were involved in the first major attempt to overturn the republic and its radical legislation. The revolt, which began on August 10, 1932, was headed by General Sanjurjo, son and nephew of prominent Carlist leaders of the 1870's, Marquis of Rif for his distinguished service in Morocco in the 1920's, and the senior officer in the army. As head of the Civil Guard during the crisis of 1931 Sanjurjo had discouraged King Alfonso's hopes of support, but now the killing and mutilation of five Civil Guards at Castelblanco by rioting peasants so appalled the general as to make him decide to be the "saviour of Spain." His exact political aims were vague, and the planning of the rising was haphazard (one plotter said he learned of the changing dates of the coup from his concierge). The insurgents seized Seville, but they were suppressed by forces loyal to the regime with the assistance of a general strike called by the anarchists. An attempt to capture the war ministry in Madrid was even more farcical. Sanjurjo, ignominiously arrested by a Civil Guard as he tried to escape to Portugal, was tried, sentenced to death, but spared with life imprisonment. Among the 144 other officers condemned to deportation were two Bourbon princes and four generals who would later gain prominence in the Franco revolt (Franco himself, commandant at Corunna, had backed out of the 1932 plot after deciding it was premature). The police suspended *Acción Española*. The Spanish people now seemed to rally to the republic more enthusiastically than before.

King Alfonso was apparently uninvolved and uninformed about General Sanjurjo's attempt to overthrow the republic, for he was traveling in Central Europe at the time. Travel had become an obsession with the restless, pleasure-loving ex-sovereign who was nearing his fifties. He still showed his sense of humor when talking about his status. "I'm a queer kind of tourist. I have no identity papers and no passport. When I come to a frontier I say to the customs officers: 'My name is Alfonso XIII and I am an undesirable.' But always they let me pass." Once he did encounter difficulties getting into Germany, carrying the day by overawing a frontier guard with the words "Look here, my man, I am an honorary admiral in your navy, a general in your cavalry, a colonel in your hussars, and I demand your salute." While usually hobnobbing with the rich and the celebrated, Alfonso also affected a kind of democratic bonhomie. During a Mediterranean cruise he startled a tourist who was taking his picture by saying, "You are the 3657th and I am not even a beauty queen. I am not even a king. I have been fired."

The ex-king kept his impressive looks, being unmistakable with his neatly trimmed dark mustache between his Bourbon nose and Hapsburg chin. Still the elegant dresser, he was wont to play the gay but courtly Lothario, and scandals were inevitable. One involved the wife of a famous Parisian jeweler who was seen with Alfonso at the racetrack and at intimate parties at the Hôtel Meurice. After intercepting letters, the husband instituted divorce proceedings, citing a "Monsieur X," but later the whole thing was dropped.

In the early 1930's King Alfonso had to face many family heartaches and disappointments. His eldest son, Don Alfonso, followed his father's example and set out to be a playboy and nothing more. In his mid-twenties, the Prince of the Asturias was strikingly handsome with his father's broad forehead and strong features and his mother's golden blond hair and rosy complexion. He was spoiled, mindless, and mercurial. The sum total of his ambitions appeared to be nightclubs and fast cars (he used to drive about with his dog, wearing sunglasses, perched on the running board). The heir's activities were circumscribed, however, by his poor health. Ever since he had to be carried into exile, Don Alfonso had many painful seizures of hemophilia. Blaming his condition on his mother, he became completely estranged from her.

While Don Alfonso was undergoing treatment in Switzerland, he contracted the first of his misalliances, ending up marrying a loving Cuban woman by the name of Edelmira Sampedro Ocejo y Robato. The marriage, which took place on June 21, 1933, was morganatic, and the prince now took the title of Count of Covadonga. Ten days earlier in a letter to his father he renounced his rights to the throne of Spain. Don Alfonso and his wife subsequently went to live in Cuba and the United States. While in Havana, he suffered for months from a bleeding abscess in his left buttock but was eventually cured by a series of transfusions of blood from people whose spleen had been removed (the theory was that such blood would coagulate rapidly, but probably any transfused blood had an antihemophiliac effect).

The day of Don Alfonso's marriage, his brother Don Jaime also sent a letter of renunciation of the throne "for me and whatever descendants I might have." King Alfonso's second son was a more attractive personality than the eldest. Facially a look-alike of his father, Don Jaime was more than six feet tall, muscular, and possessed of perfect dignity of bearing. His disposition was the most amiable, his intelligence commendable considering the physical handicaps he suffered from, complete deafness and great difficulty in speaking. In March, 1935, Don Jaime married in Rome the Countess Emanuela de Dampierre, daughter of the distinguished Pozzio family. In time they had three children, one of whom recently married Franco's granddaughter.

The older infantes' renunciations of the throne were to prove embarrassingly repudiable, but in 1933 with them confidently in hand King Alfonso wrote to his physically unimpaired third son to designate him Prince of the Asturias and his successor. Don Juan was in Colombo, Ceylon, where he was serving in the British navy. As soon as he attained his lieutenancy, Don Juan resigned and embarked on a serious program of studies in various European universities designed to prepare him for future responsibilities. Physically unlike either of his parents, the new heir had solid good looks, quite dignity, and charm of manner. His marriage on October 12, 1935, to his cousin Maria de las Mercedes in the Church of the Angels in Rome was the occasion for a rally of 10,000 enthusiastic Spanish exiles. In Spain *Acción Española* held a banquet in honor of the wedding, to which Don Juan sent a telegram. He praised the monarchist intellectuals for "showing how the sacred tradition of Spain is compatible with the most modern doctrines." This seemingly innocuous statement would serve as a platform for the man who for thirty years has been the most persistent pretender to the Bourbon crown.

King Alfonso had the satisfaction of seeing his daughters also happily wed in Italy. Doña Beatriz and Doña María Christina each married into Italian nobility. Their importance in Spanish dynastic politics ceased.

The family experienced great sorrow at the death of the youngest son Don Gonzalo at age twenty in August, 1934. The pet of his parents and the best friend of Don Juan, the youngest Bourbon was remembered for his unaffected and amiable disposition. As a student of agronomy and forestry at the School of Engineers in Louvain, he displayed exceptional ability. A hemophiliac like his eldest brother, Don Gonzalo bled to death after his face hit the windshield in a motor accident near Pörtschach in Austria. He had crashed into a wall in an effort to avoid a drunken motorcyclist.

With the prospect of a healthy, personable successor to the throne in Don Juan, monarchists in Spain took heart. In March, 1933, they founded Renovación Española, an avowedly monarchist party headed by Antonio Goicoechea and José Calvo Sotelo. Well heeled financially and well connected socially, these monarchists were able to gain forty-four seats in the elections to the new Cortes on November 19, 1933. A right-wing Catholic party, however, was able to gain 100 seats on an "accidentalist" platform, saying that whether the country was a republic or a monarchy was an accident and really did not matter. The newly founded fascist party, the Falange, although inspired by the recent triumph of Hitler in Germany, did not attract many votes (its chief idealogist was José Antonio Primo de Rivera, who was not only antileftist but bitterly antimonarchist because of the king's betrayal of his father in 1930).

The elections of 1933 signaled a general swing to the right, and the Azaña Cabinet was replaced by a conservative one. The new ministry suspended all the social reform programs, gave amnesty to General Sanjurjo, and allowed Calvo Sotelo to return from exile to write in a reopened *Acción Española*. The monarchist party offered itself now as an alternative not only to republicanism but also to rule by generals or by fascists. Nonetheless, they were not above sending Goicoechea on a mission to Mussolini in March, 1934. The Italian dictator expressed bemused puzzlement at the split between the Alfonsists and Carlists, but he promised 200 machine guns and 20,000 rifles, with more to come following a successful revolt. He allowed 400 Carlist officers to train in Italy disguised as "Peruvians." Carlist bands began drilling in Navarre, and their leadership even established a military academy. The Alfonsists were short on military cadres, longer on communiqués. King Alfonso, in his first open intervention in Spanish politics since 1931, in September, 1934, offered his services to save Spain from "revolutionary excesses." His letter to Goicoechea was published in *ABC*.

King Alfonso's declared availability caused little stir in a Spain where fascists and anarchists dominated the headlines as they vied with each other in perpetrating violent outrages. Indicative of the intense hatreds in the air was the case of a young Falangist being beaten to death in one of Madrid's parks on a Sunday afternoon following a political altercation; his eyes were gouged out and one of his tormentors, a young woman leftist, urinated in the sockets. In immediate retaliation the aristocrat of aristocrats, Alfonso Merry del Val, drove his automobile through a workers' district and indiscriminately shot several people.

Violence on a national scale broke out in October, 1934, after the ministry was reorganized to include more rightists. The anarchists and socialists called a general strike, and Catalonia declared itself an independent republic. he workers of the mining districts of the Asturias staged an armed uprising, seizing Oviedo and other cities and proclaiming *comunismo libertario* that is, a moneyless, propertyless utopia. The government was successful in crushing the various outbreaks, but in the case of the Oviedo uprising it was forced to send in General Franco's Moorish troops and the Foreign Legion, who committed atrocities that were far more appalling than anything the miners had done. As a result of the October,

1934, crisis, 40,000 people found themselves in prison, and Spain braced itself for further showdowns between an increasingly fanatical and intolerant right and left.

A decisive swing to the left occurred in the elections of February, 1936, which were "generally exemplary" for the absence of violence, according to the New York *Times*. While the exact results of the voting are disputed to this day, about 256 seats were won by a coalition called the Popular Front, which included Left Republicans, Socialists, Communists, and Anarchists. Their main opposition, which captured 143 seats, was another coalition, the National Front, including Right Republicans, a Catholic party, Alfonsist monarchists, and the Carlists. At this point General Franco was approached by various rightist politicians who wanted him to seize Madrid and annul the elections. The general privately decided the moment was premature, but the government publicly took the precaution of posting him to the Canary Islands.

The Popular Front considered that it had won a mandate for radicalism, and Azaña, once again prime minister, reembarked on a program of amnesty, Catalan autonomy, anticlerical laws, agrarian reform, and the confiscation of the estates of rebel generals. The republican leader's measures were considered too conservative by leftist extremists, who began to indulge in illegal land seizures, wildcat strikes, and church burnings. The right, which considered Azaña wildly radical, began actively to plan the overthrow of the government. General Sanjurjo, in exile in Portugal, was the coordinator of the plot, but the most active conspirator was General Mola, security chief in the last years of King Alfonso. The Carlists, led by Fal Conde and Prince Francis Xavier, promised tens of thousands of armed supporters, but they were so insistent on the uprising's being avowedly Carlist in its program that General Mola complained that "the Traditionalist movement is ruining Spain by its intransigence as surely as is the Popular Front." The generals had to salve the sensibilities of non-Carlist supporters such as José Antonio's Primo de Rivera Falange and Calvo Sotelo's Alfonsist party.

"The only thing that delayed the outbreak of the Civil War was that no party felt strong enough to begin it." Two assassinations provided the needed spark. The first victim was an army officer with socialist leanings who was gunned down by Falangists on July 12, 1936. In reprisal that very day, some leftists made the decision to kill a prominent rightist. Not finding Goicoechea, they invaded Calvo Sotelo's apartment and led him off to his death. The murder served to end the squabbling among the rightist factions. The Civil War began on July 17 with a pronunciamiento in Morocco, after which General Franco flew there from the Canaries in a private British plane hired by monarchist agents. Within days every Spanish city and town had to declare itself for the republic or for the rebels.

The Second Spanish Republic had failed, as King Alfonso had hoped and predicted. The Civil War he had sought to avoid in 1931 broke out five years later with a ferocious intensity which reflected the frustrations and hatreds accumulated by the extreme right and left in the intervening period. The failure of the republic was hardly a vindication of the monarchy, however. King Alfonso could take little credit for getting to the root of Spain's ills, or even trying to, while the regime that succeeded him had made noble efforts in the right directions. To the glory of the republic were its agrarian reform projects, its experiments with regional autonomy, and its efforts to establish civilian supremacy over the army. One can also ponder the telling statistic that in the two-year period 1931-1933 the republic built 10,000 schools, or almost as many as in the last two decades under the king.

3. The Civil War

The Spanish Civil War of 1936-1939 was one of the most fascinating and instructive events of our century. One of its dimensions was a classic struggle of social strata and institutions, in which, generally speaking, great landowners, big business, the church, and the regular army were arrayed against the masses of workers and peasants and the intellectuals. In this conflict of the privileged and the underprivileged the middle class was split.

A second dimension of the struggle was ideological. Spain offered the widest possible choice of political parties, with, for example, two kinds of monarchists on one side and two kinds of Communists on the other. The Rebels led by Franco, or the Nationalists as they preferred to be called, were not all fascists, as their opponents claimed, but included conservatives and clericals of many shades of opinion, the Alfonsist monarchists and the Carlists, as well as the Falange, which itself was split between radical and reactionary wings. One of Franco's major achievements was to establish his personal supremacy over the various factions within the Nationalist movement, to the distress particularly of the Carlists. The Popular Front parties supporting the republic called themselves Republicans or Loyalists, only to be unfairly lumped together and labeled Reds by their enemies, even though they included many supporters of capitalism, as well as socialists, anarchists, Trotskyites, and Stalinists. The Madrid government faced great difficulties restraining the anti-Establishment zeal of some of its supporters, and paradoxically the Stalinist Communists emerged as the postpone-the-revolution and win-the-war-first party, and as such they came to exert in the Popular Front a power out of all proportion to their numbers. A civil war within the Civil War developed on the Republican side.

A third dimension of the Civil War was geographical. Franco's supporters in the first week of the July, 1936, uprising were able to take over virtually all Andalusia and most of the northeast including Galicia, the Asturias, and Old Castile. The historic cathedral city of Burgos in the last-named province became Nationalist headquarters. Navarre was also pro-Franco, and this area soon fielded 40,000 red beret-wearing Carlist *requetés*, or militia (one-tenth of the population). The Basque provinces, however, although traditionally Carlist and ultra-Catholic, threw their lot with the republic, which offered them autonomy in government, and the Basque city of Bilbao was a major Loyalist stronghold. The republic also controlled New Castile, or at least all of it eastward from Madrid, and the Mediterranean provinces of Valencia and Catalonia. Catalan autonomy was the cause that made Spain's most industrialized region fiercely anti-Franco. While, roughly speaking, western Spain was ranged against eastern Spain in the struggle, behind-the-lines clashes took place on both sides. Workers took over downtown Toledo, for example, but its garrison in the Álcazar held out through a ten-week siege until relieved by the Nationalists.

Besides being a clash of classes, ideologies, and regions, the Spanish Civil War had an important international dimension. The aid of Mussolini's Italy and Hitler's Germany was absolutely decisive for Franco's victory. The fascist dictators provided the vital air transports which brought Franco's crack Moroccan troops over to the mainland in the first days, and they followed up with more help, including 70,000 Italian regulars, thousands of German specialists in such strategies as tank warfare and dive-bombing, and all the heavy war matériel to keep the Nationalists going. Britain, commercially tied to the Nationalist areas, and France, ideologically sympathetic to the Republicans but anxious to placate its British ally, appeased the dictator countries by arranging nonintervention agreements, but these only served to camouflage the huge supplies Franco received from his backers. The United States, isolationist and with President Roosevelt worried about the Catholic vote, joined the Western democracies in their shameful hands-off policy, with Congress passing a Neutrality Act which, without precedent, denied arms for a recognized, legal government to defend itself with. Only Soviet Russia supported the Spanish Republic in the form of major shipments of tanks and airplanes, losing some of its vessels to torpedo attacks by "pirate," meaning Italian, submarines. Some Russian technicians, including the future Marshal Georgi Zhukov, served in Spain, and a very important source of strength to the Loyalist military defense was the International Brigade, 30,000 strong, recruited from communists, sympathizers, and just plain idealists from all over the world. The Russian aid served to give the Spanish Communists an undue voice in the Popular Front government and an opportunity to take ugly vengeance on ideological adversaries such as the Trotskyites.

King Alfonso in exile was quick to endorse the Nationalist uprising, and in the months after July, 1936, he gave General Franco about $10,000,000 from his private fortune. "We all believed in Franco," wrote the now less than iconoclastic Infanta Eulalia. "We gave money till it hurt, even selling our jewels." Military buff that he was, the former sovereign followed the battles and campaigns with great interest. While he had new reason to indulge in dreams of the restoration of the Bourbon dynasty, Alfonso was also anxious about his ultimate responsibility for plunging Spain into such devastation and slaughter. Intimates of the king, who had never seen self-doubt in him before, were struck by his pensiveness, his loss of humor, and his expressed perplexions. For a man who considered himself a patriot above all, the presence of German and Italian soldiers on Spanish soil was particularly galling.

The former king did not chose to interfere actively and directly in Spanish affairs during the Civil War. For a while he continued his travels, one trip taking him as far as Aswan on the upper Nile, but as he entered into his fifties, he found less pleasure in being the royal tourist. He had ceased to be a novelty. Once he complained wistfully to the Duke of Windsor, who joined the ranks of ex-sovereigns in 1936, that he was no longer given a front-row seat at British polo matches but each year was asked to sit a little farther back. Finally, Alfonso settled down in a suite in the Grand Hotel in Rome, taking only a late summer holiday in Lausanne, where he would ceremoniously visit his estranged wife, Queen Ena. The king's favorite nightly pastime in Rome was playing bridge. The Italian government accorded him royal privileges and a tax-free status.

The ease of exile was not enough for Alfonso's designated heir, Don Juan, who impulsively joined Franco. His brother-in-law had joined the Nationalists earlier and had been killed at the front. Don Juan, after saying farewell to his mother and receiving his father's blessing by telephone from Czechoslovakia, waited just long enough for his wife to give birth to a daughter before crossing the frontier into Navarre on August 1. He was accompanied in his roadster by his cousin Don José. In Pamplona the infante became "Juan López" and changed into the uniform of a Nationalist volunteer. After visiting Burgos, he drove to the front, but while stopping at Aranda for a meal, he was detained for identification by the Civil Guard. Eventually a telephone call came through from headquarters saying that General Mola forbade Don Juan to stay in Spain. The obedient prince got back in his car amid cheers from soldiers and bystanders and returned to the French border, shouting *Viva España* as he left his country once more.

The following year Don Juan wrote to General Franco, man to man, without protocol. Carefully noting his experience in the British navy, he asked to be allowed to serve on the most important Nationalist warship, the cruiser *Baleares*. He promised not to take shore leave in Spanish ports and not to receive friends on board. Franco's reply of December 1 was politely negative, saying that someone in the infante's position would not be able to function as a simple officer. Earlier in an interview with *ABC* of Seville, the Nationalist leader had declared, "I have the highest regard for Don Juan de Borbón, for his ability, discretion, and feelings. . . . My responsibility is very great, and I have the duty not to put in danger his life, which someday could be precious to us." In a mood of conciliation not typical of him, Franco concluded that "if some time at the summit of the state we return to having a king, he should come in the character of a pacifier and should not be counted in the number of conquerors." Franco proved to be doubly wise, for on the night of March 5, 1938, the *Baleares* was sunk with almost all its crew by Republican destroyers in their most spectacular exploit of the war.

While Franco succeeded in keeping King Alfonso's heir at a cordial arm's length, he found his dealings with the Carlists more trying, for the Carlist *requetés* were a vital component of his army, an even more dedicated and ferocious group of fighters than the Falangist militia. For the Carlists the Civil War was simply the Fourth Carlist War or what they hoped would be the final round in the deep-rooted and dogged struggle of Spanish traditionalism against Spanish liberalism that dated back to 1833. The zeal of the Navarrese *requetés* was legendary. One recruit asked to name his next of kin named his father and his son, both of whom were already under arms. The skillful and determined political maneuverings of their chief civilian leader, Fal Conde, also furthered the Carlist cause.

The titular head of this rival line of the Bourbons was Don Alfonso Carlos, who even in his eighties breathed fire into his adherents on visits to their recruiting stations in southern France. The last of the direct line of his family going back to Fernando VII's brother Don Carlos, Don Alfonso Carlos died on September 28, 1936, after being knocked down by an automobile in front of his mansion in Vienna. He was buried with great pomp at Püccheim Castle, having named his nephew by marriage Francis Xavier "Regent" until such a time as Carlists could agree on a legitimate successor. While Fal Conde and the other Carlist politicians were away in Austria for the funeral, they heard with consternation that General Franco had proclaimed himself "Chief of State" in Spain.

Franco's success in making himself unrivaled head of the Nationalists was a result of both luck and skill. The most prestigious leader of the Nationalist uprising, General Sanjurjo, had been killed on July 20 in an airplane accident while still in Portugal. Sanjurjo, who had close ties with both Alfonsists and Carlists, had declared his intention of putting himself "at the orders of the Head of the Spanish State," when he regained his native soil. People alleged sabotage by the Republicans or even by Franco as the cause of Sanjurjo's fatal mishap, but more likely it occurred because the Portuguese authorities had insisted that his lightplane leave secretly from a hazardous little airstrip and the general had insisted on bringing with him two heavy suitcases full of dress uniforms.

Franco himself was magnificently cautious and evasive about revealing his feelings about the monarchy, his blueprint for the future of Spain, and his own ambitions. He was regarded as a soldier's soldier, admired for past bravery under fire, for success in training the formidable Moroccan Legion, and for unblinking severity as a disciplinarian. At age thirty-three in 1926 Franco had become the youngest general in the army, largely thanks to the personal intervention of King Alfonso XIII, who with Queen Ena were chief sponsors at Franco's wedding in 1928. Although he had not lifted a finger for the king in 1931 or 1934, Franco caused a stir during his tumultuous reception in Nationalist-captured Seville on August 15, 1936, when he stood on a balcony and kissed the monarchist flag with tears in his eyes. Yet later at his Burgos headquarters he allowed the rebel radio to play alternately the "Royal Anthem," the Carlist marching song, and the Fascist "Cara al Sol." Designating himself "Chief of State" on October 21 was essentially a coup d'état by Franco, plotted and engineered by his brother Nicholas in the manner of Lucien Bonaparte and Napoleon's 18th Brumaire. Franco's fellow generals in the Nationalist junta expected him to become merely "Chief of Government." Now Nicholas Franco stage-managed crowds shouting in unison "Fran-co, Fran-co" in the manner of the Italians' "Du-ce, Du-ce" for Mussolini, and propagandists bestowed on him the unusual Spanish term caudillo, or leader. With mutually hostile Falangists, Carlists, and Alfonsists to hold together, Franco told the German ambassador that he was proceeding with "kid gloves" toward creating a common ideology and was postponing any decision on the monarchy.

Franco's coup occurred after the Nationalists had succeeded in consolidating their pockets of control in western Spain. On November 6, 1936, they drove into the outskirts of Madrid. The Republican government evacuated the city, fleeing to Valencia, and on November 18 Germany and Italy formally recognized the Franco government, apparently expecting his triumphal entry into the capital at that time. Madrid's Republican militia, however, supported by its citizenry, put up a fierce and successful resistance, with the most desperate fighting taking place in King Alfonso's University City on the northwest. The siege of Madrid would continue for two and a half years.

Fighting shifted to the southeast, and Mussolini achieved one of the spectacular victories he craved when Málaga fell on February 8, 1937, to the Nationalists and the Italians. The Italian dictator tasted bitter defeat, however, when his troops were routed by the Loyalists at Brihuega on March 18 in a new effort to encircle Madrid. Some time between his victory and his defeat, Mussolini blithely proposed to Franco that he solve the problem of Spain's rightful monarch by bringing in the Duke of Aosta, cousin of Italy's Victor Emmanuel III. *Il Duce* was undeterred by the fate of Aosta's grandfather, King Amadeo I of Spain, who gave up the throne in 1873 after enduring two years of unrelenting animosity from Alfonsists, Carlists, and Republicans alike.

In April, 1937, Spanish Carlists were excited by the announcement of the formal candidacy of their "Regent" Francis Xavier. Carlist genealogists had faced serious soul-searching since the death of the last direct-line pretender, Alfonso Carlos. The easiest thing to do would have been to accept Alfonso XIII and his heirs in view of all their compounded Bourbon and Hapsburg lineage, but to do so would be to abandon their whole obsession about Isabel II and the necessity of uninterrupted male descent. Accordingly, they settled on the line of Bourbon-Parma, going back to Felipe V's son Felipe and descending through six generations to the thirty-eight-year-old Francis Xavier, an eminently handsome, energetic, and ambitious prince who was more than willing to mouth the most unyielding and reactionary traditionalist formulas. Francis Xavier had the further luster of being the nephew of two Carlist queens (his father's sister, Margarita of Parma, was the wife of Carlos VII; his mother's sister, María de las Nieves, the wife of Alfonso Carlos). Also, he gained a little Hapsburg cachet from his sister's being Zita, the last Empress of Austria. Maria Madelaine, Francis Xavier's wife, was of the distinguished house of Bourbon-Busset. What the new pretender lacked in contact with and knowledge of Spain he appeared to make up in illustrious royal associations.

Franco promptly upstaged Francis Xavier by forcing the Carlists to unite with the Falange in one party. Anti-Franco groups had existed within both parties, and not only plots but riots took place behind the Nationalist lines as rival factions jockeyed for power. One Falangist leader countermanded Franco's orders over the radio, only to be arrested as he swaggered into headquarters seeking to have a showdown with the "Chief of State." Taking the advice of his influential brother-in-law, Ramón Serrano Suñer, that the Nationalists should constitute a single party with a single ideology, Franco now established the Falange Española Tradicionalista with himself as head. By a supplementary decree he affiliated the Alfonsists with the new party, too. All Nationalists were now expected to wear the same uniform, which combined the Falangist blue shirt with the Carlist red beret. Unconsulted, Fal Conde and Francis Xavier protested helplessly at the Carlist's loss of identity, and the widow of Don Alfonso Carlos called the whole thing an "infamy."

Franco now felt sure enough of his power to tell *ABC* that he personally would decide when it was the right time to give Spain a king, and he went even further in a statement of July, 1937, declaring "should the moment for the restoration arrive, the new monarchy would be very different from that of 1931, different in constitution and in the person who would incarnate it." Either Don Francis Xavier or Don Juan could take some hope from such a position.

The Nationalists finally captured Bilbao on June 18, 1937, giving particular satisfaction to the Carlists who had signally failed to take this objective both in 1835 and 1874. Basque resistance collapsed, and the last Republican pocket in the northwest, Gijón, fell to Franco in October. The Loyalists in a major counteroffensive managed to capture Teruel in December, but their drive was stopped short soon after and their gains lost within a few months.

Franco's victories were accompanied by new disputes with the Carlists. When in December, 1936, the Carlists ventured to set up their own military academy, the dictator denounced the move as an attempted coup d'état, and he gave Fal Conde forty-eight hours to go into exile in Portugal, confiding to the German ambassador that he would have had the Carlist politician shot but for the effect on the morale of the *requetés*. Meanwhile, in France Don Francis Xavier denounced any of his supporters who took an oath to Franco without his permission. Then, in Debember, 1937, the pretender boldly decided to visit Spain in person. At a meeting with Franco in Burgos Francis Xavier grandly and bluntly told the general, "If it were not for the *Requetés* I very much doubt if you would be where you are." He went on to tour the battlefields, stirring up demonstrations in his favor in many places and receiving a hysterically enthusiastic reception in Seville, the largest Nationalist center. While Francis Xavier was trying to repeat his triumph in Granada, he received a peremptory order from Franco to leave Spain. In a final interview between the two, the Carlist idol scored a few more verbal points about Franco's hypocrisy regarding the monarchy and his dependence on foreigners, but his departure was duly enforced.

Franco confidently appointed his first regular cabinet on January 3, 1938, carefully including two Alfonsists, two Carlists, and two Falangists in the preponderance of nonpolitical experts. That summer he named himself

Captain General of the Army and Navy, a title hitherto a royal prerogative. The war continued to favor his Nationalist armies, who captured Vinaroz on April 15 and cut off from each other the Republican-held areas around Madrid and in Catalonia.

With complete victory for the Nationalists in sight, monarchist circles were startled in the spring of 1938 by an announcement from a strange quarter. From the United States King Alfonso's eldest son, Don Alfonso, declared his willingness to accept the Spanish throne if invited to it, in effect voiding his renunciation of five years previously. This announcement infuriated his father, who promptly and publicly disowned his son altogether, an unnecessary action, for the younger Don Alfonso's two brief marriages to Cuban women and his dissolute way of life were not likely to win him any public confidence. Then, on September 6, the miserable existence of the infante was tragically cut short after a car accident in Miami. The onetime Prince of the Asturias was returning from a night on the town in the company of a "Merry Mildred" Gaydon, variously described as a cigarette girl or an entertainer. She swerved to avoid a truck and crashed into a telephone pole. Alfonso sustained cuts and bruises and a broken leg, and his hemophilia caused him to bleed to death within hours. Miss Gaydon, who suffered minor injuries, wept uncontrollably at the funeral service and could not bear to go to the interment of her royal companion. There were only three mourners that day at Graceland Memorial Park where now exists the vault of "His Royal Highness Prince Alfonso de Borbón y Battenberg." Fresh flowers appear at the site from time to time.

Whatever sorrow King Alfonso and Queen Ena felt at the loss of their scandalous firstborn was mitigated that year by the birth of their first grandson to Don Juan. Don Juan Carlos came into the world on January 5, 1938, and was baptized in the Chapel of the Order of Malta by Eugenio Cardinal Pacelli, who within months would become Pope as Pius XII. The hopes and dreams of monarchists were further stimulated in December, when the Franco government decreed the restoration of citizenship to King Alfonso's family and the return of all their properties in Spain.

Barcelona fell to Franco on January 26, 1939, followed by the collapse of resistance in all Catalonia and the flight of 200,000 Loyalists to France. After Britain and France recognized the Franco regime on February 28, the republic's President Azaña resigned, and Loyalist generals began negotiations for the surrender of Madrid, which occurred on March 28. Franco presided at a huge victory parade and received congratulatory messages from many quarters, including wires from King Alfonso and Francis Xavier, who could do no more than put themselves at the dictator's service.

The Civil War cost Spain's population of 25,000,000 an estimated 580,000 dead. Of these, 100,000 perished on the battlefield, 10,000 were casualties of air raids, and 50,000 succumbed to disease and starvation. "Red terror" behind the Loyalist lines accounted for perhaps 20,000. The bullfighting term *paseo* was used to describe such executions committed out of class hatred. The fanaticism of the left, however, was more than matched by that of the right. The Nationalists killed 200,000 of their political opponents before 1939 and another 200,000 in the years after the war. One can only speculate if Spain's human losses would have been so great if King Alfonso had resorted to civil war in 1931. Nothing in the Bourbons' past suggests that, if victorious, the monarchy would have exacted such appalling vengeance as the Franco dictatorship.

XIII.
Franco and the Prospects of
the Monarchy

1. The Old Pretender

FOR thirty years after the end of the Civil War Spain suffered through a
murky drama under the iron dictatorship of Franco without knowing
what the nature of the succeeding act would be. The generalissimo was
chief actor as well as director, with few others allowed speaking parts. The
scenario was classic reaction, its tedium and oppressiveness occasionally
modified not so much in response to the restless mood of the Spanish
audience as in response to the complaints of foreign critics. In the wings
waited many would-be leads, onetime matinee idols as well as young
hopefuls, including three generations of Alfonsist Bourbons, some collateral
relations, and the ever-theatrical Carlists. Not until July, 1969, did Franco
name his understudy and successor.

"In sober truth it may be said that General Franco built the most
powerful and repressive regime to exist in Spain since the reign of Philip
II." The Spanish chief of state, forty-seven in 1939, consolidated his control
by taking advantage of the nation's willingness at any cost to avoid renewed
civil strife and devastation. Despite constant tensions and a few crises,
Franco showed a positive genius for balancing opposing groups, for
suppressing critics, for compromising on problems he could not face out,
and for keeping everyone guessing. With the Falange allowed a prominent,
if not predominant, role, observers were tempted to label the regime as
simply fascist, but actually Spain never was to indulge in the totalitarian
excesses of Hitler's Germany or even of Mussolini's Italy. Franco was more
in the tradition of the nineteenth-century Hispanic dictatorships, like those
of Narváez in Spain, Roxas in Argentina, or Díaz in Mexico. The

completeness and duration of his power would have been envied by even the most tyrannical of his Bourbon predecessors.

A critic of Franco has spoken ironically of his dynamics of "stepping courageously forward toward yesterday." Even before the fall of Madrid the general's government set out to dismantle and reverse all the reforms of the Second Republic of 1931 and even many of the freedoms gained under the restored monarchy of 1874. The military got back its captain generalcies, with their far-reaching powers in civil affairs. The Jesuits returned, and the church gained the most complete control of education it had wielded in a century. Catalonia lost its autonomous stature. The trade unions were crippled under the guise of a new Labor Charter. Land reform halted. The most vigorous censorship came back into being. In sum, the vested interests of Spain never enjoyed such privilege and security in modern times, especially the army and the church, to a lesser degree big business and big landowners. Madrid bureaucrats were free to carry to the ultimate the centralization at the expense of the northern and eastern regions begun by the first Bourbon, Felipe V.

However backward-looking and stifling his regime in internal affairs, Franco did spare Spain from the added burdens of continental and overseas adventurism, a course usually chosen by autocrats, old or new. Nor did he deeply involve Spain in the aggressions of the Axis dictators with whom he was associated in the Anti-Comintern Pact. In both cases, Franco's Falangist supporters would have had it otherwise. The party program spoke of Spain's "will to empire" and its destiny to have a "preeminent place in Europe," and the party press indulged in such fantasies as the recapture of Gibraltar, the annexation of Portugal, and the expansion of Spain's African territories. Propagandists recalled the Bourbon empire at its height, casting eyes even on the United States-held Philippines and on Latin America (the loss of the latter was blamed not on the reactionary Fernando VII but on Spanish liberals). Franco acknowledged these dreams but confined action in the 1940's to taking over the international zone in Tangier.

After the imposing victory parades of May, 1939, Franco obtained the rapid removal from Spain of the troops of his German and Italian benefactors. He paid Hitler occasional deference, as evidenced in the comic incident involving King Carol of Rumania and his mistress, Madame Lupescu. This playboy king had been driven from his country by pro-German fascists, and Franco ordered his detention in Barcelona. Later, while in Seville, Carol in his high-powered automobile was able to outdistance his Spanish police escort and cross the Portuguese border to freedom and luxury.

Franco proclaimed Spain's "neutrality" in World War II, which began in September, 1939, just as Alfonso XIII had done twenty-five years previously. The controlled press editorialized scornfully and indignantly against the Western democracies, pointing out, in the great truth learned under the Bourbon kings, that Britain had been Spain's greatest enemy by sea and France by land. During the collapse of France in June, 1940, Franco moved Spain a little closer to the Axis by announcing "nonbelligerency," but he did not perform a "stab in the back" (Roosevelt's words) against his northern neighbor as Mussolini did, and he candidly counseled his friend Marshal Henri Pétain, then ambassador at Madrid, not to return to France to be "sacrificed" as head of the puppet Vichy regime.

The one personal meeting between Franco and Hitler took place at Hendaye across the French frontier on October 23, 1940. The Spanish chief of state kept the *Führer* waiting on the station platform a full hour, and Hitler later said of Franco, "I would rather have three or four teeth out than meet that man again." With the date January, 1941, in mind, Hitler sought transit for a German army across Spain to capture Gibraltar and close the Mediterranean to the British. Franco evasively talked of Spain's desperate need for food supplies, of the honor of Spain's own army vis-à-vis Gibraltar, and of annexations of African territories still held by Hitler's Vichy French ally and also coveted by his Italian one. When the German threatened invasion, the Spaniard countered with reminders of 1808. Later at Bordighera on February 12, 1941, Franco met Mussolini, the Italian dictator's invasion of Greece having recently turned into a disaster. Mussolini feebly endorsed Hitler's plans for Spanish belligerency on the Axis side, until Franco put to him the question, "Duce, if you could get out of the war, would you?" Gesticulating and laughing, Mussolini replied, "You bet your life I would."

While Franco, Mussolini, and Pétain played mice to Hitler's cat, Spain's royalty in exile marked time, expectantly but timidly. However much his life-style had been identified with Paris and London, Alfonso XIII remained Mussolini's guest in Rome, and he did nothing to disassociate himself from the holocausts dictated from Berlin.

Then, on January 15, 1941, King Alfonso XIII created a stir by renouncing his rights to the Spanish throne in favor of his son Don Juan. The ex-sovereign in his mid-fifties had been suffering from angina pectoris for many months. His action, amounting to abdication, was very similar to that of his grandmother, Queen Isabel II, in 1870. Both had not ceded their rights at the time of their depositions; both felt that the monarchical principle precluded their resignation except to further the cause of their rightful heirs, in the one case Alfonso XII and in the other Don Juan. Ex-King Alfonso also recognized that his own restoration had become a practical impossibility since it "would appear a return to a politics which did not know how to avoid our tragedy." Don Juan, however, might make a fresh start, if Spain "judges it opportune," in the direction of a "more adequate organization of society and the state, and a more equitable participation of all in the general prosperity." The challenge to Franco was muted, indeed.

Within two months of his renunciation Alfonso XIII was dead, having endured extreme pain over a long period, just as his mother had. The doctor in attendance expressed great admiration for his patient's unfailing good humor, noting, however, that it concealed an underlying sadness for his country. A nun caring for the dying sovereign once importuned him, "Señor, forgive Spain." The reply was: "There is nothing to forgive, Sister, for Spain suffers and I will die." The end came on February 28, 1941, as the king lay in his plain iron bed over which hung a crucifix draped in Spain's national colors and the medal of the Virgin of Pilar, the only things decorating the walls. A bag containing earth from each of Spain's provinces was near at hand. Queen Ena was with her husband, as were his daughters and his surviving sons, Don Jaime and Don Juan, who later flanked the diminutive King Victor Emmanuel III at the funeral ceremonies in Rome.

The news of King Alfonso's death produced varied reactions in Spain. For days aristocratic callers lined up at Madrid's Ritz Hotel to sign the guest book as a sign of respect for the senior male Bourbon in residence in the country, Don Fernando of Bavaria. The Franco government proclaimed the day of the funeral a day of national mourning, and the balconies of the houses of the nobility were appropriately draped. In worker districts cruder memorial hangings appeared, perhaps because this was the only way the humble could register their desire for a change of political regime. The government did not, however, seek to have the former ruler interred in one of the two remaining vaults of the Pantheon of the Kings at the Escorial. Rather, Alfonso XIII was laid to rest in Rome in the Spanish Church of Our Lady of Montserrat under the urns of the Spanish Popes Calixtus III and Alexander VI.

As heir Don Juan extolled his father for "the generosity, the disinterestedness, and the self-effacement with which he always served Spain," referring in particular to the monarch's refusal to resort to arms in 1931 and his recent renunciation in Don Juan's favor. "Tomorrow, when Spain considers the moment opportune," he said to great applause, "I will be King of all the Spaniards." The Franco government ignored the pretensions of the man they referred to only as the "Count of Barcelona."

In June, 1941, Hitler invaded Russia, and Spain joined in to the extent of sending the so-called Blue Division. The regime encountered difficulties finding volunteers for this crusade against communism, even among Falangist stalwarts, and in the end ordered many regular army men to the Russian front. That year, on the anniversary of his pronunciamento of

1936, Franco made a speech that went the farthest in identifying Spain with the fortunes of the Axis. The democracies had already lost the war, he said and his belligerent tone continued after Pearl Harbor in December, 1941. Then the war situation changed drastically in 1942, with the Blue Division involved in the German defeat at Stalingrad. At the end of the year a huge Allied armada invaded French North Africa and stood poised at Spain's back door.

The possibility that the Allies might invade Spain provoked Don Juan from exile in Switzerland to raise his voice and to offer his "soldier's sword" if necessary for the defense of his country. In a declaration published in the *Journal de Geneva* on November 11, 1942, he reassured Franco that "I am not the chief of any conspiracy," but at the same time he averred: "I am sure the monarchy will be restored. When the Spanish people decide the moment has arrived, I will not hesitate an instant to put myself at its service." As for the political nature of a post-Franco regime, Don Juan was vague at this time. "It does not enter into my intentions to impose by my own authority the forms, the institutions destined to regulate the national life. My supreme ambition is that of being a King of a Spain in which all Spaniards, definitely reconciled, can live in common." The pretender did, however, address himself to the social question, in the manner of a Napoleon III writing on pauperism before he was elevated to power or of an Edward VIII telling Welsh coal miners "something must be done." The Spaniard declared: "A man of my times, whom adversity has permitted to observe directly the social inequalities engendered by the economic system of the nineteenth century, I will not neglect to consider all measures which could contribute to a more just distribution of wealth."

As the Axis began to collapse under the blows of the Allies, beginning with Italy's surrender in 1943, followed by the cross-Channel invasion of 1944, Franco tried to backtrack in his diplomacy as best he could, recalling the Blue Division and reaffirming Spain's strict "neutrality." After Germany's surrender in May, 1945, and Japan's in August, only one fascist dictatorship remained in the world—Spain. The postwar mood of triumphant idealism led the Western democracies to join the Soviet Union in openly condemning the Franco regime, and on December 12, 1945, by a vote of 34 to 6 with 13 abstentions the United Nations formally decided to exclude Spain from all its agencies and to recommend that all nations withdraw their chiefs of mission from Madrid.

Pablo Picasso attracted great publicity in 1945 by joining the Communist Party, Spain's foremost artist having opposed Franco vigorously ever since 1936. In the spring of that year Spanish guerrilla forces, which had fought with the French maquis against the Germans, invaded their homeland across the Pyrenees, but they were soon rounded up by the Civil Guard.

Then Spanish refugees in France and elsewhere proclaimed a republican government in exile, which Mexico recognized in August. Joining the chorus of anti-Franco voices for the first time, on March 19, 1945, Don Juan issued a manifesto calling for the dictator to accept the failure of the totalitarian regime, which was "contrary to the Spanish character and tradition," and demanding that Franco resign forthwith. Only the monarchy, he said, could "provide an effective guarantee for religion, order, and liberty." The Duke of Alba resigned as Spain's London ambassador, to prepare himself to serve a new master. Early the next year Don Juan moved from Switzerland, where his conservative past made him unpopular, to Estoril in Portugal, where he was but a few hours' distance from Madrid. While determined in his desire to replace Franco, Don Juan showed astute patriotism in March, 1946, by denouncing the pressure of the Western democracies as "absolutely intolerable" interference in Spain's internal affairs.

Don Juan's resounding challenge to Franco in the name of some sort of undefined liberalism made the world take a new look at the man who had been a quiescent pretender to the Spanish throne since 1941 and who was toasted at discreet monarchist gatherings as "Juan III" (the first two Juans were kings of Aragón in the fifteenth century). He had been born at La Granja on June 20, 1913, with the surname of Borbón y Battenberg, as the fifth child of King Alfonso XIII and Queen Victoria Eugenia. Through his mother he was Queen Victoria's great-grandson and through his paternal grandmother, María Cristina, he was a quarter Hapsburg. As a youngster, Don Juan was more unspoiled and outgoing than his sickly two older brothers. He most fondly recalled of his early years the delights of the Madrid circus and his pride at his first uniform in the hussars of Pavia. Another memory was of the efforts of a Miss Doherty to teach him languages; all the infantes spoke Spanish, English, French, and German in successive periods of the day. In imitation of his much-admired father he became a secret smoker. The happy, easygoing boy was not oblivious to his family's place in Spanish politics. Once awakened at midnight by his father when he had a fever, he cried out, "What! We are going already?"

Having reached his teens, Don Juan was able to fulfill the dream of the boy sailor at San Sebastián and won entrance to the Naval School of San Fernando, performing brilliantly during several hours of examinations held in public. Although the infante had a personal staff of five in Cádiz, he was readily accepted by his fellows and has kept up correspondence with several of his classmates to this day. The Revolution of 1931 cut short his contented days at the Naval School and forced him to sail off to Gibraltar and decades of exile.

As "the Prince John of Bourbon," the gregarious eighteen-year-old did well at the British naval academy at Sandwich, and his subsequent service carried him all over the globe on battleships and cruisers. After his brothers' renunciations of 1933, the British lieutenant found himself heir to the Spanish throne, and Don Juan then embarked on a systematic education for kingship, attending the universities of Florence, Lausanne, and Geneva (where he studied under the celebrated historian Henri Pirenne). In 1935 he married his cousin María de las Mercedes, with 10,000 Spanish monarchists on hand in Rome for the occasion. For their honeymoon the couple took a six-month world tour, leaving from Cherbourg, visiting in New York his ill-fated eldest brother, Alfonso, and his Cuban wife, and proceeding across the United States and on to the Far East. While being honored at a banquet by the Spanish colony in the Philippines, the prince displayed amused aplomb on hearing the band mistakenly strike up the revolutionary "Hymn of Riego" instead of the "Royal Anthem."

Returning to Europe, the young royalty in exile had barely settled down in the Villa San Blaise in Cannes when the Civil War broke out in Spain. Twice, in 1936 and in 1937, Don Juan tried to join the Franco forces fighting the Popular Front. France too had a Popular Front, and after insulting incidents in that country, Don Juan moved his family to Rome, where he was living at the time of his father's abdication and death in early 1941. Thereafter he moved to Switzerland to be near his mother, taking up residence in Lausanne in the Villa Roncailles, a simple two-story house with a private garage and a small garden. In the course of all these wanderings, which finally brought him to Estoril in 1946, Don Juan came into contact with all Europe's royalty, six French presidents, four popes, and Mussolini (but never Hitler). He developed a phenomenal memory for faces and people, a Bourbon trait his father shared.

Tall, muscular, broad-faced, the pretender had the facial features of his Bourbon grandfather. He looked less like his parents than any of his brothers. He had great dignity, but Don Juan impressed his supporters most for his quiet charm and sensitivity, his directness, and his simplicity.

He gave evidence of having his father's quick intelligence, and he was far better read. In Estoril he spent his mornings digesting the press and carrying on a large correspondence. Afternoons he lent his ear to a constant flow of visitors and on occasion welcomed delegations from Spain. The Franco government sometimes helped, sometimes hindered his contacts with people who were monarchist supporters or who were just curious. For the benefit of his Spanish visitors, Don Juan kept a portable altar in his house, encouraging them to join him in hearing a mass. Royal ceremonial at the villa in Estoril was maintained to a degree, with seventeen servants in the pretender's employ and gentlemen-in-waiting designated among Spaniards living in the vicinity.

Don Juan did not shun the image of the royal sportsman. He hunted when possible, complaining that the shooting would be better in Spain. In his father's footsteps, he was a frequent patron of the local golf club and occasionally joined in international tournaments. Sailing, however, was Don Juan's greatest passion, one he had acquired in the balmy 1920's in San Sebastián. Readers of picture magazines soon became familiar with the sight of a serious-looking, tanned, and informally dressed Don Juan at the helm of his sailing yacht *Giralda*, which he took to regattas throughout Europe. The pretender assured his supporters that even in midocean his yacht did not "cease to be an office for a constant and anxious meditation on Spanish affairs."

The pretender's outdoor interests were fully shared by his wife, who enjoyed playing cook on the *Giralda*. Doña María de las Mercedes de Borbón Orléans, Dos Sicilias y Orléans was otherwise the most regal of princesses with the most impressive of royal genealogies. Through her father, Don Carlos, accorded the rank of Infante of Spain, she was descended from the Neapolitan Bourbon royal house, while through her mother she was doubly a descendant of King Louis Philippe of France. The many-times-over Bourbon princess had been born in Madrid at Number 3 Paseo de la Castellana, but she spent much of her youth in Seville, first at the home of her grandmother, the Countess of Paris, and later at the Álcazar, when her father served as captain general of the region. She came to be known as a classic Andalusian beauty—dark-haired, bright-eyed, and voluptuous. A frequent playmate of the royal infantas and infantes, including Don Juan, just two years her elder, Doña María earned from King Alfonso XIII the title Doña María la Brava—for her lively daring at hide-and-seek. Yet so unassuming was she as a young girl that while a student at Madrid's College of the Irish Mothers she demurred playing the role of princess in a production of *Snow White. Sic transit* royalty.

Doña María and her family were in Palermo for a relative's wedding at the time of the overthrow of the Spanish monarchy in April, 1931, and she next saw her husband-to-be in Paris. There she studied at the Louvre, becoming an adept at painting miniatures. After her marriage to Don Juan, she settled into the role of mother, giving birth to two sons and two daughters. At Estoril in the 1940's Doña María took part in some charitable work but gave few audiences. The family lived in the spacious Villa Giralda, once a golf club, and the mistress of the house developed a special interest in the gardens. Generally, Doña María chose to remain in the background, a benign female presence in the traditional Spanish manner.

Tradition was the main thing Don Juan offered to Spain as an alternative to Franco in the years after 1945. He scoffed at Franco's rigid censorship, the excessive controls over trade unions, and the single party system as un-Spanish. At the same time he believed that a strong monarchy would avoid the excesses of the republic, "the synonym of chaos and unruliness" and "the political formula of anarchy," the words of the Count of Rodezno, the Carlist leader whom Don Juan had the satisfaction of welcoming to his cause in 1946. Don Juan was chary in defining his exact position, resorting to such equivocal statements as: "It is necessary to continue our history and not to pursue the impossible enterprise of stopping it, reviving some determinate moment of it, be it the year 1876 or the absolutism of the eighteenth century." He did not want to offend the Carlists by appearing too constitution-minded, and, without repudiating his father, he sought to disassociate himself from the monarchical system that led to 1931. Yet his main message was that a traditional monarchy would be progressive and liberal, above all concerned with social justice.

One political position of Don Juan was embodied in the very title he styled himself with, that of Count of Barcelona. This bow to Catalan sensibilities was in effect a repudiation of the suicidal antiregionalist politics of his father's regime. The Castilian-educated prince made a point of showing his ability to speak Catalan, a language remarkable for the frequency of the letter x.

Franco survived the condemnation of Spain in the United Nations. His regime survived the postwar economic crisis which kept Spain the poorest of the poor, even compared to the war-devastated countries of Europe (Spain received no benefits from the Marshall Plan). He survived the blandishments of the Count of Barcelona, and he ignored a petition of 450 generals and prominent citizens to restore the monarchy. The dictator did, however, declare himself a monarchist in principle on February 20, 1946, and the next year he formally made Spain a kingdom without a king. A handpicked Cortes ratified a Law of Sucession on April 1, 1947, which provided that Franco's successor as chief of state would be a "person of royal blood who shall be chosen by the combined Council of the Kingdom and Government and accepted by two thirds of the Cortes." The monarch-to-be had to be male, Spanish, Catholic, over thirty, and under oath to observe the "fundamental laws" of Spain. Aside from committing the future sovereign to the Falange-dominated state, the new law in essence made the monarchy elective. From Portugal Don Juan protested vigorously that Franco was tampering with the principle of legitimacy, and he advocated a boycott of the national referendum called to approve Franco's new dispensation. It was a futile gesture, for on July 6 the regime announced that 14,000,000 citizens had voted aye, 1,000,000 nay. That year Franco revived titles of nobility, arrogating to himself the royal right to create new grandees.

As the dreary 1940's were succeeded by the equally dreary 1950's in

Spain, Don Juan continued to confine himself to protests, manifestos, and a life of leisure. The pretender and his wife several times went big-game hunting, and the walls of the Villa Giralda became laden with trophies from Kenya and Angola. The sailor prince continued his yachting. On occasion storms forced him to put into Spanish ports, to the embarrassment of the local police, who feared popular demonstrations, but Don Juan was too gentlemanly to encourage any. The Franco government was gentlemanly also, allowing the Countess of Barcelona to come to Seville in 1949 for the funeral of her father, the Infante Carlos.

In 1958 Don Juan sailed across the Atlantic and back, following the route taken by Columbus. For the 6,000-mile voyage he forsook the *Giralda* for the 54-ton 90-foot *Saltillo*, and he had a British admiral, a Spanish duke, and a marquis among the crew, although, to her chagrin, Doña María was left behind. After making a landfall at Puerto Rico, Don Juan proceeded up the coast of the United States and then transferred from his own ship to a Coast Guard cutter so that he could be on hand to meet his son Don Juan Carlos, who was visiting this country as a cadet on the Spanish naval training ship *Juan Sebastián El Cano*. The meeting of the father and son at the Spanish embassy in Washington brought to people's attention a major new turn of affairs for the Bourbons and Spain—that Don Juan Carlos was being groomed as Franco's successor.

An amusing incident occurred during the young cadet's subsequent visit to New York City. Touring the Metropolitan Museum, surrounded by many officials and photographers, Don Juan Carlos was accosted by a young boy, who asked his name and, on being told, exclaimed, "Wow, a Prince rates everything!" (he then presented the royal visitor with his baseball and made his brother give him his mitt).

2. The Young Pretender

Those familiar with English history know of the Stuart pretenders, Old and Young. Just as James II was driven from England in 1688 without abdicating, so was Alfonso XIII from Spain in 1931. Both died thereafter in exile, both in Rome by coincidence, the one in 1701, the other in 1941. The Stuart claim was taken up by the "Old Pretender," James Edward, who on occasion enjoyed the hospitality of Felipe V of Spain and encouraged the futile efforts of Giulio Cardinal Alberoni to overthrow the Hanoverians in his favor. His son Charles Edward, who helped Carlos III of Spain win the throne of Naples, was famous as "Bonnie Prince Charlie" and the leader of the 1745 rising in Scotland in his father's name. James Edward died in 1761, after which the Young Pretender claimed the English throne in his own right. Don Juan was Spain's James Edward, and Don Juan Carlos Spain's Charles Edward, but with the great difference that Spain's Young Pretender allowed himself to be declared successor to the throne while the Old Pretender was still living, thus compromising the principle of legitimacy, doctrinally most dear to monarchists, whether Stuart or Bourbon.

Don Juan and Doña María had four children, the Infanta Pilar (born 1936), the Infante Don Juan Carlos (born 1938), the Infanta Margarita (born 1939), and the Infante Alfonso (born 1941). The family had its share of promise and tragedy, such as the previous generation of Bourbons had known. Hemophilia, however, was not a factor since the father was not a victim of it, nor the mother a carrier. Nor were there clear signs of dynastic inbreeding, although the children were descendants of Felipe V through five of their eight grandparents (Hanover, Battenberg, and Hapsburg account for the remaining three non-Bourbon grandparents).

The eldest daughter, Pilar, was perfectly healthy. The only disadvantage she had to overcome was a painful shyness as a young girl. In time she became outgoing as well as beautiful. Her coming-out party on October 15, 1954, was the occasion for a gala fiesta at the Villa Giralda attended by 2,000 Spaniards who had crossed the border despite bureaucratic difficulties put in their way by Madrid. In Estoril Pilar was seriously involved in nursing at the Hospital de los Capuchos and relaxed by hunting and moviegoing. She did not marry until she was over thirty, her husband being a Spanish noble and lawyer. Currently living in a Madrid villa the "Dukes of Badajoz" have two sons and two daughters.

The second daughter, Margarita, was born partially blind. Nonetheless, she grew up to be merry, communicative, and of exceptional intelligence, as evidenced by her command of nine languages. She is also a devoted pianist. Like her sister, she lived with her parents into her thirties, eventually marrying a Madrid heart specialist in October, 1972.

The younger son of Don Juan was called Alfonso after his grandfather, whom he came to resemble in many ways, even looking like the profiles of the boy king at various ages as commemorated on stamps and coins. Alfonso had his grandfather's incandescent brilliance and ready humor, with none of the reserve of his father and brother. He was the mischievous one as a boy (he threw paper gliders at his sister's coming out) and the pal of fishermen and taxi drivers. Then at age sixteen he killed himself accidentally: on March 29, 1956, having returned home from his first communion, he was handling a semi-toy pistol his father had given him and shot himself between the eyes with a pellet, dying instantly from the wound. This tragedy occurred on the very eve of Don Alfonso's departure for Spain to enter the same naval academy his father had attended.

The family's pride and hope, Don Juan Carlos, had been very close to his younger brother. Serious and responsible, he had warned Alfonso about playing with the gun and was an unhappy witness to the accident. At the time he was on holiday from the military academy of Saragossa, the same school where Franco had been director in the 1920's.

The decision to have Don Juan Carlos educated in Spain resulted from a face-to-face meeting between his father and Franco on August 25, 1948. Accompanied by his older brother Don Jaime, the pretender came aboard the dictator's yacht *Azor* off the Spanish coast near San Sebastián. The encounter was cordial, Franco addressing Don Juan as "Your Highness" but all the while refusing him any political recognition. Don Juan's advisers felt that such a meeting would compromise his position as claimant to the throne, but the pretender was preoccupied by a concern that his sons grow up without knowing Spain. As a result of his father's talks with Franco, Don Juan Carlos, aged ten, took the train to Madrid in October, 1948, and enrolled without fanfare at a Madrid preparatory school. In June, 1954, he successfully took the examination for the Institute of San Isidro, going afterward to El Pardo Palace to give thanks to Franco and receive his congratulations.

A second meeting between Don Juan and Franco now ensued, this time on Spanish soil, which the pretender had not been on for eighteen years. They conferred on December 29, 1954, at Las Cabezas, the *finca* of the Count of Ruiseñada near Almaraz. Again, the subject was Juan Carlos' schooling. The father expressed his preference that some of his heir's education be at a non-Spanish university, but Franco insisted that Juan Carlos attend the three academies of Spain's armed forces and then the University of Madrid over a period of six years. In return, Franco conceded that thereafter Juan Carlos would be "surrounded with the special attentions appropriate to his rank," according to the words of the terse communiqué. During the succeeding years the student infante received princely honors in public and considerable attention in the press. He swore to the colors on December 15, 1955.

Meanwhile, Franco's position had been greatly strengthened since the immediate postwar period. In October, 1950, the United Nations had rescinded its anti-Spanish resolution by a vote of 37 to 9 with 12 abstentions, the following year the United States, Britain, and others resumed sending ambassadors, and then, most important, in September, 1953, the United States pledged to Spain substantial financial aid in return for the right to establish military bases in the country.

The monarchists mollified and the republicans quiescent, opposition to Franco's policies now erupted from a strange quarter, the Falange. Even back in 1951, when Don Juan had attended the coronation of Queen Elizabeth II in the capacity of her cousin and the government had allowed several thousand Spaniards to join in the royal celebrations, the Falangists raised voices of anti-aristocratic protest. Following his second meeting with Don Juan, Franco felt impelled to set up an interview with the editor of the Falangist *Arriba* to remind people of the logic of the Referendum of 1947 concerning the monarchy. The Falangists were not reassured, and in February, 1955, their student union took to the streets with leaflets accusing the first several Bourbon monarchs of monstrous actions and the last king of even more crimes than his predecessors. In a second interview with the editor of *Arriba* Franco once again promised the Falange that there would be no return to parliamentarianism under a future monarchy, but he found many good things to say about Alfonso XIII, the king he had sworn allegiance to and had served as gentleman of the bedchamber. Soon after he led the government and diplomatic corps at a solemn requiem mass in the Escorial to honor all of Spain's past royalty. The regime made its position even more clear in a statement to the Cortes on July, 1957: "When the Generalisimo is not with us, the destinies of Spain will be directed by a Monarchy, which will be neither Liberal nor Absolute, but a Traditional Representative, and Catholic monarchy."

For his part Don Juan did not accept an indefinite future, and he was not satisfied that his son was being schooled as a possible successor to Franco. He moved to broaden his own basis of support by receiving a delegation of forty-five traditionalists at Estoril on December 20, 1957. His guests, who offered their allegiance, included a descendant of the Carlist hero Zumala-cárregui, the 1930's parliamentarian Rodezno, and the late Carlos VII's secretary Melgar. In a formal speech to them the pretender praised the "miraculous" persistence of Carlist faith in God, King, and Fatherland in the nineteenth century; he denied the "black legend" that traditionalism was "something antiquated and reactionary"; and he quoted an obscure 1896 declaration of Carlos VII regarding "social justice." Don Juan avowed that the "anonymous mass of the Spanish people" supported him, adding that "I aspire to be a human king, in contact with my people and not a symbolic mummy kept behind the curtains of court protocol." The following year he attended his first mass meeting of monarchists, mostly Carlists, at Lourdes, and his reception was so warm that he was forced to caution his audience that the restored monarchy under him would not solve all problems as if by magic. One Carlist leader enthused that Don Juan was Carlos VII "without the beard." At still another reception for Carlists at Estoril in 1961 Don Juan underlined his distinctiveness from Franco by calling for a "state structure equally distant from dictatorial totalitarianism and from dangerously weak political formulas."

The endorsement of Don Juan proved to be confined to only a portion of the Carlist movement. To others the idea of a "human king" was repugnant to their divine right ways of thinking, and "social justice" did not appeal to them either. Don Juan for all his Bourbon credentials was still in their eyes a claimant through the woman Isabel II and through the possibly illegitimate Alfonso XII, as well as being the son of the renegade Alfonso XIII and a man who had served in the navy of hated Great Britain. Unfortunately for their cause, the unrelenting Carlists could not agree on a suitable candidate of their own. Some invoked a strange "semi-Salic law" and favored a son of Carlos VII's eldest daughter Bianca. Others championed the Neapolitan line. The most vociferous Carlists supported Don Francis Xavier, the claimant who had given Franco difficulties during the Civil War. In Francis Xavier's son, the twenty-nine-year-old Hugo Carlos, they had a personable, active, and eloquent leader. Led by Hugo Carlos and two of his many sisters these Carlists staged a massive rally in May, 1959, at Montejura, the mountain battle site of hallowed memory from the First Carlist War of more than a century before. Forty thousand red berets looked on with excitement restrained only by piety as their idol made fourteen stations of the cross. All he would have needed were a white horse and halberdiers to evoke the past completely.

Franco at this time did not stop the Carlist manifestations, using them as a counter in his dealings with the Alfonsist Bourbons. He had a third meeting with Don Juan on March 29, 1960, again at Las Cabezas and amid "great cordiality." They agreed that Don Juan Carlos would continue his studies at the University of Madrid "owing to pedagogical reasons and national feeling." As a sop to Don Juan, the communiqué stated that Juan Carlos' prolonged stay in Spain "does not prejudge the succession question or the normal transmission of dynastic obligations and responsibilities."

The long, polite, but determined duel between the Old Pretender and the dictator was founded on mutual distrust. Franco associated Don Juan with some sort of fuzzy liberalism, and accordingly he sought to make sure that Spain would be spared not only the rule of the father but also the transmission of the father's ideas to the son. For his part, Don Juan feared that Franco was seeking to indoctrinate Juan Carlos with Falangist principles, to say nothing of disloyalty to the principle of legitimacy.

At age twenty-one, Juan Carlos had finished the three academies and on December 12, 1959, was accorded the rank of lieutenant in the army and air force and that of ensign in the navy (on the same day he received the rank of honorary lieutenant of the "Red Devils," or 491st U.S. Air Squadron, and also a miraculous image of the Virgin of Pilar). No one would expect that the military part of his education had been anything but provincial and mechanical. Thereafter he took graduate courses in law, political science, history, and economics. No biographer has ever claimed for him that he showed any brilliance in his studies, just conscientiousness. As for indoctrination, the prince had been little exposed to Falangist thinkers but much influenced by scholars associated with Opus Dei, a Catholic organization which attracted increasing attention in the 1950's. Opus Dei, obviously cleric-minded, was also technocratic in its outlook—that is, more concerned with economic progress than political liberty. Its managerial experts came to dominate cabinets under Franco, who was persuaded also to choose Juan Carlos' chief tutors from this group.

After completion of his studies at the university, Juan Carlos became an observer of but not a participant in the regime. The dictator said that the prince had been "placed beside me to see how government works," but in truth Juan Carlos engaged in the existence of a young-man-about-town—bachelor parties, society dances, a variety of sports including wrestling, collecting jazz records, and zooming about in fancy cars, much in the manner of his grandfather, whom the stolid, well-meaning prince little resembled otherwise. The new-generation Bourbon became an active civil pilot in both planes and helicopters.

Juan Carlos was a distinctively attractive as well as eligible young man. With wavy blond hair, a broad face, serious eyes, and a set chin, he reminded people of his grandmother Queen Ena. At six feet three he was as tall as his father, although more slender and muscular. Besides being a yachtsman and equestrian, Juan Carlos prided himself on his status as a second-class black-belt karate adept.

Both society columnists and political observers took notice when Juan Carlos married Princess Sofia of Greece on May 14, 1962. The betrothal of their eldest daughter had been announced the previous September by King Paul and Queen Frederika, the latter being credited by some commentators with overweening ambition for her Danish-German dynasty. Whether a coup for the queen or not, the match was a romantic one, Juan Carlos having pursued his courtship of Sofia in Athens and elsewhere for many months. The Spanish and Greek royal families developed the most cordial relations during the exchange of several visits, including one in Switzerland, where Queen Ena gave her blessing to her grandson's marriage. The engaged couple also called on their British relatives in Buckingham Palace. Franco registered his benevolent approval by dispatching a high minister and a Spanish warship to the wedding in Athens, having previously invested the Bourbon prince with the Grand Cross of Carlos III, an honor usually accorded by a reigning sovereign to a reigning sovereign.

In the spirit of ecumenism Pope and Patriarch authorized the couple to be wed in successive Catholic and Orthodox ceremonies. Athens' Roman Cathedral was decorated with 45,000 red and yellow carnations. Under sparkling skies Princess Sofia and her father drove from the royal palace in a carriage drawn by six white horses, with the future King Constantine escorting his sister on horseback. A guard of honor of sailors from the cruiser *Canarias* saluted them at the door of the cathedral, and then an orchestra struck up Handel's "Halleluljah Chorus." Don Juan received his bride dressed in his simple lieutenant's uniform which glittered with the orders of the Golden Fleece and Carlos III. The guests included the roster of reigning and dethroned royalty. Queen Ena and her daughter Cristina attended, and of course, the groom's parents were there, Don Juan having sailed to the Greek capital on the *Saltillo*. Also present were King Olaf of Norway, Queen Juliana of the Netherlands, ex-King Humberto II of Italy, ex-King Michael of Rumania, the Prince of Liechtenstein, Prince Rainier of Monaco with Princess Grace, the Grand Duke of Luxembourg, and Princess Alexandra of Kent. In the ensuing ceremony at the Orthodox Basilica the wedding couple had crowns held over their heads in the traditional manner and were showered with rose petals.

The extravagant wedding gifts received by Don Juan and Doña Sofia included a diamond brooch from Franco, the villa where Sofia was born from her parents, precious jewels from the Counts of Barcelona, a fabulous ruby from Queen Ena, sapphires from the Queen of Belgium, a Persian tapestry from the Shah of Iran, a clock from Switzerland, Sèvres china from President Charles de Gaulle, a yacht from the Prince of Monaco, porcelain from Chiang Kai-shek, a chest of jade and gold from the Duke of Alba, furs from Onassis, paintings from thirty-six Spanish artists, and a large sum of money subscribed by Spanish monarchists. The royal couple spent a honeymoon aboard the yacht *Eros*, sailing to Corfu, afterward being received by Pope John XXIII, having a formal dinner with Franco, and making a world tour by plane via the United States.

Juan Carlos and Sofia subsequently settled in the Zarzuela Palace, a small but elegant red brick chateau in the vast royal park west of Madrid. Their abode, as if symbolically, lay halfway between Franco's residence at El Pardo and the Oriente Palace. Madrileños began to accustom themselves to the sight of the attractive young couple at benefits and social occasions. Blond like her husband, the effervescent, ever-smiling Greek princess made an appealing contrast with the sober Juan Carlos. As the eldest daughter of King Paul and Queen Frederika, her full title to Spanish genealogists was Doña Sofia de Schleswig-Holstein-Sonderborg Glücksburg y Brunswick-Lüneburg, but her sobriquet in some of the Athens press had been the "People's Princess" in tribute to her democratic sociability, particularly in evidence during the three years she had spent in child-care nursing in an Athens hospital. Don Juan Carlos' wife was broadly educated and could claim special distinction as the author of a book on archaeological discoveries she had made.

Another Bourbon wedding attracted notoriety a short time after Don

Juan Carlos', that of his cousin and Carlist rival, Hugo Carlos, to Princess Irene of the Netherlands, the twenty-four-year-old second daughter of Queen Juliana and Prince Bernhard. Noisy demonstrations took place in Dutch cities over the prospect of their liberally educated Protestant princess marrying the scion of Bourbon-Parma, a Catholic, the junior leader of an obscurantist ideology, and a gadfly vis-à-vis a government with which the Netherlands had correct relations. Princess Irene was stubborn in her romantic desires, and the Dutch royal family acceded to her wishes. After her conversion at the hands of a Dutch cardinal, the wedding occurred on April 29, 1964, not in the Netherlands but at Santa Maria Maggiore in Rome. Fanatical Carlists turned the celebration into a political manifestation.

The Franco government was unimpressed with Hugo Carlos' pretensions and ignored his marriage. Once again the following May the red berets gathered for their annual rally at Montejura, this time in the number of 70,000 enthusiasts. Hugo Carlos was "advised" not to attend by the authorities and did not appear, but one of his chief supporters used the occasion to make a bitter and emotional denunciation of the regime for favoring the wrong monarchical claimant and party. The following year when Princess Irene came to represent her husband at the Montejura reunion, she was received with ecstatic excitement and approval. Yet the Carlists were beginning to sense in their hearts that theirs was "the most lost of lost causes."

If there was a chance for a Carlist to be put on the Spanish throne or for anyone other than Don Juan Carlos to be, the chance lay in the fact that the law of 1947 provided for election of the king by the Cortes. This consideration brought a new candidate into the field in 1964. In Paris Don Jaime, Alfonso XIII's second son and elder brother to Don Juan, repudiated his thirty-year-old renunciation of the throne as forced from him by his father. A tall, thoroughly regal figure, but virtually a deaf-mute, Don Jaime bore Felipe V's title of Duke of Anjou (since 1941) and considered himself head of the house of Spanish Bourbons and also of the French. Twice married morganatically, he was nearly sixty. He had a talented and attractive son, Don Alfonso-Jaime (born in Rome on April 20, 1936), who could argue for himself good hereditary claims to the throne on the grounds that a royal father could not renounce the rights of his children. The Falange press made something of a fuss over Don Alfonso, contrasting the hardworking position he had in a Madrid business with the gilded existence of Don Juan Carlos in the Zarzuela. Styled Duke of Burgundy and later Duke of Cádiz, Don Alfonso had studied law and political science in Italy, Switzerland, and Spain and had attained the rank of aviation lieutenant. His brother, Don Gonzalo, was a year younger.

Neither his own son's place in the limelight nor the pretensions of his elder brother and nephew deterred Don Juan from persisting in his claim to the throne. Thus, in September, 1964, when waited on by a delegation from Cádiz, the Old Pretender saw fit to declare, "I do not and I do not want to represent a doctrine or system. I represent the logic and the minimum simplicity whereby . . . the future of Spain will resolve itself in peace."

Still another generation of Spanish Bourbons came into being with the birth of the Infante Felipe to Don Juan Carlos and Doña Sofia on January 30, 1968. The christening of the child on February 7 was the occasion for an extraordinary assemblage of the dynasty in Madrid. The most honored guest was Queen Ena, eighty years old, a white-haired but spry matriarch, who had been living in Lausanne most of the years since her rude ouster from Spain in 1931—an event for which *ABC* now apologized, as well as for her near assassination at her wedding in 1906. The ex-queen readily put aside bitter memories, and when her plane arrived over Spanish soil, she toasted her adopted country in champagne. Touring Madrid, she recalled that the city had only one first-class hotel in 1906, and she made a special point of visiting her Red Cross hospital. Although Ena's visit was supposed to be a private one, crowds gathered everywhere in the rain and cold, and thousands of people sent flowers or signed the register at the Palace of Liria where she stayed. At the actual baptism ceremonies the great-grandmother carried in the child and held him thereafter. Present were Franco, his ministers and generals, Don Juan and Doña María de las Mercedes, Don Juan Carlos and Doña Sofia, the infantes Pilar and Margarita, Queen Frederika, and various other royal figures such as ex-King Simeon II of Bulgaria (who had attended Valley Forge Military Academy before marrying a Madrileña). Queen Ena's departure from Madrid's Baracas airport on February 11 saw another emotional gathering of Spaniards, who sensed that the visit had been a last one. Her son and grandson solicitously saw their grande dame into the plane.

Queen Ena resumed her retirement in Lausanne, where she lived at the villa Vieille Fontaine, white-walled like a Seville house, with golden fleur-de-lis on the gates and a host of Spanish mementos inside. She personally answered a large correspondence in English, Spanish, and other languages. Occasionally she was seen walking her basset hounds by the lakeside. She died on April 15, 1969, of a hepatitis infection and was buried in the Bois de Vaux cemetery of the Swiss city.

Within a year of the birth of his heir, Don Juan Carlos made a difficult decision regarding the future of the Spanish monarchy, and then Franco himself at last announced his definite choice. Obviously something was in the air when the newspapers published a long interview with Don Juan Carlos held on January 7, 1969, by the head of the official news agency *El*

Cifra. The meeting took place in the office at the Zarzuela, described as book-lined and somewhat disorderly because of the host's collecting manias. The questioner revealed the prince to be effusively cordial, excessively modest, and a "good man" concerned only with service to all, not ambition or intrigue. In reply to an opening question on whether the monarchy was an anachronism, Juan Carlos replied that institutions were not antique or modern, just efficient or inefficient. The crucial statement came later when he said he would fulfill his earlier soldier's oath by serving "in the post that would be most useful to the country, even though this could cost me sacrifices." Observers had previously been convinced that Juan Carlos would never usurp his father's rights in his lifetime, but now, in effect, he declared his willingness to accept the throne if offered to him. As for the question of legitimacy, he equivocated, saying, "I believe in our epoch it is better to speak of duties rather than rights." He called on "monarchist circles" also "to make sacrifices," at the same time dismissing them as a legalistic minority whose very existence was abnormal.

Predictably, the Old Pretender was furious at the action of the Young. The father reportedly refused to speak to the son when the latter called to break the news of the interview. Later Madrid newspapers published a strong letter from Don Juan in which he said that Juan Carlos was the victim of political intrigues in Madrid and that his failure to respect strictly hereditary succession would deprive the monarchy of all sanctity and effectiveness. The son stuck to his guns. Torn between filial loyalty and other considerations, perhaps ambition or perhaps a wider sense of responsibility to the Bourbon dynasty, Juan Carlos was counseled by his advisers to avoid indecisiveness. He was now thirty-one, or one year past the age of eligibility under the 1947 law, and Franco was only four years away from his eightieth birthday.

Franco had already moved to eliminate Juan Carlos' Carlist rivals from consideration. In mid-December, 1968, Don Hugo Carlos had been expelled from the country on grounds that he was engaging in political activities, illegal for foreigners in Spain. The Bourbon-Parmas were technically French citizens. A week later his father Francis Xavier was ordered to depart in twenty-four hours without any explanation being given. In retrospect, although Franco may have deliberately used the presence of the Carlist claimants as a counterfoil to the Alfonsists, he never gave them any real recognition. The Carlists' uncompromising ideology probably grated on the opportunistic generalissimo, and their appeal to Basque and Catalan regionalism offended his Spanish patriotism.

The question of his successor, which had been so dramatically raised at the beginning of 1969, was allowed by Franco to drop during the spring, and then on July 22 at a special meeting of the Cortes the dictator caught everyone by surprise by nominating Don Juan Carlos to be chief of state "in due course" when the post "became vacant." In his speech Franco noted that Juan Carlos "had given clear proofs of his loyalty to the principles and institutions of the Regime." He underlined the limitations being put on his successor by speaking of the coming "Monarchy of the National Movement," a monarchy that owed nothing to the past except the July 18 uprising. Instead of the "restoration" of the monarchy, Franco spoke of its forthcoming "installation." The Cortes approved Franco's decision by a vote of 491 to 19.

The following morning in the Zarzuela a white-uniformed Don Juan Carlos signed an act of acceptance, and in the afternoon, wearing a khaki uniform, he knelt before the deputies with a Bible in his hand and with Franco at his side to swear his loyalty to his benefactor and his regime. In his acceptance speech the prince averred: "I belong by direct line to the Royal House of Spain and in my family, by the designs of Providence, has been united the two branches." He did not offend any of his listeners by declaring, "I wish for our people progress, development, unity, justice, liberty, and grandeur." The only independent note was the clause "The cult of the past should not be a brake on the evolution of a society that is transforming itself with dizzying rapidity." The prince's speech was interrupted by cries of "Franco, Franco" from some of the deputies. There were no crowds outside the Cortes for the occasion.

From Portugal Don Juan issued the expected statement of protest, which was not published in Spain. What did surprise legitimists was the subsequent lapse of the Old Pretender into dignified silence and his authorization of the disbanding of his unofficial organization in Spain, consisting of a secretariat of sixteen members and a privy council of eighty-seven members, which had been strategically scattered all over the country. Don Juan soon afterward left on his yacht for an extended voyage in the Mediterranean, apparently unwilling to hurt his son by encouraging monarchist wranglings. He did not abdicate, however.

3. Past, Present, and Future

Since 1969 Don Juan Carlos has been at Franco's elbow on every ceremonial occasion, a somber-faced, stiff-postured figure who towers over the imperturbable, pudgy generalissimo. The protégé's new and unprecedented title *Principe de España* (rather than the traditional *Principe de las Asturias*) is a constant reminder to people that he is destined to become chief of state, but he does not yet exercise any power whatsoever (in 1969 he also became an honorary general and admiral). He will sit on the throne only if he continues to be docile, for Franco has left himself alternatives, and his scope of action when king will be rigidly circumscribed, for Franco has carefully institutionalized his present regime. As for the more remote future, no one can say if Spain will long tolerate a monarchy in the image of Franco, or a liberal monarchy, or, indeed, any kind of monarchy at all.

For years Franco himself has played king, to the annoyance of traditionalists. He follows the custom of the Bourbons by beginning each year with a resplendent reception in the Oriente Palace. The occasion is the Feast of the Epiphany on January 6, and Franco presides from a dais in the throne room as the leading Spanish dignitaries and the diplomatic corps file past him. Unlike the late Alfonso XIII, Franco does not seek to mingle with his guests. Rather he appears to be even more etiquette-conscious than royalty, once ordering the Duke of Alba from his presence because he was wearing street clothes. Another regally staged yearly function is a garden party at La Granja on July 18, the anniversary of the Nationalist Uprising. Here the guests are entertained amid the sculptured fountains of the "Little Versailles" of Felipe V. The most distinguished guests at the summer 1971 reception, which began at 7 P.M., were Vice President Spiro Agnew, wearing a cutaway and striped pants, and Mrs. Agnew, wearing a longish dark print dress and a small black hat. The American leader was passing through Spain after a global tour of dictatorial countries. Franco was also host to President Eisenhower in 1959 and to President Nixon in 1970.

For most of the year the Spanish dictator lives in relative seclusion at El Pardo Palace to the northwest of Madrid, where he imitates his royal predecessors in his avid pursuit of hunting. Not long ago he injured his hand in a shooting accident, causing a flurry of speculation about nonexistent palace intrigues.

Doña Carmen Polo de Franco also cuts an imposing figure and is frequently pictured in the press. Madrid gossips claim Franco's wife has dynastic family pretensions, and they also whisper about her using her position to promote various financial interests, notably in Madrid department stores and antiques shops. If the charges of financial speculation are true, Mrs. Franco is merely acting in the grand royal tradition of the Queen Regent Cristina a century before.

Franco reported an income of $31,000 in 1971, the first year the Spanish government decided to reveal the financial status of the 300,000 citizens who paid income taxes. (Spain collects about half the amount of taxes in proportion to national income as neighboring countries.) The Duke of Alba, the country's greatest landowner, admitted to $236,000, a leading banker $371,000, while Prince Juan Carlos put down a modest $8,000.

Across the park from El Pardo, the Zarzuela establishment of Don Juan Carlos and Doña Sofía would be described as more homey than majestic. In the 1960's the chintz-decorated rooms seemed entirely devoted to the activities of the three royal children, Princess Elena María Isabel (born December 20, 1963), Princess Cristina Frederica Victoria (born June 13, 1965), and Prince Felipe Juan Pablo (born January 1, 1968). At first the staff was small and visitors few, but since 1969 a parking lot and a suite of offices have been added. The prince has to go to a nearby private gymnasium for his exercises, which he does for an hour each day at 7:30 A.M. The rest of his mornings are spent with officials giving him briefings, and then Juan Carlos may take a helicopter to downtown Madrid to make the round of governmental departments. He and his wife frequently ride horseback late in the afternoon. For their summer recreation the royal couple acquired in 1973 the Palacio de Marivent in Palma de Majorca, a gift from the provincial deputation of the Balearic Islands. Don Juan specializes in sailing Dragon-class boats and was on the 1972 Olympic team. He is the first Bourbon to eschew hunting as a diversion, preferring the image of conservationist.

Never an issue of the royalty-loving picture magazine ¡*Hola!* goes by without photographic coverage of the public activities of *Los Príncipes de España*. They have relieved Franco of many of his ceremonial obligations (and surely the dictator must be gratified, to give a recent example, to let Juan Carlos be the one to receive a delegation of American Baptists led by "Dub" Jackson, who gave the prince a ten-gallon hat and cowboy boots before making him an honorary citizen of Texas). The serene, ever fresh-looking Doña Sofía seems to be present at every charity function, while her husband, a man without a job in a sense, appears to be endlessly busy inspecting factories, shipyards, schools, and public works. Like Prince Philip of Britain, he always gives the impression of being earnest and informed about technical processes, a man perhaps more interested in things than people. On their visitations around the country the royal couple make a point of shunning formal presentations and honorary banquets.

Besides putting themselves on view in every corner of Spain, Don Juan Carlos and his wife have represented their country on foreign tours which have taken them as far away as Teheran, Tokyo, and Addis Ababa. They made a five-day goodwill visit to the United States in January, 1971, receiving a nineteen-gun salute on arrival and full-scale ceremonial treatment thereafter, all in contrast with three earlier visits when Juan Carlos was merely the son of the pretender to the Spanish throne. The princes of Spain exchanged gifts with the Nixons, a Spanish galleon in silver for an American eagle in gold, and attended a state dinner at the White House, at which time they were hailed by Secretary of State William Rogers as the "future generation of Spain." The thirty-three-year-old Juan Carlos, who can speak fluent English, formally replied in Spanish, reminding his listeners of the contribution made by his ancestor Carlos III to American independence. When he spoke of the "even greater social well-being and political advance" in store for his own country, the press saw it as politically significant, but at a meeting with the Washington press Juan Carlos was guarded in his comments and let himself be coached by Franco's foreign minister, Gregorio Lopez Bravo. The visit also included his seeing the Apollo 14 launching at Cape Kennedy.

For all his public exposure, the character and views of Juan Carlos remain something of a mystery. Some Spaniards appraise their king-to-be as wooden and simpleminded, even dull and insipid, since they see only his public image. Foreign correspondents, however, have remarked that the prince is very amiable in private, having an earnest charm, even if lacking in the *simpático* qualities of an Alfonso XIII. His memory for names and his fluency in many languages are impressive. A less than flattering recent assessment by a New York *Times* man dismissed Juan Carlos as "a slender athletic young man whose eager cordiality seems wrenched out of a perpetual private melancholy."

Kept in a kind of gilded isolation, more seen than heard, Juan Carlos has reportedly sent out private signals that he intends to be a liberal king. In his public utterances, however, which were recently released in collected form, he is politically circumspect, leaving nothing to be read between the lines. Occasionally, foreign press interviewers have tried to corner him on specifics. In the United States, for example, when told that the Spanish press did not report his expressed hope that as king he would appeal to a wider range of Spaniards than the present regime, he hesitated and then said it was not for him to say why. On German television on October 7, 1972, in response to a question about the Spanish people wanting a "larger political participation in their destiny," he blandly responded that "the essence of our monarchy is the union of the king with his people." When the interviewer persisted by asking if he favored an interpretation of the laws "more liberal than they are given now," he retorted with serene vagueness that "it is impossible or at least unrealistic to give an exact prescription of the norms to be applied some years hence, when all the facts of the problem are not known." Generally, Juan Carlos has done nothing to disassociate himself from Franco's police state policies. His subservience, evident in constant expressions of gratitude to Franco, may simply be the better part of valor or may reflect a conditioning that has stifled any independence of political outlook.

If Juan Carlos has given no indication that he intends to rewrite the Constitution, he has gone to great lengths to say whatever sounds best. He is always telling students, "I belong to your generation." Typical was his declaration of 1969: "I am very close to youth. I admire and share its desire to seek a world more authentic and better. I know that the rebelliousness which preoccupies so many contains the great generosity of those who wish an open future, often with unrealizable dreams but always with the noble aspiration of the betterment of the people." "Accelerated progress" is a favorite phrase of Juan Carlos when he refers to the time he will replace Franco. He told a Madrid graduating class in March, 1971, "You may be sure that I will never be a dike which holds back but a channel which lets things flow in an orderly fashion." Aside from general tributes to the need for social equality and opportunity for all, matters of great concern to many Falangists, the Bourbon prince has been at pains to reassure nonaristocrats that he does not intend to play Alfonso XIII surrounded by the privileged. In his own words, "today one cannot think of a court organization analogous to that modeled on past centuries and even less of maintaining situations based on ancestral merits."

Juan Carlos has been given somewhat contrary indications of what Franco expects of him. Once the old dictator confided to the young prince that he should keep aloof from strictly movement celebrations "since you will have such a different task than mine." Yet Franco has publicly reminded him that the 1947 law gives him the right to change his mind about his successor, adding that he saw no prospects that this might be necessary.

If Juan Carlos were to get flagrantly out of line in Franco's eyes, the dictator has a ready substitute for him in the person of Prince Alfonso-Jaime de Borbón y Dampierre who on March 18, 1972, married Franco's granddaughter in an atmosphere of ostentatious social glitter and private distress among some of the members of the Bourbon dynasty. The thirty-five-year-old bridegroom was then ambassador to Sweden. His father, Don Jaime, who renounced the throne in 1933 and repudiated this move in 1964, attended the wedding after an absence from Spain of forty years. With him was his first wife and Alfonso's mother, Emanuela de Dampierre. What caused an initial sensation were the wedding invitations, which styled Alfonso "His Royal Highness," a title that was considered reserved for the children of Don Juan. Then Don Jaime proceeded to invest General Franco with the Order of the Golden Fleece, another prerogative claimed by Don Juan. The Old Pretender, infuriated, stayed in Portugal, but his son Don Juan Carlos and his wife not only attended the wedding but acted as witnesses, all the while looking rather uncomfortable.

Alfonso's bride, the twenty-one-year-old María del Carmen Martínez-Bordiu Franco, wore a Balenciaga gown and an emerald tiara. Franco wept with pleasure when she kissed him after the ceremony at El Pardo, and Mrs. Franco beamed triumphantly under her black mantilla. When their only daughter, Carmen, had married a marquis in the late 1940's, it had been a lackluster affair, but now the 3,500 guests included the most aristocratic Spanish names, the two leading bullfighters, a sprinkling of royalty, Hollywood personalities, and the international jet set. Later Salvador Dali set his stamp of approval on it all by presenting Franco with a huge surrealist portrait of the bride. The public unveiling of the portrait in the Velázquez salon of the Prado Museum was the occasion of an unprecedentedly large gathering that amounted almost to a pro-Alfonso demonstration.

The Bourbon and Franco blood lines were united in the baby born to Don Alfonso and Doña María del Carmen on November 22, 1972. The child, named Francisco, is four years junior to Juan Carlos' Felipe. Actually, neither boy would have an inherent claim to the throne, since by the 1947 law a monarch must be thirty years of age. Most important, this proviso means that if Juan Carlos died before Franco, his son could be ignored and Don Alfonso put on the throne. Franco's grandson-in-law has the image of a secret traditionalist in contrast with his cousin, and his presence is always felt as an alternative choice as successor.

Spain has had various Bourbon pretenders to a vacant throne for forty years—during the Second Republic, the Civil War, and the Franco era. In 1945 particularly, with the economy at a standstill and fascism discredited the world over, it had seemed likely that the old monarchy would shortly be brought back, but a new try at royal and constitutional politics did not come to pass. Economically, the Spain of 1973 is as different from 1945 as 1945 would be from 1845 or even 1745, and this fact now counts far more than genealogy or ideology for the country's and dynasty's future.

Spain's "economic miracle" occurred in the 1960's after Franco replaced Falangists in government with technocrats who proceeded to eliminate excessive state regulation, stabilize the peseta, and open the door to foreign capital. Economic growth has been an average 7 percent annually since 1961, with industry increasing at 10 percent, or the highest growth rate in the world next to Japan's. For the first time in history Spain has become an exporter of manufactured goods, and industry, not agriculture, is now the major employer. A solid majority of the population lives in urban concentrations, while Madrid has grown from 300,000 people to 3,000,000 since the Civil War. Economists predict that by 1980 Spain will be the world's tenth most industrialized nation with a per capita income of $2,000 (in contrast with $500 in 1950).

A considerable part of the country's new wealth comes from tourists, 31,000,000 of whom spent $2.6 billion in 1972. Spain gets hordes of package tourists, but millionaires are attracted, too. For example, Aristotle Onassis made a visit in July, 1973, to the Costa del Sol, where he is considering investments (on this occasion, incidentally, Mrs. Kennedy's second husband declared that Franco "is the world's greatest genius who has known how to organize the country and to predict the future. The example of Spain should be understood in all countries." As for Don Juan Carlos, he "is an intelligent man who has known how to adapt himself to the politics and interest of his country.")

One governmental advertising pitch to tourists has been "Spain is a luxury you can afford." A Spanish journalist dared to quip in print, "Spain is a luxury I can't afford," but the fact is that real wages increased drastically in the 1960's. Also, the state now provides a level of social services undreamed of under the old monarchy or the republic.

As Spain begins to taste prosperity, increasingly people talk of gaining even greater benefits by joining the European Common Market. Tourists from the United States are a small fraction compared to those coming from European countries, which are also contributing the lion's share of foreign investments. The Spanish government is also reconsidering its special relationship to the United States in terms of defense, symbolized by the huge United States air and naval base at Rota (in May, 1973, Juan Carlos and his wife were guests there aboard the carrier *John F. Kennedy*). These efforts at economic and diplomatic breakthroughs are frustrated by one major factor: the political backwardness of the Spanish regime. Socialist-influenced governments in the Common Market find Franco loathsome; a liberal monarchy they would probably find more palatable.

Political progress under Franco since 1939 has been minimal. Aside from his decrees on the succession, the one major development has been the Organic Law of November, 1966, providing for a few elected members in the otherwise appointive Cortes. Also, unions were to be allowed free elections, non-Catholic religions were to be tolerated, and the press was to be freed from some restraints. Hailed as a liberalization of the regime, these reforms were largely rescinded after 1969 in the face of a wave of strikes, student disorders, and terrorist acts by Basque nationalists. With martial law and executions to the fore, people have given up hope that the regime would provide an "evolution" to a liberal post-Franco monarchy. The watchword is now "continuity," meaning continued totalitarianism. Writing under a pseudonym in a magazine article of April 2, 1970, Franco declared that to bring liberal democracy to Spain would be like giving a drink to a reformed alcoholic.

Political or class organizations are banned under Article 173 of the Penal Code, except for the Falange Tradicionalista Española. The party, or movement, suffered an eclipse in the 1960's and is split into factions, some of its younger leaders being radically antimonarchist. Other political groupings exist informally or underground. Members of the semisecret Opus Dei have been credited with a large role in the economic-social progress of recent years, but this group too is split into liberal and authoritarian factions, as is the Spanish Catholic Church generally (Franco, like his royal predecessors, has had a stormy relationship with Rome and the hierarchy). The Catholics or Christian Democrats have no real political cadre, nor do the secret remnants of the socialists, the anarchists, or the Liberals. Then there are underground Basque and Catalan nationalist movements. Only the Spanish Communist Party, or at least its Moscow-oriented branch, appears to have some real organization down to local levels and on a national scale. The Communists are the one group that has consistently opposed the restoration of the monarchy, while the others—Catholics, leftists, regionalists—have agreed at informal conferences abroad to tolerate, temporarily at least, a king who would allow and arbitrate democratic elections. No political group knows quite what to expect from the masses, two-thirds of whom have known no other ruler than Franco, three-quarters of whom have no memory of the monarchy.

The army, which since 1956 no longer has Spanish Morocco to parade around in, appears to be dedicated to a smooth transition from Franco to the monarchy, as does the newly confident business community. Many in the Establishment, however, resent the political stagnation that has set in since 1969 when Franco named his successor without relinquishing power.

The kinds of problems Franco's royal heir will face are indicated by recent headline news from Spain. The country's most famous sociologist is arrested for criticizing an obscurantist speech by an army chaplain. Two outspoken oppositionists are among 104 members elected to the Cortes. One hundred and forty monarchists, Christian Democrats, and socialists are heavily fined for sending an address to visiting Secretary of State Rogers. Eight rightists, loosely connected with a group called Warriors for Christ the King, smash and steal from an exhibition of Picasso's art because they consider the painter decadent (something of a surprise was the fact that the strong-arm men were arrested). Hundreds of people, mostly students, are beaten or seized by the police in a May Day, 1972, demonstration in Madrid. Expressions of political discontent are even stronger on May Day, 1973: a policeman is killed, and 5,000 extreme rightists stage a counterprotest, clamoring against the "red priests" of Opus Dei and the too-lenient government. Basque nationalists kidnap a prominent businessman.

Franco's eightieth birthday on December 4, 1972, was also noted by the press with controlled enthusiasm, but the general remained in aloof splendor at El Pardo. One could detect from other reports—his appearing at church with Juan Carlos or his going to a bullfight—that the dictator was not exactly fading away. As recently as July, 1973, during a state visit by the President of Paraguay, Franco stood for two hours as his open car made its way through Madrid's main thoroughfares; he was escorted by a squadron of cavalry in silver helmets and white capes, with guards deployed every few feet at the curbs and more soldiers with submachine guns posted on the rooftops. Later Don Juan Carlos had more than an hour-long interview with the Paraguayan leader, but at the banquet table at the Oriente the Prince of Spain shared prominence with the Duke of Cádiz.

On the magic July 18 date in 1972, Franco designated his vice premier, Admiral Luis Carrero Blanco, as his choice for premier after his death. An Opus Dei man, Carrero Blanco was, nonetheless, considered tough, uncompromising, reactionary, and more Franco than Franco. Juan Carlos "detested" the admiral, according to reports in the New York *Times*, but he had to accept Franco's will and to face the prospect of reigning while the other ruled. In a genuine concession to the somewhat dangling Bourbon prince, Franco specified in the same pronouncement that Juan Carlos must be sworn as king within eight days of the dictator's demise. Then, on June 8, 1973, a living Franco gave over to Carrero Blanco his position as premier or head of government, all the while retaining his position as chief of state and commander in chief of the armed forces. This development enabled Carrero Blanco to relieve Franco of the burden of presiding at cabinet meetings. He promptly reorganized the ministry to have a more rightist composition, getting rid of the Foreign Minister López Bravo, friend of the Western democracies and villain to the Falange for signing treaties with the Soviet bloc.

In the first major political killing in Spain since the Civil War, Premier Carrero Blanco was assassinated on December 20, 1973. A mine in the street set by Basque nationalists blew his car five stories up in the air over the roof of the church where he had been worshiping. Rightists turned the admiral's funeral into a vociferous demonstration against "Reds" and "liberals," screaming epithets even at the Cardinal Archbishop of Madrid (that Carrero Blanco was less than universally popular was indicated by the prompt circulation of a "sick joke" renaming the church in question Our Lady of the Ascension).

On January 2, 1974 Franco swore in as new premier a kneeling Carlos Arias Navarro, a man known only as a stern police official and a loyalist of the generalissimo. The extensive cabinet reshuffle favored the Falange over Opus Dei but also younger bureaucrats over the older generation. Arias succeeded in alarming the right by promising greater freedoms on February 12 and then aroused leftist protests by allowing the execution by garroting of a Catalan anarchist on March 2. The preferred posture of the new ministry became infinitely difficult to decide in late April as a result of the military overthrow of the dictatorship in Portugal, a repressive regime long antedating Franco's. Events in Portugal have prefigured those in Spain with strange persistence, two cases in point being the male-female dynastic contests of the 1830's and the overthrow of the monarchies, 1910 and 1931 respectively. On the one hand, the Arias regime has allowed extensive media coverage of such unsettling scenes in the neighboring country as the harassment of the secret police by the people and the ovations given released political prisoners and returned exiles, including the head of the Portuguese Communists. On the other hand, the Spanish government has been assiduously arresting potential oppositionists and curbing student manifestations.

The news of the consolidation of Carrero Blanco's power and the resurgence of the right in Spain provided the focal point at a previously planned conference on "Spain in the 1970's" in Washington in June, 1973, which brought together the leading Hispanic experts from the diplomatic, academic, and journalistic communities. The consensus of the learned meeting, whose participants gathered to speculate about the future, was that Spain faced three possibilities: a bald-faced continuation of Francoism under a puppet Juan Carlos; some sort of vague liberalization under a more forceful Juan Carlos; collapse under a helpless Juan Carlos.

Calculating the Spanish Bourbons' future with less sociological cold-bloodedness and more historical mysticism, one cannot fail to be impressed by the fact that the dynasty has staged more than its share of comebacks. The founder, Felipe V, was twice driven from his capital by his Hapsburg rival and survived bouts of madness as well. The best of them all, Carlos III, went from sulk and repression to popularity and enlightenment. The wicked Fernando VII not only outlasted imprisonment by Napoleon but outfaced two moments of inspired liberalism by his own subjects. Isabel II, dethroned, enjoyed a triumphal return after the monarchy had been restored in the person of her son, Alfonso XII. The last king, Alfonso XIII, also dethroned, made no personal comeback, but he lived to see his enemies annihilated. His son, his grandson, and his great-grandson are triumphantly to the fore in 1974. Of course, there are a few brothers, cousins, and other rival claimants in the picture—that has long been the Spanish Bourbons' difficulty. Yet all of them together represent a very tenacious dynasty.

Notes

PROLOGUE: INVADERS AND DYNASTS BEFORE THE BOURBONS

15 "A savage ass": John A. Crow, *Spain: The Root and the Flower* (New York, Harper, 1963), p. 49.
16 "Those who want": *ibid.*, p. 90.
17 "Oath of the Aragonese": J. H. Elliot, *Imperial Spain 1469–1716* (New York, St. Martins, 1963), p. 18.
17 "The most glorious": Mariéjol, quoted *ibid.*, p. 115. See also Jean Hippolyte, *The Spain of Ferdinand and Isabella* (New Brunswick, Rutgers University Press, 1961).
18 "No states were more": *ibid.*, p. 167.
18 "Splendid failure": Crow, *op. cit.*, p. 169.
18 "No secretary": quoting a Spanish cardinal, Elliot, *op. cit.*, p. 252.
18 "Royal kill-joy": quoted in Thomas F. McGann, *Portrait of Spain* (New York, Knopf, 1963), p. 140.
19 "The grandest ideal": *ibid.*
20 "Superstition, sloth, and ignorance": Elliot, *op cit.*, p. 374.
20 "Universality": Salvador de Madariaga, *Spain, A Modern History* (New York, Praeger, 1958), p. 46.

I. THE CRISIS OF 1700–1714: THE CROWN DISPUTED

21 "The monarchy without a monarch": quoting the German historian Ranke, G. F. White, *A Century of Spain and Portugal (1788–1898)* (London, Methuen, 1909), p. 159.
22 "Most beautiful": John Langdon-Davies, *Carlos, the King Who Would Not Die* (Englewood Cliffs, N.J., Prentice-Hall, 1963), p. 15. The present author is greatly indebted to this brilliantly dramatic work.
22 Four generations: *ibid.*, pp. 28–29.
22 Acrocephaly: *ibid.*, p. 21.
22 "Like a caricature": Simon Harcourt-Smith, *Alberoni or the Spanish Conspiracy* (London, Faber and Faber, 1943), p. 16.
23 A modern scholar: Doris McGuigan, *The Hapsburgs* (New York, Doubleday, 1966), p. 212.
23 "A sub-human person": Langdon-Davies, *op. cit.*, p. 96.
23 "It would be difficult": Elliot, *op. cit.*, pp. 361–62.
23 "This country": John Lynch, *Spain Under the Hapsburgs* (New York, Oxford University Press, 1964–69), Vol. II, p. 280.
23 "From the poor": Gerald Brenan, *The Spanish Labyrinth* (New York, Cambridge University Press, 1967), p. 17.
23 "Of the gold": *ibid.*, p. 36.
24 "Moral and intellectual bankruptcy": Elliot, *op. cit.*, pp. 358–59.
24 "The first": *ibid.*, p. 361.
24 "Without any question": Langdon-Davies, *op. cit.*, p. 91.
25 "Of remarkable artistry": *ibid.*, pp. 91–92.

405

25 "Praecatio ejacualis": *ibid.,* pp. 122–23.

26 "A recent British biographer: *ibid.,* pp. 145–47.

26 "Nobody could call": *ibid.,* p. 157.

28 "Ghost": *ibid.,* p. 221.

28 "They will rather": A. W. Ward et al. (eds.), *The Cambridge Modern History* (New York, Macmillan, 1912), Vol. V, p. 384.

29 "Sensibly worse": Langdon-Davies, *op. cit.,* p. 238.

29 "His Catholic Majesty": *ibid.,* p. 239.

30 "Sir, it is": William Coxe, *Memoirs of the Kings of Spain of the House of Bourbon* (London, Longman, Hurst, Rees, Orme, and Brown, 1815), p. 24.

30 "Gentlemen, you see here": Ward et al., *op. cit.,* p. 395.

30 "What a pleasure": Pio Zabala y Lera, *España bajo los Borbónes* (Barcelona, Editorial Labor, 1955), p. 11.

32 "He carried idleness": Harcourt-Smith, *op. cit.,* p. 37.

32 "the king, my father": Jean-Louis Jacquet, *Les Bourbons d'Espagne* (Lausanne, Editions Rencontre, 1968), p. 28. This recent survey of the Bourbons in French is full of racy details and telling anecdotes.

32 "As if they had shot": Harcourt-Smith, *op. cit.,* p. 37.

33 "It is true": Zabala, *op. cit.,* p. 21.

33 "To be minister": *ibid.,* p. 22.

34 "From his first leap": Harcourt-Smith, *op. cit.,* p. 68.

34 "To govern": Martin Hume, *Spain: Its Greatness and Decay 1479–1788* (London, Cambridge University Press, 1913), p. 331.

35 "To maneuver": Pierre Gaxotte, *The Age of Louis XIV* (New York, Macmillan, 1970), p. 305.

37 "He had a gravity": Robert Pick, *Empress Maria Theresa* (London, Weidenfeld, 1966), p. 5.

39 "Thorns in the feet": Zabala, *op. cit.,* p. 71.

39 "Protect our *fueros*": Henry Kamen, *The War of Succession in Spain 1700–1715* (Bloomington, Indiana University Press, 1969), p. 257.

40 "Castile will never obey": Zabala, *op. cit.,* p. 15.

40 "Long live Carlos III": *ibid.,* p. 16.

41 "One can clearly": Alfonso Danvilla, *El Reinando Relámpago, Luis I y Luisa Isabel de Orléans* (Madrid, Espasa-Calpe, 1952), p. 10.

41 "Strong as a Turk": *ibid.,* p. 22.

41 "Mon fils": *ibid.,* p. 23.

42 "Rather be buried": Coxe, *op. cit.,* p. 126.

42 "Rode to Mataró": McGuigan, *op. cit.,* p. 216.

43 "Were he in the place": Ward et al., *op. cit.,* p. 423.

43 "I shall never quit": Kamen, *op. cit.,* p. 49.

44 "The country is our enemy": Harcourt-Smith, *op. cit.,* p. 78.

44 "Had been bled": *ibid.,* p. 81.

44 "Your Majesty shall": *ibid.,* p. 79.

45 "Nothing in the world": Danvilla, *op. cit.,* p. 60.

46 "The kingdoms": Zabala, *op. cit.,* p. 18.

47 "May well have shaken": Kamen, *op. cit.,* p. 181.

47 "The relatively mild": *ibid.*

II. THE MELANCHOLY KING: FELIPE V (1700–1746)

48 "Princes, are they": Louis de Saint-Simon, *Historical Memoirs* (New York, McGraw-Hill, 1967), Vol. II, p. 309.

49 "This strumpet": Kamen, *op. cit.,* p. 54.

49 "Oh, no": Saint-Simon, *op. cit.,* p. 344.

51 "Kindness and generosity": Harcourt-Smith, *op. cit.,* p. 100.

51 "Arrest this mad woman": *ibid.,* p. 101.

51 "The ocean": *ibid.,* p. 102.

51 Slave for life: Ward et al., *op. cit.*, p. 122.
51 "The Court": Kamen, *op. cit.*, p. 55.
52 "The jealousy": Harcourt-Smith, *op. cit.*, p. 112.
52 "I recognize": *ibid.*, p. 106.
52 "I'm succeeding": *ibid.*
52 "I repeated": *ibid.*, pp. 104-5.
52 "Great changes": *ibid.*, p. 119.
52 "If things": *ibid.*
53 "I wonder: *ibid.*, p. 130.
53 "Give me": Danvilla, *op. cit.*, p. 90.
54 "The only things": Harcourt-Smith, *op. cit.*, p. 108.
55 "Dictation": *ibid.*, p. 169.
55 "The whim of the Queen": *ibid.*
55 "Will allow the four corners": *ibid.*, p. 194.
55 "To grow to such": *ibid.*
56 "Human schemes": *ibid.*, p. 197.
57 "The first minister: Hume, *op. cit.*, p. 356.
58 "Confounded": Jacquet, *op. cit.*, p. 88.
58 "Black melancholy": Harcourt-Smith, *op. cit.*, p. 162.
58 "He let flash": Jacquet, *op. cit.*, pp. 88-89.
58 "He loves his wife": E. C. Orleans, *Secret Memoirs* (Boston, Grolier, n.d.), p. 252.
59 "A bed": Jacquet, *op. cit.*, pp. 89-90.
59 "*Viva la Saboyana*": Danvilla, *op. cit.*, p. 222.
59 "The Spanish do not": *ibid.*
59 "An entourage": Ward et al., *op. cit.*, Vol. VI, p. 136.
61 "Having considered": Hume, *op. cit.*, p. 360.
61 "Nobody escapes": Danvilla, *op. cit.*, pp. 227-28.
62 "Render justice": Jacquet, *op. cit.*, p. 91.
62 "They can do": *ibid.*
62 "The well-beloved": Hume, *op. cit.*, p. 360.
62 "Very ignorant": Danvilla, *op. cit.*, p. 83.
63 "He resembles": *ibid.*, p. 137.
63 "I would prefer": Jacquet, *op. cit.*, p. 93.
63 "One cannot say": *ibid.*, p. 95.
63 "She had a strong": *ibid.*, p. 93.
65 "The prince had a gay air": Danvilla, *op. cit.*, p. 194.
65 "Battles of the night": *ibid.*, p. 269.
65 "You are not the King": *ibid.*, p. 291.
66 "Poison him": *IBID.*, P. 344.
69 "Little more than a corpse": Ward et al., *op. cit.*, Vol. VI, p. 166.
69 "Since I have been": Jacquet, *op. cit.*, p. 109.
70 "All right": *ibid.*, p. 107.
71 "The sun so pale": *ibid.*, p. 107.
71 "The King himself": Harcourt-Smith, *op. cit.*, p. 221.
72 "The persistence": Hume, *op. cit.*, p. 369.
73 "They now ring": Sir Charles Petrie, *King Charles III of Spain* (London, Constable, 1917), p. 69.
75 "Almost single-handedly": Richard Herr, *The Eighteenth Century Revolution in Spain* (Princeton, Princeton University Press, 1969), p. 37. This work is cultural history at its best.
76 "Broke the gloomy spell": Hume, *op. cit.*, p. 381.
76 "Although the national renaissance": *ibid.*, p. 383.

III. THE ENLIGHTENED DESPOTS: FERNANDO VI (1746–1759) AND CARLOS III (1759–1788)

78 "The new king": Jacquet, *op. cit.*, p. 116.
78 "The most effusive": Zabala, *op. cit.*, p. 45.

79 "The new Queen": Jacquet, *op. cit.*, p. 116.
80 *falta de cabezas:* Elliot, *op. cit.*, p. 377.
80 "King Fernando": Zabala, *op. cit.*, p. 44.
81 "It is difficult": Hume, *op. cit.*, pp. 390–91.
82 "In the interests of Spain": Jacquet, *op. cit.*, p. 123.
83 "He went to bed": *ibid.*, p. 127.
83 "Here lies": Zabala, *op. cit.*, p. 54.
84 "Go forth": Petrie, *Charles*, p. 26.
85 "The notorious imbecility": *ibid.*, p. 65.
85 "The city I carry": Jacquet, *op. cit.*, p. 151.
86 "You see": Petrie, *Charles*, pp. 164–65.
87 "An uncommon command": Petrie, *Charles*,, p. 97.
88 "The Marquis Squilacci": *ibid.*
89 "Long live": Ward et al., *op. cit.*, Vol. VI, p. 371.
89 "I deserve": Jacquet, *op. cit.*, p. 161.
90 "My son": *ibid.*, p. 163.
91 "The appearance": Petrie, *Charles*, p. 118.
91 "The hand of": Zabala, *op. cit.*, p. 64.
92 "The immediate, wise": *ibid.*, p. 65.
92 "The Spaniards": Herr, *op. cit.*, p. 29.
92 "According to the lights": *ibid.*, p. 163.
93 "Subjecting the lights": *ibid.*, p. 174.
94 "I order that": *ibid.*, p. 97.
94 "The sight of poverty": *ibid.*, p. 150.
95 "Intellectually inferior": Gabriel H. Lovett, *Napoleon and the Birth of Modern Spain* (New York, New York University Press, 1965), p. 2.
95 "They are like children": Jacques Chastenet, *Godoy, Master of Spain* (London, Batchworth, 1953), p. 17.
96 "His dress: Petrie, *Charles*, pp. 164–65.
97 "O'Reilly is going": *ibid.*, p. 158.
98 "I have no doubt": *ibid.*, p. 170.
98 "Never, perhaps": Ward et al., *op. cit.*, Vol. VI, p. 276.
99 "It will soon": Petrie, *Charles*, p. 201.
99 "Gibraltar being": Ward et al., *op. cit.*, Vol. VI, p. 380.
101 "Did you think": Petrie, *Charles*, p. 229.
101 "It did not need": Chastenet, *op. cit.*, p. 27
101 "small praise": Ward et al., *op. cit.*, Vol. VI, p. 382.
101 "Among the enlightened": Herr, *op. cit.*, p. 234.
101 "He brought about": Petrie, *Charles*, p. 230.

IV. THE ROYAL CUCKOLD: CARLOS IV (1788–1808)

102 "Hale, good-humored": Lovett, *op. cit.*, p. 6.
103 "He takes no account": Chastenet, *op. cit.*, p. 97.
103 "In a world": *ibid.*, p. 19.
104 "I shall finally be": Rachel Challice, *The Secret History of the Spanish Court During the Last Century* (New York, Appleton, 1909), p. 2.
104 "Passionate, unsatisfied woman": Chastenet, *op. cit.*, p. 20.
104 "Many confinements": *ibid.*, pp. 49–50.
104 "The Queen": Lovett, *op. cit.*, p. 7.
105 "Especially from an ill": Pierre de Luz, *Isabel II, Reina de España* (Barcelona, Editorial Juventud, 1962), p. 6.
105 "Carlos, what a complete fool": *ibid.*, p. 7.
105 "Only three": Chastenet, *op. cit.*, p. 214.
106 "tall, strongly-made": *ibid.*, p. 70.
106 "A big strong": *ibid.*, p. 24.

106 "Precise but unsparkling": *ibid.,* p. 70.
106 "Bedroom prowess": Lovett, *op. cit.,* p. 9.
106 "Joined by the Queen": Chastenet, *op. cit.,* pp. 71–72.
106 "In such a corner": *ibid.,* p. 94.
107 "Sire, Mallo": Jacquet, *op. cit.,* p. 205.
107 "The principal room": Chastenet, *op. cit.,* p. 70.
107 "A girl arriving": *ibid.,* p. 71.
108 "The thing": *ibid.,* p. 96.
109 "Every day": *ibid.,* p. 26.
109 One has: Herr, *op. cit.,* p. 317.
109 "How carols": Lovett, *op. cit.,* p. 24.
110 "Both energetic and flexible": *ibid.,* p. 11.
110 "The King asks me": *ibid.,* p. 12.
110 "You are our only": *ibid.,* p. 10.
110 "The Prince saw": *ibid.,* p. 15.
110 "The Prince dispatches": Chastenet, *op. cit.,* p. 73.
110 "He seemed born": *ibid.,* p. 244.
110 "Was the crafty manipulator": Lovett, *op. cit.,* p. 16.
110 "Toy of destiny": *ibid.*
111 "Rural and humorous": Pierre Gassier and Juliet Wilson, *The Life and Complete Work of Francisco Goya* (New York, Reynal, 1971), p. 99. This huge book, which has a judicious and comprehensive text, contains reproductions of every work from Goya's pen or brush.
112 A very recent theory: New York *Times,* February 28, 1971, p. 33.
112 "A unique blend": Gassier and Wilson, *op. cit.,* p. 125.
113 "Pinned like great insects": *ibid.,* p. 148.
113 "Riot of malformation": Chastenet, *op. cit.,* p. 92.
114 "It seems": Gassier and Wilson, *op. cit.,* p. 148.
114 "The best of all paintings": Chastenet, *op. cit.,* p. 92.
114 A possible explanation: Priscilla E. Muller, "Goya's The Family of Charles IV, An Interpretation," *Apollo,* Vol. XCI (February, 1970), pp. 136–37.
115 "The Spanish people": Herr, *op. cit.,* p. 241.
115 "None of the causes": *ibid.,* pp. 233–34.
115 "all prints": *ibid.,* p. 165.
116 "Verses or any political": *ibid.,* p. 262.
116 "I belong to Godoy": Chastenet, *op. cit.,* p. 54.
116 "The grandees": Jacquet, *op. cit.,* p. 199.
116 "It would be a great mistake": Chastenet, *op. cit.,* p. 53.
117 "Will accord fraternity": Herr, *op. cit.,* pp. 272–73.
118 "After all": Peter Polnay, *A Queen of Spain, Isabella II* (London, Hollis and Carter, 1962), p. 4.
119 "The Bourbons must disappear": Chastenet, *op. cit.,* p. 59.
119 "Took up arms," Herr, *op. cit.,* p. 312.
119 "Sister republics": Herr, *op. cit.,* p. 293.
119 "It is true": Chastenet, *op. cit.,* p. 65.
119 "Even the whores": Herr, *op. cit.,* p. 325.
120 "Be assured": Chastenet, *op. cit.,* p. 67.
120 "Great Britain": *ibid.,* p. 76.
121 "If the result of peace": *ibid.,* p. 81.
121 "I shall be": *ibid.,* p. 87.
121 "Manuel, who has": *ibid.,* pp. 89–90.
123 "Of the most dazzling": *ibid.,* p. 98.
123 "The number of Godoy's": *ibid.,* p. 102.
123 "All is agitation": *ibid.,* p. 107.
123 "Do not expose": *ibid.*
124 "family of cretins": *ibid.,* p. 115.
124 "this rascally Court": *ibid.,* p. 116.

124 "threadbare": *ibid.*, pp. 125–26.
125 "We will humiliate": *ibid.*, p. 122.
126 "The dynasty of Naples": Jacquet, *op. cit.*, p. 215.
126 "A sovereign state": Chastenet, *op. cit.*, p. 146.
127 "Absolute devotion": *ibid.*, p. 153.
127 "Let me rather": *ibid.*, p. 162.
127 "False and wicked," *ibid.*, p. 165.
128 "Appalling conspiracy": *ibid.*, p. 168.
128 "Kiss the feet": *ibid.*, p. 172.
128 "Disgusting desires": *ibid.*, p. 181.

V. THE CRISIS OF 1808–1814: THE BOURBONS AT THE MERCY OF NAPOLEON

130 "Knew nothing": *ibid.*, p. 194.
130 "Desiring to command": *ibid.*, p. 190.
131 "Melt a heart": *ibid.*, p. 192.
131 "For my health's sake": *ibid.*, p. 193.
131 "Never was a monarch": Lovett, *op. cit.*, p. 101.
132 "Looked to reaction": *ibid.*, p. 102.
132 "The King of Spain": Chastenet, *op. cit.*, p. 199.
132 "I will let myself": Lovett, *op. cit.*, p. 112.
133 "The tragedy": *ibid.*, p. 116.
133 "Have you not": Chastenet, *op. cit.*, p. 206.
133 "Very stupid": Lovett, *op. cit.*, p. 117.
134 "Balconies, windows": *ibid.*, p. 144.
134 "Yesterday's affair": *ibid.*, p. 149.
134 "The blood": Chastenet, *op. cit.*, p. 210.
134 "What a mother": Jacquet, *op. cit.*, p. 218.
134 "If between now": Lovett, *op. cit.*, p. 118.
135 "Yes, I know": *ibid.*, p. 120.
135 "Rivers of blood": *ibid.*, p. 119.
135 "King Carlos": Jacquet, *op. cit.*, p. 226.
135 "Spaniards": Lovett, *op. cit.*, p. 123.
135 "Reassumed sovereignty": *ibid.*, p. 172.
136 "Happiness of": *ibid.*, p. 128.
136 "If your Majesty": Gabriel Girod de L'Ain, *Joseph Bonaparte: Le Roi Malgri Lui* (Paris, Librairie Académique Perrin, 1970), p. 197.
136 "It seems": Lovett, *op. cit.*, p. 129.
137 "Have courage": *ibid.*, p. 130.
137 "Light spirit": Girod de L'Ain, *op. cit.*, p. 25.
137 "The craft and sullen art": David Stacton, *The Bonapartes* (New York, Simon and Schuster, 1966), p. 21.
138 "At Madrid": Lovett, *op. cit.*, p. 121.
138 "I have not": *ibid.*, pp. 130–31.
139 "What struck": *ibid.*, p. 496.
139 "I prefer": Girod de L'Ain, *op. cit.*, pp. 187–88.
139 "Don José Napoleon": Lovett, *op. cit.*, p. 498.
139 "*Yo el Rey*": *ibid.*, p. 195.
139 "I am King": Girod de L'Ain, *op. cit.*, p. 242.
139 "It must not": Lovett, *op. cit.*, p. 501.
139 "The King must be": *ibid.*, p. 503
140 "He wants to be," ibid.
140 "A king": Girod de L'Ain, *op. cit.*, p. 298.
140 "He had a particular penchant": *ibid.*, p. 240.
140 "The best creature": ibid., pp. 435–36.
140 "If her departures": *ibid.*, p. 245.

140 "Pepe Botellas": Lovett, *op. cit.*, p. 493.
141 "The first cannon shot": *ibid.*, p. 186.
141 "Destiny of the world": *ibid.*, p. 322.
141 "The past": Girod de L'Ain, *op. cit.*, p. 211-12.
142 "Nothing short": Lovett, *op. cit.*, p. 359.
142 "Messieurs Monks": *ibid.*, p. 304.
142 "perfidious men": *ibid.*, pp. 311-12.
143 "My brother": *ibid.*, p. 315.
144 "Live content": *ibid.*, p. 523.
144 "E per que": *ibid.*, p. 513.
144 "The hardest": Elizabeth Longford, *Wellington: The Years of the Sword* (New York, Harper, 1969), p. 197.
144 "Poor Spaniards": Lovett, *op. cit.*, p. 496.
145 "Spaniards, rally around": Girod de L'Ain, *op. cit.*, p. 251.
145 "The crossing": Lovett, *op. cit.*, p. 528.
145 "One of the errors": Girod de L'Ain, *op. cit.*, p. 248.
145 "The way": *ibid.*, p. 252.
145 "Blazing furnance": *ibid.*, p. 254.
145 "Opinion today": *ibid.*, p. 256.
147 "When the French": Longford, *Wellington*, p. 240.
147 "Fatal mistake": Karl Marx y Friedrich Engles, *Revolución en España* (Barcelona, Ediciones Ariel, 1970), p. 76.
148 "We believed": Lovett, *op. cit.*, p. 307.
148 "The great academy": quoted in *ibid.*, p. 721.
148 "Everything was rotten": Brenan, *op. cit.*, p. 87.
148 "The nation . . . fought": Lovett, *op. cit.*, p. 659.
150 "The only true faith": *ibid.*, p. 453.
150 "To take the dregs": *ibid.*, p. 466.
150 "Sovereignty resides": *ibid.*, p. 454.
151 "I am among": Longford, *Wellington*, p. 290.
152 "How about Spain": James H. Billington, *The Icon and the Axe* (New York, Knopf, 1966), p. 652, note 67.
152 "The unfortunate Spanish war": Lovett, *op. cit.*, p. 176.
153 "The farewell plunder": *ibid.*, p. 548.
153 "Scum of the earth": Longford, *Wellington*, p. 321.
154 "Good Spaniard": Girod de L'Ain, *op. cit.*, p. 315.

VI. THE WORST KING: FERNANDO VII (1814-1833)

155 "Your Majesty, here!": *ibid.*, p. 335.
156 "If I were": *ibid.*, p. 343.
157 "If no descendant": Lovett, *op. cit.*, pp. 551-52, note 26.
157 "Thrown a kingdom": Chateaubriand, quoted in Chastenet, *op. cit.*, p. 211.
157 "A quite unimportant": *ibid.*, p. 213.
158 "How handsome": *ibid.*, p. 219.
158 "Passionate soul": Jacquet, *op. cit.*, p. 225.
158 "Friend Manuel": *ibid.*, p. 226.
158 His royal protectors: Chastenet, *op. cit.*, pp. 218 ff.
160 "That slut": Jacquet, *op. cit.*, p. 230.
160 "Hideous to look at": Chastenet, *op. cit.*, p. 116.
161 "All one could say": Lovett, *op. cit.*, p. 822.
161 "The fact is": Jacquet, *op. cit.*, p. 248.
161 "If the Prince": Lovett, *op. cit.*, pp. 119-20.
161 "I desire": *ibid.*, p. 516.
162 "Long Live Our Chains": Jacquet, *op. cit.*, p. 263.
163 "Capable only": *ibid.*, p. 289.

163 "The traditionalists": Bradley Smith, *Spain, A History in Art* (New York, Doubleday, 1971), p. 16.

164 "A social and economic reform": Lovett, *op. cit.,* p. 825. According to Karl Marx, the masses "preferred the lewd despotism of kings and monks to the sober government of the middle classes" (Marx, *op. cit.,* p. 117).

165 "The reestablishment": Lovett, *op. cit.,* p. 814.

165 "Many good": Jacquet, *op. cit.,* p. 263.

165 "My desire": Lovett, *op. cit.,* p. 825.

165 "Indescribable enthusiasm": *ibid.,* p. 826.

166 "Absolute monarchy": *ibid.,* p. 816.

166 "Kiss!": *ibid.,* p. 828.

166 "The blood": *ibid.*

166 "It is my royal will": Jacquet, *op. cit.,* p. 265.

166 "Masterstroke of treachery": White, *op. cit.,* p. 106.

167 "It was not rejoicing": Josep Fontana Lázaro, *La Quiebra de la Monarquía Absoluta* (Barcelona, Ediciones Ariel, 1971), p. 80.

167 Accounts of miracles": Frederick B. Artz, *Reaction and Revolution 1814–1832* (New York, Harper, 1934), pp. 134–35.

167 "Highly impolitic" Lovett, *op. cit.,* 840.

168 "There were simply": C. W. Fehrenbach, "Moderados and Exaltados," *Hispanic American Historical Review,* Vol. 50, No. 1 (February, 1970), p. 58.

168 "The poor generals": *ibid.,* p. 57.

169 "Buffoon parliament": White, *op. cit.,* p. 107.

170 "Centuries of slighting": *ibid.,* pp. 90–91.

171 "Failed altogether": *ibid.*

171 "Delirious": Margaret Woodward, "The Spanish Army and the Loss of America 1810–1824," *Hispanic American Historical Review* (November, 1968), p. 589.

173 "Just to give": *ibid.,* p. 596.

174 "The wishes": H. Butler Clarke, *Modern Spain (1815–1898)* (Cambridge, Cambridge University Press, 1906), p. 48.

175 "His most ardent": *ibid.,* p. 52.

175 "If the priests": Jacquet, *op. cit.,* p. 270.

176 "Little Rose": Clarke, *op. cit.,* p. 60.

177 "In perhaps no capital": Fehrenbach, *op. cit.,* p. 68.

178 "Ode to Liberty": Percy B. Shelley, *Poetical Works* (Oxford, Oxford University Press, 1970), pp. 603–4.

178 "A hundred thousand"; Clarke, *op. cit.,* p. 66.

179 "Complete and absolute": White, *op. cit.,* p. 121.

180 "Fierce and hideous": Clarke, *op. cit., p. 74.*

180 "To stamp out": *ibid.*

181 "The whole country": Polnay, *op. cit.,* p. 19.

182 "Only an instrument": Jacquet, *op. cit.,* p. 285.

182 "It was all": Nicholas V. Riasanovsky, *Nicholas I and Official Nationality in Russia* (Berkeley, University of California Press, 1916), p. 266.

VII. THE CRISIS OF 1833–1839: THE DYNASTY SPLIT

184 "I would rather": Edgar Holt, *The Carlist Wars in Spain* (Chester Springs, Pa., Dufour, 1967), p. 15.

184 "An almost indecent": Theo Aronson, *Royal Vendetta: The Crown of Spain 1829–1965* (New York, Bobbs-Merrill, 1966), p. 6. The present author is greatly indebted to this eminently readable account of the modern Bourbons which is particularly concerned with the dynastic split between the Legitimists and the Carlists.

185 "A huge fat": *ibid.,* p. 6.

185 "the veriest scold": Holt, *op. cit.,* p. 25.

185 "No more rosaries": Robert Sencourt, *The Spanish Crown* (New York, Scribner's, 1932), p. 130.
185 "This epileptic bastard": Chastenet, *op. cit.*, p. 233. *See also* Lovett, *op. cit.*, p. 11.
186 "royal coquette": Holt, *op. cit.*, pp. 27–28.
187 "The question of": Antonio Jimenez-Landi, *Una Ley de Sucesión* (Madrid, Aguilar, 1968), pp. 215 ff.
188 "What is it": Holt, *op. cit.*, p. 30.
188 "In order that": Aronson, *op. cit.*, p. 9.
188 "Lack of instruction": Jimenez-Landi, *op. cit.*, p. 230.
189 Sciocca: ibid., p. 241.
189 *"Los Manos Blancos"*: ibid., p. 242.
189 "Horrible plot": Sencourt, *Crown*, pp. 138–40.
190 "Authorized": *ibid.*, p. 36.
190 "Rights which God": *ibid.*, p. 38.
191 "My lord and king": *ibid.*, pp. 144–47.
191 "Spain is a bottle": *ibid.*, p. 137.
191 "Castile, Castile" (this is just my inference from past such ceremonies).
191 "To bequeath a civil war": Holt, *op. cit.*, p. 13.
192 "I will maintain": Clarke, *op. cit.*, 92–93.
192 "Now I am": Sencourt, *Crown*, p. 152.
193 "That man": Holt, *op. cit.*, p. 62.
193 "If Don Carlos": Polmay, *op. cit.*, p. 32.
193 "Underlying the dynastic": Gabriel Jackson, *The Spanish Republic and the Civil War* (Princeton, Princeton University Press, 1967), pp. 3–4.
194 "Comprised entirely": Aronson, *op. cit.*, p. 17.
194 "It is a Carlist invention," Marx y Engels, *op. cit.*, p. 54.
194 "Attracted to their colors": Sir Charles Petrie, *Alfonso XIII and His Age* (London, Chapman, 1963), p. 24.
194 "To change their shirts": Clarke, *op. cit.*, p. 104.
195 "A very noble": Sencourt, *Crown*, p. 155.
196 "Ducal mantle": Luz, *op. cit.*, p. 35.
196 "Chambers mildly": Clarke, *op. cit.*, p. 96.
197 "I should like": Holt, *op. cit.*, p. 15.
198 "I have no ambassador": *ibid.*, p. 50.
199 "Disgusted": Aronson, *op. cit.*, p. 21.
199 "Imbecility, cowardice": *ibid.*, p. 22.
200 "It was the turning point," Clarke, *op. cit.*, p. 111.
201 "Strange infatuation": *ibid.*, p. 78.
201 "An imbecile": *ibid.*, p. 5.
201 "A sort of cretinism": *ibid.*, p. 18.
201 "As one of the silliest": Holt, *op. cit.*, p. 18.
201 "His dark eyes": Aronson, *op. cit.*, p. 22.
202 "true masculine types": *ibid.*, p. 5.
202 "Very handsome": *ibid.*, p. 19.
202 "Has acquired gravity": Polnay, *op. cit.*, p. 32.
202 "A perfect wife": Luz, *op. cit.*, p. 105.
202 "As he never": Holt, *op. cit.*, p. 49.
203 "Wasted her time": Polnay, *op. cit.*, p. 14.
203 "John and a half": Luz, *op. cit.*, p. 39.
204 Major economic revolutions: Brenan, *op. cit.*, p. 109.
206 "She and her children": Holt, *op. cit.*, p. 146.
206 "Mama, why don't": Luz, *op. cit.*, p. 49.
206 "Success is not": Holt, *op. cit.*, p. 168.
207 "Like the people": Luz, *op. cit.*, p. 55.
207 "The hour has come": Clarke, *op. cit.*, p. 141.
208 "I would give": Luz, *op. cit.*, p. 65.

208 "The infamous traitor": Clarke, *op. cit.,* p. 155.

209 "Proved in the long run": Cánovas del Castillo, quoted in Clarke, *op. cit.,* p. 155.

VIII. THE SCANDALOUS QUEEN: ISABEL II (1833–1868)

211 "The little Isabel": Sencourt, *Crown,* p. 182.

211 "Wore out more sheets": Luz, *op. cit.,* p. 68.

212 "That is not certain": *ibid.,* p. 77.

212 "The present state": Clarke, *op. cit.,* p. 166.

212 "I have made": Polnay, *op. cit.,* p. 60.

213 "Republic on marquise": Luz, *op. cit.,* p. 82.

213 "They can read": Sencourt, *Crown,* p. 183.

214 "Condemned to read": *ibid.,* pp. 170–71.

215 "I will not": *ibid.,* p. 190.

215 "My sister Carlota": *ibid.,* p. 190.

216 "Awful night": Aronson, *op. cit.,* pp. 37 ff.

216 "We cannot refuse": Sencourt, *Crown,* p. 189.

217 "If I fail": Clarke, *op. cit.,* pp. 192–93.

218 "She is by no means": Polnay, *op. cit.,* p. 76.

218 "At this period": *ibid.,* p. 78.

219 "Olózaga insisted": *ibid.,* p. 85.

219 "The violation of": E. Jones Parry, *The Spanish Marriages* (London, Macmillan, 1936), p. 160.

219 "Royal prostitute": Luz, *op. cit.,* p. 95.

220 "Ramón, you know": *ibid.,* p. 112.

220 "My enemies?": Hugh Thomas, *The Spanish Civil War* (New York, Harper, 1961), p. 211.

222 "Let me govern": Luz, *op. cit.,* p. 106.

222 "*We* could *never*": Aronson, *op. cit.,* p. 51.

223 "Sovereign will": *ibid.,* p. 50.

223 "I will not marry": Holt, *op. cit.,* p. 207.

223 "a little insignificant": Aronson, *op. cit.,* p. 59.

224 "Madame Muñoz": Holt, *op. cit.,* p. 28.

224 "What can be hoped": Parry, *op. cit.,* p. 97.

224 "But the way": Sencourt, *Crown,* pp. 193–94.

225 "Repugnant little monster": Luz, *op. cit.,* p. 108.

225 "Wild and unmanageable": Polnay, *op. cit.,* p. 101.

225 "*La reine est nubile*": Aronson, *op. cit.,* p. 54.

225 "Married somehow and to someone": Holt, *op. cit.,* p. 210.

225 "There were blunders": Polnay, *op. cit.,* p. 108.

226 "To be sure": Luz, *op. cit.,* pp. 117–18.

226 "A dark scheme": Clarke, *op. cit.,* pp. 205–6.

227 "One of the great": Luz, *op. cit.,* p. 116.

227 "One of the most reckless": Sencourt, *Crown,* p. 199.

227 "The English": Parry, *op. cit.,* p. 319.

227 "But if your marriage": Luz, *op. cit.,* pp. 118–19.

227 "When I fall in love": Parry, *op. cit.,* p. 324.

228 "Infamous": Aronson, *op. cit.,* p. 53.

228 "The little Queen": Polnay, *op. cit.,* p. 117.

228 "Great national effort": Luz, *op. cit.,* p. 124.

228 "Rise and rally": Aronson, *op. cit.,* p. 56.

229 "What shall I say": *ibid.,* p. 58.

229 "In fact, the Spanish Marriages": Sencourt, *Crown,* p. 206.

230 "Mechanical doll": Luz, *op. cit.,* p. 83. *See also* Aronson, *op. cit.,* p. 56; Parry, *op. cit.,* p. 297.

230 "In features": Infanta, Ludwig Ferdinand, *Through Four Revolutions* (London, John Murray, 1933), p. xx.

231 "Inseparable companionship": Jimenez-Landi, *op. cit.*, p. 317.

231 "Ou est Lambert" Jacquet, *op. cit.*, p. 334.

231 "It is believed": Sencourt, *Crown*, p. 227. "She was sexually ardent, possibly a nymphomaniac" (Clarke, *op. cit.*, p. 218).

231 "The daughter of": Luz, *op. cit.*, p. 224.

232 "The young Queen": Aronson, *op. cit.*, p. 64.

232 "She was a woman": *ibid.*, p. 86.

233 "Très grand": *ibid.*

233 "Keep it": Luz, *op. cit.*, p. 166.

233 "I declare": *ibid.*, pp. 185–86.

233 "As she became": Aronson, *op. cit.*, p. 72.

233 "General Beautiful": *ibid.*, p. 55.

235 "I understand": Challice, *op. cit.*, p. 175.

235 "She is disposed": Luz, *op. cit.*, p. 130.

235 "Kick out Bulwer": Aronson, *op. cit.*, p. 66.

236 "Gentlemen": Luz, *op. cit.*, p. 133.

236 "To seize the stick": Clarke, *op. cit.*, p. 211.

236 "This night": Luz, *op. cit.*, pp. 134–35.

237 "Dear one": Aronson, *op. cit.*, pp. 60–62.

238 "If one day": Luz, *op. cit.*, p. 146.

238 "Rest from the fatigues": Aronson, *op. cit.*, p. 70.

239 "But, Mama": Luz, *op. cit.*, p. 150.

239 "I am not beaten": Sencourt, *Crown*, p. 218.

240 "You who have": Luz, *op. cit.*, p. 156.

240 "My child": Sencourt, *Crown*, p. 214.

240 "It is the king": Luz, *op. cit.*, p. 157.

241 "There is not": *ibid.*, p. 165.

242 "guilty of high treason": Sencourt, *Crown*, pp. 219–20.

242 "Sovereigns who," Luz, *op. cit.*, p. 169.

242 "Like Mahomet": Marx, *op. cit.*, p. 40.

242 "Never has anyone: Luz, *op. cit.*, p. 171.

243 *Muera Cristina*: *ibid.*, p. 172.

243 "I shall depart": Sencourt, *Crown*, p. 220.

243 "Not by day," Aronson, *op. cit.*, p. 76.

243 "Queen Cristina": *ibid.*, p. 224.

243 "Carlos V": Aronson, *op. cit.*, p. 78.

244 "Let's go": Luz, *op. cit.*, p. 176.

244 "You will not abandon": *ibid.*, p. 182.

245 "In the first rank": *ibid.*, pp. 190–91.

245 Puigmoltejo: Clarke, *op. cit.*, p. 219. This author says flatly that Puig Moltó was "presumably the real father of her son the future King Alfonso XII."

245 "You like": Polnay, *op. cit.*, p. 173.

246 "Enjoy in peace": Aronson, *op. cit.*, p. 82.

246 "National prosperity": Clarke, *op. cit.*, p. 223.

247 "A nineteenth century progressive": *ibid.*

247 "If Mexico": Luz, *op. cit.*, p. 199.

248 "Reoccupy the position": *ibid.*, p. 198.

249 "We hope": Ana de Sagrera, *Amadeo y María Victoria* (Palma de Majorca, Imprenta Mossin Alcover, 1959), p. 65.

249 "Handsome fellow": *ibid.*, pp. 66–67.

249 "Poor Isabel!": Luz, *op. cit.*, p. 209.

249 "Today it is necessary": *ibid.*, p. 216.

250 "To attest": *ibid.*, p. 215.

251 "Had Montpensier": Aronson, *op. cit.*, p. 94.

251 "Spain with honor": *ibid.*, p. 95.

251 "Who would be": Luz, *op. cit.*, p. 221.

252 "To rest," *ibid.*

252 "Shall I abdicate?": Aronson, *op. cit.,* p. 95.

252 "I thought I had": Clarke, *op. cit.,* p. 233.

252 "In 1868 she preferred": Luz, *op. cit.,* p. 222.

253 "Considered themselves": José Cortes-Cavanillas, *Alfonso XII, el Rey Romóntico* (Barcelona, Editore Juvental, 1961), p. 23.

253 "So full of incident": Zabala, *op. cit.,* p. 421.

253 "Never was a Queen": Cortes-Cavanillas, *op. cit.,* p. 16. *See also* Jimenez-Landi, *op. cit.,* p. 264.

IX. THE CRISIS OF 1868–1874: THE MONARCHY IN DOUBT

254 "Remained cheerful": Holt, *op. cit.,* p. 233.

255 "Universal republic": Brenan, *op. cit.,* p. xv.

255 "If God": Holt, *op. cit.,* p. 234.

256 "Carlism is synonymous": Aronson, *op. cit.,* p. 106.

257 "Golden cage": Sagrera, *op. cit.,* p. 116.

257 "May be summed": Clarke, *op. cit.,* p. 262.

258 "Looking for": Holt, *op. cit.,* p. 237.

259 "The day": *ibid.,* p. 240.

259 "Gentle": Sagrera, *op. cit.,* p. 118.

259 "Madame": *ibid.,* p. 119.

260 "Puffed up French": Aronson, *op. cit.,* p. 107.

261 *Olé, olé*: Sagrera, *op. cit.,* p. 119.

261 "I am still Queen": Luz, *op. cit.,* p. 226.

261 "Human weaknesses": Jimenez-Landi, *op. cit.,* p. 314.

261 "Would be a direct attack": *ibid.,* p. 313.

262 "Cage of fetters": Sagrera, *op. cit.,* p. 120.

262 "At last": *ibid.*

263 "Secret repulsion": *ibid.*

263 "Unite the friends": *ibid.,* pp. 120–21

263 "Kings can come": Jimenez-Landi, *op. cit.,* p. 274.

263 "King of the 191": Holt, *op. cit.,* p. 243.

263 "Don Amadeo": Sagrera, *op. cit.,* p. 142.

264 "How he looks": *ibid.,* p. 25.

264 "Rather than belong": *ibid.,* p. 104.

265 "I hope God": *ibid.,* p. 53.

265 "Maria will marry": *ibid.,* p. 59.

265 "She has": *ibid.,* pp. 128–29.

265 "I am royalist": *ibid.,* p. 127.

265 "I am going": *ibid.,* p. 129.

266 "Of the case": Jimenez-Landi, *op. cit.,* p. 278.

266 "The monarchy of Savoy": *ibid.,* p. 296.

266 "*Avanti*": Sagrera, *op. cit.,* p. 139.

267 "Then Your Majesty": *ibid.,* p. 140.

269 "Everyone can shout": *ibid.,* p. 232.

269 "Poor children": *ibid.,* p. 161.

269 "Almost infantile": *ibid.,* p. 188.

269 "We are all grandees": *ibid.,* p. 157.

269 "Defects": Luz, *op. cit.,* p. 229, citing Villa-Urrutia.

269 "Lady of the Balcony": Sagrera, *op. cit.,* p. 235.

270 "I feel admiration": *ibid.,* p. 187.

270 "Shorten the table": *ibid.,* p. 227.

270 "Your Majesty": Holt, *op. cit.,* p. 245.

270 "General uprising": Aronson, *op. cit.,* pp. 102–3.

271 "*Yo contrario*": Sagrera, *op. cit.,* p. 246.

271 "Here is the King": Challice, *op. cit.*, p. 234.
273 "Rabble": Sagrera, *op. cit.*, p. 312.
273 "I can do nothing": *ibid.*, p. 313.
273 "But all who": *ibid.*, p. 315.
273 "The dignity": *ibid.*, p. 322.
273 "Thank God": *ibid.*, p. 337.
273 "One of the most generous": Jimenez-Landi, *op. cit.*, p. 304.
273 *"Avanti"*: Sagrera, *op. cit.*, p. 373.
274 "If it were not easy": Luz, *op. cit.*, p. 229.
275 "Enemies of the Republic": Clarke, *op. cit.*, p. 283.
276 "Viva la Reina": Holt, *op. cit.*, p. 259.
276 "There is only one man": Cortes, *op. cit.*, p. 42.
276 "I would not like": *ibid.*, p. 61.
277 "Red gold": Brenan, *op. cit.*, p. 155.
278 "King of the Basques": Holt, *op. cit.*, p. 251.
280 "Hereditary and constitutional": Cortes, *op. cit.*, p. 291.
280 "When you receive": *ibid.*, p. 105.
281 "Sir, Your Majesty": *ibid.*, p. 102.
281 "I already": *ibid.*, p. 103.
281 "But, Alfonso": *ibid.*, p. 104.

X. THE CONSTITUTIONAL MONARCHS: ALFONSO XII (1874–1885)
AND THE REGENT MARIA CRISTINA (1885–1902)

283 "He woke up": *ibid.*, p. 22.
283 "Alfonso does not know": Aronson, *op. cit.*, p. 88.
284 "Alfonso, give Pepe": Cortes, *op. cit.*, p. 31.
284 "His Highness": *ibid.*, p. 83.
285 "If he had been": Melchor Fernández Almagro, *Historia Política de la España Contemporánea* (Madrid, Alianza Editorial, 1968), Vol. I, p. 288.
286 "Your Majesty": Cortes, *op. cit.*, p. 119.
286 "The reception": *ibid.*, p. 128.
286 "King of all Spaniards": *ibid.*, p. 124.
286 "In this manner": *ibid.*, p. 178.
287 "The wine": *ibid.*, p. 130.
287 "King of the Revolution": *ibid.*, p. 141.
287 "If you are fighting": Holt, *op. cit.*, p. 263.
288 "The more royal heads": Cortes, *op. cit.*, p. 149.
288 "I am the legitimate": *ibid.*, p. 143.
288 "I reign in": *ibid.*, p. 142.
288 "If my son": *ibid.*, p. 143.
288 *"Volveré"*: Aronson, *op. cit.*, p. 118.
289 *El rey pacificador*: *ibid.*, p. 142.
289 "Spain has returned": *ibid.*, p. 121.
289 "I have come": Brenan, *op. cit.*, pp. 3–4.
290 "No. It makes": Aronson, *op. cit.*, p. 118.
290 "If we can get": Brenan, *op. cit.*, p. 14.
290 "I never fear": Aronson, *op. cit.*, p. 139.
291 *El rey romántico*: *ibid.*, p. 142.
292 "Were you bitten": Cortes, *op. cit.*, p. 218.
292 "I will lead": *ibid.*, p. 157.
293 "There are two things": Aronson, *op. cit.*, p. 121.
293 "I have just come back": Ludwig Ferdinand, *op. cit.*, p. 57.
293 "Yesterday, Alfonso": *ibid.*
294 "My ministers": Sagrera, *op. cit.*, p. 368.
294 "Alfonso and Mercedes": Ludwig Ferdinand, *op. cit.*, pp. 68–69.

294 "She was": Aronson, *op. cit.*, p. 122.
295 "Against this horrible": Pérez Galdós quoted in Cortes, *op. cit.*, p. 172.
295 "Tell my Alfonso": Ludwig Ferdinand, *op. cit.*, p. 72.
296 "A woman as good": Cortes, *op. cit.*, p. 188.
296 "Daughter-in-law": *ibid.*, p. 193.
296 "I have little time": *ibid.*, p. 183.
297 "Everyone loved Pilar": Ludwig Ferdinand, *op. cit.*, p. 126.
297 "Señor, my great desire": Cortes, *op. cit.*, p. 196.
297 "What is too bad": *ibid.*, p. 197.
297 "I ask that": *ibid.*, p. 200.
299 "Two feet": *ibid.*, p. 213.
299 "Social troubles": Ludwig Ferdinand, *op. cit.*, p. 126.
299 "Earned his salary": *ibid.*, p. 177.
301 "You will understand": *ibid.*, p. 257.
301 "My son is dying": Luz, *op. cit.*, p. 234.
301 "Cried like a child": Ludwig Ferdinand, *op. cit.*, p. 152.
301 "Give me my sword": Cortes, *op. cit.*, p. 247.
302 "Not then, not before": Fernández Almagro, *op. cit.*, Vol. 1, pp. 257–58.
303 "Doña Virtudes": Aronson, *op. cit.*, p. 146.
304 "We have just": *ibid.*, p. 147.
304 "Some historians": Grand Duke Alexander of Russia, *Twilight of Royalty* (New York, Ray Long, 1932), p. 45.
305 "King of the children": Princess Marthe Bibesco, *Some Royalties and a Prime Minister* (New York, Appleton, 1930), pp. 3 ff.
305 "Terrible fright": Sir Charles Petrie, *Alfonso XIII and His Age* (London, Chapman and Hall, 1963), p. 47.
305 "The little King": *ibid.*, p. 48.
306 "He is good": *ibid.*, p. 49.
306 "Their little histories": Aronson, *op. cit.*, p. 155.
306 "Do not hesitate": Petrie, *Alfonso*, p. 51.
307 "I have been": *Blanco y Negro* (magazine), *Álbum Gráfico de los Reyes* (Madrid, July 5, 1959), p. 6.
307 *"Viva la República"*: Aronson, *op. cit.*, p. 154.
307 "Propaganda by deed": Brenan, *op. cit.*, p. 163.
308 "Wild beasts": *ibid.*, p. 169.
309 "This would": Aronson, *op. cit.*, p. 164.
309 "About as ill-prepared": Clarke, *op. cit.*, p. 365.
310 "I hardly": Ludwig Ferdinand, *op. cit.*, p. 243.
310 "Unhappy is the country": Aronson, *op. cit.*, p. 165.
310 "generation of 1898": Petrie, *Alfonso*, p. 60.
310 "the sum total": Brenan, *op. cit.*, p. 22.
311 "Maligned, superseded": Aronson, *op. cit.*, p. 150.
312 "The floating ease": Sacheverell Sitwell, *A Background for Domenico Scarlatti* (London, Faber and Faber, Ltd., 1935), p. 74.
313 "I have no wish": Aronson, *op. cit.*, p. 162.
314 "The small slender man": *ibid.*, p. 169.
315 "Here is one": Petrie, *Alfonso*, p. 106.
315 "The dynasty": Aronson, *op. cit.*, p. 135.
315 "The one I loved": Marino Gómez-Santos, *La Reina Victoria* (Madrid, Afrodisio, 1969), p. 221.

XI. THE PLAYBOY POLITICIAN: ALFONSO XIII (1885) (1902–1931)

316 "She was very elegant": *ibid.*, p. 222.
316 "Calf's eyes": Aronson, *op. cit.*, p. 137.
317 "Cuba was gone": *ibid.*, p. 159.

317 "I should say": *ibid.,* p. 155.
318 "King of Spain": Petrie, *Alfonso,* p. 46. See also Lovett, *op. cit.,* p. 498. For titles and genealogical data, including especially birthdates, the most comprehensive work is Francisco Xavier Zorrilla, *Genealogía de la Casa de Borbón de España* (Madrid, Editora Nacional, 1971). For the titles of Alfonso XIII, see p. 201.
318 "I swear": Petrie, *Alfonso,* p. 63.
319 "Ah, if the day": Aronson, *op. cit.,* p. 176.
319 "He will do": *ibid.,* p. 173.
319 "A supreme elegance": *Blanco y Negro, op. cit.,* p. 113.
320 "For many years": Gómez-Santos, *op. cit.,* p. 299.
320 "Consummately royal": *Blanco y Negro, op. cit.,* p. 114.
320 "I see in his eyes": Bibesco, *op. cit.,* p. 52.
320 "When Alfonso XIII": *Blanco y Negro, op. cit.,* p. 112.
321 "If his Majesty": Petrie, *Alfonso,* p. 92.
321 "Tomorrow": *ibid.,* p. 149.
321 "Very carnivorous": Gómez-Santos, *op. cit.,* p. 299.
322 "The King wishes": Aronson, *op. cit.,* pp. 173–74.
322 "He has an extreme": *ibid.,* p. 174.
322 "Very sympathetic": Petrie, *Alfonso,* p. 76.
323 "Be calm": Gómez-Santos, *op. cit.,* p. 34.
323 "Risks of the trade": Bibesco, *op. cit.,* p. 26.
323 "As if he had given": *Blanco y Negro, op. cit.,* p. 6.
323 "The word chic": Bibesco, *op. cit.,* p. 24.
324 The tabulation in *ABC*: Gómez-Santos, *op. cit.,* p. 52.
324 "Alfonso of Spain": Seymour Berkson, *Their Majesties!* (New York, Stackpole, 1938), p. 322.
324 "Hopelessly in love": Gómez-Santos, *op. cit.,* p. 62.
324 "And who is": *ibid.,* p. 39.
324 "Who have": Petrie, *Alfonso,* p. 185.
325 "Rebaptism": *ibid.,* p. 73.
325 "Don't come whining": Aronson, *op. cit.,* p. 179.
325 "The impulses": Petrie, *Alfonso,* p. 86.
325 "If the princess": Gómez-Santos, *op. cit.,* p. 86.
326 "Very fine": Petrie, *Alfonso,* p. 89.
326 "Probably because": Gómez-Santos, *op. cit.,* pp. 130–31.
326 "Open the doors": Petrie, *Alfonso,* p. 88.
327 "Naturally on their return": *ibid.,* p. 90.
327 "The swine": *ibid.,* p. 91.
327 "Alfonso XIII": Gómez-Santos, *op. cit.,* pp. 177–78.
328 "For God's sake": *ibid.,* p. 144.
328 "Picture book": Aronson, *op. cit.,* p. 179.
328 "I can think": *ibid.,* p. 199.
328 "She was by far": Grand Duchess Marie of Russia, *A Princess in Exile* (London, Cassell and Co., 1932), pp. 209–10.
329 "Twenty-four years": Gómez-Santos, *op. cit.,* p. 221.
329 "No, no, never": *ibid.,* p. 398.
330 "National asphyxiation": *ibid.,* pp. 235–36.
331 "Constant and intimate": Petrie, *Alfonso,* p. 92.
331 "Joke": Miguel Maura, *Así Cayó Alfonso XIII* (Barcelona, Ariel, 1966), p. 14.
332 "I am King": Petrie, *Alfonso,* p. 104.
332 "Until the Spanish Government": *ibid.,* p. 193.
333 "I saw a man": *ibid.,* p. 104.
334 "There is no one": Brenan, *op. cit.,* p. 58.
336 "I have immense faith": Aronson, *op. cit.,* p. 193.
337 "If I had to paint": Petrie, *Alfonso,* p. 154.
338 "I am not": *ibid.,* pp. 164–65.

338 "I see you": Bibesco, *op. cit.*, p. 64.
338 "I want": Grand Duchess Marie, *op. cit.*, pp. 210–11.
339 "A paradise": *ibid.*, p. 208.
339 "It was terrible": Gómez-Santos, *op. cit.*, pp. 299–300.
339 "The long years": quoted in Aronson, *op. cit.*, p. 188.
339 "A perpetual young man": quoted *ibid.*
339 "The most elegant": *ibid.*, p. 202.
340 "I would say": Gómez-Santos, *op. cit.*, p. 297.
340 "He tires": Aronson, *op. cit.*, p. 198.
340 "Not a model husband": *Blanco y Negro*, *op. cit.*, p. 114.
341 "Aunt Eulalia": Aronson, *op. cit.*, p. 191.
341 "Who is this": *ibid.*, p. 198.
341 "Spain is great": *ibid.*, p. 194.
342 "Do as I tell you": Brenan, *op. cit.*, p. 75.
342 "From tomorrow": Petrie, *Alfonso*, p. 170.
343 "With the generals": Aronson, *op. cit.*, p. 195.
343 "It was a hard": Petrie, *Alfonso*, p. 184.
343 "You have got": *ibid.*, pp. 174–75.
343 "We must govern": *ibid.*, p. 175.
344 "Professional politicians": *ibid.*, pp. 177–78.
344 "Very amateurish": *ibid.*, p. 181.
345 "Tonight everyone": Thomas, *op. cit.*, p. 17.
345 "*Naipes, mujeres*": Petrie, *Alfonso*, p. 180.
345 "Heathful and happy vacation": Maura, *op. cit.*, p. 41.
345 "Less a nuisance": Petrie, *Alfonso*, pp. 194–97.
346 "This is my Mussolini": Aronson, *op. cit.*, p. 196.
346 "If like another Urban II": Petrie, *Alfonso*, p. 185.
348 "The last two years": Brenan, *op. cit.*, p. 84.
349 "And now": Thomas, *op. cit.*, p. 17.
349 "El Salvador": Aronson, *op. cit.*, p. 203.
349 "Primo's enemies": Ludwig Ferdinand, *op. cit.*, p. 349.
349 "King Fernando Seven": Aronson, *op. cit.*, p. 203.
349 "the revolution": *ibid.*, p. 205.

XII. THE CRISIS OF 1931–1939: THE DYNASTY OVERTHROWN

350 "*Dicta-blanda*": Maura, *op. cit.*, p. 5.
351 "Delenda est monarquia": Thomas, *op. cit.*, p. 17.
351 "I am no longer": Aronson, *op. cit.*, p. 206.
351 "While I live": Maura, *op. cit.*, p. 50.
351 "The Army": Petrie, *Alfonso*, p. 217.
351 "Worst mistake": Brenan, *op. cit.*, p. 85.
352 "With this man": Vincente R. Pilapil, *Alfonso XIII* (New York, Twayne, 1969), p. 179.
352 "I thought I was": *ibid.*, p. 180.
352 "I had the impression": Petrie, *Alfonso*, p. 220.
352 "What more crisis": Pilapil, *Alfonso*, p. 188.
353 "Go home": Ludwig Ferdinand, *op. cit.*, p. 357.
353 "Before sundown": Jackson, *op. cit.*, p. 723.
353 "On taking leave": Pilapil, *Alfonso*, p. 194.
353 "An act of humanity": Jimenez-Landi, *op. cit.*, p. 331.
354 "The elections": Petrie, *Alfonso*, pp. 225–26.
355 "Excuse me": Pilapil, *Alfonso*, p. 198.
355 "Take care of": Gómez-Santos, *op. cit.*, p. 285.
356 "Queen Victoria Eugenia": Pilar of Bavaria and Major Desmond Chapman-Huston, *Every Inch a King* (New York, Dutton, 1932), pp. 375–76.
356 "I thought": Aronson, *op. cit.*, p. 209.

356 "My husband": Petrie, *Alfonso,* p. 225.
356 "Those who leave": Pilapil, *Alfonso,* p. 196.
356 "The monarchy": Maura, *op. cit.,* p. 8.
357 "The times": Petrie, *Alfonso,* p. 238.
357 "Whether from love of power," Brenan, p. 24.
358 "Let them come": Gómez-Santos, *op. cit.,* p. 283.
358 "Monarchists who wish": Petrie, *Alfonso,* p. 229.
359 "Long live": Thomas, *op. cit.,* p. 38.
360 "The antithesis": Aronson, *op. cit.,* p. 186.
360 "You or one": Thomas, *op. cit.,* p. 61.
360 "Don Jaime and Don Alfonso": Ramón Sierra, *Don Juan de Borbón* (Madrid, Afrodisio, 1965), p. 37.
361 "Splendidly anachronistic," Aronson, p. 214.
361 "My beloved cousin": *ibid.,* p. 75.
361 "Acts of rebellion": Petrie, *Alfonso,* p. 230.
361 "Republic of workers": Jackson, *op. cit.,* p. 45.
362 "Saviour of Spain": Thomas, *op. cit.,* p. 62.
362 "I'm a queer kind": Berkson, *op. cit.,* pp. 318–19.
363 "For me and whatever": Sierra, *op. cit.,* p. 65.
364 "Showing how": José Gutiérrez-Ravé, *El Conde de Barcelona* (Madrid, Prensa Espasa, 1963), pp. 11, 71.
365 "Peruvians": Jackson, *op. cit.,* p. 246.
365 "Revolutionary excesses": *ibid.,* p. 146.
365 *Comunismo libertario*: Jackson, *op. cit.,* p. 160.
366 "Generally exemplary": Thomas, *op. cit.,* p. 93.
366 "The Traditionalist": *ibid.,* p. 119.
366 "The only thing": Brenan, *op. cit.,* p. xiv.
369 "We all believed": Aronson, *op. cit.,* p. 219. *See also* Jackson, *op. cit.,* p. 417.
370 *Viva España*: Sierra, *op. cit.,* pp. 88 ff.
370 "I have the highest": *ibid.,* p. 95.
370 "Chief of State": Jackson, *op. cit.,* p. 296.
371 "At the orders": Thomas, *op. cit.,* p. 162.
371 "Fran-co, Fran-co": *ibid.,* p. 286.
371 "Kid gloves": *ibid.,* p. 91.
373 Falange Española Tradicionalista: *ibid.,* p. 415. *See also* Jackson, *op. cit.,* pp. 356–58.
373 "Infamy": Thomas, *op. cit.,* p. 416.
373 "Should the moment": Aronson, *op. cit.,* p. 219.
373 "If it were not": Thomas, *op. cit.,* p. 483.
374 "His Royal Highness": this was verified by a friend of the present author who made a trip to the grave.
374 The Civil War cost: Jackson, *op. cit.,* p. 589.

XIII. FRANCO AND THE PROSPECTS OF THE MONARCHY

376 "In sober truth": Jackson, *op. cit.,* p. 422.
377 "Stepping courageously": Crow, *op. cit.,* p. 13.
377 "Will to empire": Thomas Hamilton, *Appeasement's Child, The Franco Regime in Spain* (New York, Knopf, 1943), p. 76.
378 "Sacrificed": George Hills, *Franco* (New York, Macmillan, 1967), p. 341.
378 "I would rather": *ibid.,* p. 337.
378 "Duce, if you": *ibid.,* p. 351.
378 "Would appear": Sierra, *op. cit.,* pp. 101–2.
379 "Señor, forgive": Gómez-Santos, *op. cit.,* p. 295.
379 "The generosity": Petrie, *Alfonso,* p. 235.
380 "Soldier's sword": Sierra, *op. cit.,* pp. 110–11.
380 "I am not the chief," *ibid.*

381 "Contrary to the Spanish character": Hills, *op. cit.,* pp. 388–89.
381 "Absolutely intolerable": Gutiérrez, *op. cit.,* p. 15.
381 "What! We are going": Sierra, *op. cit.,* p. 44.
383 "Cease to be": *ibid.,* p. 168.
383 "Doña María la Brava": *ibid.,* p. 182.
384 "The synonym": *ibid.,* pp. 148–49.
384 "It is necessary": *ibid.,* p. 117.
384 "Person of royal blood": Aronson, *op. cit.,* p. 221.
387 "Surrounded with the special": Sierra, *op. cit.,* p. 175.
388 "When the Generalisimo": Aronson, *op. cit.,* p. 221.
388 "Miraculous persistence": Sierra, *op. cit.,* p. 154.
388 "Without the beard": Aronson, *op. cit.,* p. 222.
388 "State structure": Gutiérrez, *op. cit.,* pp. 227–28.
389 "Semi-Salic": *ibid.,* p. 226.
389 "Great cordiality": Sierra, *op. cit.,* p. 177.
390 "Placed beside me": Vincente R. Pilapil, "Franco, the Monarchy, and Juan Carlos," *Contemporary Review* (July, 1971), p. 5.
392 "Advised": Aronson, *op. cit.,* p. 223.
392 "The most lost": *ibid.,* p. 224.
393 "I do not": Sierra, *op. cit.,* p. 169.
394 "Good man": Juan Carlos de Borbón, *Por España, con los Españoles* (Madrid, Editorial Doncel, 1973), p. 124.
394 "In the post": *ibid.,* pp. 128–29.
395 "In due course": Richard Comyns-Carr, "Succession to Franco," *Contemporary Review* (June, 1970), pp. 11–12.
395 "Had given clear proofs": Pilapil, "Franco," p. 4.
395 "I belong": Juan Carlos, *op. cit.,* p. 135.
395 "Franco, Franco": Jacques Georgel, *El Franquismo* (Paris, Ruedo Iberico, 1971), p. 300.
396 Franco reported: New York *Times,* March 7, 1971, p. 3.
397 "Future generation": New York *Times,* January 27, 1971, p. 45.
398 "Even greater social": *ibid.*
398 "A slender athletic": Richard Eder, "Spanish Joke," *New York Times Magazine* (August 27, 1972), p. 52.
398 "Larger political participation": Juan Carlos, *op. cit.,* p. 189.
398 "I belong": *ibid.,* p. 34.
398 "I am very close": *ibid.,* p. 136.
399 "Accelerated progress": *ibid.,* p. 44.
399 "Today one cannot think": *ibid.,* p. 190.
399 "Since you will have": Eder, *op. cit.,* p. 52.
399 "His Royal Highness": New York *Times,* March 9, 1972.
400 "Is the world's greatest": ¡Hola!, July 14, 1973.
401 "Spain is a luxury": Eder, *op. cit.,* p. 8.

Bibliography

ACTON, HAROLD, *The Last Bourbons of Spain*. London, Methuen and Co., 1961.

ALCALÁ GALLIANO, ANTONIO, *Recuerdos de un anciano*. Madrid, 1878.

ALEXANDER, GRAND DUKE OF RUSSIA, *Twilight of Royalty*. New York, Ray Long and Richard R. Smith, Inc., 1932.

ALFONSO XIII, KING OF SPAIN, *Diario Íntimo*. Madrid, Biblioteca Nueva, 1961.

ALMAGRO SAN MARTÍN, MARQUÉS DE, *Crónica de Alfonso XIII y Su Linaje*. Madrid, A. Aguado, 1946.

ALTAMIRA, RAFAEL, *Historia de España y de la Civilación Española*. Barcelona, 1913. 4 vols.

ANSALDO, JUAN ANTONIO, HEREDEROS DE J. GILI, *Mémoires d'un Monarchiste Espagnol*. Monaco, Editions du Rocher, 1952.

ARMSTRONG, EDWARD, *Elizabeth Farnese*. London, Longmans. Green, and Co., 1892.

ARONSON, THEO, *Royal Vendetta: The Crown of Spain, 1829–1965*. New York, Bobbs-Merrill, 1966.

ARTOLA GALBGO, MIGUEL, *La España de Fernando VII*. Madrid, Espasa Calpe, 1968.

ARTZ, FREDERICK B., *Reaction and Revolution 1814–1832*. New York, Harper, 1934.

ATKINSON, WILLIAM C., *A History of Spain and Portugal*. London, Penguin Editions, 1960.

BALLESTEROS Y BERETTA, ANTONIO, *Historia de España y Su Influencia en la Historia Universal*. Barcelona, Salvat Editores, S.A., 1922. 12 vols.

BATCHELLER, TRYPHOSA BATES, *Royal Spain of Today*. London, Longmans, 1913.

BERKSON, SEYMOUR, *Their Majesties!* New York, Stackpole Sons, 1938.

BERMEJO, ILDEFONSO, *La Estafeta de palacio*. Madrid, Carlos Bailly-Bailliere, 1872.

BEYERSDORF, EUNICE SMITH, *A Rediscovered Portrait of Godoy, Minister to Charles IV*. New York, The Hispanic Society, 1962.

BIBESCO, PRINCESS MARTHE, *Some Royalties and a Prime Minister*. New York, Appleton, 1930.

BLACKBURN, HENRY, *Travelling in Spain*. London, Sampson Low, Son, and Marston, 1866.

Blanco y Negro (magazine), *Album Gráfico de los Reyes*. Madrid, July 5, 1969.

BLASCO-IBÁÑEZ, V., *Historia de la Revolución Española*. Barcelona, La Enciclopedia democrática, 1890.

———, *Alfonso XIII Unmasked*. New York, E. P. Dutton and Company, 1924.

BOETZKES, OTTILIEG, *The Little Queen: Isabella II of Spain*. New York, Exposition Press, 1966.

BOLIN, LUIS, *Spain, The Vital Years*. London, Cassell, 1967.

BORKENAU, FRANK, *The Spanish Cockpit*. London, Faber and Faber, Ltd., 1937.

BORROW, GEORGE, *The Bible in Spain*. Philadelphia, J. M. Campbell and Co., 1843.

BOWERS, CLAUDE, *My Mission to Spain, Watching the Rehearsal for World War II*. New York, Simon and Schuster, 1954.

BRAVO MURILLO, J., *Política y Administración en la España Isabelina*. Madrid, Narcea de Ediciones, S.A., 1972.

BRENAN, GERALD, *The Spanish Labyrinth: An Account of the Social and Political Background of the Civil War*. New York, Cambridge University Press, 1967.

BURGES, ELLEN, *Viscaya or Life in the Land of the Carlists*. London, 1874.

BURGO TORRES, JAIME, *La Primera Guerra Carlista*. Pamplona, Diputación Foral, 1973.

CALLEJA, JUAN L., *Don Juan Carlos: ¿Por Qué?* Madrid, Libros Directos, 1972.

CANCIO, RITA MARIA, *The Function of Maria Christina of Austria's Regency (1885–1902) in Preserving the Spanish Monarchy*. New York, Eliseo Torres, 1956.

CARLOS VII, *Memorias y Diario*. Madrid, Europa, 1957.

CARMEN VELÁZQUEZ, MARIA DEL, *La España de Carlos III de 1764 a 1776 Según los Embajadores Austríacos: Documentos*. Mexico, Universidad Nacional Autonóma de Mexico, 1963.

CARR, RAYMOND, *Spain, 1808–1939*. New York, Oxford University Press, 1966.

CASTILLEJO, JOSÉ, *War of Ideas in Spain*. London, 1937.

CASTRO, AMERICO, *The Spaniards: An Introduction to Their History*. Berkeley, University of California Press, 1971.

CHALLICE, RACHEL, *The Secret History of the Spanish Court During the Last Century*. New York, Appleton and Co., 1909.

CHASTENET, JACQUES, *Godoy, Master of Spain, 1792–1808*. London, The Batchworth Press, 1953.

CHRISTIANSEN, E., *The Origins of Military Power in Spain, 1800–1854*. New York, Oxford University Press, 1967.

CHURCHILL, WINSTON S., *Great Contemporaries*. New York, G. P. Putnam's Sons, 1937.

CIERVA, RICARDO DE LA, *Historia de la Guerra Civile Españole, Antecedentes Monarquía República, 1898–1936*. Madrid, San Martín, 1969.

CIGES APARICIO, MANUEL, *España bajo la Dinastía de los Borbones*. Madrid, Aguilar Editor, 1932.

CLARKE, H. BUTLER, *Modern Spain*. Cambridge, Cambridge University Press, 1906.

COLLIER, WILLIAM MILLER, *At the Court of His Catholic Majesty*. Chicago, McClurg and Co., 1912.

COMELLAS, JOSÉ LUIS, *Los Primeros Pronunciamentos en España*. Madrid, Consejo Superior de investigaciones cientificas, Escuela de historia moderna, 1958.

COMYNS-CARR, RICHARD, "Succession to Franco," *Contemporary Review*, Vol. 216 (June, 1970).

CONNELLY, OWEN, *The Gentle Bonaparte*. New York, Macmillan, 1968.

CORONA BARATECH, CARLOS E., *Revolución y Reacción en el Reinado de Carlos IV*. Madrid, Editorial Rialp, S.A., 1957.

CORTES-CAVANILLAS, JOSÉ, *Alfonso XII, el Rey Romántico*. Barcelona, Editorial Juventud, S.A., 1961.

———, *Alfonso XIII, Vida, Confessiones, y Muerte*. Madrid, Editorial Prensa España, 1959.

COURCY, LE MARQUIS DE, *L'Espagne après la paix d'Utrecht*. Paris, Librairie Plon, 1891.

COXE, WILLIAM, *Memoirs of the Kings of Spain of the House of Bourbon*. London, Longman, Hurst, Rees, Orme, and Brown, 1815.

CROW, JOHN A., *Spain: The Root and the Flower*. New York, Harper and Row, 1963.

DANVILLA, ALFONSO, *El Reinado Relámpago, Luis I y Luisa Isabel de Orléans, 1707–1742*. Madrid, Espasa-Calpe, S.A., 1952.

DESCOLA, JEAN, *A History of Spain*. New York, Alfred A. Knopf, 1963.

DÍAZ-PLAJA, FERNANDO, *La Vida Española en el Siglo 18*. Barcelona, Editorial Alberto Martín, 1946.

———, *La Historia de España en Sus Documentos*. Barcelona, Ediciones G.P., 1969.

DOMÍNGUEZ ORTIZ, ANTONIO, *The Golden Age of Spain, 1516–1659*. New York, Basic Books, 1971.

DUMAS, ALEXANDRE, *Adventures in Spain*. New York, Doubleday and Co., 1960.

ECHEVARRÍA, TÓMAS, *El Pacto de Territet: Alfonso XIII y los Carlistas*. Madrid, Editorial E. Janzer, 1973.

EDER, RICHARD, "Spanish Joke," *New York Times Magazine* (August 27, 1972).

EGIDO LÓPEZ, TEOFANES, *Opinión Pública y Oposición al Poder en España del Siglo XVIII (1713–1759)*. Valladolid, Editorial Severcuesta, 1971.

ELLIOT, J. H., *Imperial Spain 1469–1716*. New York, St. Martins, 1963.

EPTON, NINA, *The Spanish Mousetrap: Napoleon and the Court of Spain*. London, MacDonal, 1973.

ERSKINE, MRS. STEWART, *Twenty-nine Years: the Reign of King Alfonso XIII of Spain*. London, Hutchinson and Co., 1931.

EULALIA, *Memoirs of Her Royal Highness the Infanta*, translated by Phyllis Megroz. London, Hutchinson and Co., 1936.

FEHRENBACH, C. W., "Moderados and Exaltados; The Liberal Opposition to Ferdinand VIII 1814–1823," *Hispanic American Historical Review*, Vol. 50, No. 1 (February, 1970), pp. 52–69.

FERNÁNDEZ ALMAGRO, MELCHOR, *Historia Política de la España Contemporánea.* Madrid, Alianza Editorial, 1968, 3 vols.

——, *"Alfonso XIII,"* Blanco y Negro (February 26, 1966), pp. 60–65.

FERNÁNDEZ-RUA, JOSÉ LUIS, *España Secreta (1868–1870).* Madrid, Editorial Nacional, 1970.

FIELD, HENRY M., *Old Spain and New Spain.* New York, C. Scribners Sons, 1888.

FONTANA LÁZARO, JOSEP, *La Quiebra de la Monarquía Absoluta, 1814–1820,* Barcelona, Ediciones Ariel, 1971.

FORD, RICHARD, *A Handbook for Travellers in Spain.* London, J. Murray, 1847.

GALINDO HERRERO, SANTIAGO, *Historia de los Partidos Monárquicos, bajo la Segunda República.* Madrid, Ediciones Rialp, S.A., 1956.

GALLO, M. MAX, *Histoire de l'Espagne Franquiste.* Robert Laffont, Paris, 1969.

GARCÍA-NIETO, MARÍA CARMEN, *Bases Documentales de la España Contemporánea.* Madrid, Guadiana de Publicaciones, S.A., 1972. 8 Vols.

GASSIER, PIERRE, and WILSON, JULIET, *The Life and Complete Work of Francisco Goya.* New York, Reynal and Co., in association with William Morrow and Co., 1971.

GAXOTTE, PIERRE, *The Age of Louis XIV.* New York, Macmillan, 1970.

GEORGEL, JACQUES, *El Franquismo: Historia y Balance 1939–1969.* Paris, Ruedo Ibérico, 1971.

GIROD DE L'AIN, GABRIEL, *Joseph Bonaparte: Le Roi Malgré Lui.* Paris, Librairie Académique Perrin, 1970.

GLYN, ELINOR, *Letters from Spain.* London, Duckworth & Co., 1924.

GÓMEZ-SANTOS, MARINO, *La Reina Victoria, De Cerca.* Madrid, Afrodisio Aguado, S.A., 1969.

GRIBBLE, FRANCIS, *The Tragedy of Isabella II.* London, Chapman and Hall, 1913.

GUTIÉRREZ-RAVÉ, JOSÉ, *El Conde de Barcelona.* Madrid, Prensa Espasa, S.A., 1963.

HALL, GEOFFREY F., *Moths Around the Flame: Studies of Charmers.* New York, Holt, 1936.

HAMILTON, GERALD, *Blood Royal.* London, A. Gibbs & Phillips, 1964.

HAMILTON, THOMAS J., *Appeasement's Child: The Franco Regime in Spain.* New York, Knopf, 1943.

HARCOURT-SMITH, SIMON, *Alberoni or the Spanish Conspiracy.* London, Faber and Faber Ltd., 1943.

HARGREAVES-MAWDSLEY, W. N. (ed.), *Spain Under the Bourbons 1700–1833.* London, Macmillan, 1972.

HAVERTY, MARTIN, *Wanderings in Spain in 1843.* London, 1844.

HAY, JOHN, *Castilian Days.* Boston, Jas. R. Osgood and Co., 1872.

HENDERSON, N., "Charles III of Spain: An Enlightened Despot," *History Today,* Vol. 18 (October–November, 1968), pp. 673–82, 760–68.

HENNESSY, C. A. M., *The Federal Republic in Spain: Pi y Margall and the Federal Republican Movement 1868–1874.* Oxford, Oxford University Press, 1962.

HERR, Richard, *The Eighteenth Century Revolution in Spain.* Princeton, Princeton University Press, 1969.

———, *Spain.* Englewood Cliffs, N.J., Prentice-Hall, 1971.

HILLS, GEORGE, *Franco: The Man and His Nation.* New York, Macmillan, 1967.

HILT, DOUGLAS, "Manuel Godoy: Prince of Peace," *History Today* (December, 1971), pp. 833–38.

HIPPOLYTE, JEAN, *The Spain of Ferdinand and Isabella.* New Brunswick, Rutgers University Press, 1961.

HOLT, EDGAR, *The Carlist Wars in Spain.* Chester Springs, Pa., Dufour Editions, 1967.

HUME, MARTIN, *The Court of Philip IV: Spain in Decadence.* London, Eveleigh Nash, 1907.

———, *Spain: Its Greatness and Decay 1479–1788.* London, Cambridge University Press, 1913.

IRVING, WASHINGTON, *Letters from Sunnyside and Spain.* New Haven, Yale University Press, 1928.

IZQUIERDO HERNÁNDEZ, MANUEL, *Antecedentes y Comienzos del Reinando de Fernando VII.* Madrid, Ediciones Cultura Hispánica, 1963.

JACKSON, GABRIEL, *The Spanish Republic and the Civil War 1931–1939.* Princeton, Princeton University Press, 1967.

JACQUET, JEAN-LOUIS, *Les Bourbons d'espagne.* Lausanne, Éditions Rencontre, 1968.

JIMENEZ-LANDI, ANTONIO, *Una Ley de Sucesión y Quince Siglos de Historia.* Madrid, Aguilar, 1968.

JUAN CARLOS DE BORBÓN, PRINCIPE DE ESPAÑA, *Por España, con los Españoles.* Madrid, Editorial Doncel, 1973.

KAMEN, HENRY, *The War of Succession in Spain 1700–1715.* Bloomington, Indiana University Press, 1969.

KIERNAN, V. G., *The Revolution of 1854 in Spanish History.* Oxford, Clarendon Press, 1966.

LANGDON-DAVIES, JOHN, *Carlos, the King Who Would Not Die.* Englewood Cliffs, N.J., Prentice-Hall, 1963.

LEWIS, W. H., *The Sunset of the Splendid Century.* New York, William Sloane, 1955.

LIDA, CLARA E., and ZAVALA, IRIS M., *La Revolución de 1868: Historia, Pensamiento, Literatura.* New York, Las Americas, 1970.

LIVERMORE, HAROLD, *A History of Spain.* New York, Minerva Press, 1968.

LONGFORD, ELIZABETH, *Queen Victoria, Born to Succeed.* New York, Harper and Row, 1964.

———, *Wellington: The Years of the Sword.* New York, Harper and Row, 1969.

LÓPEZ SANZ, FRANCISCO, *Carlos VII, Rey de los caballeros y caballero de los Reyes.* Pamplona, Editorial Gómez, 1969.

LOVETT, GABRIEL H., *Napoleon and the Birth of Modern Spain.* New York, New York University Press, 1965. 2 vols.

LUDWIG FERDINAND, HER ROYAL HIGHNESS, PRINCESS OF BAVARIA, INFANTA OF SPAIN, *Through Four Revolutions*. London, John Murray, 1933.

LUZ, PIERRE DE, *Isabel II, Reina de España (1830–1904)*. Barcelona, Editorial Juventud, S.A., 1962.

LYNCH, JOHN, *Spain Under the Hapsburgs*. New York, Oxford University Press, 1964–69. 2 vols.

MADARIAGA, SALVADOR DE, *Spain, A Modern History*. New York, Praeger, 1958.

MARIE, GRAND DUCHESS OF RUSSIA, *A Princess in Exile*. London, Cassell and Co., 1932.

MARIÉJOL, JEAN HIPPOLYTE, *The Spain of Ferdinand and Isabella*. New Brunswick, Rutgers University Press, 1961.

MARTÍN, CLAUDE, *José Napoleón I*. Madrid, 1969.

MARTÍ, GILABERT, FRANCISCO, *El Motín de Aranjuez*. Pamplona, Ediciones Universidad de Navarra, 1972.

MARX, KARL, Y ENGELS, FRIEDRICH, *Revolución en España*. Barcelona, Ediciones Ariel, 1970.

MAURA, MIGUEL, *Así Cayó Alfonso XIII*. Barcelona, Ediciones Ariel, 1966.

McGANN, THOMAS F., *Portrait of Spain: British and American Accounts of Spain in the Nineteenth and Twentieth Centuries*. New York, Knopf, 1963.

McGUIGAN, DORIS, *The Hapsburgs*. New York, Doubleday, 1966.

McKUSICK, VICTOR A., "The Royal Hemophilia," *Scientific American*, Vol. XX (August, 1965), pp. 88–95.

MENÉNDEZ PIDAL, RAMÓN, *The Spaniards in Their History*. New York, W. W. Norton & Co., 1950.

MERCADER RIBA, JUAN, *José Bonaparte, Rey de España 1808–1813*. Madrid, Editorial Elexpuru Hnos., S.A., 1971.

MOSS, ROBERT, "Spain After Franco," *World Today*, Vol. 12 (August, 1973), pp. 324–36.

MULLER, PRISCILLA E., "Goya's The Family of Charles IV, An Interpretation," *Apollo*, Vol. XCI (February, 1970). Reprinted by the Hispanic Society.

OMAN, CHARLES, *A History of the Peninsular War*. Oxford, Clarendon Press, 1902–1930. 7 vols.

ORLEANS, E. C., *Secret Memoirs of the Court of Louis XIV and of the Regency*. Boston, Grolier, n.d.

ORLEY, WALTER J. P., *Monarchs in Waiting*. New York, Dodd, Mead, 1973.

ORTEGA Y GASSET, JOSÉ, *Invertebrate Spain*. New York, W. W. Norton and Co., 1937.

OYARZUN, ROMÁN, *Historia del Carlismo*. Madrid, Editora Nacional, 1944.

PARRY, E. JONES, *The Spanish Marriages 1841–1846*. London, Macmillan and Co., 1936.

PAYNE, STANLEY G., *Falange*. Palo Alto, Stamford University Press, 1961.

———, *The Spanish Revolution*. New York, W. W. Norton, 1970.

———, "In the Twilight of the Franco Era," *Foreign Affairs* (January, 1971), v. 49, pp. 153–159.

PETRIE, SIR CHARLES, *Alfonso XIII and His Age*. London, Chapman and Hall Ltd., 1963.

———, *King Charles III of Spain*. London, Constable, 1971.

PICK, ROBERT, *Empress Maria Theresa: The Earlier Years 1717–1757*. London, Weidenfeld and Nicolson, 1966.

PILAPIL, VINCENTE R., *Alfonso XIII*. New York, Twayne Publishers, 1969.

———, "Franco, the Monarchy, and Juan Carlos," *Contemporary Review*, Vol. 219 (July, 1971), pp. 1–7.

PILAR OF BAVARIA, HER ROYAL HIGHNESS, PRINCESS, and CHAPMAN-HUSTON, MAJOR DESMOND, *Every Inch a King*. New York, E. P. Dutton, 1932.

PI Y MARGALL, *El Reinado de Amadeo de Saboya y la República de 1873*. Madrid, Seminarios y Ediciones, S.A., 1970.

POLNAY, PETER, *A Queen of Spain, Isabella II*. London, Hollis and Carter Ltd., 1962.

POLT, JOHN H. R., *Gaspar Melchor de Jovellanos*. New York, Twayne Publishers, 1971.

PRIETO, INDALECIO, *Con el Rey o Contra el Rey*. Mexico, Ediciones Oasis, S.A., 1972.

QUIN, MICHAEL, *Visit to Spain*. London, Hurst, Robinson, & Co., 1824.

ROBINSON, RICHARD A. H., *The Origins of Franco's Spain: The Right, the Republic, and Revolution 1931–1936*. Pittsburgh, University of Pittsburgh Press, 1971.

RODEZNO, CONDE DE, *Carlos VII, Duque de Madrid*. Madrid, Espasa-Calpe, S.A., 1944.

ROMANONES, CONDE DE, *Notas de Una Vida 1868–1901*. Madrid, Renacimiento, 1934.

SAGRERA, ANA DE, *Amadeo y Maria Victoria, Reyes de España 1870–1873*. Palma de Majorca, Imprenta Mossin Alcover, 1959.

———, *La Reina Mercedes*. Madrid, Blanco de Puejo, 1951.

SAINT-SIMON, LOUIS DE ROUVROY, *Historical Memoirs of the Duc de Saint-Simon*, edited and translated by Lucy Norton. New York, McGraw-Hill, 1967. 3 vols.

SANZ DE BREMOND, EMILIO OLIVER, *Castelar y el Periodo Revolucionario Español (1868–1874)*. Madrid, G. del Toro Editor, 1971.

SHNEIDMAN, J. LEE (ed.), *Spain and Franco 1949–1959*. New York, Facts on File, 1973.

SENCOURT, ROBERT, *The Spanish Crown 1808–1931: An Intimate Chronicle of a Hundred Years*. New York, Scribner's, 1932.

———, *King Alfonso*. London, Faber and Faber Ltd., 1942.

SERRANO, CARLOS SECO, *Alfonso XIII y la Crisis de la Restauración*. Barcelona, Ediciones Ariel, 1969.

SEVILLA ANDRÉS, DIEGO, *Historia Política de España 1800–1967*. Madrid, Editora Nacional, 1968.

SIERRA, RAMÓN, *Don Juan de Borbón*. Madrid, Afrodisio Aguado, S.A., 1965.

SITWELL, SACHEVERELL, *A Background for Domenico Scarlatti.* London, Faber and Faber, Ltd., 1935.

——, *Spain.* London, B. T. Batsford, 1950.

SMITH, BRADLEY, *Spain, A History in Art.* New York, Doubleday, 1971.

STACTON, DAVID, *The Bonapartes.* New York, Simon and Schuster, 1966.

SUÁREZ, FEDERICO, *La Crisis Política del Antiguo Régimen en España (1800–1840).* Madrid, Editorial Rialp, 1958.

—— (ed.), *Documentos del Reinado de Fernando VII.* Pamplona, Ediciones Universidad de Navarra, S.A., 1970.

SZULC, TAD, *Portrait of Spain.* New York, American Heritage Press, 1972.

TAXONERA, LUCIANO DE, *Felipe V.* Barcelona, Editorial Juventud, 1956.

THOMAS, HUGH, *The Spanish Civil War.* New York, Harper and Row, 1961.

TREND, J. B., *The Origins of Modern Spain.* New York, Macmillan, 1934.

TRYTHALL, J. W. D., *El Caudillo: A Political Biography.* New York, McGraw-Hill, 1970.

VALLOTON, HENRY, *Alfonso XIII.* Madrid, Editorial Tesoro, 1945.

VICENS VIVES, JAIME, *Approaches to the History of Spain.* Berkeley, University of California Press, 1967.

VILAR, PIERRE, "El Motín de Esquilache," *Revista de Occidente,* Vol. 36–37 (February, 1972), pp. 83–91.

VILAR, SERGIO, *Les Oppositions à Franco.* Paris, Éditions Denoël, 1970.

VOLTES, PEDRO, *Carlos III y Su Tiempo.* Barcelona, Editorial Juventud, S.A., 1964.

VRIGNAULT, HENRI, *Généalogie de la Maison de Bourbon.* Paris, Henri Lefebvre, 1957.

WHITE, G. F., *A Century of Spain and Portugal (1788–1898).* London, Methuen and Co., 1909.

WOODWARD, MARGARET, "The Spanish Army and the Loss of America 1810–1824," *Hispanic American Historical Review,* Vol. 48 (November, 1968), pp. 586–607.

ZABALA Y LERA, PÍO, *España bajo los Borbones.* Barcelona, Editorial Labor, S.A., 1955.

ZORRILLA Y GONZÁLEZ DE MENDOZA, FRANCISCO XAVIER, CONDE DE LAS LAMAS, *Genealogía de la Casa de Borbón de España.* Madrid, Editora Nacional, 1971.

Index